Modern British Drama

A revised and updated version of *Modern British Drama, 1890–1990*, now covering the whole twentieth century, this is the first one-volume analysis of English play writing to cover the most exciting and productive period in British Theatre from its inception to today. Through detailed discussions of major dramatists and plays, Innes traces the evolution of modernism from Bernard Shaw to Patrick Marber and Sarah Kane, and theatrical developments over the whole century. Information is included on the social and political environment surrounding the plays, first productions, and critical reception, plus chronology, illustrations from key performances, lists of playwrights and works, and selective bibliographies. The book is an invaluable guide for students, theatre-goers and theatre historians.

CHRISTOPHER INNES is one of the leading experts in the field of modern British drama studies, and he has written and published extensively in this and related areas. His books include *Piscator's Political Theatre*, *Modern German Drama*, *Holy Theatre*, *Edward Gordon Craig*, *Avant Garde Theatre: 1892–1992*, and *A Sourcebook on Naturalistic Theatre*, as well as *Modern British Drama: 1890–1990*. Professor Innes also serves as the General Editor for the Cambridge University Press series Directors in Perspective, and holds the Canada Research Chair in Performance and Culture.

Modern British Drama

The Twentieth Century

CHRISTOPHER INNES

PUBLISHED BY THE PRESS SYNDICATE OF THE UNIVERSITY OF CAMBRIDGE
The Pitt Building, Trumpington Street, Cambridge, United Kingdom

CAMBRIDGE UNIVERSITY PRESS
The Edinburgh Building, Cambridge CB2 2RU, UK
40 West 20th Street, New York, NY 10011-4211, USA
477 Williamstown Road, Port Melbourne, VIC 3207, Australia
Ruiz de Alarcón 13, 28014 Madrid, Spain
Dock House, The Waterfront, Cape Town 8001, South Africa

http://www.cambridge.org

First published 2002

Printed in the United Kingdom at the University Press, Cambridge

Typeface Minion 10.5/13.5 pt   *System* LATEX 2$_\varepsilon$ [TB]

A catalogue record for this book is available from the British Library

Library of Congress Cataloguing in Publication data

Innes, C. D.
Modern British drama : the twentieth century / Christopher Innes.
p.   cm.
Includes bibliographical references and index.
ISBN 0 521 81651 3 – ISBN 0 521 01675 4 (pb.)
1. English drama – 20th century – History and criticism.   I. Title.
PR736 .I53   2002
822′.9109–dc21   2002071567

ISBN 0 521 81651 3 hardback
ISBN 0 521 01675 4 paperback

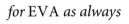

for EVA *as always*

Contents

Illustrations

Illustrations are taken from the first performances, except for numbers 5, 13 and 14, where later productions have special relevance.

I should like to thank the following individuals and institutions for permission to reproduce the photographs: illustrations 1, 2, 4, 12: The Raymond

Mander and Joe Mitchenson Theatre Collection; illustrations 3, 13: photo: Houston Rogers, from the collections of the Theatre Museum. By courtesy of the Board of Trustees of the Victoria and Albert Museum; illustrations 5, 14, 15: photo: Zoe Dominic; illustration 6: photo: Chris Davies; illustration 7: photo: John Haynes/The Raymond Mander and Joe Mitchenson Theatre Collection; illustrations 9, 16, 20: photo: John Haynes; illustrations 10, 19, 21: © Donald Cooper, Photostage; illustrations 17, 22: photo: Geraint Lewis.

Acknowledgements

This study could not have been achieved without the active help and support of many individuals and institutions. The willingness of dramatists, directors and designers to submit to interviews and supply information was invaluable; and I should particularly like to thank Edward Bond and David Edgar, Max Stafford-Clark and Jocelyn Herbert. Staff at the National Theatre and the Theatre Association Library provided essential details, and guided me through their archives. In addition, many colleagues offered valuable advice and criticism, which materially contributed to the shaping of the book, as well as guiding my judgements. Sarah Stanton and Vicki Cooper at Cambridge University Press fostered the original work, and were unflagging in suggesting revisions. Vicki Cooper also has my sincere thanks for freely offered assistance with this new version. Hersh Zeifman and Peter Holland helped me to rethink my arguments, and redefine the structure of the whole – while Ronald Bryden deserves particular thanks for supplying facts and insights from his long experience of British theatre, correcting my mistakes and giving encouragement. Without his illuminating commentary my analysis would be considerably poorer, although any errors, omissions and tendentious opinions remain entirely my responsibility.

On a more material level, this project could not have been undertaken without the exceptionally generous funding for research and release time provided by the Social Sciences and Humanities Research Council of Canada, as well as by the Faculty of Arts at York University, both to the original *Modern British Drama* and to this updated text. I am especially grateful for this support and for the continued confidence shown in my scholarship. I should also like to thank St John's College, Cambridge, for electing me to the Benian's Fellowship, which allowed me to complete the research and writing of the first version of this book, and the Killam Foundation of the Canada Council that provided the time to produce this new version.

Christopher Innes
Toronto, 2001

Chronology

While extensive, this is not intended to be a complete listing of plays staged over the century, nor of the total output of each dramatist discussed. It shows the chronological relationship between those plays mentioned in the different chapters, and includes some of the major historical and theatrical events of the period as reference points. The dates given here in the Chronology, and in the list of plays included with each section on a specific playwright, are those of the first professional English productions.

1889	First English performance of Ibsen's *A Doll's House*	
1890	Shaw: *Quintessence of Ibsenism* published	
1892	Grein's Independent Theatre opens	Shaw: *Widowers' Houses*
1893		Pinero: *The Second Mrs Tanqueray*
1894		Shaw: *Arms and the Man*
1895	Trial of Oscar Wilde	Wilde: *The Importance of Being Earnest*
1896	Jarry's *Ubu roi* performed in Paris	
1897		Shaw: *Candida* *The Devil's Disciple*
1899	Boer War begins	Maugham: *Marriages Are Made in Heaven*
	The Stage Society founded	Shaw: *You Never Can Tell*
1900		Shaw: *Captain Brassbound's Conversion*
1901	Queen Victoria dies	

1902	Boer War ends	Granville-Barker: *The Marrying of Ann Leete*
		Barrie: *The Admirable Crichton*
		Housman/Craig: *Bethlehem*
		Shaw: *Mrs Warren's Profession*
1903		Craig/Ibsen: *The Vikings at Helgeland*
		Maugham: *A Man of Honour*
		Shaw: *Man and Superman*
1904	Barker's first Court Theatre season	Barrie: *Peter Pan*
		Shaw: *John Bull's Other Island*
1905	Craig's *Art of the Theatre* published	Granville-Barker: *The Voysey Inheritance*
		Shaw: *Passion, Poison and Petrifaction*
		The Philanderer
		Major Barbara
1906		Galsworthy: *The Silver Box*
		Robins: *Votes for Women!*
		Shaw: *Caesar and Cleopatra*
1907	First Repertory theatre founded in Manchester	Granville-Barker: *Waste*
		Garnett: *The Breaking Point*
1908	Actresses' Franchise League founded	Masefield: *The Tragedy of Nan*
		Maugham: *Jack Straw*
		Lady Frederick
		The Explorer
		Mrs Dot
		Shaw: *Getting Married*
1909		Granville-Barker: *The Madras House*
		Galsworthy: *Strife*
		Maugham: *Smith*
1910	Workers' Theatre Movement founded	Galsworthy: *Justice*
		Masefield: *The Tragedy of Pompey the Great*
		Shaw: *Misalliance*
		The Dark Lady of the Sonnets
1911	Prison Reform Bill	Shaw: *Fanny's First Play*
		Galsworthy: *The Eldest Son*

1913		Maugham: *The Promised Land*
		Shaw: *Pygmalion*
1914	First World War declared	Shaw: *Androcles and the Lion*
1915	Granville-Barker's final Court Theatre season	
1916	Easter Uprising in Dublin	Yeats: *At the Hawk's Well* (Plays for Dancers)
1917	Russian Revolution	Barrie: *Dear Brutus*
	Proletkult Movement founded in Russia	Maugham: *Our Betters*
1918	Women granted the Vote First World War ends	
1919		Shaw: *Heartbreak House*
1920	Irish Civil War	Barrie: *Mary Rose*
1921		Masefield: *Esther*
		Maugham: *The Circle*
		Shaw: *The Shewing-Up of Blanco Posnet*
1922	Irish Free State established	Galsworthy: *Loyalties*
		Maugham: *East of Suez*
		Shaw: *Back to Methuselah*
1923		Coward: *The Young Idea*
		Flecker: *Hassan*
1924		Coward: *The Vortex*
		Easy Virtue
		O'Casey: *Juno and the Paycock*
		Shaw: *Saint Joan*
1925		Coward: *On With the Dance*
		Hay Fever
		Galsworthy: *The Show*
		Travers: *A Cuckoo in the Nest*
1926	General Strike	Lawrence: *The Widowing of Mrs Holroyd*
	Workers' Theatre Movement revived	Maugham: *The Letter*
		Travers: *Rookery Nook*
1927		Corrie: *In Time of Strife*
		Travers: *Thark*
1928	Full emancipation for women	Coward: *This Year of Grace*
		Maugham: *The Sacred Flame*

		Sherriff: *Journey's End*
		Travers: *Plunder*
1929	The Great Depression Wall Street Crash	Coward: *Bitter Sweet*
1930		Coward: *Private Lives* Maugham: *The Breadwinner*
1931		Coward: *Calvalcade* Priestley/Knoblock: *The Good Companions*
1932	Doone's Group Theatre founded Littlewood's Theatre of Action founded	Coward: *Words and Music* Maugham: *For Services Rendered* Priestley: *Dangerous Corner* Shaw: *Too True To Be Good*
1933	Hitler comes to power in Germany Dukes founds Mercury Theatre	Coward: *Design for Living* Maugham: *Sheppey* Priestley: *The Roundabout* Shaw: *On the Rocks* Travers: *A Bit of a Test*
1934		Auden: *The Dance of Death* Eliot: *The Rock* *Sweeney Agonistes* Priestley: *Eden End* Theatre of Action: *John Bullion*
1935	Theatre of Action reorganized as Theatre Union	Coward: *Point Valaine* Eliot: *Murder in the Cathedral* Housman: *Victoria Regina*
1936	Spanish Civil War begins	Auden and Isherwood: *The Dog Beneath the Skin* Lodge and Roberts: *Where's That Bomb?* Rattigan: *French Without Tears*
1937		Auden and Isherwood: *The Ascent of F6* Priestley: *Time and the Conways* *I Have Been Here Before*
1938		Priestley: *Music At Night* Spender: *Trial of a Judge* Travers: *Banana Ridge*

1939	The Group Theatre closes	Auden and Isherwood: *On the Frontier*
		Coward: *This Happy Breed*
	Spanish Civil War ends	Eliot: *The Family Reunion*
		Priestley: *Johnson Over Jordan*
	Hitler invades Poland	Theatre Union: *Last Edition*
1940		Priestley: *The Long Mirror*
1941		Coward: *Blithe Spirit*
1942	Hitler invades Russia	
1945	Hiroshima: Second World War ends	Duncan: *This Way to the Tomb*
	Browne's first Pilgrim Players season at the Mercury Theatre	
	Littlewood's Theatre Workshop founded	
	Labour government elected	
1946		Fry: *A Phoenix Too Frequent*
		The Firstborn
		Priestley: *An Inspector Calls*
		Rattigan: *The Winslow Boy*
1947	Final Pilgrim Players season	Priestley: *Ever Since Paradise*
1948		Fry: *The Lady's Not for Burning*
		Rattigan: *Playbill*
1949		Eliot: *The Cocktail Party*
		Rattigan: *Adventure Story*
		Shaw: *Shaks versus Shaw*
1950	The Group Theatre revived	Fry: *A Sleep of Prisoners*
	Shaw dies	*Venus Observed*
1951	Festival of Britain	Coward: *Relative Values*
		Whiting: *Saint's Day*
1952		Rattigan: *The Deep Blue Sea*
		Whiting: *A Penny for a Song*
1953	Theatre Workshop moves to Stratford East	Beckett: *Waiting for Godot*
		Eliot: *The Confidential Clerk*
		Thomas: *Under Milkwood*
1954	The Group Theatre closes	Coward: *After the Ball*
		Chapman: *Dry Rot*

		Fry: *The Dark is Light Enough*
		Rattigan: *Separate Tables*
		Whiting: *Marching Song*
1955	Beckett: *Waiting for Godot* performed in London	
1956	The English Stage Company founded	Osborne: *Look Back in Anger*
	Berliner Ensemble in London	
	Suez Crisis	
	Russian Invasion of Hungary	
1957		Arden: *The Waters of Babylon*
		Live Like Pigs
		Beckett: *Endgame*
		Osborne: *Epitaph for George Dillon*
		The Entertainer
		Pinter: *The Room*
1958	English Publication of Artaud's *The Theatre and Its Double*	Beckett: *Krapp's Last Tape*
		Bolt: *Flowering Cherry*
		Delaney: *A Taste of Honey*
		Eliot: *The Elder Statesman*
	CND movement founded	Jellicoe: *The Sport of My Mad Mother*
		Pinter: *The Birthday Party*
		Rattigan: *Variations on a Theme*
		Shaffer: *Five Finger Exercise*
		Wesker: *Chicken Soup with Barley*
1959		Arden: *Serjeant Musgrave's Dance*
		Osborne: *The World of Paul Slickey*
		Simpson: *One Way Pendulum*
		Wesker: *The Kitchen Roots*
1960	Centre 42 founded	Bolt: *A Man for All Seasons*
		Delaney: *The Lion in Love*
		Pinter: *The Caretaker*
		The Dumb Waiter
		Rattigan: *Ross*
		Wesker: *I'm Talking About Jerusalem*
		(*Trilogy* performed)

1961	US invasion of Cuba (Bay of Pigs)	Beckett: *Happy Days*
		Cooney: *One for the Pot*
		Jellicoe: *The Knack*
		Osborne: *Luther*
1962		Bond: *The Pope's Wedding*
		Osborne: *Cry for Love*
		Rudkin: *Afore Night Come*
		Wesker: *Chips With Everything*
1963	National Theatre opens	Arden: *The Workhouse Donkey*
		Ironhand
	President Kennedy assassinated	*Ars Longa, Vita Brevis*
		Beckett: *Play*
		Littlewood/Theatre Workshop: *Oh, What a Lovely War*
		Pinter: *The Lover* & *The Connection*
		Priestley: *A Severed Head*
		Rattigan: *Man and Boy*
1964	Brook's Theatre of Cruelty season	Arden: *Armstrong's Last Goodnight*
		Cheeseman: *The Jolly Potters*
		Osborne: *Inadmissible Evidence*
		Orton: *Entertaining Mr Sloane*
		Shaffer: *The Royal Hunt of the Sun*
1965	Theatre in Education Movement founded	Arden: *Left-Handed Liberty*
		Barnes: *Scelerosis*
		Beckett: *Come and Go*
		Bond: *Saved*
		Coward: *A Song At Twilight*
	Vietnam War begins	Orton: *Loot*
		Osborne: *A Bond Honoured*
		A Patriot For Me
		Pinter: *The Homecoming*
		Shaffer: *Black Comedy*
		Wesker: *The Four Seasons*
1966		Mercer: *Belcher's Luck*
		Stoppard: *Rosencrantz and Guildenstern are Dead*

		Wesker: *Their Very Own and Golden City*
1967	Orton murdered	Jellicoe: *The Rising Generation*
		Orton: *Crimes of Passion*
1968	Abolition of Censorship in England	Arden: *The Hero Rises Up* *Harold Muggins is a Martyr*
	Russians invade Czechoslovakia	Barnes: *The Ruling Class* Bond: *Narrow Road to the Deep North*
	Student Revolt in Paris	*Early Morning*
		Hampton: *Total Eclipse*
	Royal Court D.H. Lawrence season	Osborne: *Time Present/Hotel in Amsterdam*
		Stoppard: *The Real Inspector Hound*
	Red Ladder Stage Company founded	*Enter a Free Man* Travers: *Corker's End* Tynan: *Oh! Calcutta!*
1969	US Moon Landing	Ayckbourn: *How the Other Half Loves*
		Barnes: *Leonardo's Last Supper/ Noonday Demons*
		Brenton: *Christie in Love* Nichols: *The National Health* Orton: *What the Butler Saw* Pinter: *Landscape* and *Silence*
1970	Women's Liberation Group and Gay Liberation Front founded	Bolt: *Vivat! Vivat Regina!* Bond: *Black Mass* Brenton: *Fruit* and *Wesley* Edgar: *The National Interest* Fry: *A Yard of Sun* Hampton: *The Philanthropist* Hare: *Slag* Rattigan: *A Bequest to the Nation* Shaffer: *Shrivings* Stoppard: *After Magritte*
1971	McCrath's 7:84 Theatre Company founded	Brenton/Hare/Edgar: *Lay-By*

		Brenton: *Scott of the Antarctic*
		Bond: *Lear Passion*
	General Will Theatre	Griffiths: *Occupations*
	Company founded	Osborne: *West of Suez*
		Pinter: *Old Times*
1972		Arden: *The Island of the Mighty*
		The Ballygombeen Bequest
		Ayckbourn: *Absurd Person*
		Singular
		Brenton: *Hitler Dances*
		Brenton/Edgar/Hare: *England's*
		Ireland
		Brenton/Hare: *Brassneck*
		Churchill: *Owners*
		Strachan/Coward: *Cowardy*
		Custard
		Hare: *The Great Exhibition*
		Osborne: *A Sense of Detachment*
		Stoppard: *Jumpers*
		Artist Descending a
		Staircase (radio)
		Wesker: *The Old Ones*
1973		Ayckbourn: *The Norman*
		Conquests
		Beckett: *Not I*
		Bond: *The Sea*
		Brenton: *Magnificence*
		Griffiths: *The Party*
		McGrath: *The Cheviot, the Stag*
		and the Black, Black Oil
		Rattigan: *In Praise of Love*
		Shaffer: *Equus*
1974	Association of Community	Ayckbourn: *Absent Friends*
	Theatres founded	Barnes: *The Bewitched*
		Bond: *Bingo*
		Gems: *Go West Young Woman*
		Hare: *Knuckle*
	Joint Stock company founded	Nichols: *Chez Nous*
		Rudkin: *Ashes*

	Women's Theatre Group founded	Stoppard: *Travesties*
1975		Ayckbourn: *Bedroom Farce*
		Arden: *The Non-Stop Connolly* *Show*
		Brenton: *A Saliva Milkshake*
	Fall of Saigon	Frayn: *Alphabetical Order*
		Gray: *Otherwise Engaged*
		Griffiths: *The Comedians*
		Hare: *Fanshen* *Teeth 'n Smiles*
		Pinter: *No Man's Land*
		Travers: *The Bed Before Yesterday*
		Wesker: *The Journalists*
1976	Gay Sweatshop founded	Beckett: *That Time/Footfalls*
		Bond: *The Fool*
		Brenton: *Weapons of Happiness*
		Churchill: *Light Shining in* *Buckinghamshire* *Vinegar Tom*
		Edgar: *Destiny*
		Frayn: *Clouds*
		Osborne: *Watch It Come Down*
		Rudkin: *Sons of Light*
		Stoppard: *Dirty Linen*
		Wesker: *The Merchant*
1977		Bolt: *State of Revolution*
		Frayn: *Make and Break*
		Gems: *Queen Christina* *Dusa, Fish, Stas and Vi*
		Nichols: *Privates on Parade*
		Rattigan: *Cause Célèbre*
		Stoppard: *Every Good Boy* *Deserves Favour*
1978		Ayckbourn: *Joking Apart*
		Barnes: *Laughter*
		Bond: *The Bundle* *The Woman*

		Edgar: *The Jail Diary of Albie Sachs*
		Gems: *Piaf*
		Hampton: *Tales from the Vienna Woods*
		Hare: *Licking Hitler Plenty*
		Laverty: *Time Gentlemen Please*
		Pinter: *Betrayal*
		Stoppard: *Night and Day*
		Wandor: *Whores d'Oeuvres*
1979	Thatcher government elected	Ayckbourn: *Sisterly Feelings* *Taking Steps*
		Bond: *The Worlds*
		Churchill: *Cloud Nine*
		Frayn: *Liberty Hall*
		Shaffer: *Amadeus*
	Miners' strike in Britain	Sherman: *Bent*
		Wandor: *Aurora Leigh*
1980	Reagan elected President of the USA	Brenton: *The Romans in Britain*
		Edgar: *Nicholas Nickleby*
		Russell: *Educating Rita*
1981	Greenham Common Peace Camp	Beckett: *Rockaby*
		Bond: *Restoration*
		Brenton: *Thirteenth Night*
		Nichols: *Passion Play*
		Rudkin: *The Triumph of Death*
		Wesker: *Caritas*
1982		Beckett: *Catastrophe*
		Bond: *Summer*
	Falklands War	Churchill: *Top Girls*
		Frayn: *Noises Off*
		Stoppard: *The Real Thing*
1983	Thatcher re-elected	Ayckbourn: *Intimate Exchanges*
		Barker: *A Passion in Six Days*
		Beckett: *What Where*
		Churchill: *Fen*
		Daniels: *Masterpieces*
		Edgar: *Maydays*

1990	Thatcher resigns	Barker: *Scenes from an Execution*
		Barnes: *Sunsets and Glories*
	Reunification of Germany	Brenton/Ali: *Moscow Gold*
	Gulf War	Churchill: *Mad Forest*
		Eagleton: *Saint Oscar*
	Gorbachev awarded Nobel	Edgar: *The Shape of the Table*
	Peace Prize	Frayn: *Look, Look*
		Griffiths: *Piano*
	Paris Summit marks the end	Hare: *Racing Demon*
	of the Cold War	Nicholson: *Shadowlands*
1991		Ayckbourn: *The Revengers' Comedies*
		Steven Berkoff: *Kvetch*
	Boris Yeltsin elected President	Dorfman: *Death and the Maiden*
	of Russia	Gems: *The Blue Angel*
		Hare: *Murmuring Judges*
	Soviet Union replaced by	Pinter: *Party Time*
	Commonwealth of	Wertenbaker: *Three Birds Alighting on a Field*
	Independent States	
1992		Brenton: *Berlin Bertie*
	Major wins fourth consecutive	Isitt: *You Never Know Who's Out There*
	Conservative govt.,	
	defeating Kinnock	John Osborne: *Déjàvu*
	War in Bosnia	Theatre de Complicité: *The Street of Crocodiles*
1993	IRA bomb London's financial	Ayckbourn: *Time of My Life*
	district	Barker: *The Europeans*
		Hare: *The Absence of War* (*Trilogy* performed)
		Johnson: *Hysteria*
	Britain ratifies the European	Pinter: *Moonlight*
	Union Treaty	Shaffer: *The Gift of the Gorgon*
		Stoppard: *Arcadia*
1994	Genocide in Rwanda	Ayckbourn: *Communicating Doors*
		Barker: *Bite of the Night*
		Berkhoff: *Acapulco*
	'Chunnel' completed	Churchill: *The Skryker*
		Edgar: *Pentecost*

		Hampton: *The White Chameleon*
		Theatre de Complicité: *The Three
	Russia invades Chechnya	Lives of Lucie Cabrol*
1995		Hare: *Skylight*
		Kane: *Blasted*
		Marber: *Dealer's Choice*
		Stoppard: *Indian Ink*
1996	Prince Charles and Princess	Barker: *(Uncle) Vanya*
	Diana divorce	Barnes: *Corpsing*
		Elton: *Popcorn*
		Gems: *Stanley*
	Royal Court Theatre moves	*Marlene*
	to West End	Griffiths: *Who Shall Be Happy...?*
		Kane: *Phaedra's Love*
		Marber: *After Miss Julie*
		Pinter: *Ashes to Ashes*
		Ravenhill: *Shopping and Fucking*
1997	Sheep named Dolly cloned	Churchill: *This is a Chair*
	Blair forms Labour govt.	*Blue Heart*
	Princess Diana killed	de Angelis: *Playhouse Creatures*
	Mother Theresa dies	Hare: *Amy's View*
	Scotland and Wales vote for	Marber: *Closer*
	Devolution	Stoppard: *The Invention of Love*
		Wesker: *When God Wanted a Son*
1998		Ayckbourn: *Things We Do For
		Love*
	General Pinochet detained	Bartlett: *Seven Sonnets of
		Michelangelo*
	Reform of House of Lords	Brenton/Ali: *Ugly Rumours*
		Frayn: *Copenhagen*
		Gems: *The Snow Palace*
	US President Clinton	Hare: *Via Dolorosa*
	impeached	*The Judas Kiss*
		The Blue Room
		Kane: *Cleansed*
		Pritchard: *Yard Gal*
		Ravenhill: *Handbag*
		Wesker: *Letter to a Daughter*

1999	NATO bombs Kosovo	Ayckbourn: *House* and *Garden*
		Barnes: *Dreaming*
	Kane commits suicide	Brenton/Ali: *Collateral Damage*
	Global celebrations mark the	Theatre de Complicité: *The*
	new Millennium	*Vertical Line*
2000		Kane: *4.48 Psychosis*

Contexts

The twentieth century is one of the most vital and exciting periods in English drama, rivalling the Elizabethan theatre in thematic scope and stylistic ambition. It has produced a wider range of plays than any previous era: both developing and cutting across traditional genres, as well as extending the subject-matter of the stage. The massive social changes resulting from two world wars, the need for national reappraisal with loss of Britain's imperial role, together with the effects of technological advances and increasing urbanization, have had a continuing creative impact on the theatre. Stimulated by new ideologies, from Fabian socialism to Marxism and more recently feminism, playwrights achieved a public voice. The social importance of their work has been acknowledged by Nobel Prizes (for Shaw, T.S. Eliot and Beckett) as well as more recently a number of knighthoods awarded to major playwrights, from Noel Coward – belated because of his sexual reputation – and Terence Rattigan, to Alan Ayckbourn, Tom Stoppard, and even a dramatist with a radical reputation, David Hare. To put this in context one must remember that Henry Irving was the first theatre artist of any sort to be knighted, and for the first half of the century, with the exception of J.M. Barrie, the honour was limited to actors and theatre-managers.

More significantly, their political and cultural impact is marked by the successful campaigns for the abolition of censorship and the founding of a National Theatre, each of which began at the turn of the century and reached fulfilment in the 1960s. Awareness of the theatre's potential for influencing audiences has raised questions about the function of drama, the nature of its reception and the relationship between form and content – all of which have fuelled the intellectual dynamism and artistic significance of British theatre throughout the modern period. In short, in this century the stage regained its position as a forum for public debate, which it has retained despite the drawing power of new media. Film and television reaches an infinitely broader

1

audience and may have the capacity to represent social reality more completely, or intervene in topic issues with far more immediacy. But the direct contact with spectators on the live stage has continued to attract major talent. Almost all the leading dramatists, directors and actors have done extensive work for film or television, yet their main focus has remained the theatre.

And unlike France or Germany, where theatrical developments (with the signal exception of Bertolt Brecht) have been driven largely by directors, in Britain throughout the century it has been a playwright's theatre. Indeed here, far more than elsewhere, dramatists have also worked as directors – from Shaw and Granville-Barker during the early decades of the century who directed their own plays, as Alan Ayckbourn has also done, up to Harold Pinter, Edward Bond, or David Hare who generally stage the work of other playwrights. It is also significant that when major stylistic advances became widely adopted in English theatre, most importantly in the 1950s with the impact of Brecht and Beckett, these new dramatic forms came from playwrights (even if Brecht in particular had also established himself as one of the leading German directors and manager of the world-famous Berliner Ensemble).

This is not to minimize the role played by the Royal Court, first in the Granville-Barker/Vedrenne seasons near the beginning of the century, then under William Gaskill and Max Stafford-Clark from the mid-1950s on, the Royal Shakespeare Company which in the 1970s began to include new plays in its repertoire, or the National Theatre and the role played by Richard Eyre in promoting Hare's plays. And there have been many distinguished as well as path-breaking directors, without whom the dramatists could not have flourished – though it is perhaps indicative that the most important British director, Peter Brook, has chosen to pursue his career in France. Yet it was Bernard Shaw's influence and example that formed the main shaping force in British theatre all the way through 1950 (when he died) and beyond; while William Gaskill saw his task as specifically encouraging new English dramatists, and when his breakthrough came in 1956 it was identified with John Osborne and other playwrights. So it is appropriate to focus specifically on drama, rather than on the theatre history of the modern period.

It may seem arbitrary to look at a period bounded by a century. And indeed British drama flows back across the year of 1900, as it looks forward to the future in 2000. Playwrights like Arthur Pinero and actors or theatre-managers like Sir Henry Irving remained active through the first decade of the Twentieth Century, while the younger playwrights who have just established their careers in the last decade, like Patrick Marber or Mark Ravenhill, can be expected to develop well beyond Arthur C. Clarke's canonical year of 2001. Indeed (as I have argued before) the beginning of modern drama in England can be dated in 1890 when Bernard Shaw gave his lecture on 'The Quintessence of Ibsenism', which marks a watershed between traditionalism and new politicized forms of drama. And it is true that the ferment of the modern era was already breaking the mould of Victorian certainties during the final decade of the Nineteenth Century. Yet while the boundaries may be blurred, these divisions are not artificial.

As we have very recently experienced, a real popular consciousness of coming to the close of an era grew overwhelmingly as the millennium approached. Books appeared with titles like *The End of History*, while movements for change emerged and took to the streets to challenge global institutions like the IMF and the WTO. The same was true in the last years of the Nineteenth Century, with the rise of the symbolically named *fin de siècle* movement (epitomized in Oscar Wilde's version of *Salomé*), concurrently with a socialist like Bernard Shaw (or in more utopian novelist terms, William Morris with *News from Nowhere*) writing for change. And undeniably there is a tangible difference between Victorian attitudes and the modernist aesthetic that defines artistic progress as a radical opposition to the past, as in the equally symbolically named *Art Nouveau* movement.

This can be illustrated by the contrast between Shaw and Pinero: the major dramatists who bridge the divide between the two centuries. Pinero, whom even Shaw's collaborator William Archer praised for his 'serious treatment of serious themes', believed that the proper function of drama was 'giving back to the multitude their own thoughts and conceptions illuminated, enlarged, and if needful purged'.[1] Not surprisingly Pinero became the main target in Shaw's campaign to promote the 'new' drama (which of course he identified with his own plays); and he singled out *The Second Mrs Tanqueray*, Pinero's most widely recognized social tragedy, as an example of 'Sardoodledom' (Shaw's term for the conventional morality embodied in the Well-Made Play formula identified with the French playwright Sardou). Even so, although Shaw had already written six plays by 1899, these are mainly reprises of the kind of plays he aimed to displace – varieties of melodrama in *Arms and the Man* (1894) and *The Devil's Disciple* (1894) or domestic comedy in *Candida* (1897) – and formed mirror-images of these traditional forms. In a very real sense it was not until the turn of the new century with plays like *Mrs Warren's Profession* (1902) or *Man and Superman* (1903) that Shaw struck out in a completely new direction.

It is also symptomatic of what might be called centennial consciousness among the dramatists themselves that so many films and plays, particularly in the last decade, have dealt with a highly symbolic figure from the end of the previous century: Oscar Wilde. Starting with Terry Eagleton's *Saint Oscar*, directed by Trevor Griffiths in 1989, this trend reached a peak with David Hare's *The Judas Kiss* exploring Wilde's motives for sacrificing himself, and Tom Stoppard's *The Invention of Love* in which Wilde appears to interrogate the poet A.E Houseman, together with the movie *Wilde* starring Stephen Frye, which had been released in 1997. All were running simultaneously in London during the spring of 1998; and it is no accident that such a quintessentially *fin de siècle* playwright is used to reflect on the failure of humanism and modernism at the end of the millennium.

1.1 Defining British drama

Theatre has always crossed boundaries, and in the Nineteenth Century there was relatively little difference between drama in Manchester or Moscow. The balance might shift between Romantic tragedy, melodrama and the well-made play. The level of sophistication in the staging might vary. But the way life was represented looked much the same. It is usually assumed that Naturalism brought nationalism to the stage, splitting this homogenized European culture into clearly identifiable entities distinguished by language. Although naturalistic drama was indeed used to express and foster national-ist sentiment at the turn of the last century, in fact it was no less international. Its search for specifics was the same whether in Norway or Ireland, however different the locale depicted.

Similarly the series of reactions against Naturalism that followed spread from Scandinavia to Spain, even though their form might vary from country to country. The nature and function of theatre has been questioned, disman-tled, redefined in a process of continual revolution: Symbolism, Expression-ism, Surrealism, Dada, Futurism, Antonin Artaud's 'Theatre of Cruelty', the Absurd. All these *avant-garde* factions share a rejection of logical structures and reason, which are seen in Artaud's phrase as 'chains that bind us in a petrifying imbecility'. The history of modern European theatre is largely the record of these extreme and short-lived movements; and it is noticeable that from this *avant-garde* perspective Britain barely rates a mention. Al-though continental trends have been imported by the occasional British or Irish playwright or director – Symbolism with Yeats and Gordon Craig; the expressionistic experiments of O'Casey, Auden and Isherwood; Theatre of

Cruelty in the post-1964 work of Peter Brook or the plays of David Rudkin – they have exerted relatively little influence on the development of British drama as a whole. Its evolution has been markedly different.

Significantly, the only European stage form that has had more than a passing effect is Brechtian 'Epic Theatre'. In the late 1950s and through the 1960s Brecht's work acted as a catalyst for everything from Shakespearean productions to the plays of Osborne, Arden or Bond; and its influence is still clearly discernible in the work of the younger generation of contemporary dramatists. However, Brecht's impact was hardly coincidental. English theatre had already been conditioned to appreciate intellectual drama. The consistency and sophistication of Brecht's approach might be novel. But its rationalism, with its demystifying of the stage, its anti-illusionistic theatricality or its thematic emphasis on the linkage of character and social context were not new.

These elements paralleled and extended the essential thrust of Bernard Shaw's work. Picking up on Ibsen's brand of Naturalism, which he reinterpreted to form the basis of a rational drama dealing with social issues, Shaw defined modernism in a way that became standard for mainstream British theatre. The artistic ethos he promoted was antithetical to that of the European *avant-garde*; and his career spanned the whole of the first half of the century, giving his principles a continuing influence. It is largely due to Shaw that British drama in the twentieth century is distinct from the European tradition, rather than being the effect of cultural, or even linguistic differences. Thus, the development of modern drama has been different in America, or even Ireland – though in both English is the standard stage language.

Ireland is something of a test case for defining British drama, since the relationship with English theatre is so close. At the beginning of the period, with the whole of Ireland still under British rule, Irish-born would-be writers, in particular Oscar Wilde and Bernard Shaw (like Sheridan or Dion Boucicault in the Eighteenth and Nineteenth Centuries), naturally pursued their careers in London as the only available theatre centre. Their subject was primarily English society. Even when Shaw takes Ireland as his theme in a play like *John Bull's Other Island*, he is explicitly addressing the British Establishment. By almost any criteria these nominally Irish playwrights count as part of the English dramatic tradition, as does T.S. Eliot, despite his American background.

Synge, who died before independence, and W.B. Yeats are to some extent transitional figures. Developing a literary language based on the speech of

Arran peasants, as Synge did, or using traditional Irish legends and contexts, their work was designed as the expression of a national consciousness that would be clearly distinguishable from England. They have therefore been excluded from this study, as has Sean O'Casey. Even though O'Casey's later plays were written in England, to which he had retreated from the hostility of the Dublin public, all his work is specifically addressed to an Irish audience. His classic trilogy, in particular *The Plough and the Stars* and *Juno and the Paycock* may have won significant popularity on the English stage. But these fall outside the British theatre, being largely appreciated in a touristic fashion – in contrast to the riot that greeted the first performance of *The Plough and the Stars* in Ireland.

However, Samuel Beckett is a special case: perhaps the one truly international figure in contemporary theatre. Self-exiled from Ireland, the roots of his drama are in the Existentialism of Sartre and Camus, picking up on the Surrealism of Andre Breton or Roger Vitrac in the 1920s. There is also a link with Antonin Artaud's experiments in subliminal theatre through Roger Blin, Artaud's collaborator in the 1930s, who directed Beckett's early plays. Indeed, all his longer plays were originally written in French; and up until the 1970s, when he started creating pieces for particular actors and directors – Billie Whitelaw, Patrick Magee and Jack MacGowran, or Alan Schneider – Beckett continued to use French and English interchangeably.[2] Beckett (like O'Casey) abandoned Ireland, and prohibited performances of his plays there in protest against the Irish ban on O'Casey's work. And while many of his dramatic characters possess a recognizably Irish background and sometimes consciousness, Beckett consciously deals in universal themes, and (with a few exceptions like his radio play, *All That Fall*) avoids any specifically Irish locality or political theme. As an exile writing primarily in French, Beckett would be categorized as European, if the way he redefined the essence of drama had not conditioned the basic approach of practically all present English playwrights, as well as prompting Stoppard to write for the stage or causing Harold Pinter to send his plays for Beckett to comment on before production. He is therefore very much a part of twentieth-century British theatre – and indeed his work, which first appeared in London in the same season as the Berliner Ensemble, had as much if not more impact on British dramatists, even than Brecht.

Other Irish playwrights, including those from Northern Ireland, belong to a separate cultural framework. Even when their plays transfer successfully to the London stage, as with Brian Friel, Brendan Behan or Thomas Kilroy, there has been little cross-fertilization. They too are addressing specifically

Irish themes in a recognizably different way, and building on an increasingly well-established national tradition. It is therefore ironic that it should be an expatriate Irishman, Shaw, who was instrumental in giving British drama its own identity.

1.2 Patterns of development and organizing principles

The large number of serious writers attracted to the stage, the richness and variety of their dramatic output, and the consistent challenging of accepted norms, make historical developments particularly complex. Although Bernard Shaw dominates the theatre from 1890 right through to the Second World War, and his influence can still be felt up to the mid-1950s, there is no single line of evolution in British drama. Nor is there a distinct succession of periods.

Critical studies customarily treat the century as if it were composed of distinct units – such as the decade following 1956 (John Russell Taylor's *Anger and After*, published in 1962), or the generation between the two world wars (Laurence Kitchin's *Mid-Century Drama*,1960). Yet even those periods bounded by major historical events are not self-contained. Each war certainly produced a theatrical hiatus, with escapist or patriotic entertainment (satirically reflected in Joan Littlewood's *Oh, What a Lovely War* or Peter Nichols' *Privates on Parade*) replacing serious drama. New playwrights emerged in the aftermath of both: Noel Coward expressing the febrile disillusion of the 1920s; Christopher Fry reflecting the desire for colour and affirmation in the 1950s. Even so, Shaw, banished from the stage during the 1914 18 War because of his iconoclastic attitude to the conflict, continued to restate his pre-war concerns in a darker and more evangelical light during the 1920s and 1930s. Similarly Coward, having contributed to the 1939–45 war effort with flag-waving films, returned to the theatre in the 1950s, while Terence Rattigan's post-war attack on moral conventions was the lineal descendant of Granville-Barker's Edwardian social criticism.

John Osborne and the group of so-called 'kitchen-sink' realists, who emerged in the 1950s, were hailed at the time as a revolutionary force on the English stage. But they can be shown as extending the principles established by Shaw and Galsworthy; and their new Naturalism was anticipated by D.H. Lawrence's plays from almost forty years earlier. Not only that: one of the influences that was to displace 'kitchen-sink' appeared in the same year as Osborne's breakthrough, with the visit of Brecht's Berliner Ensemble, while the other had already made its mark with the production of Beckett's

Waiting for Godot the year before. The ideologically defined 'social realism'
of the post-1968 generation seemed an equally radical departure. But their
extreme politicization of English drama took its starting point from the
Agitprop theatre of the 1930s. And in each case, the new forms can be seen
as reaffirming the modernist values that Shaw had formulated, although in
different terms.

Even within a single generation there are contrasting lines of development;
and there are seldom clear-cut breaks between them. The influence of Brecht
and Beckett coexists. Pinter appears alongside Wesker. Rudkin and Stoppard
occupy the same time frame as the Social Realists. John Arden and Edward
Bond form a bridge from Osborne to the 1980s. Noel Coward and Ben
Travers, whose works characterize mainstream theatre between the wars,
were still producing popular new plays in the 1960s.

The century itself is not a self-contained unit. The ferment of the modern
era was already present in the final decade of the Nineteenth Century, breaking the mould of Victorian certainties. Issues like women's rights or class
justice, which have become major contemporary themes, were already
finding reflection on the stage. The year 1890 marks the beginning of modern drama in England, as the date of Bernard Shaw's lecture on 'The
Quintessence of Ibsenism'. This can be seen as the watershed between traditionalist and modern perspectives, with its call for a revolution in the nature
and function of the dramatic experience.

The lack of clear temporal signposts makes a straight chronological treatment of twentieth-century British drama artificial. Shaw's central position,
the length of his artistic career spanning over half of the whole period, and
his continuing influence, mean that any study of modern English dramatists
has to begin with his work. However, developments can best be understood
through grouping other playwrights under separate, fairly flexible head-
ings. These correspond to three major types of theatre, defined equally by
stylistic approach and thematic focus: Realism; Comedy; and Poetic Drama.
If stressing the unity of form and content is one characteristic of modern
drama, another is the rejection of traditional genres, so that these categories
are unconventional. They reflect the nature of the work.

'Realism' is generally used as a synonym or derivative of 'Naturalism':
a critical label describing the objective reproduction of ordinary contemporary life. Given the loosening and merging of stylistic divisions that is one of
the hallmarks of modernism, 'realism' only continues to have relevance as
a way of defining focus rather than form. The key qualities become type of

subject and authorial intention, so that the term applies to all playwrights who describe their work as Social/Socialist Realism, even when it does not fit naturalistic criteria. They deal directly with political issues, typically addressing questions of justice or calling for revolutionary change. Their aims differ in degree, but are comparable in range: from presenting ethical challenges to the audience to raising ideological consciousness, or from working to correct abuses within the system to inciting violent action against it.

As consensus disintegrates during the 1930s and again in the 1970s, the stance of such playwrights becomes more extreme, and their approach less naturalistic. Agitprop produces one-dimensional characters, using direct address and melodramatic simplification for agitation and propaganda. Epic Theatre exposes stage illusion, separating actor from role. It replaces cause-and-effect plot with montage structure, and works to alienate the audience. Yet these stage forms are not opposites of 'realism', even though Brecht defined his Epic Theatre by contrast to Ibsen and Stanislavski. Rather they should be seen as alternative modes of portraying society in terms of politics. Episodic collage, interjected songs, even verse dialogue and historical subjects can all be considered part of this line, as long as the social relevance is immediate and the perspective specifically political.

Comedy is different in kind, intrinsically distancing and depending on stock formulae to produce humour. Although traditionally reflecting society and embracing social criticism, it works obliquely and through distortion. This distinguishes comic from realistic playwrights, even when their drama becomes progressively more radical and their aims equally political. Again the breaking down of conventional boundaries makes a narrow generic definition inappropriate. Paradox gives way to polemics. Laughter is used against the audience. Standard comic techniques are applied to horrific or physically repulsive material. In the Sixties, satire is transformed into farce, with its emphasis on the grotesque, and comedy itself becomes an object of attack. At the same time, an element of artifice is always present. Traditional forms, modified by the intersection with ideological activism or even inverted, remain recognizable.

At times these two categories overlap. Shaw occupies a middle ground, using both forms interchangeably. Comic techniques are frequently employed in Agitprop, while a highly politicized social realist like Edward Bond has written plays that are formally comedies. But in Agitprop, as in Bond's plays, the comic elements are subordinated to a direct depiction of social issues. The overall focus is realistic. On the other hand, although a playwright like Peter Barnes deals with typically political themes, his treatment transposes history into farcical fantasy and turns even the victims of Auschwitz into tap-dancing clowns. Similarly, Pinter's late plays are overtly political, while his early drama has been interpreted as part of the existential Absurdist movement. Yet the overriding tone of his work as a whole is comic, and even his political pieces retain an undidactic detachment. Only in the case of Oscar Wilde does a dramatist's work split into quite separate categories – the poetic symbolism of *Salomé* being incompatible with his satiric social comedies in style as well as focus.

Contrasting with the primarily social concerns of realistic and comic drama, there is a third line of development represented by playwrights whose values are existential or spiritual. From this universal perspective, materialistic questions or political solutions are largely irrelevant. Their characters tend to be mythic or, like Beckett's figures, to embody 'all mankind'. Alternatively their themes are religious, whether dealing with martyrdom or questioning the existence of God. This is the area traditionally associated with poetic drama, although increasingly towards the end of the Twentieth Century – particularly with the feminist assertion that the personal is political – poetic plays have taken on political dimensions.

Up to the end of the Nineteenth Century, poetry had been accepted as the only proper medium for treating significant moral issues on the stage. The rationalism and political focus that Shaw promoted effectively marginalized this mythic or religious drama; and it is the one type of British theatre where Shaw has had no influence. Instead, these playwrights almost all turned to European *avant-garde* models. Although their work is broadly speaking 'poetic' in subject matter or theme, it is not necessarily written in formal poetry. Verse has become only one option among alternatives that include Symbolism, Surrealism and fantasy. As with the other generic categories discussed – Realism and Comedy – conventional ideas of Poetic Drama have broken up under the impact of modernism. So these quasi-poetic dramatists use a variety of styles to communicate their vision.

Here too there are points at which this type of theatre approaches the other forms. Indeed, Christopher Fry's plays are specifically comedies; yet their essential characteristics are verse dialogue and religious themes. Beckett uses farcical elements. Auden and Isherwood, or John Whiting present a strong political aspect, as do playwrights such as Caryl Churchill or Sarah Kane (whose work is treated in this category since doing so offers fresh insights, although it might normally be thought of as an extension of the naturalistic/political line in British drama). But in Beckett's plays, or even in Auden and Isherwood, these qualities are incorporated in a psychological landscape, or given a surreal dimension.

1.3 Critical treatment

These three categories form the structure for this study of twentieth-century British drama. After opening with Shaw, we examine the development of realism from the turn of the last century to the present – by far the most significant genre, corresponding to the highly politicized nature of a century marked by global wars and ideological revolutions – followed by discussions of comedy, then the varieties of poetic drama. Both return to 1900, tracing the way these forms respond to the changing social context through the century. The outlines that emerge in the shape of recurrent subjects or motifs, as well as patterns of influence, far outweigh the resulting separation of playwrights who, although contemporaries, are working in different styles. However, these historical relationships are indicated by the chronological table, which prefaces the text.

In addition to novels and poetry, many of the playwrights covered have written for other media besides the stage: Arden for radio, Griffiths and Hare for television, Pinter and Edgar for film, Beckett and Stoppard for all three. However, these new media have different formal criteria from the theatre. Thus, radio or film scripts are usually only mentioned in passing since the focus here is theatrical. Similarly, taking drama as the subject has meant excluding musicals, pageants (which were a popular vogue in the first decade of the century), or – with some exceptions – unscripted performance art.

History is by nature selective, the past always a foreign country where the landscape becomes increasingly simplified with distance. Particularly with such a transient art form as theatre, where a play only reaches its full expression in performance, the majority of what occupies the stage at any given time vanishes from view almost as soon as the final curtain comes down. So in general when one travels back through the decades, only those whose plays continue to be revived remain visible. By contrast, the present appears so crowded that it is sometimes hard to tell the wood from the trees. One function of an overview is to correct this imbalance. A leading Edwardian like Somerset Maugham, though now usually remembered solely as a novelist, gains in significance. By contrast some contemporary drama-tists seem to have less intrinsic interest, and become omitted or barely rate a mention. The wide-angle lens imposes such discriminations, but what goes into or gets left out of the critical picture is necessarily a question of personal judgement.

At the same time, any historical continuum – even one conceptually bounded by a complete century – is open-ended. Although hindsight appears to offer some certainty about the situation in 1900, this may be challenged by revisionists who reveal the importance of plays that have been overlooked (as has happened to some extent with recent feminist re-evaluations of women dramatists at the turn of the last century). And of course new plays are continually appearing. These may well alter the critical judgement of some contemporary playwrights, while those who are now at the beginning of their careers will alter the picture as they become established. In that sense, this book – like its predecessor, *Modern British Drama: 1890–1990* – should be read as a report-in-process.

Notes

1 William Archer, review of Pinero's *The Profligate* in *The World*, 1 May 1889; Pinero, 'The Modern British Drama' in *The Theatre*, 1 June 1895, p. 347.

2 For a discussion of Surrealist drama and Beckett's position in the French *avant-garde*, see Christopher Innes, *Holy Theatre*, Cambridge, 1981, pp. 72ff and 202ff. Beckett's emphasis on inner reality, creating a drama of the mind, is typically Surrealist. Although Beckett's stasis is the antithesis of Artaud's visionary violence, he shares Artaud's aim of creating a dramatic form 'fixed in its least details . . . as strict and calculated as any written work', working on the same principle that 'the theatre, less than any other means of expression, will not suffer improvisation' – which motivates Beckett's notorious control over directorial interpretation of his plays (Antonin Artaud, *The Theatre and Its Double*, New York, 1958, p. 111 and *Oeuvres Complètes*, Paris, 1961–74, vol. III, p. 206). Since the focus of this study is British drama, only the English texts (in Beckett's own translation) will be discussed.

2

Defining modernism:
George Bernard Shaw (1856–1950)

If any single person set the course of British drama over the last hundred years, it was Shaw. Through longevity and the sheer volume of his dramatic as well as critical writing, reinforced by a carefully cultivated public image and a talent for controversy, he occupied a central position from the opening of the modern period to his last play in 1950. He not only influenced the general direction taken by other British dramatists, particularly in the early formative decades, but was largely responsible for defining its terms. Where the trend-setting landmarks of modernism in France were Maeterlinck's *La Princesse maligne* in 1889 or Jarry's *Ubu roi* in 1896, and in Germany Wedekind's *Spring's Awakening* in 1892, the corresponding shift in English theatre was represented by Shaw's lecture on 'The Quintessence of Ibsenism' (1890) and *Widowers' Houses* two years later.

As a result Ibsen – or rather Shaw's perception of his work – became the decisive factor. Elsewhere in Europe symbolic or psychological themes predominated. By contrast, the mainstream of serious English drama has continued to reflect the realistic treatment of social questions that Shaw promoted; and Shaw continued to acknowledge Ibsen's example throughout his career. Not only was a bust of Ibsen given a dominant place in the central scene of *The Philanderer* (written in 1893, though not performed until 1905), but the Norwegian dramatist is canonized as 'Saint Ibsen' in the utopian future of *Back to Methuselah* (1923). Underlining the connection, Shaw even specified 'Ibsenite whiskers' for his own *alter ego*, Captain Shotover, in his 1929 production of *Heartbreak House* for the Malvern Festival.[1]

2.1 The reinterpretation of Ibsen

Shaw's debut as a dramatist was closely linked with the hotly debated introduction of Ibsen's naturalistic works to the English stage. 'The Quintessence' followed closely on the first English performance of *A Doll's House* in 1889 by Janet Achurch, who also acted the lead roles in several of Shaw's plays, including *Candida* (1897). Archer, who suggested the plot of Shaw's first play, established his reputation as the leading theatre critic of the period by championing Ibsen; while it was J.T. Grein's Independent Theatre – which was modelled on Antoine's Théâtre Libre and had opened in 1892 with the English première of *Ghosts* – that produced *Widowers' Houses* the same year. Both plays attracted similar terms of abuse from morally outraged critics; and in categorizing early works like *Widowers' Houses* and *Mrs Warren's Profession* (1902: written 1894) as 'Unpleasant' Shaw was consciously aligning them with Ibsen in stressing the way an explicit depiction of 'crimes of society' was intended 'to force the spectator to face unpleasant facts' by recognizing 'his own photograph'. Yet at the same time, as Archer later remarked, though Shaw was 'in some sense [Ibsen's] disciple . . . as for imitating him – well, I can only say I wish he had'.[2]

Shaw's perceptive, if idiosyncratic analysis in 'The Quintessence of Ibsenism' focused on the iconoclastic aspect of Ibsen's themes: his attack on life-denying idealism, and his constructive employment of internal contradictions. In particular, it pointed to an overall pattern in Ibsen's work, where a secondary problem in one play became the main subject of the next, or an apparently positive stance (such as the moral principles of Dr Stockman in *An Enemy of the People*) was subsequently revealed as negative (Gregers Werle's destructive 'demand of the ideal' in *The Wild Duck*). What Shaw singled out was a strategy for trapping the audience through sequentially manipulating their responses, discrediting socially conditioned reflexes, exploding the conventional moral categories of hero or villain, and forcing spectators to re-evaluate their assumptions about the world around them: 'so that Ibsen may hunt you down from position to position until you are finally cornered'.[3]

This was to become Shaw's characteristic technique. As an analysis of Ibsen's dramaturgy it may be misleading. But it is an accurate description of Shaw's own use of inversion to reveal the contradiction between accepted systems of belief and actual behaviour. As he defined it, 'I deal in the tragic irony of the conflict between real life and the romantic imagination'. In addition to this thematic overlap, Ibsen's characterization provided the fundamental principle on which both Shaw's criticism of Victorian drama and his own dramaturgy were based: that realistic play construction or settings were invalidated unless each of the figures was represented from his or her own perspective, independent of moral stereotyping.[4]

This can be seen particularly clearly in *Saint Joan* (1924), even though as 'a Chronicle' its form is very different from naturalistic drama. The whole action is structured by the reversal of expectations. In scene 1 a lord of the manor, the conventional strong man, is cowed by 'a slip of a girl'; in scene 2 the helpless and cowed Dauphin is transformed into a prince; in scene 3 certain defeat by the English 'Goddams' becomes victory; and in scene 6 Joan is burnt despite the Inquisitor's conviction of her innocence and the saving compromise worked out by the ecclesiastical court. At the same time, as Shaw pointed out in a programme note for the London première, 'it cannot be too clearly understood that there were no villains in the tragedy of Joan's death. She was entirely innocent; but her excommunication was a genuine act of faith and piety'.[5]

The 'Quintessence' was more a manifesto for Shaw's approach than an objective appreciation of Ibsen. The true nature of his debt can be illustrated by *Candida* (1897, written 1894), which he later described as 'a counterblast to Ibsen's *Doll's House*, showing that in the real typical doll's house it is the man who is the doll'.[6]

There seems to be very little connection between the two plays on the surface. Ibsen's heroine, treated as a doll by her hypocritical husband, sees through the sham of a marriage founded on mutual deceit. Although Nora flirts with a family friend, he is dying of inherited syphilis and offers no way out of her predicament. She opts for independence, walking out on husband and children despite the warning of her confidante, who has experienced the demeaning loneliness of a single woman in a male-dominated society. By contrast to the shocking nonconformity of Ibsen's resolution, Shaw described his dramatic situation as 'absurdly commonplace'. Candida is the centre of a love triangle. Married to an earnest and prosaic clergyman, she is adored by a youthful and idealistic poet, who urges her to fulfil her spiritual potential by running away with him. Morell is a muscular bourgeois, idolized by all the women in his congregation. Eugene Marchbanks is the unworldly and over-sensitive son of an Earl, who plays on Candida's maternal instincts. Where Ibsen's play has a melodramatic plot, with forgery, blackmail and a fatal letter, Shaw's drama is almost completely discussion. As he summed it up:

the plot – what there is of it – consists mainly in the persistent efforts of Eugene to attain his object, and the growing fear of Morell – the clergyman – that he may succeed . . . Morell finally decides to ask his wife to decide between them . . . And the wife replies that she will 'choose the weaker'.[7]

In both plays the set is dominated by a painting of the Virgin, but its thematic significance is very different. The first production of *A Doll's House* had a picture of Mary with the infant Jesus, symbolizing the sentimental idealization of Motherhood that Nora must reject to find personal fulfilment. Shaw uses Titian's *Assumption of the Virgin* to represent the true spiritual potential of his heroine. In a theatrical review written shortly after completing the play, he cited Titian's painting as the supreme example of 'a union of the flesh and the spirit . . . triumphantly beautiful', and at the climax of the action his stage direction specifies that Candida '*goes to the fireplace* [directly beneath the picture] *and stands there leaning with her arm on the mantlepiece, and her foot on the fender*'.[8] Since Titian portrays the Virgin with her hands raised, one foot lifted and her face turned up towards God, the pose is as close as could be presented in a naturalistic context.

The visual parallel is clearly intended to indicate that the archetype is incarnate in the human reality of the character. Instead of condemning social morality and its theological patterns as enslaving illusions, as Ibsen did, Shaw reinterprets the ideal in recognizably religious terms. On the surface, Candida's clergyman husband may appear the 'pompous windbag' that Nora's husband is indeed revealed to be. But Morell's virtues of Christian socialism are real, as is his dependence on his wife; and Candida chooses to stay with him, rather than embracing the romantic fulfilment offered by the young poet.

Both plays are designed to challenge conventional assumptions. However, where Ibsen denies the audience's moral expectations, Shaw discredits expectations derived from literary norms. The outcome of *Candida* denies both the Tristan and Isolde/Antony and Cleopatra ideal, where the world is well lost for love, and the conventions of nineteenth-century Domestic Comedy, in which the husband would have proved his superiority to the poetic lover. Here it is not romantic escapism (poet and aristocrat versus materialistic respectability) that attracts Candida, but Marchbank's emotional need for her, while she chooses her husband because he is the weaker of the two men. At the same time, this resolution also inverts the *Doll's House* model, where emancipation is a door slammed on domesticity.

Two additional points underline the difference from Ibsen. Instead of being integrated in the naturalistic background, Shaw's picture of the Virgin dominates the setting by its scale and central placing. Its symbolic significance is also made explicit. Similarly Shaw's play is programmatic in the way the figure of the poet is treated. Hypersensitive, fearful, physically puny, Marchbanks is a typical Shavian contrast to the conventional hero. Yet he represents both the idealist and an ideal. Rejected by Candida, the mother/madonna who has inspired him, his sentimental poetic fantasies are transformed into a selfless quest for perfection. His rival, her unromantic clergyman-husband, may embody socially responsible morality, but Marchbanks stands for the vision that informs it. In him is seen the 'promise of higher powers than [a practical reformer, even if he is also a professional 'man of God'] can ever pretend to . . . it is in the poet that the holy spirit of man – the god within him – is most godlike'.[9] Although the poet's art is not to be mistaken as a substitute for political action, it provides the essential motives for social change. By creating images of a more desirable state, Shaw (like Marchbanks) follows Shelley in serving as a 'legislator of mankind'.

Beneath the realistic surface, Shaw's thrust is allegorical, and in other plays this is given even more direct expression through his use of mythological archetypes as the basis for the action. The Galatea theme, for instance, not only underpins *Pygmalion* (1914) but resurfaces in the short farce *Passion, Poison and Petrifaction* (1905) and in the concluding section of *Back to Methuselah* (1922) as well. Its treatment, too, is less unconventional than it might seem initially. In the original myth the sculptor's love for his statue was a punishment for his scorn of living women, and his penitential faithfulness was rewarded by reciprocated love once the statue came to life. In Shaw's versions the Pygmalion figure is either rejected when the artificial woman he has shaped achieves real consciousness, transformed into a statue himself, or killed by physical contact with his creation. Even though the established pattern is denied, the effectiveness of the inversion depends on maintaining the symbolic significance of the original. The distance between this intrinsically allegorical type of drama, and naturalistic theatre, is indicated by Shaw's response when he saw Antoine's production of *The Wild Duck*: 'there was no character in the acting at all as we understand it, but it was a bustling piece of work (to conceal Ibsen's deficiencies, no doubt)'.[10]

When Shaw outlines his 'formula of making the audience believe that real things are happening to real people', it may sound like a typically naturalistic principle; and on one level his plays present an apparent transcription of reality.

Historical fact is stressed in the prefaces to *Caesar and Cleopatra* (1906) and *St Joan* (1924). His advice to a director staging a revival of *You Never Can Tell* in 1922 was 'Don't muddle about mid-Victorian costumes, take the exact date [1895, the year the play was written] and look up . . . the fashions'.[11] In addition, as well as the satiric portraits scattered through Shaw's plays, major characters are frequently based on well-known people. Candida's husband is based on James Mavor Morell, a Scottish theologian and friend of Tolstoy's , while the Oxford phonetician Henry Sweet appears as Professor Higgins in *Pygmalion*, the classicist Gilbert Murray as Cusins in *Major Barbara* (1905), and T. E. Lawrence as Private Meek in *Too True to Be Good* (1932). Similarly, the underlying context of *Caesar and Cleopatra* (1906) is British Imperialism in Africa, while *Saint Joan* (1924) reflects the contemporary struggle for Irish independence beneath the quasi-nationalist war in fifteenth-century France. Joan's martyrdom parallels the execution of Roger Casement, the Anglo-Irish patriot, while her canonization in 1920 – which was the overt inspiration for the play – also contains a modern political reference, La Pucelle having been the major propaganda symbol used by the French military during the First World War.

Yet Shaw's aim is not documentary. The inclusion of recognizably real figures or immediately relevant political contexts in his plays is seldom more than a way of gaining credibility for fundamentally artificial situations. Alternatively, the factual references are designed to lend conviction to an intellectual proposition that the action is designed to illustrate.

The distinction between this use of fact, and documentary theatre, can be seen in Shaw's use of settings. In the Darwinian terms of naturalistic drama, the material environment conditions an individual's personality. It is both an active agent determining the characters' fates and authentication of it. However, rather than focusing on the social milieu, Shaw's rooms represent their inhabitants' philosophical context or signal their intellectual capacity. For instance, the statuette of Shakespeare together with the engravings of theatrical personalities, Henry Arthur Jones and Pinero '*but not Eleanora Duse nor anyone connected with Ibsen*' in Act I of *The Philanderer*, not only contrasts with the bust of Ibsen in Act II, but represents a very different mental attitude to the anatomical display and the Rembrandt 'School of Anatomy' (specifically a photograph) of Act III. Similarly the heads of John Bright and Herbert Spencer that decorate Ramsden's study in *Man and Superman* are the physical signs of his political and scientific opinions, while the single shelf of cheap French novels – outnumbered by hunting trophies – in the so-called 'Library' of *Arms and the Man* all too accurately represents the intellectual pretensions of the Petkoffs. In fact the oblique relationship between Shaw's drama and more usual naturalistic forms can be summed up by the way he defined *Major Barbara* in the author's statement that opens the 1944 film version: 'It is a *parable*... Some of the people in it are real people, whom I have met and talked to. One of the others may be YOU. There will be a bit of you in all of them.'[12]

A further example of the way Shaw diverged from Ibsen while apparently following his example is the emphasis on discussion. In Shaw's view, Ibsen's major innovation was taking the exposition-complication-development-crisis-denouement structure of the Scribean Well-Made Play, and substituting discussion for the denouement. The value of this change for modern drama lay in the necessity of presenting opposing viewpoints of equal weight – the precondition for any real argument – which precluded simplistic moral judgements and left the audience with questions rather than the illusory satisfaction of artificial closure. Shaw went on to observe that discussion need not be limited to the conclusion, but could interpenetrate the plot. This indeed was so characteristic of his own approach, that William Archer felt it necessary to warn Shaw against a tendency to 'non-stop logomachy', and complained he was misinterpreting Ibsen's plays to legitimize his own practice: 'it suits you to call them unconstructed, whereas in fact they are the most complex jigsaws ever invented'.[13]

The verbal focus of Shaw's drama is underlined by his descriptions of *Misalliance* (1910) as 'A Debate in One Sitting' or *Major Barbara* (1905) as 'A Discussion'. It reflects a preference for ideas over incident, for a rational theatre, the object of which was explicitly to make people think. In this he can be seen as continuing the line of 'prose preachers' (the phrase of Francis Jeffrey, editor of *The Edinburgh Review* from 1802 to 1829) that ran from Carlyle and Ruskin to H. G. Wells and G. K. Chesterton, and extended into the twentieth century through the *New Statesman* (which Shaw helped to found).

Instrumental in furthering political causes, such as the abolition of the slave trade or parliamentary reform, *The Edinburgh Review* embodied the nineteenth-century faith in the spread of knowledge and the power of argument as the motor of social progress. Like the French *Encyclopédistes*, its contributors established something approaching a secular religion, based on a belief in reason and the perfectibility of man. Carlyle, whose concept of grand historical patterns led him to attack the individualistic rationalism of *The Edinburgh Review*, projected the image of the writer as sage and prophet. Ruskin's writings, which were more concerned with ethics and spiritual salvation than their ostensible subjects of painting and architecture, established a moral framework for art as well as proposing art as an antidote to the materialism of the Victorian age. In addition, there was the liberal ideal of debate as the highest form of social enjoyment, which came from John Stuart Mill (whose Dialectical Society was one of the many discussion clubs Shaw attended in his London youth).

The way Shaw brought these polemic and contradictory principles together is characteristic, and helps to explain the combination of his logical and rationalistic style with romantic evolutionary ideas derived from Schopenhauer and Nietzsche. The key is his confidence in the progressive force of intellectual enlightenment which – despite their ideological differences – he shared with H. G. Wells. For Wells, the purpose of writing the *Outline of History* was to create a 'directive synthesis'; and it is the same belief in moulding the future by exposition and exhortation that is expressed in Shaw's prefaces. For him, the stage was a pulpit. Yet, although more than one of his plays is described as a 'Sermon' in its original subtitle, the propaganda is for rationalism – while the underlying message is romantic, and the discussion-play principle of multiple viewpoints is inherently dynamic, engaging the emotions. As Shaw himself defined it:

My plays do not consist of occasional remarks to illustrate pictures, but of verbal fencing matches between protagonists and antagonists, whose thrusts and ripostes, parries and passados, follow one another much more closely than thunder follows lightning. The first rule for their producers is that there must never be a moment of silence from the rise of the curtain to its fall.[14]

What this implied in terms of performance was essentially anti-naturalistic. Having begun his career as a music critic, Shaw worked for melodic rhythm and 'wrote long rhetorical speeches like operatic solos, regarding my plays as musical performances'. When he was able to exercise control over productions, he insisted that the speeches should contrast in tone and pitch, and selected actors for the musical quality of their voices. In *Arms and the Man* (1894) this set a soprano as Raina against a contralto as Louka. In the Hell sequence of *Man and Superman* (1903) Shaw annotated the speeches with different musical keys, crochets and crescendos for the actor playing Don Juan. Even in an apparently more naturalistic play like *Pygmalion* (1914) his rehearsal notes specify 'Tenor register' or 'Andante tranquilo'.[15]

The common view of Shaw as a mere verbal artist, one-sidedly rational, and therefore sexless or mechanically clever, is mistaken. Quite apart from his emphasis on emotive musicality, his prompt books show a deep concern with precise movements and spatial relationships. His view of the right balance between physical representation and dialogue can be indicated by his comment that 'staging the play . . . positively takes longer than writing it'. As a result, directors and designers from Sir Lewis Casson to Harold Clurman and Jocelyn Herbert have testified that his stage directions – which were frequently rewritten to incorporate the precise way the action was realized in production – provide the optimum physical dimension for his plays.[16]

In fact Shaw's stage pictures and subtext frequently undermine his verbal emphasis. For example, while rehearsing *Man and Superman*, Shaw turned around a suggestion from Robert Loraine (playing Tanner to Lillah McCarthy's Ann Whitfield), who 'wanted to deliver the great speech about the tyranny of mothers enthroned in the motor car, with Lillah somewhere under the wheels with her back to the audience'. Shaw reversed this to create a visual image of biological drive as superior to intellect: 'I immediately saw the value of the idea, and put Lillah in the car in a fascinating attitude with her breast on the [steering] wheel, and Loraine ranting about on the gravel'. Placing the woman literally in the driving seat revealed the irrelevance of male rhetoric, pointing up the dismissive line of the chauffeur as 'the new man' – 'Never you mind him . . . He likes to talk. We know him, don't we' – which is restated more explicitly over a quarter of a century later in the final stage direction of *Too True To Be Good* (1932). After the concluding sermon by the Clergyman-Burglar, in which he declares 'I must preach and preach and preach no matter how late the hour and how short the day', Shaw draws an ironic parallel to his own practice: *'But fine words butter no parsnips... The author, though himself a professional talk maker, does not believe that the world can be saved by talk alone. He has given the rascal the last word; but his own favorite is the woman of action'.*[17]

Such a statement is clearly borne out by the number of female protagonists in Shaw's plays and by their status as embodiments of human vitality against an artificial system of morality. From *The Philanderer* (written in 1893), where the emancipated woman is the sexual aggressor, through *Saint Joan* (1924), where she is 'an illusionproof genius', to *The Millionairess* in 1936, these figures are conceived in opposition to conventional norms. In Shaw's view it was false idealism – translated into politics, ethics or religion – that prevented social progress by distorting reality; and the root of this idealistic perspective lay in the sentimental values of 'the romantic imagination'. These were encapsulated in literature. So it is quite logical for his most illusion-proof man of destiny to approve the burning of a library that contains 'the memory of mankind' in *Caesar and Cleopatra*. For Shaw's Caesar, books substitute dreams for doing, so that (anticipating the epigraph of Jarry's *Ubu enchaîné*, published only one year later) it is necessary to 'destroy the past... and build the future with its ruins'. Though Shaw never took his iconoclasm to Jarry's extreme, his work was explicitly designed as a liter-ary antidote, replacing the simplifications of melodrama with 'a genuine scientific natural history'.[18] In practice, however, this meant using pre-existing conventions rather than experimenting with new forms, as the subtitles to many of his plays indicate: 'An Almost Historical Comedietta', 'An Intentionally Unfinished Comedy', 'A Brief Tragedy'.

2.2 Refurbishing nineteenth-century styles

The most appropriate way of attacking misleading values was to under-mine the standard dramatic forms through which they were expressed and promoted. For Shaw, the most glaring example was the romantic inflation of Shakespearean 'Bardolatry' (his term for the exaggerated nineteenth-century respect for the Bard's poetic genius). And *Caesar and Cleopatra* (written 1898, first public production 1906) is designed as a disillusion-ing contrast to both *Julius Caesar* and *Antony and Cleopatra*, which he saw as shedding fictitious glory on robbery, starvation, disease, crime, drink, war, cruelty, cupidity, and all the other commonplaces of civilization that drive men to the theatre to make foolish pretences that such things are progress, science, morals, religion, patriotism...[19]

The comparison set up by the title is reinforced by the preface with its assertive title of BETTER THAN SHAKESPEARE? Shaw claims to be following Shakespeare's precedent in portraying historical figures from a specifically modern perspective. But taking his portrait of Caesar from the nineteenth-century German historian Mommsen has quite different implications from the way Shakespeare used Plutarch as his source. The contrast emphasizes that Shakespeare's interpretation is determined by the ideas of a particular time, rather than having the status of universal truth. It also implies that from a historical perspective the views of the past have been superseded.

The equivalent theatrical updating would have replaced Shakespeare's bare stage and imaginative evocation by the type of scientifically objective naturalism that marked Shaw's preceding plays. Instead, *Caesar and Cleopatra* reproduces the visual spectacle typical of the late-Victorian actor-managers' Shakespearean productions. With its crowd scenes and elaborate scenery, it echoes Beerbohm-Tree's staging of *Julius Caesar* in Alma-Tadema's monumental settings, or the production of Tennyson's *The Cup*, a Roman spectacular produced by Henry Irving in the same year (1898) that Shaw's play was written.

Although Shaw's spectacle gives a public dimension to the action, re-minding the spectator that Caesar controls the armies and the destiny of nations, it is in fact treated ironically. For instance, in the programme he drew up for the copyright performance (15 March 1899), Shaw listed two spectacular scenes – The Burning of the Library and The Capture of the Pharos – as if they were actually to be presented, even though these actions are off-stage. Typical of nineteenth-century advertisements for popular his-torical or military melodramas, the spectacle also corresponds visually to the pseudo-poetic language of the Egyptians in the play, and it contrasts with the down-to-earth common sense of Shaw's Caesar in the same way that their linguistic inflation is undercut by an outsider. The original opening gave an example of this process in miniature:

BELANZOR By Apis, Persian, thy gods are good to thee.
THE PERSIAN...Double or quits!

The explicit contrast is with Shakespeare, ridiculing his idealization of tragic figures who are incapable of distinguishing 'between life and rhetoric'

(Brutus) or degraded by romantic self-indulgence (Antony). But the form of the play provides a critical perspective on the popular historical dramas of the time. Deriving from Sardou, these represented the debased end-product of the Shakespearean ethos, 'in which love is . . . alleged as the motive of all the actions presented to the audience', trivializing significant events while creating heroic acting parts out of histrionics. Shaw's deflationary treatment of Caesar is as much a deliberate antithesis to this tradition as his alteration of history to omit any possibility of Cleopatra bearing Caesar's son (Caesarion) by making her a pre-pubescent girl. The emphasis on Cleopatra's childishness rules out any love interest. Indeed, the sole purpose of having Caesar forget to even say goodbye to Cleopatra in the final scene is to poke fun at such romantic expectations.[20] He also refuses the other typical action of a melodramatic hero: revenge. The target of the play is as much what Shaw called Sardoodledom as Bardolatry.

The emphasis of the revised prologue is on the relevance of this 'History Lesson' (as Shaw subtitled his play) to the contemporary audience. Unlike escapist romances – and indeed costume-play treatments of Shakespeare – where remoteness lends the characters a spurious grandeur, to the author/ god figure of the 1912 prologue 'men twenty centuries ago were already just such as you'. At first glance this looks similar to the later Brechtian use of history, and Shaw's anachronisms function in much the same way as Brechtian alienation effects. But while Brecht's staging devices remove the illusion of reality from the performance, the crowd's cry of 'Egypt for the Egyptians', Apollodorus' motto of 'Art for Art's sake', or the report of Caesar 'settling the Jewish question' jar us into recognizing the topicality of the past.[21] (Although these wordings may sound startlingly modern, Shaw stresses that all the apparent anachronisms can be justified historically.)

Conversely the debate on colonialism and carving up Africa, at its height when the play was written, is reflected in the imperialism of Classical Rome. The audience are required to put themselves in the position of the colonized through the figure of Brittanus, Caesar's morally self-righteous secretary with his philistine '*eye-to-business*'. At the same time they are shown their responsibility as members of a colonial power to subjugated peoples who (like the Egyptians) may have a civilization of their own that is superior to that of their conquerors, however childish or immoral it may seem to outsiders. Similarly in Shaw's other Roman play, *Androcles and the Lion* (1913), the persecution of the Christians clearly parallels the suffragette struggle for female equality. Shaw's point is that the essential issues do not change. The counter-productive multiplication of the revenge ethic, the limits of controlling society through force, or the need for realism in a ruler are universal truths.

As Shaw has his protagonist say in *Caesar and Cleopatra*, to break the spiral of violence a 'man will have either to conquer the world as I have, or be crucified by it', which explains why Caesar consciously goes to his death in Rome. The methods of the man of action are ambiguous, since Caesar's power for clemency is based on the blood shed by his agents. The deed for which he condemns Cleopatra's murderous servant to death parallels the expedient killing of Pompey by his own henchman. What makes him superior is the ability to judge 'independently of convention and moral generalization'; and the play's counterpoint to Shakespeare – as well as its ironic use of nineteenth-century spectacle – is intended to give the audience an equivalent perception by showing 'old facts in a new light'.[22]

However, the use of 'old' dramatic forms for this purpose was intrinsically problematic. Duplicating a conventional model was all too liable to reproduce its effect as well. As Shaw openly acknowledged, a play like *The Devil's Disciple* (1897) 'does not contain a single even passably novel incident. Every old patron of the Adelphi pit would... recognize the reading of the will, the oppressed orphan finding a protector, the arrest, the heroic sacrifice... the courtmartial, the scaffold, the reprieve at the last moment'. What was intended to make these melodramatic elements appear unnatural was the rationale given to the characters. Dick Dudgeon does not sacrifice himself for love (unlike Dickens' Sydney Carton in *A Tale of Two Cities*) – instead, he allows himself to be mistaken for Judith's husband because the British would execute him in any case once they found out who he was. The husband in whose place he has been arrested docs not follow the expected pattern, in which he would give himself up to save his substitute. The British general turns out to be human rather than the tyrannical monster of rebel propaganda; and Dick is set free. Beneath the reversed clichés is a drama of conversion, allegorically represented by the exchange of coats – the patriotic rebel turns into a preacher; the parson becomes a revolutionary soldier. Yet the conventional expectations were so strong that it was all too easy for productions of the period to reverse this inversion, returning the action to straight melodrama, as Shaw complained.[23]

To avoid such misrepresentation, he found it necessary to resort to broad parody, as in *Androcles and the Lion*. In the 1913 Granville-Barker/Shaw production, Lillah McCarthy was cast as Lavinia, to underline the contrast between Shaw's independent-minded heroine and the tragic Christian maiden in *The Sign of the Cross* (1895), which had been one of her most popular roles. But the massacre of Christians in the Coliseum was presented as 'music hall, with a very casual call boy, who announces the number of each turn'.[24]

In *Arms and the Man* (1894) the 'glaringly artificial devices' that Archer deplored were less liable to being misunderstood than they were in *The Devil's Disciple*. But they were also perhaps less appropriate as examples of the turn-of-the-century audience's moral clichés since – in place of the 'hackneyed ones of our own time' – here the 'stage tricks' were, as Shaw himself remarked, the 'forgotten ones' of the 1860s.[25] The conventions being played on are those of Military Melodrama, in which the brave win the fair, love incites heroism and romantic passion rewards gallantry.

The opening of *Arms and the Man* appears to substantiate this idealism, with the starlit snows of the mountains outside the window and the figure of '*a young lady, intensely conscious of the romantic beauty of the night, and of the fact that her own youth and beauty are part of it*', who proclaims 'that the world is really a glorious world for women who can see its glory and men who can act its romance! What happiness! What unspeakable fulfilment!' Reports of a victory appear to validate these 'heroic ideals'. Even the entry of a fugitive officer from the defeated enemy through the bedroom window is a stock plot device of the genre.[26] There are undermining touches, even in this first scene: the presence of cheap Western manufactured objects in the oriental exoticism of the setting, the implication that Raina is aware of herself as the image of a romantic heroine, a slightly exaggerated enthusiasm in her exclamation marks and an implied question in her assertion 'that Sergius is just as splendid and noble as he looks!' Yet the audience are clearly expected to take this picture at face value. By creating identification, Shaw is able to attack the spectators' 'romantic imagination' in revealing the pretentious unreality of the characters' ideals. At least, this is the overt intention.

The deceptively simple action, which is forwarded by conventional mechanisms like a misplaced love-message, revolves around two interlocking triangles. In each Sergius, presented literally as the picture of a hero in the opening scene, is set against a materialist: a cynical servant and a defeated mercenary. In the first triangle, the servant Nicola's willingness to give up his fiancee to Sergius for financial independence, preferring to have her as a paying customer than as a wife, would mark him as despicable. Yet his renunciation of 'the higher love' is the only realistic option, given Louka's clear attraction to Sergius. So the audience is forced to agree with Bluntschli, the Mommsenite anti-hero, who hails Nicola as 'the ablest man . . . in Bulgaria'. However, it is worth noting that we accept this unconventional judgement only because our sentiment is appealed to.

Similarly, although Shaw inverts conventional expectations in Bluntschli's approach to war as a trade, revealing his cowardice as intelligent self-preservation, the action is resolved by a second reversal that restores cliché in a slightly modified form. What had been presented as the actions of a realist are exposed as

An incurably romantic disposition ... I climbed the balcony of this house when a man of sense would have dived into the nearest cellar. I came sneaking back here to have another look at the young lady when any other man of my age would have sent the coat back.[27]

In the second triangle, the apparently unmilitary Bluntschli, whom Raina despises in the opening scene for carrying chocolates instead of cartridges and for admitting to fear as a reason for not preserving her reputation by climbing back down the drainpipe, accepts Sergius' challenge to a duel over Raina with equanimity because of his skill as a fencing instructor.

But Shaw not only reverses stereotypes like this; following Oscar Wilde, he inverts his reversals. The realistic Bluntschli dismisses Sergius' operatic cavalry charge as suicidal – yet his own 'correct principles of scientific warfare' led to regiments being routed and major-generals killed.[28] Even though openly acknowledged as fraudulent posturing, Sergius' heroic attitudes are approved because they cut through class barriers and unite him with the servant-girl. Instead of the immature seventeen that Bluntschli (and the audience) have taken her for, Raina is revealed as twenty-three – and, as a mature woman, her romanticism has to be taken seriously. Changing the subtitle to 'An Anti-Romantic Comedy', as Shaw did, may have made the play's intentions clearer. Yet it could be adapted to an Opera Bouffe (as indeed it was in *The Chocolate Cream Soldier*) without making any major changes in action or situation.

Shaw's reliance on romantic convention is a long way from the 'genuine scientific natural history' claimed in the preface. His inversion of clichés creates a kind of double meaning that reintroduces sentimental values beneath the rational surface, and sets up a counter-current of emotion which undercuts the logic of the play. This contradicts the view of Shaw as a purely rational writer, sexless and mechanically witty: as he pointed out, 'any fool can make an audience laugh. I want to see how many of them ... are in the melting mood.'[29]

So all the characters of *Arms and the Man* vindicate romanticism. Even the realist Bluntschli falls in love; and though his sentiments will always be tinged with scepticism, he offers Raina a true basis for the sublime fantasies she has renounced. Sergius becomes a genuine hero and patriot when he finds a girl who knows what patriotism is since she has no property to confuse it with and believes in him as a man, not an ideal. In the same way, the stock formulae of melodrama ridiculed in *The Devil's Disciple* are also used to create serious emotional moments. Even in *Caesar and Cleopatra* the promise of Antony's coming hints at alternative values to Caesar's political world, giving his rationalism a tinge of sadness since he can only fulfil Cleopatra's longings through a proxy who will throw away everything for which he is sacrificing himself. This double vision is built into the subversive use of obsolete dramatic forms that Shaw invented with *Arms and the Man*.[30] The costume sketches Shaw prepared for the first production not only demonstrate his concern for naturalistic detail, but act as a touchstone to show how far from Naturalism his dramaturgy actually was. In choosing the contemporary Serbo-Bulgarian war as a setting, he paid careful attention to factual accuracy, yet in itself this was characteristic of Victorian imperial melodramas about the Crimea or the Sudan, where 'local colour' was part of the romantic attraction. It only served to mislead critics into believing the satire was directed against unsophisticated foreigners in the far-off Balkans (i.e., confirming the superiority of a London audience), while the discrepancy between the heightened acting Shaw demanded and the deflationary characterization was simply perceived as 'grotesque'.

Here operatic style was part of what was being burlesqued. It was inherent in the dramatic context. (One of Shaw's rehearsal notes to Lillah McCarthy advised that 'what Raina wants is the extremity of style – style *Comédie Française*, Queen of Spain style...', while he required the actor playing Sergius on a Vedrenne-Barker tour to 'act...as if he were acting Hamlet...Let him read Byron – Sarah – the Corsair, etc. etc. – and play and feel like that, leaving the irony to come from the words.') However, the style he wanted for all his plays was rhetorical and exaggerated. He criticized Barker's production of *Androcles and the Lion* as being too quiet, slow and detailed, and a rehearsal picture clearly shows the flamboyant display he valued in 'the drunken, stagey, brass-bowelled barnstormers my plays are written for'.[31]

Shaw may here be following his own advice that a director should exaggerate in demonstrating to avoid imitation from the actor. Yet he consistently rejected the understated naturalistic approach: 'My plays require a special technique of acting and, in particular, great virtuosity in sudden transitions of mood that seem to the ordinary actor to be transitions from one "line" of character to another.' Actors who worked with Shaw testified to his reliance

1 A demonstration of operatic acting: Granville-Barker, Lillah McCarthy and Shaw, in rehearsal of Shaw's *Androcles and the Lion* at the Court, 1912

on traditional 'stage speech' that used a wide range of pitch and melody together with 'rhetorical punctuation' to convey meaning. However, this calculated stylization was capable of giving 'the illusion of "natural" speaking, though with far more significance'. It corresponded to Shaw's conscious sacrifice of verisimilitude for veracity in making his characters more articulate than their real-life counterparts although it also gave an automatic comic emphasis that was sometimes inappropriate. In the first production of *Saint Joan*, for instance, his direction of the Epilogue resulted in 'overplaying . . . that . . . shocked the audience far more than was necessary'.[32] But in general the heightening of gesture and diction gave an intrinsic theatricality to the otherwise static Discussion Play, where the dynamism comes from ideas rather than physical action.

Shaw directed most of the first London productions of his major plays from *Arms and the Man* in 1894 to *Saint Joan* in 1924, frequently in collaboration with others who became the director of record – Granville-Barker, Beerbohm Tree, Lewis Casson – and was thus able to set the performance style for his work. Though this may seem an early example of a particularly modern practice, which points forward to Bond and Hare's productions of their own work and (again) parallels Brecht, the trend towards replacing the actor-manager by the dramatist-director was already established. Shaw was following Henry Arthur Jones, Boucicault and Pinero, the same dramatists whose plays he inverted to attack romantic idealism. In almost every way, therefore, his work has to be seen as an extension of the nineteenth-century theatre, though antithetical to its ethos.

As Shaw comments in a prologue, written for a 1916 performance of *Fanny's First Play* (1911), which parodies the critics' response to his work:

I loved the actors; copied all their ways;
But oh! I got so tired of the plays,
Always the same . . .
Not one of them a bit like real life . . .
Just think! In real life what is it touches us?
Stories about ourselves, not about duchesses.[33]

The reference is to *Pygmalion* – and to Boucicault's *Grimaldi; or The Life of an Actress* (1862), elements of which had reappeared in Pinero's *The Times* (1891). In Boucicault's comedy an old stager trains a Covent Garden flower-girl as an actress, introduces her to high society at a garden party, and makes her a duchess (by revealing himself as a Neapolitan duke and adopting her as his heir) so that she can marry into the aristocracy. The title of both plays refers to the transformer rather than the transformation on which the action focuses, and it can hardly be coincidental that the flowers Shaw specifies for Eliza's basket are violets, Violet being the name of Boucicault's heroine.

By contrast with a play like *Saint Joan*, which depended for its effect on public belief in 'the melodramatic legend of the wicked bishop and the entrapped maiden' that it countered, here Shaw's model would have been generally unfamiliar. Instead, *Pygmalion* presents an antitype of the popular Cinderella story, which had been reworked so many times that it had achieved the status of social myth. The essential strategy of the play is still the denial of expectations, but these have to be raised before they can be undercut. So both halves of the contradiction are built into the plot.

Eliza does not pass herself off as a lady at the first social test (Mrs Higgins' 'At Home' day). But rather than realizing her origins, the representatives of society are misled by snobbery into taking her conversation about an aunt being 'done in' and even her use of 'bloody' as the height of fashion. We are not shown her triumph at the Ambassador's garden party – despite Barrie's reproaches to Shaw about lost opportunities, and the insistence of Beerbohm Tree, who co-directed as well as playing the part of Higgins. Such a spectacular vindication is avoided precisely because it would have been the pivot of a conventional drama. And in particular, Eliza does not marry Higgins, although Shaw had to add a sequel to underline this because 'people in all directions . . . assumed, for no other reason than that she became the heroine of a romance, that she must have married the hero of it'.[34]

The necessity for reasserting what the revised last line explicitly states – that Eliza marries Freddy – is by no means due only to the way Beerbohm Tree contradicted Shaw's intentions, signifying his romantic attachment by throwing flowers to Eliza as the curtain fell. Shaw may claim that the popular misreading was merely further evidence of 'imaginations enfeebled by their lazy dependence on the ready-mades and reach-me-downs of the ragshop in which Romance keeps his stock of "happy endings" to misfit all stories'.[35] But the play is in fact ambiguous. This is partly because Shaw's desire to create false expectations led him to focus on the relationship between Eliza and Higgins in a way that forecasts romantic fulfilment. In the original text, Eliza not only searches for, but keeps the ring that Higgins had hurled into the fireplace, while at the end Higgins remains confident of her return. Beyond this, even the revised ending retains a sense that life has passed Higgins by when Eliza walks out, leaving him isolated and sterile. She is becoming Superwoman, while he can only imagine the Superman.

The anti-romantic intention also contrasts with the thrust of Shaw's previous plays. Higgins has demonstrated his need for Eliza, and it was precisely this quality that won Candida for her husband, while as one critic commented, 'everybody who . . . has read or seen his classic on the duel of sex, "Man and Superman", could guess . . . the way in which such a Galatea plays cat and mouse with her fore-doomed Pygmalion'. More significant still, the drama of conversion is incomplete. Higgins quite clearly represents a mechanistically distorted view of life, with '*a life-size image of half a human head, shewing in section the vocal organs*' occupying a prominent place in his laboratory, and his reductive dismissal of beautiful women as 'blocks of wood'.[36]

The imaginative balance of the drama requires his humanization, emotional depth added to clinical intellect, as a counterpoise for Eliza's transformation in which understanding and culture are added to the physical warmth and feeling of the gutter. Not surprisingly, stage photos from a 1914 Polish production to a 1954 London revival show Higgins and Eliza clasping hands with soulful looks or smiling into each other's eyes. In fact, the 1938 film of the play, which Shaw approved, ended with Eliza's reappearance in Wimpole Street and Higgins demanding 'Where the devil my slippers are!' It is a relatively short step from this to the affirmation of romantic values in the musical adaptation of *My Fair Lady*. Yet the real centre of Shaw's play is social, not sentimental.

In passing off the cockney flower-girl as his 'creation of a Duchess Eliza', Higgins' experiment demonstrates the artificiality of class distinctions. Society defines peoples' value by externals, and the Eynsford-Hill family show the stupefying repression of keeping up appearances. Their pretensions rule out any useful employment, and the only 'respectable' option open to Eliza as a lady is the equivalent of prostitution: selling herself in marriage. The moral superiority of 'the undeserving poor' is pointed up by the parallel transformation of her father (appropriately named Doolittle) from a dustman to a middle-class lecturer on ethics. Wealth forces him into hypocritical conformity, which negates the very originality that qualified him for the position.

This contrast between social appearances (form) and personal integrity (content) is inherent in Shaw's use of language as a metaphor for civilization. Higgins claims that 'to take a human being and change her into a quite different human being by creating a new speech for her' abolishes 'the deepest gulf that separates class from class and soul from soul'. But in this he confuses signifier and signification. As a phonetician, all he can teach is pronunciation and grammar, and in doing so he transforms a feeling individual into a statue (by definition appreciated for solely external qualities). For Shaw, 'Galatea comes to life' only 'when Eliza emancipates herself' from Higgins.[37] There is no essential difference between the gaudy ostrich feathers of the dressed-up flower-girl and the bejewelled finery of the 'duchess'. The real transformation is internal, the realization of spiritual being or – in semantic terms – sense, and this independence comes from the self-respect fostered by Pickering, Higgins' *alter ego*, who as author of 'Spoken Sanscrit' is concerned with linguistic meaning rather than the social geography of vowel sounds.

2.3 Thesis drama and metaphysical comedy

Throughout his career Shaw's treatment of plot, situation and character was conditioned by his attack on the fallacies of the sentimental or melo-dramatic imagination. However, his real target was not the outdated dra-matic forms themselves, which he drew on for so much of his material, but their political dimension. In his analysis, capitalism imposed such ignorance through division of labour that 'we should die of idiocy through disuse of our mental faculties if we did not fill our heads with romantic non-sense out of illustrated newspapers and novels and plays and films. Such stuff . . . falsifies everything for us so absurdly that it leaves us more or less dangerous lunatics in the real world'. On the other hand, his social focus, which in *Widowers' Houses* had been immediate and specific – 'to induce people to vote on the Progressive side at the next County Council election' – broadened into the metaphysical.[38] This shift was already established in the play that greeted the new century, *Man and Superman* (1901–3). Subtitled 'A Comedy and a Philosophy', it also encompasses the whole range of Shaw's dramatic strategies.

Only about 40 per cent of the total text of *Man and Superman* is drama in any conventional sense. A symbolic dream sequence takes up approximately another 30 per cent, and the remainder is devoted to the prose appendages. These offer a direct statement of Shaw's thematic aims, theses and theatrical tactics. The Preface outlines the premise of the play, and revolves around three paradoxes. Social change is indispensable, but progress depends on two incompatible urges. The ethical imperative of the artist, 'selected by Nature to carry on the work of building up an intellectual consciousness of her own instinctive purpose', conflicts with the biological drive to evolution through reproduction. The essential quality of the Don Juan figure is, like the diabolism celebrated in *The Devil's Disciple*, 'a sense of reality that dis-ables convention' and makes him the antagonist of religious orthodoxy or the nonconformist bourgeois conscience which has superseded it. As always in Shaw, the biological role of women makes them the aggressors, and by definition the victors in the duel of the sexes. So Don Juan's sexual pursuit is illusory. It has therefore become replaced by a dedication to ideas. The immoralist is now the moral revolutionary. At the same time this affirmative position is undercut because the intellectual, whether a modern Don Juan or the Shavian artist, has to be immune from the 'tyranny of sex' in order to express 'the philosophic consciousness of Life'. Being atypical, his analysis of sexual relationships is necessarily distorted. As a result, any play where these are specifically the subject can only be a record of personal illusions, which have no validity except in 'providing data for [a] genuine scientific psychology'.[39] The paradoxical nature of this argument is clearly designed to challenge the reader into thinking, rather than providing a direct commentary on the play. It is an intellectual exercise, conditioning potential spectators to approach *Man and Superman* as the 'pit of philosophers' that Shaw wanted for his drama.

This is also the only one of all Shaw's dramatic prefaces to address an individual. In calling it 'An Epistle Dedicatory' Shaw is evoking seventeenth- and eighteenth-century literary practice, presenting himself in the character of 'Author' (and representing the 'Patron' he addresses as the amoral wit incorporated in the traditional Don Juan figure). He also identifies himself with the protagonist so clearly that in the 1905 première Granville-Barker acted the part of Tanner as a recognizable image of the youthful Bernard Shaw. In short, the Preface is conceived in dramatic terms and referred to as no less 'suitable for immediate production at a popular theatre' than the philosophic fantasy of the detachable third Act dream sequence. It serves as an ironic demonstration both of Shaw's assertion that the 'argument' (the old-fashioned word for the 'plot' of a literary work) was the soul of drama, and of the challenge to melodramatic moral categories inherent in the play of ideas.

As Shaw remarks in connection with 'The Revolutionist's Handbook' (supposedly written by Tanner and printed as an appendix to the play), 'all my characters, pleasant and unpleasant . . . are right from their several points of view; and their points of view are, for the dramatic moment, mine also. This may puzzle people who believe that there is such a thing as an absolutely right point of view, usually their own.'[40] However, such a statement is more a tactical description than a declaration of principle. To the extent that Shaw is adopting a self-projection in aligning himself with the persona of Tanner, the thrust of the complete *Man and Superman* text is openly didactic. Even in an almost farcical comedy like *Arms and the Man*, the weighting of the action clearly indicates which set of attitudes or opinions are 'right'; and here we are given a compendium of aphoristic maxims that explicitly illustrate the intellectual genius of the protagonist.

The main thesis of 'The Revolutionist's Handbook' is that social progress can only be achieved by the systematic evolution of the whole human population into 'Supermen' through eugenics. It establishes one half of the argument that has served as a touchstone for serious political drama throughout the century: social structures reflect the nature of a people, so that transforming man is the first requirement for changing the world. The counter-proposition is the Darwinian one espoused by Brecht: that environment determines personality, and political change is therefore the precondition for reforming human nature. From this standpoint 'Vital Economy is the Philosopher's Stone', while social economy, the Fabian politics of persuasion Shaw had supported, and the violence of class warfare that he opposed, are equally dismissed as 'fundamentally futile'.[41] Over-statement, used for shock effect, is characteristic of Shaw's bravura style. But here this has been inflated into extravagant simplification, in character with the fictional mask of Tanner that Shaw has adopted – an ironic *alter ego*, whose intellectual rhetoric is exposed by the comic action as a form of sexual display, dismissed by the woman as irrelevant once its purpose has been served in winning her.

Shaw defined the business of an original thinker as being the testing of outworn codes, and Tanner's theories should be read as provocative propositions rather than dogmatic solutions. Paradoxically, the thesis of *Man and Superman* can only be realized by the 'defeat' of its proponent. The evolution Tanner calls for subjugates him to the biological urge, which negates his intellect.

In contrast to the usual Shavian approach, in this play the stock formulae of nineteenth-century theatre on which the social comedy is based are not inverted. Deriving the motive for the action from a will – although here Tanner inherits an unwanted guardianship over Ann Whitfield, the woman who is determined to marry him, rather than money – is a deliberate cliché. So is the overt use of coincidence, which makes the chance-met bandit Mendoza the lover of Straker's sister and Violet's father-in-law an investor in his brigandage, or the recognition scene in which the pregnant Violet's apparently immoral love affair is revealed to be with her 'missing husband'. The motorcar that struck the 1905 audience as such a novelty is not only a piece of Belasco-realism, but typical of the melodramatic deployment of nineteenth-century technology like railway trains on the stage. Even the mainspring of the action, the reversed love chase where woman is the aggressor, has its antecedents not just in Shakespeare (as the Preface claims), but in the superannuated contralto maidens of Gilbert and Sullivan. The only change, as Shaw himself points out, is that 'the jests of Mr W.S. Gilbert' are treated

'seriously'. The conventional comedy is 'the jam that has carried the propaganda pill down' (Shaw's description of his dramatic method in defending
what he insisted were 'music hall entertainments, thinly disguised as plays'
against complaints about his didacticism).[42] The plot follows completely
traditional patterns. The apostle of 'the Life Force', as well as the unmarried
mother-to-be whom he (mistakenly) claims as an example of the higher
morality of biological instincts, are paired off in conventional couples.

In fact, all nonconformist positions represented in the play are subverted.
The philosopher proposes to replace sex by intellect, extending the 'knowledge of ourselves' that 'creates new minds as surely as any woman creates
new men'. As the embodiment of 'Vital Genius', Ann is predatory, ruthlessly
entrapping the chosen male. Marriage is not a question of love, but the eu-
genic basis for evolving the future 'Supermen' of the play's title. However,
all these potentially shocking elements are undercut. When Tanner tries to
justify Violet, she repudiates his doctrine of free love, while Ann's mating
with Tanner occurs within a socially sanctioned framework.

Even the structure of the play is not nearly so unconventional as it seems.
The incompatibility of extended philosophical discussion and courtship
comedy has a thematic rationale, although it was responsible for the mixed
response to the first production. Indeed, those critics who condemned
Tanner as a 'glib anarchistic babbler' whose speeches distracted from 'amus-
ing perplexities', or dismissed *Man and Superman* as 'talk, talk, talk', were
repeating the judgement of the last lines.[43]

Shaw constructed the play so that it could be performed without
Act III, claiming the dream sequence could only be staged at Bayreuth or
Oberammergau. It was omitted by the Stage Society première in 1905, but
even at that date he was discussing ways of realizing 'the void' in performance:
'with top lighting in the manner of Craig' (whose 1903 production of *The
Vikings at Helgeland* had been praised for its 'strange supernatural element'
that 'utterly precludes any notion of realism') and black velvet, draped over
stools to merge with the black backdrop, for achieving the effect of figures
'seated, absurdly enough, on nothing'. And he directed the dream sequence
himself only two years later as an independent one-act drama. In the preface
Shaw had referred to this as the essence of the play, and although the comedy was already being criticized as dated by the time of the 1911 revival, the
Hell scene became one of Shaw's most popular pieces. The 1907 première
was hailed as 'very much the best thing that Mr. Shaw has done'. Charles
Laughton's US tour in the 1950s drew a better box office than even such
a successful musical as *South Pacific*, which was touring at the same time.

Indeed the response to the 1981 National Theatre staging of the complete text, with Daniel Massey, was that the comedy had dated badly, but this third act retained effective dramatic life because of its verbal brilliance.[44]

The dream sequence reverses the picture of Tanner. Where the worldly comedy deflates his heroic pretensions, hell reveals his true moral stature; and – as with all Shaw's inversions – we are given an example within the script to alert us to the thematic reversal. Borrowing from another Mozart opera, *The Magic Flute*, in hell an elderly crone is transformed into a youthful ideal and revealed as Ann's *alter ego*. The Papagena motif also serves to challenge expectations on a further level, implying that the Dona Ana whose revenge forms the main action of *Don Giovanni* is the true soul-mate of Don Juan. In fact the essence of the underworld is that it apparently turns everything inside out. 'Hell is the home of honour, duty, justice, and the rest of the seven deadly virtues. All the wickedness on earth is done in their name.' It is also 'the home of the unreal and of the seekers for happiness', conditions that breed the false romantic vision of 'universal melodrama'.[45] And the bandit-as-businessman, who justifies highway-robbery by spurious socialist principles, is its logical overlord. Mendoza, Mammon and the pleasure principle go together: the Devil incarnate. The opposite state, to which Shaw's Don Juan escapes (exchanging places with Mozart's statuesque Commendatore who prefers the home comforts of hell) is a purely intellectual heaven.

This division of the dramatic world into three levels points to the moral nature of Shaw's dramatic universe; and the way this conditioned his analysis of society can be illustrated by *Major Barbara* (1905), the play Shaw was writing at the time he directed *Man and Superman*. Here the elegant drawing-room of Act I stands for the hell of unreality. Beneath the naturalistic veneer its upper-class inhabitants, freed from the cares of existence to indulge their sentiments and aspirations to virtue, are those without purpose, and their life of ease is financed by the devil figure of a merchant-of-death arms-manufacturer. Earth, where people who 'play at being heroes or ... saints' are 'the slaves of reality' and subject to 'hunger and cold and thirst, age and decay and disease', is clearly the Salvation Army shelter for the economically exploited of Act II. Heaven is represented by the utopian factory of the last scene, in which 'the masters of reality ... work instead of playing' and 'face things as they are'.[46] The identification of the idle pleasures of the cultured classes with a state of spiritual damnation becomes a constant reference in Shaw's plays, reaching its fullest expression in *Heartbreak House*.

Yet beneath this judgemental consistency his moral valuations are characteristically relative. Compare the treatment of the Devil in *Man and Superman* and *Major Barbara*. Both are explicitly Mephistophelean (a reference underlined by Shaw's directions to Louis Calvert, who played the original Undershaft), and serve the same function as 'cunning tempter'. But where the first actually is the devil in Shaw's terms, being the anarchist of the pleasure principle, the other is 'the Prince of Darkness' only from the illusory perspective of the socially moralized people who inhabit 'hell' (and have therefore not only made evil their good, but by definition mistake good for evil). The cynical and self-indulgent projection of Mendoza has a red halo. By contrast, Calvert's Undershaft was made up to look like Shaw, a tradition continued by Robert Morley in the 1944 film version of *Major Barbara*. Indeed, the image of Undershaft as a diabolical trombonist leading the Salvation Army in a Dionysian march was based on Shaw's own appearance at the 1905 Salvation Army festival in the Albert Hall, where he won their approval for his play by joining the hymn singers on the stage.

To the operatic devil of *Man and Superman* – who espouses the enjoyment of life – evolution is an illusion, and the dominant human drive is a death wish. By contrast, Undershaft – whose business promotes death – is 'the instrument of a Will or Life Force' at the controls of the engine of social progress (whereas the Salvation Army is the tool of enslaving exploitation).[47] Although some of the reviewers identified him with Carnegie, this seems as far from the mark as Shaw's clearly mischievous and misleading claim that Undershaft was the double of the Turkish Ambassador. Being an instrument of the Life Force, and as a devilish creator of paradoxes, Undershaft is filling the role of Shaw as a dramatist. If he represents anyone else, it is the Swedish industrialist Nobel, whose actions parallel the Undershaft argument that the capacity for destruction promotes equality and social progress. Nobel, who endowed his Peace Prize in 1901 with the profits from nitroglycerine, the most advanced high explosive of the time, specifically founded the prize as a challenge to the world to solve the problems his inventions created. And, indeed, Undershaft's thesis was supported by an analogy even closer to home, since *Major Barbara* was written the year of the Russo-Japanese war, in which the Imperial Russian fleet was sunk by armaments supplied by the British firm, Vickers: a tangible demonstration of a small nation defeating a colossus through modern weaponry, and one which could be interpreted as an oppressed people liberating themselves from colonialism.

The way Shaw reversed conventional views on arms-manufacturers (evil) and religious charities (good) was equally provocative in its attack on the audience's moral assumptions. The prominence of the artillery gun and the dummy soldier, sprawled '*like a grotesque corpse on the emplacement*' in the final scene, underlines Undershaft's earlier description of himself as 'a profiteer in mutilation and murder'. The destruction of human life clearly has to be swallowed if the worker's paradise is to be accepted. However, the shocking demonstration of the cost is almost over-successful as an alienating device. Gilbert Murray, the classical scholar who provided the model for Cusins, pointed out that 'the audience tended to feel the end as merely a giving up of all religion, and morality, too, for that matter, instead of realizing that it was a change from one system to another'. In response Shaw declared Undershaft was unequivocally 'in the right', and his film version added a scene to clarify this:

CUSINS Nitrates to make explosives
UNDERSHAFT Or sulphates to fertilize fields...Come Euripides, you think that nitrates are good for nothing but death. Now I'll show you the sort of life they produce...

after which the camera cuts simplistically to happy children playing in lush countryside.[48]

The abandonment of ironic ambiguity in this late reworking of the text indicates the significance that the biological doctrine of 'Life's incessant aspiration to higher organization, wider, deeper, intenser self-consciousness, and clearer self-understanding' held for Shaw. As his 1933 postscript to *Man and Superman* states, 'the evolutionary theme of the third act...was resumed by me twenty years later in the preface to *Back to Methuselah*, where it is developed as the basis of the religion of the near future'.[49] This evangelical line is a fundamental quality of Shaw's work. Religious idealism, perhaps the inheritance of his Irish background, combines with secular belief.

2.4 Symbolism and politics

Perhaps surprisingly for a comic playwright, who consistently debunks establishment creeds, the underlying motive of Shaw's drama is evangelical. This tends to be overlooked by criticism that fails to distinguish between orthodoxy, and the religious instinct. In fact, Christ is a recurring reference in Shaw's work. Barbara speaks the last words from the cross against the accompaniment of the Salvation Army marching band; and the doubly ironic choice of music here (not only opera, representing worldliness, but the tune of the chorus celebrating that most disastrous of all marriages from *Lucia di*

Lammermoor) underlines the parallel between the despairing Barbara and the forsaken Christ. Saint Joan, risen again from the dead after being cruci-fied at the stake for her belief in individual and national self-determination, also repeats Christ's words. In *Back to Methuselah*, the brothers who develop evolutionary theories are evangelists spreading 'the Gospel'. The 1933 preface to *On the Rocks*, which follows Shaw's principle of representing 'exponents of the drama as saying . . . the things they actually would have said if they had known what they were really doing', even includes the trial scene for 'a modern passion play'. In this Jesus is Shaw's spokesman against Pilate's ar-gument that stable government brings progress, presenting the doctrine of evolution in traditional religious terms: 'I am the embodiment of a thought of God . . . God is within you.'[50]

Almost all Shaw's social comedies are dramas of conversion. Although this is not religious in any conventional sense, the symbols that express such existential changes frequently are. For example, the thematic basis of *Pygmalion* is represented in the set for the opening scene, where the juxtaposition of church and market embodies the contrast between material and spiritual values. However, this straight use of religious symbolism is atypical. More usually its meaning undergoes a radical transformation, as with the reinterpretation of biblical figures in *Back to Methuselah*. Here the Serpent (like the 'diabolist' Undershaft) is the agent of evolution, and specifically female – as are almost all Shaw's characters standing for creative consciousness: 'You imagine what you desire; you will what you imagine; and at last you create what you will.' By contrast, Cain is the father of 'civilization' (as defined in the aftermath of the 'Great War' by twentieth-century political leaders in Part II of the play).

This unwieldy 'metabiological pentateuch' takes Shaw's approach to its log-ical conclusion. From his early dramatic criticism, which he viewed as 'a siege laid to the theatre of the XIXth Century by an author who had to cut his own way into it at the point of the pen', to his theatrical inversion of stock situations and standard figures, Shaw was attempting to explode the conventional limits of the British stage.[51] In *Back to Methuselah* this polemic aim produced a five-part, eight-hour history of the world from the Book of Genesis to 'As Far As Thought Can Reach' (or an arbitrary AD 31,920). Even with extensive doubling, any performance requires a minimum cast of twenty-six and elaborate multiple sets. So the expense of producing this epic is almost prohibitive, while the demands on audience stamina make wide public appeal unlikely. It must be counted the most ambitious work of twentieth-century theatre; and its relative popularity is a vindication of

Shaw's drama. The première was in New York, at the Theatre Guild (1922), rather than England. The Birmingham Repertory production which followed in 1923 was successful enough to transfer to London; and the complete play has been revived with surprising frequency: at the Court in 1928, the Arts Theatre in 1947, at the National Theatre in 1971 (although the two-evening performance was condensed to one during the run), and in Canada at the Shaw Festival in 1986.

In portraying the triumph of mind over matter it is the most intellectual of Shaw's plays; and in accordance with his focus on thought, conventional plot elements are completely absent. Events, whether the murder of Abel or the First World War, are not just off-stage, but in the past. They serve only as a basis for discussion. Cain may threaten violence, but obeys the command to 'sit and listen'. The Napoleon of the future gives up his pistol without a struggle. The euthanasia of an anachronistic Elderly Gentleman, who suffers terminal culture shock from his contact with the higher beings into whom humanity has evolved, is carried out painlessly by telepathy. The whole cycle, which Shaw (the 'perfect Wagnerite') compared to Wagner's *Ring*, is structured by thematic *leitmotifs* instead of plot.

The most significant of these through-lines were reinforced in the Theatre Guild production by Shaw's suggestions for doubling combinations. With the same actor playing Cain, Burge, Burge-Lubin, Napoleon and Ozymandias (Shelley's 'King of Kings'), one polarity is established. Each of these represents different aspects of the popular misconception of the 'Superman' in progressively more parodied forms, from the heroic conqueror to the general whose fame is measured by the numbers of his own men killed, or the statesman whose principles are self-interest, both of which are combined in the final megalomaniac puppet. The counterpoint to this is the female representative of the Life Force: Eve as the primal mother, Mrs Lutestring who becomes the first tricentenarian, the Oracle, the She-Ancient. This linkage of characters provides a multidimensional, developing image of conceptual archetypes. Yet at the same time, as the same actor reappears, the roles become successively less individual. Characterization vanishes along with plot. By the final section the figures are purely symbolic – the classically pastoral Strephon and Chloe – while in place of a fully developed dramatic action the audience are warned, 'This is going to be a busy day. First the birth. Then the Festival of the Artists.'[52]

The play not only explicitly preaches a 'religion that has its intellectual roots in philosophy and science just as medieval Christianity had its intellectual roots in Aristotle'. It presupposes the effectiveness of Shaw's evangelical aims, since ideas have demonstrable effects in this dramatic world and simply overhearing or reading about the Brothers Barnabas' 'gospel' is not only sufficient to 'unconsciously convert' characters. It also acts as a trigger for biological change, and all Shaw's techniques of persuasion are deployed – clearly with the hope of evoking a comparable process in the audience. (As Shaw's *alter ego* argues at the pivotal point of the play, 'We can put it into men's heads that there is nothing to prevent its happening ... Spread that knowledge and that conviction; and as surely as the sun will rise tomorrow, the thing will happen.') And it is hardly coincidental that Shaw has named his visionary believers after the First Century Cypriot missionary, Barnabas, a companion of St Paul.[53]

In addition to teaching-by-example, almost the complete gamut of Shaw's comedy is introduced. The intellectual challenge of the familiar Shavian inversion, the insertion of anachronisms to imply that modern attitudes are barbaric, the satiric diminution of authority figures on stage to give spectators a sense of superiority – all are explicitly used as functional tools, since 'Creative Evolution doesn't stop while people are laughing. Laughing may even lubricate its job.'[54] As a result the manipulative basis of Shaw's comedy is more obvious than in his other plays. The parody of contemporary 1920s politicians (Lloyd George and Balfour) in Part II may be an effective way of gaining assent for the propositions of the Barnabas brothers. But accepting an idea simply because demonstrable fools miss the point does not make it either rational or necessarily true. The farcical childishness of the governing figures of the immediate future, the representatives of ordinary humanity a thousand years later, or even the idealized youths and nymphs of the final section, is intended to create identification with the 'longlivers' and the 'ancients', who otherwise are conceived as being by definition beyond our comprehension.

The inherent flattery of this characteristic (though usually more disguised) approach is even explicit at one point, where the English are proposed as 'potentially the most highly developed race on earth', and thus the natural genetic pool for the evolutionary 'miracle' precisely because 'we are just a lot of schoolboys', who never reach maturity during the normal life span. However, this technique is also integral to the major theme. If the syllogism is followed through, convincing the audience that they have the potential for genetic evolution is sufficient to initiate the 'new departure in the history of the race'; and the audience's ability to associate with these 'supermen' is an implicit confirmation that the change has occurred.[55]

Specific details of Shaw's science fiction have of course been outdated. Both the pace and direction of modern progress are very different from the future projected for AD 2170. Generally his forecasts underestimate technological advances and social development, as with assumptions about the continued existence of the British Empire, school-leaving ages (rising to 13), communications and transport based on the telephone operator and the parachute, or farmers in smocks. Conversely, changes in the quality of life are wildly overestimated in the picture of a society without class or colour discrimination, poverty or war. On one level, whether these predictions are right or wrong is irrelevant. They reflect Shaw's bias towards internal change as the measure of progress, and express the mind over materialism theme of the cycle. However, along with the comic treatment of any figures who oppose evolution, they undercut credibility. And although in other contexts this might not matter, here Shaw has deliberately raised the imaginative stakes by making intellectual conviction such an essential part of the theme itself.

In a comparable way, the further Shaw projects his thesis into the future, the more archaic it appears. The miniature classic temple and the dress of the idealized youths and maidens dancing in the groves of 30,000 years hence, which '*resembles Greece of the fourth century B.C., freely handled*', is not even an original cliché. The perfect inhabitants are echoes of H. G. Wells' dumb Arcadians at the end of *The Time Machine*, while the overall picture is unmistakably reminiscent of the dance dramas mounted by Dalcroze at Hellerau before 1914.

Even so, Shaw's thesis has a compelling visionary quality. The premise of 'The Gospel of the Brothers Barnabas' is that human history has been one continual descent 'down all the steps of this Jacob's ladder that reached from paradise to a hell on earth', marked by progressive reductions in life span.[56] Since the nadir has been reached in the Twentieth Century, man's choice is between extinction – or Shaw's 'evolutionary fable', in which humanity regains immortality and the maturity that it allows. On a literal level, the final state envisaged is in fact a return to the primal state of innocence: a utopian Garden of Eden without sex, science or animal life forms, where even the Serpent is a ghost. As a symbolic statement, it indicates that the play itself is returning to the level of myth in presenting Man as God, supremely rational and consciously fulfilling his evolutionary destiny. Yet at the same time – as in *Arms and the Man* or *Pygmalion* – there is an emotional counter-current to this apotheosis of intellect. From the viewpoint of this perfect future, the passionate sexuality represented by Cleopatra makes her a malign puppet, incompatible with the artist who resurrects her and dies on coming into contact with her. Yet, as in the episode of the Elderly Gentleman, the underlying tone of the ending is loss. Like him, the unregenerate audience could never feel at home in such a completely sane world, where there is no place for Shakespeare's poetry. Shaw is revealed as the last of the Romantics.

There is, of course, a great deal of wish-fulfilment in such a formulation. Yet the hope that the cycle so confidently expresses is a useful antidote to the usual view that Shaw's career is marked by stages of increasing despair as the prospect of reforming society along Fabian principles receded with the Boer War, then vanished into the mud and slaughter of the First World War. *Back to Methuselah* should not only be seen as an extension of *Man and Superman*, but as a counterpoint to the play that immediately preceded it, *Heartbreak House*, which was completed in the depths of the war and has been called 'The Nightmare of a Fabian . . . a picture of failure'.[57] There may indeed be a failure of vision in Shaw's portrayal of the future, which makes the optimism of *Back to Methuselah* seem unconvincing. But its idealism informs his criticism of the present.

Heartbreak House (1919) is a compendium of all Shaw's major themes. Plays like *Getting Married* (1908) and *Misalliance* (1910) anticipate its picture of terminal decline in Edwardian England. It extends ideas which had been expressed in *Man and Superman:* that even a superman with all the power and prestige of the state at his command 'cannot raise a people above its own level'; that competitiveness and its extreme form, war, although 'instruments of selection and evolution in one epoch, become ruinous instruments of degeneration' at the next stage of development; and that seeing any advance in present conditions as progress is 'the Illusion of Illusions'.[58] The education of Ellie Dunn, which is the through-line of *Heartbreak House*, starts at the disillusion with romantic love of Raina in *Arms and the Man* or Judith Anderson in *The Devil's Disciple* (Act I), and passes through Major Barbara's conversion to Undershaft's values in the misalliance with Mangan (Act II). The repentant burglar, who makes his profit from being caught in the act, is yet another variation on the Doolittle figure in *Pygmalion*. The play can therefore be seen as the culmination of Shaw's work, even though he continued writing for over thirty years after its completion. Indeed, right at the end of his career, in the *Shakes versus Shav* puppet play (1949), Shaw asserted that *Heartbreak House* was his *King Lear*, the masterpiece by which his achievement should be measured.

The preface claims Chekhov as the model for depicting the moral vacuum of English society, but the play bears much the same relationship to *The Three Sisters* as *Candida* did to Ibsen's *A Doll's House*. *Heartbreak House* may also have two sisters and a potential sister-in-law. However, the parallel between Shaw's Ellie Dunn and Chekhov's lower-class Natasha, both of whom take over the household into which they marry, is offset by the Shakespearean

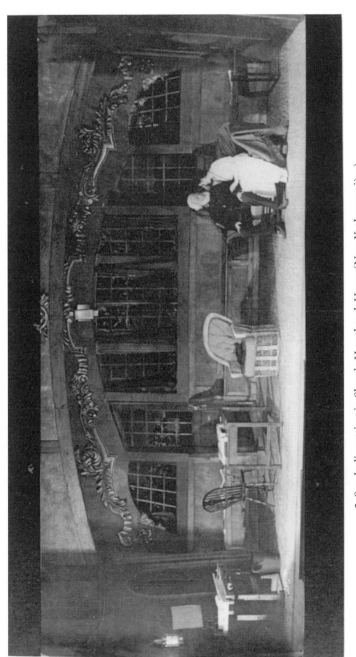

2 Symbolic setting in Shaw's *Heartbreak House* (New York première)

analogy. Here, Ellie represents Cordelia to the Goneril-and-Regan daughters of Captain Shotover, Hesione Hushabye and Lady Utterwood, whose names are representative rather than realistic. Her eventual marriage is purely mystical; and the fatal duel that destroys one sister's hopes in Chekhov's play is here imaginary, with Hesione's husband shadow-fencing against himself. Although the dialogue proceeds along Chekhovian non-logical, musical lines, the subtext that is so central to Chekhov's drama is completely absent. The characters' inner states are the subject of obsessive conversation. The surface realism may be similar to Chekhov, from the detailed country house setting to the presentation of a composite picture, in which the social group as a whole is the protagonist and the focus on trivialities exposes the emptiness of the characters' idle existence. Yet both the figures and their physical context are openly allegorical in a way that Chekhov's never are.

The interior of Captain Shotover's home is recognizably nautical, his workroom being the stern galley of what is explicitly referred to as 'this ship we are all in. This soul's prison we call England', while the contemporary reviewers were quick to spot 'one of our Premier's Cabinet supermen' (Lord Devonport) in Mangan. On the symbolic level this is clearly the ship of state. But despite the specifically English context and the obvious relevance of the image to a maritime power (Britannia ruling the waves), Shaw sees his aimless, self-alienated family as a microcosm of 'cultured, leisured Europe' as a whole, metaphorically fiddling while their civilization burns.[59] The Chekhovian reference has a purely thematic function. Echoes of *The Cherry Orchard* or *The Three Sisters* are used to expand the play's focus. And simply showing that 'the Russian manner' is appropriate to the English scene – Russia being not only the most distant area of Europe, but a country in which revolution had already changed the face of society – is a way of demonstrating that all the traditional ruling classes are in the same boat.

Shaw's subtitle, 'A Fantasia in the Russian manner', expresses the true style of the play. Chekhovian naturalism is contradicted by a symphonic structure: a fantasia being a musical composition in which form is subservient to fancy, a dream vision. Quite apart from the symbolism, the perspective is so intrinsically poetic that at one point the dialogue can shift into chanted verse without breaking the tone. Similarly the action falls into three moods or movements, in each of which Ellie is paired with a different man. Romantically attracted to the storybook Marcus Darnley whom Hector pretends to be, she learns that his boasted exploits are imaginary, and that he is prosaically married to Hesione. Disillusioned, she renounces love for money in the repulsive shape of Boss Mangan, the tycoon who has ruined her father. When he is shown up as equally hollow, she links her fate with her 'soul's captain', only to find that Shotover's spiritual powers are merely spirituous. In fact, the apparent naturalism of the play is ironic since everything in it is illusory. As Ellie discovers,

> Marcus's tigers are false; Mr Mangan's millions are false; there is nothing really ... true about Hesione but her beautiful black hair, and Lady Utterwood's is too pretty to be real. The one thing that was left to me was the Captain's seventh degree of concentration: and that turns out to be –
> CAPTAIN SHOTOVER Rum.

On one level *Heartbreak House* is straightforward social satire. Much of Shaw's verbal wit is comparable to Oscar Wilde, and the paradoxical balance of the characters' repartee is typical of Wilde's comedy, as in a sequence like

MRS HUSHABYE Well, why shouldn't my husband be a handsome man?
RANDALL ... One's husband never is, Ariadne.
MRS HUSHABYE One's sister's husband always is, Mr Randall.[60]

However, as here, the satiric tone is exaggerated, verging on self-parody; and the characters are both more artificial than Wilde's, with non-individual names – Hushabye, Utterwood, Shotover – and more sentimental. The inversion of cliché, structurally as well as verbally, in Shaw's early comedies clearly comes from Wilde. But where Wilde's work harks back to Restoration models, Shaw's comic momentum carries his drama towards a much more modern form.

In *Misalliance*, first performed in 1910, two years before Ionesco's birth, the commonplace reality of a Surrey mansion is shattered by an aeroplane crashing through the glass roof of the conservatory, out of which steps an elegant Polish female acrobat, while a shy and timid clerk emerges from a portable Turkish bath as a revolutionary, bathetically declaiming 'Rome fell. Babylon fell, Hindhead's turn will come.'[61] So in *Heartbreak House* the acceptance of arbitrary situations suddenly makes normal life look wildly irrational. Indeed, at moments the action qualifies as a prototype for Theatre of the Absurd. The Napoleon of industry who controls governments '*begins to cry like a child*', and is only barely prevented from stripping naked. The Captain 'is trying to discover a psychic ray that will explode all the explosives' in the world, and no one shows the least surprise to find him carrying sticks of dynamite around the house. Characters are inflicted with mistaken identities: Lady Utterwood's father and sister are both incapable of recognizing her, while the victimized and respectable Mazzini Dunn is persistently confused with a piratical boatswain of the same name, who unexpectedly turns up as a burglar.

Coincidence reigns, and behaviour continually explodes in bizarre farce. The Burglar not only makes his nefarious living from blackmailing the guilty consciences of the rich, rather than stealing their possessions, but turns out to be the Captain's old boatswain and the Cook's missing husband. The romantic Hector makes an appearance in full Arab costume. Though antedating Ionesco's plays by over a quarter of a century, such elements are recognizably comparable to his dramatic world. Even 'the very burglars can't behave naturally in this house', and by the end of the play the Zeppelin overhead seems equally absurd.[62] Not only is it totally unexpected, no enemy even having been hinted at earlier, but the equanimity with which characters respond to its doomsday appearance is even greater than their acquiescence in all the other improbabilities.

Thus war is made to seem both the logical extension of these characters' self-destructive lives, and completely irrational: something no sane civiliza-tion could believe. Yet the play's ending is very closely based on an actual incident. When the first German raids occurred, aircraft were such a novelty they were greeted with excitement. A workman near Ayot, Shaw's home, even lit a flare to attract a Zeppelin – and was killed by a bomb dropped from it – while on another occasion one that had passed right over Shaw's house was shot down close by, and the characters' response in the play almost exactly mirrors his own feelings.

What is hardly credible, but true, is that the sound of the Zepp's engines was so fine, and its voyage through the stars so enchanting, that I positively caught myself hoping next night that there would be another raid ... One is so pleased at having seen the show [watching the airship burn] that the destruction of a dozen people or so in hideous terror and torment does not count. 'I didn't half cheer, I tell you' said a damsel at the wreck. Pretty lot of animals we are.[63]

In the context of this play, the more directly reality is transcribed, the more ironic it becomes, because the world depicted is explicitly 'a madhouse' and the inmates – who 'haunt' rather than inhabit it – are 'all heartbroken imbeciles'. However, each of the vital members in this group are acutely aware of the lunatic nature of their society, and their zany behaviour can be seen as a deliberate attempt to conform to its reality. With madness and sanity having become reversed, there is no possibility that the saviour Ellie is searching for can emerge from within the group. Mangan is completely the victim of the system he controls, Horseback Hall (the natural home of the Utterwoods) is no alternative to the Bohemian romanticism of Heartbreak House, and Captain Shotover is metaphorically steering the ship of state 'on the rocks': the title of Shaw's 1933 'Political Comedy' dealing with the Depression and the General Strike. Consequently, as the characters conclude, 'one of two things must happen. Either out of that darkness some new creation will come to supplant us as we have supplanted the animals, or the heavens will fall in thunder and destroy us.' On the surface it is the second prediction that is fulfilled; and the double irony in the music of 'Keep the Home Fires Burning', which forms the theme of the finale and closes the curtain, points directly to the coming holocaust. Yet the declaration that 'there is no sense in us. We are useless, dangerous and ought to be abolished' is the judgement of Hector, the archetypal romantic.[64] It is inherently false, romantic ideals that lead to nihilistic pessimism; and the ending shows that the either/or forecast is an incorrect alternative.

Significantly, it is 'the two practical men of business' who act according to common sense and are the only ones completely unconscious that their own behaviour is irrational, Mangan and the Burglar, who are blown up together with the clergyman's house.[65] In addition, it is the explosion of Captain Shotover's dynamite that kills them – and it does not seem too far-fetched to associate the bomb which acted as a catalyst with the 'mind ray' he hopes to invent. What has been removed are the twin pillars of society, the economic structure of Capitalism and the conventional morality of the Church establishment that sanctified it. Destruction is seen as a liberating force.

As early as 1914 Shaw had put forward the idea of war as a potential agent for social change in a pamphlet that outraged public opinion. The argument, which caused H. G. Wells to vilify Shaw and his fellow playwrights to demand his resignation from the Dramatists Club, was that there was nothing to choose between England and Germany. Both sides were equally militaristic and the moral justifications that legitimized the war – Save Little Belgium, etc. – were hypocritical pretexts for attacking a competitor to secure the continuance of British supremacy. But *Commonsense About the War* also made a series of suggestions ranging from a trade union for soldiers to peace terms anticipating the League of Nations. Under the guise of methods for waging war more efficiently, these were clearly ways of shifting society towards socialism; and Labour politicians were urged 'to take advantage of the war emergency' to win parliamentary reforms that would transfer power to the people. The point was made explicit in the preface to a post-war reprinting: 'I felt as if I were witnessing an engagement between two pirate fleets . . . All the ensigns were Jolly Rogers; but mine was clearly the one with the Union Jack in the corner.' And if the war had not accomplished the necessary social revolution, at least it had changed the terms of the struggle. 'There are only two flags in the world henceforth: the red flag of democratic socialism and the black flag of capitalism, the flag of God and the flag of Mammon.'[66]

From this perspective it becomes clearer why Shaw referred to *Heartbreak House* as the work that 'has more of the miracle, more of the mystic belief in it than any of my others'.[67] Reviewers of the 1919 première, in the immediate aftermath of the war about which Shaw was writing, found the comic approach incompatible with the seriousness of the subject. But to the atomic age the apocalyptic elements make it the most relevant of his plays.

While the allegory has been recognized, the parable is generally missed. Ellie's role of Cordelia to Captain Shotover, who like Lear demonstrates reason in madness, affirms the possibility of redemption in her choice of him as her 'spiritual husband and second father'. In Shaw's conception she combines 'immaculate virginity' with (another Shakespearean reference) the strength of character of a 'Lady Macbeth', and his rehearsal notes for a 1932 revival of the play stress her status as an outsider: 'Ellie's skirt – black – ugly – should contrast well with scene.' Unlike the natural inhabitants who 'in this house . . . know all the poses', she breaks through illusions.[68] Where Hector's turning the house into a beacon for the bombs expresses the romantic's death-wish, her desire to set fire to it is the opposite.

The society of *Heartbreak House* is identical to the abstract vision of hell in *Man and Superman*. As Shaw noted in the programme for the 1907 première of the Dream sequence

Modern theology conceives heaven and hell, not as places but as states of the soul . . . This world, or any other, may be made a hell by a society in a state of damnation: that is, a society so lacking in the higher orders of energy that it is given wholly to the pursuit of immediate individual pleasure, and cannot even conceive the passion of the divine will.

So in *Heartbreak House*, renewal can only come through clearing away the rotten timbers that imprison the souls of its living-dead inhabitants; and Shaw's advice to the French translator of the text stresses the positive nature of Ellie's final state. 'Après la reveille de Mangan, jusqu'à la fin de la pièce, Ellie est une figure de poésie . . . quoique toujours forté'.[69] The musical reference at the end of the play is not Wagner but Beethoven, whose characteristic theme is the Ninth Symphony's affirmation of the future, rather than the *Götterdämmerung*.

Not surprisingly, perhaps, since the Shavian *alter ego* here is presented as senile and the play's statement is carried by symbolism and evocative

atmosphere, *Heartbreak House* has attracted more different critical interpretations than any other of Shaw's works. At least its ambiguity serves to
counteract the common view that, starting with *Major Barbara* in 1905, he
increasingly 'tended to over-emphasize the polemical ... at the expense of
the character drawing and drama'.[70] Even at the time their political or social
polemics were widely accepted, and certainly today Shaw's theories are no
longer novel. His quasi-millenarian utopianism may seem as dated as his
topical satire, while his attack on Darwinism has become respectable and
social changes have outstripped his attacks on sexual mores, medical ethics
or censorship. But the terms in which his themes are expressed, the inversion
of norms and theatrical wit, is still just as effective in challenging the preconceptions of an audience. In that sense his plays have been successful in
transforming drama into a vehicle for ideas. His prefaces and sense of ethical
purpose provide a model for Edward Bond. His intellectual comedy, and the
verbal brilliance he shares with Wilde, look forward to Tom Stoppard. His
intention, 'to write something that would be so simple that the dullwitted
would understand, and so real that life would be stripped thereby of all sham
and a new conception of it created' demarcates the territory of all serious
drama in the century, although his terms are intellectual while theatre has
become increasingly politicized.[71]

As the most prominent playwright in the trend-setting Court Theatre
seasons, with eleven of his plays in the repertoire between 1903 and 1907
occupying almost two-thirds of the total performances, Shaw established
the criteria for twentieth-century British drama in its formative phase.
His work provided a staple for the emerging Repertory Theatre movement – in addition to representing modern British theatre abroad, with
seasons of his plays from Pasadena, USA to Kobe, Japan – and the continuing popularity of his work means that it still provides a standard. The
Malvern Festival (inaugurated in 1929) staged the premières of six Shaw
plays and sixteen revivals, *Man and Superman* was restaged professionally
over twenty times (including productions of the Dream sequence) up
to 1951, while the Shaw Festival in Canada has celebrated its thirtieth
anniversary.

Notes

1 Shaw, *Back to Methuselah*, p. 121 (unless otherwise indicated, quotations are
taken from the Standard Edition of *The Works of Bernard Shaw*, London,
1930–1950); Rehearsal Notes for *Heartbreak House*, BL Add. 50647.

2 *Plays Unpleasant*, pp. xxii–xxiii and *Widowers' Houses*, Independent Theatre edition, 1893, p. 118; William Archer, *The Old Drama and the New*, Boston, 1923, p. 307.

3 *The Quintessence of Ibsenism*, London 1913, p. 203.

4 *Three Plays For Puritans*, p. xxxvi. See also *Plays Pleasant*, pp. i–iii and Shaw, *Our Theatres in the Nineties*, London, 1932, II, pp. 4–5.

5 *Saint Joan*, p. 4; Letter, 1944, cited in Mander and Mitchenson, *Theatrical Companion to Shaw*, London, 1954, p. 43.

6 Shaw, *Evening Standard*, 28 November 1944.

7 Shaw, Author's Note in *Collected Plays*, London, 1970, I, pp. 596–7.

8 *Our Theatres in the Nineties*, I, p. 82; *Candida*, p. 145. (Although the painting of Virgin and Child is not specified in the scene description of *A Doll's House*, it was a central part of the setting both in Ibsen's own first production of the play and Achurch's staging.)

9 *Candida*, p. 104.

10 Letter, 1906, in *Bernard Shaw's Letters to Granville-Barker*, ed. C. B. Purdom, London, 1956, p. 63.

11 'The Art of Rehearsal', London, 1928, p. 4; letter, 1922, in *To A Young Actress: The Letters of Bernard Shaw to Molly Tompkins*, ed. P. Tomkins, New York, 1962, p. 19.

12 *Plays Unpleasant*, p. 73; *Major Barbara* (filmscript), cited in Donald Costello, *The Serpent's Eye*, London, 1965, p. 96 (my italics).

13 Letter to Shaw, 20 June 1923, BL Add. 50615.

14 Shaw, *Malvern Festival Book*, 1931.

15 *Shaw on Theatre*, p. 220 (see also, letter to Cecil Lewis 1932, *ibid.* p. 280, & Winifred Loraine, *Headwind: The Story of Robert Loraine*, New York, n.d., p. 90).

16 Letter 1904, *Bernard Shaw's Letters to Granville-Barker*, p. 30. For commentary on the practical difficulty of changing Shaw's stage directions, cf. Jocelyn Herbert, *Plays and Players*, March 1983, p. 12.

17 Shaw, *Letters to Granville-Barker*, p. 85 (1907); *Man and Superman*, Harmondsworth, 1946, p. 51, and *Too True to be Good*, pp. 107–8.

18 These points are made continuously in Shaw's prefaces, and the quotations are taken from *Saint Joan*, pp. 14 & 21f., *Plays Pleasant*, p. 15, *Caesar and Cleopatra*, p. 132, and *Major Barbara*, p. 10.

19 Preface, *Plays Pleasant*, p. xviii.

20 *Caesar and Cleopatra*, p. 91; *Three Plays for Puritans*, pp. xvi, xxxv. For a fuller discussion of the relationship between Shaw's play and Victorian historical drama, see Martin Meisel, *Shaw and the Nineteenth-Century Theatre*, Princeton, 1963, pp. 355f.

21 *Caesar and Cleopatra*, pp. 89, 119, 138, 188, 181.

22 *Ibid.*, pp. 124, 201; notes to the 1901 edition of *Caesar and Cleopatra*, and Preface, *Three Plays for Puritans*, p. xxxv.

23 *Three Plays for Puritans*, pp. xxii & xxvii. For details on the way *The Devil's Disciple* was conventionalized in production, see Archibald Henderson, *George Bernard Shaw: Man of the Century*, New York, 1956, p. 450.

24 *The Era*, 3 September 1913.

25 Archer, letter to Shaw 1923, BL Add. 50615; *Three Plays for Puritans*, p. xxiii.

26 *Arms and the Man*, pp. 14 & 17–18. (For a fuller discussion of the sources for these stock situations, see Meisel, *Shaw and the Nineteenth Century*, pp. 186–94.)

27 *Arms and the Man*, pp. 80–2.

28 *Ibid.*, p. 41.

29 *Three Plays for Puritans*, p. 16; *Plays Pleasant*, p. xv.

30 This emotional ambiguity in Shaw was first noted by Edmund Wilson in *The Triple Thinkers*, London, 1938.

31 *The Times*, 23 April 1894; Lillah McCarthy, *Myself and Friends*, New York, 1933, p. 94; *Letters to Granville-Barker*, pp. 134 (1908) and 93 (1907).

32 *Shaw on Theatre*, p. 287; Edith Evans and Lewis Casson, cited in Mander and Mitchenson, *Theatrical Companion*, pp. 291–2 & 18. See also, *Saint Joan*, p. 98. *New York Times*, 12 July 1927.

33 In F. E. Lowenstein, *Rehearsal Copies of Bernard Shaw's Plays*, London, 1930, p. 19.

34 Preface to *Saint Joan*, p. 24; *Pygmalion*, p. 244. See also, pp. 251–2. The changes introduced by Tree are amusingly presented by Richard Huggett, *The First Night of Pygmalion*, London, 1970, pp. 70f., and see also Henderson, *Shaw*, p. 730.

35 Preface to *Pygmalion*, p. 32.

36 *The Illustrated London News*, 18 April 1914; *Pygmalion*, p. 50.

37 *Pygmalion*, pp. 264, 220 & 256; letter to Mrs Patrick Campbell, cited by Bernard Dukore in *Shaw's Plays in Performance*, ed. Dan Leary, Pennsylvania, 1983, p. 139.

38 *Fabian Essays*, London, 1962, p. 38; preface to *Widowers' Houses*, in *The Complete Prefaces of Bernard Shaw*, London, 1965, p. 703.

39 Preface to *Man and Superman*, Harmondsworth, 1946, pp. 20, 18, 21 and 37.

40 *Ibid.*, pp. 28, 27 & 26. Despite Eric Bentley's assertion that Tanner's physical appearance duplicates one of Shaw's political antagonists, H. M. Hyndeman (*Bernard Shaw: A Reconsideration*, New York, 1976, p. 55), the reviewers of the time had no doubt that Barker was made up to resemble Shaw himself (see *The Illustrated London News*, 27 May 1905).

41 *Man and Superman*, pp. 264 and 233.

42 *Ibid.*, p. 24; letter to Vedrenne, 1907, in *Bernard Shaw's Letters to Granville-Barker*, p. 77.

43 *Man and Superman*, pp. 62 and 54; *Theatre Magazine*, October 1905 and *New York Sun*, 25 October 1905.

44 Letter to Florence Farr, 1905, in *Letters*, ed. Clifford Bax, New York, 1942, p. 43; Max Beerbohm, *The Saturday Review*, 28 April 1903 and 12 June 1907. See John Elsom, *The Listener*, 24 January 1981.

45 *Man and Superman*, pp. 127, 138–9.

46 *Ibid.*, pp. 127, 138–9. See *Bernard Shaw's Letters to Granville-Barker*, p. 50, and *Shaw on Theatre*, p. 107.

47 *Major Barbara*, pp. 334, 323.

48 *Major Barbara*, pp. 317, 261; letters, Shaw/Murray and Murray/Shaw 1905, cited in *Bernard Shaw's Plays*, ed. Warren Smith, New York, 1970, pp. 382 & 397; *Major Barbara* (screen version), Harmondsworth, 1945, pp. 135–6.

49 *Man and Superman*, pp. 151 & 37–8.

50 *On the Rocks*, pp. 175, 180.

51 *Back to Methuselah*, V, p. 207; *Our Theatres in the Nineties*, I, p. v.

52 *Back to Methuselah*, I, p. 9; V, p. 217.

53 As suggested by my copy-editor Sue Dickinson.

54 *Ibid.*, II, pp. 79, 81 & 86.

55 *Ibid.*, III, p. 128.

56 *Ibid.*, V, p. 119; II, p. 82.

57 Bentley, *Bernard Shaw: A Reconsideration*, p. 140.

58 'The Revolutionist's Handbook' in *Man and Superman*, pp. 224 and 235.

59 *Heartbreak House*, pp. 106, 96; *The Illustrated London News*, 29 October 1921.

60 *Heartbreak House*, pp. 30, 68.

61 *Misalliance*, p. 7.

62 *Heartbreak House*, pp. 32, 81, 117.

63 Letter to the Webbs, October 1916, in Henderson, *Shaw*, pp. 378–9.

64 *Heartbreak House*, pp. 96, 101–2, 90, 110.

65 *Ibid.*, p. 90.

66 Shaw, *What I Really Wrote About the War*, London, 1931, pp. 86 & 2.

67 Shaw, *The Dramatic Heritage*, New York, 1953, p. 127.

68 *Heartbreak House*, pp. 98 & 83; Letter to Lillah McCarthy (cited in *Myself and Friends*, p. 204) and to St John Ervine, 28 October 1921 (Hanley Collection).

69 BL Add. 50644; ms. note in typescript of the French translation, cited in Louis Cropton, *Shaw the Dramatist*, Lincoln, Nebraska, 1969, p. 164.

70 Sir Lewis Casson, in Mander and Mitchenson, *Theatrical Companion*, p. 289; Archer, letter, 1921, BL Add. 50615.

71 Shaw, letter, 1927, cited in *Shaw's Plays in Performance*, p. 164.

3

Social themes and realistic modes

3.1 Shavian influences and the question of censorship

The links with Shaw's drama of ideas extend throughout the century. They are most obvious in the work of naturalistic playwrights, and direct influences can be traced in his contemporaries, Harley Granville-Barker and John Galsworthy, right through Noel Coward and Terence Rattigan, as well as in Irish dramatists like Sean O'Casey. However, he serves as a reference point for John Osborne, and so indirectly conditions the wave of new drama that burst on the scene in 1956, after his death. So Edward Bond is following Shaw in his stress on 'Rational Theatre', as well as in his practice of accompanying plays with analytical prefaces, while Tom Stoppard's brand of highly intellectual comedy combined with stylistic experimentation is very much a contemporary equivalent of Shaw. This does not mean that those who come after are in any sense subordinate to Shaw: their work stands on its own merits. It extends the boundaries of English drama far beyond forms evolved by Shaw, cutting his umbilical link with the nineteenth century.

The very real significance of Shaw's impact is shown by the way writers like John Galsworthy, D.H. Lawrence, Somerset Maugham or later J.B. Priestley, all of whom already had leading reputations as novelists, turned to the stage in order to address topical issues directly. In the nineteenth century the trivialization of theatre (partly due to the lack of copyright protection, which Shaw was instrumental in changing) had made novels the main vehicle for social comment. Now the situation was reversed. And in claiming a direct social function for theatre, Shaw not only gave a strong political cast to the mainstream of English drama, but set its stylistic terms. Dramatists working in this line were effectively faced with the choice of reforming society by depicting its evils in naturalistic detail, or by attacking its ethos through the representative nature of a character or group. So Galsworthy and Lawrence

55

write even more photographically than Shaw in his early 'Unpleasant' plays; and the same realistic emphasis carries through to the 'kitchen-sink' drama of Osborne's early plays, Arnold Wesker and Shelagh Delaney in the late 1950s. Alternatively the Agitprop movement of the 1930s, Joan Littlewood, and the younger generation of 'Socialist Realists' who developed out of Agitprop in the 1970s, together with English followers of Brecht – John Arden and Edward Bond, as well as less politically motivated populists such as Robert Bolt and Christopher Hampton – all stripped the stage of detail to present a moral or ideological analysis of society that goes beyond Shaw's later, more symbolic plays. In both these contrasting types of theatre, due to the immediacy of the dramatic subject or political aims, the question of censorship becomes an important factor.

This tension between realism and epic forms is the background for social drama throughout the period. On the one hand there is the naturalistic depiction of society, which always risks becoming too individual and specific to rouse general indignation. On the other, there is the Brechtian, which tends to lose sight of the society to be reformed in reducing scenery and specific circumstances to abstract issues. At its extreme this leads to the kind of expressionistic drama represented by Auden and Isherwood's plays or Howard Barker, which although it retains a strong political emphasis turns to poetic imagery and even verse forms.

Shaw's breakthrough to public acceptance was largely due to Granville-Barker, the initiator and driving artistic force of the Court Theatre seasons between 1903 and 1907. The significance of this joint venture with J.E. Vedrenne can hardly be overstated. Together with the subsequent repertory seasons directed by Granville-Barker under Charles Frohmann's management (1908–10) and with Lillah McCarthy (1910–15), it provided both the catalyst for a provincial Repertory movement and a model for the long-delayed National Theatre. Granville-Barker originally planned 'to run a stock season of the uncommercial drama: Hauptmann – Sudermann – Ibsen – Maeterlinck – Schnitzler – Shaw – Brieux etc . . . stake everything on plays and acting – not attempt "productions"'.[1] This clearly followed the line originally set by J.T. Grein's Independent Theatre in 1891, which had mounted the first English performances of Ibsen as well as Hauptmann and Shaw. In fact, out of over fifty plays produced at the Court Theatre from 1903 to 1915 – ranging from Euripides (in Gilbert Murray's translation) and Shakespeare to Galsworthy, John Masefield or James Barrie – eighteen were by Shaw. And these provided over half of the total performances.

The impetus for the Court Theatre seasons came from the Stage Society, which succeeded Grein's Independent Theatre in 1899. This was founded to give private presentations of socially significant plays that were either uncommercial or censored, and continued to fulfil an important function in championing new drama – including the plays of D.H. Lawrence and R.C. Sherriff – up to 1939. The Stage Society won audiences for both Ibsen (*The League of Youth*) and Shaw's *Candida* (1900). It gave exposure to Somerset Maugham's first and most problematic play, *A Man of Honour* (1903), as well as allowing limited performances of Granville-Barker's banned play *Waste* (1907 – first public performance 1936). It is hardly coincidental that Granville-Barker, whose acting career had begun in 1899 with Mrs Pat Campbell's revivals of *The Second Mrs Tanqueray* and *The Notorious Mrs Ebbsmith*, played leading roles in all four of these productions. His transition from Pinero through Ibsen to Shaw and Maugham indicates the direct connection between the nineteenth-century problem play, Naturalism, and the challenge to establishment (in this case Victorian) ethics. Both Arthur Wing Pinero and Henry Arthur Jones were founder-members of the Independent Theatre – as was Laurence Housman, whose poetic and religious drama had also been banned, together with more natural supporters like Galsworthy or Maugham. And all joined with Shaw and Granville-Barker in their campaign against censorship of the stage. Indeed the conventional problem play still occupies a central place in serious mainstream drama, whether dressed up with a realistic environmental portrayal of characters, or disguised in the Brechtian/'Epic' style.

These continuities have been disguised by the almost complete triumph of the modernist critique formulated by Shaw, which has come to be generally accepted as an unquestionable premise, however dated Shaw's own works may now seem. His attack on the type of play that underpins conventional morality by judging outcasts from a standard social perspective, instead of undermining clichés by presenting society from the outcast's viewpoint, has carried all before it. For well over fifty years it was all too easily accepted that there are fundamental differences in approach between the older playwrights (identified with the previous century, even if like Pinero they remained active as late as the 1920s) and the New Drama promoted by Shaw. His dismissive comment that 'in fact these so-called problem plays [of the 1890s] invariably depended for their dramatic interest on foregone conclusions of the most heart-wearying conventionality concerning sexual morality', led to their almost complete banishment from the stage – although there has recently been a revival of interest in Pinero and Tom Robertson.[2] It also conditioned the rejection of Terence Rattigan in the mid-1950s, and has resulted in an implicit equation between any play that does not overtly challenge the status quo, and conventional/outdated drama. Conversely, plays that were censored are almost automatically assumed to be both 'modern' and moral.

In itself censorship may be no guarantee of social significance, let alone artistic quality. Among the plays refused a performance licence in 1907 was *The Breaking Point* by Edward Garnett, which Granville-Barker himself had rejected as melodramatic, with its suicide of a seduced girl, two-dimensional characterization and sentimental tone. But the fight against censorship can be seen as a measure of the politicization of modern drama. The original law restricting the public presentation of theatrical work had been framed to silence criticism of Walpole's government in the time of Fielding and John Gay (*The Beggar's Opera*, 1728). Its essential provisions were retained unchanged in the 1843 Theatres Act, placing the licensing authority with the Lord Chamberlain: a royal official with no public accountability. This remained the situation up until the banning of Edward Bond's *Early Morning* finally brought an end to the Lord Chamberlain's control of the stage in 1968. Obvious symbols of authority, monarchs or the Holy Family were automatically censored, from Housman's *Bethlehem* in 1902 and *Victoria Regina* (even though laudatory) in 1935, to Bond's vitriolic lampooning of Queen Victoria, her consort Albert and Florence Nightingale in *Early Morning* (1968). And although plays in the Twentieth Century have generally been banned on moral grounds of sex or violence, it is noticeable that those which have become test cases all contain radical political implications.

The terms of the furore about Granville-Barker's *Waste* in 1907 were remarkably similar to the battle over Osborne's *A Patriot for Me* and Edward Bond's *Saved*, in 1965 and 1966. In each case the official cause of objection was secondary to the play's real theme. The abortion (*Waste*), homosexuality (*Patriot*) or baby battering (*Saved*), which formed the justification for censorship, symbolize the decadence of the social establishment or the human cost of an oppressive political system. They are not presented as salacious entertainment. The drag ball in Osborne's play, for instance, may be spectacular but the surface attraction is undercut by grotesqueness. Similarly, in *Saved* the placing of the murder in an early scene – together with the biblical metaphor implicit in casting stones at a baby – transfers the focus from the act itself to causes and the question of responsibility.

As Galsworthy pointed out in a 1909 pamphlet (the year two further plays of Shaw's were banned, *The Shewing-Up of Blanco Posnet* – for blasphemy – and even a trifling pastiche like *Press Cuttings*), 'censorship . . . is not concerned with the essential matter of the play, but with the presumed taste and feeling toward it, of the majority'. He showed convincingly that the result was to encourage plays 'treating vice in a light attractive way' while censuring those 'following out its consequences with grim indelicacy, or . . . offering severe criticism of current standards of morality'.[3] It was specifically the notion of theatre as a tool for social reform (NOT the more personal demands of free expression in *avant-garde* art) that fuelled the fight against censorship. The point is made by Galsworthy, who compared the function of drama not only to religion in its moral force, but to science in its potential for changing material conditions.

This is explicitly the theme of Granville-Barker's *Waste* (1907). The protagonist Trebell is a key figure in the political Establishment, who holds the balance of power. His price for supporting the government of the day is the disestablishment of the Church, freeing resources for a secular system of universal education. Linking this with the funding of old-age pensions from income tax and the nationalization of medicine, the play outlines a socialist programme that was almost exactly fifty years ahead of its time. And it would seem more logical to conclude that it was the propagation of such ideas that caused its banning, rather than any embarrassment of parliamentary leaders by presenting a politician who is involved in adultery. The aim of the playwright and his protagonist are identical: in Trebell's words, to 'preach revolution'.[4] Granville-Barker's play offers a paradigmatic example of the naturalistically oriented, socially engaged line in English drama. At the same time, the religious sense of mission and reliance on verbal persuasion incorporated in the concept of *preaching* social change bridges the apparent gap between Shaw and later hard-Left playwrights.

Notes

1 Barker, letter to Archer, 1903, BL Add. MS 50534. For detailed discussion of these issues and Barker's leading role in their development, see George Rowell and Anthony Jackson, *The Repertory Movement*, Cambridge, 1984 (in particular pp. 22–34), and Dennis Kennedy, *Granville-Barker and the Dream of Theatre*, Cambridge, 1985 (in particular pp. 190ff.).

2 Shaw, Preface to *Three Plays for Puritans*, p. xi.

3 John Galsworthy, A *Justification* of *the Censorship of Plays*, London, 1909, pp. 11 & 12. (His examples range from Sophocles' *Oedipus Tyrannus* to Ibsen, Shaw and Brieux.)

4 Kennedy's suggestion, *Granville-Barker*, p. 85. The official objection to *Waste* was the explicitness with which sexual relations were depicted, and the reference to

'a criminal operation' (cf. C.B. Purdom, *Harley Granville-Barker*, Westport, 1971, pp. 73–4) but these elements were so central to the plot that omitting them would make nonsense of the play. *Plays by Harley Granville-Barker*, Cambridge, 1987, p. 182.

3.2 Intellectual drama versus public theatre: Granville-Barker and John Galsworthy

Psychological realism: Harley Granville-Barker (1877–1946)

CHECKLIST OF GRANVILLE-BARKER'S MAJOR PLAYS

The Marrying of Ann Leete, 1902	*The Madras House*, 1909
The Voysey Inheritance, 1905	*The Secret Life* (1923; perf. 1988)
Waste, 1907	*His Majesty*, 1928

The influence of Shaw is clear in all Granville-Barker's work. Reviewers of *The Voysey Inheritance* (1905) immediately drew the connection between its heroine, who takes the lead in proposing marriage, and the 'New Woman' of *Man and Superman* (1903, restaged one month earlier with Barker acting the part of Tanner), while Edward Voysey is exactly the same theatrical antitype as Cusins in *Major Barbara* (also 1905). The plot is propelled by his indecisiveness and self-questioning doubts, and the characterization explicitly counters 'the superstition' (found, as Granville-Barker complained during rehearsal, even in the actor playing Edward) 'that a good man on the stage must always be a strong one, and that a sensitively weak character cannot be interesting'.[1] Even the basic concept – an apparently respectable solicitor who defrauds his clients, and whose family wealth comes from his (and his father's) speculations with the Trusts they administer – is a variation on *Mrs Warren's Profession* (1902), with theft replacing prostitution as the essence of capitalism. The most obvious comparison, however, comes in the substitution of discussion for action, which Granville-Barker took even further than Shaw.

The settings for both *The Voysey Inheritance* and *Waste* (1907) are designed to limit movement in ways that emphasize dialogue by filling the stage with furniture. Seating the actors round a dining room table that filled the acting area for three acts of the first play turned them into debaters. The way furnishings were placed formalized the verbal quality of the conflict, like the pair of settees positioned back-to-back to divide the stage in the second act, specifically designed 'to form a tennis net, something to keep the two factions in the scene separate, and for them to fight across'. This was reinforced by the conceptual nature of Granville-Barker's productions, which in *The Madras House* (1909) led to conducting rehearsals on a stage cloth marked out in one-foot squares for exact blocking, so that as one actor reported 'every move was part of a pattern, so was every gesture, every speech'.[2]

However, despite the extreme of intellectual drama this implies, Granville-Barker's characters habitually act on the basis of unconscious instincts that by definition cannot be verbalized. This internal contradiction is partly responsible for the confused response his plays have aroused. For example in his first play to reach the stage, *The Marrying of Ann Leete* (1902), the 'new woman' who breaks out of social convention for 'a new world' is motivated by an unexpressed sexual attraction to a young and virile male: her father's gardener. This proto-Lawrentian drive becomes the tragic equivalent of fate in *Waste*, where the urge to reproduction is completely divorced from personal emotion. For the characters, 'Nature's a tyrant'. When Trebell seduces a married woman she becomes pregnant while literally unconscious, having fainted under his kisses. Granville-Barker's vision is summed up by Trebell's question to her: 'Wouldn't any other woman have served the purpose – is it less of a purpose because we didn't know we had it?'

This is a radical reinterpretation of Shaw's Life Force. Being female is 'worse off than an animal'. Although Granville-Barker's women are the sexual aggressors, their vulnerability is presented as a 'physical curse', while the male – for whom intellectual creativity replaces children, as in Shaw's *Man and Superman* – is metaphorically sterile.[3] Trebell's excessive rationality drives his mistress to the abortion that kills her. This nullifies his proposed reforms by discrediting him, and drives him to suicide. Yet he is also emotionally obsessive. It is not guilt, but the total commitment to his political programme that causes him to take his own life.

On one level, *Waste* is a critical riposte to *Man and Superman*. The two 'Revolutionists' are directly comparable (and each is also a projection of his author). But Tanner flees from sexual pursuit into a comic opera fantasy of foreign countries, and Shaw gives him the escape of a conventional ending – even though marriage undercuts his professed principles. By contrast Trebell's situation is conceived realistically, and there is no way of avoiding the consequences of seduction. As a director, Granville-Barker promoted Shaw's work, but although they held similar political views he established his drama by opposition to Shaw's ideas.

Even if, from today's perspective, Granville-Barker's stature as a playwright is completely overshadowed by Shaw, at the time the relationship seemed far less one-sided. Indeed, *Misalliance* (1910) and *The Madras House* (1909) are companion-pieces, Shaw's play being written in response to the first draft of Barker's script, while Granville-Barker includes references to Shaw's play in the dialogue of his final version.

Shared concerns and close career links have generally meant that Granville-Barker is undervalued as a mere follower of Shaw. However, his theatrical approach opposes Shaw's no less than his themes, as even the early and in some ways atypical *Ann Leete* indicates. Where Shaw embedded stock nineteenth-century plot situations in contemporary contexts to expose the falsity of melodramatic ideals, giving a histrionic quality to his plays, here strikingly modern characterization is combined with a historical setting. The realism of indirect dialogue and unexplained behaviour is designed to reveal the conditional nature of social structures, making the form (as costume drama) itself a thematic statement. So the moral attitudes of the age – and by implication those of the twentieth-century audience as much as the eighteenth-century characters – are seen to have as little intrinsic validity as fashions of dress. The juxtaposition of antiquated behaviour and contemporary attitudes presents 'civilization' as a state where 'one grows into a ghost . . . visible . . . then invisible. I'm glad [cosmetic] paint has gone out of fashion . . . the painted ghosts were very ill to see.'[4]

The effect is not only a subtler form of naturalism than Shaw, but a subjective, almost introvert tone that finds its fullest expression in *The Madras House*, Granville-Barker's most characteristic play. Substituting structural patterning almost completely for plot action and making its thematic point through juxtaposed impressions rather than statement, this brings together all the major motifs of his earlier work. Philip Madras is an ironic variant on Trebell, having 'got . . . the Reformer's mind', and each act illustrates a different aspect of the position of women in a male-dominated society.[5] The business Philip inherits, like Voysey's, makes its profits from hypocrisy, but as a fashion-house it is one that directly exploits sexuality. His uncle's family of six unmarried daughters advancing into a middle-aged wasteland of rigid respectability – the first segment of society put under the microscope – are paralleled with the closely supervised and segregated salesgirls who are forced to 'live in' the establishment that employs them, even when married: a state they must conceal to keep their jobs. One of these employees is the centre of a scandal, having become pregnant but refusing to name the man responsible. This, it turns out, is Philip's father.

A convert to Mohammedanism, who abandoned his wife over twenty years before to live in an Arab village, old Madras has returned now only to sell off the business he founded. He initially serves the same classic role of objective commentator as Goldsmith's satiric eighteenth-century Chinaman. Distance shows up unquestioned norms as irrational and indefensible, allowing him 'to discover . . . with a stranger's eye . . . that Europe in its attitude towards women is mad'. But simply being the moral opposite of an evil society is no guarantee of sanity. In fact, since his claim to superiority is that he practises openly what the English hypocritically disguise, apparent opposites are identical. He may attack the clothing industry as 'an industrial seraglio', an image that relates back to the literal (though virginal) harem of unmarried daughters, but he is a practising polygamist. He attacks the Protestant ethic embodied in the Madras business, under which women are depersonalized, reduced to economic units. Yet, as a Mohammedan, he sees them solely in terms of 'perpetuating [the] race'.[6]

This demonstration that Shavian eugenics are as reactionary as the most rigid Victorian morality is accompanied by an attack on Shaw's ideal of the superior attraction of ideas over sexual pursuits. Granville-Barker specifies that Philip Madras is '*cold, capable of that least English of dispositions – intellectual passion*' and even undercuts his example of sexual equality (treating women 'as a man would treat another man') by implying that it is the result of an upbringing that has made him 'dislike men and despise women'. The point is that sexual conditioning in this society bars any viable relationship between the sexes. Philip's wife expresses equal contempt for men, and even a philanderer admits 'I don't like women and I never did'.[7] The mechanism that creates and perpetuates this negative situation is brilliantly illustrated in the climatic third Act set in the showroom of the fashion-house.

Mannequins parade across the stage while the American purchaser of the firm and its owners discuss price and business philosophy: living illustrations of the hypocrisy of their principles. The most blatantly commercial of the men (an American) refers to women in terms of Goethe's 'eternal feminine'. He rhapsodizes about the spiritually purifying effect of the female ideal, while the three models are treated as characterless extensions of the dresses they are displaying. Professionally silent marionettes whose facial expressions, stance and style of movement are completely artificial, they are reduced to mere sex objects. And the dialogue underlines the irony that the wives and daughters – who, as the previous scenes illustrated, were expected to behave with the most rigid propriety – are persuaded to dress as prostitutes, fashions being set by French whores. An earlier stage direction juxtaposes '*a photograph of the premises – actual; and an advertisement sketch of them*'; and the focus is on the distorting gap between commercialized ideals and human realities. This is epitomized by the contrast between the fake exoticism of quasi-Moorish decor in the showroom, heightening the illusion of voluptuous curves created by fashion, and the actual girl: '*The vision becomes once more a ridiculously expensive dress, with a rather thin and shivering young person half inside it.*'[8]

The scene provides a remarkably clear model of the way people are packaged by the marketing of sex as a commodity. It is designed to go beyond discussion into tangible demonstration, acting as a touchstone of spectators' sexist attitudes. As Philip's wife points out in Granville-Barker's 1925 revision of the text, 'You men parade in words just as fantastically as we do in our fashions.' The fakeness of the female images on display is intended to react on the intellectual male discussion in the foreground, making the audience recognize the falsity of their arguments. However, the success of this technique is debatable. In Granville-Barker's 1910 production the images appear to have been all too seductive; and the reviews singled out the 'beautifully dressed and superbly shaped young ladies'.[9]

As in the best of Shaw's work, the audience are continually persuaded into false positions and forced to revise their opinions. In *The Madras House* each definition of emancipation turns out to be a different form of slavery – to male-created moral standards, wage exploitation, biological demands or manufactured self-image – while the final decision reached by the protagonist is a non-decision. The ending is left open in an unfinished conversation, refusing any easy solution. The subject allows for dramatically flamboyant even grotesque touches. Yet the effect is extremely realistic, lending the social criticism additional conviction which reinforces the challenge to the audience. *The Madras House* is clearly a thesis play. However, the message is left for spectators to define, in contrast to other contemporary dramas on the same theme (for instance Elizabeth Robins' *Votes for Women!*, produced by Granville-Barker in 1906 and famous for its recreation of a Trafalgar Square suffragette rally on stage).

Indeed, the implications of *The Madras House* are far more radical than simply a demand for political equality, although the apparent objectivity makes its case unarguable. As a result it is perhaps the most effective feminist drama before Caryl Churchill's plays. However, it has had little influence, perhaps because presenting its naturalistic cross-section of society requires so large a cast as to be beyond the range of almost any stage but the National

Theatre (for which, at least in a notional form, Granville-Barker was writing, and which successfully revived the play in 1977).

Granville-Barker's significance is generally considered to be as a director, or as a scholar who was instrumental in defining the modern approach to Shakespeare. But his three major plays show the potential of a dramatist who might have been more significant even than Shaw in the development of English theatre, if he had not effectively abandoned the stage after the First World War. His subsequent output was limited to translations of Spanish popular drama and two plays that remain unproduced. These each take the contrasting elements of his drama to an extreme. One moves towards a completely internal and psychological theatre, for which the title of *The Secret Life* is indicative. The other, *His Majesty*, is pure spectacle, with eighty speaking parts. Both represent a refusal of action – even though the King reaches a decision, it is at such a deep level of his being as to be almost inexpressible – and qualify as 'anti-theatre'. Although intended 'to set actors new problems and to widen the theatre's appeal', they have tended to confirm the misleading view of Granville-Barker as an academic playwright, whose focus is intellectual rather than dramatic.[10]

The stage as political platform: John Galsworthy (1867–1933)

CHECKLIST OF GALSWORTHY'S MAJOR PLAYS

The Silver Box, 1906	*The Mob*, 1914
Strife, 1909	*The Skin Game*, 1920
Justice, 1910	*Loyalties*, 1922
The Eldest Son, 1912	*The Show*, 1925
The Fugitive, 1913	*Exiled*, 1929

Within the conceptual premises common to all naturalistic drama – the integral relationship of environment and character, motivated action allowing the exploration of causes, a quasi-scientific evaluation of plays by their contribution to social progress – Granville-Barker's work is at the subliminal end of the spectrum. In contrast to his emphasis on the psychological aspect of generic problems, seeking to foster a sea-change in society by moulding the attitudes of individuals, Galsworthy's *Justice* (1910) was designed to have an immediate public impact and mould legislation. And it is noteworthy that even such a well-known novelist as Galsworthy would turn to the theatre for his vehicle – even though he continued to write novels, with his most famous work *The Forsyte Saga* only appearing in 1922.

The subject of *Justice* is a specific, clearly defined issue, and the action was distilled from factual documentation and extensive interviews with convicts. Directed by Granville-Barker, it is one of the few plays where the connection between performance and a significant alteration in the contemporary political situation can be proved. Its opening coincided with a new Liberal government's first days in office; and the depiction of prison conditions was powerful enough for several of the reviews to suggest that members of parliament should see the play, as indeed the new Liberal Home Secretary Winston Churchill did four times. Also in response to the play, Churchill reportedly received a flood of letters protesting against solitary confinement. After confirming the facts, he announced a programme of prison reform less than five months later. The play not only focused public opinion, but had a central role in political decision-making: a fact confirmed by Churchill's arranging an introduction to Galsworthy while Asquith, the Prime Minister, personally informed Galsworthy of the government proposals in advance.[11]

These links to the Establishment are indicative of Galsworthy's approach, which attempted to change the system from within. In political terms the role of his theatre was that of a 'loyal opposition'.[12] It worked for reform through criticism that assumed shared moral principles – not for revolution through the explicit rejection of social structures. This was standard for all main-stage English dramatists before the 1970s, and shows the extent to which Shaw continued to dominate English theatre. It expresses a Fabian perspective. (Indeed in 1909 Beatrice and Sidney Webb, the intellectual leaders of the Fabian movement, had tried to persuade both Granville-Barker and Galsworthy to dramatize their Minority Report on the Poor Law Commission.)

Although the emphasis placed on realistic transcription and topical detail in Galsworthy's plays now makes them period pieces, the power they retain comes from their objectivity. He consistently attacked social injustice and the double standards of class (*The Eldest Son*, 1912), or gender (*Loyalties*, 1922). But in all his plays the desired moral response is evoked by structuring the dramatic situation, rather than by weighting the characterization. This avoidance of bias is already set in his earliest play *The Silver Box* (1906) and forms the whole basis for his best play *Strife* (1909) where Galsworthy makes it the central theme. Embodying the value of compromise that is the underlying theme, it sets up a gripping dialectic.

Based on the premise that opposites are identical, *Strife* charts the progress of an industrial strike. This is fuelled by the intransigence of two men: John Anthony, the company chairman, standing out against socialism; David Roberts, the local strike leader, refusing to give in to capitalism. Neither the Union intent on imposing its authority on the workforce, nor the management concerned with responsibility to the shareholders, supports their extreme positions. However, the deadlock can only be broken melodramatically. News of his wife's death – a victim of the deprivation caused by the strike – causes Roberts to rush out of a crucial union meeting; and the workers are swayed by moderates in his absence. At the same time, old Anthony is forced to resign from the board. Opposed by his son-in-law who argues that the sufferings of the strikers' wives and children outweigh economic or political considerations, he is outvoted by the other directors. Yet the outcome is ambiguous. The final settlement is exactly the same as the terms rejected by both sides four months earlier. Annie Roberts' death and the breaking of 'the two best men' (in the first version Anthony collapsed with a stroke, and the uncharacteristic passivity of both is simply a more naturalistic equivalent) has all been literally for nothing.

From one angle it is (the final) compromise that makes the sacrifice pointless. From another it was (the original) refusal to compromise that sacrificed everything, even itself, to moral principle. Only the structure indicates that there is an alternative to the hubristic fanaticism of the protagonists. Compromise is represented in the balance between the scenes: the manager's house, then Roberts' cottage; the strike meeting/the boardroom discussion. This also underscores the value of objectivity in implicit contrast to the protagonists' passionate conviction. In this play parallels have been sharpened into polarities, but Galsworthy emphasizes that there is no distinction between them in human terms. Defeated, the two antagonists look each other in the eye and nod in mutual respect.

From a modern and more ideological perspective, *Strife* seems a conflict of will rather than a portrayal of class struggle. But unlike Granville-Barker's characters, whose inner life determines their fate, Galsworthy's figures exist almost exclusively in the public sphere. Each of his plays revolves around a mass scene: the stage filled with shouting strikers, swayed as a group by passionate orators in *Strife*; a police court in *The Silver Box*, where a continual procession of witnesses and prisoners emphasizes that the individual case of the protagonist is routine. Galsworthy stressed that he was 'dealing in types'. And even Annie Roberts' death is designed as 'the crystallization of all the sufferings and fears that each man and his family have been through', not as a catalyst for revealing the personal emotions of a central figure.[13]

This is true even in *Justice*, where the focus is on the rights of the individual. When solitary confinement drives the convicted protagonist to madness, the whole climactic scene is performed in silent mime – the image of man reduced to an animal by inhuman treatment – and as he beats on the door of his cell the sound of his fists is echoed by the hammering of other prisoners. The one stands for the many; and the play's circular action emphasizes that there is nothing unique about the case even in terms of an individual life. It ends in the lawyer's office where it began, with Falder committing suicide rather than face re-imprisonment. Again the treatment is objective, and it is the lack of any overt bias that makes the play so powerful. Falder is guilty of the fraud for which he is convicted. The judge's summing up is impartial and unemotional. The prison governor is humane. The scrupulous 'justice' with which the dramatic case is presented makes the demonstrated injustice of the system unarguable.

At the same time, Galsworthy's adherence to the principle of 'furthering with each thread the harmony and strength of a design to which all must be subordinated' limits the resonance of his drama. There is always a sense in which the specificity of a play's political aim or social purpose limits its depth, the extreme example being Agitprop, and this is reinforced by Galsworthy's schematic approach. Even though his drama has an almost documentary quality, the reliance on formal set scenes limits the impression of realism by contrast with a younger contemporary like D.H. Lawrence. And a later play like *The Show* (1925) is revealingly aware of its own superficiality. In exposing the inhumanity of not only the judicial system but journalism, the bottom line that 'everything's a show nowadays' implicitly refers back to the theatre – particularly to the type of drama that, like a living newspaper, deals with public events through the photographic reproduction of human anguish. As one of the characters remarks at the conclusion of an inquest on the suicide of a high profile adulterer, 'There's nothing like real life after all. Beats the theatre hollow.'[14]

Notes

1 Letter to William Archer, BL Add. MS 45290, 1905.
2 Granville-Barker, letter to Michael MacOwen, 1936, cited in *Plays and Players*, July 1955, p. 7; Lennox Robinson, *Curtain Up*, London, 1942, p. 26.

3 *The Collected Plays of Granville-Barker*, London, 1967, I, p. 168; *Plays by Harley Granville-Barker*, pp. 188–90.

4 *The Collected Plays*, I, p. 69.

5 *The Madras House*, London, 1977, p. 5.

6 *Ibid.*, pp. 93, 101, 96.

7 *Ibid.*, pp. 4, 134, 121.

8 *Ibid.*, pp. 65, 37, 87.

9 *Ibid.*, p. 134; *Bystander*, cited in Dennis Kennedy, *Granville-Barker and the Dream of Theatre*, Cambridge, 1985, p. 113.

10 Letter to St John Ervine, Humanities Research Centre, Texas. (For a statement of the case against Granville-Barker, see John Russell Taylor, *The Rise and Fall of the Well-Made Play*, London, 1967, pp. 112f.)

11 See letters to Edward Garnett, 7 September and 19 December 1909, in *Letters from John Galsworthy 1900–1932*, ed. Garnett, London, 1934, pp. 172, 174.

12 *The Life and Letters of John Galsworthy*, ed. H.V. Marrot, London, 1935, p. 192.

13 *Letters from John Galsworthy 1900–1932*, pp. 175 & 157.

14 Galsworthy, 'On Expression', English Association, July 1924, p. 15, and *The Plays of John Galsworthy*, London, 1929, pp. 891, 901.

3.3 Realism versus Agitprop: D. H. Lawrence (1885–1930) and the Workers' Theatre Movement

D. H. Lawrence

CHECKLIST OF LAWRENCE'S MAJOR PLAYS

(Since the first production of almost all Lawrence's plays was so widely separated from the original social circumstances surrounding their composition, the date of writing is also given in brackets.)

> *A Collier's Friday Night* (1909), 1968
> *The Widowing of Mrs Holroyd* (1911), 1926
> *The Daughter-in-Law* (1912), 1967
> *David*, 1927

Although both came to theatre through the novels that in each case established their reputation, unlike Galsworthy, D.H. Lawrence's plays show no sense of the problematic aspect of recreating actuality on the stage. Opposing Shaw and Galsworthy equally for their rationalism and on

principle – 'bloodless . . . rule and measure mathematical folk . . . We have to
hate our immediate predecessors, to get free from their authority' – Lawrence
offers a very different perspective on the same material as Galsworthy's *Strife*.
A strike occurs in both *The Daughter-in-Law* (1912, first staged at the Royal
Court in 1967) and *Touch and Go* (1920, unperformed). But it is kept off-
stage and in each case we only see one side. As a result there is no explicit
political dimension. Deliberately presenting the 'single human individual' in
opposition to 'all these social beings' of Galsworthy's, Lawrence concentrates
exclusively on personal relationships and passions.[1]

The fact that these are far more convincing in the miner's cottage of
The Daughter-in-Law than the mine-owner's offices of *Touch and Go* is not
simply the result of foreign exile cutting Lawrence off from his roots: the
usual critical explanation for his later plays' conventional characterization
and drop in intensity. It comes equally from a bias inherent in his concept
of realism. This is part of Lawrence's own mythology and continues to
influence the popular imagination – being exemplified, for example, in
Bond's contention that the only viable culture comes from the uneducated
working classes (discussed below, p. 168). For Lawrence, coalminers and
peasants are vital figures, being close to nature or associated metaphorically
with the subterranean world of the instincts, while sophistication is suspect
and intellectual logic a symptom of decadence.

A variant on the Rousseauesque idea of the Noble Savage, this has since acquired proletarian sanctification. Whatever its ideological appropriateness,
the net effect is a severe limitation in dramatic material. Cultural or social
conditioning is assumed to dehumanize an individual: education that emphasizes mind over body, behaviour that deadens the emotions to facilitate
exploitation of one's fellow-beings, religion enslaving the psyche with guilt.
So it becomes impossible to portray members of any but the working class in
realistic terms. And the essential romanticism of this approach can be indicated in Lawrence's most characteristic play, *The Widowing of Mrs Holroyd*,
which was rejected by Granville-Barker in 1911 and only staged in 1926.
The climax of a Nottinghamshire trilogy that includes *A Collier's Friday
Night* (written in 1909, unperformed until 1968) and *The Daughter-in-Law*,
it presents a detailed slice of working-class life with strong autobiographical
elements.

Each of these plays explores the marriage of a strong-willed woman who
thinks herself superior to her husband, as in Lawrence's own family; and
the increasingly destructive effect of educational or cultural pretensions

defines the theme. *A Collier's Friday Night* sets the pattern, showing that the relationship between wife and husband repeats that between mother and father. The woman's contempt drives the man to the drinking that makes him despicable in her eyes. His drunken assault on her provides ammunition for the woman's next attack – but underlines that her rejection is the cause of his brutality. In this vicious circle the almost complete lack of action indicates there is no escape. This situation of mutual misery, here presented as typical, is intensified in the succeeding plays: first by being set in a context of industrial unrest; and finally by a mine accident, in which the husband's death is taken as 'a judgment' on the woman.

In *The Widowing of Mrs Holroyd*, the wife's lack of emotional fidelity and support is seen as responsible, both for her husband's isolation from the rest of his shift, and for the despair that saps his will to survive. According to the men who bear his body back from the mine, he made no effort to escape the rock fall. On the surface, this demonstrates the truth of her earlier complaint that 'there's nothing at the bottom of him . . . no anchor, no roots'. Yet his lack of a spiritual core is due to her emasculation, usurping his place as head of the household, then deciding to leave him for another man. As she comments, 'I never loved you enough . . . you didn't try'. The irony is perhaps over-obvious. Despising his physicality, which she dismisses with 'There's just his body and nothing else', all she is left with is his corpse.[2]

Today, when even more explicit examples of poverty and sexuality have become common in realistic drama, it may be difficult to appreciate how unconventional such a depiction of human existence would have seemed to Lawrence's contemporaries. The sharp contrast with the sanitized image of the worker in more traditional plays – including those of Galsworthy – was intended to shock (and may have contributed to keeping Lawrence's work unperformed). In this blood-and-soil naturalism the emphasis on basic daily activities shows where the values of Lawrence's drama lie.

The preparation of food or ironing of linen that fill the stage are not simply documentary. The kitchen may be literally where poor families live; but it is also where the body is fed. The point is that the meals cooked are *not* eaten by the husband; washing does *not* keep out a rat on the search for food. Everything has metaphoric significance. Food stands for sex, the rodent for a coldly manipulative rival who 'filches' the wife, obsessive cleanliness for assumed moral superiority. However, even if it is given symbolic resonance, the real is not idealized. The harshness of working-class life is emphasized.

Yet by itself this is endurable, even admirable. What makes it unbearable are pretensions: Mrs Holroyd's snobbery about 'common' women; her rejection of her rough but virile husband for a man who 'hates mess of any sort' and whose idea of physical contact is holding hands; above all, spurious gentility that leads her to prefer an electrician (as a 'tradesman') to the miner (as a 'labourer').[3] And these minimal class distinctions also represent traditional power sources versus new technology, bread earned with strength and black face versus cleverness and clean hands.

At first glance the conflict appears to be balanced, with Holroyd's drunkenness and violence justifying his wife's decision to leave him, although (as in the preceding parts of the trilogy) there is the clear implication that his behaviour is an inarticulate response to her inability to appreciate his real qualities. However, beneath the personal level *The Widowing of Mrs Holroyd* presents a negative case study, as the title itself suggests. Socially conditioned standards (by which the husband is found wanting) are self-defeating, with his wished-for death bringing her a bleak awareness of loss, rather than liberation. The misery depicted in the play comes from accepting false ideals and a morality that denies the body. It implies that the potential for an undistorted relationship exists, but only in proletarian terms. Indeed, the tragic power of the ending comes from the awareness of this unrealized alternative as we watch the ritualistic washing of the dead man's body.

Lawrence avoids any explicit message. His realism documents the wretchedness of working-class existence and the evil of bourgeois values. However, when a specifically proletarian drama emerged in England, it shared the same Rousseauesque social perspective, but aimed for an even more direct political effect than Galsworthy had achieved with *Justice*. The result is Agitprop theatre at the opposite stylistic extreme to Lawrence. With only the workers being portrayed realistically, the worlds of government, industrial management or corporate finance come to be dramatized according to abstract theory, without a human dimension. Even living up to Shaw's criterion of allowing each individual a personal justification for their actions is considered the mark of a reactionary. Instead, decision-makers are reduced to caricature, creating a schematic picture of the social system that is convincing only to the already converted. The result may be a gain in moral fervour; but its stridency alienates significant sections of the public and although in the mass unemployment of the Thirties Agitprop could claim to be the voice of the working class, with the young playwrights radicalized by the 1968 student revolution the same tone increasingly became an expression of political frustration.

The Workers' Theatre Movement

The Workers' Theatre Movement (1926–35) was founded to 'conduct working-class propaganda and agitation through...dramatic representation'. Agitprop theatre originated in the aftermath of the Russian Revolution as a substitute for newsprint, to spread information and the party line through a widely dispersed and largely illiterate population; and the typical form of short sketches illustrating political commentary was developed by the 'Blue Shirts' troupe, an offshoot of the Russian Institute of Journalism. Picked up by Erwin Piscator in Berlin during the 1920s, and used by Brecht as the basis for his short didactic pieces, it became a logical model for Joan Littlewood and Ewan McColl's Manchester 'Theatre of Action' (1932–4). The most theatrically developed group in the WTM, this evolved from McColl's 'Red Megaphones' (a typical Agitprop label), which had specialized in four-minute topical sketches. These were performed outside factory-gates to groups of strikers, or on the streets for the unemployed and the hunger-marchers of the time. Sometimes little more than choral declamation or political rewordings of popular songs, simplicity was the key factor in these street-scripts, since the group had 'to be able to move into position, to perform...and be away before the cops got onto you'.[4]

Agitprop was deliberately minimalist drama that rejected literary standards, intellectual subtleties and structural complexity, along with theatrical illusion. The aim was to take performances directly to the working people, and presentational simplicity became an ideological value in itself. The plays corresponded to an ideal of proletarian art, by definition the opposite of traditional ('bourgeois') forms. Although the WTM also performed work such as *In Time of Strife* – an intensely realistic 1927 depiction of starvation in Scottish mining communities by Joe Corrie, a Fifeshire miner – Naturalism was rejected as 'a mere photographic view of things as they appear on the surface'. In its place came what Tom Thomas, the one dramatist to emerge from the WTM, defined as 'Dialectical Realism': 'the X-Ray picture of society and social forces'. In practice this led to melodramatic simplifications of social reality, presenting the devil as a top-hatted financier with money-bag paunch, opposed by virtuously muscular proletarians, or Hitler as the embodiment of Capitalism. And the dominance of cartoon imagery is indicated by the way it conditions even a 1936 Unity script, *Where's That Bomb?*, which attempts to counter the distortions of such images by changing the Bolshevik villain (with the bomb) into a worker-hero.

Reacting against this, McColl, who had become aware that 'limitations in production ideas were an implicit feature of Agit-Prop theatre', defined the Theatre of Action's aim as being to develop a theatrical form 'sufficiently flexible to reflect the constantly changing twentieth-century political scene'.[5] Agitprop elements were retained, particularly its conceptual simplification, stereotype characters and concision. But either these were set in a sophisticated structural frame (influenced by the American example of Clifford Odets' *Waiting for Lefty*, pirated by Unity Theatre in 1935), or they were combined with 'scientific' stage machinery and techniques adapted from Vakhtangov or Meyerhold, as with *John Bullion*, a stock WTM script.

In Joan Littlewood's 1934 version of the script, *John Bullion* – reduced from an hour and a quarter performance time to 18 minutes – became 'a constructivist ballet with words'. Cartoon characters, photographic projection, and a 'mutograph' (an electric news board) combined to illustrate the thesis that big business is responsible for war; and war is presented as a witchdoctor's dance of death. Sentimental or ironic contrasts (such as the sound of gunfire drowning out off-stage children's voices singing 'All things bright and beautiful', or mannequins in bathing costumes and gas masks) are brutally obvious. Grotesque automatons, and driving rhythms (Mossolow's 'concrete' music) punch home the message, which culminates in a typically Agitprop utopian catharsis. On the declaration of war the dancing Capitalists freeze. Headlines announce ' FRENCH WORKERS DEMONSTRATING FOR PEACE – BRITISH DOCKERS REFUSE TO LOAD MUNITIONS – GERMANY PARALYSED BY MASS STRIKES... REVOLUTION IN SPAIN ... ANTI-WAR ORGANIZATIONS ISSUE ULTIMATUM' Then 'the INTERNATIONALE flowers into several languages. Workers march onto the stage from all sides', while the Capitalists 'collapse like deflated balloons in a heap'.[6]

Beneath this utopian stridency, the use of caricature, cartoon elements and rapid pacing form the basis for Joan Littlewood's work following the Second World War (see below pp. 121–22). Indeed, even at this point there was a move towards conventional drama. By 1935 the Theatre of Action had been reorganized as Theatre Union, and transferred to a fixed stage, where they performed radical classics – *Lysistrata*, and Lope de Vega's *Fuente Ovejuna*, which had been given new political relevance by the outbreak of the Spanish Civil War – as well as the occasional straight contemporary play, such as the première of O'Casey's *The Star Turns Red* (1940). However, these productions still retained Agitprop elements; and the immediacy of street performance was replaced by improvisation. This was embodied both in acting and scripts, which were continually changed to reflect the headlines of the day. As McColl commented, 'we never stopped working on any of the scripts. And this went on right through Theatre Workshop [in the 1960s], until it became an absolute barrier [with the more complex dramatic requirements of conventional theatre] – you never knew where you were, you never knew which script you were working from. But ... conditions and political situations might change overnight.' Reflecting this, their repertoire continued to include 'Living Newspaper' pieces such as *Last Edition* (1939).

As a tool for creating political consciousness with journalistic origins, the establishment-controlled news media (being direct ideological competition) has been a continual target for Agitprop drama and its derivatives, from Tom Thomas' 1929 sketch, *Suppress, Oppress, Depress*, to Howard Brenton and David Hare's full-length polemic *Pravda* in 1986. *Last Edition* was typical, being at once based on and parodying news reports. It presented the Munich agreement and Germany's invasion of Czechoslovakia as a gangster-slapstick (anticipating Brecht's *Arturo Ui* by over a decade) with political commentary interjected in songs: elements that characterized the Littlewood/McColl brand of Agitprop. And during the Second World War, Littlewood returned to Agitprop parody with a Marx brothers Macbeth/ Lady Macbeth in *The Strange Case of Sigismund McHess and the Weird Sisters*, and again in *The Sleepwalker* (The Strolling Players 1943) which included such lines as 'Out damned spot! ... Shall ruined Stalingrad, a spot upon the map, defy a score of my divisions?'

Addressing the masses and working outside both the theatrical and political system, this type of drama is the opposite of Galsworthy's in approach, just as much as it departs from Lawrence's realism in style. Its aim is the abolition of an inequitable system as a whole, not its reform through the correction of specific injustices; and it works through highlighting class divisions and economic disparities. As with the gap between political forecast and historical actuality in a script like *John Bullion*, the simplified analysis of the Agitprop mode turns its dramatic statement into wish-fulfilment. Even in the widespread unemployment of the Thirties it had little demonstrable political effect. McColl later commented that plays performed by the Theatre of Action and Unity Theatre might have 'changed the class of heroes and villains ... but ... even when they were successful they weren't successful in our terms – in changing the nature of the *audience*'.

However, by developing Agitprop elements within the resources of the conventional stage, the Theatre Workshop remained a model for counter-theatre. When radical playwrights emerged in the early 1970s with the aim of making drama a weapon for class conflict, they turned again to Agitprop.

Notes

1 D.H. Lawrence, *Selected Literary Criticism*, ed. Anthony Beal, London, 1961, pp. 132 (1913) and 122.

2 *The Widowing of Mrs Holroyd*, London, 1965, pp. 56, 389, 57–8.

3 *Ibid.*, p. 39.

4 Tom Thomas, cited in Raphael Samuel, Ewan McColl and Stuart Cosgrove, *Theatres of the Left 1880–1935*, London, 1985, p. 34, and McColl, p. 230. (For a comprehensive discussion of The Workers' Theatre Movement, its international ramifications, and evolution into Community Theatre, see David Bradby and John McCormick, *People's Theatre*, London, 1978.)

5 Tom Thomas, *Daily Worker*, 8 February 1930; Samuel, McColl, and Cosgrove, *Theatres of the Left*, p. 247. These aims were directly repeated in the London Unity Theatre manifesto, which declared that only by using 'the most recent scientific and technical developments can we create a theatrical form sufficiently flexible to reflect the rapidly changing twentieth-century scene'.

6 This script and subsequent material cited from Joan Littlewood and Ewan McColl is from typescripts held by Clive Barker, University of Warwick.

3.4 Terence Rattigan (1911–77): updating the Well-Made Play

CHECKLIST OF RATTIGAN'S MAJOR PLAYS

French Without Tears, 1936

Flare Path, 1942

Love in Idleness, 1944

The Winslow Boy, 1946

Playbill, 1948

(*The Browning Version/*

   Harlequinade)

Adventure Story, 1949

The Deep Blue Sea, 1952

Separate Tables, 1954

(*The Table in the Window/*

   Table Number Seven)

Variations on a Theme, 1958

Ross, 1960

Man and Boy, 1963

A Bequest to the Nation, 1970

In Praise of Love, 1973

Cause Célèbre, 1977

Terence Rattigan was widely admired and set the tone for serious English the-atre in the decade after the Second World War, only to be relegated to critical oblivion at the height of his career. As he commented, 'There I was in 1956, a reasonably successful playwright with *Separate Tables* just opened, and sud-denly the whole Royal Court thing [George Devine's 'new writers' season that produced John Osborne] exploded, and Coward and Priestley and I were all dismissed, sacked by the critics.'[1] Despite the continuing popularity of his plays on the stage, Rattigan is still ignored in most discussions of modern English drama, or dismissed disparagingly as an anachronism.

Today, Rattigan's work has gained new significance as a forerunner of 'Gay drama'. But his concern not to alienate the general public that his work was designed for, and which he christened 'Aunt Edna', led him to generalize the underlying homosexual themes of his most characteristic plays, turning them into a plea for the sexually outlawed or disabled of all genders. This fictional image of a 'respectable, middle-class, middle-aged, maiden lady' demanded 'lowbrow' entertainment, emotional satisfaction and suspense.[2] He supplied it, producing a modern equivalent of Pinero's Problem Play. Rattigan's themes are subtly subversive, his plots revolve around widely relevant moral issues, and his characters have considerable depth. But because he had become identified with this average spectator, his plays suddenly seemed dated when *Look Back in Anger* appeared in 1956.

Although Osborne is discussed in detail below, it is worth noting here how ironic it was that *Look Back in Anger* should have relegated Rattigan to critical darkness, since its dramatic situation is almost identical to the first half of *Separate Tables* (which opened twenty months before and was still running). Rattigan's play is composed of two contrasting one-act pieces set in the same locale, *The Table in the Window* and *Table Number Seven*. In one, a hotel manageress finds herself abandoned by the resident she loves: an incognito Labour politician, driven out of public life after being convicted of assaulting his wife, who is now desperate for a reconciliation. The other playlet traces the relationship between two victims of society: a fading spinster, dominated by the mother who has infantilized her – a situation borrowed in turn from Noel Coward's *Point Valaine* (1935, first London performance 1947) – and a nonentity whose low estimate of self worth has caused him to masquerade as a retired major and molest women in the darkness of local cinemas, leading to the ignominy of a trial that exposes his pretentious upper-class accent and claimed military background as fraudulent.

Both *The Table in the Window* and *Look Back in Anger* deal with a triangular relationship in which a cool and self-possessed woman (the manageress/Alison's best friend) fails to replace the upper-class wife of a socialist from a proletarian background (the ex-politician/Jimmy Porter). Each marriage has erupted in violence, which leads to separation, but the battered wives' emotional needs drive them both back into their husbands' arms. Surface detail may be slightly different. Osborne's setting is a seedy provincial flat instead of a shabby Bournemouth hotel. Jimmy is a university graduate without a job, not an ex-cabinet minister reduced to hack journalism; and he is presented as the victim of society in general, rather than being forced to hide his identity because of a prison sentence, while his cruelty is mental instead of physical. Yet the fundamental similarities are striking. The wives in each play are beautiful, accused of sexual frigidity and characterized as 'predictable' (Rattigan) or 'pusillanimous' (Osborne). It is also the revelation of weakness beneath their apparent dominance, their abasement that finally wins back the husbands. The description of 'a genuine, live, roaring savage from the slums of Hull' is equally appropriate to both males, who share much the same passionate verbal monologues and political commitment.[3] What is different is primarily Rattigan's objectivity.

Where Osborne shows the world through his protagonist's angry eyes, the *Look Back in Anger/Table in the Window* story is only half of Rattigan's action. It is balanced by the contrasting vignette of the two sexually repressed emotional cripples in *Table Number Seven.* On the surface the two situations are mirror opposites. Instead of a forceful and strongly masculine person-ality of working-class origins and prime minister potential, we are shown a fearful nonentity whose boasts of sexual prowess and upper-class extrovert appearance are fake. Similarly, the focus shifts from the epitome of female elegance and poise in both the politician's wife and the manageress, to the nadir of insecurity and clumsy inarticulacy in the child-like daughter. But it is not only a shared setting (the ironically named Beauregard Private Hotel) that unites the two halves into a single play.

A retrospective action, uncovering the past, is followed by the tentative beginnings of a new relationship. The same minor figures who formed an almost anonymous background to the first half, develop into individualized characters, capable of catalysing the dramatic situation and determining its outcome. Both male protagonists have taken refuge in pseudonyms and false identities. One has been sentenced to jail for causing his wife grievous bodily harm, while the other pleads guilty to minor sex crimes. The women in each half can also be seen as equivalents, with an appearance of self-assurance covering despair in the first, while real weakness is finally provoked into self-assertion in the second. Such role-playing is intrinsically theatrical; and even more significantly, both pairs are designed to be played by the same actors (originally Eric Portman and Margaret Leighton).

At first glance, the two halves seem out of order. The rhetoric of passion is followed by the unstated suggestion of a minimal commitment. The cowed and retarded daughter defies her censorious mother in refusing to ignore the pitiful figure of the exposed Major. He in turn has found the courage to stay where his real personality is known, rather than running away to continue living a lie in another rootless place where 'beau regard' can be sustained. But given their deficiencies, there can be little future for the pair. This almost anticlimactic reversal is an expression of the value Rattigan placed on 'the implicit rather than the explicit that gives life to a scene and, by demanding the collaboration of an audience, holds it, contented, flattered, alert and responsive'. The quality of understated suggestion, which Rattigan repeatedly emphasizes, links his work both to Granville-Barker's barely verbalized impressionism, as a way of embodying an inner or 'secret life', and to Harold Pinter's use of silences to carry emotional meaning.[4] On another level, this obliqueness has an unsettling effect, using the contrast with standard patterns of domestic drama – avoiding a rising action and unified plot, denying a clear resolution – to question moral norms.

At the same time, Rattigan avoids overt confrontation with the values of an average spectator by emphasizing the entertainment quality of performance. Unlike, for example, Somerset Maugham's *Lady Frederick* (discussed below, pp. 256–57), where make-up transforms an aging woman into an apparently youthful beauty to show the falsity of ideals and the illusory nature of theatrical performance, Rattigan's role changes serve to display the expertise of the performers. Rather than questioning the image of beauty established in the first half, the actress' subsequent pitiful appearance implies that there is the potential for loveliness even in the most ugly or inept. However, all these elements are highly effective dramatically; and beneath the apparent lack of intellectual challenge there is a subtle probing of the spectators' responses. The structural complexity gives thematic depth to what might otherwise be a conventional type of play.

Separate Tables is both Rattigan's most popular and characteristic piece, articulating his typical themes of loneliness, inarticulacy, and above all the twin poles of sexual obsession and repression. Apart from *The Winslow Boy* (1946), almost every one of his plays revolves around the conflict between these two states. Both are seen as equally damaging, while true strength is defined as asexual 'self-sufficiency . . . being alone, that's the real blessed state – if you've the character for it'; and indeed this is reflected in the way Rattigan sets up his plays. The more urgent the need or violent the passion, the more rational and verbal the characters' expression of emotion. This goes along with the formal patterning of the action; and in the assessment of David Rudkin – whose poetic and visionary drama is so different (see below, pp. 495ff.) that it lends his positive assessment particular weight – both elements are sublimations of Rattigan's homosexuality: 'The craftsmanship . . . seems to me to arise from deep psychological necessity, a drive to organize the energy that arises out of his own pain. Not to batten it down but to invest it with some expressive clarity that speaks immediately to people, yet keeps himself hidden.'[5]

This is also expressed in the theme of disguised personality, which is one of Rattigan's dominant motifs. It recurs in *The Browning Version* (1948), as well as in both halves of *Separate Tables* (1954), reaching its fullest statement in *Ross* (1960), where it is the explicit subject of the play. Lawrence of Arabia is dramatized as 'a legend', a malarial dream that initially looks 'phony and posed' versus the 'vision ... of the truth' about himself, which has been revealed by the homosexual assault of his Turkish torturers. And this is framed in his final search for 'peace' (the last word of the play) in the ranks of the airforce under the successive aliases of Ross, then Shaw, and finally a totally anonymous number.[6]

T.E. Lawrence's changing of identities is the crux on which the plot turns in *Ross*. The same switch, in sexual terms, was typical of Rattigan's writing methods up until 1956. The Major in *Separate Tables*, and the suicidal heroine of *The Deep Blue Sea* (1952) were both originally conceived as homosexual figures. The way they have been transposed into male and female heterosexuals, while retaining the identifying qualities of 'perversion' (from the narrow viewpoint of the moral majority) or victimization, was not due simply to censorship. The boundaries of 'allowable' subject-matter had been pushed back inch by inch in the early 1950s by imports from America, such as *A View from the Bridge* or Julien Green's *South* (mostly performed under club licence). But Rattigan's metaphorical masking was a form of generalization that had distinct theatrical advantages, adding depth though indirection, and increasing intensity by setting up barriers to direct expression. Removing the necessity for disguise made Rattigan's drama less – not more – effective when he turned to explicit treatments of homosexual characters or relationships in *Variations on a Theme* (1958) or *Man and Boy* (1963). Indeed Shelagh Delaney wrote *A Taste of Honey* (1958: see below, p. 233) to correct what she perceived as insensitivity in the way Rattigan portrayed homosexuality.

As in his earlier plays, Rattigan's primary concern was still what the average spectator accepted as 'normal'. After 1956 there was a clearly discernable liberalization of public attitudes, fostered by the 'new wave' playwrights: Osborne, Wesker and Arden, as well as Delaney. His change in focus can be seen as responding to this. Since 'Aunt Edna' was now 'classless, rejuvenated' and 'of some sexual experience', a more open treatment of his dramatic material was possible. Yet at the same time, the sense that Rattigan is sacrificing integrity to popularity tends to undercut his characters' main concern 'of learning ... to know yourself as you really are'.[7]

Even so, compromise is not necessarily a bad thing in theatrical terms. Any type of drama that loses touch with its public rapidly ceases to have any vitality (a case in point being Edward Bond's later and increasingly strident political plays – discussed below, pp. 156 and 173); and to the degree that all art is self-selective in the type of spectator it attracts, drama necessarily reflects the majority opinions of its audience. So a performance may provide a rallying cry, as with Bond's anti-apartheid or nuclear disarmament sketches, written for specific protest meetings. But plays are most effective as agents of change in articulating a deeply felt but as yet unfocused idea. The wider drama's appeal, the broader its social influence. Thus Rattigan's concern with reflecting behavioural norms can be defended as formulating a theme in the most universal terms, where the emotional quality of a relationship is more significant than its specific sexual orientation.

His public rejection of the 'Theatre of Ideas' in 1950 began a debate that drew attacks from the whole spectrum of dramatists at the time, from Christopher Fry to Sean O'Casey and, of course, Bernard Shaw himself. However, Rattigan's defence that 'plays should be mainly about people and not mainly about things' is a useful corrective; and it is revealing that his rejection of intellectual drama is stated in terms of style rather than content:

It's only Aunt Edna's *emotions* that a playwright can hope to excite ... She is bored by propaganda, enraged at being 'alienated', loathes placards coming down and telling her what is going to happen next, hates a lot of philosophical talk on the stage with nothing happening at all, enjoys poetry only when it is dramatic.

Even Brecht would have agreed that 'entertainment *per se*' was not 'necessarily an unworthy object of drama'. The danger is that if plays are 'designed principally ... to entertain' (as Rattigan defined his aim) this effectively reduces any thematic statement to a lowest common denominator.[8] But Rattigan's drama consistently raises significant questions, and by dealing with them in human terms causes the audience to identify with the problems faced by his characters.

An example of this is the double action of *Separate Tables*, which was Rattigan's standard structural form throughout his career. Contrasted one-act plays are also paired in *Playbill* (*The Browning Version* and *Harlequinade*, 1948) and *In Praise of Love* (1973). The same structure recurs in full-length plays like *Adventure Story* (1949), where action is set against philosophical discussion, or *Cause Célèbre* (1977), in which two different plots are juxtaposed and interwoven. The doubleness is designed to make audiences continually re-evaluate their attitudes, as with *Separate Tables*, where the spectator instinctively associates ex-politician and fake major, sophisticated beauty and faded innocence, seeing each in terms of the other. In addition, in *Separate Tables* the initial impressions of each character are deliberately misleading – a typically Shavian approach, almost a distinguishing technique of serious social drama in England. At the same time, the doubling generalizes the individual case, allowing the wider moral issues to emerge.

The Winslow Boy (1946), written before Rattigan had evolved his characteristic structure with *Playbill* and *Separate Tables*, shows this technique applied to a political issue, rather than moral questions. It was based (like *Cause Célèbre*) on an actual case from 1908, the two-year long Archer-Shee trial against the Admiralty to establish the innocence of a young naval cadet expelled from his training school for theft. Developing this documentary material to show the denial of 'a fundamental human right', Rattigan's subtext is the significance of individual liberty versus global problems that threaten the stability of society itself (the coming First World War).

The reactionary and despotic nature of the Establishment is represented by the lawyer for the defence. A totally unsympathetic figure, self-serving and supercilious, he is presented as 'always speaking against what is right and just', and held responsible for the suicide of a radical Trades Union leader whom he had prosecuted for embezzlement. However, shifting blame onto an individual allows Rattigan to switch his attack from an easy political target (the late-Victorian Establishment) to the public tendency for censuring people on insufficient evidence. The audience's preconceptions are challenged, when the lawyer is revealed to be emotionally committed to the cause of innocence and deeply idealistic – to the point of refusing an appointment as Lord Chief Justice. His 'cold...logic' turns out to be only a mask, adopted as the one way to 'Let right be done.'[9]

Despite some similarities to Galsworthy's *Justice* (1910), Rattigan's model is Pinero's *Benefit of the Doubt* (1895), where the course of an off-stage trial is reported by a series of messengers to display its impact privately on a family. So here, the action is kept entirely outside the courtroom on which it centres, substituting a series of personal interrogations in each act. The father ascertains the financial state of his daughter's fiancé. The lawyer cross-questions the boy, and declares him innocent in the face of the evidence. The mother challenges the father's motives for sacrificing his family and his health to continue the case. Finally the daughter establishes the lawyer's true nature.

This private focus diverts attention from the system to a purely human dimension. At the same time the action affirms the essential humanity of nine out of every ten people – the exact number of the cast, counting the reporter and photographer as a composite figure of the Press (and precisely the same ratio as in *Table Number Seven*). Each of the play's four scenes closes with one of the opposing forces converted to the cause of Justice. Innocence is both vindicated and preserved. And in the immediate post-war context this has a double relevance. It relates to the surprise election of a Labour government in 1946, serving as reassurance that this will be only a passing trial, while the 'moral' referred to in the dedication of the play translates the triumph of right in 'the Winslow boy' affair into the defeat of Nazi Germany. So the battle against an apparently unjust Establishment in the original court case becomes a demonstration of the social order's continuing validity that enlists the spectators' emotions of victory over Hitler:

ARTHUR ... perhaps brute stubbornness isn't such a bad quality in the face of injustice?
CATHERINE Or in the face of tyranny.[10]

The omission of any reference to anti-Catholicism, which made the historical Archer-Shee trial an equivalent to the anti-Semitic Dreyfus case, underlines the thrust towards generalization. Rattigan is clearly defining his theme in terms with which most people will be able to identify; and it is mainly this that links Rattigan to the traditional Problem Play of Pinero and the nineteenth-century Tom Robertson. However, where their characters were manipulated to demonstrate a moral, Rattigan's principle was always that 'subject matter stems from people'.[11]

To the extent that his plays reflected the psychological repressions and hypocrisy of post-war Britain, they came to epitomize the evasion of emotion that seemed to characterize the society Osborne castigates – even though Rattigan's own play *In Praise of Love* condemns precisely this lack of personal feeling as the real '*vice Anglais*' (a term usually applied to homosexuality). Rather than any failure of dramatic integrity, this sense of his work as period pieces, and his identification with the Establishment (signalled by a knighthood), was what made him the primary target for a younger generation of playwrights.

It was perhaps specifically in reaction to Rattigan that Osborne proclaimed the purpose of his drama was to 'give lessons in feeling' or Wesker's characters declared 'if you don't care, you'll die', just as *A Taste of Honey* (1958) was explicitly written in reaction against Rattigan's *Variations on a Theme*.[12] The fact that this was Shelagh Delaney's only successful play is some indication of the way the new wave dramatists required a representative of traditionalism to define their drama against. A decade later Rattigan's work was still fulfilling the same function; and it could be argued that paradoxically this opposition makes him one of the more influential post-war playwrights.

Even John Arden, whose style and themes (discussed below, pp. 132ff.) were already well-developed, made use of his work in this way. His parodistic treatment of Nelson in *The Hero Rises Up* (written in collaboration with his wife, Margaretta D'Arcy, 1968) was a deliberate counterpoint to Rattigan's *A Bequest to the Nation*. Originally produced on television as *Nelson: A Portrait in Miniature* in 1966, revised for the stage in 1970, then filmed with Glenda Jackson in 1973, Rattigan's play was written at the Duke of Edinburgh's suggestion. Although this seemed to associate it with Establishment values, Rattigan's focus is more radical than it appears.

Rattigan and the Ardens both highlight the gap between the mythical image and the human reality. Typically Rattigan reinforces the heroic stature of his protagonist – in the personal terms of his capacity for emotion, ability to rise above moral convention and self-sacrifice – while the Ardens deny and invert it. However, beneath the Brechtian pyrotechnics of *The Hero Rises Up*, their attack on the connection between war and the exploitation of the poor, or on hero-worship and the perpetuation of the status quo, is not the antithesis of Rattigan's play. Exactly the same criticism forms the subtext of *A Bequest to the Nation*:

Pressed means kidnapped... knocked on the head and thrown into a life as brutal and slavish as any in the world... If you were British seamen would you break your hearts if the revolutionaries won their war against us or the guillotine were set up in Piccadilly?

Rattigan's explicit suggestion that the masses are fighting against their real interests throws a highly ambivalent light on the national hero, whose capacity to inspire devotion is the cause of victory. Rattigan's characters may declare: 'Nelson. That's your answer.'[13] But as a whole, the play makes such certainties questionable. Overtly a salute to Establishment values, its true implication is subversive.

This is expressed with typical obliqueness that marks Rattigan's modernization of the Well-Made Play. Social issues are translated into personal terms – as with the exclusive family focus in *The Winslow Boy*, or the central emphasis on Nelson's adulterous relationship with Lady Hamilton in *A Bequest to the Nation*. This affirms the value of individual experience. The naturalistic surface of his plays, blending into period pieces with his historical subjects, gives his work an anachronistic flavour. Yet Rattigan's use of masking and the thematic displacement, which disguises his homosexual concerns, corresponds to the contemporary sociological analysis of role-playing in social behaviour. Indeed his 'Aunt Edna' reappears triumphant in Barry Humphries' 'Dame Edna Everage'. And where the Sardou/Pinero plotting of crisis and denouement imposes a melodramatic vision, Rattigan's double structures express the modern perception of relativity. At the same time, his obliqueness was drowned out in the strident tone introduced by Osborne. In the context of direct emotional activism established by the younger generation of dramatists, his plays appeared to have little relevance.

Notes

1 Rattigan, interview in *The Times*, 9 May 1977.

2 *The Collected Plays of Terence Rattigan*, Preface to vol. II, London, 1953, p. xii. For an example of the analysis of Rattigan's work as specifically homosexual material, see Benedict Nightingale, *An Introduction to 50 Modern British Plays*, London, 1982, pp. 249ff.

3 Osborne, *Look Back in Anger*, London, 1957, p. 22, and *The Collected Plays of Terence Rattigan*, III (1964), pp. 129 & 132.

4 Rattigan's comments on the importance of 'dramatic implication' (*Collected Plays*, I, p. xx) – as summarized by a more minor but in some ways comparable playwright, William Douglas Home: *The Times*, 10 February 1978. For a comparison to Pinter, see Susan Rusinko, *Terence Rattigan*, Twayne, 1983.

5 *Collected Plays*, III, pp. 142–3; Rudkin, in *Plays and Players*, 25, 5, February 1978, p. 23.

6 *Collected Plays*, III, pp. 332–3, 395 & 418.

7 *Collected Plays*, III, pp. xxii & 386.

8 *Ibid.*, III, pp. xxvii & xvii. See also *The New Statesman*, 13 May 1950, pp. 545–6.

9 *Collected Plays*, I, pp. 397, 450, 401, 354.

10 *Ibid.*, p. 444.

11 Interview, *Theatre Arts*, November 1956, p. 22.

12 Osborne, in *Declaration*, ed. Tom Maschler, London, 1957, p. 65; *The Wesker Trilogy*, Harmondsworth, 1960, p. 76.

13 Rattigan, *A Bequest to the Nation*, London, 1970, p. 41.

3.5 John Osborne (1929–94): the rhetoric of social alienation

CHECKLIST OF OSBORNE'S MAJOR PLAYS

Look Back in Anger, 1956	*Hotel in Amsterdam*, 1968
The Entertainer, 1957	*West of Suez*, 1971
Luther, 1961	*A Sense of Detachment*, 1972
Inadmissible Evidence, 1964	*Watch It Come Down*, 1975
A Patriot for Me, 1965	*Déjàvu*, 1992
Time Present, 1968	

Like certain other plays – Noel Coward's *The Vortex* in 1924, Edward Bond's *Saved* in 1965 – *Look Back in Anger* had an impact out of all proportion to its dramatic quality. More than any other single work in the century, it was a sociological phenomenon. Theatre historians were quick to point out that its production in May 1956 'marks the real break-through of "the new drama" into the British theatre' (despite the fact that the first performance was poorly received, with members of the audience, including the West End impresario Binkie Beaumont, walking out), sweeping away Terence Rattigan's problem plays and Noel Coward's later comedy (discussed below, pp. 262ff.). More traditional in tone, these suddenly seemed superficial by comparison. Largely because of a single review – by Kenneth Tynan, who declared that the play 'presents post-war youth as it really is' concluding 'I doubt if I could love anyone who did not wish to see *Look Back in Anger'* – the passion of Osborne's dialogue, together with a deliberately unglamorous depiction of everyday urban life, established fresh criteria for authenticity and contemporary relevance.[1]

Hailed by Arthur Miller as 'the only modern, English play', *Look Back in Anger* was accepted as 'a land-mine' that exploded all the old theatrical conventions. By contrast with sophisticated intrigue in the Coward manner or a plot based on significant public events, as in Rattigan's dramatizations of famous trials, Osborne's characters are defined by their inability to act. Since 'there aren't any good, brave causes left', social frustration is taken out on personal relationships.[2] The movement in the play is one of progressive isolation, with the protagonist driving each of his companions away. Denied political opportunities for changing the world around him, the consciously proletarian Jimmy Porter is reduced to verbal assaults on his pregnant wife, whose Establishment background makes her a surrogate for the class system. Having idealized Alison, Jimmy is incapable of appreciating her real qualities.

His violence drives her to return to her family, as well as (implicitly) causing her miscarriage. This love/hate dependency is replayed with a substitute from Alison's circle, driving out the working-class friend who shares the flat and is alienated by the lack of emotional integrity in this new relationship. She too leaves when Alison returns, in pain and unable to conceive any more children, trapping Jimmy in a sterile and regressive childhood fantasy.

The polemical dominance of the long invectives given to Jimmy, his isolation and the transposing of class struggle into the war of the sexes, presents politics as passion. Such emotional emphasis makes the impression of authenticity particularly important; and this is underpinned by the strongly autobiographical basis of the play.

The dramatic situation reflects Osborne's marriage to the actress Pamela Lane, whom he describes in exactly the same terms as Jimmy applies to Alison – 'Pamela's refusal to be drawn was the power of her sphynx's paw' – while the woman who takes her place corresponds to Jill Bennett, Osborne's lover at the time. Yet author and protagonist are mirror-opposites. Whereas Jimmy mistakes loving selflessness for unfeeling passivity, Osborne 'interpreted [Pamela's] bland complacency for the complaisance of a generous and loving heart'.[3] Like Alison she became pregnant, had an abortion and left him, while her parents disapproved so strongly of their engagement that they had Osborne followed by a private detective. Even the presence of a third person in the Porter *ménage* is not simply a dramatic convenience, providing a counterweight to the over-articulate author-figure. It too has autobiographical justification, since Osborne and his wife lived with Anthony Creighton (who collaborated on Osborne's early plays) in his flat.

These autobiographical elements helped to identify Osborne with his protagonist; and the catchphrase of 'angry young men' was coined to describe both. (In fact, typical of the hype that surrounded the play, this phrase had been coined by the press-officer of the Royal Court.[4]) Yet Jimmy is not just Osborne's mouthpiece, as this assumes. From the opening stage-direction, with its references to pride, cruelty, malice and 'apparent honesty', he is presented with ambiguous irony. His passion is undercut by lack of awareness: particularly his ignorance of Alison's pregnancy, but also the inability to understand that her father's Edwardian values are comparable to his own. His political claims are made questionable by his failure to see that her friend Helena is in fact the depersonalized product of an Establishment upbringing that he has mistakenly accused Alison of being. Self-pity is deliberately substituted for commitment; and the ending can hardly be classified as

wish-fulfilment – even if it corresponds exactly with his earlier hope that
Alison 'could have a child, and it would die'.[5]

In fact, beneath the autobiographical realism *Look Back in Anger* has
a symbolic structure. The four main characters are clearly divided on class
lines, in which sex equals status. Honest and male proletarians are set against
beautiful, but repressed or immoral – and female – gentry, with social conflict represented by the sexual battleground of Jimmy Porter's marriage to
the upper-class Alison, and his seduction of her more self-assured counterpart, Helena. Society is characterized by Alison's apparent avoidance of
commitment, which in Jimmy's view equals an inability to feel emotion,
being 'Pusillanimous. Adjective. Wanting of firmness of mind, of small
courage' – though Osborne himself saw the part still more negatively as
'a study of the tyranny of negation'. Epitomized by her symbolically absent
Brother Nigel, this vacuum of insensitivity is what enables the Establishment
to continue their traditional exploitation of the working classes. And even
towards the end of his life Osborne continued to insist on the validity of
this critique, excoriating Jill Bennett (the original of Helena) for avarice and
heartless narcissism in leaving all her money to the Battersea dog's home
when she committed suicide in 1990.[6]

Against this, as a note in the acting edition indicated, the play was designed
to give 'lessons in feeling' and Osborne's criterion for success was provoking
the audience to walk out during the performance. The rhetoric is powerful,
and the most common reaction to the play focused almost exclusively on
Jimmy's tirades, to the point where his voice became identified totally with
Osborne's. The political metaphor breaks down, however, precisely because
the play is not a monologue. The centrality and articulacy of the protagonist
may be overwhelming, with the other characters acting as feeds when Jimmy
is on stage, while off-stage he serves as the chief topic of their conversation.
Yet Alison's Edwardian-colonel father arouses sympathy and respect, instead
of substantiating Jimmy's invectives against the bourgeoisie. Jimmy's companion asserts his independence, while Alison comes to dominate Jimmy.
Her self-controlled reserve turns out to be a pose; and the audience is clearly
intended to empathize with her as a suffering individual. When that point
comes, she ceases to represent anything.

Rather than any political insight, it was this negativism that made
Osborne's protagonist the spokesman for the young generation, eliciting
comparisons with James Dean in *Rebel without a Cause* (1955). But in *Look
Back in Anger* the rebellion is purely verbal. It is a psychological truism that
forceful expression can be a cover, compensating for impotence; and Jimmy

Porter is accurately summed up in the stage direction 'to be as vehement as he is to be almost non-committal'. He even explicitly makes the connection between being 'angry and helpless', although in context this equation of passion and powerlessness is typically a weapon to force another character into submission, and therefore ambiguous.[7] Indeed the extent to which the rhetoric is divorced from any political commitment is illustrated by Osborne's reprise of *Look Back in Anger* in his last play *Déjàvu* (1992), where the aging Jimmy Porter's vituperation is directed against all left-wing causes.

Given the way Osborne's protagonist dominates the dialogue, which was reinforced by the strength and attractiveness of the actors who played the role, like Richard Burton in the film version of *Look Back in Anger*, it was easy to overlook these ironies and ambiguities. Instead, the shabby disorder of the set and the ordinariness of the characters' occupations (reading Sunday newspapers, ironing clothes) were taken to represent a new level of social realism, ushering in an era of 'kitchen sink' drama. However, as the Royal Court 1968 revival of *A Collier's Friday Night* (1906, first produced 1965) and *The Widowing of Mrs Holroyd* (1914, first produced 1926) reminded, D.H. Lawrence had already given more authentic pictures of working-class kitchens on stage.

In fact, Osborne emphasizes realistic details for thematic rather than factual reasons. This was brought out in the first production by the use of a sky-cloth in place of a ceiling. That it is always Sunday not only implies the missing spiritual centre in these characters' existence, but provides an image of stasis and displacement. In this context all actions are repetitive, ritualized and pointless. The ironing is never finished and the clothes they wear are never clean. Their lives have as little reference to reality outside the theatre, as the 'Flanagan and Allen' routine (Act III, scene 1) does to the real situation within the play. For all its comic verve, this music-hall turn not only lacks spontaneity, but marks the break-up of the partnership it celebrates.

The circularity of the action (which in some ways echoes *Waiting for Godot*, staged in London the preceding year) underlines the image. Act III mirrors the opening, confirming the point made by Alison to her father: 'You're hurt because everything is changed. Jimmy is hurt because everything is the same . . . Something's gone wrong.' The ending seems to offer a decisive break in the pattern with Alison's suffering, which finally destroys her neutrality and qualifies her as 'a human being' in Jimmy's terms. But the only possible response is a retreat to the sentimental substitute of 'Bears and Squirrels', which has earlier been defined as 'a silly symphony for people who couldn't

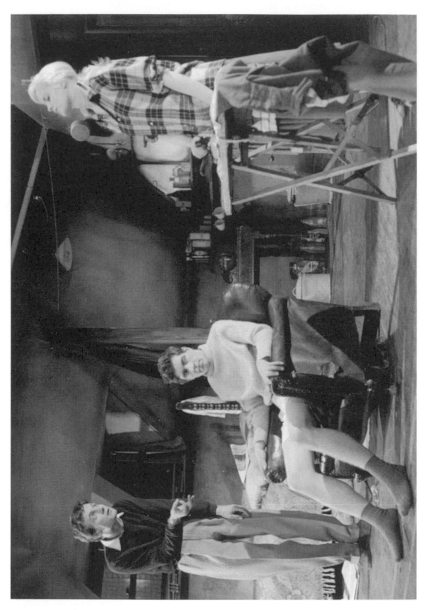

3 The social realism of everyday activities in Osborne's *Look Back in Anger* at the Royal Court

bear the pain of being human beings any longer'.[8] Although this resolution is too unstable to last, the dramatic statement it makes is bleak: there is no possibility of meaningful social change – no child of the future – and idealism equals self-destructive fantasy.

The title of *Look Back in Anger* defines the underlying theme of all Osborne's plays. Each is motivated by outrage at the discovery that the idealized Britain, for which so many had sacrificed themselves during the war years, was inauthentic. All in one way or another express the conviction that the national cults of Royalty, Our Finest Hour, Westminster as the Mother of parliamentary democracy – peddled by the jingoistic Tory tabloids that had formed Osborne's beliefs as a child – are fraudulent betrayals. Jimmy Porter, Archie Rice (the disillusioned comedian of *The Entertainer*, 1957), and Bill Maitland (the isolated lawyer, who becomes incapable of dealing with reality in *Inadmissible Evidence*, 1964) represent increasingly severe cases of alienation. Having seen through their society, they can no longer live or be sustained within it.

The impulse to pull down sham façades, to explode the psychologically crippling Establishment myths, is what marks *Look Back in Anger* as the prototype for the more radical drama of Arden, or Orton's farce, and links it to the work of Brenton and Hare in the following generation. But Osborne's disillusion also reflects a sense of disappointment that the traditional values are not true: a desire for lost certainties, which leads to the nostalgic portrayal of Edwardian figures like Alison's father.

Ironically, for a play hailed as ' . . . Then, on 8 May 1956, came the revolution . . .', *Look Back in Anger* is also retrospective in stylistic terms. As Osborne himself acknowledged, *Look Back in Anger* is 'a formal, rather old-fashioned play'.[9] Indeed, it is remarkably derivative. There are distinct parallels with Rattigan's commercial success of the time, *Separate Tables* (see pp. 77–8 above), which was precisely the kind of drama Osborne superseded, and had itself been derived from a Noel Coward play. In addition the setting – 'a fairly large attic room, at the top of a large Victorian house' – echoes Ibsen's *Wild Duck*, which also deals with the destructive effects of idealism; and at one point the text refers to Shaw.

'Proper little Marchbanks, you are!' may be ironic. Yet, Osborne was consciously using the same approach as Shaw in describing the rhetorical eloquence of his protagonists as 'arias'. He also drew a direct comparison in *Epitaph for George Dillon* (one of his earlier collaborations with Anthony Creighton which only reached the stage in 1958), where the playscripts written by the title-figure are clearly similar to his own: 'Dialogue's not bad, but these great long speeches – that's a mistake. People want action, excitement. I know – you think you're Bernard Shaw. But where's he today? Eh? People won't listen to him.'[10]

The parallel with Shaw is not coincidental. Osborne is consciously part of the mainstream theatrical tradition. Shaw had taken Ibsen as his starting point in 1890; and Osborne's admiration for Ibsen led him to adapt *Hedda Gabler* (1972). There are also clear echoes of D.H. Lawrence in *Look Back in Anger*. The Jimmy/Alison relationship reflects Lawrence's marriage to Frieda, as well as Osborne's own marriage, while the sparks coming from Jimmy's hair and his love/hate attitude to a dying aristocracy are typically Lawrentian.

Osborne's ambivalence about the outdated Edwardian Establishment – admiring their style while rejecting the values incorporated in it – recurs in his next play, *The Entertainer* (1957), as well as in a late play like *West of Suez* (1971). It is also reflected in his dramaturgy. Osborne's earlier work reproduced the conventional type of drama offered by the touring companies that he was stage-managing and acting in at the time. For instance *Epitaph for George Dillon* prompted comparisons with Scribe and a minor Edwardian farce like *Company for George* from 1910 when it was produced in 1958. And Jimmy Porter's personality closely parallels George Dillon, whom Osborne characterized as 'a walking confliction' of lethargy and passion, dishonesty and candour.[11]

Indeed, the artist manqué anti-hero, reduced to impotence or mediocrity by a vapid society, was already a cliché. Similar characters had appeared in Somerset Maugham; and the type is present even in Osborne's earliest play, *The Devil Inside Him* (1950, revived under a pseudonym as *Cry For Love* in 1962). What was new and struck the public nerve in *Look Back in Anger* was the sense of naked honesty that came from the identification between author and protagonist, and the tone of self-lacerating (but generalized) anger.

This figure of a creative personality, marginalized or corrupted by a philistine and class-ridden society, forms a central motif in Osborne's plays right up to *West of Suez, Watch It Come Down* in the 1970s and *Déjàvu* (1992). It is given its fullest treatment in Archie Rice, the broken-down comic of *The Entertainer*, which had already been half-completed before Osborne came to be widely acclaimed as the spokesman of angry youth with *Look Back in Anger*. The form of this play also derived from the touring shows on which he had worked. In particular it was inspired by the 'music-hall drama' that Osborne defined as a straight dramatic piece containing 'very simple appeals to emotions like jealousy, crude patriotism, lost love, poverty, death', but presented in 'short scenes of melodramatic information, sentiment and broad humour'.[12]

At the same time, Osborne's reputation effectively disguised the conventional nature of his drama in the 1950s; and the myths that came to surround the first performance of *Look Back in Anger* are a testimony to its impact. The 'angry young men' catchphrase gained rapid currency as the defining image of a 'lost generation', and in doing so distorted the actual statement of his plays, though the concept was also self-fulfilling in the sense that it imposed a particular role on Osborne. Since he had been elected the spokesman of 'the new wave', the reviews of *The Entertainer* all ascribed its music hall format to Brecht. This gave essentially traditional elements a gloss of topicality. The Berliner Ensemble's first London performances in the same year as *Look Back in Anger* – and Kenneth Tynan's enthusiastic reception of both – associated Epic Theatre with revolutionary social consciousness, although at the time this was related solely to style since few in the English audiences understood German.

Not surprisingly perhaps, Osborne's following play, *Luther* (1961), was consciously aligned with the expectations imposed by his proclaimed role: an overtly Brechtian treatment of a young rebel whose anger and commitment changes history. Simultaneously his polemic invectives on the hypocrisy of English society ('Epistle to the Philistines', 1960, and 'Letter to My Fellow Countrymen', 1961) played up to the image; and the same qualities can be seen in *The World of Paul Slickey* (1959). A protest play with interspersed songs, this was specifically designed to provoke the maximum hostility from the Establishment by insulting the critics (as its representatives) and dedicated 'to their boredom, their incomprehension, their distaste'. Anger is also the basis of *A Bond Honoured* (1966), an adaptation of Lope de Vega commissioned by Tynan. This combined a primitive distancing effect of having the whole cast seated round the acting area as on-stage observers, with an 'extremely violent' style of presentation: 'pent-up, toppling on and over the edge of animal howlings and primitive rage'.[13]

Neither of these latter plays was successful. Although the personal significance of *Slickey* is indicated by the fact that Osborne directed it himself, the anger appears as unfocused spleen. The political attack on the ruling classes, the Church and the media is undermined by contempt for the common man, and defused by the crudity of the lampooning. Similarly, Osborne's treatment of Lope de Vega was so careless and exaggerated in its vituperation and anti-social gestures (Osborne's protagonist has raped his mother, and lives incestuously with his sister who is also his daughter) that it becomes almost a self-parody.

In short, the imposed image detracted from Osborne's real dramatic strengths. The mask of anger was unsustainable. He had already returned to the real themes of *Look Back in Anger* – isolation and social alienation – with *Inadmissible Evidence* in 1964. Yet the assault on his audience recurs even as late as *A Sense of Detachment* (1972). In this play Osborne sets out to generate hostile reactions from the public artificially in order to justify the play's attack on their philistinism. It deliberately denies basic expectations of drama by being without plot or coherent characters; and the script transposes dramatic conflict into antagonism between actors and spectators, incited by 'interrupters' planted in the auditorium.

The gap between Osborne's reputation as the spokesman for a politically conscious younger generation, and the real roots of his drama can be illustrated by *The Entertainer* (1957). Rather than being influenced by Brecht, its subject as well as its overriding metaphor comes from a 1956 BBC radio series, *The Boy in the Gallery*, devised by Colin MacInnes and Charles Chilton (who later scripted *Oh, What a Lovely War* for Joan Littlewood – discussed below, pp. 121–22). This series presented the vanished music hall as the authentic, populist culture of the British working class, dealing with topics from bankruptcy to mothers-in-law through a compilation of comic turns, melodramatic sketches and ballads. And Marie Lloyd's 'The Boy in the Gallery', which forms the one moment of authenticity in *The Entertainer*, was the theme-song of the series, as well as its title. Indeed the underlying tone of Osborne's play echoes J.B. Priestley's nostalgic novel about the variety circuit at the outbreak of the First World War, *Lost Empires*: a parallel underlined by the recent television dramatization in which Olivier, who created the role of Archie Rice, plays the doomed comedian Harry Burrard. But above all, Osborne's setting is reminiscent of Shaw. The dilapidated music-hall stage presents the same kind of metaphor for the state of England as the symbolic ship of *Heartbreak House*.

Yet the comparison with Shaw defines an essential difference because the theatrical context of *The Entertainer* 'cuts right across the restrictions of the so-called naturalistic stage. Its contact is immediate, vital and direct.' In exactly the same way that Shaw had borrowed from nineteenth-century theatre to challenge its premises, Osborne inverts the Shavian model. For him Shaw represents an intellectual extreme calling for a purely rational response – to Osborne an evasion of reality: 'Shaw avoided passion almost as prudently as Coward. Frigidity and caution demand an evasive style and they both perfected one.' Thus the references to Shaw within Osborne's plays are designed to emphasize the contrast, his aim being 'to make people feel, to give them lessons in feeling. They can think afterwards.'[14]

The same technique of establishing a jarring contrast between the immediate expectations of a dramatic form and the actual content is even more obvious in Osborne's *Luther* (1961). But it led reviewers to judge the play by the wrong standards in criticizing the lack of identifiable historical context or objectivity. Here, the Brechtian framework associated with rationality and detachment is filled by impassioned outpourings, violence and an obsessive physicality designed to produce an immediate gut reaction.

The bare stage and episodic structure, the contemporary resonance in a historical subject, the use of the Knight from Act III to announce the time and place of each scene in the first production of *Luther*, together with the Renaissance context, all set up a recognizable parallel to Brecht's *Galileo*. Osborne's psychological emphasis comes from Eric Erickson's Freudian study, *Young Man Luther*. The movement of the play is from up-stage/subjective, to down-stage/public, with the theatre becoming the world in Luther's trial before Charles V. The oration of Tetzel, the 'ecclesiastical huckster' selling salvation, is balanced against Luther's sermon; and the authority figure of Staupitz reappears in the final scene to justify Luther's idealism, even though Staupitz was in fact dead by the time Protestantism had been established in 1530.

The external struggle against the papacy is treated as a mirror image of the psychological conflicts within Luther himself. His rebellion against the pope repeats the rejection of his father, while the bloodshed of the Peasants' Revolt is an extension of the epileptic fit he suffers when celebrating his first mass. This denies the political dimension of the subject; and the symmetrical structuring of the historical scenes undercuts chronological development. As Osborne acknowledged, 'the historical character is almost incidental'. Luther's achievement is limited to individualism, the value of the personal conscience versus social authority, and his revolt offers a self-justifying archetype for 'the angry young man':

to me there are three ways out of despair. One is faith in Christ, the second is to become enraged by the world and make its nose bleed for it, and the third is the love of a woman. Mind you, they don't all necessarily work.[15]

The third alternative (sexual love) had already been dismissed by *Look Back in Anger*, while Luther replaces faith with doubt. The play itself supports the second option. The violence of the imagery and the excremental emphasis, which locates the spirit in bowel movements and bile, were clearly intended to outrage the sensibilities of the audience. The deliberate avoidance of wider issues, for instance Luther's role as a political revolutionary, or the social change that occurred as a result of the Reformation, not only made intellectual analysis problematic. It also diminished the traditional religious significance of the protagonist. The unpleasantness of the physical symptoms associated with Luther's uncompromising rebellion – sweat, stench, constipation, vomit – are part of this iconoclasm; and the acting style developed by Albert Finney in response to the demands of the part emphasized emotional intensity. He found that the only possible approach was to 'take the peaks and valleys of a performance, the ups and downs of a character as written and push them even further apart' to make 'the climaxes higher and the depths lower than you feel is possible in the text'.[16]

Luther is the only Osborne anti-hero who qualifies, however ambiguously, as successful in smashing a complacent society. A class-ridden and decadent civilization is on the edge of self-destructing in *A Patriot for Me* (1965), which ends in 1913 on the eve of world war and focuses on a historical figure who could be held partly responsible for the fall of the archaic Austro-Hungarian Empire. Yet, rather than emphasizing Colonel Redl's role as a revolutionary catalyst, Osborne shows his protagonist as the product of a corrupt society and its scapegoat. From *Inadmissible Evidence* (1964), through *A Patriot for Me*, *Time Present* and *Hotel in Amsterdam* (1968), to *West of Suez* (1971), *Watch It Come Down* (1975) and *Déjàvu* (1992), Osborne's later works chart progressive depths of disillusion.

With the exception of Maitland, the lawyer on trial for irremediable mediocrity in *Inadmissible Evidence*, all these deal with actors or writers of plays, films and novels. Even Redl is a performer, whose public role as a Hapsburg intelligence officer conceals his lower-class origins, Jewish background, and the unwilling treachery that is scripted by his Russian opposite number. By definition the actor (like the spy) lives a lie. Wearing costumes, pretending passion, 'making sweeping, spurious gestures all over the place', even using a fake stage-name, the characters of *Time Present* are alienated from themselves (as is Redl). The plays in which they appear have titles like 'The Call of Duty' (from the scrapbook of Pamela's dying father), and substitute form for substance, being 'well-constructed... Like a travelling clock. You can see all the works. That way you know it must keep the right time.' Alternatively they are 'full of erudite banalities... a posture... written by someone thinking about writing it instead of thinking about whatever it's about'. In

addition to being an attack on the type of theatre Osborne finds spurious
(Terence Rattigan; Harold Pinter), this dramatic reference has a wider thematic purpose. *Time Present* sums up the actor's art as 'The Real Thing'
(anticipating Stoppard), not only in the occasional ability to communicate
true emotion, but because the pretence and alienation in acting reflects the
essence of contemporary society.[17]

Helena's perception in *Look Back in Anger* that 'You're all of you in Show-
Business now. Everybody . . . Books, politics, journalism' is more than just a
cliché for Osborne. It becomes the basic measure of decadence in *A Patriot
for Me*, where the action pivots around two contrasted scenes of spectacular display. For all their superficial difference, the rigidly formal Court Ball
and the grotesque homosexual Drag Ball in turn-of-the-century Vienna
are identical. Many of the participants are the same, while in both scenes
appearances are illusory. The transvestite pretence of the second both retro-
spectively reveals the authoritarian respectability of the first as hypocritical
pretence, and symbolizes its inner corruption. In both, theatre substitutes
for reality. The two images overlap. An archduke at the head of an empire
becomes indistinguishable from a fancy-dress tsarina, who is only a queen
in the homosexual sense. The same officer's uniform which in one context
stands for patriotism and honour – though worn by a traitor who is a social
misfit – is nothing but a costume in the other.

For Osborne, what makes homosexuals significant is that, like the Jews
under the Austrian Empire, they are 'outsiders, so their whole creed of life
must be based on duplicity – by necessity'. But the actor/homosexual is
not simply rejected by society. Like any scapegoat he epitomizes it. As one
Viennese aristocrat in drag satirically describes it, he is 'a warning symptom
of the crisis in, oh, civilization, and the decline in Christian whatnots'.[18] And
in terms of the play the homosexual is a symbol of the isolation and sterility
of the individual in modern civilization, as Osborne portrays it.

The Entertainer provides the most fully developed use of this show-business
metaphor. The Music Hall is both a frame for the action and an image
of Britain, in which the debased state of popular culture is a direct representation of social decadence. Once a vital theatrical form, by the middle
of the century the Music Hall was almost extinct, displaced by television
sitcoms and bingo. Even so, Laurence Olivier was able to prepare for the
title role by attending a variety bill at the Collins Music Hall in Islington,
which combined traditional cross-talk and comic monologue with nudes
and rock-and-roll numbers, exactly as Osborne does in *The Entertainer*.

While Joan Littlewood and the Theatre Workshop returned to the Music Hall's Edwardian heyday to provide an image of robust proletarian culture in *Oh, What a Lovely War* (1963), Osborne selects only those elements that have been downgraded by being updated. Through the figure of Billy, the one-time star of the earlier generation long since retired, he emphasizes this devaluation. Setting up the past as a standard is open to misinterpretation as sentimental nostalgia: a frequent criticism against Osborne. But the intention is to provide a sharper focus on the present. What remains of the traditional form, as represented by the routine jokes in Archie's script, is no less threadbare than the 'ordinary, tatty backcloth and draw-tabs'; as anti-illusionistic/disillusioning as the crude lighting. Contemporary innovations are even less attractive, with the rock music specified as 'the loudest, the worst', and the nudes superannuated and 'sagging a bit'. This is theatre as entertainment at its lowest level, and its corruption is explicitly due to public demand: 'They don't want real people ... human beings. Not any more'.[19]

The structure is designed to bring home exactly who is responsible for this social decay. The (serious-minded, Royal Court) audience for straight drama, represented by the domestic scenes in the Rice household, are placed in the uncomfortable role of (uneducated, provincial) spectators at the seediest of vaudevilles. In terms of the performance, it is the lewd patter and nude tableaux they/we are waiting for; and the double focus puts them/us in the position of voyeurs while watching the distinctly unfunny off-stage private life of the impoverished comedian. The role the spectators are co-opted into playing can be seen as the thematic centre of the drama as a whole. It is only when their response to Archie Rice is embarrassed, their laughter mechanical that his ironic injunctions, 'Don't clap too hard – it's a very old building', have any point or the self-destructive contempt for his public comes across.

The music-hall frame acts as a barrier to identification with the conventionally serious family drama, which is reinforced by the nature of the characters. As Archie sums them up, 'we're dead beat ... We're something that people make jokes about, because we're so remote from the rest of ordinary everyday, human experience. But we're not really funny. We're too boring' – and the play substantiates this. Even the two apparently worthwhile exceptions, Archie's father and his daughter, are undercut. Old Billy's frequently referred-to dignity and self-respect are a hollow cover for snobbery and racist attitudes, while Jean's social commitment is empty. She admits to loathing the Youth Club kids she teaches; and although her refusal to compromise over taking part in an anti-war rally breaks her engagement (to a clone of Alison's Brother Nigel), the truth is that 'I don't even know what I'm feeling. I don't even know if I do at all.'[20]

Together with the way Archie's professional technique carries over into the family scenes, this conditions the audience's response to an intrinsically powerful situation that reflected a well-publicized incident in the contemporary Suez crisis. The execution of a captured war-hero, seen through the shock and grief of the Rice family who represent a complete spectrum of attitudes from imperialistic jingoism to pacificism, is highly emotive material. Indeed this emotion is heightened by reversal, with the news of the son's death coming at the climax of a party celebrating the prospect of his triumphal return, and by the use of alcohol as a release from inhibitions.

Yet these conventional means of intensification are so exaggerated – the reversal is extreme, all the characters are inebriated to some degree right up to the final scenes – that the actual effect is ambiguous. In addition to making it difficult to empathize with such individuals, Osborne has relegated this dramatic situation to a secondary position in the structure of the play as a whole. We are deliberately being prevented from emotional participation. If the capacity to care defines 'real people', then the (imposed) non-involvement of the spectators disqualifies them.

The method may be artificial, but it is entirely appropriate. It demonstrates Osborne's point about the uncaring nature of the Establishment (rather loosely represented by the audience), which has corroded the common people's culture and sense of national life into a vulgarly inauthentic charade – and it does so on the pulses, rather than through an intellectualized statement from the stage. 'Old Archie, dead behind the eyes, is sitting on his hands, he lost his responses on the way'; and we are intended to recognize ourselves in this figure we reject. Whether the Blues sung by Archie in reaction to his son's death demonstrates the capacity for real feeling, or is merely a ritualized pretence (a conscious imitation of the negress' expression of fundamental emotions that he has just recalled), depends of course on the way it is performed. In a sense, precisely because he was the most powerful tragic actor of his time who had no previous experience of comedy, Olivier was perfectly cast; when the part was played by a professional comedian in a 1974 revival Osborne himself pointed out that 'the problem with Max Wall, who is a comic genius, is that people might laugh the moment he comes on. Which is what you don't want of course; you want absolute deadness.'[21]

The title role was clearly intended to set the tone. And, paradoxically, the criticisms levelled against *The Entertainer* when it was first performed demonstrate how effective Osborne's manipulation of the audience was.

Reviewers typically complained that they were 'not excited by Archie Rice's family affairs' because those sequences were 'not very ably constructed', that Billy is 'a bore', Jean 'a nullity', and that the final back-stage scene of the old man's funeral at which she rejects her fiancé was 'a welter of sentimentality'. By contrast the identification with Archie in the music-hall numbers was very strong, though this was generally held to be a unique actor's triumph over a flawed script: 'a thin enough business . . . impossible to imagine without the presence of Olivier'; 'Sir Laurence holds the part firmly to the stage, but it begins to lose its hold over our minds.'[22]

In fact the revivals, not only in 1974 but most recently 1986 – which make this the most popular of Osborne's work after *Look Back in Anger* – have shown that its effectiveness is not dependent on a specific performer. Assuming Osborne's apparent 'inability' to give his characters 'the emotional weight where it is needed if they are to affect us' was intentional, the fact that the reviewers were evidently bored by the emotional content and concentrated almost exclusively on empty form – Archie Rice's performance, which although less than one tenth of the total script carries the main thematic weight – demonstrates precisely Osborne's point about society. The reviewers, and the audience they represent, have been shown up as no less emotionally bankrupt than the tired clown who entertains us by his failure. And the final ironic lines not only assert the equal inauthenticity of our lives outside the theatre. They challenge us to refute Archie's theme song: 'Let me know where you're working tomorrow night – and I'll come and see YOU . . . *The orchestra goes on playing:* 'Why should I care'; *suddenly, the little world of light snaps out . . .*'[23]

The Entertainer is Osborne's most developed and technically inventive play. Although he successfully experimented with expressionistic dream-sequences in *Inadmissible Evidence*, his later work is mainly naturalistic and tends to restate the same themes. In particular, Osborne's plays after 1966 pick up on the problematic relationship between the nonconforming writer, and the society he addresses which co-opts the artist through commercial success. Since this mirrors Osborne's own career, his plays increasingly become a form of navel-gazing. His writer-figures are escapist, fleeing across the channel to gain a fleeting and illusory independence from the constricting pressures of the commercialized media (*Hotel in Amsterdam*, 1968), or living as a tax-exile in the insular remnants of Empire like Wyatt in *West of Suez* (1971). Since Osborne himself at one point made a much-publicized departure to live in Australia, the autobiographical relevance is inescapable.

Indeed, the figure of Wyatt can be taken as an explanation of why *West of Suez* was Osborne's last major play for twenty years. Hardening of the arteries saps idealism; socialism has been sold out to material comfort; public recognition has compromised the commitment that gained it. Providing 'lessons in feeling' – Osborne's earlier definition of his aims – becomes increasingly problematic because distance does not bring political objectivity, but intellectual detachment. Vituperation and the capacity for insult are retained, but now these are purely verbal: form without passion. The anger that should fuel it has passed to a younger generation still, and their representative in the play is portrayed unsympathetically. This new activist is a philistine. His violence is crude, rejecting all cultural aspirations, including the rhetorical control and capacity for language that made Osborne's protest as an 'angry young man' effective. As he tells Wyatt: 'There's only one word left, and you know what it is? It's fuck . . . Or maybe shit. Because that's what we're going to do on you. Shit.'[24]

Wyatt is shot dead by the Caribbean islanders he has insulted; and *Watch It Come Down* (1975) completes the picture, since all the arts are represented: a film director, his father who writes biographies, his novelist wife and her painter sister – living as a transient commune in a converted country railway station, together with assorted wives and lovers (both homosexual and lesbian as well as heterosexual). Like Wyatt, they have opted out of a society they find intolerable. But here the invective of Osborne's characters has become routine, an 'unlistening, constant rant'; and society – or their own futility: the cause of what happens is unclear – takes its revenge. The biographer who has outlived his ability 'to show us what we are' dies, while the girl representing artistic inspiration throws herself under the wheels of the last goods train to pass through the station.[25] Finally the building itself is demolished by unseen 'yobbos', who riddle the film-director's body (and the girl's corpse) with bullets just as, earlier, the local landowner had shot his dog.

The melodrama is a giveaway. Where earlier protagonists such as George Dillon, Archie Rice and Bill Maitland fight with increasing desperation against the censorious forces of society in the shape of police arrest, the tax-man or the hook that drags the unpopular comedian off the stage, the writer-figures in Osborne's later plays self-destruct. And in his final play Osborne demolishes his own public image in a return to the world of *Look Back in Anger*. The young firebrand Jimmy Porter has grown into an establishment figure – J.P. now residing in a country mansion (doubtless acquired with the fortune Osborne made from his film of *Tom Jones*) – whose anger now is directed at anyone with a 'cause': vegetarians, animal rights, political correctness, feminists and gay crusaders, trendy bishops, striking miners, 'progressives, futurologists and illiterates' – and even the Royal Court Theatre, which was so closely associated with Osborne's reputation. His pregnant daughter, also named Alison, takes refuge behind the kitchen ironing board in the same way and is replaced by a friend (again called Helena) who has an affair with J.P. Once more there are clear autobiographical echoes: J.P's first wife, the original Alison, is an amalgam of Osborne's second wife Mary Ure (who created the original role) and Jill Bennett, who briefly became his fourth wife, while the second Mrs J.P. is described in exactly the same terms Osborne used for his third wife, Penelope Gilliatt, in the second volume of his autobiography, *Almost a Gentleman*. As J.P. gloomily remarks, with the Sunday newspapers scattered round his feet, 'I feel: very Dayzhar Voo.'[26] All too obviously, the imposed role of spokesman for the alienated younger generation of the 1950s has become an artistic cul-de-sac, cutting Osborne's drama off from the contemporary scene.

Notes

1 John Russell Taylor, *Anger and After*, London, 1962, p. 37; the *Observer*, 13 May 1956 (reprinted in Kenneth Tynan, *A View of the English Stage*, London 1975, pp. 176f).

2 Arthur Miller (1957) and Alan Sillitoe (1966), in *John Osborne: Look Back in Anger: A Casebook*, ed. John Russell Taylor, London, 1968, pp. 193 & 185; Osborne, *Look Back in Anger*, London, 1957, p. 84.

3 Osborne, *A Better Class of Person*, London, 1981, pp. 239 & 245.

4 As Osborne himself acknowledged, but only long after the fact: see his autobiography *Almost a Gentleman*, London, 1991, p. 20.

5 *Look Back in Anger*, p. 37.

6 *Ibid.*, p. 22; *Almost a Gentleman*, pp. 17 & 255–9 (for his diatribe on the obituaries of Jill Bennett).

7 *Look Back in Anger*, pp. 10, 58.

8 *Ibid.*, pp. 68 & 47.

9 *Anger and After*, p. 28; 'That Awful Museum' (1961), in *John Osborne: Look Back in Anger: A Casebook*, p. 66.

10 *Anger and After*, p. 28; *Look Back in Anger*, p. 18; *Epitaph for George Dillon*, London, 1958, p. 75.

11 *Epitaph for George Dillon*, p. 29. Osborne's autobiography indicates the conscious use of melodramatic elements, as well as the influence of Pinero: see *A Better Class of Person*, pp. 194ff & 255.

12 *A Better Class of Person*, p. 174.

13 *The World of Paul Slickey*, London, 1959, p. 5; acting note in *A Bond Honoured*, London, 1966, p. 15.

14 *The Entertainer*, London, 1957, introductory note; *A Better Class of Person*, p. 257; *Declaration*, ed. Tom Maschler, London, 1957, p. 65. (For a comparison of the comic patterns in Shaw and Osborne, see Katharine Worth, *Revolutions in Modern English Drama*, London, 1973, ch. 5.)

15 'That Awful Museum', p. 67; *Luther*, London, 1961, pp. 95–6.

16 Albert Finney, cited in Bryan Forbes, *That Despicable Race: A History of the British Acting Tradition*, London, 1980, p. 295.

17 *Time Present and Hotel in Amsterdam*, London, 1968, pp. 38, 52, 70, 73.

18 *Ibid.*, p. 48; *A Patriot For Me*, London, 1966, pp. 90 & 74.

19 *The Entertainer*, pp. 11–12, 86, 18.

20 *Ibid.*, pp. 59, 86 & 59.

21 *Ibid.*, pp. 54, 72; *The Sunday Times*, 24 November 1974.

22 *The New Statesman*, 20 April 1957, p. 512; *The Times*, 11 April 1957; *Tynan on Theatre*, Harmondsworth, 1964, p. 49; *Drama*, Summer 1957, p. 18; *The Illustrated London News*, 27 April 1957.

23 That similar opinions were expressed by Kenneth Tynan and J.C. Trewin (respectively Osborne's most enthusiastic supporter and vociferous attacker) reinforces this analysis of audience response. *The Entertainer*, p. 89.

24 *West of Suez*, London, 1971, p. 84.

25 *Watch it Come Down*, London, 1975, p. 56.

26 *Déjàvu*, London, 1991, p. 19.

3.6 Arnold Wesker (1932–): utopian realism

CHECKLIST OF WESKER'S MAJOR PLAYS

Chicken Soup with Barley, 1958

The Kitchen, 1959

Roots, 1959

I'm Talking About Jerusalem, 1960

Chips with Everything, 1962

Their Very Own and Golden City, 1965

The Four Seasons, 1965

The Friends, 1970

The Old Ones, 1972

The Wedding Feast, 1974

The Merchant, 1976

The Journalists, 1977

Caritas, 1981

Annie Wobbler, 1984

Blood Libel, 1996

When God Wanted a Son, 1997

Wesker and Osborne are almost exact contemporaries, and their drama follows very similar patterns of development. Osborne was twenty-seven at the time *Look Back in Anger* hit the Royal Court; Wesker twenty-six when his first play, *Chicken Soup with Barley*, was performed two years later in 1958 at Coventry. They share the conviction that politics is a question of emotional commitment, equating socialism with the capacity to care. Both became key contributors to the repertoire of The English Stage Company, established by George Devine at the Royal Court. In name as in policy, this company emphasized 'a visionary pedigree [that] stretches back to the early champions of an exemplary theatre'; and Devine was consciously following the line Granville-Barker had promoted on the same stage half a century before: to foster new drama that would be 'an essential part of society, a major educative force, a potential agent of political change'.[1]

Wesker's plays in the first half of his career shared the tone of crusading radicalism set by Osborne, although his work in that period remained strongly rooted in Naturalism, rather than experimenting with expressionistic or music-hall/Brechtian elements. His working-class trilogy – *Chicken Soup with Barley*, *Roots* (1959) and *I'm Talking About Jerusalem* (1960) – compares in many ways with D.H. Lawrence (see pp. 70–2 above), a parallel emphasized by the Royal Court staging of Lawrence's trilogy in 1968. Indeed, the detailed realism and autobiographical basis of *The Kitchen* (1959) and *Chips with Everything* (1962) has been described as 'théâtre trouvé', implying that Wesker transcribes lived experience without restructuring or fictionalization.

Like Osborne too, Wesker's later plays show a perceptible loss of political purpose and dramatic coherence, with the turning point for both playwrights coming in the mid-1960s. The causes were different, but the effect on their work was similar. Where Osborne suffered from being typecast in the role of 'angry young man' and missed the guidance of Devine, whose last acting role before his early death was in *A Patriot for Me* (1965), Wesker was frustrated by his failure to win trades union support for the performance space in London, of which he was founder-director: Centre 42, named after the number of a resolution passed by the Trades Union Congress in 1960. Although this clause committed the TUC to developing socialist art for the working-class public, they never backed up their words with sufficient money.

Wesker's disillusion was reflected in *Their Very Own and Golden City* (1965); and his alienation from the Labour movement led to a more introverted and symbolic drama in *The Four Seasons* (1965) or *The Old Ones* (1972), which verges on abstraction in *Caritas* (1981). Even when he returned to major social themes in *The Journalists* (1975) or *The Merchant* (alternatively titled *Shylock* – first staged in Scandinavia in 1976) these plays remain unperformed in London, and almost all his later work has had to wait for many years before being produced. *The Journalists* is a good example of the difficulties he has faced. The play was written in 1971–2; but its production scheduled by the RSC for October 1972 was cancelled – followed by Wesker suing for breach of contract – and when finally staged in 1977 it was by an amateur group in Coventry, with the first professional performance only appearing in 1981 and in Germany. Similarly *When God Wanted a Son* (1997) was already published in 1990, and even though specially commissioned by the Nottingham Playhouse *Blood Libel* (1996) took five years to reach the stage. This is at least partly due to an increasing sacrifice of character and plot to a thesis, and possibly to the increasing stridency in Wesker's specifically Jewish themes, which has also been one of the factors in marginalizing the work of his contemporary Bernard Kops. At the same time from the early 1980s on Wesker has focused on short one-woman plays: *Yardsale*, *The Mistress*, *Annie Wobbler*, *Four Portraits of Mothers*, his most recent work *Letter to a Daughter* (performed at the Edinburgh Festival in 1998) and in a return to redressing a perceived bias in Shakespeare, *Lady Othello*. As monologues, in a very real sense these mark a withdrawal from the theatre, although he directed a selection of them under the title of *Three Women Talking* in Chicago in 1991, while two others were produced as a double bill by Michael Bogdanov in Cardiff in 1997. And if these too have been presented so seldom it is partly because in dealing so exclusively with female experience they compete with the wave of feminist plays that had reached mainstream theatre by the 1980s (see below, pp. 233–38) and which are felt to have more validity as gender statements, being by women-writers.

As with Osborne, the seeds of this regression were already present in Wesker's early work. Beneath its documentary surface his drama is even more clearly autobiographical than Osborne's *Look Back in Anger*. In his Trilogy, for example, all the major characters are 'total recreations' of his family.[2] Wesker's father was a Jewish tailor like Harry, and his mother a communist like Sarah, Ronald's parents in *Chicken Soup with Barley*. His wife, like the heroine of *Roots*, left Norfolk to work as a waitress. *I'm Talking About Jerusalem* repeats the experience of his sister and her husband – while the link figure in the three plays is Wesker himself, Ronald being an obvious anagram for Arnold. And when Ronnie reads aloud from Harry's notebook, Wesker is quoting verbatim from his own father's unfinished autobiography.

What balances these strongly subjective elements in the Trilogy – first performed in Coventry, where they seemed to presage the growth of a new regional drama, and staged as a whole by the Royal Court in 1960 – is the sense of gritty realism that echoes Lawrence's drama. The play that seems most Lawrentian, with its inarticulate working-class characters and gutter-documentary emphasis, is *Roots*. The setting of rural poverty is at first glance strikingly similar to a play like *The Widowing of Mrs Holroyd* (1926), Norfolk farm labourers substituting for Nottinghamshire coal miners. Indeed, opening as *Roots* does with a woman at the sink washing dishes in two out of three Acts and progressing through bread-baking, potato-peeling and table-laying, folding laundry and heating buckets of water for a bath, it is hardly surprising the new wave represented by Wesker, Bernard Kops or Shelagh Delaney was labelled 'kitchen-sink drama'.

Yet the comparison shows Wesker as the mirror-opposite of Lawrence. Anti-cultural proletarianism is presented as '*lumpenproletariat*' brutishness, and education proposed as the tool for change. In effect Wesker inverts Lawrence's thematic values. The isolated Norfolk cottages are a micro-cosm for regressive attitudes (picked up again a generation later in Caryl Churchill's *Fen*, 1982). The crude physical existence that Lawrence prized is presented as an emotionally crippling form of slavery. Drudgery has de-humanized the characters, who 'live in the country but . . . got no majesty. Your mind's cluttered up with nothing and you shut out the world.'[3]

These farm labourers are culturally and intellectually dispossessed. They are in the most traditional of occupations, yet without roots – an irony not only signalled by the title but explicitly underlined in the dialogue – and the girl who liberates herself does so through mastering language. Having adopted the socialist attitudes of her intellectual lover, whose words she parrots without making any effort to understand their meaning, she is already alienated from her family. So that when he breaks off the relationship in despair of overcoming her mental apathy, she is finally forced to find her own voice (the roots of her personal being).

Taken on a solely naturalistic level, *Roots* seems naive; and the kind of individual transformation depicted has been criticized as inadequate for changing society: 'Beatie is saved because she happens to have attracted a proselytizing thinker into a love affair. How many in need of salvation can hope for that?'[4] However, this type of literal interpretation is a misreading of Wesker's dramatic intentions. Despite the almost exaggerated naturalism of the environment, the action is in fact symbolic: a paradigm for the social problem and the solution that Centre 42 was intended to translate into reality.

Founded in specific response to lobbying of the TUC from Wesker, this arts centre was established as a cultural arm of the Union movement for the 'direct promotion of plays, films, music, literature and other forms of expression . . . of value to its beliefs and principles'. The extent of Wesker's involvement is reflected in several of his plays. He has pointed out that the exploration of death in *The Friends* (1970) expressed his consciousness 'of the failure to make Centre 42 work'.[5] And the connection in *Roots* is even more direct.

Centre 42 was designed to function exactly as the absent Ronnie does in the play, with Beatie representing the working classes. Artists, controlling 'their own channels of distribution' and speaking directly to a mass audience, would enable 'the public to see that artistic activity is a natural part of their daily lives'. By replacing the mindless and belittling escapism of the commercial 'slop songs and film idols' with a socialist vision that challenges the working 'millions' into 'asking questions, all the time', instead of 'taking the easiest way out' (as the play puts it), artists might overcome the barrier of education that separated them from working-class audiences, and serve as a catalyst for true proletarian art.[6] Indeed, the central significance of the aspirations of Centre 42 to *Roots* (and the comparative irrelevance of the Norfolk background) can be indicated by the way Wesker's theme and heroine have subsequently been transposed into an Open University setting with Willy Russell's *Educating Rita* (1980).

The stage-set in the Royal Court production pointed explicitly to the fact that (like the other parts of the Trilogy and indeed all Wesker's early work) *Roots* is only superficially a slice-of-life. Instead, following much the same approach as Sean O'Casey, Wesker makes the environment overtly symbolic. This was brought out by reducing the house walls to an outline and a single chimney stack against a backcloth of bare, simplified tree branches, while the use of common elements – low ceiling beams, window frame and sink – for the country-kitchens in both *Roots* and *I'm Talking About Jerusalem* under-lined the universalization. The first and most naturalistic part of the Trilogy, *Chicken Soup with Barley*, has recognizable parallels to *Ghosts* and compares with Ibsen in the extended flow of its action and its avoidance of sensationalism. Yet even here the Kahns' East End basement apartment opened up above into a panorama of slum tenements, balancing the internal focus of the play against its exterior context. Significantly, Jocelyn Herbert's settings became progressively more schematic as the Trilogy progressed, ending with a semi-abstract silhouette of house and barn through which a blurred and featureless landscape could be seen in *I'm Talking About Jerusalem*, and bringing out the thematic implications of the time sequence.

Chicken Soup presents three snap-shots at intervals of a decade, starting at 1936 with the first year of the Spanish Civil War, and its reflected microcosm in the London riots between parading socialists and Moseley's Blackshirts. Act II marks the election of a Labour government in 1946. The final act sets this against the Russian invasion of Hungary in 1956. (It is no coincidence that David Edgar's survey of the causes for contemporary disenchantment in *Maydays*, 1985, takes these two later dates as its starting point. Indeed, Edgar's play can be seen as a direct continuation of Wesker's Trilogy: see pp. 186–90 below.) Spain marked the first major setback for communism; and Wesker passes over the eventual defeat of fascism with a dismissive stage direction – '*June 1946 – the war has come and gone*' – to provide a study in progressive disillusionment.

From an extreme socialistic standpoint, working through parliamentary democracy can only compromise revolutionary principles. The disintegration of idealism is already evident in the first act of *Chicken Soup* with Dave, whose experience as a volunteer in Spain has 'killed any illusions... about the splendid and heroic working class'.[7] And the nadir of despair is then reached in the example of armed Soviet oppression. *Roots* is a continuation of *Chicken Soup*, set three years after the last act to make the action exactly contemporary with its production. *Roots* serves both as a commentary on the earlier play, and as a touchstone for *I'm Talking About Jerusalem*. Documenting the failure of a William Morris alternative socialism, this concluding drama in the Trilogy covers the period from the first scene of the middle Act in the opening play (1946) to a point following the end of *Roots* (1959–60). Where Beatie learns to unite speech with action, the utopian aspirations of the romantic dropouts in the last play are only 'talking'.

The chronological duplication offers more than a shift of perspective on historical events. Like overlapping exposures in photography, it makes material realities seem insubstantial and imposes a sense of relativity. This reinforces the way the two extended cross-sections of family life in *Chicken Soup* and *Jerusalem* pivot round the concentrated affirmation in *Roots*, which forms the thematic centre of the Trilogy. The effect is to show the disillusionment generated by events on a political level through a prism that states the potential for internal change. A declaration like 'It's always only just beginning for the Party. Every defeat is a victory and every victory is the beginning', may be ironic in its immediate context. Yet it also accurately describes Beatie's ecstatic apotheosis, which arises out of despair: 'it's happening to me, I can feel it's happened, I'm beginning . . .' as she '*stands alone, articulate at last –* '.[8]

In the ideological argument over whether social revolution is an essential first step to reforming people – the Marxist position – or the net result of changing the attitudes of individuals, Wesker is firmly on the side of liberal socialism. As he commented in 1977, he was then 'and probably always have been, an old-fashioned humanist'. Such individualism requires realistic characterization; and his success can be measured by reviews claiming that (before 1960) 'nobody else has ever attempted to put a real, live, English Communist family on to the stage, and the important thing . . . is that they *are* real, and they *do* live'.[9] The key to this impression of reality, reinforcing the linguistic theme of the plays, was Wesker's dialogue. At the time, when Osborne's – and even Lawrence's – figures spoke standard English, his use of country dialects and identifiably ethnic traits was striking.

Yet beneath the superficial appearance of individuality given by the way they speak, Wesker's characters are illustrative, tied to their author's thesis. Even the most vital figure, Sarah, is limited by her thematic function. As the archetypal mother, an embodiment of emotional commitment, 'for her the world is black and white . . . It was all so simple.'[10] Although in the play this criticism is voiced as a self-serving excuse by a former comrade, who has abandoned socialist principles, it is also a valid criticism of the way she has been characterized by Wesker.

The same kind of simplification also affects the thematic crux of the Trilogy as a whole: the personal transfiguration in *Roots*. The change in Beatie is even greater than the contrast between first and last states of Ibsen's feminist prototype in *A Doll's House* (a parallel stressed by the dance with which Wesker ends the second Act). The implication is clearly that Beatie's conversion will have as wide-ranging social significance as the classic slamming of the door by Ibsen's heroine. However, although Nora's Tarantella reveals her inner turmoil and forecasts her rebellion against convention, it is performed as a set piece to demonstrate her marital subjugation. By contrast, Beatie's grotesque mixture of sailors' hornpipe and Cossack leaps comes straight from the heart. It is a proclamation of independence, even if this temporarily turns out to be a delusion. The lack of inner complexity gives an unconvincing air of didacticism; and indeed the whole Trilogy demonstrates a thesis that is summed up in the cry that ends the first play: 'if you don't care you'll die' (underlined by repetition).[11]

There is a straight equation between communism and the capacity for emotion. Apathy, in the example of Ronnie's father, is indistinguishable from mortal illness. *Roots* underlines the effectiveness of feeling versus political activism by showing the truth of Ronnie's assertion that 'You can't alter people . . . You can only give them some love and hope they'll take it.' In turn Beatie's triumph over the apathy of her environment becomes a pattern for the conversion of Ronnie. *Chicken Soup* ends with his disillusioned withdrawal from politics, which reduces his writing to posturing lyricism like 'the pool of my smile – a very lovely metaphor'. Beatie's example is the active factor in reawakening the emotional commitment that will finally make him (Ronald/Arnold) the 'socialist poet' capable of creating the Trilogy – and so, by extension, passing on the ability to care to society as a whole. In fact, one of the dominant images in the Trilogy is that of soapbox oratory, even if the context makes it partly ironic:

BEATIE [*standing on a chair*]: I don't care if you call me a preacher . . .

As a result, Wesker felt it necessary to emphasize (specifically for 'Actors and Producers') that these 'people are not caricatures. They are real (though fiction)'.[12]

As the obvious echo of Blake's song in the title suggests, *I'm Talking About Jerusalem* is really a parable beneath its naturalistic surface. Consequently it has generally been seen as a transition to Wesker's later, more structured and imagistic works like *The Four Seasons* or *Their Very Own and Golden City* (both 1965). Yet even in Wesker's earliest and apparently most naturalistic play *The Kitchen* (first staged in 1959, though written before *Chicken Soup*), the documentary impression is deceptive.

The basis of *The Kitchen* may be autobiographical, written 'in between serving sweets at the Hungaria Restaurant', but the characters are all types, one from each European nation. The setting is explicitly a microcosm, with Wesker's introductory note that 'The world might have been a stage for Shakespeare but for me it is a kitchen' indicating the seriousness attached to a speech like 'This stinking kitchen is like the world – you know what I mean?' The symbolic nature of the action was emphasized by John Dexter's choreography in the 1961 production, which turned the hectic movements of cooks and waitresses into a highly stylized ballet. In fact, spectators are specifically expected to see the material reality of the kitchen as questionable, replaceable, since it represents a model of industrial capitalism for which they are being asked to substitute a socialist alternative. As the restaurant owner says in response to his employees, frustrated discontent, 'This is life, isn't it? . . . What is there more?', to which a stage direction in the first version of the play replied '*We have seen that there must be something more.*'[13]

In Wesker's later work the same subordination of plot and character to idea is even more marked. *The Old Ones* (1972) is a barely illustrated debate about the value of life, asserting the meaningfulness of struggle in the face of its negation by death. The central figures in *The Merchant* (first English-language production, New York, 1977) are characterized mainly in terms of their philosophical positions. Despite the difference in context between contemporary London and sixteenth-century Venice, *The Old Ones* and *The Merchant* are companion pieces. Both focus on the relationship between two elderly men who represent contradictory attitudes: disillusion versus optimism in defiance of the facts. In each a lonely bachelor is drawn out of isolation by the life-giving force of an extended (Jewish) family.

As a radically different re-telling of *The Merchant of Venice*, any audience is forced to respond to *The Merchant* on an intellectual level in drawing continual comparison with Shakespeare.[14] For Wesker, Shakespeare casts a dark shadow in the light of twentieth-century history. Belmont is bankrupt and the ideal of mercy proclaimed by *The Merchant of Venice* 'seemed hollow – after the holocaust', to which the image of Shylock is seen as directly contributing. Shaw had attacked Shakespeare's poetic vision as a dangerous distortion of reality; and Wesker takes Shaw's argument to its logical conclusion. There is a clear Shavian echo in his characterization of Portia, who introduces herself with 'I-am-the-new-woman-and-they-know-me-not!' Wesker's play is a point-by-point reversal of its source, justified as 'accurately reflecting historical reality' which was the opposite of Shakespeare's 'racist fantasy'. But as a conscious rebuttal of the Shakespearean archetypes, the focus of *The Merchant* is literary; and the action never rises above an abstract drama of ideas.[15]

Much the same is true of *Blood Libel* (1996), though it is based on a historical incident and gained chilling specificity from being performed on almost the exact spot where the actual event had occurred a thousand years before: the medieval murder of a 12-year-old boy, William of Norwich. His rape, torture and killing – falsely attributed to the Jews and used (according to Wesker's take on history) by the Church as an excuse for a pogrom in order to qualify the dead child for a commercially exploitable sainthood – is replayed three times during the highly ritualized action, where stylized presentations of the community working or dancing, liturgical chants and processions overwhelm the argument between a lone priest who stands up for reason against the religious fervour of all the rest of the characters.

Only in *When God Wanted a Son* (written in 1986 though not performed until 1997) does Wesker return to family drama, presenting his perennial theme – encapsulated in a quotation from the Bishop of Birmingham, 'anti-Semitism has never been far below the surface of English life', reprinted in the programme for the New End production – through a mixed marriage between a Jewish professor and his Anglo-Saxon wife. Unusually for Wesker there is a strong vein of humour in the dialogue, since the daughter (in a variation on Trevor Griffiths' *Comedians* – see pp. 365–67) is an unsuccessful stand-up comic agonizing over her repertoire of Jewish jokes. But the characters turn out to be types, with the divorced wife being demonized as 'a tight-arsed, gold-plated, thin-lipped, sanctimonious bitch' (in the words of her returned ex-husband) who is goaded into declaring that it's 'them and us', betraying the anti-Semitism that her daughter describes as dividing the world into 'those that are clever and die, and those who are stupid and do the massacring'.[16] As a result, despite the intensity and seriousness of the argument, this three-member family is too symbolically weighted for their relationship to be convincing.

As here – and even more so in *The Merchant* or *Blood Libel* – the balance between naturalistic and allegorical levels in Wesker's later full-length plays is all too often problematic, with the symbolic reference making the characters unconvincing, or the ordinariness of the situation trivializing the general image. In addition, as he turned to dramatizing generalizations, Wesker's language has a tendency to become inflated. This gap between specific and universal was one of the reasons for the failure of *The Friends*. In fact – apart from *Chips With Everything* (1962) – Wesker's plays have never been commercially successful on the English stage. The RSC and the National dropped their options on later works such as *The Journalists* and *The Old Ones* without producing them, although the National Theatre did commission *Caritas* while *The Old Ones* was given a short run at the Royal Court. *The Merchant* failed disastrously on Broadway. Even *Roots* folded after a short run when it was transferred to the West End, despite the triumph of a star actress like Joan Plowright in the lead role and acclaim for the Trilogy from reviewers.

By contrast, Wesker's critical status has been exceptionally high. He is the only playwright of the 1950s to be included in a selection from *Theatre Quarterly* titled *New Theatre Voices of the Seventies*. Yet already by the end of the 1950s the initiative in English political drama had passed from the kind of Naturalism his work represents, to playwrights like John Arden, who take their lead from Brecht. It is the Brechtian model that has provided a catalyst for some of the most innovative drama over the last three decades, from Arden, through Edward Bond to Caryl Churchill.

Notes

1 *At the Royal Court*, ed. Richard Findlater, London, 1981, p. 10.

2 Wesker, cited in Ronald Hayman, *Arnold Wesker*, London, 1970, pp. 2 & 4.

3 *The Wesker Trilogy*, Harmondsworth, 1960, p. 127.

4 Glenda Leeming and Simon Trussler, *The Plays of Arnold Wesker*, London, 1971, p. 58.

5 Centre 42, 'Annual Report 1961–2', cited in *Theatre Quarterly*, 18 May 1975, p. 40; Wesker, in *New Theatre Voices of the Seventies*, ed. Simon Trussler, London, 1981, p. 147.

6 Centre 42, 'Annual Report 1961–2'; and *The Wesker Trilogy*, pp. 147–8. For the radical left-wing analysis of the reasons for the failure of Centre 42, see Catherine Itzin's summary of John McGrath's 1970 attack on Wesker as a 'cultural imperialist': *Stages in the Revolution*, London, 1980, pp. 103ff.

7 *The Wesker Trilogy*, pp. 36, 42. For a comparison between *Chicken Soup* and *Ghosts*, see Glenda Leeming and Simon Trussler, *The Plays of Arnold Wesker*, London, 1971, pp. 44f.

8 *The Wesker Trilogy*, pp. 41, 147.

9 Wesker, *Theatre Quarterly*, 6, no. 28, p. 20; Kenneth Tynan, *The Observer*, 12 June 1960.

10 *The Wesker Trilogy*, p. 62.

11 *Ibid.*, p. 76.

12 *Ibid.*, pp. 56, 48–9, 111, 56, and 'Author's Note' (n.p.).

13 Wesker, interview in Hayman, *Arnold Wesker*, p. 2; *The Kitchen*, in *Penguin Plays* 2, Harmondsworth, 1964, pp. 5, 19, 78–9, and in *New English Dramatists* 2, Harmondsworth, 1960, p. 61.

14 The intellectualized nature of the response is illustrated by the tone of the Broadway reviews: 'Intelligent but Weak'; 'Merely Bloodless' (*The New York Times*; *New York Post*, 17 November 1977).

15 Arnold Wesker, in *Theatre Quarterly*, 7, no. 28, pp. 22–4, and *The Merchant*, London, 1983, p. 28.

16 *When God Wanted a son*, in *Lady Othello and Other Plays*, Harmondsworth, 1990, pp. 173, 134, 126.

3.7 Brechtian influences: Epic stagecraft and British equivalents

Brecht's plays had first appeared on the English stage in the 1930s, with Lotte Lenya's performance of *The Seven Deadly Sins of the Bourgeoisie* (under the title of *Anna, Anna,* 1933), and Unity Theatre's production of *Senora Carrar's Rifles* (1938). But in the 1950s the exposure to Brecht's acting company in his own productions of his plays was a revelation. The Berliner Ensemble's first London performances in 1956, the same year as *Look Back in Anger* – and Kenneth Tynan's enthusiastic reception of both – associated Epic Theatre with the new wave of English drama.

Brecht's use of a bare stage, clinically bright and non-atmospheric lighting from clearly visible lamps and spotlights, placards to indicate location or state the essential point of a scene, as well as a half-curtain, above which set changes could be seen, were strikingly different from anything in the London theatre of the time. These techniques exposed the mechanics of performance that naturalistic dramaturgy concealed. The style of demonstrative acting developed by the Berliner Ensemble, in which performers overtly presented the characters instead of identifying with their roles, was designed to promote a critical attitude to the action. The use of episodic montage where self-contained scenes were juxtaposed, in place of conventional cause-and-effect plot-development, emphasized thematic relationships. Vividly contrasting with the naturalistic approach that had dominated the British stage since Shaw, Brecht's work offered an anti-illusionistic model for theatrical immediacy and directness.

At the same time, since Brecht's writings were not yet available in translation, and few London spectators of the Berliner Ensemble productions understood German, the politics of his drama was obscured. As a result, its influence was primarily on production values and ways of playing; and this one-sided adoption was further promoted by the close connections between Epic Theatre and Shakespeare. In developing his concept Brecht was borrowing from the Elizabethans; and Tyrone Guthrie's Shakespearean productions had already introduced similar elements during the previous decade. And the Hall/Barton years at the RSC, which were marked by heavily Brechtian productions like the monumental *Wars of the Roses* (1963), made bare stages and broadly Epic elements part of mainstream British theatre. This encouraged the general adoption of Brecht's dramaturgy, while also emphasizing its purely stylistic aspect – and a second visit by the Berliner Ensemble in 1964 attracted still more attention.

This formed the background for the new dramatists who emerged in the late 1950s. George Devine, the founder of the English Stage Company was one of the first to experiment with Brecht's techniques, as well as staging several notable productions of his plays starting with *The Good Woman of Setzuan*. William Gaskill, who succeeded Devine in 1965, was already known for his Brechtian approach; and the Royal Court became very much identified with the British brand of Epic Theatre.

It is no coincidence that following *Look Back in Anger* Osborne's next plays, *The Entertainer* and particularly *Luther* both used Brechtian techniques. And the major political dramatists of the 1960s and 1970s, John Arden and Edward Bond, were attuned to the principles underlying Brecht's radical stage form. They extended his Epic Theatre, adapting and updating it to fit contemporary social conditions that were very different from those of Weimar Germany, which had conditioned Brecht's approach. Their work is discussed in the following sections. However, there was also a wide range of superficially Brechtian drama that appeared on the English stage at the same time. This severed Epic techniques from the Marxist analysis of society that they were designed to express; and the effects can be seen in the plays of Robert Bolt, Joan Littlewood's Theatre Workshop and Peter Nichols, as well as those of Christopher Hampton.

Far from being inseparable from revolutionary political consciousness, Brecht's work fulfilled the requirements of what he himself would have dismissed as 'culinary theatre'. Structurally his plays had a 'chunky classical four-square quality', while his staging techniques were identifiable enough to serve as instant clichés.[1] Just as Shaw could use nineteenth-century melodrama to make an anti-romantic statement, so Brechtian episodic play-construction and framing devices can be borrowed for drama that is apolitical or conservative in supporting the status quo. The historical emphasis of Brecht's drama also lent itself to portraying ethical issues in universal terms, so it is not surprising that Rattigan's successor, Robert Bolt, was initially hailed as the British Brecht.

Adopting the Epic Style: Robert Bolt (1924–95)

CHECKLIST OF BOLT'S MAJOR PLAYS

> *Flowering Cherry,* 1957
> *A Man for All Seasons,* 1960
> *Vivat! Vivat Regina!,* 1970
> *State of Revolution,* 1977

Robert Bolt's career overlaps with Terence Rattigan, Rattigan's film script for *Lawrence of Arabia* – which formed the basis for his play, *Ross* (1960) – being rejected in favour of Bolt's version of T.E. Lawrence's biography. Even though

Bolt formed part of the anti-nuclear protest movement with Wesker, and donated the fee for *Lawrence* (filmed in 1962) to Centre 42, he is addressing the same public as Rattigan. The 'Common Man' in Bolt's most popular play, *A Man for All Seasons* (1960), is the equivalent of Rattigan's 'Aunt Edna', anti-intellectual and apolitical. Bolt's approach is the same in catering to 'a straight-forward, childlike, primitive desire to be told'; and although his emphasis on 'what can be abstracted from the pattern of events' implies a more intellectual purpose, his focus too is on the individual.[2] *A Man for All Seasons* epitomizes this in the figure of Thomas More, Henry VIII's Chancellor. Faced with the demand that he approve the King's divorce (prohibited by the Church), which means supporting royal will against papal authority, Bolt's hero goes to the block rather than compromise his personal integrity.

At the same time the value given to the individual is programmatic, rather than carrying through into Bolt's characterization. For instance, although the focus of *A Man for All Seasons* is on More's crisis of conscience, the figure who in fact dominates the play's action is the ubiquitous Common Man – who takes all the servants' and ordinary citizens' roles, as well as stage-managing the scenes. He is explicitly an abstraction, illustrating the lack of identity that comes from equivocating, or from defining humanity solely by physical externals. As an empty husk, he is nothing but a symbol. Hence Bolt's opening comparison of the Common Man to Adam, and his chameleonlike ability to wear any hat: steward, innkeeper, jailer, foreman of the jury, executioner. This unhistorical non-personality serves as a common denominator for a range of characters whose behaviour is self-defeating in being self-serving: the short-sighted pragmatists Cromwell and Chapuys, neither of whom can appreciate that there may be a 'third alternative' to their positions; and the opportunist Richard Rich, More's clerk who literally sells his soul for material self-advancement.[3] Against this group stands Sir Thomas More, who sacrifices everything, including his life, to preserve his moral being.

Despite the religious vocabulary and tone of discourse, which comes from using More's actual words as well as the sixteenth-century context, Bolt is not concerned with the historical issue of belief, nor with religious faith. As in his films, from *Lawrence* and *Doctor Zhivago* to *The Mission*, he is concerned with 'morally accountable individuals, trying to hold true to their [humanistic] beliefs against the mindless violence of ideological genocide or religious fanaticism'.[4] So in *A Man for All Seasons*, the demands of Church and State are not the opposites their functionaries proclaim, but equal threats to the protagonist's integrity. And the central conflict is not between Chancellor and King, but between More and the ubiquitous Common Man.

According to Bolt, the play's premise 'was not just that it's the individual that counts but that the individual is all there *is*'. Certainly its whole structure revolves around the fundamental question put to More at the beginning: 'What are you?' A range of possible ways in which this might be answered are successively tested, from defining a person by his 'shape', or by his knowledge and experience, to the proposition that 'a man's soul is his self'. Paradoxically (since the historical Thomas More stood for Catholicism against the claims of individual conscience inherent in the protestant Reformation), for Bolt's protagonist 'what matters to me is not whether [a doctrine is] true or not but that I believe it to be true, or rather not that I *believe* it, but that *I* believe it'.[5]

A Man for All Seasons is a secular equivalent to T.S. Eliot's *Murder in the Cathedral* (1935: discussed below, pp. 465–68). For More's sacrifice to be justified, he must define the reason for it correctly. Rich's first words, 'every man has his price', echo throughout the action. Wealth and power are no temptation to More. The real lures parallel those of Eliot's martyr, Thomas à Becket – that More might be bought 'with suffering', or that he is driven by pride – and Bolt's problem is the same as Eliot's. Motivation on this level is so hard to define that although More may assert 'I oppose it – *I* do – not my pride, not my spleen, nor any other of my appetites but *I* do – *I*!', yet the only way it can be embodied in the action is through a negative: the refusal to state his opposition to the King's divorce. In effect, the search for an intrinsic core of personality leads to all the attributes of individuality being stripped away, until a 'constant factor' emerges.[6] This may be dramatically convincing. But if it is unpredictability and inconsistency that gives a character its uniqueness, as Bolt's hero asserts, then the play's argument undermines its own premise.

Bolt's use of Brechtian techniques intensifies the problem. Anti-illusionistic staging tends to transform the particular into the general, since even unconcealed lighting and open scene changes are a constant reminder that the figures on stage are actors playing roles. This is underlined in *A Man for All Seasons* by the setting: a stylized Elizabethan stage. It is also reinforced by the emphasis on performance in combining direct address with the use of the Common Man as a stage-hand – for instance in the shift from jail to trial scene, where he

Fetches from the wings his prop basket ... enter CROMWELL. *He ringingly addresses the audience (while the* COMMON MAN *is still bustling about his chores) ...*

indicating the descending props...
What Englishman can behold without Awe
The Canvas and the Rigging of the Law![7]

The clear symbolism that such a speech points up is extended from things to people: the 'rigged' nature of the trial is reflected in the way the jury-men are presented as a row of hats suspended above the jury stools. Such elements break the naturalistic surface of the dialogue, transposing the historical action into an illustration of a general thesis. Despite Bolt's stress on individualism, individuals become secondary to the demonstration of a model situation.

The same problematic individualism becomes a moral standard for evaluating the significance of world events in a later play, *State of Revolution* (1977). This picks up on Bolt's argument in the Preface of *A Man for All Seasons* that

'Religion' and 'economy' are abstractions which describe the way men live. Because men work we may speak of an economy, not the other way round. Because men worship we may speak of a religion ... And when an economy collides with a religion it is living men who collide, nothing else ...[8]

Instead of the focus on a single heroic protagonist such as Sir Thomas More or a contrasted pair (like Mary Queen of Scots and Elizabeth I in *Vivat! Vivat Regina!*, 1970) the action covers the whole sweep of the Russian Revolution from Lenin's arrival at the Finland Station to the final betrayal of its principles with Stalin's rise to supreme power. Again, there is direct address from a choric figure – but here Bolt's handling of Epic techniques is far freer and more thematically relevant. The character who introduces the events and comments on them is not an abstraction, but a historical person: Lunacharsky, who became Lenin's Commissar for Culture. The action is framed by his lecture, in which the audience are cast as 'Young Communists'; and the scenes (in the form of his reminiscences) increasingly diverge from the Party line they are overtly designed to illustrate. As a result, his interspersed commentary not only bridges gaps, and identifies the rapidly changing locale. It also sets up a series of dialectical tensions that challenge an audience to measure theory against political practice.

What *State of Revolution* specifically contradicts is the Marxist thesis that 'The personal of course is marginal. The historically determined movement of the masses is alone decisive', which Lunacharsky enunciates in a last-ditch attempt to convince himself, not the audience for his lecture.[9] If this can be shown to be true, then he is absolved from responsibility for the bloodshed and cruelty epitomized in Stalin. But his agonizing contortions are a more convincing rebuttal of this ideology than any speeches attacking the revolution.

Free will versus determinism is, of course, a religious opposition – and if these philosophical positions are portrayed in terms of the individual versus fate, as in *State of Revolution*, then they correspond to Aristotelian tragedy. This is explicitly a thesis drama, illustrating the argument set out in the Preface. What it focuses on are the disproportions between ideals and results, the demands of the historical moment and the capacities of those who believed they controlled the course of events. Such conflicts contain the classic elements of hubris, reversal and recognition; and Bolt's aim is clearly to reproduce in the audience his own response to the subject: 'overwhelmed by primitive pity and awe'.[10]

To achieve this Aristotelian catharsis, he relies on empathetic characterization, and the intrinsic significance of events that literally shaped the modern world. Thus, the factual nature of the material is stressed by using visual echoes of famous photographs in the staging, by cataloguing dates, quotations and historical data in the programme, and by establishing a tone of clinical objectivity. Although the reviewers' response in general was summed up in 'Character is swamped by event, as it was bound to be', Bolt's principle of selection convincingly implies the opposite.[11]

Large-scale happenings are always presented indirectly in private discussions between the central figures, so that events are seen through the perspective of how decisions were reached or personal reactions to their results. Famine or the massacres of peasants during collectivization are reported as first-hand experiences, either anecdotally or through reading out a letter from an eyewitness. World war is relegated to the background; and the crushing of revolutionary sailors at Kronstadt is only suggested impressionistically: '*The guns roar, blackness falls*'. In contrast, the assassination attempt against Lenin by a single woman is acted out. Although the dialogue never resolves the question of whether men are the instruments of history or events are determined by great men, the focus graphically demonstrates the supremacy of individuals. The outcome of the action answers the question stated in the first scene:

LENIN If [Stalin's] needed he'll be there. If we had more men like him and fewer
    men like you . . . the revolution would succeed.
GORKI Perhaps. But Vladya, what would it succeed in doing?[12]

However, the nature of the facts undermines the high value placed on
the individual. The actual implications are that history is more the result of
human weakness than personal will. The outcome of the Russian Revolution
is shown to be the result of Lenin's brain degeneration. The triumph of Stalin
is due to Lenin destroying Trotsky's self-confidence. This is accompanied
by characterization that distinguishes the figures thematically through a
contrasting range of attitudes to revolution. Dzerzhinsky, the founder of
the communist secret police, is the revolutionary as romantic; Lunacharsky,
the revolutionary as aesthete and enthusiast. Women such as Krupskaya
or Kollontai show the emotional aspects of pity and passion. Gorki, as an
author, represents the conscience of the revolution. Together they make
up the complete revolutionary, and they are also paired thematically: the
mother figure versus the exponent of free love, the humanist versus the man
forced to suppress his humanity.

Although a dramaturgically neat way of structuring such an overwhelming mass of documentary material, this patterning is comparable to the
psychomachia of a Morality Play – an effect reinforced by the specifically
theatrical definition of 'great men' Bolt employs. Stalin is a melodramatic
villain, complete with references to 'sulphurous operatic grandeur' and Ivan
the Terrible. Lenin and Trotsky are contrasted types of tragic hero: the moral
man so obsessed by an ideal that ends are sacrificed to means, and the poly-
math paragon whose awareness of superiority becomes a fatal flaw. The
magnitude of what they are attempting is itself hubristic, while Stalin triumphs because driven by a sense of inferiority. So the Russian Revolution
itself becomes a tragic action, where noble qualities abdicate to a brutal
clown. The dramatic premise may be that 'an idea which excludes the man
cannot be right'.[13] Yet the tragic treatment tends to symbolic abstraction,
and the effect of personalizing history is reductive.

For all the religious dimension in Bolt's plays, his drama remains firmly
on a social, not a metaphysical level. As an ex-communist, who broke with
the Party 'after asking a lot of naive questions about freedom', his intention in *State of Revolution* was to bring out the 'terrifying parallels with
the way we live now'. Using history as a prism for evaluating the present
is the point where Brecht's concept of Epic Theatre and traditional drama
overlap; and Bolt's comment that 'To me the ideal audience reaction is not

"My goodness, I would never have expected that", but "Oh my God, of course"...' is an almost exact inversion of Brecht. It signals a return to 'Aristotelian' (or traditional) aims within a specifically modern and politicized frame.[14]

Music-hall parallels: Joan Littlewood (1914–97) and Peter Nichols (1927–)

CHECKLIST OF NICHOLS' MAJOR PLAYS

A Day in the Death of Joe Egg, 1967	*Born In The Gardens*, 1980
The National Health, 1969	*Passion Play*, 1981
Chez Nous, 1974	*Poppy*, 1983
The Freeway, 1974	*Piece of My Mind*, 1986
Privates on Parade, 1977	

By contrast to Bolt's melodramatic morality-play version of Brechtian drama, Joan Littlewood evolved a theatrical form that duplicated Brecht's aims, while avoiding his methods. Instead, a familiar British model was adapted in a way that made it a home-grown equivalent. Taking its cue from Osborne's association of the Edwardian Music Hall with Empire in *The Entertainer*, her Theatre Workshop production of *Oh, What a Lovely War* (1963) presented the carnage of the First World War in terms of '*a pierrot show of fifty years ago with red, white and blue fairy lights, twin balconies left and right and coloured circus 'tubs', which are used as seats, etc.*'.[15] This linked the present performance with the past, and prevented pathos. It provided a distancing device that had the same effect as Brecht's 'Alienation', but was identified with popular tradition.

Familiar songs of the 1914–18 period – 'Pack Up Your Troubles In Your Old Kitbag', 'Belgium Put The Kibosh On The Kaiser', 'The Ragtime Infantry' – presented a specifically working-class culture, as they had in the 1956 BBC radio series, 'The Boy in the Gallery' devised by Charles Chilton, who collaborated with Littlewood on the text of *Oh, What a Lovely War*. This nostalgically attractive expression of the common people's spirit and indomitable humour offered a positive standard to set against the Establishment responsible for the war. The Pierrot costume, with tin helmets for ordinary soldiers or Sam Browne belts for generals, focused on the wider thematic significance of the scenes beyond the personality of the historical figures. A constant reminder of the characters' representative status, it denied the 'great men' theory of history, while justifying caricature as the clowns'/ common man's perspective.

The value placed on the collective by the theatrical form was emphasized by Littlewood's stress on the communal nature of both text and production. It also embraced the audience. Replaying the recruiting shows of 1914–15, girls threw white feathers into the auditorium, after which the spectators were cast as troops in the trenches by using a 'plant' to set up a dialogue with the 'soldiers' on the stage, as well as being called on to join in choruses of the songs.

At the same time this overt theatricality was counterpointed by documentary fact (a technique that Bolt repeated in *State of Revolution*). Photographs of infantry advancing, corpses in the mud, 'walking wounded', were projected – three-times life-size – on a screen behind the actors representing them. Slides of posters and advertisements from the era set the action in the context of the period as a whole. A Newspanel gave a running commentary on the scenes with dates and statistics. Thus the ironic theme song of 'Oh It's A Lovely War' was juxtaposed with APRIL 22 ... BATTLE OF YPRES ... GERMAN USE POISON GAS ... BRITISH LOSS 59,275 MEN ... MAY 9 ... AUBERS RIDGE ... BRITISH LOSS 11,619 MEN IN 15 HOURS ...'.[16] Reduced to bare facts, the documentary level of the performance lent a stark reality to the song and dance, mime and revue-like sketches that interpreted it. These techniques of caricature and short scenes, each designed to illustrate a single point, like the collective evolution of a script and even the Newspanel, all come from Littlewood's Agitprop work in the 1930s. Now, developed through their incorporation in the Music Hall, they gained resonance and offered a new theatrical dimension, capable of popularizing political drama.

The playwright who picked up most directly on the potential of *Oh, What a Lovely War* was Peter Nichols. His work has alternated between naturalistic domestic drama, such as *Chez Nous* (1974) and *Passion Play* (1981), and didactic comedies that use epic techniques to portray historical or social themes, such as *The National Health* (1969) and *Poppy* (1983). In *The National Health* or *Privates On Parade* (1977) music-hall techniques are inserted both within the naturalistic context of the action and as external commentary. The central figure in *The National Health* is a male nurse, whose jokes and comic routines serve as therapy for the depressed patients, trapped in a dehumanizing healthcare system. He also steps forward to address the audience directly through revue turns that comment on the characters, and to draw connections with the hospital and society. In the

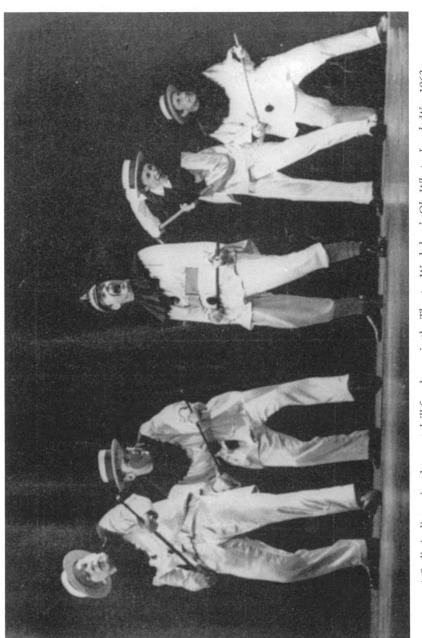

4 Stylistic distancing: bayonet drill for clowns in the Theatre Workshop's *Oh, What a Lovely War*, 1963

later, more commercially popular *Privates on Parade*, the music-hall form
is even more closely integrated with the dramatic situation. Using an ENSA
troupe of army entertainers, touring South-East Asia during the Vietnam
War, gives Nichols a dramatic rationale for the continual interpolation of
song and dance, or stand-up comedy.

This military context also adds psychological credibility to the stark contrast between presentation and content, embodied in the punning title
of *Privates on Parade*, which is characteristic of Nichols' work. The lively
lightness of performance numbers is set against the increasing bleakness
of the troupe's off-stage lives. The war destroys each performer in some
way – but the show has to go on. However, the way in which the theatrical frame is turned into the focus of the play to some extent defused the
intended political impact. For instance the final scene, where the troupe
parade in a high-kicking chorus line on the dockside as they prepare to
leave for Blighty, plays as a conventional comic ending. Yet, as Nichols has
pointed out,

It's pretty stark if you think about it. The girl's pregnant, one of the men has had
his balls shot off. The boy friend of another man is dead, and [their leader] is under
police escort. Whenever I see that scene in rehearsal, it's stronger than I expected,
but in performance it changes. By that time so much goodwill has been generated
[by the musical numbers] amongst the audience that it prevents them seeing what
a trenchant scene it is.[17]

In *Poppy* (1983), Nichols turns this problem of perspective into a thematic
strength by reversing the relationship between reality and the theatrical
format. Instead of using the revue as a frame while the weight of actuality
was placed on the performers' lives, here real events are the subject of an
ironic pantomime.

The characters are the stock figures of (female) Principal Boy, (male)
Pantomime Dame, comic servant and (two-man) Pantomime Horse. This
arcane stereotyping, developed during the nineteenth century, is not only
appropriate for portraying Victorian imperialism – emphasizing the element of sexual fantasy points up the way history is all too often distorted
through nostalgic mythologizing. 'Panto' is also the modern extension of
the popular culture once embodied in the vanished Music Hall, accounting
for as much as one fifth of all live-theatre attendance in Britain today. In addition, pantomime was originally a vehicle for satiric, even anarchic, social
criticism; and Nichols restores the anti-Establishment focus by treating its
conventions seriously.

When the obviously male Dame and Obediah Upward (a Gilbert-and-Sullivan tycoon in Union Jack waistcoat) become lovers, the effect is grotesque. But on another level the attraction between them is entirely credible, being mercenary not sexual: 'a title, a country house' on one side, and 'poppy ... in the bank' on the other. 'Poppy' being money in Cockney slang, the logical connection with the poppies from which opium is produced becomes a multiple pun (as well as the play's title). The link to 'mud' – the term for opium in its untreated state – leads into 'nostalgie de la boue': the seamy preference for the gutter. And this provides the theme of a musical number, modelled on Brecht's 'Song of Sexual Dependency' from *The Threepenny Opera*, in which the pair celebrate their unnatural relationship. Looking at 'Lady Whittington coming down the grand staircase for the finale in a diamanté crinoline and Sir Richard (Dick Whittington) in a close-fitting bodice, fishnet tights and high-heeled shoes', as the Dame comments, 'You may be wondering who does what to whom'. But Nichols' point is that this 'perverse tradition' symbolizes a vicious social structure.

Good honest folk subliminally know
That romance helps maintain the status quo
         ... to understand
The real preoccupations of our land
[we] could do worse than spend a little time
Deciphering the British pantomime.[18]

This effect is achieved by playing on the gap between conventional expectations, and Nichols' exposure of the nineteenth-century drug trade: the financial basis of the Indian Empire and the cause of the Opium War that destabilized China (and annexed Hong Kong). The contrast is summed up in the image of 'CHORUS GIRLS *as British tars danc[ing] across with their chests of opium and barrowloads of Bibles*'. Patter songs, comic turns, apparently idyllic scenes and the theatrical glitter that goes with pantomime, all seduce spectators into an initial approval of what outside the theatre they would unhesitatingly condemn as evil – only to discover the cost to them as an audience in terms of entertainment.

The standard audience repartee and sing-along is used inventively as a measure of the switch in perspective. Being asked to help the characters, in the conventional 'boys and girls' formula at the beginning, the public are associated with their activities by responding to the familiar cues: as the honest servant exclaims, 'they're going to be on our side'. And before it becomes clear that the Old England is to be rescued from bankruptcy through drug trafficking, the trade with China is explained in terms of an everyday product, which has become the most basic staple of British life:

UPWARD (*partly to the audience…*) Your cuppa's what it's all about. Your English cuppa China tea.

Who could disapprove of the national drink? However, by the end of the play, the massive guns of the British fleet that impose trade on the Chinese are turned threateningly on the auditorium, while the '*rousing music-hall number*' that the audience are required to join in singing is a song of looting the Summer Palace.[19] And the dialogue assumes that now no spectator participates.

In this updated version of the Dick Whittington rags-to-riches story, where Queen Victoria doubles as the Fairy Godmother, the innocent village maiden-heroine is used as an idealistic front for economic exploitation. In the traditional pantomime scenario she would become Dick Whittington's 'natural' wife. But here the pattern is shockingly broken, using our disappointed expectations to persuade us both of the unnaturalness of the society depicted, and the falsity of such sentimental visions of the past as conventional pantomime represents.

Dick has become Sir Richard, the original Whittington's easily corrupted descendant, who puts wealth before our heroine. Following him as a missionary, she takes refuge in opium when he rejects her. The final wedding-scene is thus a hollow mockery. The Principal Boy has chosen the 'wrong' wife; and the heroine, horrifically revealed in the last stages of physical decay – with '*ashen face. Blackened gums*' – as the end-product of the drug trade, is literally a 'spectre at the feast'.[20] Instead of symbolizing a future of social happiness, this celebration marks a marriage of convenience between business and the aristocracy, which Nichols presents as the basis of the contemporary Establishment in a final transformation scene.

Everything has been sacrificed to 'poppy'. The romantic characters are destroyed, even the pantomime horse (satirically playing on English sentimentality over animals) is shot for food during the siege of the Cantonese trade missions. Political relevance has been injected into a highly traditional form of drama. Yet its popular basis made *Poppy* a long-running West End hit, which also transferred successfully to Broadway (even though the specifically British terms of Nichols' attack on society were far less relevant to American spectators). Like *Oh, What a Lovely War*, its theatricality and ironic depth attracted a broad mainstream audience, normally antagonistic to straight political drama.

Dramatizing Brecht: Christopher Hampton (1946–)

CHECKLIST OF HAMPTON'S MAJOR PLAYS

When Did You Last See My Mother, 1966	*Tales From Hollywood,* 1983
	Les Liaisons dangereuses, 1987
Total Eclipse, 1968	*The White Chameleon,* 1991
The Philanthropist, 1970	*Sunset Boulevard,* 1993
Savages, 1973	*Alice's Adventures Underground,*
Treats, 1976	1995

With the adoption of Brechtian models for essentially mainstream drama, it was only a matter of time before Brecht himself appeared on the English stage – as he already had in Germany with Günter Grass' play, *The Plebeians Rehearse the Uprising* (1966), in which Brecht is critically presented as a theatrical 'Boss', bought out by an oppressive communist government that discredits the Marxist principles of his drama. And it is logical that the playwright to do this should be Christopher Hampton (although Howard Brenton also later used Brecht's name as the alias used by an East German secret policeman in *Berlin Bertie* – see p. 217 below.)

Like his contemporaries, David Hare and Howard Brenton, Christopher Hampton had been exposed to the Brechtian approach while resident dramatist at the Royal Court, which staged *Total Eclipse* (1968), his black picture of Rimbaud and Verlaine – the artist-as-outcast/homosexual, victimized by a materialistic society – and a satire on modern intellectual life as a moral vacuum, based on Molière, *The Philanthropist* (1970). Unlike other Royal Court playwrights, however, Hampton rejected left-wing ideology, and avoided polemics. Indeed his one foray into topical issues with *Savages* (1973) – which deals with the psychology of hostage-taking – clearly shows the contempt of Marxist revolutionaries for the common people (in this case South American Indians) whom they claim to be liberating. Both his early plays were based on his university experience and study of modern languages, which led him to translating modern classics, in particular Ibsen, and the Austrian dramatist Odōn von Horváth, and more recently the contemporary French playwright Yasmina Reza (*The Unexpected Man*, 1998).

Since leaving the Royal Court these translations, or adaptations like the script for Andrew Lloyd Webber's musical version of the Billy Wilder classic film about Hollywood, *Sunset Boulevard* (1993) or *Alice's Adventures Underground* (NT, 1994) have formed the majority of Hampton's theatrical output. Although he has also written polished comedies, and an openly auto-biographical play, *The White Chameleon* (1991) Hampton's most successful play has been one of his translations: the 1987 dramatization of Laclos' novel, *Les Liaisons dangereuses*. The explanation for dealing with experience as it were at second-hand, through the medium of others' work, is given in *The White Chameleon* where he presents himself as a child trying, like the animal of his title, to disappear into his surroundings, in this case the alien landscape of Egypt in the years leading up to the Suez crisis. According to the narrator – the grown-up Christopher Hampton – the discovery of a coolly detached observer inside himself was what made him a writer; and this is very close to the objectivity demanded by Brecht (who of course also made a practice of rewriting others' plays).

Odōn von Horváth was a particularly important model for Hampton, having developed an alternative type of Epic Theatre in the early 1930s. This substituted ironic structuring for Brecht's alienation techniques: an approach echoed in Hampton's *Tales from Hollywood* (National Theatre, 1983). Its title deliberately parallels Horváth's *Tales from the Vienna Woods* (translated by Hampton in 1977), in which brutal reality and sentimental lyricism are counterpointed to expose the psychology of fascism in the Vienna of 1931. Hampton transfers this criticism to wartime America, the starting point of his play being the death of Horváth, who was about to leave for America when killed by lightning on the Champs-Elysées the year before war broke out. Hampton's play imagines what might have happened if he had survived to join the circle of German émigrés there.

The device fictionalizes a historical reality, and – in centring the action on a non-existent figure – provides a telling image of moral emptiness. Both qualities are, of course, typical of Hollywood, which is presented in terms of Brecht's vision (cited in the programme notes): 'In these parts . . . heaven . . . /Serves the unprosperous, unsuccessful/As hell'.[21] The exiles are also displaced persons, dispossessed in a world of material luxury, and dependent on a system that alienates them. *Tales from Hollywood* is dedicated to the memory of David Mercer, whose plays (such as *Belcher's Luck*, 1966) express a similar sense that when it is a question of the survival of the fittest, the fittest to survive are the least admirable.

Hampton's focus is on the destruction of Nellie, the wife of Heinrich Mann, who was the original model for the role played by Marlene Dietrich in *The Blue Angel*. In 1932, as the embodiment of socialist integrity, Mann had been called on to run against Hindenburg in the German presidential election. In the commercialized Hollywood context he is as much spiritually as financially impoverished, while Nellie's extrovert vitality is perverted into alcoholism, promiscuity and ultimately suicide. The survivors are Heinrich's brother Thomas Mann, the Nobel prizewinner, who has become reduced to a plaster image of the man of principle by selling out to materialism, and Bertolt Brecht, who cynically exploits the system.

The play is a counterpart to Klaus Mann's novel *Mephisto*, which embodies the moral corruption of Nazi society in Gustaf Gründgens (presented as a soulless mask: Mephistopheles as the damned Faust). Hampton substitutes Thomas Mann for Hitler's favourite actor, and capitalism for fascism. He copies Horváth's episodic structure, although the average British spectator would have taken this as Brechtian imitation. He also sets quasi-naturalistic scenes against his character Brecht's on-stage demonstration of anti-illusionistic theatre, as an equivalent to the contrast between the self-deception of false ideals and brutal realism in Horváth's drama.

However, the result is a drama of mirrors, where the social criticism is only apparent, and all the cross-references relate back to theatre. Everything regresses to fantasy in a play based on a play, with a situation derived from a novel that first appeared as a film, and characters who – almost without exception – are novelists, playwrights and performers. In addition, the actuality of the scenes is not only undercut by the imaginary status of the main character (already dead before the events occur). It is also devalued by the anti-illusionistic theory of drama presented during the play by the figure of Brecht, the social as well as theatrical antagonist, in which he ridicules the way these scenes are being presented. To the degree that the play identifies with its dramatist-protagonist, it presents a self-cancelling statement. As a ghost, Horváth is literally incapable of intervening in the historical events; and this ironically undercuts the belief in a dramatist's ability to influence society, a belief which is typified by Brecht.

In *Tales from Hollywood*, Hampton has Brecht step out of the historical context (though not out of role), to lecture the modern audience on the reality principle that Epic stagecraft represents – thus reducing the descriptive placard, bare stage and exposed lighting of the scene to stylistic tools that can be applied interchangeably with the naturalistic format of the rest of the play. As with *A Man for All Seasons*, the effect is simply to signal that the playwright's intentions are 'political' in the sense of dealing seriously with a socially significant theme. These techniques of 'distancing' have no ideological content. Indeed, the critical attitude to a performance that the Epic Theatre supposedly induces does not prevent empathy. It may even intensify the emotional response by the shift in emphasis from a character's feelings to his/her existential situation. Spectators naturally find personal analogues for the circumstances that trap Thomas More, Trotsky or Nellie Mann, and identify with them as individuals, rather than concentrating on the political causes of their plight, which requires taking an objective view. And this is as true of such characters from Brecht's own repertoire as Grusche in *The Caucasian Chalk Circle* and Kattrin or the title-figure of *Mother Courage*, all of whom contain a high emotional charge.

Brecht developed his approach in response to a new perception of the determining factors in modern society:

Just the grasping of a new range of material requires a new dramatic and theatrical form. Can we speak about finance in heroic couplets? . . . Petroleum struggles against the five-Act form . . . The dramatic technique of Hebbel and Ibsen is totally insufficient to dramatize even a simple press release . . . Indeed one no longer dares to offer [drama] in its old form to grown-up newspaper readers.[22]

From such a perspective, Epic techniques can be seen as an extension of Naturalism, rather than its opposite. Although their means may be different, the aim of both these types of drama is essentially the same: to enable the major socio-political issues of the time to be dealt with directly on the stage. Ibsen's dramaturgy presupposes that the key to social progress was the family, where Darwinian factors of environment and heredity combine; Brecht's that the active forces were those of the market and industrial technology. But in contemporary theatrical terms they are equal alternatives.

As in the Royal Court productions of Wesker's Trilogy, Epic design can be applied to essentially naturalistic material. Or Brechtian technique can be juxtaposed with other styles, as in *Tales from Hollywood*. What links Granville-Barker or Galsworthy at the beginning of the century (discussed above, pp. 60ff.) with John Arden or Edward Bond, the two English playwrights who have most consciously built on Brecht's dramaturgy and are closest to his political position, is the desire to use theatre as a fulcrum for change. The stylistic differences between the naturalistic followers of Shaw, and the Brechtian dramatists of the 1970s, relate to differences in era and audience expectations. Any theatrical form appears realistic as much by contrast with the existing norm, as for any intrinsic qualities; and once established as the new standard it too becomes 'conventional', associated with conservatism, cliché and the commercial stage, leading to the adoption of a new style.

So the shift away from Naturalism on the modern English stage can be seen as a sign of continuity – and already Brecht's influence has spread from designers such as Jocelyn Herbert and directors like Joan Littlewood through a whole range of dramatists from Osborne to Caryl Churchill, to general standards of production. With the exception of spectacular musicals, illusionistic staging is now an exception. Even in the commercial theatre, the box set that dominated the first half of the century has been replaced by semi-abstract, representational or overtly theatrical scenery. It is in the context of these developments that the work of Arden and Bond should be seen, together with the following generation of political dramatists, such as David Edgar, Howard Brenton and David Hare.

Notes

1 Bolt, interview in Ronald Hayman, *Robert Bolt*, London, 1969, p. 8.

2 *Ibid.*, p. 5; *A Man for All Seasons*, London, 1963, p. 58.

3 *A Man for All Seasons*, p. 63.

4 David Puttnam (director of *The Mission*), RSA journal, March 1989, p. 226.

5 Bolt, cited in Hayman, *Robert Bolt*, p. 7; *A Man for All Seasons*, pp. 10, 93, 53.

6 *Ibid.*, pp. 2, 72, 45.

7 *Ibid.*, p. 88.

8 Preface, *A Man for All Seasons*, p. x.

9 *State of Revolution*, London, 1977, p. 29.

10 *Ibid.*, p. 17.

11 *New York Times*, 19 June 1977 (see also *The Times*, 19 May 1977: 'one is mainly conscious of the sheer weight the piece has to carry').

12 *State of Revolution*, pp. 78 & 39.

13 *Ibid.*, pp. 21 & 17.

14 Bolt, in *The Times*, 25 May 1977, and in Hayman, *Robert Bolt*, p. 14. (For comparison, see *Brecht on Theatre*, ed. John Willett, New York, 1964, p. 71: 'The spectator of the epic theatre says: "I'd never have thought it – That's extraordinary, hardly believable – It's got to stop . . ."')

15 Theatre Workshop, *Oh, What a Lovely War*, London, 1967, p. 7.

16 *Ibid.*, p. 44. (These running news-flashes are a direct development from Littlewood's use of the 'electric newspaper' in her 1930s Agitprop play, *John Bullion*: see above, p. 73.)

17 Peter Nichols, interview, *Plays and Players*, March 1978, p. 15.

18 Peter Nichols, *Poppy*, London, 1982, pp. 35, 50 & 111, 31.

19 *Ibid.*, pp. 88, 8, 45, 109.

20 *Ibid.*, p. 112.

21 Brecht, *Hollywood Elegies*. For a discussion of Horváth's work, see Christopher Innes, *Modern German Drama*, Cambridge, 1979, pp. 219ff.

22 *Brecht on Theatre*, p. 30. For an extended discussion of the emotional content of Epic Theatre, both in early productions under Brecht's own direction and in the Berliner Ensemble, see John Fuegi, *Bertolt Brecht* (Directors in Perspective), Cambridge, 1987, pp. 30ff and 123ff.

3.8 John Arden (1930–): the popular tradition and Epic alternatives

CHECKLIST OF ARDEN'S MAJOR PLAYS

The Waters of Babylon, 1957	*Left-Handed Liberty*, 1965
Live Like Pigs, 1958	*The Hero Rises Up*, 1968
Serjeant Musgrave's Dance, 1959	*The Island of the Mighty*, 1972
The Happy Haven, 1960	*The Ballygombeen Bequest*, 1972
The Workhouse Donkey, 1963	*The Non-Stop Connolly Show*, 1975
Armstrong's Last Goodnight, 1964	*Little Gray Home in the West*, 1981

John Arden's early plays, starting with *The Waters of Babylon* in 1957, were produced by the Royal Court like Osborne's, and derive from the same tradition as *The Entertainer* (staged the same year). But where Osborne uses the Music Hall as an explicit symbol, and as a frame for naturalistic scenes that divide 'back stage' from 'on stage' (see above, pp. 98–99), Arden integrates music-hall techniques in the action. He uses dance routines, sentimental or satirical songs, comic monologue and direct address to the audience, or pantomime gags. However, these are inserted into plots revolving around social problems: a neighbourhood conflict produced by housing policies (*Live Like Pigs*, 1958), the institutionalizing of the aged (*The Happy Haven*, 1960), or local government corruption (*The Waters of Babylon*, 1957; *The Workhouse Donkey*, 1963).

Live Like Pigs, for example, takes a typically naturalistic theme. A family of gypsies are forcibly re-housed on a council estate. The audience are initially led to identify with the ordinary housewife next door, whose socially approved standards of order and cleanliness are threatened by the gypsies' scavenging, anarchistic life style – only to be shown that her 'respectable' behaviour is even more repellent than the most anti-social member of the gypsy group: Blackmouth, a howling drunk who has murdered a warder to escape from prison. She '*roars in her throat like a bull*' and, along with other women from the housing estate, tries to tear the gypsy's son to pieces for presumed rape. The police, who stop the riot, effectively carry out the mob's intentions by other means when they find stolen goods in the gypsies' house. The youth flees, and his father's leg is broken in obstructing the police's attempt to prevent his escape.

In the 1958 Royal Court production the characters were treated psychologically, rather than as stock types, while the setting – a cutaway of the two up/two down council house – emphasized the fourth-wall convention. Although the journalistic subject lends itself to such an interpretation, this kind of presentation effectively disguised the music-hall elements. It distorted the real nature of the play: a model of social interaction, designed to reveal the dehumanizing pressures and superficial nature of 'respectable' values, which are discarded in their own defence.[1]

The focus on a general analysis of social attitudes, of which the specific action and figures in *Live Like Pigs* were intended as examples, is underlined by the ballad that prefaces each scene. This is a typically Brechtian approach, with the ballad singer presenting the episodes as illustrative material.

Indeed, references to Brecht's plays are common in Arden's early work. The epilogue of *The Good Woman of Setzuan* (1940) is directly echoed in the rhyming couplets that end *The Waters of Babylon*:

So, with only a few minutes to live,
I must see can I not give
Some clearer conclusion to this play
To order your lives in the neatest way . . .

The name of this dying protagonist, Krank, and that of Feng, the police chief in *The Workhouse Donkey*, parallel names like Garga or Schlink from Brecht's *In the Jungle of Cities* (1923). Indeed, the basic situation of *The Workhouse Donkey* is identical to that of Brecht's play. Butterthwaite, the corrupt Napoleon of municipal politics, and the rigidly moral Feng each destroy the other in a struggle for control of the town; and Arden gives 'the fell and calamitous grinding of two mighty opposites' (Feng being named after Hamlet's uncle in Saxo Grammaticus) a mock-heroic tone.[2] Similarly, King John's paradoxical legal precedents in *Left-Handed Liberty* (1965) are a direct copy of Azdak, the people's judge, who achieves true justice by reversing the law that protects the status quo in Brecht's *Caucasian Chalk Circle* (1945). Even *Serjeant Musgrave's Dance* (1959), Arden's most successful play, can be seen as paralleling Brecht's adaptation of *The Recruiting Officer* (*Trumpets and Drums*, 1952); and Arden gave it a typically Brechtian subtitle: 'An Unhistorical Fable'.

Arden has listed Brecht as the most important of his literary models, along with Lorca and Ben Jonson. But instead of uncritically adopting the external characteristics of Epic Theatre, he has attempted to find contemporary equivalents drawn from familiar British models, seeing Brecht as

limited by the conditions and prejudices of his time. The methods of a poet like Brecht cannot be expected to eliminate these barriers. But to follow his methods is to become . . . aware of the *existence* of the barriers.[3]

One of Arden's alternatives is a calculated refusal to provide simple answers to complex issues. The ambiguities of his plays up to *Left-Handed Liberty* – that is, before he began collaborating with his wife, Margaretta D'Arcy – are designed to make a spectator conscious of unexamined assumptions, leading them to question the principles on which society is based, as in *The Workhouse Donkey*. There the electoral tactics of both Tory and Labour are equally self-serving and unscrupulous; and although the plot revolves around the corruption of those in power, the opposition has no quarrel with the effect of the others' policies on the town: 'Oh, it's not exactly misgoverned. It's just the wrong lot are the governors, that's all.'[4] If the system rules out meaningful change, the audience are being challenged to find a different system.

As with Shaw's reinterpretation of the quintessence of Ibsenism to fit his own drama, Arden's analysis of Brecht describes his own aims, rather than Brecht's achievement. According to Arden, Brecht

believed that [theatre] was a potential instrument of social progress; and that the playwright, by reflecting in his work the true image of human society, assisted the members of that society to diagnose the defects in the image and thence to improve the reality.[5]

Where Arden is most Brechtian is in his use of anti-illusionistic theatricality (underlined in the title chosen for his collection of critical and theoretical writings, *To Present the Pretence*).

The most formally 'Epic' of Arden's dramas is *The Hero Rises Up* (written in collaboration with his wife Margaretta D'Arcy, 1968). It corresponds to the Brechtian didactic model in theme, selection of material, and technique. As with Brecht's version of *Coriolanus*, it stands as a counter-text to another drama that represented an Establishment view of history: Terence Rattigan's 1966 television play, *Nelson: A Portrait in Miniature*, which had been written at the suggestion of the Duke of Edinburgh (see above, pp. 84–85). The demythologizing of Nelson ('the last uncontested hero-figure of our own history') in *The Hero Rises Up* is a variation on the central thematic paradox of Brecht's *Galileo* (1947) 'Unhappy the land that breeds no hero'/'Unhappy the land that needs a hero'. As in their other collaborations, Arden and D'Arcy also use a whole range of Brechtian devices. Placards objectify the content of a scene or set the action in an ironic perspective, as with 'THE BLIND EYE' at the Battle of Copenhagen, or 'THE FATHER RETURNS TO HIS CHILDREN' when Nelson crushes a popular republic in a neutral state to restore the tyrannical King of Naples, whose only concept of ruling is revenge.[6] Street ballads sum up the underlying significance of historical events. Exaggeratedly baroque arias stress the artificiality of the performance. The story continually resolves into third-person narrative, and is structured episodically. Conventionally dramatic situations are undercut, as in the Battle of Copenhagen where the only conflict presented is between Nelson at one side of the stage and Admiral Parker at the other; and victory is represented by a procession of dead and wounded seamen.

However, all these anti-illusionistic techniques fit into the overall frame of the nineteenth-century military melodrama that the play was advertised as:

THE HERO RISES UP
contains *many* and *varied* Stage-Spectacles of sensational splendour:
including –
(1) The Resurrection of the HERO NELSON from the *Dead* . . .
(8) The HERO *ascends* into His *Fitting* Paradise . . .

* * *

DO NOT FAIL to see What Once We Were: DO NOT FAIL to make the Dismal Comparision with What We Are Now!!

The pastiche evokes the qualities it parodies, which precisely mirrors the ambivalence of the authors.

On one hand Nelson is seen as admirable: an anarchic individualist of 'asymmetrical "curvelinear" temperament to an unusually passionate degree', who successfully challenges moral and military authority. Indeed, an 'Asymmetrical' preface identifies the loose structure, clashing styles and consciously tawdry 'two-pence coloured' tone of the play itself with Nelson. And these qualities were reflected in the Ardens' production. This was designed as an anarchic defiance of a 'rectilinear' theatre establishment, which the Ardens rejected as having an 'inevitable subservience to a military requirement'.[7]

On the other hand, Nelson is presented as an instrument of oppression, the exploiter of the common people. The fleet Nelson commands becomes an image of Britain, with its pressgangs and brutal discipline being interchangeable with Newgate Gaol. Each of his victories is shown as repetition of his cynical massacre of revolutionary citizens at Naples:

> He ordered in his red marines
> Sing ho for liberty
> And he smashed them all to smithereens
> All for to make them free.[8]

The irony, underlined by the contrast between the words and a cheerful sea-chanty tune, is the key to the play's vision.

In this light Nelson, as the originator of the concept of total war, is explicitly paralleled with Napoleon. The reputation of both is based solely on the successful organization of slaughter, and Nelson's famous flag-signal is shown to be exactly the same as the inscription on a French medal ('*La France expectera que tous les hommes allons faire leur devoir*'). Hero and villain are indistinguishable; and Nelson's final apotheosis is bathetic, with its fake mermaids and baroque marine chariot in the shape of a gilded seashell hoisted up, not to the heavens, but to the top of Nelson's column. The point is made explicit by a dissenting commentator, in the shape of Nelson's disillusioned stepson who resigned his naval commission:

> Equality, Fraternity, and so on never came:
> And what we were then, now we are just the same . . .
> All of us, for whom he died,
> Have no reward, because we never tried
> To do without him on our own.[9]

At the same time, this choric figure's motivation for revealing the anti-heroic truth undercuts his statements. His reason for leaving the navy is explicitly to enrich himself from the commercial opportunities offered by the war.

The same contradictory valuations recur throughout the play. Nelson's adultery is clearly approved. Yet the demythologizing presents Emma as a prostituted puppet (performing nude 'Attitudes'). Indeed, the parody of academic analysis in the prologue – spoken in production by Arden himself – explicitly satirizes the play's theme and didactic drama as a whole. Any imposed meaning would conflict with the anarchic freedom which the production both promoted and exemplified, and which was also given expression by letting the public in without payment.

The opposition between positive anarchy and negative order is basic to almost all of Arden's drama. Anarchy is approved as Dionysian (*The Workhouse Donkey*), individualistic (the 'kink' in perfect philosophical circles, *Left-Handed Liberty*), intuitive, asymmetrical and curvelinear (*Ars Longa Vita Brevis, The Hero Rises Up*), a Celtic and female principle (*Island of the Mighty*) – all adjectives which recur in Arden's critical writing. By contrast, order includes rationalism and logic, which are characterized as rectilinear, Roman and masculine, as well as moral repression and religious or class hierarchies.

If Brecht was one major influence on Arden, Sean O'Casey is another. *The Ballygombeen Bequest* (1972) is a direct reworking of O'Casey's *Purple Dust* (1945), while *The Non-Stop Connolly Show* (1975) builds on the situation of *The Star Turns Red* (1940). In singling out the 'mythological landscape of popular imagery' created by O'Casey's amalgam of 'medieval morality play, Shakespeare, Bunyan and Victorian popular melodrama . . . the jokes and word-play of the building site, the street-ballad', Arden defines the stylistic aim and tools of his own drama – particularly *Serjeant Musgrave's Dance*, which O'Casey in turn hailed as 'far and away the finest play of the present day, full of power, protest and frantic compassion'.[10]

Serjeant Musgrave's Dance, which established Arden as a leading figure among the new group of English playwrights when it was produced in 1959, forms a reference point for all his subsequent work. It is the most complex formulation of Arden's conflict between order and anarchy.

The nineteenth-century Serjeant is obsessed by an idea of Old Testament justice and military discipline: 'It's got a strong name – duty. And it's drawn out straight and black . . . a clear plan'. He stands for 'Numbers and order. According to Logic'; and in purely abstract terms his purpose is rational. The murder of one soldier on foreign service led to the killing of five natives in revenge. So executing twenty-five of the leading citizens in the dead man's birthplace will literally bring home the cost of colonialism by exacting its blood-price from the colonizers. Musgrave is, as numerous references imply, taking the place of God, and his multiplication can only work by ignoring any human element. The fact that one of his squad has murdered an officer, or that they 'accidentally' kill one of their own number who tries to desert from this band of deserters, is – like any questioning of his purpose – dismissed as 'not material'.

Against this blinkered vision is set 'life and love' in the shape of the two women in the play: qualities which he labels 'crooked, dirty, idle, untidy . . . anarchy'. But the action supports what one of the women points out: in reality 'it's arsy-versey to what you said'.[11] The only outsider Musgrave recruits is Crooked Joe, a sinister barge-man who is motivated by prospects of rape and pillage that are the exact opposite of order and justice. The Serjeant's precision is the real anarchy, and his logic is explicitly insane.

However, as even such a schematic outline indicates, the play itself is as structured and logical as its protagonist's design. The elements of the action are precisely balanced in parallels and inversions; and the treatment of the story is linear. The young soldier shot in the back by anti-colonial rebels, whose skeleton Musgrave has brought back to his home town, was the lover of the barmaid. The affection she gives to the youngest of the deserters leads to him being bayoneted in the stomach by his fellow rebels against colonialism. The image of Crooked Joe is superimposed on the straightest Serjeant of the line in the Graveyard scene of the first Act, where the Bargee mimics Musgrave's gestures and attitude behind his back. Two scenes later this situation is reversed when Musgrave, unnoticed, watches the Bargee's mock drill of some drunken colliers. The parody of military discipline is an image of the reality behind the supposed recruiting party: 'The effect should be, not so much of three incompetents pretending to be soldiers, but of three trained soldiers gone mad.'[12]

The same precision and balance can be seen in the colour symbolism that runs throughout the play. Analysing O'Casey's stagecraft, Arden underlined the dramatic significance of colours for evoking mood and giving themes visual definition. In *Serjeant Musgrave's Dance*, colours are also emblematic, being restricted to primary tones of black, red and white. The visual contrast expresses a conceptual unity. All three colours stand for death – white for winter and the skeleton of Billy Hicks, black for the grave, red for murder – and are brought together in the central figure. Black Jack in his scarlet uniform is said to have been 'got . . . in a cold grinding' by 'the North Wind in a pair of millstones'.

The symbolic parallels proliferate. The parson's gown and Musgrave's Bible are black, as are the pit-men and the coal fields. The mine-owner Mayor's robe is scarlet, as are both the tunics of Musgrave and his squad, and the jackets of the dragoons who restore order at the end. Musgrave's demonic Dance of Death beneath the skeleton, which he hoists on the town flag-pole to signal the start of his revolutionary revenge, is set against the people's dance celebrating the lifting of his threat to society – yet this is specifically

5 Shock effect: threatening the audience in Arden's *Serjeant Musgrave's Dance*
(Royal Court revival, 1965)

'*not a dance of joy*'. The status quo is saved by shooting and executions; and the pit-men are 'back where we were': starvation and lock-out.[13]

The almost uniformly unfavourable reviews of the first production in 1959 were largely due to incomprehension. The allegorical elements led critics to expect an explicit moral. Since this was denied by Arden's ambiguous conclusion, the critics concluded that the play was about 'the brutalizing effects of war': a statement they dismissed as cliché.[14] This is certainly one aspect of the play. However, Arden's comments in the preface about the difficulty of pacificism set the anti-war theme in a wider context of institutional violence, and the means of bringing about social change.

Part of the confusion about the play came from Arden's reliance on shock effect for the climax. In order to preserve the element of surprise for the hoisting of the skeleton in place of a flag, all references to Musgrave's plan up to that point are left oblique. Yet the simplicity of the storyline is designed to make the real situation clear in retrospect. The opening lines present a capsule summary in the metaphor of a card game: 'The black spades carry the day. Jack, King and Ace. *We* throw the red Queen over.' The focus is on revolution; and war is meant to be seen as a symptom of the class structure – both an instrument of exploitation, with recruitment being used to remove the leaders of any popular opposition (as the Mayor proposes), and a definition of the relationship between the Capitalist Establishment and Labour (as in the final re-imposition of 'order' by Dragoons). From this political perspective, colonialism is the extension of an unjust social system. The treatment of its own working people is identical to that of foreign natives in a 'Protectorate' – a point explicitly argued in *The Non-Stop Connolly Show* sixteen years later.

Arden suggested that these implications were unclear because the re-sources of the Royal Court only allowed for two Dragoons, instead of a visually overwhelming force to demonstrate 'that even the most sympa-thetic of the colliers, who nearly sides with Musgrave, has no alternative but to take part in the dance'.[15] But the real problem is the role assigned to the audience, who are collectively taken to represent society.

Following the same pattern as *Live Like Pigs*, in the first half of the play sympathy is channelled to Musgrave, who appears the image of social order. The inhumanity of his logic is concealed, while the logical structuring of the action serves as a subliminal reinforcement of Musgrave's morality. When he trains the Gatling gun on the auditorium, the spectators' identification with the exploiters and the establishment becomes overt; and to bring this home the Mayor, Parson and Constable are lined up '*downstage to stand facing the platform and covered by the gun*'. The historical parable breaks through into the present. What had appeared safely distanced, suddenly applies to us. The shock effect coupled with the revelation of Musgrave's insanity, the '*frantic*' tone of his threat to shoot and the pacifist throwing himself in front of the muzzle, are clearly intended to produce a feeling of real fear.

The aim is to make the spectators directly aware of their responsibility, and so bring them to reject their assumed authoritarian thought patterns. This is the 'seed' referred to in the final song. The 'flourishing tree of fruit', which this notional seed may sprout into, is the peaceful social revolution that such a change in attitude would bring about – and the last line explicitly presents the experience of watching Musgrave's failed rebellion as a prophylactic paradigm: 'They're going to hang us up a length higher nor most apple trees grow, Serjeant. D'you reckon we can start an orchard?'[16]

However, the emotional threat blurs the intellectual content of the play. It is not just the authority figures on the stage, but the audience who are 'saved' by the Dragoons at the end. Paradoxically, *Serjeant Musgrave's Dance* is a play where the power of a performance bears an inverse ratio to its political effectiveness. The more convincing the violence of the climax, the less likely a spectator is to accept Musgrave's 'order' as an image of his own attitudes, or to reject the forces of 'law'.

Serjeant Musgrave's Dance is also an example of Arden's attempt to create a popular stage form, equivalent to Lorca's plays where 'apparent simplicity . . . is set against the suggestively rich imagery of their dialogue and the twopence coloured decor to produce the genuine effect of peasant art'. The symbolism of primary colours, focus on plot at the expense of motivation, use of stock situations (like the eleventh-hour arrival of the cavalry in a Western) and simplified characters in Arden's play are typical of the traditional ballad, with its typified figures and poetic crystallization of basic issues. These qualities are also comparable to mummer's plays, where 'the Turkish Knight kills St George, only to find an interfering doctor who raises him from the dead again'.[17]

The strip cartoon can be seen as a modern variant of peasant art, and this forms the basis of later plays like *Harold Muggins is a Martyr* (1968). Written for CAST (Cartoon Archetypal Slogan Theatre), one of the earliest alternative/explicitly socialist performance groups, and taking over the Muggins figure they had developed as 'the English archetype of the bloke who does everything and gets no reward . . . the working class', it is the Ardens' first openly propagandist play. The exaggerated simplification of cartoons is carried over into political analysis, with businessmen as gangsters and a sleazy nightclub as a microcosm of proletarian revolt.

This was picked up again in *Henry Dubbs* (California, 1973): an extended sequence of songs and sketches, illustrating the history of the American labour movement through figures drawn from cartoons in the Socialist Party of America newspapers around the time of the First World War. In addition to Dubbs – 'the archetypal non-unionised chauvinist "backward worker"' – the Ardens borrowed Grabitall, a universal 'boss-figure' wearing different masks to represent a Capitalist, a General, or President Nixon.[18] In fact, they developed a standard repertoire of depersonalized stock characters. Grabitall reappears in their 1976 quasi-documentary, *The Non-Stop Connolly Show*, together with a pair of choric 'Employers' from the Agitprop script for *Two Hundred Years of Labour History* (written for a Socialist Labour League rally, 1971). So do Hook and Crook, a music-hall duo of sleazy fixers whose names change to MacHook and MacCrook or O'Hookey and Crookey depending on national context, as well as abstract symbols like a WAR DEMON (male) or OPPRESSED NATIONS (female) that were repeated from an anti-Vietnam *War Carnival* (New York, 1967).

This shift to Agitprop theatre marks a distinct change in Arden's approach. Ambiguity vanishes along with individualized characterization. Ironic paradox and objectivity are replaced by simplistic ideological divisions; and the change coincides with his collaboration with his wife, Margaretta D'Arcy.

There are clear thematic continuities with Arden's early plays. Lindsay, the poet-narrator of *Armstrong's Last Goodnight* (1964) who is driven to the butchery that he has set out to prevent, betraying his humanistic idealism, reappears as Merlin, the liberal who sells his poetic gifts to the establishment, and is driven mad by political realities in *The Island of the Mighty* (1972). Both these plays project modern society into a similar military-feudal system, while the image of soldiers as 'bloodred roses' serving the 'red Queen' carries over into *The Non-Stop Connolly Show* (1975), which Arden conceived as 'a kind of inside-out version of my invented Black Jack Musgrave'. The historical Connolly is also an army deserter, and his revolution fails for similar reasons – 'the inability of British Labour to understand the political implications of Irish Separatism' mirrors Musgrave's incomprehension of 'the political implications of the labour movement (the striking pitmen)'.[19]

However, in the early plays the dark side of anarchy is shown as well as the celebration of liberty, while the repressive pole is also portrayed as progressive. As Arden remarked in 1965, discussing the 'ferocious integrity' of Feng, the Police Chief of *The Workhouse Donkey*,

if you dramatize a conflict and you say, one side in my opinion is white, the other side is black, and you underrate the strength, integrity and commonsense of the black side, then you will give your side an easy walkover ...
It wouldn't be necessary to make this propaganda if there wasn't a serious struggle involved – therefore why not be fair?[20]

By contrast, in *The Island of the Mighty*, where the context is mythological, and the conflict is conceived in terms of symbols, these polarities are simplistic and heavily weighted. King Arthur is intended to be 'a disruptive figure, both reactionary and revolutionary at one and the same time'. But the action ignores this ambiguity. The Balin/Balan story offers an emblematic preview: two brothers are manipulated into participating in a primitive ritual, where the lamed king of the past year is killed by his successor, and both

die. Similarly, the struggle for supremacy between Arthur and his illegitimate son destroys existing authority; and the political vacuum is filled by
the proto-feminist revolution that transforms society into an antediluvian
utopia where

... land was held in common, no landlord gathered his gold,
All of the people ate what all of the people did grow...
Once more shall the life of the Island of the Mighty be exactly as I have told.[21]

In *The Non-Stop Connolly Show*, the bias is even more one-sided: individualized characters versus stereotypes. Anarchy is simplistically equated with
political freedom, order with reactionary repression.

There is a comparable shift in the relationship between social reality and
stage image. *Serjeant Musgrave's Dance* and *Armstrong's Last Goodnight* are
both based on contemporary documentary sources: news reports of Cypriot
civilians having been indiscriminately killed in an army round-up after a
soldier's wife was shot by terrorists in the late 1950s; and the memoirs
of Conor Cruise O'Brien, dealing with the operation carried out by the
UN during the civil war in the African Congo during the early 1960s. Each
distances the event by transposing it into a historical context. The incident in
Cyprus provides the background for Musgrave's revenge on Victorian society
in the microcosm of an isolated town, cut off by snowdrifts. A parallel to the
secession of a Congolese province, and the murder of its leader, is found in
a sixteenth-century Border Scots epic, with O'Brien paralleled in the poet-
diplomat Lindsay, whose political morality play *The Thrie Estates* served as
a model for Arden's dialect language in *Armstrong's Last Goodnight*. In both
plays the reference to contemporary problems is oblique, and the audience
are left to draw the connections.

That was hardly the case when *Serjeant Musgrave's Dance* was adapted to
refer unequivocally to the events of Bloody Sunday (when mourners at an
IRA funeral were killed in Londonderry), and to the contemporary Miner's
Strike, for a 1973 production in Northern Ireland. The changes brought
Musgrave into line with the Ardens' later work where documented facts are
treated directly, as in *The Ballygombeen Bequest* (1972). There the competitive machinations of the local contractor with IRA connections and the
English landlord, which leads to the dispossession of a peasant family, and
the death of their Marxist son at the hands of British security forces, is a transcription of an actual case. This was underlined in the original Edinburgh
production by distributing leaflets to the audience. These gave the name, address and phone number of the absentee landlord in the process of evicting

a tenant family in the neighbourhood of the Ardens' western Ireland home, against whom they had been campaigning. Indeed, their dramatic material was sufficiently factual for a writ for libel to be granted, which stopped performances until 1981 (when a slightly revised version was produced under the title of *The Little Gray Home in the West*). Similarly, *The Non-Stop Connolly Show* presents the facts of the historical protagonist's life in extensive detail, using direct quotation from the speeches of specific figures like Rosa Luxemburg as well as Connolly himself, and citing documentary sources in the published preface.

At the same time, the political relevance is made explicit in Arden's later plays. In *The Island of the Mighty*, a dedicatory poem states the intended parallel between the mutually destructive Arthur/Medraut warfare, and the contemporary Edward Heath/Harold Wilson electoral conflict (both Labour and Conservative being equally oppressive from a Marxist point of view). In addition, to prevent audiences from interpreting the dramatic situations as merely historical or local, the Ardens' stage presentation becomes crudely symbolic.

In *The Little Gray Home in the West* the landlord is a satiric caricature even less individualized than in the original 1972 version, which placed him in a melodramatic green spotlight. The economic competition between landlord and contractor is reduced to custard pies in the face, and the story is presented through a narrator: the politically aware ghost of the victim, whose motto is Lenin's 'Educate, Agitate, Organize'. 'Drawing a significant analogy', the tenant (whose rights are unratified by the law) is not only said to be 'like the Irish Free State, as it was then, I mean, within the British Empire', but takes on the character of Collins, one of the executed Irish republican leaders – while the landlord (who employs the secret service and the British Army as his instruments) appears as Lloyd George, the British Prime Minister.

Slogan scene-titles, such as 'THE LAST OF THE IMPERIALISTS CON-FRONTS FACE-TO-FACE THE LAST OF THE SONS OF THE SOIL', and songs expand the reference to the whole of the third world:

The fat men of the fat half-world
Had food on every plate.

The lean men of the naked world
Grew leaner every day
And if they put their faces up
Their teeth were kicked away.[22]

This may reflect the Ardens' perception of political reality – after a visit to India, where they became involved with radical activists and were arrested, Arden declared that his future writing would be from the perspective of an Indian revolutionary. But the step from the specific incident to the universal stretches credibility because it is externally applied, not grounded in the dramatic situation.

The disjunction of presentation and subject is even more marked in *The Non-Stop Connolly Show*. The Capitalist is explicitly the villain from melodrama:

GRABITALL (*Lunges forward*) Ha ha, ha ha...
MOTHER CONNOLLY Proud demon avaunt! You can and shall be beaten!

An election is portrayed as a tag-wrestling match with candidates in different coloured singlets; ideological conflicts are simplified to Keystone Kops slapstick with the British Prime Minister Asquith chased through the auditorium by Trades Union leaders waving the red flag, Connolly by whistle-blowing policemen, Grabitall by the common people. This traditional farce, and the juxtaposition of historical with cartoon figures, is extended into symbolic abstraction with the entry of 'the War Demon'. And it finally becomes open allegory in the mythical prologue to Part Six: the story of an ancient Irish king, Conaire, killed 'Because he...tried to turn the whole world upside down'. Conaire/Connolly's self-sacrifice both serves as an inspiration for the future, and in a quasi-magical way ensures the eventual achievement of liberty: 'He broke his prohibitions and so prevails...'[23]

In *Connolly*, the contrast between documentary situation or dialogue, and cartoon/slapstick treatment, is designed to reflect the ideological perspective of the protagonist. The Irish Trades Union leader Connolly, shot for his part in the Easter 1916 uprising, had been selected as a subject for drama as much because his life exemplified the Marxist thesis that what an individual does is determined by class position, as for his historical significance. Thus the physical imagery, intended as an objective representation of 'the huge movement of class-forces', is also the expression of Connolly's vision.

Increasingly in the later sections of the play he is present as an observer, interposed between symbols and spectator; and the less realistic a scene is, the more obvious his presence becomes. At the beginning of Part Six, for example, where the First World War is presented by a dance – Grabitall gyrating with the War Demon and the symbolic figures of Oppressed, Controlling and Neutral Nations – Connolly is seated 'wearily' at his desk 'with his head in his hands'.[24] The parallel to Goya's well-known etching 'The Dream of Reason produces Monsters' may not be intentional, but it implies that (as in Goya) the scene is the fantasy of a disturbed mind, which invalidates the Ardens' political analysis. The only factor offsetting such an interpretation is the assumed audience-identification with the central figure. The first performance took place in the headquarters of Connolly's Irish Transport and General Workers' Union and on the 1975 Easter anniversary of his death, with the sponsorship of Sinn Fein, the political arm of the IRA. In such a context, the required 'atmosphere of unity and solidarity' was practically ensured – but it is not easily duplicated.

By contrast to earlier plays written for conventional theatre, whether commercial or subsidized, where the spectators had been presumed members (or at least unwitting associates) of the Establishment, *Connolly* was 'aimed directly at audiences of Socialists and Republicans'. Instead of conversion, the intention becomes to affirm existing commitment; and as the action progresses the text clearly assumes that the preceding sections have been effective in achieving this. Passages of direct address to the audience presuppose specific responses. We are expected to have identified with the 'Socialist Hero', as in 'The ultimate tribunal to which we appeal is not, of course, this court, but the verdict of the class to which we [ie. the audience] belong' – and automatically to reject representatives of the status quo, as in

BISHOP . . . We appeal to all charitable and catholic organizations to do their utmost at once to relieve this dreadful suffering . . . ! *He repeats his appeal several times, moving about the hall. There is dead silence . . .*

CONNOLLY (*After a slight pause*) The church of Christ has failed the test: the brotherhood of man must carry on.[25]

The most obvious theatrical prototype for this six-part, ten and three-quarter hour drama (depending on performance: in London, eleven hours and forty minutes; in Dublin, with interspersed films such as Eisenstein's *Strike* and *Battleship Potemkin* plus choral interludes, twenty-six and a half hours) is the medieval Mystery Play Cycle. The history of socialism replaces divine history from the Creation, with Ireland claimed as the birthplace of revolutionary consciousness:

before Marx grew his beard
Fintin Lalor put forth this demand –
'The entire soil of a country belongs of right to the people of that country'.

Here, too, martyrdom is the prerequisite for salvation; and there is even justification by faith in the sense that historical figures are evaluated by their doctrinal purity, while audiences are expected to affirm the overtly 'partisan conclusion' of the cycle.

Ideological commitment and religious belief lend themselves to the same dramatic treatment. Moral absolutes lead to the interpretation of society in terms of '*essential* (or *emblematic*) *truth*', while the Ardens' consciousness of the significance of their subject – conceived as determining 'the entire future of the human race' – demands 'a traditionally heroic scale'.[26]

As the subtitle to the cycle indicates, the performance of *The Non-Stop Connolly Show* is intended to form an image of 'Continuous Struggle'. Each section follows the same pattern, ending with an apparent defeat which hardens the protagonist's resolve and illustrates that 'the failure of a revolution is the springboard of the next success' – as the audience are exhorted 'above all' to remember. This repetitive structure replaces conventional plot. The struggle between Capital and Labour, simplified to an archetypal opposition of '*Evil and Good* or *Darkness and Light*', is hardly more than a context for programmatic statements given the premise that the eventual triumph of socialism is preordained.[27] The speed of presentation, required by short episodic scenes, is intended to reflect the irresistible forces of history that shape Connolly's career. The use of multiple stages translates the documentary montage into concrete terms; and the physical involvement of the audience in the action serves as an external sign of the political solidarity, which a performance is intended to produce.

Although the completely conventional nature of the symbolism is typical of Agitprop plays from the 1930s, like Joan Littlewood's *John Bullion* (see p. 74), *The Non-Stop Connolly Show* has been described as 'the major theatrical development in Britain in the 1970s'.[28] Yet the cycle has remained almost unperformed, despite the fact that its various parts were designed as self-contained entities capable of being put on separately and with minimum physical resources. After its initial production (and the performance of selected episodes in Catholic 'ghettoes' of Belfast and as 'street plays' around Dublin), it has only been presented three times: in a lunch-time series of staged readings at the Almost Free Theatre (1976), as an experimental exercise for university drama students (1983), and at an academic conference where Arden and D'Arcy were present.

In effect, the Ardens have deliberately withdrawn from the conventional theatre – although they claim that the professional theatre's rejection or dilution of their later and explicitly Marxist plays reveals its continued subjugation by reactionary forces in society through commercial pressure, government subsidy or inherently conservative dramatic criticism. Even though the Lord Chamberlain's control over theatrical scripts was removed in 1968 after the furore over Edward Bond's early plays, civil servants, trained by the military in techniques of media propaganda, are said to have exercised indirect censorship through 'remote control'. According to Arden, 'dramatists will rarely be told: "Your play is *subversive*: we are imposing a political restriction upon its performance": an aesthetic or bureaucratic reason will rather be advanced . . .' Thus the system operates through the 'emasculating elevation of the Director above the Playwright', which ensures that even if a doctrinaire play reaches the Establishment stage, its statement will be distorted.[29]

This conspiracy theory of artistic politics is self-justifying. It effectively rules out normal criteria for evaluating drama, and turns the failure of any production into an example of social repression that demonstrates the play's message. Transforming the theatre itself becomes an image of revolution. The focus shifts from dramatic product to process, so that (at its extreme) the primary aim of a production becomes to 'challenge' the theatrical 'structure – with all its political and financial and artistic implications', rather than being to achieve a successful performance.[30] The public quarrel with the management in the foyer of the Roundhouse during the première of *The Hero Rises Up* in 1968 followed this scenario, as did the picket-line mounted by the authors outside the Aldwych during rehearsals and previews of *The Island of the Mighty*, and on its opening night in 1972.

In the first instance, where Arden and D'Arcy had directorial control over the production of *The Hero Rises Up*, the economic consequences of 'free' performances, and problems of overcrowding in the Institute of Contemporary Arts, forced the management to cut their financial losses by closing the show after four performances. Arden claimed that they were 'genuinely – if naively – flabbergasted by the sudden and fearful rigidity of the ICA officials', which revealed 'the limitations of such bodies as the midwives of free experiment'. But the incident could also be seen as deliberately orchestrated, as a way of illustrating the premise of their play. The Advertisement had summed this up as 'the Individual' asserting 'his *potential* God-like Glory in the face of Established Financial Malice, the Merciless Use of the *Bludgeon* for the sake of Law-and-Order, and the Cold Concretion of Bureaucracy' – and referred specifically to the ICA ('*having, as is sadly admitted, certain unavoidable Connexions with the Bureaucracy aforesaid*').[31]

In the second case, Arden and D'Arcy's unsuccessful attempt to substitute an on-stage public discussion for one of the previews led them to take 'industrial action' against the RSC. Picketing the production was presented as their only recourse against fundamental disagreements with the director's interpretation of *The Island of the Mighty*, although they may have had other strictly political motives. According to Ron Bryden, the RSC literary adviser at the time,

there really weren't any fundamental disagreements about staging – I kept asking Arden throughout the rehearsals if he'd had any unhappiness, and he said no. The day Margaretta left Dublin to join him in London was the day the Government arrested Sean MacSeafoin (John Stevens), then head of the Provisional IRA, and huge crowds protested outside his prison while he went on hunger strike. The day John and Margaretta ended their picketing of the Aldwych was the day MacSeafoin broke his fast and alienated his IRA following. Margaretta was looking for an institution of British tyranny to parade against, and the RSC was the handiest...[32]

Similar difficulties arose even with a radical Left troupe like CAST. According to its director, Ronald Muldoon, the result of 'internal rows' with Arden and D'Arcy about the literary style of the script, the use of nudity, and the production style in *Harold Muggins is a Martyr*, was that 'we haven't worked together since. We said, never again'. It should also be noted that after *Serjeant Musgrave's Dance* no Arden plays appeared at the Royal Court, even though William Gaskill provided a platform for alternative performance groups such as John McGrath's radical 7:84 Company, or Portable Theatre (which had been founded specifically because leftist authors were ignored by mainstream stages: 'the bastards won't do our plays, we'll do them ourselves... it was boiling for a fight against the established values in the theatre').[33]

Instead, the Ardens moved away from the conventional stage altogether into short pieces for political demonstrations, outsize Agitprop, and street theatre – concluding with a 1978 incident, when D'Arcy was arrested for painting an inflammatory slogan on the Ulster Museum walls during a poetry reading. The point was not her disruption of socially approved art, nor even to put across her verbal protest, but the action that followed. In her words,

I deliberately made a technical assault on these men [representatives of authority: the attendants who intervened, and the police] in order to demonstrate...how suppression of free speech will lead to violence. I would have preferred the members of the public to have asked them to leave me alone... But as it was I was compelled to carry my little improvised play to the end... to create a very small and imperfect work of art showing how much more important works of art had been censored because they referred to military violence, police repression, erosion of civil rights, etc.[34]

The theatricalizing of politics replaces the politicization of theatre – and the audience's antagonism in this case, expressed in their refusal to intervene on her behalf, is significant.

Arden's development encapsulates many of the main issues that have faced the younger generation of political playwrights, such as Howard Brenton, David Hare or David Edgar. In particular, it defines the problem of treating political material realistically. If ways of depicting actuality are ideologically determined, then Naturalism (as the norm of establishment theatre) expresses the mind-set of the society that endorses it as an accurate reflection of itself. For a dramatist who rejects the social system it therefore becomes necessary to formulate a completely different style.

Brecht rejected Naturalism because it reinforced the status quo in leading an audience to accept the fate of its characters as unchangeable through empathy, and because its domestic focus was irrelevant to the forces controlling modern history. Arden's critique is even more radical. Any conventionally accepted style of portraying life (in particular the naturalistic norm) automatically expresses the Establishment view of reality. According to the protagonist/commentator of *The Little Gray Home in the West*,

... not one of us can see
What we look at, except
As our class-role may direct.[35]

Following this argument, a style that reflects a proletarian perspective is more 'realistic' since (as the final line of the same play states) 'There are more of us than them!' The medium is literally the message. Hence the use of techniques borrowed from Music Hall – as the last form of people's theatre – or cartoon figures from socialist newspapers.

The appropriateness of a 'proletarian' style is limited to that section of the population whose world view it expresses, which almost by definition leads to a withdrawal from mainstream (i.e. bourgeois) theatre. It also shifts the political aim of a performance from conversion to confirmation. The kind of Aristophanic comic-strip drama embraced by Arden in the 1970s assumes an audience that completely shares the political views of the play. The effect is a tendency to substitute wish-fulfilment for social analysis, so that proclaiming revolution on the stage becomes an end in itself. Theatrical pretence becomes confused with reality. Yet, as the Ardens are well aware,

When you act in a play it is easy to say
That we shall win and never be defeated
When you go from here it is not so clear
That power for the people is predestined...[36]

Notes

1 John Arden, *Three Plays*, Harmondsworth, 1967, p. 175. According to Arden, *Live Like Pigs* was intended to be 'not so much a social document as a study of differing ways of life brought sharply into conflict and both losing their own particular virtues under the stress of intolerance and misunderstanding' (*Three Plays*, p. 101).

2 *Three Plays*, pp. 101, 96. (Compare Bertolt Brecht, *Parables for the Theatre*, trans. Eric Bentley, Minneapolis, 1965, p. 96.) For a full treatment of the music-hall elements in Arden's early plays, see Albert Hunt, *Arden: A Study of His Plays*, London, 1974, pp. 38–52.

3 Arden, *To Present the Pretence*, London, 1977, p. 40.

4 *The Workhouse Donkey*, London, 1964, p. 12.

5 *To Present the Pretence*, pp. 37–8.

6 Bertolt Brecht, *Seven Plays* (trans. Eric Bentley), New York, 1961, p. 392; *The Hero Rises Up*, London, 1969, pp. 14, 72, 30.

7 *The Hero Rises Up*, p. 7.

8 *Ibid.*, p. 31.

9 *Ibid.*, pp. 98 & 101.

10 Arden, 'Ecce Hobo Sapiens' in *Sean O'Casey: A Collection of Critical Essays*, ed. Thomas Kilroy, Englewood Cliffs, NJ, 1975, pp. 68–9; O'Casey, *Blasts and Benedictions*, pp. 73–4.

11 *Serjeant Musgrave's Dance*, London, 1960, pp. 51, 101, 102.

12 *Ibid.*, pp. 52, 26.

13 *Ibid.*, pp. 102, 99.

14 *The Times*, 23 October 1959.

15 *Serjeant Musgrave's Dance*, p. 9; *Encore*, July–August 1961, p. 31.

16 *Serjeant Musgrave's Dance*, pp. 85, 104.

17 *To Present the Pretence*, pp. 22, 108. Arden himself pointed out that one of the inspirations for *Musgrave* was an American film, *The Raid*, in which disguised Confederate soldiers occupy a Northern town (*Encore*, July–August 1961, p. 26), while the soldiers – originally 'The Joking Soldier' or 'The Surly Soldier' like 'The Slow Collier' or 'The Pugnacious Collier' – were only given individual names during rehearsal at Lindsay Anderson's insistence (*ibid.*, pp. 38–9).

18 Arden in *Encore*, May–June 1960, p. 25; Roland Muldoon (CAST) cited in Catherine Itzen, *Stages in the Revolution*, London, 1980, pp. 14, 15.

19 *Serjeant Musgrave's Dance*, pp. 9–12 (see 'The jacket of the blood-red Queen as red as any rose', *The Non-Stop Connolly Show*, London, 1977, I, p.23); *To Present the Pretence*, p. 155.

20 *Encore*, September–October 1965, p. 16.

21 *The Island of the Mighty*, London, 1974, pp. 13, 175.

22 *The Little Gray Home in the West*, London, 1982, pp. 50, 31, 30, 34 & 41.

23 *The Non-Stop Connolly Show*, London, 1977–8, I, p. 1; V, pp. 5–6.

24 *Ibid.*, VI, p. 7; *To Present the Pretence*, p. 97.

25 *To Present the Pretence*, pp. 118, 119; *The Non-Stop Connolly Show*, V, pp. 66, 75.

26 *Ibid.*, III, p. 16; *To Present the Pretence*, pp. 137, 131, 98.

27 *Connolly*, IV, p. 40; II, p. 34.

28 Albert Hunt, *New Society*, 18 January 1979.

29 *To Present the Pretence*, pp. 157, 177.

30 *Ibid.*, p. 212.

31 *Ibid.*, p. 84, and *The Hero Rises Up*, p. 10.

32 Ronald Bryden, letter to the author, January 1990. In Bryden's view, although 'It wasn't a great production, and it lacked lightness...the way [*The Island of the Mighty*] leads its modern British audience to identify with the ancient, primitive British and poor divided Arthur, and so to enter into the state of mind of their own imperial subjects in the Third World, not to mention the minds of women, seemed and seems to me...one of Arden's major achievements'.

33 Ronald Muldoon and Howard Brenton, cited in Itzen, *Stages in the Revolution*, pp. 22–3 and 189.

34 Margaretta D'Arcy, interview, *Tribune*, 29 December 1978, p. 13.

35 *The Little Gray Home in the West*, p. 21.

36 *Ibid.*, p. 73.

3.9 Edward Bond (1934–): rationalism, realism and radical solutions

CHECKLIST OF BOND'S MAJOR PLAYS

The Pope's Wedding, 1962	*The Bundle*, 1978
Saved, 1965	*The Woman*, 1978
Early Morning, 1968	*The Worlds*, 1979
Narrow Road to the Deep North, 1968	*Restoration*, 1981
	Summer, 1982
Lear, 1971	*The War Plays*, 1985
The Sea, 1973	*Jackets II*, 1990
Bingo, 1974	*In the Company of Men*, 1996
The Fool, 1976	

Just as Osborne can be paired with Wesker, so Bond's development as a dramatist broadly parallels Arden's. All four were born within five years of each other, from 1929 to 1934, growing up through the Depression and the war against Hitler. Like Osborne and Arden, Bond's career began at the Royal Court. Like Arden too, he went on to write for both left-wing fringe companies and the National Theatre in the 1970s, becoming increasingly radical and didactic, although he has not gone so far as to completely reject mainstage theatre.

Also, even more clearly than Arden, Bond has adapted Brecht's principles. Beginning at the Royal Court with exercises in Epic dramaturgy, he updated Brecht's *Roundheads and Peaked Heads*, and arranged an evening of Brecht songs (which have strong similarities in style and sound to his own poetry). But his stylistic solutions to creating a non-naturalistic, political drama have been consistently more experimental and inventive than Arden, covering almost the whole modern spectrum. Surreal fantasy, Brechtian parables, stripped-down realism, Shakespearean revisionism or Restoration parody, the historical epic and even opera librettos – all are interchangeable moulds for his political message.

Yet beneath this eclecticism, there is an unusual degree of intellectual consistency. Bond's major works, from *Saved* in 1965 to *The Woman* in 1978, form a double series, with the second being consciously designed to echo the first sequence of plays. In each, bleak condemnations of society end in a positive statement of hope.

Saved and *Early Morning* (1968) – which in conjunction with Osborne's *A Patriot for Me* led to the abolition of censorship – go together with *Narrow Road to the Deep North* (also 1968), *Lear* (1971) and his comedy *The Sea* (1973). *Saved* opens the series with a hyper-realistic example of contemporary urban dehumanization. Moving in the next two plays through symbolic depictions of the roots of this modern violence in Victorian morality, Bond then generalizes his attack on the forces of social injustice and oppression in an anti-Shakespearean model of power structures and their corrupting effect. The final play returns to the early twentieth century, with redemptive sacrifice and youthful love affirming the possibility of change, and echoes of Greek myth.

The second series picks up on themes from the earlier plays. Shakespeare appears as the protagonist of *Bingo* (1974); and the next play explores the predicament of the socially-conscious writer under an unjust society through the fate of a nineteenth-century poet, John Clare, in *The Fool* (1976). This is followed by two quasi-mythic demonstrations of successful revolution: *The Bundle* (1978 – a rewriting of *Narrow Road to the Deep North* that omits the Victorian reference of the earlier play); and *The Woman* (1978), which uses material from classical Greek tragedy. The impression of logical

continuity is reinforced by the coherence of Bond's prefaces, which repeat
and elaborate a highly specific social analysis. It is also underlined within
the second series by giving each play a parallel subtitle: 'Scenes of Money
and Death', 'Scenes of Bread and Love', 'Scenes of Right and Evil', 'Scenes of
Freedom'.

Each of these plays is a variation on a single theme, analysing the causes of
contemporary violence, and showing its psychological effects. Since four out
of the nine have poets or playwrights as their central figures, while another
(*The Sea*) includes an on-stage play within the play, they also offer a unique
insight into the function of political drama, and the equivocal position of a
dramatist alienated by his commitment from the society he addresses. This
consistency is expressed too by the way the same images surface throughout
the two series – in particular, Bond's central thematic symbol: a double
character, one being the corpse, *alter ego* or anti-type of the other.

The first of these symbiotic pairs appears in *The Pope's Wedding* (Bond's
earliest play, though only performed in 1962), where the young Scopey
takes the place of the hermit whom he has murdered: an action that makes
him what he hated and feared. Similar figures recur in almost all Bond's
plays, from the Siamese twins of *Early Morning*, through the mad king
and dead pig boy of *Lear*, to the mutual dependency of the central female
characters, Hecuba and Ismene, the one-time Trojan and Greek Queens,
in the second part of *The Woman*. These couples are a literal embodiment
of Ibsen's *Ghosts*, where moribund beliefs shackle the living, except that
Bond's 'ghosts in chains' are less alive in a moral sense than the corpses to
whom they are bound. Since no one can escape the deadly effect of social
conditioning, in Bond's terms 'The pro-life half of the pairs...has been
killed off like the others...but not completely killed'. Yet the possibility for
survival, or even renewal, is still present; and Bond's plays are progressively
more optimistic – though to reach positive conclusions he withdraws from
the present into myth.

At one extreme is Len's minimum of 'restless curiosity' in *Saved*, which
has to be seen as highly ambiguous: a morbid and voyeuristic fascination
with murder. But for Bond, this 'amounts to the search for truth, and in
the contexts in which [Scopey and Len] find themselves it's miraculous!'[1]
At the mid-point on the scale are symbolic acts of resistance which function
as moral examples: Arthur's refusal to participate in the cannibal competitiveness of *Early Morning*, or the deposed Lear's final gesture of dig-
ging up the wall of oppression that he had built as king. At the other

extreme, the interaction between living-dead pairs produces revolutionary change, as with the assassination of Heros, the symbol of male authority in *The Woman.*

As Bond has put it, concluding his first group of plays with *The Sea* was 'meant to reassure the audience they can cope with the problems dealt with in the series'. By comparison, he has described *The Woman*, the play with which his second group culminates, as a 'rhapsody...in praise of human beings. In it right triumphs over bad'. In structure as well as intention, it contrasts 'the carnage and waste of war' against an idyllic vision of renewal to celebrate 'human tenacity and insight'. Both plays end with conventional romantic affirmations. In the first, a young man frees himself from his dead 'other' – his commitment to a drowned friend whose body is washed up on the beach – and liberates the girl who plays Eurydice in an amateur pageant from the underworld of her class-ridden village. They leave together to 'find...answers' and 'change the world'.[2] In the second, Ismene is brought back to life rescued from being buried alive in the wall of Troy – while a 'dark man' has escaped from underground slavery in the Athenian silver mines. He overcomes his physical disabilities to kill Heros, her former husband and the symbol of authority, after which they become lovers.

There is a real difference between the reassurance in *The Sea* and the celebratory ending of *The Woman*. 'Rhapsody' has overtones of enthusiastic extravagance, emotionalism and wish-fulfilment – qualities indeed reflected in the second half of the latter play, where the ideal society is presented as a Golden World of peasant innocence. This is not only a somewhat impractical alternative to the modern situation, but one that Bond had earlier dismissed as illusory escapism in *Lear*. It marks a distinct change from the qualities of 'analysis' or 'social realism' which Bond typically stressed in his earlier plays.

This corresponds with a shift in moral outlook. All Bond's plays are explicitly preoccupied with 'violence [that] shapes and obsesses our society', and which he therefore claims to write about 'as naturally as Jane Austen wrote about manners'.[3] In the series ending with *The Sea*, violence is shown as the tool and symptom of an unjust society. Using force to counter this violence only perpetuates a vicious circle that, in the atomic age, will inevitably lead to the annihilation of mankind. Even in Agitprop pieces for specific political occasions – such as *Black Mass* (for an Anti-Apartheid Rally in 1970) or *Passion* (performed on the Alexandra Park Race Course in 1971) – radical pacifism is presented as the sole way of breaking the mould of violence. As with Arden, the pacificist response is problematic, but the refusal of easy answers gives a burning sense of real human issues.

After 1973, this position becomes reversed as the second series progresses, until in *The Woman* answers are substituted for problems, and ideological affirmation replaces questioning.

In subsequent plays, violence is adopted as the only way of promoting social change. *The Worlds* (1979) justifies the 'execution' of businessmen by radical terrorists, on the ground that a company chairman is a criminal who 'depends on force as much as any terrorist'. The equation originates from Brecht, but lacks the provocative complexity that Brecht's formula has in *The Threepenny Opera*, where 'what is robbing a bank compared to the founding of one?' is offered as a rationale by habitual thieves. (A later formulation of the same Brechtian phrase appears when a destitute servant is bribed to murder his ex-master with the injunction 'Don't rob – earn', to which he responds 'I'll rob – an keep my self-respect': *In the Company of Men*, 1996.) Bond has argued that the shift to extremism and direct statement are a response to 'the desperation of the situation', in which increasing violence and the closeness to annihilation rule out compromise or subtlety.[4] However, the note of urgency pre-empts argument.

So in *The Worlds*, when the striking factory workers refuse to help fulfil the conditions for the release of their boss by returning to the production line, and a working-class chauffeur (abducted in mistake for another company executive) is also threatened with death, the ethical implications are left unexplored. Instead, the chauffeur is shot by the chairman – rescued from the terrorists, but driven insane from being ousted by rivals on his board, who have taken advantage of his kidnapping. The play ends with the declaration: 'When they ask me to condemn terror I shall say: no. *You* have no right to ask. You [i.e. those who implicitly support the status quo by rejecting violence] are a terrorist.' 'The Activists Papers' (appended to *The Worlds* in the same way as Shaw's 'Revolutionist's Handbook' to *Man and Superman*) asserts that 'revolution . . . is the good use of weapons', while *The War Plays* (1985) assumes that even atomic apocalypse will serve the revolutionary cause.[5]

However radical this change in outlook, it is clearly foreshadowed in the way Bond depicts the writers in his earlier plays. The social role of art being his primary concern, Bond focuses on the figure of a poet as early as *Narrow Road to the Deep North* in 1968. Basho is an idealist who, in using the abstract ideals of art as an excuse for non-involvement, becomes responsible for atrocities. When the abandoned baby he leaves to die on his quest for 'Enlightenment' survives to revenge himself on society by seizing power, Basho brings in colonial overlords, ending up as the figurehead of an evil regime. He represents false culture; and as the only outright 'villain' in Bond's early plays, he reflects the strength of Bond's conviction that art must be politically committed. There is even the suggestion that if there were no injustice or oppression, then there would be no reason for art at all: 'In an ideal society . . . [Basho] would have picked that baby up, gone off the stage and there would have been no necessity for a play'.[6]

The Bundle (1978) makes the point even clearer. Instead of an itinerant seeker of 'Enlightenment', Basho has become rich: the active agent of oppression, rather than merely its apologist. This time the abandoned baby turns into a revolutionary leader, radicalized by Basho's lack of principle; and the victory of the common people destroys Basho. He is merely a polemic figure.

Bond's second series of plays deals with the problem facing a writer in depth, starting with Shakespeare in *Bingo* (1974). Unable to reconcile the demand for sanity and justice in his art with his complicity in an unjust and irrational social order, Shakespeare is driven to suicide. Bond presents him as the type of artist who sells out morally, invalidating everything he writes because he separates art from life. The birth of Capitalism can be traced to the land enclosures of the Elizabethan period. So Bond is showing Shakespeare as ultimately responsible for the oppressive state of modern Britain. It is because he might have changed the course of events by speaking out in his plays that he is destroyed by guilt. Instead, he sacrifices his artistic integrity by profiting from this misappropriation of communal property. This is hardly a new accusation – as Shaw remarked in the preface to his play about Shakespeare, *The Dark Lady of the Sonnets* (1910), it had already been raised by turn of the century 'land nationalizers' – and Bond's condemnation depends on the unhistorical assumption that contemporary moral attitudes are universal.

However, what makes Shakespeare's moral blindness criminal in Bond's eyes is his genius as a dramatist. Bond's earliest experience of theatre was a performance of *Macbeth*, which moved him so strongly he could not understand how anyone continued to live in the same way after seeing the play. And it is his admiration for Shakespeare's 'intellectual strength and passionate beauty', however compromised by 'the [dishonest] reconciliation' that he created on the stage, which animates *Bingo* by making Shakespeare a complex figure. It was also the purely aesthetic response of audiences to Shakespeare's plays, which means 'you . . . don't have to question yourself, or change your society', that led Bond to adapt *King Lear*.[7]

Having been selected precisely because of its status as Shakespeare's masterpiece, Shakespeare's original text remains only as a paradigm of false culture. Basic elements are retained: blindness representing insight, and sanity appearing in madness; two monstrous daughters whose unnatural treatment of their father is the extension of his own behaviour, and a third daughter who stands as a moral contrast (though here rather than rejected she is no relation). But the tone and plot of Bond's *Lear* are so different as to be unrecognizable. The violence is unremitting; and the darkness of the vision is summed up in the dominant image of man as a mad animal trapped in a cage.

This Lear is obsessed with defending his kingdom by encircling it with a monstrous wall: the symbol both of his power and its paranoia. He abdicates because his daughters defeat him in civil war, and is himself blinded (in place of Shakespeare's Gloster) as well as going mad. The Edgar figure is the ghost of a young peasant, who was killed for sheltering Lear. This pig-boy's wife, raped and brutalized by the murdering soldiers, replaces Cordelia. But the proletarian revolution that she leads turns out to be no less ruthless than the previous regime; and the building of the wall continues. The sanity Lear finally achieves is – by the perverted standards of this society – madness. Recognizing his responsibility for the cycle of fear and oppression, he pays for it with his life in attempting to break down the wall: a symbolic gesture that is the opposite of the acceptance of suffering proposed by the final lines of Shakespeare's play.

Following on from *Bingo*, Bond presents the counter-type to Shakespeare in *The Fool*, which uses John Clare as the example of a poet who refuses to compromise. But the ending is equally bleak because moral commitment is not enough. The artist has to have an ideological programme, which he can use to change political institutions. Otherwise, the pressures to conform, together with the outrage and frustration of his moral sense by the society of which he is a part, will drive him mad. Here Bond is paralleling Peter Weiss, whose play about Hölderlin (written four years before *The Fool*) deals with exactly the same subject: a proto-Marxist poet without a revolution who is driven mad by the irrationality he increasingly perceives around him.

In Bond's early plays, what is important is to free the individual from social repression. Any solution in the form of a political programme is seen as simply an alternative structure of coercion. So the endings of his plays are left deliberately ambiguous; and if a character reaches a positive conclusion, he is parodied – as in *Early Morning*, where the protagonist's final apotheosis is a satiric echo of Christ's ascension. At that stage, Bond rejected leaders along with uniforms and flagpoles, declaring in 1969: 'No, I've no Utopia, no image of the society I want to see emerge. It would simply be people being themselves.' Indeed, *Narrow Road* implies that there is little to choose between Russian Communism and Western democracy – the dictator Shogo (a primitive Stalin who enslaves his citizens by naked force) and the imperialist missionary Georgina (with her subtler but more insidious psychological intimidation) being equally condemned. And in 1970, he commented that 'there is no viable political system in existence in the world at this moment'. So in *Lear*, not only the old King and his monstrous daughters with their palace revolution, but also Cordelia and her peasant revolutionaries, are all corrupted by power. Those who over-throw the system by violence perpetuate it, and even preaching a clearly defined political vision will create precisely the oppression it is designed to avoid. 'We do not need a plan of the future, we need a method of change.'[8]

But while working through this dilemma of ends and means, in *Bingo* Bond sets Shakespeare up as the representative of his own earlier viewpoint, which was that 'you can change the world simply by being rational' – and shows that this attitude contributed to Shakespeare's suicide. As he com-mented: 'I wish that were true, but I don't think it is true... it is not possible to reach a rational world by wholly rational means'. So in *The Bundle*, the writer's role has been taken over by the revolutionary activist, who spreads political consciousness specifically through actions, not words. The ending, where the revolutionary throws a baby into the river as a conscious political act that the dramatic context supports, graphically reverses the standpoint of his earlier plays. It denies what Bond had previously declared 'evident moral truths... things that are simply wrong in themselves. For example, it's evidently wrong to kill someone.'[9]

In response to the shift to the right in Britain during the late 1970s and 1980s, which caused other left-wing playwrights like Hare or Edgar to question the effectiveness of political drama, Bond took an increas-ingly radical position. Instead of persuading people to behave rationally, the tools for achieving 'a classless society' become 'the frustration... aggression and... political violence' produced by the violent nature of 'class society'. So ends vindicate means: 'left-wing... violence is justified when it helps to create a more rational society'.[10] In *The Bundle*, this takes the form of guerrilla warfare to overthrow the landowner; and violence is justified by a utopian outcome. The liberated peasants are shown communally plan-ning a system of dykes and locks to control the river-floods that (like the rapacious exploitation of their rulers) had continually reduced them to starvation.

Despite this change in Bond's position, all his plays are based on the same political analysis. Social institutions, originally developed for the protection of individuals, become self-perpetuating. Law and religion, mores and morality, now have no function but moulding individuals to serve their needs. Repression leads to aggression, and this aggression is the driving force behind social progress. Thus, all social activity is presented as moralized violence. The sack of Troy that the authorities condone in *The Woman* and the politically justified killing of children in *Narrow Road*, or the anarchic murder and rape of civil war in *Lear* and the stoning of a baby in *Saved*, which society condemns – all are treated as actions of exactly the same kind and status. For Bond, violence is not an aberration but a general symptom. The infanticide, for which the baby's father is sent to prison in *Saved*, is no different from his beating by ordinary housewives, who represent the moral outrage in the judicial system. Indeed, the way Bond manipulates such parallels makes the point overly obvious:

FRED Bloody 'eathens. Thumpin' and kickin' the van . . . I don't know what'll 'appen. There's bloody gangs like that roamin' everywhere. The bloody police don't do their job.

The same point is made by the way clichés about disciplining children and toilet-training are parroted during the baby-killing sequence itself in *Saved*. Indeed, infanticide is a symbol of what social conditioning does to us all. Bond's parade of children who are stoned, put to the sword, or thrown from the battlements of an emblematic Troy is literally 'the Massacre of the Innocents'. For Bond, 'All our culture, education, industrial and legal organization is directed to the task of killing [people psychologically and emotionally] . . . Education is nothing less than corruption, because it's based on institutionalizing the pupil, making him a decent citizen.'[11] By extension, we are all victims; and the rulers are as repressed as those they exploit. In fact, aggressors need to be even more strictly conditioned than the oppressed if they are to continue functioning while doing such violence to their innate humanity. So where Bond creates symbolic authority figures, like the monstrous imperialist Georgina of *Narrow Road to the Deep North*, they are presented as insane.

Saved, Bond's first play produced at the Royal Court (1965), examines this system in terms of its victims. The characters are all unemployed teenagers or their working-class parents, brutalized by poverty and the brick desert of their London environment. The baby is an unwanted encumbrance to its promiscuous unmarried mother, who ignores its screaming and abandons it to the unwilling father's care in the local park. Its murder is completely gratuitous: a game of 'rock-a-bye baby' turns into a competitive test of manhood between its adolescent father and his street gang. By placing this climax of violence in the first half of the play, Bond intends the act itself to become subordinate to its social context. His focus is on its cause; and this is emphasized by the role of Len. As an outsider who has witnessed the violence, he questions Fred obsessively. In his quest for understanding, he foists himself on the family of the girl, with whom he too has had a brief sexual relationship.

By contrast with the other youths, Len consistently avoids action. He remains passive when the girl's slatternly mother attempts to seduce him. And when her decrepit husband invades his bedroom with a knife at night – having been hit over the head when he interrupted the seduction – Len disarms him, but does not take the anticipated revenge. The old man's nightshirt and bandaged head make him yet another of Bond's ghost-doubles: the image of what Len will become if he takes his place (and wife) by killing him. In such a context, doing nothing is the only possible virtue. It allows a break in behaviour patterns that have not only been shown as the norm of this society, but are implied to be archetypical by the Oedipal resonance. Len's lack of response to provocation finally exhausts the family's resentment of his presence, and the final image is of him awkwardly mending a chair surrounded by silence – the achievement of community at its most minimal level.

However, these positive aspects hardly came across in performance. By the time it was revived in 1969, the public had become more acclimatized to Bond's work. But members of the audience at the first production protested against the play as 'obscene', while reviewers attacked it as 'not . . . the feeblest thing I have seen on any stage, but . . . certainly the nastiest', with 'characters who, almost without exception are foul-mouthed, dirty-minded, illiterate and barely to be judged on any recognizable human level at all'. Bond's defence was that 'Compared to the "strategic" bombing of German towns' – a parallel raised by the old man's memories of serving in the war – the death of a single baby 'is a negligible atrocity; compared to the cultural and emotional deprivation of most of our children, its consequences are insignificant'.[12] But the initial outrage was in response to the deliberate absence of any condemnation in the way infanticide was depicted, not (as Bond's statement implies) at the depiction of the act itself. Combined with the bleakness of a bare stage and the reductionism of stunted, basic dialogue, which gave an impression of unredeemable factuality, the apparent gratuitousness of the violence obscured the intended social criticism.

This was even truer of *Early Morning* (1968), which extended Bond's analysis of oppression by exploring its mentality. The resulting fantasy elements led to considerable misunderstanding, compounded by the defamatory caricatures of respected figures from the past: not only Queen Victoria, but Lloyd George and even Florence Nightingale. These were taken as attacks on the historical individuals, rather than as the distorted images of moral attitudes. Perhaps as a result the following play in the series, *Narrow Road to the Deep North* (also 1968), dealt with the mechanics of oppression, rather than the oppressors.

Here the action is carefully distanced as an unhistorical fable of an alien country: Japan, in which another abandoned baby – left by a river bank to die – grows up to become a tyrant. The twin pillars of Establishment power, religion and armed force, are presented as caricatures of nineteenth-century imperialism in a British admiral and his missionary sister, Georgina. Instead of the physical enslavement of feudalism, they subjugate the population psychologically through a repressive morality. Since they legitimize their authority by using the last emperor's child as their puppet, when the tyrant temporarily re-conquers his city and is prevented from identifying the young emperor, he puts all the children to the sword. But using straw dummies to represent the children avoided the emotional disturbance of *Saved* by making the action clearly symbolic.

As William Gaskill (whose directorial imprint defined the other works in Bond's first series, as well as *The Pope's Wedding*) later pointed out, what he 'took to be realistic plays' and interpreted as such, were in fact using 'symbolism and allegory as part of [their] working method'. Their symbolic basis was disguised by the Royal Court productions. However, the non-naturalistic basis of Bond's drama was particularly obvious in the Coventry première of *Narrow Road*, where the unusual width of the Belgrade Theatre stage meant that 'the picture-book element in the play was . . . brought out in the right way – the actors were able to work in *demonstrated* relationships'.

Even so, in *Narrow Road* the weight of violence in the action again overruled an intended positive final image, where four contrasting figures are presented. The dead tyrant's dismembered body is displayed; Georgina, driven insane by the sexual repression of her religion, fantasizes rape by Basho's disciple, who is committing *hara-kiri*; while a man drowning in the river calls for help. The symbolic self-destruction of the forces of exploitation is set against the naked man struggling from the water. This was 'meant to suggest . . . a sense of rebirth' – 'though [as the director, Jane Howell, acknowledged] this didn't really work properly in my production'.[13]

Given such graphic images of death, possibly no production could make the final optimistic message convincing. This is symptomatic of the way Bond's choice of material distorts the intended audience response through its sheer emotional power, which is particularly obvious in *Early Morning*. There the grotesque images are so evocative that the political relevance of the play was almost completely overlooked. Naming the protagonist Arthur (after Queen Victoria's son who died in infancy) signals that this is not a historical documentary; and the figures are nakedly symbolic. When his twin brother is mistakenly killed in an assassination attempt on himself, Arthur remains umbilically linked to a gradually disintegrating corpse. Len reappears from *Saved* – but here he is a murderer who has eaten his victim. Prince Albert, forced to drink the poison he had prepared for Queen Victoria, rises from his tomb in a parody of Hamlet's father's ghost. Arthur, driven insane by the pressure to conform, deliberately massacres the whole population by arranging a farcically treacherous tug-of-war on the cliffs of Dover. They all appear in a cannibal heaven, where bodies regenerate after they have been eaten – and Florence Nightingale, who has been raped by the lesbian Victoria and has taken the job of public hangman, hides Arthur's decapitated but still-speaking head beneath her starched crinolines.

Not surprisingly, the play has been interpreted as a fantasy: 'a dream world of infant sexuality'. The cannibalism was seen as an 'expression of the earliest infantile sexuality, oral eroticism', and the Siamese twins as 'an image of . . . sibling rivalry'.[14] In reaction against such Freudian readings, Bond labelled *Early Morning* 'social realism', in order to stress that the action is intended as a documentation of the psychology that perpetuates and justifies political power structures.

The term 'social realism' usually applies to naturalistic drama, Here it is extended to encompass an objective record of subjective illusions:

What we perceive really isn't a straight transcription of reality, and because people do live in fantasy worlds that is part of social reality. If we could understand our problems, we wouldn't have any need of mythologies and absurd religions to close that gap . . . I am writing about the pressures of the past that are mis-forming our present time, and that's where it received its public image and its normative values.[15]

Victorian morality is attacked because it underpins contemporary political and economic institutions. The Siamese twins are intended to symbolize the social (conforming and therefore dead) versus the individual (anarchist and so positive) halves of a single person, while Queen Victoria's lesbianism stands for the perversion of personality by power. 'Heaven' is the popular concept translated straight into socio-economic terms: a state in which those desires designated as 'good' by the inverted morality of society can be indulged without consequence.

On one level, the structure of the play is a straight-line story. Starting with Albert's palace revolution, it progresses through civil war and the deaths of all the characters, to after-life and Arthur's final liberation.

On another level, the structure corresponds to the maturing moral vision of the protagonist. Act I, where Arthur can make no sense of the self-destructive repressiveness of the Establishment or its equally appalling alternatives, represents childhood; Act II, adolescence. At this point, having lost the last remnant of his twin (i.e. being now completely conditioned), Arthur carries the social principles he has adopted to their logical extreme: literally the 'final solution', which also stands for the holocaust of nuclear war that Bond sees as the inevitable consequence if aggressive societies continue along their present lines. Act III, where Arthur recognizes the true nature of society and rejects it, represents adulthood.

But Bond's aim is to take the audience 'through the learning process of the characters' lives'. *Early Morning* reflects this directly in being written from Arthur's viewpoint. Act I is deliberately bewildering because 'he is bewildered by the political set-up and his own emotional involvement in it'; Act II, grotesque because he is mad; and Act III, 'simple and direct ... because ... Arthur recovers his sanity'.[16]

Thus, on a third level, this final act is a symbolic restatement of the earlier scenes. Having been shown particular examples of society in action, we are then given a universalized analysis of their inner meaning. The after-life of reciprocal cannibalism, which Arthur repudiates, is both an image of capitalist free enterprise and a symbol of the way 'people consume each other emotionally ... in a society where there's only taking'.[17] The moral challenge posed by Arthur threatens this inverted idyll, but is removed by eating him up completely. At which point his soul is released, and rises from its coffin (nailed shut with Victoria's teeth) to ascend to another – presumably humanitarian/socialist – sphere of existence.

However, these superimposed levels to the action cancel each other out in a confusion of categories. The first two Acts illustrate that there is no escape from or exception to the deadening emotional distortion of the individual under Capitalism. The common people are completely brutalized, killing and devouring a man, simply because he pushes in front of them in the queue for pornographic movies. A proletarian attack on the power structure (led by a caricature of Lloyd George) is only a dog-eat-dog takeover bid. Arthur, the only one to question the system, literally becomes the dead twin who represents his socialized *alter ego*. Yet on the symbolic plane, the very character who takes the death principle of society to its ultimate conclusion, is the only one able to refuse to eat. Not only that: by apparent osmosis or some undefined form of sympathetic magic, his passive example spreads temporary indigestion (or pangs of conscience) through the whole (dead) society. In addition, it starts a chain reaction of conversion with Florence, who is brought to question society's assumptions – 'Perhaps I'm alive, perhaps we needn't be like this' – and ends by also finding excuses for not eating other people.[18]

This conversion is intended, of course, as a model for the future behaviour of Bond's audience. Yet all the preceding events have demonstrated the inevitability of the corruption, perversion or destruction of any instinctive moral goodness by social conditioning. So much so, that the very existence of a positive character in the context Bond has created means that either the case against society is overstated, or his solution must be seen as wish-fulfilment.

Bond's drama is openly didactic: in his terms 'rational theatre'. This definition is a clear restatement of Shaw's 'drama of ideas', though in a more polemic form. It also echoes Brecht, and Bond has defined *Narrow Road* and *Saved* as 'somewhat Brechtian in shape'. He has also explicitly labelled his recent work 'Epic theatre', declaring that 'the form of the new drama will be epic'.[19] In addition, the characteristic tone of Bond's drama was established by the style in which his early plays were staged. Gaskill, who directed them all with the exception of the first production of *Narrow Road*, described his approach as being 'as clinically accurate as possible ... a legacy from the influence of Brecht'. Even *Early Morning* was staged in this way; and although some critics found 'brechtian sparseness' incongruous, demanding 'more visual fantasy', Bond himself insists that in *Early Morning* 'Very little scenery should be used, and in the last six scenes probably none at all', limiting even the throne-room to 'a bench, upstage, and downstage two chairs or a smaller bench'.[20]

A bare stage is the hallmark of Bond's own productions of his plays. The visual images that provide the driving force of his drama are created by the figures of the actors themselves: Lear holding the entrails of his daughter, or climbing the wall he has built in order to demolish it; the starving peasants in *The Fool* clutching at a naked priest's fat body (the flesh stolen

6 Dance patterns on the bare stage: Bond's *The Woman* at the National Theatre

from them); or the counterpoint between the poet John Clare (struggling to preserve his identity from aristocratic patrons) and a brutal boxing match in the background. The clearest example of his style is the National Theatre production of *The Woman*, where the action was described as having 'a sweep of great power on a bare circular stage ... Bond, as director, gives us some unusual effects, such as counterpoint of conversation against actions and voices, and scenes that end anti-theatrically. The action is also in many places choreographed almost like a dance.'[21]

Bond's consistent principle is simplification and imaginative suggestion – rather than Brecht's undercutting of illusion, in which the stage machinery is exposed and actors step out of role. Brecht's objectivity and distancing were specifically 'a withdrawal course for emotional drug addicts': an antidote to the rhetorical emotionalism and sentimentalized heroic posturing of the Nazis. Writing for a later generation that appeared to accept violence with complacent calmness, Bond found Brecht's treatment of the audience 'outdated'. And the way he developed Brecht's Epic principles closely parallels that of German dramatists in the 1970s, such as Franz Xavier Kroetz or Heiner Müller.

As Manfred Wekwerth, one of the younger directors who worked with Brecht at the Berliner Ensemble, pointed out: 'Brecht's figures are so fluent', having 'a fund of language ... which is not in fact conceded to them by their rulers', that 'the way is open to a positive utopia, to revolution'. By contrast Kroetz's characters use a truncated and brutalized dialogue very reminiscent of the barren language in *Saved*. In both cases the 'speechlessness' of the socially exploited makes them unable to manipulate or even recognize their political situation. Similarly, Müller (who became director of the Berliner Ensemble in 1992) rejected Brecht's rational objectivity in favour of violent images that generated immediate, emotional reactions because 'the time for intervening to alter something is always less. Consequently there is really no more time for discursive dramaturgy, for a calm presentation of factual content.' Like Bond, Müller has not only followed Brecht in updating Shakespeare. He has also turned to Greek classics for dramatic material as well as transcribing contemporary society in subjective, surrealistic terms. And commenting on his own version of *Lear*, Bond referred to precisely the same sense of urgency: 'Shakespeare had time. He must have thought that in time certain changes would be made. But time has speeded up enormously, and for us, time is running out.'[22]

Traditionally seen as a 'moral tribunal', German theatre has tended to confront political issues more directly than the British stage; and Bond is closer to its combination of polemic ideology and stylistic experiment than any other English playwright. Not surprisingly perhaps, his drama has been more popular in Germany than at home.

For Bond, what defines art is 'rational objectivity, the expression of the need for interpretation, meaning, order – that is: for a justice that isn't fulfilled in the existing social order'.[23] His statement could be laid out as a syllogism: art is objective/attacks on social injustice are objective/all attacks are art. (And conversely, no work that accepts the existing social order can qualify as art.) In other words, objectivity is not impartial. It comes from a particular political bias, while a 'rational' theatre is a theatre of political persuasion.

But if we are all socially conditioned victims, exploiters and exploited alike, and therefore functionally insane, whom can he address? Bond implies that only those, like himself, who have escaped the educational process, are capable of perceiving reality. According to him, the fact that he was prevented from taking the grammar school qualifying exam at the age of eleven 'was the making of me . . . after that nobody takes you seriously. The conditioning process stops. Once you let them send you to grammar school and university you're ruined.'[24] Yet, almost by definition, the audience for main-stage theatre is educated. So Bond is preaching to the unconvertible (in his terms). As a result his approach is contradictory. He labels his work 'rational theatre', yet madness is one of his major themes, and his images are almost unprecedented in their visceral effect. His function as a playwright becomes comparable to Arthur's in the heaven of *Early Morning*: not rational persuasion, but causing extreme moral discomfort.

The way he uses farce shows his approach at its clearest. Unlike *The Sea*, where the comedy is a traditional 'intellectual medium, demanding detachment', the treatment of the Warrington torture scene in *Lear* is characteristic.

FONTANELLE Use the boot! (*SOLDIER A kicks him.*) Jump on him ! (*She pushes SOLDIER A.*) Jump on his head!
SOLDIER A. Lay off, lady, lay off! 'Oo's killin' im, me or you?
BODICE (*knits*) One plain, two purl, one plain.
FONTANELLE Throw him up and drop him. I want to hear him drop . . .
BODICE (*to SOLDIER A*) Down on your knees.
SOLDIER A Me?
BODICE Down! (*SOLDIER A kneels.*) Beg for his life.
SOLDIER A (*confused*) 'Is? (Aside) What a pair! – O spare 'im, mum.
BODICE (*knits*) No.
SOLDIER A If yer could see yer way to. 'E's a poor ol' gent, lonely ol' bugger . . .
BODICE It s my duty to inform you –

SOLDIER A Keep still! Keep yer eyes on madam when she talks t'yer.

BODICE – that your pardon has been refused... (*She pokes the needles into WARRINGTON's ears.*) I'll just jog these in and out a little. Doodee, doodee, doodee, doo.

The incongruity of juxtaposing heartless farce and human suffering is explicitly intended to be highly disturbing. As Bond has said, 'the effect' of such an 'inappropriate' tone 'is very cruel'. Indeed, Bond's use of farcical comedy has to be seen as an extension of his naked images of violence. For example, on a thematic level, the baby-killing in *Saved* may be a symbol for social pressures; but in terms of dramatic function, its value is primarily that it provokes extreme reactions in an audience. As Bond commented: 'everybody's reaction is different... people came out absolutely shaking and other people can't even watch it. So it's their reaction, I mean they must ask themselves, not ask me what I think about.'[25]

In fact, the change from bleak realism in *Saved* to the Grand Guignol of *Early Morning* or *Lear* is only a response to the public's capacity for accommodating themselves to violence. As Bond admits: 'If I went on stoning babies in every play then nobody would notice it anymore. I had to find [continually new] ways of making people notice, of making those things effective.' This is what he has labelled 'the aggro-effect' in deliberate distinction from the Brechtian 'alienation effect':

In contrast to Brecht, I think it's necessary to disturb an audience emotionally to involve them emotionally in my plays, so I've had to find ways of making that 'aggro-effect' more complete, which is in a sense to surprise them, to say 'Here's a baby in a pram – you don't expect these people to stone that baby.' Yet [snapping his fingers] they do.[26]

By most standards, the public's emotional reaction to his plays was all that Bond could have wished. In one of the *Lear* previews, 'When the Ghost says "People will be kind to you now, surely, you've suffered enough", a departing gentleman in the stalls was heard to remark: "Yes, so have we!".' With *Saved*, one critic 'spent a lot of the first act shaking with claustrophobia and thinking I was going to be sick'. Indeed, this sort of response became exactly what productions of *Saved* aimed at, and the American première was described by its director as a 'complete success' on the grounds that 'the walkout rate after the first half was the highest the theatre has ever had, and I have never seen an audience at a traditional play so disturbed'.[27]

But for any propagandist, simply provoking a rejection of his message would be obviously counter-productive. So Bond uses farce to control the violence 'by irony, so that it would become a focus to jolt the audience into thinking'. This underestimates the intensity of his fragmented scenes, and the immediacy of his images of violence, which tend to produce a form of emotional overkill that makes thought almost impossible. But clearly Bond sees outraging the audience emotionally as a sort of shock therapy designed to galvanize their consciences into life and provoke them into viewing society 'objectively' and 'rationally' (that is, from his perspective). For him, the degree of violence is nothing more than a measure of urgency, and he denies any 'desire to shock':

The shock is justified by the desperation of the situation or as a way of forcing the audience to search for reasons in the rest of the play. If you have the effrontery to say, 'I am going to use an aggressive "aggro-effect" against an audience', if you have the impertinence to say that – and I've just said it – then it must be because you feel you have something desperately important to tell them. If they were sitting in a house on fire, you would go up to them and shake them violently . . . And so it's only because I feel it is important to involve people in the realities of life that I sometimes use those effects.[28]

Thus the violent nature of his dramatic material is offset by the production techniques Bond has evolved for his plays, which require a conceptual approach on the actors' part. Directing *The Woman* at the National Theatre in 1978, Bond found himself 'astonished at the way the acting forced the play into the ground, buried it in irrelevant subjectivity', because the characters were being portrayed in naturalistic emotional terms. So he imposed 'a new sort of acting', directly modelled on Brecht's practice: 'Put roughly and briefly, it's this. A concept, an interpretation [of the situation, not the character] must be applied to an emotion, and it is this concept or interpretation or idea that is acted. This relates the character to the social event so that he becomes its story teller.' However, this abstracting, intellectualizing quality is modified by Bond's rejection of 'anybody who imagines the answers to life are cerebral and that the problems are cerebral'. It is limited to the presentation. For the audience, 'Theatre involves the whole person . . . Ideas are two-dimensional . . . involvement on the stage is a three-dimensional process'.[29]

The Woman (1978), the final and most ambitious play in Bond's double cycle of major works, recapitulates all his major thematic points, and gives them a mythic dimension through the archetypal story of the fall of Troy. Warfare is explicitly presented as not only the product of class society and that society's way of perpetuating itself, but also as absurd since 'even victory would cost ... more ... than defeat at the beginning'. And indeed, the Greek conquerors are forced into dehumanizing atrocities, in order to reassert their authority over troops demoralized by the long siege. The last surviving Trojan prince, a young boy, is thrown off the battlements, combining the image of the Massacre of the Innocents with the wall from *Lear*. Heros (the Greek general) has his wife Ismene walled up alive in its stones for having tried to stop the slaughter by revealing the truth – calling on the Greek soldiers to rebel because their officers are only using the war to enslave them. The Statue of Good Fortune, for which the Trojan War is being fought in Bond's symbolic version of history, stands for the counterfeit ideals that legitimize an unjust society and trap the oppressors who rule through them, destroying the leaders even more than the masses whom they exploit. Arthur's madness, leading him to believe that a leader who kills everyone is the greatest benefactor, recurs in Hecuba's son who is torn apart in the mob violence he incites. Arthur's parodic ascension is echoed at the end of the play in an even more grotesque form, with Hecuba being sucked up high into the air by a waterspout that 'ripped out her hair and her eyes. Her tits were sticking up like knives.'[30]

The first half of the play is the most graphic of all Bond's depictions of the paranoid effect of power and the self-destroying violence inherent in a social system based on inequality, culminating in the sack of Troy. But the second half offers an explicit solution that anticipates the argument in *The Worlds* (his next play).

The Statue of Good Fortune is lost at sea when the ship transporting the blinded Hecuba and Ismene (rescued from the wall, but reduced to dumbness and the mental level of a child by the social insanity she has confronted) to slavery in Greece is wrecked. The two helpless women, reduced to the most basic level of existence and forgetting their former enmity in mutual dependence, have found refuge in a bucolic fishing community. A dark man, crippled by years in the Athenian mines – the opposite to classical ideals of beauty and proportion – escapes to the island, followed by Heros and his forces in search of the statue. Hecuba, now a priestess because her sightlessness has brought her the reputation of a seer, promises that it will be restored to Heros if he wins a race against the cripple. In this variation of Aesop's fable the tortoise beats Achilles (possibly by taking a short cut, though this is never made clear). Then, when Heros, duped into believing the cripple's victory to be a miracle performed by 'the goddess', commands his soldiers to disarm, the dark man stabs him with a sword hidden under

Hecuba's skirt. Assassination renders the forces of tyranny impotent, and they carry their leader's body away, leaving the villagers to celebrate the resumption of their natural existence.

Such a resolution embodies the change in perspective signalled by Bond's assertion that 'We mustn't write only problem plays, we must write answer plays.'[31] However, peasant innocence is hardly a convincing alternative to the problems of modern urban society; and the dramatically unjustified way the action is resolved discredits the proposed solution. For the crippled slave to win a race against Heros, who is all that his name implies, demands a deliberate mystification of the audience. A man who is capable of transforming Athens into a tyranny with himself at the top, but succumbs to such religious idealism that he orders his guards to throw away their weapons, is credible only on a purely symbolic level. Nothing we have seen of the Greek soldiers prepares us for an ending in which they are so dispirited by the death of their leader that they simply leave without any acts of revenge.

In addition to this obvious manipulation of the dramatic action, Bond even has to stretch the logic of his symbols to make the play prove what he intends. The slave's deformed body stands explicitly for the effect of social repression, which works on a mental level. In all Bond's other plays, a character's physical state represents his/her psychological condition. Yet here the slave's moral sense, articulacy and kindness remain untouched by his upbringing and exploitation.

Such inconsistencies are disguised and to some extent offset by the mythical basis for the play, which draws on practically the whole range of Ancient Greek tragedy, from echoes of Aeschylus (*The Persians*, the earliest surviving drama, as well as *Suppliant Women*), to Sophocles' *Philoctetes*, and Euripides' *Helen in Eygpt* and *Iphegenia in Tauris* – in all of which heroines believed killed during the Trojan War are revealed to be alive – together with Euripides' *Trojan Women*. This forms Bond's major source for the first half of the action; and his title-change to *The Woman* is indicative of the play's thematic simplification. Here it is specifically men who set up the repressive structures of a violent society. Women (leaving aside the monstrous regiment from Bond's earlier plays: Victoria, Georgina, Bodice and Fontanelle, *et al.*) keep their maternal instinct, and so have the capacity to reject irrationality.

Even so, in *The Woman* more than any other play, Bond comes closest to achieving what he has defined as politically significant theatre, fulfilling the 'need to set our scenes in public places, where history is formed, classes clash and whole societies move. Otherwise we're not writing about events that most affect us and shape our future.' The price of this is a sacrifice of individual characterization and identifiable social reality to the extent that 'the world is . . . put forward as a moral example' while the figures 'stand for various forces in history'.[32] However, in later plays this ideological reduction makes the dramatic conflict increasingly external, and though Bond's images are still visually effective they no longer contain the psychological dimension that gave them such emotional power in *Early Morning* or *Lear*.

The switch from 'question' to 'answer plays' is more than just a change in material. As the 'answers' become more explicit, the audience is required to accept them without questioning – a shift signalled in particular by characterization. In *Bingo* (1973), for example, Shakespeare is depicted as inherently admirable and sympathetic. This makes his inability to rise above the inhuman standards of his time a condemnation of the unjust social system, which is as convincing as it is disturbing. By contrast, later protagonists are all too often totally black or flawlessly white. In *Summer* (1982), the main figure is an outright villainess. Not only typecast as evil (having collaborated in wartime atrocities as a former Balkan fascist), she is arrogant and completely egoistic, even where her own daughter is concerned, as well as being trivialized by limiting her horizons to Harrods (presented as the shopping heaven of the mindless rich). Conversely, in *Human Cannon* (1985, unperformed) the peasant heroine is literally the weapon of the title, unhistorically defeating the reactionary forces in the Spanish civil war. Similarly in *Jackets II* (1990) the authorities restoring order in a riot-torn 'city in modern Europe' are 'Them' – army officers depicted as genocidal hypocrites to whom the common soldiers are only 'the lowest of the low, vermin, scum' to be callously sacrificed as an excuse for reprisals, and a clergyman exhorts the fall-guy to 'Arise! go forth! Be shot!' – while the looters and armed insurgents are presented as 'Us'.[33]

The only play to rise above this simplification in the recent phase of Bond's career is *Restoration* (1981), where a parodistic form offsets the melodramatic division between the evil exploiting rich and virtuous victimized poor. The preening self-admiration of the aristocratic anti-hero, his purely aesthetic view of poetry and his Hoyden-like fiancée's wish to become an instant widow, together with a 'ghost' episode – though here it is transposed from bedroom to breakfast, and results in her death instead of seduction – all come from Vanbrugh's *The Relapse*: a particularly appropriate Restoration comedy since its subtitle 'Virtue in Danger' could stand for both plays. But here the danger is social, not sexual. Bond's aim is to show that social oppression only exists through the complicity of the oppressed. The class system depends on the active co-operation of the slaves – all they have to do is be aware of their chains, 'Then you'd be free: you'd know what you are.'[35] And the setting is the eighteenth century, as a period when class contrasts were not only extreme, but (in the shape of aristocrat and peasant) obvious.

A good-hearted servant is duped into confessing to the murder of his mistress (actually committed by his aristocratic master) and kept quiet, even on the scaffold, by his master's promise of a pardon. The action clearly demonstrates the message of the final song 'Man is what he knows.' Learning to read in prison, the innocent hero laboriously spells out the same statement, while his illiterate mother cannot recognize his pardon, and ignorantly burns it when the sardonic aristocrat hands the paper to her for a firelighter. Believing (despite the evidence of his senses) that 'every Englishman is free ... England is the home of liberty', the hapless servant is incapable of escaping, even when nothing bars his way. His loving wife (a black serving-maid, whose slave-plantation background qualifies her as the voice of political consciousness) uses her knowledge of the law that 'No one can benefit from his own crime', as well as her perception that greed is the only motive of the rich, to persuade the dead girl's mine-owner father to accuse the real murderer, since he will then be able to reclaim her dowry. But, being unaware of his real reason for arranging the marriage – to get the coal beneath the aristocrat's estate – her information only allows him to make a better bargain: mineral rights for silence.

The didactic nature of the play is emphasized by the frequency with which the actors step out of role in songs, which recapitulate points already made in the scenes or draw mainly redundant contemporary parallels. And the audience are clearly expected to echo the bereaved black girl's closing line: 'What have I learned? If nothing, then I was hanged.'[36] In addition, in the 1987 RSC revival of the play, the text was altered to make the suicidal cooperation of the innocent Bob (renamed 'Boob' by his villainous master) directly relevant to the Falkland War.

However, this didactic overkill is offset by Bond's pastiche of Restoration drama. Because the caricatures of the rich are recognizable comic types, their antics become appreciated rather than condemned, while the innocent simplicity of the servant also corresponds to a stock figure: the naive fall-guy, whose predicament is deserved by stupidity. Objectively, Lord Are may be the 'arse' into which his servants change his name. But in the context of Wycherley and Congreve, his marriage solely to pay off his debts becomes acceptable, as it was for the rakes of their plays, while his obsession with fashion – an exaggeration of Vanbrugh's already excessive Lord

Foppington – is not read as the intended sign of heartless superficiality. Instead his pursuit of style appears as self-awareness that gives his figure the attraction of an actor; and the element of conscious performance removes moral judgement of his actions. When withholding his servant's pardon (obtained by Old Lady Are to discredit the son she hates), his cry of 'What, no lightning stroke? No thunder?' has the vitality of Jonson's Volpone (on whom the speech is modelled).

So Lord Are's declaration that 'The Boob must hang for the public good', because 'In my person I am society, the symbol of authority, the figure-head of law and order', is not taken as the straight social criticism Bond clearly means it to be. Instead, his claim, that the revelation of his villainy would bring revolution, becomes a self-mocking hyperbole. Indeed reviewers found 'Lord Are so charming... that we are likely to extend all the grace in the world to a witty sinner', who is 'despite all the awful things he does to the downtrodden peasantry, carrying off' his crimes 'with such gleeful resource that, as with all the best villains, you really want him to get away with it'.[37]

Here, ideology is subsumed in theatre. Elsewhere in Bond's recent work polemics tend to displace drama. But his most powerful plays balance the political and the personal. The creative tension in those has given his drama much the same weight as Shaw's at the beginning of the century, even if the uncompromising nature of his vision means that his plays will never attain the same popularity. Indeed, the importance Bond gives to prefaces links him directly with Shaw; and one of his most recent plays, *In the Company of Men*, is an updated version of Shaw's *Major Barbara* dealing with an adopted son's plot to take over his father's armaments firm. Following Shaw, too, this is a comedy, but here the son is anything but an ethical professor of classics and the villain is no visionary standing against the false ethics of an unjust society. Instead the conflict over the company is a competition between evils. The 'merchant of death' father only saves himself from being murdered by dying first; and the rival entrepreneur who blackmails the son, who owes him millions from his ruthless takeover of an engineering firm, is a predator whose only aim is to dominate the market and sees himself selling guns along with butter to the Third World.

Although in contrast to Arden, Bond is still an active force at the close of the century, like Wesker his ideology now seems dated. Indeed *In the Company of Men* (directed by Bond himself for the RSC in 1996) was the first new play of his to be produced in the professional theatre for fourteen years, and took seven years to reach the stage. And although *Coffee* (1997) appeared at the Royal Court – marking a return to the theatre that had made him the most subversive playwright of the 1960s – it was performed by a small Welsh community theatre (albeit one that clearly indicates his continuing influence in its name: the Rational Theatre Company) and almost completely ignored. The single review dismissed it as a confused and impenetrable failure, pointing out that its equation of the hollowing out of small Welsh villages under the pressures of modern life to the Babi Yar massacre, where in 1941 30,000 Jews were shot by the SS, had no justification or contact with reality.[38] Even so, the politics that make Bond's plays flawed are also what gives them such moral force that they demand to be taken seriously; and the stylistic issues raised in them have defined the arena for contemporary British political drama.

Notes

1 Edward Bond, letter, 7 January 1970, in Malcolm Hay and Philip Roberts, *Edward Bond: A Companion to the Plays*, London, 1978, p. 43.

2 Bond, letter, 28 July 1977, in Hay and Roberts, *Bond: A Companion*, p. 75, and interview, *Canadian Theatre Review*, no. 23 (Summer 1979), p. 108; *The Sea*, London, 1973, p. 65.

3 Preface to *Lear*, London, 1971, p. 11.

4 Bond, *Plays: 5*, London, 1966, p. 419.

5 *The Worlds*, pp. 84 & 114.

6 Bond, interview in *Gambit*, 5, no. 17 (1970), p. 9.

7 *Plays: Two*, London, 1977, pp. ix, and Bond in *Gambit* (1970), p. 24.

8 Bond, interview in *The Observer*, 16 March 1969, and in *Gambit* (1970), p. 8 (see also Richard Scharine, *The Plays of Edward Bond*, Lewisburg, 1976, p. 147); *Lear*, p. 11.

9 Bond, cited in Hay and Roberts, *Bond: A Companion*, pp. 61–62, and in *Theater Heute*, November 1969.

10 *Plays: One*, London, 1977, pp. 14 and 17.

11 *Saved*, in *Plays: One*, pp. 83 & 85; Bond, in Hay and Roberts, *Bond: A Companion*, pp. 43–4.

12 Letter on *Saved, Plays and Players*, Feb. 1966, p. 6, *Illustrated London News*, 13 November 1965, and *Daily Express*, 4 November 1965; Bond, Preface to *Saved*, London, 1966, p. 6.

13 William Gaskill, interview, *Plays & Players*, July 1982, p. 12; Jane Howell, *Plays and Players*, October 1968, pp. 70 & 71.

14 Martin Esslin, *Plays and Players*, 15 (June 1968), p. 26.

15 Bond, interview in *Canadian Theatre Review* (1979), pp. 109 and 111.

16 Bond, letters, 14 January 1977 and 6 November 1969, in Hay and Roberts, *Bond: A Companion*, pp. 67 & 50.

17 Bond, in *Theater Heute*, November 1969.

18 *Early Morning*, in *Plays: One*, pp. 211 & 223.

19 Bond, interview in *Canadian Theatre Review* (1979), p. 112, and in *Gambit* (1970) (see also Richard Scharine, *The Plays of Edward Bond*, p. 147), p. 35; *The Worlds*, pp. 129, 108.

20 Gaskill, interview in *Gambit* (1970), p. 41; Ronald Bryden, *Observer*, 16 March 1969 (cf. also Esslin, *Plays and Players*, May 1969, p. 26); Bond, Note to *Early Morning*, p. 138.

21 Note to *Early Morning*, p. 146; *Where To Go*, 14 September 1978.

22 Bertolt Brecht, quoted by Manfred Wekwerth in *Theater Heute*, February 1968, p. 17; Bond, in *The Times*, 25 September 1969; Franz Xaver Kroetz, *Süddeutscher Zeitung*, 20/21 November 1971; Heiner Müller in *Theater 1975* (*Theater Heute Sonderheft*), p. 120; Bond, quoted in Hay and Roberts, *Bond: A Companion*, p. 18.

23 Edward Bond, *Plays: Two*, London, 1978, p.xiii. This, of course, is the same definition used by Peter Weiss in *Dramen 2* (Frankfurt, 1968), pp. 468–9, and by Mao Tse-tung in 'Talks at the Yenan Forum of Art and Literature' (1942): according to Mao, what 'showing both sides of the question' means, is that 'every dark force which endangers the masses must be exposed, while every revolutionary struggle of the masses must be praised'; and art is 'good...if it opposes retrogression and promotes progress' (cited in *Drama in the Modern World*, ed. D.A. Heath, New York, 1974, pp. 560 & 558).

24 Bond, quoted in Hay and Roberts, *Bond: A Companion*, p. 7. (Before comprehensive education was introduced, all children in the state system were streamed into academic – grammar-schools, or technical – secondary – schools by an exam called the 11+.)

25 Scharine, *The Plays of Edward Bond*, p. 253; *Plays: Two*, pp. 28–9; Bond, letter, 25 January 1977, in Hay and Roberts, *Bond: A Companion*, p. 72, and cited, p. 10.

26 Bond, in *Canadian Theatre Review* (1979), pp. 112 and 113.

27 Gregory Dark, 'Production Casebook No. 5: Edward Bond's "Lear" at the Royal Court', *Theatre Quarterly*, January–March 1972, p. 31; Penelope Gilliatt, in *Contemporary Theatre*, ed. Geoffrey Morgan, London, 1968, p. 41; Michael Feingold, *Plays and Players*, May 1969, p. 65.

28 Bond in *Canadian Theatre Review* (1979), p. 113. Bond's reuse of the image of 'a house on fire' from an interview in 1971, shortly after *Lear*, in an interview eight years later – when he was working upon *The Woman* – indicates the consistency of his approach to the audience.

29 Bond, *Plays and Players*, October 1978, pp. 8–9; in *Gambit* (1970), p. 19, and *Canadian Theatre Review*, (1979), p. 112.

30 Bond, *The Woman*, London, 1979, pp. 27, 108.

31 Letter, 28 July 1977, in Hay and Roberts, *Bond: A Companion*, p. 75.

32 Bond, *Plays and Players*, October 1978, p. 8, and in *Socialist Challenge*, 28 September 1978.

33 *Jackets II*, London, 1990, pp. 62, 68, 69.

35 *Restoration*, London, 1981, p. 34.

36 *Ibid.*, pp. 42, 33, 28 & 42.

37 *Ibid.*, pp. 38 & 25; *Drama*, Winter 1981, p. 33, and *Plays and Players*, October 1981, p. 25.

38 See Adrian Turpin, *Independent*, 28 May 1997.

3.10 David Edgar (1948–): from Agitprop to Social Realism

CHECKLIST OF EDGAR'S MAJOR PLAYS

Destiny, 1976

The Jail Diary of Albie Sachs, 1978

Mary Barnes, 1978

Nicholas Nickleby, 1980

Maydays, 1983

Entertaining Strangers, 1985

Heartlanders, 1989

The Shape of the Table, 1990

Pentecost, 1994

The social misery of the Depression, the Nazi holocaust and the bombing of the cities in the Second World War, together with high expectations of the Labour government swept into power at the war's end had been the formative experiences for Osborne, Wesker, Arden and Bond. However, the following generation of English playwrights was radicalized by the students' revolt, which reached its high point in Paris in May 1968 with the takeover of the French National Theatre. The exhilarating demonstration of people-power, focused by the widespread rejection of the Vietnam War, appeared to signal the breakdown of discredited establishments. Revolution seemed a real and immediate possibility. Idealistic certainties (and the abolition of theatrical censorship in the same year) spawned a range of counter-theatre groups and mobilized young dramatists like David Hare, Howard Brenton, David Edgar and Howard Barker, as well as Trevor Griffiths and a primarily comic writer such as Peter Barnes.

Out of the 1968 experience came a wide range of counter-theatre perfor-mance groups. The type of drama they produced is accurately summed up in the name chosen for the earliest of these, The Agitprop Street Players. This troupe, which developed into Red Ladder (named after the stage prop that became their trademark), was rapidly followed by many others: among them The Welfare State, The General Will (for which Edgar's early pieces were written), the Pip Simmons Theatre Group, and Portable Theatre founded by Hare. These combined with a growing number of socialist theatre groups with strong regional affiliations, such as North West Spanner and Hull Truck, in which drama merged with other forms of political activity. Initially, all targeted disadvantaged sections of society, or industrial labourers. For instance, John McGrath's 7:84 Company was named to highlight the statistics of social inequality: in 1971, the year of its founding, seven per cent of the population owned eighty-four per cent of Britain's wealth. Most of these Agitprop troupes were relatively short-lived. However, the Scottish branch of 7:84 is still operating, while Welfare State International has moved into large-scale stagings of environmental events.

They all began by returning to the same principles of agitation and propaganda on which the work of Joan Littlewood and Ewan McColl had been based in the 1930s (see above, pp. 73–75). As then, the conditions of performance ruled out thematic subtlety or character development; and the only criterion of effectiveness was political not theatrical. Designed for picket-lines, public meetings, street or shop-floor presentation, they were limited to poster-and-slogan style, and used little or no scenery. The scripts Edgar wrote for The General Will Company in 1971–2, such as *The National Interest, Rent, or Caught in the Act* or *State of Emergency*, were fairly typical. Straight Agitprop pieces, these employed direct imagery, simple caricature and short episodic sequences to present issues of immediate topical interest for working-class audiences: the Industrial Relations Act, the Housing Finance Act, and the 1973 coalminers' strike. Others were aimed at wider audiences. *Lay-By* (1971, on which Edgar collaborated with six other writers, including Brenton and Hare) and *England's Ireland* (1972, co-written by Edgar, Brenton and Hare as well as Snoo Wilson and others) offered a more synoptic view of society in the same dramatic form.

Such plays were generally short sketches, communal or improvised in nature, and rewritten for each performance to take account of daily events or the local context. As a result most of the texts are of sociological, rather than dramatic interest, although some of Edgar's early pieces have been revived – notably plays using sexual metaphors for social problems, like *The National Theatre* (1975 – England as a strip-club) or *Saigon Rose* (1976 – American commercial influence as VD). An exception is McGrath's plays, such as *The Cheviot, The Stag and the Black, Black Oil* (1973) or *The Imperial Policeman* (1984), which extended the music-hall approach that Joan Littlewood had developed in *Oh, What a Lovely War* (discussed above, pp. 121–22). Combining song and dance with current issues of public concern in an extended Epic structure, these have continuing political vitality and popular appeal.

As even such a brief overview indicates, this Agitprop movement was not homogeneous. The various groups shared similar stylistic qualities, since the Agitprop form had become identified with a Marxist ideological line. But their aims ranged from providing information (for instance, on the social and economic implications of new laws), through moulding political consciousness (promoting support for industrial action, or exposing Establishment corruption), to aggressive protest (using violent images to bring home the corrupting effects of pornography, or to assert the public's complicity in the bloodshed of Northern Ireland).

At one end of this Agitprop spectrum the material was that of a 'living newspaper', where the sketches were compiled and the stage images distilled from press clippings, with topical references being updated daily. David Edgar's work between 1970 and 1972, in particular, drew from his early experience as a journalist and was based on factual research – as in *The Case of the Worker's Plane*, a piece about the manufacture of the Concorde. *Rent*, devised for presentation to tenants' groups, illustrated how the Housing Act applied to individual situations through the format of early Victorian melodrama. Its pre-set emotional values in the persecuted poor (Honest Tom and the Harddoneby family) versus villains (landlords and a lawyer from the firm of Devious, Devious & Downright Dishonest) were transposed into the contemporary scene of squatters and high-rise apartments. But in Edgar's view, even if *Rent* might have been his 'most successful agitprop play' in reaching 'exactly the audiences it wanted and was intended for', the less popular *Dunkirk Spirit* ranked higher 'because in two hours you actually got through the most massive amount of extremely complex material'.[1]

At the other end of the spectrum, although a piece like *Lay-By* also derived from a newspaper article, the kind of material selected was very different: a tabloid rape-story rather than economic or legal reports. It used scenes of nudity and dismemberment as shock tactics in 'group warfare', culminating in the trashing of even the main characters' corpses.[2]

Whether the emphasis was on propaganda or on agitation, these pieces shared one other characteristic of the news media. Created in response to specific issues and designed for immediate effect, they dated as rapidly as any conventional journalistic items. Utility was their criterion. So, if they contributed to changing a specific situation they became redundant; if social circumstances remained the same they were irrelevant. Once the Housing Act was repealed, for example, *Rent* lost its function. Alternatively, where there was no immediate or obvious effect, the classic Agitprop finale of flag-waving victory for the people was reduced to empty rhetoric. As Edgar put it, 'when the actors having shown yet another great working-class defeat, stand with clenched fists singing a song about how it'll be alright next time', that 'is the moment when many people crawl under their seats' with embarrassment.[3]

A few playwrights remained in Agitprop after the 1980s, the most notable being John McGrath. However, Edgar, along with Hare and Brenton, had already come to challenge the assumptions of Agitprop drama by the mid-1970s. In 1968 the political situation had seemed as clear as the struggle for democracy against fascism of the 1930s. But it had become increasingly obvious that caricature and slogans failed to match social reality. Even during his Agitprop work, Edgar had been aware that 'there were plays weaving through [his dramatic material] which the form couldn't take'. And although he continued to write in this mode – *Wreckers* for the 7:84 Company, or *Our own People* for the Pirate Jenny Company (both 1977) – this led him to develop Agitprop elements into an essentially new style of drama in his first full-length piece, *Destiny* (1976).[4]

The original text of *Destiny* – which would have taken over seven hours to perform, being almost three times the length of the final version – was designed schematically. The initial outline was not a sequence of actions, but a series of political observations, abstracted from two years of factual research. The plot – revolving around a parliamentary election in which an unofficial strike of immigrant workers becomes the dominant issue – was then constructed to illustrate these points. For instance, in the central scene of a local Party meeting, where a patriotic protest movement is manipulated into a neo-fascist rally, Edgar has pointed out that on the page 'the scene looked as if it had been written from a chart, which, as it happens, was the case'. However, in performance the recognizable reality of the context, evoked by rows of almost empty seats, embarrassing silences and feedback from a badly adjusted microphone, made the dramatic situation entirely credible. Reflecting this, criticism that 'the politicians of all three parties are purely stereotype figures, their dialogue is carried on in clichés' was balanced against comparisons to Galsworthy on the grounds that the grass-roots level of politics 'has never been drawn so accurately before'.[5]

Edgar has argued that this combination of an Agitprop approach with naturalistic detail creates a distinctively new theatrical form. The fundamental element of any type of drama is characterization, since the way people are depicted defines the way society is perceived, and determines the kind of statement a playwright can make. A photographic reproduction of individual behaviour (to which Naturalism leads) is the opposite of the two-dimensional class figures (characteristic of Agitprop). In one, the factors that determine how people act are psychological and environmental. In the other they are economic or historical necessity. And each style distorts reality. The primarily personal emphasis of the first rules out the objective overview necessary for dealing with the political issues, while the ideological focus of the second ignores the subjective reactions of the participants. The solution is 'a synthesis... of the surface perception of Naturalism and the social analysis that underlies Agitprop plays'. Such a combination is possible because both types of characterization imply that the way people act in a given set of circumstances can be accurately predicted. And the resulting 'dialectical' tension between subjective and objective factors creates a form of true 'Social Realism', that allows public events to be handled on an epic scale, without (at least in theory) sacrificing the human dimension.[6]

Spanning two continents and nearly thirty years, from 1947 to the date of its first performance, *Destiny* is a prototype of this Social Realism. Its episodic framework interweaves the experience of three sets of people, who come together as the nucleus of a potential fascist future: the Conservatives, whose traditional principles have become irrelevant; the military, with their ideals of authoritarian order; and the dispossessed, whose livelihood or status is threatened by social developments. But these general groupings are presented through individual case studies that explore the complexity of their personal motives. An old-style Conservative MP laments the decay of traditional values – but his death precipitates the by-election; and his heir, who takes his place as the Party candidate, is a callous technocrat. An ex-Army major is radicalized by the killing of his son in Belfast – yet the speech declaring his commitment to 'an iron dawn' is designed to make the audience empathize with his grief. Sympathy is elicited even for the election candidate of the neo-fascist Nation Forward Party (a clone for the National Front), because we see how being bankrupted by the shady property speculations of an investment company fuels his frustrated anger.

To defeat the Labour candidate, these right-wing figures form an alliance of mutual convenience, which lends the fascists a gloss of respectability, and makes them a real political danger – and the play ends on the disillusion of the Nation Forward candidate, when he discovers it is the investment company responsible for his bankruptcy that finances his political party. Edgar's aim is summed up in the final lines, spoken by the voice of

Adolf Hitler: 'Only one thing could have stopped our Movement: if our adversaries had understood its principle.'[7]

To this end a large part of the dialogue is concerned with neo-fascist theory. But what these discussions demonstrate is that fascism appeals to individual fear and despair. It is not ideological. So the subject requires precisely the synthesis on which Edgar's Social Realism is based; and the need to provide an insight into personal motives was reinforced by the targeted audience – the middle-class theatre-goers most susceptible to right-wing extremism. This meant creating 'characters that the audience could relate to and in a way that they could confront in themselves'.[8] Hence, Edgar considered that the transfer of the RSC production to a West End theatre (where it was seen by 20,000 people) had more significance than the television showing of the play, which reached a far larger, but more socially diverse audience. And indeed the stage performances struck a public nerve, making it one of the few British plays that have caused the same sort of riots as those caused by the plays of Synge or O'Casey in Dublin. Taken on by the RSC specifically because a by-election in the West Midlands had just marked the emergence of the National Front as a potential political force, *Destiny* became the focus of a violent street demonstration by neo-fascists on the last night of the London performance, and again when it was revived in 1985 at the Half Moon Theatre in London's East End.

At the same time, in *Destiny* the formal problems are not completely resolved. The historical background is encapsulated in Kiplingesque verse monologues, one for each of the main figures. The representational basis of the action makes the plotting too neatly coincidental, with the right-wing protagonists and the Asian who leads the strike, all appearing as members of the same regiment at the time of Indian independence: Colonel, Major, Sergeant and Sikh orderly. Similarly, two youths working in the same shop take exactly contrasting, but equally extreme political lines. Both are arrested at the same picket-line incident, and the parallel is emphasized by dialogue:

PAUL...it was like looking in a mirror, looking at him, me old mate, Tony. All
    correct, the same, identical. Just one thing wrong. Left's right. Class – race. As
    different as can be. The opposite. The bleeding wrong way round...[9]

Adapting *Nicholas Nickleby* for the RSC (1980) helped Edgar to overcome these problems, and develop techniques for dealing with a broad social panorama that did not sacrifice either objective or subjective perspectives. The nineteenth-century novel required handling large blocks of material;

and this offered a graphic demonstration of the potential in his new style of theatrical realism. Although there was no direct contemporary reference, it was conceived as 'a play about Dickens that criticized his form of social morality, rather than a straight dramatization of the novel'.[10]

The attractiveness of Dickens' hero was compromised by his adaptability to any circumstances. So Edgar shifted the focus to the crippled Smike. Even if some critics felt the bravura performance of the role unbalanced the piece, Smike's distorted figure set the line followed (in a more popularized form) by the Lloyd-Webber musical spectacular, *The Phantom of the Opera*. Smike's physical shape embodied the deforming effects of an unjust society, whose inhumanity was represented by the Dickensian gallery of caricatures. The audience's initial revulsion at the grotesquely contorted and drooling Smike, which associated them subliminally with the oppressors, intensified their reactions as they discovered the victim's humanity. So emotions evoked for the individual were almost automatically turned against the system responsible for his condition. Hence the spontaneous nightly applause at the point when Nicholas rescued Smike from the sadistic schoolmaster, which (unusually for the conventional theatre) signalled approval for the action, rather than appreciation of the performer.

As in Agitprop staging – though here entirely in context, given the Victorian acting company embalmed in the novel – there was no scenic illusion. A few basic props, carried on by the actors, defined each locale; and the level of reality was always that of performance. The whole cast were continually on stage, observing the events from an upper level of the set. The actors stepped out of role to explain the inner feelings of their characters. Edgar's treatment provided a strikingly theatrical experience – even if the difficulty in dramatizing such wide-ranging picaresque material was still obvious from the two nights required to stage the whole story. But by any standards it was a successful exercise in the manipulation of contrasting viewpoints. In many ways it anticipates the physical theatre of Simon McBurney (see pp. 537ff.); and the effectiveness of unison acting and improvisational scenes can be contrasted with Edgar's later dramatization of another Victorian novel, *The Strange Case of Dr Jekyll and Mr Hyde* (also for the RSC, 1991). Edgar had already focused memorably on the theme of the divided self in a previous adaptation of a psychiatric case history, *Mary Barnes* (1978) – but here the setting overwhelmed the action, with its vistas of elaborate houses in Victorian London on a revolve. His addition of a psychiatric history of childhood sibling rivalry and Oedipal fixation for Dr Jekyll, as well as characters who represent the economic exploitation of Victorian (and by extension contemporary) society, to Robert Louis Stevenson's tightly focused tale of psychological repression also dissipates the narrative drive that makes his adaptation of *Nicholas Nickleby* so compelling.

The panoramic focus, physical theatricality and narrative format of *Nicholas Nickleby*, coupled with the documentary basis of *The Jail Diary of Albie Sachs* (1978), eventually led Edgar into 'community festival' pieces like *Entertaining Strangers* (directed by Anne Jellicoe for the citizens of Dorchester in 1985) or *Heartlanders* (co-written with the Irish playwright Anne Devlin and mounted in Birmingham in 1989). Initiated by Peter Cheeseman with *The Jolly Potters* at Stoke-on-Trent in 1964, the local involvement and documentary emphasis of Community Theatre has formed one of the main counterweights to the centrifugal culture of the London stage – and is still a vital force at the end of the century with the work of groups like the Cornish Kneehigh Theatre. Over the last twenty-five years this company has been a vehicle for one of the leading regional playwrights, Nick Darke, who deals specifically with Cornish history: most recently *The King Of Prussia* (1996) based on the brandy-smuggling and rise of Methodism at the end of the eighteenth century, or *The Riot* (1999) reconstructing an actual incident from the fishing wars of 1896. The Kneehigh company is typical of Community Theatre in its integration with the locality, performing on cliff-tops and in quarries, as well as in its physical style of acting where the cast all play multiple roles. And Darke's plays are equally typical in their working-class perspective, and in the parallels drawn with the present. Thus the 'King' of the smugglers lives up to his principle that 'if you break the law you've got to be honest' while the wealthy are corrupt, exploiting the poor. At the same time *The King Of Prussia* is a clear critique of Capitalism, while *The Riot* plays off current predatory over-fishing by the Spanish and – echoing the politicizing of the millennium – the characters continually use the 'upcoming nineteen undreds' as rhetoric to disguise commercial self-interest.

These elements made Community Theatre a logical continuation of Edgar's work for the conventional stage, though it took community involvement to a new level. Indeed, his first drama of this kind, *Entertaining Strangers* which centred on the great cholera outbreak of 1854, was specifically written for the townspeople of Sherbourne to perform – although it was later adapted for production at the National Theatre in 1987 (as was Nick Darke's *The Riot*, staged as a co-production by Kneehigh and the National Theatre in 1999). Reflecting the local knowledge of the inhabitants and with some 170 speaking parts, *Entertaining Strangers* was designed to 'revitalize' the community by generating social consciousness in a direct way that extended the aim of Edgar's earlier plays. It also offered 'a vision of theatre and art which is part of life'.[11]

However, the immediate results of the experience gained from adapting Dickens can be seen in *Maydays* (1983), which has an even greater historical scope than *Destiny* or even *Entertaining Strangers*. Dauntingly, *Maydays* spans political developments on the left from Moscow to California, in a chronological sequence that begins with a May-Day rally in London celebrating the victory over Nazi Germany in 1945 as the start of a socialist millennium, and ends with the Greenham Common anti-nuclear protest: a radical feminist 'peace camp' encircling a US Airforce base, which was much in the news during the play's performance.

As in *Destiny*, the situation is defined by parallel characters, but now the patterning only becomes clear in retrospect. A framework of expectations is established through the figure of Crowther. A working-class Marxist who proclaims the 'New Jerusalem', he breaks with the Party over Hungary in 1956, then rejects the anti-intellectualism of the 1968 student revolution, and ends up as the leading theorist in a right-wing think tank. His final conclusion is that 'our disease is not too little freedom but too much' – which is a near-quotation of an extract from *Conservative Essays* (Peregrine Worsthorne, 1978) cited in the RSC programme for the first production. This is the complete reverse of his original politics. But, as with the paired youths from *Destiny*, his opposite positions are in some aspects identical. Crowther's motivation remains the same throughout: the need to resolve the 'fundamental contradiction between the urge to make men equal and the need to keep them free'.[12] He has merely substituted liberty for liberation.

Crowther's switch from hard-Left to extreme Right is reinforced by another example from an older generation and a different society. The American father of a radical hippy appears as an apologist for Latin American military dictatorships, and a proponent of the Friedmanite economics that underpin the Conservative revival in Britain. However, we learn that the compromise with McCarthyism, which led him to this position, was in response to disillusion at the pogroms and death-camps in Stalin's Russia. Like Crowther in 1945, the American professor too began as a Communist in the 1930s. The parallel extends Crowther's progress from a personal change to a general trend. It thus becomes the standard against which the political development of the young protagonist is measured.

Born on 2 May 1945, the central figure of *Martin Glass* is metaphorically the child of the utopian vision announced in the opening. His name indicates both his function as a mirror of the times, and the way he sells out first libertarian comrades for the Marxist party line, then the doctrinaire Party for humanism, only to turn – a barometer of the political shift in society – to conservatism: 'Comrade Glass goes all transparent, and you cannot see him any more.' Closely based on Edgar's own experience as a political activist reacting against a privileged background, which he sees as representative of the 'many middle-class people [who] become revolutionaries simply through an *instinct* against social injustice', Glass also incorporates details from the lives of Edgar's contemporaries. For instance, the scene that introduces him as a schoolboy disciplined for pinning a Nuclear Disarmament badge on to his cadet uniform duplicates an early protest of David Hare, who wrote 'a letter of complaint to *Peace News*... because I wasn't allowed to wear my CND badge' during compulsory military training at his school.[13]

Up to the last scene, the positions Glass takes up are explicitly out of synchronization with Crowther. When Crowther becomes disillusioned with Soviet Communism, Glass quotes his own earlier Marxist affirmation back at him. When Crowther adopts the right-wing rhetoric of authoritarian discipline, along with the reintroduction of the death penalty, corporal punishment and military conscription that it implies, Glass uses Crowther's reason for rejecting the Marcusian revolutionaries of 1968/9 to define an antithetical stand. Conversely, Crowther justifies his reactionary Conservatism with the quotation that, for Glass, had summed up what was wrong with the ideology of the hard Left: 'Is it not Leon Trotsky who reminds us, there is such a thing as human dust?'[14] The intention is clearly to give a graph of ideals betrayed in the name of principle.

The cynicism of Glass's ultimate stance as the author of Conservative manifestoes is implied by the omission of any motivation for this final betrayal. But Edgar's moral weighting was generally overlooked. This was partly because of the autobiographical elements of the early sections, the hard-line Socialist Vanguard being clearly based on the International Socialists that Edgar joined in the early 1970s. However, the confusion is also due to Edgar's objectivity in analysing the causes of the general shift in society away from Socialism during the late 1970s and early 1980s, which is reflected in his characters.

The value of Crowther and Glass to the Right is that they are 'expert witnesses' who 'have *seen* the [Marxist vision of the] future, and ... *know* it doesn't work'; and the play was seen as offering the same 'testimony'. The

American professor is presented as 'a defector who would stand up publicly and argue not for the roll-back of the state but for the reassertion of its full authority'; and Edgar was considered to be filling the same role. As a result, Conservative reviewers hailed Edgar's apparent dismissal of 'the moral validity and relevance of Marxism' as 'an ideological breakthrough in the monolithic thinking processes of our Left-oriented theatre establishment', while the Left accused Edgar of 'no longer writing . . . for socialists. The majority of the [bourgeois] audience at the Barbican was having its prejudices confirmed.'[15]

For Glass, the uncritical adoption of Marxist ideology means that 'as once again the proofs pile up that we are catastrophically wrong, we change the question . . .' – so that 'to be a communist you must purge yourself of the instincts and beliefs that made you one'.[16] Yet the fact that his denunciation is indeed amply demonstrated by the action does not imply that Edgar approves his protagonist's switch to the extreme Right. The real theme of the play is embodied in the wider structure of the action, which contradicts the political pattern exemplified by the main characters.

The history of revolutionary activism in London or California is paralleled by scenes of dissent behind the Iron Curtain. The spectacle of Russian troops crushing the Hungarian uprising provides a direct commentary on the London radicals' affirmation that Communism means the liberation of the exploited. The empty spot in Red Square, where a handful of demonstrators against the suppression of freedom in Poland and Czechoslovakia have been beaten and arrested by the KGB, is juxtaposed with a student demonstration at the University of Leeds. And both are dismissed as 'ridiculous' by characters who claim to sympathize in principle.

The development of the central figure in these scenes runs counter to Glass's progress. An officer in the Russian army, who finds it impossible to reconcile the Soviet role in Budapest with his conscience, he becomes a dissident. Imprisoned, he is exiled (like Solzhenitsyn) to the West, where he joins Crowther, Glass and the American professor on the platform for authoritarian government. Realizing the repressive basis of 'The Committee in Defence of Liberty', however, he discards the speech supporting it, which has been written for him. Instead, he takes a moral stand against 'the same variety of people – who applaud' the coercive control of the population 'on their own side – but oppose it on the other'.[17]

At the same time Glass is contrasted with the female activist, who leads him into joining the Socialist Vanguard. Although rejecting the party for exactly the same reasons, she maintains her idealism. Linked with the Russian dissident through her commitment to remembering 'the superhuman things that human beings can and have achieved . . . when for a moment they forget what they've been told they are' (which directly anticipates Glass's final declaration of his Conservative principles), she becomes a radical feminist. And the last scene brings her into direct conflict with what Glass has come to represent. Whereas his first gesture of protest had been in the cause of nuclear disarmament, now (as the owner of his parents' house adjoining Greenham Common) he opposes the women camped outside the cruise missile base.

Her declaration of the necessity for resisting 'a world that is demonstrably and in this case dramatically wrong and mad and unjust' is theatrically underlined by the sirens and searchlights of a practice alert, creating the threatening impression of mobile launchers driving forward towards the audience behind the wire fence of the base. Simultaneously the possibility of positive action, even in the most unfavourable circumstances, is indicated by a final glimpse of two Russians in Moscow, preparing to distribute a manifesto 'For our freedom – and for yours', despite the certain knowledge that they will be imprisoned for doing so.[18]

Within this structure of contrasting parallels, mirror images and inversions, repeated phrases serve as thematic leitmotifs. Betrayal, and the inhuman principle of ends justifying means, are encapsulated in 'Red Barcelona' and the 'Five Days in May', when the Communists liquidated their Catalonian anarchist allies. These slogans are set against the short-lived Paris Commune and the 'Nine Days in May' of the 1926 General Strike in Britain, which represent utopian possibilities of establishing a Socialist state. 'Kronstadt' (where the Russian sailors who had overthrown the Tsar were slaughtered to ensure the complete control of the Soviets) stands for the crisis of conscience that leads each of the protagonists to reject doctrinaire Communism.

The meaning of these clusters of ideas expands with each recurrence, serving as keys for evaluating the morality of an argument or action: in particular, Trotsky's phrase 'human dust'. So 'Revolutions are the festival of the oppressed and the exploited' – quoted out of context, Lenin's original comment being that although revolutions might seem like festivals, their consequences are catastrophic – changes its significance as the blindness of revolutionary enthusiasm becomes clear.

The ambiguity of the play's title, explicitly played on at the close of the first section where 'all the May Days' of socialist triumph and martyrdom are balanced by the cry for help of 'Mayday Mayday', is resolved in the

'Maybe..."May Days"' of the last line. For Edgar the conclusion was an 'unambiguous, untrammeled confirmation of what I believe which...sits itself firmly down on our [feminist/socialist] side of the Greenham Common wire'.[19] But in place of direct statement imposing a 'correct' interpretation (as, say, in Arden's or Bond's later plays), the structure is designed to guide spectators into arriving at the right conclusion individually. And this is signalled by deploying an exaggeration of conventional Agitprop endings – *'Red flags fly, red banners swirl, red streamers billow. "The Internationale" plays'* – as the opening scene, which the subsequent action progressively undercuts.

In *Destiny*, the situations were intended to 'force people to think in the theatre like they think when they watch current affairs programmes on television or read the newspapers'. More clearly still, the dynamics of *Maydays* confront an audience (who are assumed to have lived through the same period as the protagonist) with their own emotional response to the events. The blend of fictional characters into factual situations corresponds to what Edgar has defined as 'faction', in being 'based very closely and authentically on real subject matter'.[20] This objectivity (indicated by the reviewers' freedom to interpret the play according to individual prejudice) even carries through into the affirmative conclusion, with a question mark being set against the positive action of the feminists by their sacrifice of personality to militant aims. Their declaration that 'we have no names' is backed by the anonymous designation of 1ST, 2ND and 3RD WOMAN in the script. Yet the weight of the action has clearly defined liberty in terms of the value of individuals. *Maydays* fulfils Edgar's prescription that socialist drama should move from

The macrocosm to the microcosm, from the unequal relations of classes to the unequal relations of individuals...if the left is seriously to address society's present and its own recent past, then personal behaviour cannot remain off political limits. After all, the connection between the two was *our* slogan, *our* insight...[21]

Edgar's move after this into Community Theatre represents a return to the social macrocosm in a very direct way, but his next play for the conventional stage returned to the questioning of the socialist movement and its personal dimensions. Rather than the panoramic view of *Maydays*, *The Shape of the Table* (1990) deals with an immediate current event: the collapse of Communism in Eastern Europe. In doing so Edgar was paralleling Howard Brenton, whose *Moscow Gold* (with Tariq Ali) had appeared earlier the same year – but in sharp contrast to their cartoon treatment. Edgar, while fascinated by 'the great events in the streets; bells in Prague, the flags with the holes cut in the middle in Romania', focuses on 'the detailed reality of the negotiations . . . going on in the meeting rooms' and his presentation is completely naturalistic. The only overt symbolism comes from the table of the title, a single cloth-covered expanse of crisp white laid with formal settings in the first half of the play, standing for the sham purity of the Communist regime, its apparent monolithic unity and its rigidity, which is revealed to be made up of '*a number of smaller tables of modern manufacture*' once the revolutionaries enter and the cloth is stripped away. These are progressively separated in each of the following scenes, representing the fragmentation of the one-Party system and forming patterns that reflect the manoeuvres in the developing struggle for power. As the soon-to-be ousted Prime Minister (characterized by Edgar as a 'reasonably liberal-minded but basically machine Communist') remarks, 'things aren't always what they seem'.[22]

Setting the 1989 events in the context of an uprising a generation earlier that had been violently suppressed by the Russians – Hungary in 1956, or Poland in 1981 – he comments that 'As Marx perceptively reminds us, the events of history occurring twice. First time as tragedy, the second time as farce'. The phrase is clearly meant to be a valid judgement (Edgar having taken it as the title for his book *The Second Time as Farce: Reflections on the Drama of Mean Times*); and the play is intended to support the deposed First Secretary, who declares that Communism did not fail because 'the working class weren't up to it. It was that we weren't up to it . . . It was pilot error. Nothing wrong with the machine.' He is given moral weight by the past, when he faced the Nazis across the same room and suffered as a political prisoner in Buchenwald for his vision of 'futures of unimaginable scale and splendour, in which the immense and boundless untapped energies and talents of the masses would be liberated' – and while this may now look like a 'fairytale', the new forces of liberation are explicitly shown to have no compelling alternative. Although Edgar defined the theme of the play as an open question, 'what is it that has failed: a system, or individuals, or a whole idea of human nature?', the vision and even the system are validated.[23] It is individuals (again following his principle of expressing the political in terms of the personal) who are responsible; and indeed, as so often in Edgar's plays, apparent opposites are paralleled. The Communist leader and the poet at the head of the democratic movement who replaces him both make identical gestures. At the beginning the poet had burned a pardon, preferring to stay in prison than compromise his ideals; and at the end the former First Secretary does exactly the same. But while creating viable drama, here this focus on the individual becomes a substitute for political analysis, although some balance is created by subtextual imagery with the mirrors that lined the walls of the Nazi era being replaced by the dirty windows that shut the Communist regime off from the people, rioting in the streets, and the poet-leader of the democratic revolution having earned his living as a window-cleaner. At the same time, this is clearly meant to be an archetypal representation of ideas, rather than a dramatization of specific events. The new President of this unnamed East Bloc country is modelled on Vaclav Havel of Poland, while the old liberalizer whose revolution was crushed by Russian tanks is the equivalent of Dubcek in Hungary, and the name of the opposition grouping (Public Platform) echoes the Civic Forum of Czechoslovakia. And as a debate on the transfer of power the play gained coincidental relevance from the forced resignation of Mrs Thatcher, which occurred during its run at the National Theatre.

In *The Shape of the Table* Edgar forecasts the democratic movements of the former Communist Bloc descending into racist violence and anti-Semitism. *Pentecost* (1994) picks up on this – in the year of Sarajevo – and offers tentative hope of a possible solution. Like David Hare's *The Bay at Nice* or Alan Bennett's *A Question of Attribution*, it merges intellectual discussion about the authenticity of art with topical politics. Here the painting provides a visually dominating and imaginatively precise symbol for Edgar's major themes. The fresco, and the church itself in which it has been discovered, incorporate the concepts of history as a palimpsest, culture transcending boundaries, and the utilitarian functions of art. The building's chequered past, from a place of Christian worship (Catholic as well as Orthodox) and a mosque, to a Nazi holding cell for Jews being transported to the death camps, or simply a storehouse for potatoes, sums up the disastrous national experience of what a young female art curator from its National Museum calls an 'ugly and pathetic' country on the edge of Europe; and this is inscribed on the wall, where a typical social realist image of heroic workers triumphantly waving a huge red flag has been painted over a twelfth-century mural of the Lamentation of the Virgin. The iconography of this original work, subtly different from the painting by Giotto which first introduced perspective into Western art, leads to the conclusion – through an etymological discovery of the word 'rock' in Italian being the same as one for 'Star' in an ancient Eastern language (in fact invented by Edgar) – that the artist was an Arab, influenced by Islam. In turn this graphically illustrates the thesis that cultural advances come from cross-fertilization and that the major innovators are outsiders. As one of the art experts points out, perspective in painting marks the start of the Renaissance and the modern worldview that 'not God but Man is the measure of all things'; and since (in Edgar's parable) it also pre-dates Giotto, the fresco's discovery means rewriting the whole history of Western civilization. As such it will give this tiny unnamed country (now revealed as the true birthplace of the Renaissance) a national identity to stand against Hollywood culture and Coca Cola-colonialism, or if removed, as the Minister of Preservation wants, to the National Museum it will attract tourist dollars to solve the bankrupt country's economic problems – functional values trumping aesthetics, as they do later in the play when the painting becomes a 'hostage' for refugees seeking citizenship in the West. However, ironically, for the fresco to serve any ulterior purpose, recent history in the shape of the Communist mural has to be erased, and with it the names scratched on the plaster by the Jewish prisoners. And as the magistrate deciding whether the fresco should stay in the church or be removed to the National Museum powerfully argues:

Worst story that I ever hear, in second world war, Serb children are transport to camp at Jansenovac, and they are so hungry that they eat the cardboard tags around their neck. Which is their family, their age, their name. They eat their history. They die and nobody remember them . . . we must remember. We must not eat our names.[24]

Yet the lesson drawn by the curator, that 'We are the sum of all the people who've invaded us', takes on unexpected meaning. The present bursts violently in on this consideration of the past: first in the invasion by armed refugee-terrorists, whose multilingual group stands for the new Diaspora. With each a different nationality – a single Sri Lankan, an African, a Kurd, and a Turk, along with a Bosnian gypsy family, led by a Palestinian girl, all speaking their own tongues to add to the language of the fictional country (for which Edgar uses Bulgarian) – the church becomes a tower of Babel, where the only communication can come through English spoken imperfectly as a second language. This, Edgar implies, is the new world order indicated by the play's title. It is the contemporary equivalent of Pentecost, which in the Bible celebrates the descent of the Holy Spirit on Christ's disciples, allowing all to understand without giving up their own linguistic identity. It is also in total contrast to the failed ideal of Communism, that Edgar defined as 'a sort of Esperanto, trying to create a perfect language without any of the problems existing in language'.[25] And at the end, after the final and even more cataclysmic irruption by German-speaking assault troops (ironically ordered in by the Minister for Preservation) who break through the wall, completely destroying the fresco itself and shooting one of the hostages they are meant to liberate, the surviving art expert and the curator begin painstakingly learning a common language by reading single words from a book: 'huddled'; 'yearning'; 'free' – which echo the inscription on the Statue of Liberty, 'Give me your huddled masses, yearning to breathe free.'

Different languages and individual identity are assumed to be inseparable; and Edgar explicitly made the point in a BBC interview that while Marxism was heroic in its attempt to create a mutual dependence between all people, it had failed because this meant pretending that differences between people didn't exist. Yet this theme in the play is undercut by the symbolic weight placed on clothing. A hostage is shot because the refugees had forced him, and the others, to exchange clothes with them – and this forces them to see things from the viewpoint of their captors. Towards the end the point is reinforced by the magistrate, who suggests 'national costume' for the 'march to next millennium' and explains 'How Communism strip away all culture from our past, and clothe us all instead in uniform' – a speech given particular weight by Edgar's reuse of the imagery on television: 'Communism attempted to strip us all down to nakedness and start again. The solution was putting people in uniform as opposed to working with . . . the accretion of clothes, things we have developed over time'.[26] Other symbols too are overweighted with meaning that turns out to be contradictory. One of these is the wall carrying the superimposed paintings. As the curator removes bricks a hole appears in the red flag of the workers' mural, in a vivid reminder of all the flags with the Communist symbols cut out of the centre during the overthrow of the system in 1989. Once the refugees break in we are faced with the question of whether art has any value when living people are literally up against the wall. And finally, when the commandos burst through leaving a gaping hole, we are meant to see this simultaneously in terms of the collapse of the Berlin Wall, the oppression of the East and the gratuitous destruction of culture and history by the West (far worse than the Communists, who only painted over the fresco), and a window of opportunity for creating something new by people who have been completely liberated from the past.

Despite all this symbolism, and the stereotypical nature of the refugees, the major figures who present the arguments of *Pentecost* are fully individualized; and playing on the artistic perspective that opened up the Renaissance, audiences are presented with constantly shifting perspectives that unite form and theme. At the same time the emotions generated by the ending – elation (in the discovery of the origin of the fresco, a moment of unity between hostages and refugees and of love between the curator and the more sympathetic of the art experts) immediately followed by loss (his death as well as the destruction of the art that has been given increasing importance) – are powerfully effective. And the combination of these elements makes it Edgar's most successful play. As his last work to date it also rounds out a career in following exactly the same performance pattern as his first public success, *Destiny*: both being staged first at the small Other Place theatre in Stratford, then transferring to a long run in London.

In all of Edgar's later plays theme and dramatic form overlap. The intended nature of the audience response is echoed in the way they focus on the subjective reaction of representative figures. A broad analysis of society is achieved without sacrificing individual detail. These qualities substantially justify Edgar's claim to have created a new style of realism, where spectators 'would recognize the characters from the inside, but be able, simultaneously, like a sudden film-cut from close-up to wide-angle, to look at how these individual journeys were defined by the collective journey of an epoch'.[27] And the fact that Hare's *Map of the World* (staged in the same year as *Maydays*) incorporates precisely this kind of cinematic montage, is no coincidence. Indeed in many ways Edgar's development parallels Hare; and while his dramatic output has been far less, his indirect influence may prove to have a greater impact on English theatre in the new millennium since from 1989 on he has run courses on playwriting at Birmingham University. And these gained a reputation that attracted several promising dramatists.

Notes

1 Edgar, *Tribune*, 22 April 1977, where he defines 'providing information' as the primary function of his Agitprop drama; and in *New Theatre Voices of the Seventies*, ed. Simon Trussler, London, 1981, p. 162.

2 Brenton, *Theatre Quarterly*, 17 (1975), p. 18. (For a full discussion of British Agitprop theatre in the 1970s, see Catherine Itzen, *Stages in the Revolution*, London, 1980.)

3 Edgar, in *New Theatre Voices of the Seventies*, ed. Trussler, p. 171. (Although not referring specifically to Arden's later work, the comment relates directly to *The Ballygombeen Bequest* or *The Non-Stop Connolly Show*.)

4 Edgar, in *New Theatre Voices of the Seventies*, ed. Trussler, p. 167.

5 Edgar, 'Public Theatre in a Private Age', BTI/DATEC no. 1, Autumn 1984 (as he also commented, 'that is a technique of agitprop writing': cited in Itzen,

Stages in the Revolution, p. 146); *Financial Times*, 29 September 1976, and *Drama*, Summer 1977, p. 58.

6 Edgar, in BTI/DATEC.

7 Edgar, *Destiny*, London, 1976, pp. 70, 96.

8 Edgar, in *Tribune*, 22 April 1977.

9 *Destiny*, p. 84.

10 Edgar, interview with the author, April 1986.

11 Anne Jellicoe, Preface to *Entertaining Strangers*, London, 1986, pp. 5 and 3.

12 Edgar, *Maydays*, London, 1983, pp. 74, 122.

13 *Maydays*, p. 86; Edgar, *New Theatre Voices of the Seventies*, ed. Trussler, p. 159, and Hare, *ibid.*, p. 111.

14 *Maydays*, pp. 97–8.

15 *Ibid.*, p. 120; *Standard* and *Tribune*, reprinted in *London Theatre Record*, 8–21, 1983, pp. 911 and 906.

16 *Maydays*, p. 140.

17 *Ibid.*, p. 137.

18 *Ibid.*, pp. 60, 138, 146, 141.

19 *Ibid.*, pp. 60 & 147; Edgar, in BTI/DATEC.

20 *Maydays*, p. 14; Edgar, cited in Itzin, *Stages in the Revolution*, p. 145, and in *New Theatre Voices of the Seventies*, ed. Trussler, p. 168.

21 *Maydays*, p. 145; Edgar, 'The Morals Dilemma' in *The Second Time as Farce: Reflections on the Drama of Mean Times*, London, 1988, p. 53.

22 Edgar, 'Ideology in the Red' in the *Guardian*, 3 May 1990; *The Shape of the Table*, London, 1990, pp. 8, 48; and Edgar, cited in *Plays and Players*, November 1990, p. 7.

23 *The Shape of the Table*, pp. 80, 89, 79; and Edgar, interview in *Independent on Sunday*, 4 November 1990.

24 *Pentecost*, London, 1994, pp. 38, 10, 75.

25 *Ibid.*, p. 104; Edgar, cited by Susan Painter in *Edgar the Playwright*, London, 1996, p. 150.

26 Edgar on The Late Show, BBC2, 9 November 1994; *Pentecost*, p. 104.

27 *Maydays*, p. 145; Edgar, in BTI/DATEC.

3.11 Howard Brenton and David Hare: utopian perspectives on modern history

By contrast to other Agitprop groups that emerged after 1968, Portable Theatre had 'a *very* bad record with working class audiences', as David Hare himself acknowledged. Their touring performances in factories and workers' clubs came to be seen as 'aggro dates': arousing mutual hostility instead of political solidarity.[1] Unlike John McGrath's 7:84 Theatre or The General

Will Company, which picked issues of direct relevance to their immediate audience, their focus tended to be cultural. David Edgar's scripts for The General Will picked up on the economic concerns of specific social groups (as in *Rent*, which was staged for local Community Associations, and *The Case of the Worker's Plane*, performed for aircraft machinists, 1971–2). Hare's plays from the same period – *Slag* (1970), *The Great Exhibition* (1972) – deal with female teachers at a private girls' school, who protest against social injustice by renouncing sex, and with a Labour MP who opts out of the parliamentary system in a futile attempt to escape from public corruption.

Although both Hare and Brenton collaborated with Edgar and other straight Agitprop playwrights of the time on group scripts, such as *Lay By* (1971, about the relationship between capitalism and pornography) and *England's Ireland* (which used British imperialism to illustrate the oppressive nature of class society, 1972), they had already moved away from the informational/poster-and-slogan playlets of their radical contemporaries. Instead, Brenton and Hare formed a fifth column within the conventional theatre. Consciously developing the aggression that their Portable work had produced, to express 'a basic contempt for people who go to the theatre', they acted as a catalyst at the Royal Court (where Hare served as literary manager in 1969) by mounting plays to attack the 'humanist tradition' of social drama. *The Great Exhibition*, for instance, parodied the archetypal Royal Court play, while even *Lay By* juxtaposed 'every phoney humanistic statement that you could hear in the theatre from our elder playwrights' (e.g. Osborne and Wesker) with images of sexual violence.[2]

Turning performances into acts of provocation like this expressed a sense of outrage – and frustration – as the revolution promised by 1968 failed to materialize. Social protest turned in upon itself, to become an attack on mainstream theatre and its audience; and the confusion of aims was graphically (if unintentionally) expressed in the ending of Brenton's *Fruit* (1970). Proposing petrol bombs as the right way to destroy the political system, the activist in the play constructs one on stage, giving technical instructions while he does so. Brenton's intention is clearly to enable spectators to go home and make their own – yet the petrol bomb is thrown through the proscenium arch at the audience. The potential fellow revolutionaries are the ones assaulted. At the same time, the destructive properties of an actual explosion were trivialized as pyro-technical effects, implying that violent revolution could be painlessly achieved.

Over the following decade, the effectiveness of direct activism on the stage was denied by political events – in particular the fragmentation of the Left, and the repeated election of Thatcher's Conservatives: a government that, viewed from a socialist perspective, was even more reactionary than its predecessors. Not only had Agitprop plays failed to change the power structure. Judging by the shift in voting patterns they could actually be seen as counter-productive in their basic aim of fostering political awareness. This was underlined by David Hare during a conference on political theatre at Cambridge in 1978 (announcing the demise of the Agitprop movement, ironically at the very moment when, after ten years, it had gained academic recognition). As Hare pointed out,

consciousness has been raised in this country for a good many years now and we seem further from radical political change than at any time in my life. The traditional function of the radical artist – 'Look at those Borgias; look at this bureaucracy' – has been undermined. We have looked. We have seen. We have known. And we have not changed.[3]

The more directly the stage attempted to intervene in reality, the further it became reduced to theatrical gesture, as with *Fruit*. And this realization has even led Brenton to an outright rejection of Agitprop in *Greenland* (1988). There a street performance by a radical feminist group is presented as farce, and shown to be motivated by personal rancours that marginalize any political relevance.

In addition, Hare (like Edgar) had come to realize that 'the values of presentation' in conventional theatre 'were actually enabling writers to say richer and more complex things than they would have been able to if, like me, they were bundling an exhausted travelling company out of a van and on to an open floor'.[4] Dealing with broader social questions than the single-issue Agitprop required more sophisticated techniques and equipment. To offset the increased investment in time and production costs, a wider public forum was needed in place of the immediate contact with small groups of localized spectators. This automatically led back to mainstream stages, or even to the commercially dominated medium of television. After having plays produced at the Royal Court, Edgar began writing for the RSC, while Hare moved to the National Theatre, and Brenton has worked for both companies. Even so, this shift marked a change in means rather than aims. Their political perspective remained the same, Marxist-radical, and their formative experience in the Agitprop movement continued to influence their drama, effectively redefining realism on the stage.

In the long rhetorical tradition of theatre, Naturalism is to some extent an aberration, although it became the dominant style for plays on social themes from Robertson's 'cup-and-saucer' drama in the nineteenth century to Rattigan or Wesker. It had long been recognized that Ibsen's aim 'to create the illusion of reality' was paradoxical. With the impact of the events of May 1968 and exposure to the French Situationists, for whom all public appearances were a sham and social norms simply promoted class interests, any mimetic representation on the stage had become questionable. The naturalistic attempt to persuade audiences that a scene was an actual place, or a performance a slice of life, was rejected as corresponding to the Establishment's political deception of its public. Authenticity demanded stylistic integrity. This meant avoiding theatrical illusion, and exposing the stage as the realistic basis for any image of society. It justified characterization by social attitude (instead of individualized traits of personality), and the structuring of scenes to express a thematic statement (rather than according to the internal logic of the action).

Hare's *Fanshen* (1975) demonstrates these elements in an extreme form, combining Documentary with Agitprop. The actors not only introduce the figures they represent, but emphasize that they are re-enacting historical events by giving the source from which the material is taken:

(*holding up a copy*): This is the book *Fanshen* by William Hinton./I am Yu-Lai, an ex-bandit . . . This is a record of one village's life between 1945 and 1949. Many of the characters are still alive.[5]

The concern for accuracy was reflected by the way the original focus of Hare's script (the intrinsic human need for justice and desire for a just society) was changed because it did not correspond to Hinton's views (that morality is class-determined and justice a bourgeois concept).

Conventional dramatic conflict was restricted to ideological tensions, with statements of principle being set against observed practice. There were no protagonists. Indeed, individuals were indistinguishable from the community; and this absence of personal characterization was emphasized by extensive doubling, with facial transformations and simple changes of cap or sash indicating the switch between the various parts taken by each performer. The dialogue avoided linguistic richness, verbal irony and rhetoric, being restricted to 'the meaning of what is being said' in order to create an English equivalent of 'Ur Chinese'.[6] The stage was an empty space, the floor of a hall surrounded by spectators on three sides in close proximity to the actors, with a raised platform for mimed scenes. There were no lighting

7 Minimalist staging and group characterization: the Joint Stock production of Hare's *Fanshen*

changes to indicate distinctions between day and night, interior or exterior. Sets were limited to placard-slogans designating activities – 'Asking Basic Questions'; 'They Talked For Three Days' – and banners carrying texts that summarized the political point of a scene. There were only the minimum of stage props: material goods, the possession or lack of which determines the different figures' attitude to social change. In the context of rural China these could be convincingly limited to a small number of basic objects, such as a pair of buckets hung from a shoulder-yoke, a sack of grain or a hoe. Their simplicity not only illustrated the poverty of the peasants that brings them to revolt against their exploiters, but provides a tangible image of the dialectical materialism that underlies the play.

The sparse minimalism served as a continual reminder that the audience are watching a model: not the reproduction of real life, but a theatrical demonstration. On the most obvious level the Chinese revolution – and the argument in the play – concerns the redistribution of property, with the criteria of class rights being replaced by need, then communal ownership. This leads to the recognition that control of resources is a tool for creating equality, not the result of it. 'Land reform can't be a final solution to men's problems. Land reform is just a step opening the way to socialism. And socialism itself is transitional'.[7] The title encompasses change in its broadest sense. The word 'Fanshen' (literally meaning to turn the body) relates political revolution to a traditional Chinese metaphor where the peasant with a hoe, bowed over by the weight of three symbolic mountains on his back (war, landowners and bureaucracy), only has to change his physical posture to free himself. This image frames a play in which material things are literally subordinated to ideas.

The opening scene of a peasant hoeing in the field is repeated at the end, but we see it differently: the physical figure is the same, but internally everything has changed. Almost the only real-time action occurs in the violence at the beginning. Later scenes of physical conflict are presented as silent tableaux, illustrating an objective narration of the events, so that the focus is on discussion. Classification meetings define attitudes; leaders confess mistakes at public tribunals, only to have the judgement of the people overturned as counter-productive; repeated debates educate the peasants. In the cause of remaking the community everything is open to examination: 'How are we to make sure this time, in this tight circle, the overturning holds?/The difference is, this time, we think. We ask questions.'[8]

The structure of the play, where exposition is followed by example, is highly intellectual; and the questioning attitude was also carried through in rehearsals, establishing a process that became standard practice for Joint Stock Company productions and influenced Caryl Churchill's early work (see below, pp. 235–36). To overcome the difficulties of presenting such un-conventional material, where the characters had little personality and much of the dialogue appeared static, the techniques of self-criticism and demo-cratic discussion typical of the Chinese Revolution were applied to the acting group. As the nominal directors William Gaskill and Max Stafford-Clark tes-tified, this forced the performers to abandon characterization as the source of their roles. Instead they substituted the political process documented by the action, replacing directorial authority with the evolving consciousness of the group. As a result, the values of the drama were 'reflected in the show that emerges', and 'vindicated in the end product' to such a degree that Hare came to view this working method as inseparable from the play:

the production of this play must involve you in the continual definition of your objectives and the continual asking of questions ... the production techniques must mirror the fanshen itself.[9]

Even the typical Agitprop finale was tailored to fit this requirement, despite its ecstatic appeal in 'a superb massive groundswell of music that consumes the stage', backed by banners flooding the acting area with red and daz-zling light that blurred the figures of the triumphant Chinese villagers. The Agitprop enthusiasm expresses the feelings of the characters. It remains within the dramatic context of the Chinese revolution, rather than becom-ing a proclamation by the actors. And the audience are left with general questions to crystallize their response to the action.

Tell me.
Let me know what you think.
What do you think about this?

Although the aim was clearly to evoke emotional affirmation for the 'positive models for change' incorporated in the action, there is no attempt to draw comparisons to contemporary British society. The distant foreign environ-ment is itself an 'alienating' factor that encourages spectators to 'make their own analogies, about political leadership'.[10]

Precisely because it lay so far outside the audience's experience, the Chinese revolution could be taken as a positive model from which general political principles were to be deduced. But this in itself created difficul-ties, since it ignored the expectation (specifically catered to, for example, in Brecht's historical parables) that drama should in some way project the immediate social context. It also raised a deeper problem of authenticity. The desirability of revolution in England, posited by the play, is 'proved' by the Chinese example. Yet, as Hinton himself discovered on revisiting the area, his Chinese informants had lied to him when he was there in the 1950s, falsifying the story of the village's communization described in his original book. Despite contact with Hinton, Hare appears not to have known this, although Hinton's sequel revealing the deception was published shortly after the first production. But if the 'facts' are wrong – even though they may have been honestly believed by the Joint Stock Company – this discredits the political conclusions drawn from them.

Fanshen was a one-off experiment, despite its effectiveness as a play. Productions were mounted in Germany, the United States and Canada, while it reached a wide English audience through a televised performance. However, along with Brenton, Hare himself moved in a different direction; and their development is well illustrated by their second major collaboration (the first being *Brassneck*, an attack on local government corruption which they co-wrote in 1973). This was *Pravda* (1985), where they anatomized the corruption of truth by the newspaper establishment, combining Agitprop characterization with far subtler techniques of structure and presentation.

Subtitled 'A Fleet Street Comedy', *Pravda* follows a well-meaning journalist's career from cub-reporter on a small, family-owned provincial daily, to prize-winning editor of the leading national paper: a position he attains as a reward for first going along with the sell-out of his first boss to a foreign tycoon (loosely modelled on Rupert Murdoch), then supporting the tycoon's duplicitous takeover of the Fleet Street flagship (clearly analogous to *The Times*). Goaded by his wife, the daughter of the provincial newspaper-owner, Andrew decides to print a leaked government document (echoing a well-publicized incident of the time). The rabidly right-wing tycoon, who fires him on the spot, makes his moral stand pointless by preventing its publication; and Andrew helps to found an independent paper dedicated to printing the truth, in competition. But his obsession with revenge loses him his wife (one of Hare's many idealistic female figures of conscience) and causes him to print libellous fabrications, which put him at the tycoon's mercy. And he ends up compromising totally with the system – as the only game in town – running the sleaziest of the gutter tabloids, a broken shell. Each step has been a descent, from the pastoral opening to a manic hell.

This morality-play progress is used to expose various degrees of untruth from factual inaccuracy, through editorial distortion, to forged evidence and outright lies. In the picture given of the Press, style and layout are more important than substance; circulation and sensationalism have become the only criteria. Information is strangled by deadlines, or stifled by government pressure. Reporters are corrupted by ambition and the fear of losing their jobs. The Press Barons are power-mad crypto-fascists who exercise total control, while the print unions are industrial wreckers (though their self-serving practices are here justified by the cynicism of the material printed and its opposition to their political interests).

Such accusations are hardly new. Similar points had been made in Osborne's *World of Paul Slickey* twenty-five years before, while 'the foundry of lies' depicted in the final scene is almost a parody of *The Front Page*: an exposure of American popular journalism by Ben Hecht and Charles MacArthur staged in 1928. Even the underlying critique of *Pravda* had already been defined by Arnold Wesker, although his dramatization of the way lies distort the personalities of those who promote them (*The Journalists*, 1975) had not been staged in London: 'The cigarette packet warns that smoking can be dangerous to health; no newspaper carries the warning, daily, that "selective attention to data herein contained can be a danger to your view of the world".'[11]

However, in this case the real target is Capitalism. By showing how journalists co-operate in their own enslavement, Hare and Brenton intend to make the audience realize that only the public's active complicity – whatever their profession – makes the system possible. Fleet Street is only a metaphor; and this is underlined by Hare and Brenton's reversion to cartoon characterization. Names that stand for social type or stock attitude – Fruit-Norton, Quince, Fantom, Scroop, 'Whipper' Wellington, or Whicker-Basket – correspond to traditional farce, while the demonic villain 'totally without morality' is straight Agitprop. The racist South African entrepreneur, Le Roux, belongs to nineteenth-century melodrama. Unredeemably evil, he is also omnipotent. Those who stand out against him are fired, and he dominates the political establishment through his support for the status quo. His combination of ruthless brutality and malicious cunning is demonstrated when he wishes to get rid of competition. Instead of buying up a newspaper that provides an opposing political line, in order to close it down, he manipulates the journalists he has dispossessed into acquiring it, plays on their hatred to feed them false information about his past, then bankrupts their paper with a libel suit.

At the same time, this kind of melodramatic farce undercuts the serious social criticism. The open analogy between Murdoch as the owner of *The Times*, and the colonial capitalist Le Roux, is trivialized by the degree of exaggeration, which also rules out any convincing dramatic conflict. The name of Andrew May implies that the (anti-) hero is a potential for change – and this is reinforced by Le Roux's acknowledgement that 'from you alone there is a trace of resistance'. Yet the dominance of the villain and the plot-line, which depends on Andrew's abandonment of one principle after another, reduce the claim that *Pravda* depicts the true state of affairs to an empty gesture.

The aim of the play is to reveal the reality of the system, by embodying it in a corporate megalomaniac; and the title points to its double focus. As the official Soviet news-organ, 'Pravda' not only compares the situation in England to the USSR, where at the time the Press was a totally State-controlled propaganda sheet. In Russian it also has the literal meaning of 'the truth'. As Hare commented, Fleet Street is intended as an example of 'the political climate, where competition reigns unchecked'; and again this is made explicit by the villain.

No one tells the truth. Why single out newspapers? Why there? 'Oh! A special standard!' Everyone can tell lies except newspapers. They're the universal scapegoat for everybody else's evasions and inadequacies.[12]

Yet symbolizing Capitalism in a stock figure makes the general analysis un-convincingly simplistic, breaking the connections between the news industry and the political whole.

Despite this, the technique gives *Pravda* a compelling theatrical vitality. Under Hare's direction Le Roux's role was a *tour de force* of manic energy and simian brutality, clearly intended to provoke the audience's repulsion: the Capitalist as psychopath. So that his henchman's judgement, 'I've never met one who didn't go crazy. It's power. He's developed extra-ordinary physical aggressiveness. He hits people with poles. Literally' – will be unquestioningly accepted by the spectators, just as it is by Andrew.

This knee-jerk response, calling on political clichés, is deliberate. Seeing the tycoon as an insane villain, puts spectators in the same position as the dispossessed journalists whose emotions warp their perception of reality. As Le Roux himself explicitly states,

You never began to try and understand me. To see what I wanted. Which was quite simple. To show you all reality. So much easier to believe that I was a criminal. I'm no criminal. Your judgement went. The very thought of me drove you mad . . . See things as they truly are. I bring you reality. None of you admits it. See it as it is. To everyone I pose a question. I am the question.

ANDREW And what is the answer?
LE ROUX People like you.

The accusation is levelled equally against the audience.

In Hare's opinion, plays have taken over the function of the Press since 'journalism, however intelligent, will always fail you. It is glib by nature. Words can *only* be tested by being spoken. Ideas can *only* be worked in real situations. That is why the theatre is the best court [of justice] society has.'[13]

Howard Brenton (1942–): authenticity and alternative politics

CHECKLIST OF BRENTON'S MAJOR PLAYS

Christie in Love, 1969
Fruit, 1970
A Sky Blue Life, 1971
Hitler Dances, 1972
Magnificence, 1973
Brassneck (with Hare), 1973
The Churchill Play, 1974
A Saliva Milkshake, 1975
Weapons of Happiness, 1976
Epsom Downs, 1977
The Romans in Britain, 1980

Thirteenth Night, 1981
Bloody Poetry, 1984
Pravda (with Hare), 1985
Greenland, 1988
Iranian Nights (with Tariq Ali), 1989
Moscow Gold (with Tariq Ali), 1990
Berlin Bertie, 1992
Ugly Rumours (with Tariq Ali), 1998
Collateral Damage (with Tariq Ali, Andy de la Tour), 1999

Expressed in bare stages and episodic action, on the surface Brenton and Hare's work appeared Brechtian: an impression reinforced by the stage design of Hayden Griffiths. Developing a spartan, presentational style under Jocelyn Herbert, whose work on Osborne and Arden at the Royal Court had been influenced by the Berliner Ensemble, Griffiths provided the settings for Brenton's *Weapons of Happiness* (1976), Hare's *Plenty* (1978), *A Map of the World* (1983) and his collaboration with Brenton in *Pravda* (1985) – as well as the designs for many of Bond's major plays, from *Narrow Road to the Deep North* in 1968, through *Bingo* (1974) and *The Woman* (1978), to *Restoration* in 1981. Despite the superficial similarity this imposed, comparisons with Brecht (or Bond) are misleading. Brenton in particular had already rejected Brecht by the end of the 1960s (although he later adapted Brecht's *Galileo* for the National Theatre).

Finding Brecht's Epic theatre too limiting and artificial, Brenton was experimenting with very different standards of stage realism at the same time as his Agitprop work with Portable Theatre. Indeed, Portable took an essentially anti-Brechtian position that theatre was a bear-pit – not a place for ideas. At its simplest, Brenton's concept of theatrical authenticity was based on integrating performance space and dramatic material. *Wesley* in 1970 was specifically designed for a large traditional Methodist chapel, *Scott of the Antarctic* (1971) was written for an ice rink.

What marks Wesley and Scott was their 'attempts to drive a straight line through very complex situations' – whether geographically across the polar icecap, or morally through a corrupt society.[14] The protagonists of Brenton's following full-length plays for the conventional theatre – the wartime heroine in the French underground of *Hitler Dances* (1972), or Jed, the out-of-work squatter turned terrorist, in *Magnificence* (Royal Court, 1973) – were conceived in the same mould. All have an obsessive singleness of purpose; and all fail. The forces, which propel these figures to self-destruction, or pervert aims that in other contexts might have been admirable, are outside their comprehension. It is the characters' ignorance, rather than explicit commentary or songs (as in Agitprop), that makes the political point. Where slogans are used in *Magnificence*, these are turned into graffiti, spray-painted on the walls of the set by one of the squatters. As with one such slogan, 'WEAPONS OF HAPPINESS', they have no direct connection with the action. When another character asks what these weapons are, the question goes unanswered – though the words provide the title for Brenton's next major play three years later.

In Brenton's early work criminal violence is purely a symptom of social injustice. For instance, in *Christie in Love* (written for Portable Theatre, 1969) the police resurrect a serial killer, who dismembers his women, only to find that the notorious Christie is a completely ordinary person. His sexual needs are no different from those of the apparently respectable middle classes; and the style of the play reinforces this moral inversion. The 'villain', depicted naturalistically, is presented as 'normal' – and more liberated – while the policemen, representing the public revulsion produced by such crimes, were played as surrealistic figures. Mass-murder is not seen as an aberration, but as typical of a society that sets up such guardians of law and order. Indeed it is implied that even the most horrific killer is preferable to the forces of morality, Brenton's intention being to 'give an audience a sense of moral vertigo'.[15]

Similarly, criminal violence is transposed into political activism in *Magnificence*, where gelignite is strapped round the head of a former Tory minister, taken hostage in response to a brutal eviction of squatters by the police. But instead of blowing up the representative of authoritarian violence, the explosive destroys his idealistic captor. Brenton:

A lot of the ideas in *Magnificence* came straight out of the writing of that time in Paris, and the idea of official life being like a screen... May 1968 disinherited my generation in two ways. First, it destroyed any remaining affection for the official culture... But it also, secondly, destroyed the notions of personal freedom... It was defeated. A generation dreaming of a beautiful utopia was kicked – kicked awake and not dead. I've got to believe not kicked dead. May 1968 gave me a desperation I still have. It destroyed Jed...[16]

Where this play documents defeat, *A Saliva Milkshake* (1975) opens with the successful assassination of the Home Secretary. But Brenton's focus is on an intellectual sympathizer, who helps the police to arrest the friend responsible. In fact Brenton has always shown a certain scepticism about the writer's political responsibilities, with Maxim Gorki in *A Sky Blue Life* (1971) insisting on writing stories about the hard life of the peasants instead of 'The true literature of revolution' defined – in Lenin's words – as 'Lists. Those to be shot, those to be fed. Corpses and potatoes'.[17] And in *Weapons of Happiness* (1976), which takes the slogan from *Magnificence* as its theme, the only political action open to the characters is ineffectual and irrelevant. Disenchanted workers in a potato-crisp plant assault the boss, and when the papers in his stolen briefcase reveal that he plans to sell off the machinery and remove their jobs, all they can do is occupy the bankrupt factory.

The failure of this hopeless attempt at revolution is set in context by a series of dream sequences, which parallel the main action. The foreground group of socially alienated youths, one of whom is deaf and dumb, another illiterate, includes an outsider in the central figure of Josef Frank. On a naturalistic level he is a political refugee, who has turned down a position teaching modern history at Cambridge to bury his guilt and betrayed idealism in manual labour. But he is also literally the ghost of the past. The historical Frank – as both the programme of the first performance and a note in the published text underline – was hanged in 1952. A working-class champion of workers' rights, convinced Stalinist and one-time volunteer in the International Brigade, who became Assistant Secretary of the Czechoslovakian Communist Party after the 1948 coup that brought the Communist minority to power, Frank was one of the twelve victims of the first Stalinist show-trial generated by anti-Semitism. Along with Slanksy and Clementis (who also appears in the play), he was posthumously rehabilitated in May 1968. This fortuitous connection with the student revolution may be Brenton's rationale for choosing Frank to represent the history of Soviet tyranny. But the true significance of linking Frank with the events of 1968 is that barely a month after his rehabilitation Russian tanks invaded Czechoslovakia (taking advantage of the student disruptions in Europe, as they had of Suez in crushing liberalization in Hungary a decade earlier).

The figure of Frank is correspondingly ambiguous. Directly comparable to the dead soldier of Wolfgang Borchert's expressionistic classic *The Man Outside* (1947), who acts as a moral touchstone for the hypocrisy of post-war German society, Frank serves as a catalyst in Brenton's depiction of contemporary Capitalism. The run-down factory, producing tasteless and unwanted consumer goods, is clearly intended as a microcosm of the British economic system; while Frank's memories reveal parallels between Communist dictatorship and the supposedly democratic society in Britain. Questioned by the police as a witness to the mugging of his boss, his remembered vision of interrogation through torture is superimposed on the everyday factory office of the present. The apparently well-meaning and ineffectual factory-owner doubles as the Russian controller, while the police inspector and a trade union organizer (one being the instrument of the Establishment, the other its collaborator) turn into Czech secret policemen.

Frank also injects political consciousness into the workers' unfocused protest. He provides the missing historical perspective for a confused, but idealistic rebel who 'couldn't understand a word' of all the Russian propaganda she has read – 'but I believed in it'. He persuades her uneducated comrades that attempting to take over the system (in the sense of running the factory as a workers' co-operative) is counter-productive:

FRANK... *takes hold of* KEN's *ears from behind and puts his knee in his back...*
You do not have the chance for revolt often. And, often, it is ridiculous.
Fleeting. Difficult to think through. But it is rare. And not to be thrown away...
KEN If we could take things all apart. Put 'em all agether again. There is a way, sometimes I do see it, like with words. And it gets blurred.
A pause

The silence of recognition underlines that for Brenton this is the key to the play. The scene 'becomes an enormous position of force. Hopefully at that point there is a visible political shift.'[18]

Yet Frank is also a negative figure. His dying hallucination – in which he throws a coat over the muzzle of an advancing Russian tank's gun – is hardly an effective gesture, as Stalin's laughter emphasizes. And he reaffirms that the Party was justified in brainwashing him to get a false confession, since the rights of the individual in the present (as in the past) are immaterial compared to the future potential in socialism.

The gap between ideology and political realities is brought into sharp focus by Frank's assertion that 'They wanted to make a new human being' (the ultimate aim of Marxism) through torture. His resulting mental state and physical decay demonstrates that means invalidate ends, while his justification of the Communist system is based on the story of the Grand Inquisitor from Dostoyevsky – a cliché for totalitarian double-think to an audience familiar with modern English classics like Aldous Huxley's *Brave New World* or Orwell's *1984*. Yet it is his experiences that give purpose to the naive hunger for revolution in Janice, the girl who organizes the factory workers. Her closing eulogy – 'He was a communist' – is not in fact contradicted by Stalin's dismissive epitaph for him: 'Incurable romantic'.[19] The two labels go together. Even though the monstrous and cynical Stalin embodies what State Communism has become, Marxism is identified with idealism.

Such ambiguity proved highly confusing, causing critics to lament the absence of any 'discussion of the issues, no articulate collision of socialist ideas'. The general consensus was that the author had been reduced to taking 'the same way out as his driven girl, and to demand[ing] blind faith in an undefined concept'. Yet for Brenton, any realistic analysis of the contemporary situation demanded this lack of articulation. The conditions for revolution were present, but not revolutionary consciousness: 'in the play the distorted revolution [of Eastern Europe] awakens the sleeping revolution [in England] – or begins to, just begins to'.[20] The title comes from a Czech writer (cited in the programme for the first production), 'All the bright weapons of happiness wait only for a sign', which defines the intended function of the drama. Like Frank, the play itself should provide a catalyst for the audience – leaving them, like Ken, with a vision of the potential for social change, and challenging them to 'think through' the difficulties posed by the past.

Written for the National Theatre, elements of *Weapons of Happiness* were also designed to echo the context of the performance in a similar way to Brenton's early ice rink and chapel experiments. It presented 'an international culture, which this building was deliberately meant to be about, with people who live barely half a mile away' as its subject.[21] Programme notes tied the dramatic situation into current issues, citing a leaflet (that was currently being distributed on the streets outside the theatre) campaigning against proposed changes to the criminal trespass act: 'YOU COULD BE ARRESTED

8 Neighbourhood graffiti as social imagery for Brenton's *Weapons of Happiness*
at the National Theatre

for taking part in occupations at work.' The stage was left bare, and real objects like a motorbike were brought on to it, while elaborate graffiti painted on the rear wall of the theatre reproduced a factory wall in the neighbourhood.

In such a realistic context, where conventional illusion was introduced – as with a scene at the London Planetarium – it made the whole situation seem false. This particular scene, where Janice seduces Frank in public on the Planetarium floor while the constellations revolve on the dome above, is in any case given too much symbolic weight to be dramatically convincing. Copulating represents Frank's liberation from the paralysing distortion of history. It also represents the integration of naive idealism (embodied by Janice) into a revolutionary tradition. And reproducing the Planetarium show inflates sex into rhetorical hyperbole, with a spectacular projection of Mars (the 'red' planet of a Communist future) – plus a 'quadrophonic, exultant' musical climax for their love-making.[22] Despite such occasional unevennesses, *Weapons of Happiness* marked a distinct advance in Brenton's dramaturgy. A dialectical structure is created by juxtaposing contrasted scenes to express thematic oppositions. For instance, the grave that swallows a Czech martyr becomes the drain through which the revolutionaries escape from the authorities surrounding the occupied factory. The same white sheet that outlines a snowy Moscow square in 1947 covers the deserted English countryside of the present. The characters are both naturalistic and openly representative. Completely convincing as inarticulate street kids, the workers stand for a spectrum of typical attitudes: from the illiterate youth, to whom industrial action means physical violence, through a guitarist whose concept of revolution is limited to the utopianism of Bob Dylan, to Janice, the Marxist with no sense of history. On the opposite side of the political coin, the individual traits of their boss become heightened into caricature that marks him as the symbol of Capitalism.

This broad picture, linking contemporary social problems with political events from a quarter-century before, was extended to truly epic scope in *The Romans in Britain* (1980), which parallels Julius Caesar's crushing of resistance by Celtic Britain in 54BC, brutal Saxon/'English' invasions in the Dark Ages, and highly topical military activities by the British against the IRA in Northern Ireland. In some ways it echoes *The Island of the Mighty*, and although – in contrast to Arden's mythmaking – Brenton based his play on extensive and detailed historical research, it suffered much the same fate. While the front-stage copulation in *Weapons of Happiness* had raised few eyebrows, a scene graphically depicting the rape of a young Celtic priest by a Roman soldier (reduced to '*attempts to bugger him*' in the revised version of the text) led to outrage in the Press and a highly public trial in which the director of the National Theatre production, Michael Bogdanov, was tried for procuring an act of gross indecency under the Sexual Offences law. Although the case was eventually withdrawn, the lack of final judgment left any future production open to prosecution; and apart from a single amateur student performance in 1989, the play has remained unstaged.

The reaction can be seen as a measure of the change in public attitudes that had brought in the first Thatcher government just a year earlier. In addition, requiring 30 actors for the over 60 parts, the only companies with the resources to present it were the National (already burnt by the reaction to the première) and the RSC. It was also clear that the explicit sex, along with extremely violent action, had almost completely overwhelmed Brenton's actual theme of Imperialism and displaced the highly topical political debate the play was intended to generate. Perhaps as a result Brenton changed his approach to criticizing contemporary society.

Instead he picked up on the theme of utopian potential, against which the present is measured and found wanting. Already introduced in *Weapons of Happiness*, this utopianism underlies the bleak depictions of exploitation, oppression and corruption in *The Romans in Britain* and *Thirteenth Night* (1981); but with *Bloody Poetry* (1984) it forms the main subject. Focusing on the relationship between Byron and the Shelleys, Brenton explicitly explores Shelley's claim that 'Poets are the unacknowledged legislators of mankind.'[23] These nineteenth-century libertarian rebels justify their verse in terms of its social function; and Brenton's prefatory character-sketches stress that Shelley's work was an inspirational influence on the formation of trades unions.

However – reflecting the position of radical playwrights in the increasingly conservative 1980s – as exiles without a contemporary revolutionary movement to write for, Byron and Shelley are reduced to silence. Reactionary forces have clamped down in the post-Napoleonic era, and working-class protest leads to the Peterloo massacre (in a rather simplistic parallel with Thatcher's Britain, and contemporary battles between police and miners' pickets). Their only recourse is to live out their free-thinking utopias in their personal lives. But even they have to admit that as a pattern for the future their experiment in inventing a new society is fatally flawed, resulting in the sacrifice of children and personal cruelty.

In Brenton's view, the intense individualism of Romanticism divorces the poetic ideals of even these politically committed Romantics from the social needs of the time. And by extension, the same dissociation of words and actions affects the modern political dramatist. Indeed, the text implicitly challenges the status of the play itself as a diversion of political energy into aesthetics: 'All this writing about tyranny, eh? In the end you get itchy fingers. Violent verses pale. You want to actually put a bullet in a fat neck.'[24]

At the same time, this rejection of art is modified by the central image in *Bloody Poetry*: Plato's cave, in which mankind sits by a small fire, with his back to the light of truth outside, mistaking the shadows cast on the rock-walls for reality.

On one level the Platonic metaphor represents the restrictions of society, the mental chains that make any philosopher or poet the prisoner of his epoch. This is exemplified by the contemptible figure of Polidori, Byron's secretary, who claimed to have provided Mary Shelley with the plot for *Frankenstein*. As a physician, he represents the scientific side of Romantic aspiration, which allowed itself to be harnessed by industrialism.

Yet if what people take to be actuality is only illusory, like the stage performance itself, then the poetic vision is no less real than physical misery. Plato's image implicitly answers Mary's question: 'endless-hopeless – schemes and dreams – and . . . What have you achieved, Bysshe . . . Is the price of a poem – the death of our child?' In the interpretation given by Shelley, if the reactionary codes of the past (the fire) that determine our perception of present conditions (the shadows cast on the cave wall) are to be replaced by new forms of society ('the future of mankind . . . the absolute good'/the true sun that lights the world outside Plato's cave), then it is writers like these whose images show this true reality. As individuals they are bound to fail, literally haunted by personal responsibilities in the shape of the ghost of Shelley's first wife, who commits suicide in despair. But the pyre that burns the drowned corpse of Shelley is clearly intended as a beacon to the future. Despite Byron's nihilistic 'Burn him! Burn us all!' it is 'A great big, bloody, beautiful fire!'[25]

Byron himself is at the point of setting off for Greece: and one is reminded that, as a symbol, his death (from fever, before striking a single blow) was of more service to the cause of Greek freedom than any heroic action he might have accomplished. The assumption – emphasized in the play – that ideas can kill provides a moral imperative for literature. Either poetry works directly to change the world through redefining human nature, or it blinds people and serves as an instrument to enslave them.

As historical individuals, Brenton's proto-revolutionary heroes are hardly paragons. The Promethean ideal is by no means easy to achieve. '*Bloody*' *Poetry* sums up the contradictions in the writer's position and the human cost of acting as the conscience of society. Yet, however ironic it may seem in the context of the deaths surrounding its composition, Shelley's refusal to compromise results in his poem, 'The Triumph of Life'. The title of this poem represents the moral goal of literature. Shelley's writing served as an inspiration to the working-class movement later in the Nineteenth Century: as the characters proclaim, 'The men and women of the future will thank us. We are their great experiment.'[26]

If so, even though Shelley produced no social change in his own lifetime – then, the play implies, modern political drama may also serve as a catalyst for coming generations. This theme is picked up directly in *Greenland* (1988), which forms the final part of a 'Utopian Trilogy' (the previous plays being *Thirteenth Night* and *Bloody Poetry*) and followed through in *Berlin Bertie* (1992). The title of *Greenland* has the same Romantic resonance, with its Blakean echoes of a New Jerusalem though here the positive figures are from a post-revolutionary future instead of the historical past.

In *Greenland*, present-day society seems to offer no positive alternatives. Radical theatre (satirized in the kind of Agitprop troupe Brenton had long since distanced himself from) and socialist politicians are both rejected. Labour parliamentary candidates despise the single representative worker, who is presented as a 'dirty, lazy bugger'. However, his drinking is an escape from a society that holds no promise of a future for him. As in *Weapons of Happiness*, it is the force of repressed desires that holds the potential for real political change. The worker's frustrated idealism qualifies him as the only character from the present to find a home in the future utopia. Again, too, the structure of *Greenland* is created by contrasts, with visions from another time breaking through the contemporary scene as ghosts: projections of the characters' psychological needs. But here, in the distant (and imaginary) future, the social ideal is finally achieved. And the vision of it, gained by the present-day characters – and the audience – who make the temporal transition, but are too imperfect to stay in paradise, is what will make its realization possible.

Unlike Brenton's previous 'Utopian' plays, *Greenland* lacks any ambiguity. It is split into two halves: 'US' (here and now – 'people at their worst') and 'THEM' ('how I hope my children, or my children's children's children will live'). It is also openly symbolic. The characters have little individuality, the thirty-two roles being specifically designed to be 'performed by a company of four men and four women'; and the merging of a naturalistic depiction of society with inner reality is specifically labelled 'psycho-drama' by one of his future beings. Indeed, it is telepathy that makes them superior to twentieth-century man (an evolution strikingly similar to Shaw's projection in *Back to Methuselah*). They are able to shape the material world through purely mental powers. The political statement has become equally direct: the eventual triumph of Russian Communism that the play envisages is explicitly condemned as 'Enlightenment lost. Dark ages . . . interminable decades, brutish, censored, authoritarian', while the New Jerusalem has only been achieved by a 'mass defection' from politics.[27]

If this marks the end of the 1968 line, *Berlin Bertie* is an attempt to come to terms with the collapse of Communism and the challenge it posed to radical socialists in the West (like Brenton himself). Based on a story told to Brenton during a visit to Berlin in 1990, it deals directly with the loss of faith – not only in Marxism, but in Christianity and social commitment. These are represented respectively by an ex-Stasi officer from the former GDR who has come to England and sets up a business in pornographic videos; the British wife of an East German pastor, a psychologist who has left her husband after the Stasi officer showed her his file, demonstrating that he was a State informer; and her sister, a social worker whose negligence (specifically dreams of a more fulfilling life) has led to the brutal murder of a baby in her care, and who has taken refuge in drug addiction. As the psychologist remarks, each in their own way 'were the technicians for DOING GOOD' who 'wanted to put the world to rights', and are now 'fugitives from great faiths'.[28]

Superimposing a trashed London flat, filled with the detritus of con-sumerism – empty coke cans and leftovers of Chinese takeaways, piles of old newspapers, a grimy TV set – on a backdrop of a South London housing estate, which could double for East Berlin (indeed more than one reviewer of the original Royal Court production identified it as Berlin), the play equates conditions in England with the despair and cynicism of East Germany in the immediate aftermath of the fall of the Berlin Wall. For this parallel to be convincing, we would need to accept the social worker, crushed by de-spair and guilt, her unemployed lager-lout boyfriend and a waif-like teenage Goth and would-be mime artist suffering from gonorrhoea, whom she has given refuge to, as standing for Britain as a whole. But despite having the one-time secret policeman ask questions like 'Are these conditions represen-tative of British working-class housing?' as he gazes at the squalor, following his earlier practise of Agitprop exaggeration Brenton makes the situation too extreme.[29] It was because she allowed herself erotic fantasies, which she still harbours, about the baby's father (sex in an aeroplane lavatory high over the Pacific) that the social worker allowed the infant to be left with par-ents who didn't just abuse, but murdered it in a horrific litany of violence.

And the ending is a return to utopia, though here the vision is both more limited and openly fantastic. The three women – all in flight from social conditions summed up as moral failure, faith betrayed and sexual disease – leave together to tour the Continent as a mime troupe, energized by the teenager's hope that if they dress as nuns they will generate enough faith in their audiences so that they will actually be able to fly.

An emphasis on female idealism and redemptive power is typical of almost all the radical drama in the Twentieth Century. It goes all the way back to Shaw, and is a major theme throughout David Hare's plays. However, in more recent decades women have increasingly been presented as victims – as here, where they have found themselves incapable of changing social conditions, and any redemption now can only be on a personal spiritual level.

Berlin Bertie is also an explicit rejection of Brechtian drama. Although including flashbacks, Brenton's style is grittily naturalistic, with individualized characters designed to arouse empathy; and the title comes from the code name taken by the Stasi agent: Bertold Brecht. As a playwright Brecht stands for ideological certainty, with his open theatricality assuming the effectiveness of rationality, and his anti-traditional staging standing for the new socialist society his plays were intended to create. That vision is no longer supportable; and as Brenton is implicitly recognizing, Brecht's ideal society turned out to be a prison, requiring secret police and a population of informers as well as a wall. *Berlin Bertie* is as much about dramatic approaches as politics, but its insights are clearly too self-defeating for Brenton since they do not carry through into his other work during the 1990s. Collaborations with another veteran radical, the socialist historian Tariq Ali, not only *Iranian Nights* (1989) and *Moscow Gold* (1990) but also *Ugly Rumours* and to some extent *Collateral Damage* written after *Berlin Bertie* (1998 and 1999), all revert to his previous quasi-Brechtian cartoon style.

Each is highly topical: responding to the plight of Salman Rushdie shortly after the Fatwa calling for his death was issued; Gorbachev's power-struggle with Yeltsin; Tony Blair's 'Third Way' style of socialism; the NATO bombing of Belgrade over Kosovo. Indeed *Moscow Gold* is explicitly based on Vsevolod Meyerhold's concepts of circus-theatre and living history (history being written as it is made), with Meyerhold being quoted during the play, while *Collateral Damage* was written in just nine days. The overall theme is a lament for the loss of true socialist ideals, and they are equally nostalgic in style. Despite the immediacy of their subjects, and an elaborate RSC staging for *Moscow Gold*, none of these collaborative plays was successful. Part of the problem is their topicality (a frequent comment in reviews of *Moscow*

Gold was that the analysis in the play added little to news reports of the time) but in addition the satiric characterization that had appeared so colourful in a play like *Pravda* a decade earlier now seemed a crude copy of the highly successful TV show, *Spitting Image* (a comment made by several reviews of *Ugly Rumours*, which presented Cherie Blair as Cherry-Pop, the Prime Minister as Tony Boy and his press secretary, Peter Mandelson, as a female spin-doctor called Polly Mendacity who runs a Department for Treachery and Influence, plus caricatures of Mrs Thatcher as a ghost in Blair's cellar, Richard Branson as Biggles and – an echo of *Pravda* that underlines the loss of focus – the media tycoon, Rupert Murdoch, with a koala bear).

David Hare (1947–): subjective solutions for social decay

CHECKLIST OF HARE'S MAJOR PLAYS

Slag, 1970	*Pravda* (with Brenton), 1985
The Great Exhibition, 1972	*Secret Rapture*, 1989
Brassneck (with Brenton), 1973	*Racing Demon*, 1990
Knuckle, 1974	*Murmuring Judges*, 1991
Fanshen, 1975	*The Absence of War* (*Trilogy*), 1993
Teeth'n Smiles, 1975	*Skylight*, 1995
Plenty, 1978	*Amy's View*, 1997
Licking Hitler, 1978	*The Judas Kiss*, 1998
A Map of the World, 1983	*Via Dolorosa*, 1998

David Hare's work, which has earned him the leading position in the post-1968 generation of dramatists, in many ways parallels Brenton's development. He collaborated with Brenton on several plays, from *Lay-By* in 1971 to *Pravda* in 1985, and directed the National Theatre production of Brenton's *Weapons of Happiness* (1976). His equally bleak depictions of modern British society are also conditioned by a similar utopianism. This was already reflected in the idealization of Maoist revolution, and the way its process was duplicated in the rehearsals for *Fanshen* (1975). Like Brenton too, Hare has turned to Brecht, adapting *The Life of Galileo* (1994) and *Mother Courage* (1995). But his range has been wider, including Chekhov, Pirandello and Schnitzler, with translations or modernizations of *Ivanov* (1997), *The Rules of the Game* (1992) and *La Ronde* (*The Blue Room*, 1998). And unlike Brenton, whose figures from the past tend to be ghost-like mental projections in the consciousness of the present, Hare's approach is strongly historical. Indeed much of his later work retains the documentary basis he developed in *Fanshen*, so much so that the Trilogy was treated as 'faction' with *The Absence of War* (1993) being mined for backroom information about the Labour Party's defeat in the 1992 election, and the dialogue derived from conversations with people in Israel that formed the basis of his most recent play *Via Dolorosa* being shown to the speakers 'to ask them whether they felt I was being fair'.[30] However, after *Fanshen* this factual evidence is increasingly subsumed in a symbolic structure.

Starting in 1978 with *Plenty* and *Licking Hitler*, Hare uses documented facts as the underpinning for plots that trace the roots of the oppression and corruption, which he sees in contemporary England. Yet the meaning is embodied by certain types of figure, who carry significant emotional weight. Thus well over two-thirds of Hare's plays centre around a female idealist, and these are presented even more explicitly than in Brenton's work as the embodiment of utopian principle, providing the moral standard by which society is judged. Typically in Hare's earlier plays these women are killed or driven mad; and their destruction condemns the forces they fight against, while both *Plenty* and *Secret Rapture* (1989) end with a dreamlike affirmation of their vision. Indeed, as the social context of Hare's plays grows increasingly darker during the 1980s, his utopian thrust becomes more explicit. So in *Secret Rapture* the selflessly socialistic heroine's murder converts her rigidly self-righteous and grasping sister (Minister of State in the Conservative government: a Thatcher-clone). Despite her monstrosity, this power figure is transformed by remorse, at which point the ghost of the dead girl reappears, her spirit vindicated. The play's title relates her victimization and final apotheosis to spiritual love and Christian martyrdom. Similarly *Racing Demon* (1990) merges politics and religion through examining the crises of conscience in the Anglican clergy of a blighted inner-city poverty trap; and the ending affirms the relevance of spiritual belief. Indeed, as Hare explicitly stated in *Via Dolorosa* (1998), his one-man autobiographical examination of the Israeli/Palestinian conflict, 'for some time my subject as a playwright has been faith'.[31]

The spiritual theme, of course, is openly utopian. But in a major distinction with Brenton's drama (which focuses primarily on characters representing social evils) this leads Hare to state that 'My subject is goodness.' In a typical reversal of normal expectations, he goes on to define this focus as showing 'what choices good people might have to make in order to survive' in a social context hostile to their values, and 'how goodness can bring out the worst in all of us'.[32] And this conditions Hare's characterization: except for his collaborations with Brenton and perhaps *Secret Rapture* there are no real villains in his mature plays, while even the idealized figures of female goodness are flawed.

His work for Portable Theatre had already defined an interest in 'closely knit social situations in a process of extreme decay' and the warping of personality in 'self-enclosed societies'.[33] *Knuckle* (1974) portrays a dystopia, where cynicism is the only method of self-preservation in a corrupting materialistic context. Hare presents Guildford through the lens of Raymond Chandler's Los Angeles in the search for a missing girl. The simplistic moral frame of private-eye fiction is used to measure the hypocrisy of an apparently civilized suburban community, whose real values are those of financial dealing and property speculation.

In this context, idealism is suicidal. It causes the disappearance (and presumed murder) of a socially committed girl. As her stock-broker father sums it up in recounting their final conversation:

Those who wish to reform the world should first know a little about it. I told her some stories of life in the City … take-over bids, redundancies, men ruined overnight, jobs lost, trusts betrayed, reputations smashed, life in that great trough called the City of London, sploshing about in the cash. And I asked, what I have always asked: how will that ever change?

The absence of ideals and death of innocence in modern society is symbolized by the vanished girl. Her brother, who acts the role of detective, has escaped from commuter-belt hypocrisy by becoming an arms merchant – the only way of defeating the Establishment being to turn its own weapons of ruthlessness and brutality (his 'guns') against it. But the cynicism of all the characters is also a way of demonstrating the need for an alternative. It challenges the audience to find a morally acceptable method of change. Awareness of the problem is the first step, provided by the play where 'greed and selfishness and cruelty stand exposed in a white neon light'.[34]

The difficulty here is that the reflection of social cynicism in the Mickey Spillane format undercuts any impression of objective analysis. *Plenty*, which covers the same ground through a psychological exploration of the idealist, gains documentary conviction by its subjective accuracy. Together with its companion piece, *Licking Hitler* (1978), *Plenty* also embodies the themes of Hare's earlier plays in their most fully developed form.

A BBC television Play For Today, *Licking Hitler* traces the roots of decay in the contemporary social fabric back to the betrayed ideals of the Second

World War. Present problems are analysed through the microcosm of a 'black propaganda' unit, manufacturing and broadcasting fabricated news reports to destabilize Nazi Germany from an isolated English country house. This commandeered mansion stands for the nation in much the same way as Shaw's shiplike 'Heartbreak House' – an image already picked up in the final song from *Teeth 'n Smiles* (1975) where Hare presents *The Titanic* as the emblem of a sinking Britain. The atmosphere of lies in this secret military unit corrupts the characters' personalities and destroys any possibility of truthful emotional relationships. We watch the psychological disintegration of Archie, a journalist who identifies with Goebbels and comes to feel he has betrayed his slum background, through the eyes of an innocent girl; and she sums it up in a final letter: 'none of us had the whisper of an idea as to what we were fighting for'. And 'whereas we knew exactly what we were fighting against', what they hate is precisely what they become.

However, instead of letting the self-enclosed situation speak for itself, a postscript summarizes the characters' subsequent careers in order to point out the effect of the 'thirty-year-old deep corrosive national habit of lying'. Archie turns to making films that sentimentalize his childhood in the Glasgow slums. After an advertising job – the commercial equivalent of wartime disinformation – the girl drops out to join the radical protest movement. In the television performance this epilogue, delivered by Hare himself, was sharply criticized as intrusive moralizing: an equivalent to the discredited wartime propaganda that 'crippled' the play.[35]

The starting point of *Plenty* (1978) is another aspect of the secret war, which picks up on Brenton's *Hitler Dances* (1972): the undercover agent in German-occupied France. Hare's female protagonist here also comes to work in advertising. And the parallel to *Licking Hitler* was emphasized by Hare's choice (as the director of each piece) of Kate Nelligan as the actress for both leading roles. Although the focus is on losing the peace, rather than winning the war, the context is the same. As Susan laments, looking around at the gulf between post-war realities and her success as an advertiser: 'In France . . . I told such glittering lies. But where's the fun in lying for a living? . . . Sold out. Is that the phrase?'[36]

Having been a heroine of the Special Operations Executive, Susan is herself a subject of national advertising copy: a symbol of valour and moral action, which she co-operates in promoting through her distortions of memory. (What a 1943 flashback actually shows is by no means a glorious reality, but paralysing fear and conflict with the French resistance.) The episodic scenes begin with the break-up of her marriage, presenting the audience with an initially unexplained image of a naked man in a room that has been stripped bare. They then move chronologically from wartime 1943, through her first meeting with her husband when she reports the death of her married lover to the Brussels embassy, up to 1962 – by which time the opening situation, and her reasons for walking out on her empty home, have become clear – ending in an unsuccessful attempt to find sexual fulfilment at a rendezvous with her ex-wartime colleague, and a visionary return to 1945 when victory seemed to herald the dawn of a new age.

Each scene turns on hypocrisy and self-deception. Her relationship with Brock, the diplomat whom she marries, begins by persuading him to preserve appearances by lying; and on a world scale the pivot of the personal action is Suez, 'a fraud cooked up by the British as an excuse for seizing the canal'. But each of the situations is deliberately ambiguous. Is a lie justified when it saves a widow from learning that her husband was with a mistress when he died? Does an ambassador's resignation – because his government misled him into believing he was telling the truth by denying Britain's involvement in Suez – make him an honourable man, when he would have defended the invasion of Eygpt, even though he believed it to be wrong, just so long as it had been 'honestly done'? The world of diplomacy that is the setting for Susan's psychological disintegration not only epitomizes 'a profession in which nobody may speak their mind' and 'there is little to believe in. Behaviour is all.' It also – in a statement that could stand as a motto for Hare's theatre as a whole – provides 'perspective . . . Looking across distances. For instance we see England very clearly from [Iran].'[37]

These ambiguities come to a focus in the figure of Susan herself. As Brock points out, whenever she refers to the war it signals that she is about to deceive someone. Yet her undercover experience is the touchstone of truth against which the corruption of the post-war period is measured.

From one viewpoint Susan is an idealist, who refuses to compromise with hypocrisy. Frustrated by society's resistance to change, her desperation 'to feel I'm moving on' is a moral imperative. From another perspective, Hare intends the audience to see that Susan is driven mad by being sane in a mad society, and to share her rejection of all the socialized figures. However, it is also possible to view her as a ruthless manipulator of others, made incapable of intimacy or self-fulfilment by attitudes that – however necessary for survival in occupied France – are destructive in a normal context. Like a latter-day Hedda Gabler, Susan plays dangerously with a revolver kept as a wartime memento; and her actions are powerfully condemned by her long-suffering and rejected husband: 'You claim to be protecting some personal ideal, always at a cost of almost infinite pain to everyone around you. You are selfish, brutish, unkind . . . Admit it. Then perhaps you might really move on.'[38] Yet her accuser, Brock, has already been discredited by his own compromises with the truth, which lead to his alcoholic breakdown.

Hare commented 'that people do go clinically mad if what they believe bears no relation to how they live'; and he directed the National Theatre production to bring out the intelligence and waste of potential in Susan. The emptiness within material plenty is stressed in the text; and the barrenness of the present is indicated by the recurring theme of children. Several of the scenes concern Susan's desire to have a baby. Brock's impotence leads her to pick up a working-class stud – but she is unable to conceive. She pays for a young girl's abortion. And the only mothers seen in the play are unmarried, social rejects to whom she offers her empty house as a communal home. The contrast with the final retrospective vision of the future in which 'things will quickly change. We have grown up. We will improve our world' is all too clear – even though this 1945 flashback is a drug-induced hallucination.[39]

However, although the play details Susan's growing hysteria and mental instability, it is ultimately left for the viewer to decide whether her view of society is distorted, or social pressure has warped her personality. Hare intends the blame to be put squarely on capitalist society. As with the heroine in his 1980 television drama, *Dreams of Leaving*, Susan's character is based on an imagined form of political anorexia, produced by reacting against materialistic greed and consumption. Since the medical causes of such an illness are different, this metaphor perhaps confused the issue. Faced with uncomprehending audiences, even Kate Nelligan found it difficult to play Susan as totally right in her absolute rejection of post-war society. Instead, when the play reached New York she was showing Susan as an unreliable witness, pitiably half-aware of the unfairness in her outbursts against society.

At the same time, this kind of ambiguity is also built in to Hare's dramatic approach. *Plenty* reflects his 'belief that people died literally in vain. That the upsurge of radical feeling in the war and post-war years was a genuine outcome of their experiences.' However, Hare had come to recognize that 'if a play is to be a weapon in the class struggle, then that weapon is not going to be the things you are saying; it is the interaction of what you are saying and what the audience is thinking'.[40]

As in his earlier Agitprop polemic, *Fanshen*, scenes are organized as illustrations of different stages in a social process, rather than a naturalistic cause-and-effect sequence. Clusters of examples with wide gaps of time between are juxtaposed. The style of the two plays is also similar in the sense of spartan clarity that comes from reducing each situation to its essentials; and the visionary ending of *Plenty* is comparable to the flag-waving Agitprop apotheosis with which *Fanshen* concludes, though subtler and more complex in its effect. But *Plenty* analyses society through exploring its moral impact on an individual in subjective terms. It is a psychological study, and designed to evoke a corresponding subjective response in spectators. As Hare commented in a note for other directors of the play: 'The audience is asked to make its own mind up about each of the actions. In the act of judging the audience learns something about its own values.'[41]

This creative use of ambiguity reaches its fullest development in *A Map of the World* (1983). The play's cinematic montage echoes David Edgar's approach, where spectators 'would recognize the characters from the inside, but be able, simultaneously, like a sudden film-cut from close-up to wide-angle, to look at how these individual journeys were defined by the collective journey of an epoch'.[42] The context of the action is the filming of a novel by one of the characters, which is based on an incident he has lived through; and on-camera scenes are intercut with the re-enacted memories of the actual participants. The apparently objective eye of the lens is fictionalized by subjective corrections. The foreground of the 'on-screen' action, which we initially take for reality, differs recognizably from the book that it is supposedly reproducing. Both quasi-documentary versions are contradicted by those who were there, while their claims are not always consistent.

This constantly varying 'truth' forces the spectators into a continual re-evaluation. Seated in a theatre, they initially believe they are watching a play, only to find the stage scene was a film-showing. The seemingly real context of the cinema is then revealed to be the set of a movie studio, which in turn gives way to the actual presentation of events described in the book. The conventions of minimal set design allow the environment to be sufficiently unspecific to correspond to each level of reality, and the original production sought to integrate the audience into the technical process of representation, making them 'pan the shot: they are made to feel that they're the cameraman' by using 'different moving elements, including lights tracking – and the actors, as they play, are moving on a revolve'.[43]

It is a short step from the analogies drawn between the stage and journalism, and the use of media techniques in *A Map of the World*, to taking the Press as a theme – and in Hare's usual treatment of his dramatic subjects, as a metaphor for the state of British society – as in his next play, *Pravda*. And the abuses of today's newspapers recur as a secondary focus in later plays from *Racing Demon* (where a gay clergyman is hounded out of Britain by sensationalist tabloids) to *Amy's View* (in which the philistine representative of all that is meretricious in Thatcher's England graduates from journalist and art critic to a director of violent schlock films). There is also a logical progression from mapping the international scene, to anatomizing Britain, as Hare proceeded to do in his Trilogy covering the fundamental institutions of the nation, the Church, the Law, and Politics: *Racing Demon, Murmuring Judges* and *The Absence of War* (1990, 1991 and 1993).

The Trilogy was widely hailed as finally making the National Theatre – for which it had specifically been written – a platform for national debate. Epic in scale (as well as staging, with spectacularly realistic representations of the tightly interconnected centres of power in the Savoy Hotel, the Royal Opera House, the Lobby and Chamber of the House of Commons and the Cenotaph outside, plus introducing a real London taxi) together the plays add up to a devastating picture of a morally bankrupt society that has lost its spiritual way and corrupted or co-opted any potential forces of idealistic renewal. In a sense, like Edgar's *Maydays*, the Trilogy is a lament for the loss of socialist faith. It opens with a priest kneeling on a stage shaped like an empty cross and staring up at a shaft of light to cry out despairingly 'God. Where are you? . . . There are an awful lot of people in a very bad way. And they need something beside silence' in the first scene of *Racing Demon*, and culminates in *The Absence of War*, a title explained as meaning that in an election campaign (like a battle) lack of conflict means losing;[44] as Labour lost in 1992 – according to the play because its leader (Neil Kinnock, lightly disguised as a self-schooled Cockney) sacrificed his political principles in a vain attempt to make his party electable.

Each of the plays was based on extensive documentation, with no fewer than four researchers credited in the programme and the facts they had gathered being published separately in *Asking Around*, a handbook to the plays. As a result they attracted attention in the regular news columns as well as standard drama reviews; with the Bishop of London writing a piece acknowledging that *Racing Demon* offered 'valuable insight into how life is in the Church of England', paralleling the findings of an official Church enquiry, *Faith and the City*. Similarly, a leading female QC pointed out that the legal community had packed the seats at the production of *Murmuring Judges* and recognized that it accurately reflected 'a crisis of public confidence in the law', although it was denounced as a pantomime travesty by a former Attorney-General.[45] In particular *The Absence of War* was commented on by a Leader in the *Times* and by political editors of the *Sunday Express* and *Daily Telegraph*, as well as by senior Labour politicians and insiders (notably Roy

Hattersley – who appears as a character and who also criticized it on radio – and Peter Mandelson). Indeed since Hare had been given almost unlimited – and unprecedented – access to Labour politicians including Kinnock, and to backroom discussions throughout the election, the play was mined for inside information on Labour's campaign while the plot, in which the leader is misled by his PR team and stabbed in the back by his shadow-chancellor, was widely taken as 'faction'.

The central action in each of the other plays is also based on recognizable events, though more loosely, with the planting of false evidence on a robbery gang in *Murmuring Judges*, and the unsafe conviction of an Irish labourer who has only turned to crime as a last resort to support his handicapped child, being more a distillation of well-known cases like the Guildford Four or the Birmingham Six (Irish people convicted for IRA bombings, but later found to have been innocent). Here by contrast the criminals have been caught in the act; and although in the 1993 version explosives had been planted by the police, to create a closer parallel, in the original text it was cocaine – or rather an innocuous white powder, since even the police are treated sympathetically. Indeed Hare makes it clear that the detective had the best of motives for tampering with evidence: persuading the gang to become informers in order to catch far more violent armed criminals; and in sharp contrast to *Pravda* or even *Secret Rapture*, the Trilogy contains no villains at all.

Even though the Labour leader may have betrayed the socialist principles of the Party, he is treated as a tragically noble figure sacrificing personal convictions for what he is persuaded to be a greater good, and reduced to tortured silence in a climactic election speech when he finds himself unable to mouth the slogans that are so far from his real beliefs. The Bishop in *Racing Demon*, an authority figure that might well have been demonized in Hare's earlier plays, condemns the clergyman who has abandoned faith for social work as he dresses in formal Episcopal robes, in a clear echo of Brecht's *Galileo* where a sympathetic Cardinal is shown taking on the official attitudes of the Church as he dons the papal vestments. In fact if anyone, it is an idealist – the ambitious and fanatical born-again curate with his belief that faith alone can cure all problems including Aids – who might be seen as corresponding to the title of the play. But it's worth noting that 'Racing Demon' is the name of a card game, while the title of *Murmuring Judges* refers to an antique law against criticizing the judiciary that the play as a whole is guilty of, rather than any of the characters in it. Hare's focus is on the political system as a whole, and its terminal condition as 'a cartel.

Based on a massive failure of nerve' (and that this statement is given to the bigoted curate shows his objectivity), all of which would be undermined by loading the responsibility on to individual figures, however symbolic, or implying that it was the result of evil.[46] Even the most powerful are prisoners of the system, and all are shown as acting with good intentions, even if misguided.

In each play – as in all his other work – a single female character acts as the voice of conscience. But here, as with the absence of villains and in line with the perception that only a complete cultural shift can change an institutionalized system, they are marginalized in the social context and the dramatic action. The agnostic advertising-woman in *Racing Demon* may voice the need for kindness and human love, but is rejected by the curate (her fiancée before abandoning her for evangelical passion) and finds herself fending off an adulterous advance from the hapless liberal clergyman she wants to save from dismissal. One well-meaning PR girl cannot stave off electoral defeat in *Absence of War*. The black female barrister – a nod perhaps to the outsider/ex-slave activist in Edward Bond's *Restoration* (see p. 174 above) – who takes up the case of the convicted Irish prisoner in *Murmuring Judges*, falls in love with him. Despite all her criticism of the legal system, the best she can do is get his five-year sentence (which is out of all proportion for a first-time offender) reduced by just six months. But she also manages to persuade another woman, an idealistic young detective and the lover of the policeman who fabricated evidence, to act according to her conscience. In the final moment of the play she is poised to reveal her lover's illegal act to her superior, while the prisoner takes up a book on Irish history to learn about the IRA. Still the ending remains open: cracks may be showing in the system, but there is no sign that whistle-blowing or even bombs will overcome the inertia of the status quo.

The Trilogy presents an uncompromisingly objective commentary on the State of the Nation, challenging the audience to accept the necessity of change precisely because Hare represses easy solutions. The plays are all argument, issue-oriented, with each situation being thematically focused and almost every speech presenting a position. As such they reclaimed the public arena for theatre that Shaw had occupied at the beginning of the century; and indeed Hare's techniques are very much an updating of the Shavian dramatic approach. Yet although there have been various productions of *Racing Demon*, the Trilogy is a one-off – too huge an undertaking for any commercial theatre, and too quickly dated by its journalistic basis (particularly *Absence of War*, with the reversal of New Labour's fortunes under Tony Blair)

9 Symbolic conflicts: distorted idealism versus the female conscience in Hare's *Racing Demon*

to be restaged – and in his subsequent work Hare chose to work on a smaller intimate scale.

In *Skylight* (1995), there are just three characters; *Amy's View*, which marked the close of his highly productive partnership with Richard Eyre at the National in 1997, revolves around a single actress and her family. And the three plays staged in 1998 were all written for small alternative theatres, with *The Judas Kiss* (the Almeida) presenting just two entirely personal episodes in the life of Oscar Wilde, and *Via Dolorosa* (the small stage at the Royal Court) being an individualistic monologue performed by Hare himself, while *The Blue Room* (Donmar Warehouse) – for all its multiple pairings – is designed for just two actors. And the contrast with his previous epic treatment of public themes is underlined by the fact that the first three of these are intended to form another Trilogy, but one focused on sacrificial love. However, as *Skylight* shows, the personal is political. Its theme is a replay of *Secret Rapture*, which Hare at the time had called his 'most personal and private' play[47] – here transposed to a completely intimate scale, where all political reference is submerged in an anatomy of the relationship between two individuals.

In this argument between public morality and private fulfilment, the lines drawn are between individual passion, sexual and selfish but redemptive, versus a generalized love for humanity, self-sacrificing but committed to 'clear[ing] out society's drains'. The protagonists are classic Hare extremes: a self-made entrepreneur and insensitive sexist, who epitomizes right-wing selfishness; and a younger idealistic woman, who possesses high mathematical talent but chooses to teach in a slum-area comprehensive. Yet here the view is balanced. These opposites attract, indeed the embers of an affair between them some years ago still burn. Then, too, the grasping capitalist (who as a restaurant owner represents the ego-driven consumerism of Thatcher's Britain through the 1980s, the period of his rise to wealth) has an attractive appetite for living life to its fullest, as well as deep emotional pain. And his capacity for feeling is also expressed in telling invective against the lack of personal love, even the avoidance of any meaningful relationship in the girl's dedication to improving society: for example, when she asserts that the people who matter to her are the poor whom she meets on her daily bus journey, his response is all too accurate in suggesting she loves 'the people on the bus because in three minutes you can get off'.[48] Lost after the death of his wife (to comfort whose long final illness he built a sickroom with the skylight of the title) he needs her to put his life back together. But the mutual guilt of their past adulterous relationship finally prevents these two polarized experiences of contemporary Britain from reuniting; and although the long night ends with the woman sharing a symbolic dawn alongside the younger generation of the future, represented by the tycoon's son, the daylight is grey and uncertain.

The other plays in this second trilogy are equally bleak, as is *The Blue Room* beneath its glitzy hedonistic surface. Amy, who espouses unconditional love, dies of an unexpected hemorrhage having been abandoned by her husband and finding herself unable to embrace her mother. Oscar Wilde is shown being betrayed not once, but twice by his aristocratic lover Bosie (Lord Alfred Douglas) and ends up isolated, unable to write and waiting for death. But increasingly in his recent work Hare turns to the discussion of art, and its function in the modern world. It could be seen as a retrospective stocktaking of his theatrical career at the close of the millennium.

The Blue Room is a reworking of a play from exactly 100 years before, updating Schnitzler's *fin de siècle* Vienna of 1898 to the amoral neon-lit luxury of London in 1998; and Hare changes the original pairings to introduce a seduction between a narcissistic playwright and a West End actress. There are also echoes of earlier drama in the other plays, with *Skylight* in a sense being an updated version of Noel Coward's *Brief Encounter*; and *Amy's View* paralleling Coward's *Hay Fever*, the title of which is even mentioned explicitly in the dialogue, opening as it does at the country house of a famous but somewhat dated actress who is confronted with an unwelcome young guest romantically involved with her daughter. *The Judas Kiss* is full of theatrical references, with Bosie complaining 'I feel like an actor cast in the wrong role'; and Wilde, 'trapped in the narrative' and welcoming 'the chance to play tragedy'. In addition he is shown consciously turning his life into art, organizing his experience into a secular crucifixion and orchestrating the biblical gesture of betrayal signalled in the title. Even *Via Dolorosa* contains an argument about art (focused on 'the falsity of the art-works in the Holocaust Museum').[49] And the theme of artistic relevance and authenticity is central to *Amy's View*, where the main figure of the actress progresses under the pressure of losing everything she has, from being a West End star of fashionable comedy who is 'best at playing genteel . . . Layers. I play lots of layers' to going 'down to the core' in a 'young' play at an alternative theatre.[50]

Hare sets her against her daughter's husband (who for Amy represents the future) who once saw theatre as 'really exciting' – presumably in the politically radicalized period of Hare's early career, when 'it still had something to say' – but now asserts it is irrelevant to a modern video-oriented world where 'the image has taken the place of the word', and takes up making Tarantino-like films featuring graphic pictures of brains exploding under the impact of a bullet. In the scheme of the play 'he's lost ... It's like he's spun off his axis'; and as such he represents the false values of contemporary Britain. The action spans almost two decades, from 1979 (the year Margaret Thatcher was first elected) to 1995 (when it became obvious that the Conservative Party was falling apart) offering a view of a society who – just like him – 'no longer know who they are' and who live in a sham world of traditionalism epitomized by the Lloyd's débâcle, 'England as sheer bloody theatre', in which the actress loses everything she owns. Yet in doing so she regains the authenticity of her art, which moves even the film director to recognize the capacity of live theatre to communicate spiritual experience as an 'extraordinary phenomenon'.[51] And the ending presents an image of hope once illusions and material goals have been discarded, which is clearly intended to have political as well as artistic resonance: in a ritual of baptism, she and her young fellow-actor (stripped down to the basics '*like Poor Tom in* King Lear') pour water over each other, and stand alone, blue with cold on stage as the curtain rises on their play.

Notes

1 Hare, in *Plays and Players*, January 1972, p. 18.

2 Brenton, in *New Theatre Voices of the Seventies*, ed. Simon Trussler, London, 1981, p. 91; Hare, in *Plays and Players*, January 1972, p. 20; Brenton, *Theatre Quarterly*, 5, 17 (1975), p. 18.

3 Hare, 1978 lecture (Cambridge), published as an afterword to *Licking Hitler*, London, 1978, p. 61.

4 Hare, in *At the Royal Court, 25 Years of the English Stage Company*, Amber Lane Press, 1981, p. 142.

5 Hare, *Fanshen*, London, 1976, p. 15.

6 Hare, in *New Theatre Voices of the Seventies*, ed. Trussler, p. 120.

7 *Fanshen*, p. 83.

8 *Ibid.*, p. 21.

9 Gaskill in *Plays and Players*, May 1976, p. 11, and Hare, Preface to *Fanshen*, p. 9.

10 *Fanshen*, pp. 21, 24 & 84; Preface, p. 7; Hare, in *New Theatre Voices of the Seventies*, ed. Trussler, p. 119.

11 *Pravda*, London, 1985, pp. 119, 124; Wesker, *Journey Into Journalism*, London, 1977, cited in the National Theatre programme for *Pravda*.

12 *Pravda*, pp. 118, 113; Hare, cited in Herb Greer, *Encounter*, September/October 1985, p. 37.

13 *Pravda*, pp. 105, 103, 116–17; Hare in *New Theatre Voices of the Seventies*, ed. Trussler, p. 118.

14 Brenton, in *New Theatre Voices of the Seventies*, ed. Trussler, p. 93.

15 *Magnificence*, London, 1973, p. 15; Brenton, in *New Theatre Voices of the Seventies*, ed. Trussler, p. 97.

16 Brenton, in *Plays and Players*, February 1972, p. 16.

17 *Three Plays*, ed. John Bull, Sheffield, 1989, p. 45.

18 *Weapons of Happiness*, London, 1976, pp. 34 & 69–70; Brenton, in *Time Out*, 17 July 1976.

19 *Weapons of Happiness*, pp. 73, 79 & 75.

20 *New Statesman*, 23 July 1976, and *Drama*, Autumn 1976, p. 37; Brenton, on 'Kaleidescope', BBC Radio 4, 16 July 1976 (script, National Theatre archives).

21 David Hare (Director of *Weapons of Happiness*), cited in *The Guardian*, 9 July 1976.

22 *Weapons of Happiness*, p. 48.

23 Shelley, cited in Brenton, *Bloody Poetry*, London, 1985, p. 70.

24 *Ibid.*, p. 82.

25 *Ibid.*, p. 74, 38, 77.

26 *Ibid.*, p. 14.

27 Howard Brenton, *Greenland*, London, 1988, pp. 18, 3, 12, 37 & 53–4.

28 *Berlin Bertie*, London, 1992, p. 58.

29 *Berlin Bertie*, p. 16.

30 Hare, *Acting Up*, London & New York, 1999, p. 233.

31 *Via Dolorosa*, London, 1998, p. 6.

32 Hare, *Writing Left-Handed*, London, 1991, p. 159.

33 Hare, in *Plays and Players*, February 1972, pp. 20 & 18.

34 Hare, *Knuckle*, London, 1974, pp. 48, 39–40.

35 *Licking Hitler*, London, 1978, p. 54; Peter Ansorge, *Plays and Players*, April 1978, p. 13.

36 *Plenty*, London, 1978, p. 44.

37 *Ibid.*, pp. 53–4, 72, 65.

38 *Ibid.*, pp. 29, 78–9.

39 Hare, in *Time Out*, 29 August 1975; *Plenty*, p. 86.

40 Hare, in *Time Out*, 7 April 1978, and 'A Lecture', in *Licking Hitler*, p. 63.

41 *Plenty*, p. 87.

42 Edgar, in BTI/DATEC no. 1, Autumn 1984.

43 Hayden Griffiths, in *Plays and Players*, February 1983, p. 13.

44 *Racing Demon*, London, 1990, p. 1.

45 Helena Kennedy QC, and The Rt Rev. David Hope, *Sunday Times*, 10 October 1993, Lord Rawlinson, *Daily Telegraph*, 17 October 1991.

46 *Racing Demon*, p. 58.

47 *Writing Left-Handed*, London, 1991, p. 158.

48 *Skylight*, London, 1995, pp. 80, 88–9.
49 *The Judas Kiss*, New York, 1998, pp. 111, 36, 40; and *Acting Up*, p. 127.
50 *Amy's View*, London, 1998, pp. 16, 114.
51 *Ibid.*, pp. 52, 87, 47, 99, 116.

3.12 The feminist alternative

Apart from some minor exceptions, such as Elizabeth Robins' *Votes for Women!* (1906), female playwrights have been conspicuous by their absence from British theatre up until the late 1950s. Even then, Anne Jellicoe found the commercial stage inappropriate to her feminist aims (see below, p. 496), while Shelagh Delaney's only success was a compromise with popular taste. *A Taste of Honey* (1958), produced when Delaney was barely nineteen years old, marked out some of the dramatic material that has become characteristic of women's drama over the last two decades. The off-beat heroine, born of a chance encounter between her music-hall tart of a mother and a mental defective, is uninhibited and sexually liberated. Pregnant by a Negro sailor, who has deserted her, she sets up house with a maternally inclined homosexual: a paradigm of alternative lifestyles. But the challenge to conventional morality is undermined by comic treatment – exacerbated by Joan Littlewood's influence, which inserted knockabout farce and music-hall repartee with the audience – and defused by a sentimental ending, in which the girl and her mother join to bring up the baby without male support. Kenneth Tynan, the critical standard-bearer of the new dramatic movement, hailed *A Taste of Honey* as 'both comic and heroic' with 'the smell of living', and labelled Delaney 'a portent'.[1] Yet her follow-up drama, *The Lion in Love* (1960), only achieved a limited run; and Delaney abandoned the stage for film-writing.

By contrast, the women playwrights who followed consciously explored areas of experience that the stage traditionally ignored, and developed styles designed as a radical contrast to the standard dramatic forms. Indeed, from a feminist viewpoint the category of 'woman-writer' defines 'a species of creativity that challenges the dominant image', since 'the very concept of the 'writer' implies *maleness*'. It is claimed that simply by gaining public recognition, the female dramatist 'reorients our perspective'; and writing as a woman 'will itself introduce new concepts of subject matter'. Conventional plot structures, such as sequential scenes or patterns of cause and effect, are rejected. So is the type of conflict that represents a duel between equals, and integrated characterization that implies the dominance of individuals over their social context, since all of these conventional dramatic elements are seen as 'expressing systems of ideas in which the male concern is the norm'.[2]

The concept of writing plays about uniquely female (as against general or masculine-oriented) topics, and specifically for women performers, can be traced back to suffragette theatre, or groups such as the Actresses' Franchise League, at the turn of the century. But feminist drama only evolved as a distinct form in the mid-1970s. Allied with the Gay Liberation Front, and followed by the rise in Black militancy, its roots were in the alternative theatre companies that proliferated after the student revolution of 1968. Indeed, despite underlying ideological incompatibilities, Marxist and sexual revolutionaries at first worked together – as in a group like The General Will, which was taken over by homosexual activists in 1977.

All these radical groups tended to perform for sharply defined audiences. Left-wing Agitprop was designed for a specifically working-class segment of the population, touring outside the standard stage circuit; regional groups identified themselves with a local context, and reflected the lives or immediate concerns of their spectators. These aspects of self-selection, limited focus, and an unusual degree of unity between dramatic subject, performer and public – together with the militant radicalism of the average socialist counter-theatre – formed the basis of the new feminist drama. But the sexually defined groupings turned out to be qualitatively different from the straight political theatre troupes of the time. As titles such as Welfare State or The General Will indicate, socialist groups aimed to address society as a whole, so that they led naturally to all-inclusive Community Theatre championed by Anne Jellicoe or Peter Cheeseman (see above, p. 185). And most of the (predominantly male) playwrights, who began their career writing for Welfare State or The General Will, made a transition to main-stage drama. By contrast, titles such as The Women's Theatre Group, The Monstrous Regiment (named after the misogynist pamphlet by the sixteenth-century preacher John Knox), or the Gay Sweatshop, are implicitly exclusive. Feminist and homosexual groups have proved to be as sectarian as the Black Theatre Co-operative, which is restricted to ethnic interests and all-black audiences. Social divisions of class, wealth or status, which politically motivated drama aims to change or abolish, are extrinsic and variable. Gender and race are innate as well as visible distinctions; and in general the underlying objective of plays produced by sexually defined groups is to confirm their separateness.

Thus from the first The Women's Theatre Group prohibited male participation. When the similarly named Women's Theatre Company staged one of Pam Gems's early plays, *Go West Young Woman* (1974), the performance was interrupted by two different bands of more radical feminists objecting to the presence of men in the cast. Even a decade later a black feminist like Jacqueline Rudet was declaring it 'a mistake having a man direct' her play, *Money to Live* (1984), on the ground that 'what women create in life, men destroy'. Much of the dramatic material and the way it is staged also deliberately excluded spectators of the opposite sex, while performances depicting heterosexual relationships or romantic fantasy, such as Bryony Lavery's cabaret, *Time Gentlemen Please* (1978), were stopped by activist protesters. During these early years male characters (or in the case of Black theatre, whites) were typically presented as repugnant and evil. Even those sympathetic to their aims tend to be excluded: as Caryl Churchill noted, supportive 'men in particular were upset' by her play *Vinegar Tom* (1976) because 'they were definitely placed outside the experience of the female characters'.[3]

Similarly, there is a tendency among some of the more extreme feminists to dismiss any negative commentary as 'misogynist', thus exempting their work from criticism.[4] Their premise is that the theatrical Establishment is intrinsically hostile to any female concerns. But by ignoring the degree to which reviewers reflect the opinions of the wider public, such an attitude marginalizes their drama.

The extremism of these special-interest groups led to further fragmentation, with Gay Sweatshop splitting into separate homosexual and lesbian factions, or Imani-Faith emerging in 1983 as an off-shoot of both feminist and Black theatre movements to present plays by, about, and exclusively for black women. Inevitably, the more narrowly focused and nonconformist groups limited themselves to small-scale fringe performances. Certainly an occasional mainstream play emerged from this marginalized background, such as Sarah Daniels' radical lesbian *Masterpieces* or *Neaptide* (which won the George Devine Award in 1982, although it only reached the stage – at the National Theatre – in 1986), or Martin Sherman's melodramatically inflated equation of homosexual persecution with the Holocaust and Nazi death-camps in *Bent* (1979). Yet in general the dramatists working in such confined contexts deliberately avoided making the transition to main-stage theatre because their search for alternative modes of theatre rules out such compromise with the Establishment almost by definition.

However, to some extent the reason why so few significant playwrights emerged from these groups is related to the communal script creation, which became an intrinsic aspect of this movement. The effect of the abolition of censorship in 1968 was far more wide-reaching than simply lifting restrictions on subject matter. Instead of a complete text having to be submitted to the Lord Chamberlain's office, which once approved could not be changed in rehearsal or performance, plays could now be based on improvisation and altered to include topical reference, or in response to the performers' views. Collaborative working methods replaced the hierarchy of dramatist–director–actors. The author lost creative independence to the group; and the notion of the text as the intellectual property of the writer was rejected as not only analogous to class divisions, but associated with the male power structure.

Collective creation became the sign and example of female, as well as socialist, principles. The way scripts were evolved by a company like the Joint Stock theatre collective – which produced most of Caryl Churchill's major plays, as well as Hare's *Fanshen* (1975: see above, pp. 199–203) and Howard Barker's early pieces – is representative: 'One . . . to expose ourselves and our problems /Two . . . to create a play about it /Three . . . to rehearse and perform that play'.[5] Closely associated with the Royal Court, and with the script produced by specially commissioned writers on the basis of workshop improvisation around a set theme – rather than being devised and written by the acting company as a whole – the Joint Stock is unique in nurturing new mainstream dramatists. Yet even here the ensemble principle, with its requirement of equal parts for all, rules out the creation of large central roles whom the audience can follow.

However desirable as a political paradigm, the approach thus has certain theatrical limitations; and these were compounded by the more extreme collective process, in which the script tended to be so conditioned by the personalities of the particular performers that the roles became untransferable. At the same time, the emotional charge of working collectively and the discovery of shared ideas could be highly creative. As Churchill commented, 'my attitude to myself, my work and others had been basically and permanently changed' by writing for Monstrous Regiment and Joint Stock.[6] However, dependency on the process automatically kept playwrights on the fringe. So during the late 1970s there were just two women-writers whose work became an important and influential part of the general repertoire: Caryl Churchill and Pam Gems; and it was not until the 1990s that any number of feminist or gay writers followed them out of the closet of special-interest groups. Prominent among these are Shelagh Stephenson, whose first play *Memory of Water* (1996) was immediately picked up on both sides of the Atlantic and given major productions, or the brutally shocking work of Sarah Kane; and Neil Bartlett whose translations of Racine and Marivaux were staged at the National, and who took over the Lyric Theatre where he has directed several of his own plays as provocative stagings of gay sensibility, from his adaptation of Wilde's *The Picture of Dorian Gray* in 1994 to *Seven Sonnets of Michelangelo* (1998).

Although this next generation of playwrights all continue to present specifically female or gay experience and deal with society in terms of gender issues, they are addressing the general public. This is perhaps a measure of the broad shift in social attitudes over the last decades. By contrast both Churchill and Gems had to consciously distance themselves from the radical feminism of the 1970s; but the distinction made by Churchill is as much a key factor for these contemporary writers as it was in opening up her own work: 'what I feel is quite strongly a feminist position and that inevitably comes in to what I write. However, that's quite different from somebody who is a feminist using writing to advance that position.' Similarly, Gems declared that 'the phrase "feminist writer" is absolutely meaningless because it implies polemic, and polemic is about changing things in a direct political way. Drama is subversive.'[7]

Both developed their vision and theatrical techniques through dealing with historical subjects; and their example has been influential, making the history play characteristic of women's drama. Indeed history has particular significance for the feminist movement. As the traditional form of commemorating public events in a society almost exclusively ruled by men, it is seen as promoting a male system of values. Women, relegated to the private sphere, become invisible, reinforcing their subservient status. Just as Marxist historians have focused on the common people, instead of their rulers, so Gems asserts that 'We have our own history to create, to write.'[8] The tension between received ideas of the past, and the very different feminist perspective, contributes to thematic complexity. And perhaps because of this, the majority of women's plays that have been popularly successful on the mainstream stage are historical: perhaps the best example being Timberlake Wertenbaker's *Our Country's Good* (1988), which was developed by Max Stafford-Clark as a companion piece to the Royal Court production of Farquhar's Restoration classic, *The Recruiting Officer*, and has been widely staged internationally.

One aspect of this focus on history – establishing a female literary tradition through rediscovering 'plays from the past either by or about women', for which a group like Mrs Worthington's Daughters was founded – is represented by Michelene Wandor's *Aurora Leigh* (1979). Retaining the iambic pentameter form of Elizabeth Barrett Browning's verse novel, it illustrates two models of female independence in a barely sketched Victorian context. The semi-autobiographical heroine wins emancipation through her writing. Her artistic achievement demonstrates the falsity of masculine prescribed norms, that require women to be 'chaste wives/Sublime Madonnas... If your sex is weak/for art, it is all the more fit and strong/For life and duty.'[9] Converting the male-chauvinist who earlier offered her marriage in these terms, Aurora's literary prestige and independent income make a positive relationship between the sexes possible. The alternative example is a raped servant girl's choice of prostitution to raise her illegitimate son, existing completely outside the male-dominated society in the only role it has left her: a formula which recurs in many feminist plays – where prostitution is presented either as an assertion of sexual liberation, a way of achieving financial independence (as in Rudet's *Money To Live*), or as epitomizing the exploitation of women (as in Wandor's *Whores d'Oeuvres*, 1978).

However, while coming out of the same movement, and both dealing with historical themes, Gems and Churchill are stylistically quite distinct. Each marks out a different approach to the past: exposing the gender bias in received images of well-known women, versus reinterpreting history from a female perspective. And where Gems typically uses a modified form of realism, which links her work with the dominant line of social drama, Churchill tends to deal with the psychology of politics. Her plays are increasingly imagistic, and fall more into the category of poetic drama.

Notes

1 *The Observer*, 1 June 1958.
2 Michelene Wandor, introduction to *Plays by Women*, I, London, 1982, pp. 8, 11, and *Carry On, Understudies*, London, 1986, p. 31.
3 *Plays by Women*, V, London, 1985, p. 180; Caryl Churchill, in *Plays by Women*, I, p. 41.
4 See *Carry On, Understudies*, pp. 117–18.
5 Max Stafford-Clark, unpublished Rehearsal Diary for *Cloud Nine*, 3 January 1979. (It is worth noting that in its fifteen years of operation, Joint Stock only mounted four collectively written pieces.)
6 Caryl Churchill, *Plays: One*, London, 1985, p. 131.
7 Churchill and Gems, in *Time Out*, 27 October 1977.
8 Gems, in *Plays by Women*, I (afterword to *Dusa, Fish, Stas and Vi*), p. 73.
9 Programme for Mrs Worthington's Daughters, 1979, cited in *Carry on Understudies*, p. 84; *Plays by Women*, I, pp. 110–11.

Pam Gems (1925–): reinterpreting the stereotype

CHECKLIST OF GEMS'S MAJOR PLAYS

The Amiable Courtship of *Ms Venus and Wild Bill*, 1975	*Loving Women*, 1984
Queen Christina, 1977	*The Danton Affair*, 1986
Dusa, Fish, Stas and Vi, 1977	*The Blue Angel*, 1991
Piaf, 1978	*Stanley*, 1996
Camille, 1984	*Marlene*, 1996
	The Snow Palace, 1998

Like many women dramatists, Pam Gems came to the theatre late, after twenty years of marriage and child-raising. Starting on the fringe, her early work for feminist theatre groups included an autobiographical piece, together with two monologues about female isolation and abortion (1973), and a satiric pantomime (1975). However, *Queen Christina* (1977), her first major play, struck a new note and established all her central themes.

As in this play, Gems's most characteristic work dramatizes the human reality of women who have been transformed into cultural symbols. These range from the seventeenth-century Swedish Queen who renounced her crown, to a nineteenth-century courtesan, and modern artists: a singer, an actress and a (male) painter obsessed by images of women. In each case the character is set against a familiar and highly romanticized picture. The counter-source for the earliest of Gems's historical dramas was the classic Greta Garbo film of an ethereal and intellectual beauty, who abdicates for love, then finds consolation in religion when the man for whom she has sacrificed everything is killed in a duel. *Piaf* (1978) turns from Hollywood myth to the sanitized commercial image of a vulnerable street-sparrow, a purely emotional being whose songs are the direct expression 'of unhappiness . . . of being made helpless by love . . . of being alone'. *Camille* (1984) is a reversal of both Dumas' sentimentally tragic *Dame aux camélias* and Verdi's operatic idealization in *La Traviata*. *The Blue Angel* (1991) and *Marlene* (1996) both play off Heinrich Mann's novel *Professor Unrat* and the 1930 film of it that made Marlene Dietrich's reputation, as well as her Hollywood image as an icon of sexuality.

The opposition between what is depicted on the stage and the audience's expectations is most obvious in *Piaf*, where incidents from the Parisian singer's life are interpolated with renditions of her popular lyrics. The gutter milieu, cheap prostitution and involvement in murder, violence, drunkenness and drugs undermine the glittering public persona. Piaf is

shown as disintegrating under the contradiction; and when the gap between idol and real woman can no longer be disguised, society preserves the
false image by divorcing musical soul from female body – a male fan's typical
response being 'Madame may be a vicious and foul mouthed slut . . . but I
salute the artistry.'[1]

At the same time, the way the songs rise out of the scenes emphasizes that
Piaf's unconventional art and her physical crudity are inseparable. Her rise
to stardom is a process of continual exploitation by the men who manage
or marry her, and by her public (by extension the audience for Gems's play)
who project their desires on to her. Yet it is also her status as a star that
enables her to assert a personal autonomy, however provisional. This is
expressed through her sexual freedom, which overturns all the moral codes.
And the same reversal of conventional values is reflected in the play itself,
which shows Piaf not only copulating but ostentatiously pissing on stage.
Physicality at its most basic (a stock way of representing reality) demolishes
the socially acceptable female stereotype, promoted and imposed by men,
and thus provides an example of alternative values.

Gems explicitly explores these alternative values in her following play,
Camille (1984), where the only women presented are prostitutes, and the
completely male-dominated class system is corrupt and depraved. Radically
changing the moral context of Dumas' romantic story, Marguerite's background is one of poverty and unremitting sexual exploitation. She is raped by
the men in her family from the age of five, and made pregnant by a Marquis
who not only employs her as a housemaid while still an innocent girl, but
also (melodramatically) turns out to be the father of Armand, the young
man she loves. Her only choices are self-destroying enslavement in the kind
of marriage available to her: 'Seven pregnancies in nine years? Arms swollen
with soda from washing other peoples' linen? Ask my mother.' Or 'To be
a huntress, a marauder', bartering her body for independence (echoing the
servant-girl's option in Wandor's *Aurora Leigh*).[2]

But Gems shows even this limited form of emancipation to be illusory
by making a clear association between a prostitute's lifestyle, and the consumption which eventually kills her. Armand too is a victim of this vicious
society. Naive innocence, such as Dumas and Verdi portrayed, cannot exist
in such circumstances; and Armand is not only debauched but homosexual,
living with a degenerate Russian prince.

Retreat to a utopian countryside offers redemption to both; and Armand
outlines an idyllic future of mutual support and equality. 'We'll work
together, side by side. Without ambition, except to excel, without greed,

except to offer the best of ourselves . . . our aim. To live – to support our children – to read – to think – and to be as clear as we can.' But this vision of a different relationship between the sexes is destroyed by financial and emotional blackmail: the effete Prince slashes his wrists in an attempt to persuade Armand not to leave him, and the Marquis threatens to disown and bankrupt him, or to have Marguerite imprisoned. Her family are dependent on her earnings as a prostitute, and the Marquis kidnaps his illegitimate child from her, offering to adopt and educate the boy if she renounces Armand and returns to her previous way of living. All elements of society collaborate against the pair; and the accusation levelled at the 'respectable' gathering of the Establishment by Armand in the epilogue underlines the point.

You killed her. Were we so threatening? One man? One woman? It was the wrong transaction. There was a chance . . . for something real . . . There was respect. Honour. Possibility. But you don't want that. What do you want?[3]

The deforming pressures of society are most fully explored in *Queen Christina* (1977), which focuses on gender roles. Here the historical figure provides a test-case for issues of sexual definition, biological determinism and social programming. As the sole heir to a kingdom at war, the young Queen has been 'reared as a man . . . And then, on her accession, told to marry and breed, that is to be a woman. By which time, of course, like males of her era, she despised women as weak, hysterical, silly creatures.' For Gems 'It is a confusion which seems as apposite as ever.'[4] And the opening demonstrates this by challenging the audience's stereotypes.

Spectators are faced with an elegantly dressed, classically feminine beauty and the muddy, slouching figure in groom's clothes who follows her on to the stage. Like the waiting royal suitor, we are tricked into mistaking the wrong one for the Queen, whose arrival has just been announced. And the incongruity of conventional expectations is underlined by comedy: after a demonstration of physical superiority in which she '*thumps the* PRINCE *genially on the shoulder, sending him reeling*', the masculine-looking Christina '*takes the* PRINCE*'s nerveless arm and stands beside him in wifely stance*.'[5] But beneath this parodistic reversal lies personal tragedy. The irreconcilable contradiction destroys her.

Christina hunts, decides military strategy and state policy, as well as bedding other young women – such as Ebba, the beautiful lady-in-waiting – and her success as a substitute male ruler incapacitates her for fufilling the female requirement to ensure political stability by procreation. Her intimidating intellectual equality, as much as her plainness (accentuated by physical deformity), repels men who have been conditioned to see women as submissive sex-objects. The handsome courtier she picks prefers the conventionally feminine Ebba. So she abdicates rather than demean herself by marrying someone only interested in the crown.

Searching Europe for a way of life in which she can be herself, Christina is shown coming to terms with her sexual identity. She is hailed as 'an inspiration' to man-hating feminists (in the shape of eighteenth-century French 'blue-stockings') in their campaign for control over their bodies through abortion. But finds herself repulsed by their life-denying warfare against the opposite sex, which she recognizes as the mirror-image of male domination. Seeking spiritual emancipation in the Catholic Church, she finds that although the Pope denounces sexuality as denying 'both justice and the inner life' by treating 'other people as a means to an end', his interest is only in exploiting her conversion for religious propaganda; and spurning celibacy, she asserts that 'We won't deny the body.' Offered the kingdom of Naples, she attempts to return to her masculine role. But when it forces her to kill her lover for betraying her invading armies, she rejects the whole male ethos, setting herself against domination in all its forms, master/servant as well as man/woman. Finally – when too old to bear children – she discovers the value of maternal instincts and affirms her biological nature.

This wide-ranging epic action is set in the context of 'the new scepticism' that, fuelled by Galileo's astronomy and Descartes' rationalism, overturns all traditional assumptions about the meaning of existence. As Christina asserts:

to believe we're here *because*... or *in order to* – why that's to accept the most horrifying malignancy or the most unbelievably inept! Pestilence!... The murder of children – by design?... I begin not to believe in anything.[6]

The analogy to the present is clear (as with the French 'blue-stockings') and Christina's identity crisis epitomizes the predicament of modern women, confused by the mixed signals of romantic novels, women's magazines and advertising, all of which promote images of traditional femininity along with the feminist assertion of equality and sexual revolution. And it is these images that are centre-stage in both *The Blue Angel* and *Marlene*.

While incorporating the songs from Sternberg's classic film, Gems's version of *The Blue Angel* is more savage, returning to the far darker tone of Mann's original 1905 novel while updating it to Hamburg in the 1920s. In its original RSC production, the setting echoed the angular distortions of expressionist films like Murnau's *Cabinet of Dr Caligari*; and here the self-righteous and rigidly repressed schoolmaster – who believes it within his power to save the soul of another human being, only to destroy himself through his obsession with a nightclub singer – viciously takes revenge by blackmailing the hypocritical society that casts him out when he marries her. Prostituting the singer as bait, he exposes their moral corruption in a series of vignettes that are presented as cabaret turns on the nightclub stage, but, losing the evidence, is reduced to abject humiliation: forced to caper crowing like a cock before the people he hates, in a clown costume with a pig's snout for a nose on his whitened face. The political dimension of the play is carried by the grotesque cabaret performers, modelled on the deformed and monstrous figures of expressionist painters like George Grosz or Otto Dix, who stand as a distorted mirror of the greed and brutality of the Weimar bourgeoisie – and by extension of contemporary Capitalism. But the main focus is on the economics of glamour, with the singer (significantly named Lola after Dietrich's film role, rather than the Rosa of Mann's novel) being indeed the 'whore' the Professor calls her.

Rather than the slow smoky rhythms of Marlene Dietrich's famous interpretation, Gems's characterization of Lola, ruthless and predatory as well as vulnerable and victimized, is designed to reveal the way such an icon of female sexuality is shaped by and reflects the society that creates her. And it is as the icon that Dietrich herself – impersonated by Siân Phillips, for whom the play was written – appears on stage in *Marlene*, a title that plays not only on the first-name status of the star but on one of her signature songs, 'Lily Marlene'. Echoing Dietrich's well-known manipulation of her own public image, the backstage view shows a different but equally calculated myth to the famous persona. Although presented at the age of sixty-plus, frail and nervous in preparing for her comeback in Paris in the 1960s, her private character is depicted as no less dominating than her charismatic stage performance. Behind the glittering trademark gown of the star, Marlene is indomitable. From her opening exclamation, 'Did I have a good trip? Is Bismark a herring?' the emphasis is on her eccentric wit and arrogant candour, which carries over even into traditionally female tasks like housekeeping when we are shown Marlene (obsessed with cleanliness, as Dietrich was known to be) scrubbing the floor of her dressing room. Critics dismissed the play as merely a star vehicle, which indeed on one level it is, or even as a hagiography with no critical edge. But this misses the point that *Marlene* is the portrait of a positive feminist ideal. Not only a

10 Expressionist distortions: the male gaze and woman as sex icon – the image of
Marlene Dietrich in Gems's *The Blue Angel*

survivor – unlike the, in many ways, similar figure of Piaf – she triumphs over circumstance, enjoys complete sexual freedom while retaining her personal independence.

Marlene is intended as an icon of female empowerment as well as sexuality and stardom. But Dietrich was too unique to serve as a general model. And in *The Snow Palace* (1998) Gems's returned to the issue of the personal cost for women in taking control of their own lives through the example of a young Polish writer from the 1920s (Stanislawa Przybyzewska) who died of hypothermia at the age of 33, having cut herself off in an abandoned and unheated school, sustained by morphine, to write a 600-page play about the French Revolution – which Gems had already used as the basis for *The Danton Affair* in 1986. That had been her only play with a male protagonist, until *Stanley* in 1996. Here Gems's theme is art and the sources of creative inspiration, explored through the rural bohemian Stanley Spencer, who died in 1959 and whose paintings transformed the very solid flesh of English country people into contemporary versions of biblical myth. Spencer celebrated the working class, portraying the strongly physical inhabitants of Cookham, his home village, as taking part in *The Last Supper* or *The Resurrection. Cookham* (which filled the set in the original National Theatre staging). But although in this production the figure of Spencer dominated with Antony Sher in the role, again the real focus is on women and how they are portrayed, since the source of Spencer's visionary art was (notoriously) sexuality. The emotional centre of the play is Stanley's first wife Hilda, dying of cancer after being abandoned for an upper-class lesbian who only seduces and marries Stanley to finance her mediocre career as a painter, then returns to her lover, the artist Dorothy Hepworth.

The play supports Stanley's belief that sex is the essence of religion and that his paintings 'reveal the nature of the world through love', making the point that the task of the artist is to mediate between God and man in a long final monologue. However, there is an all too real contradiction in his belief that 'the erotic is the essence of religion', which leads him to assert that 'The whole of my life in art has been a slow realization of the mystery of sex.' Carrying this divine 'passion' through in his private life, he insists with appalling insensitivity that earth-mother Hilda, whom he has betrayed and divorced, return to live with him and his new wife. And his naive but naked egoism is all too clear when he demands 'What I want to know is why must a man have only one woman? Apart from the expense.' Indeed the play holds Stanley responsible for Hilda's illness; and he himself realizes the destructiveness of his behaviour when after her death Hilda returns as his muse.[7] At the same time the exposed, even ugly, flesh portrayed in Spencer's art is set as a positive image of women against the standard (and blatantly false) icon of sexuality in the male gaze: the fetishistic body in black underwear displayed by the lesbian to attract Stanley.

For Gems, 'Whichever way we look at it, the old norms won't do any more.' But the new radical feminism is seen as taking over precisely those qualities that distort relationships between the sexes in the male-dominated system. By juxtaposing the two most extreme positions, *Queen Christina* asks what it means to be 'female'. And although *Marlene* offers a triumphant image of what this might be, Christina's example implies that a valid definition can only be reached through 'the creation of a society more suited to both sexes' – which Gems described as her aim in writing. Her concept of drama as subversive, rather than confrontational, means working on public consciousness indirectly. In line with this, her eighteenth-century protagonist comes to realize that positive change can only be achieved through the specifically female, undervalued qualities of 'weakness', non-violent resilience and maternal nurture.

Must it always be the sword? By God, half the world are women . . . they've learned subversion . . . why not try that? Half the world rapes and destroys – must women, the other half, join in?[8]

The final question of *Queen Christina*, as in *Camille*, is addressed more to the audience than to the historical characters. And Gems's two present-day, non-biographical plays deal directly with the creation of a new relationship between the sexes. *Dusa, Fish, Stas and Vi* (1977) demonstrates the tragic breakdown of conventional patterns, while *Loving Women* (1984) proposes a positive alternative.

The four title characters of the first play represent a complete spectrum of female experience. Dusa, whose identity is rooted entirely in maternal instincts, embodies woman's biological nature, while the theme of sexual stereotyping is demonstrated through Stas – a physiotherapist moonlighting as a call-girl to finance her training as a marine biologist: 'before our eyes she transforms herself from an unremarkable female employee to a glittering, heavy-headed, mesmeric-eyed Klimt painting'. Fish, who is modelled on Rosa Luxemburg (the German pacifist and revolutionary leader, shot by reactionary forces after the First World War), represents politically conscious feminism. Although apparently liberated, all are casualties of 'the antagonism between the sexes' which for Gems is 'an indictment of our age'.[9]

Vi, a teenage refugee from the slums, has aborted an unwanted baby; and the anorexia she almost dies from is a symptom of her alienation. Dusa, whose vengeful husband abducts her children when she divorces him, tries to throw herself out of the window, having lost her reason for living. Even Stas, to whom sex is simply a business proposition, contracts venereal disease from her customers. For these women marriage is no longer a viable possibility since wives 'end up skint, abandoned and hooked on valium', while any emotional involvement with men is 'pain, when was it anything else?'[10]

Fish's moral strength and capacity for caring, which holds this female commune together and brings the others through their different crises, makes her experience a touchstone for the audience. Her platform speech on the modern relevance of Rosa Luxemburg is the central point in the play. Offering an alternative to the (male-dominated) politics of confrontation, she outlines an ideal of men and women 'breaking moulds together'. But her socialist lover turns out to be incapable of responding to this vision. Unwilling to relinquish the male advantages in traditional roles, he rejects her for a conventionally submissive, dependent, sensual woman. Isolated, unable to fulfil her emotional needs, and with her political commitment to changing society as a whole discredited by her inability to put her ideals into practice on a personal level, Fish kills herself. Her suicide note spells out a position of despair: 'There's no love, and I can't face the thought of fighting . . . We won't do as [men] want any more, and they hate it. What are we to do?'[11]

Loving Women suggests an answer to precisely this question. Again the man chooses physical attractiveness and housewifely comfort over an ideologically demanding feminist. However, here this is the opening situation; and the options are not closed off melodramatically by death. Instead a dialectic is created between socialist principle and sexuality.

In the second Act Frank, married to a beautiful but unintelligent working-girl, has abandoned his revolutionary idealism and the Theatre in Education group that he ran with Susannah. Having sold out to socially conformist roles of schoolteaching and fatherhood, he rejects their previous political activism as intellectually dishonest, quasi-fascist and working against the real interests of the underprivileged. Unable to answer his criticism, Susannah preserves her commitment by leaving to work in the Third World. In the last Act, some years later, the positions are reversed. Frank is once more dedicated to changing society, which has led him to neglect his marriage. Susannah's exposure to the extreme deprivation of South American peasants has convinced her that sacrificing individual fulfilment for an ideological programme is self-defeating. Now she wants to fulfil her biological nature by raising a family with the man she still loves.

For Frank, Thatcherism has intensified the urgency to 'influence, subvert, create models, communicate – God knows the channels are open now. Anything's possible, d'you see? Because everything's collapsed. Politics – religion – imperialism. At least it makes for clarity.' This corresponds exactly to Gems's dramatic approach, and serves as an accurate description of her aims.

The disintegration of traditional values is depicted in the breakdown of Frank's marriage; and the play's resolution offers a new model of personal relationships. Unlike Susannah, Frank's hairdresser-wife is incapable of satisfying his intellectual requirements, while he cannot accept the sexual freedom she demands. However, neither are prepared to give up their children in a separation – and Susannah refuses single parenting on the ground that fathers are a child's right, which takes precedence over the woman's 'right to choose'.[12] The impasse is resolved by the two women deciding to set up a communal home in which Frank can act as father to an extended family, and they will each cater to his different needs, while being liberated by the other's presence.

Apart from *Marlene, Loving Women* is the only one of Gems's plays that does not end with a question, requiring the audience to reevaluate their attitudes to sexual norms that have been shown as untenable. And it is significant that both these plays are conventionally naturalistic, as well as each presenting a similar dialectical pattern of thesis, antithesis, synthesis. By contrast almost all Gems's other work qualifies as 'uterine' drama – her description of *Queen Christina* – where the Naturalism implied by this biological focus is consistently modified by structures that represent a 'female' approach.

In *Camille*, the woman's tragedy is seen through the agonized consciousness of Armand as a disjointed series of retrospective vignettes. *Piaf* intercuts scenes and songs, personal life and popular image to form a fluid collage. And a quotation (pointedly from the scientific journal, *Nature*) in *Dusa, Fish, Stas and Vi* suggests that intuitive, lateral forms of drama correspond to the essential nature of reality: 'Helium three becomes a superfluid because of the weak attractive force between its atoms ... the dynamic tension between attraction and repulsion keeps the paired atoms at a distance. That is the unique property of the helium system.'[13] Applied to scene-structure, the analogy provides a general model for feminist theatre up to the mid-1990s.

Notes

1 Pam Gems, *Three Plays*, Harmondsworth, 1985, pp. 43 (an extract from a review of a Piaf performance, read out by her agent), 61.
2 *Ibid.*, pp. 108–9.
3 *Ibid.*, pp. 131, 152–3.
4 Gems, Afterword to *Queen Christina*, in *Plays by Women*, V, p. 47.
5 *Plays by Women*, V, p. 19.
6 *Ibid.*, pp. 36–7, 30, 21.
7 *Stanley*, London, 1996, pp. 2, 60, 55.
8 *Ibid.*, pp. 48 (Afterword) and 44–5.
9 Gems, in *Plays by Women*, I, pp. 47 and 71.
10 *Dusa, Fish, Stas and Vi*, in *Plays by Women*, I, pp. 52, 60.
11 *Ibid.*, pp. 68, 70.
12 *Three Plays*, pp. 199 and 198.
13 Gems, in *Plays by Women*, V, p. 47; and I, pp. 55–6.

4

The comic mirror – tradition and innovation

Many of the dramatists discussed in the previous section have turned to comedy as one of the possible weapons in their political armoury. Agitprop characterization, with its cartoon simplification and symbolic types, is basically comic. Both Peter Nichols and Edward Bond specifically labelled some of their plays as comedies. John Arden's first plays have an intermittently comic tone, and some of his later drama incorporates farcical routines, while Howard Brenton was concerned with the structure of jokes in his early work. However, in each case their overall focus is realistic, or these elements are secondary to the direct depiction of political issues. By contrast, the playwrights in this section have concentrated on the comic mode, with its essentially artificial patterning and oblique social commentary.

Although Somerset Maugham's themes became increasingly bleak, he still retained a basically comic format. Similarly, while Joe Orton focuses deliberately on material that in traditional drama would be treated tragically – rape, incest, necrophilia, even violent death – he presents this in the stock forms of Farce. Similarly Samuel Beckett, who pioneered the new comic tone, applied structures, figures and word-play of Farce and Music Hall to bleak existential themes. Harold Pinter, explicitly following Beckett, presents a slightly different case. His work, which has generally been confused with the Absurdist movement – leading his later political plays to be mistakenly seen as a radical departure – gains fresh coherence when viewed in the evolving context of English comedy.

Indeed, none of the writers or directors in the century has been isolated from the art of their contemporaries. There are continual crossovers, with themes from one type of drama being picked up and reflected in another. This is particularly true of comic dramatists, humour being so closely associated with popular taste; and since the 1960s the different theatrical genres have increasingly merged as society has became more radicalized.

Peter Barnes's comedy, for example, is so ferocious and its choice of subjects for humorous treatment deliberately outrageous – the Plague, torture at the hands of Ivan the Terrible, Jack the Ripper, the gas chambers at Auschwitz – that it moves the boundaries. As does Trevor Griffiths's most significant play (*The Comedians*, 1975), which is why his work is discussed under this heading, even though his other plays form part of the same political movement marked by Howard Brenton and David Hare who also use farcical techniques in some of their plays, such as *Pravda* or *Moscow Gold*.

As the most socially dependent of all dramatic forms, the definition of comedy shifts continually; and in the modern era the change has been particularly extreme. In the Eighteenth Century Henry Fielding ridiculed the idea that anything horrific or unnatural could ever be a theme for comedy (using the example of Nero, ripping out his mother's belly, to illustrate the incongruity). Towards the end of the Nineteenth Century W.S. Gilbert played with precisely such a notion in *The Mikado* (1885), where tortures are imagined as 'a source of innocent merriment'; and although these are only imaginary and never executed, the incongruity between the grotesque and laughter is still used for comic effect. From the 1930s onwards, this type of subject has increasingly become the basis for comedy, with Pinter's 'Comedies of Menace' in the late 1950s, or Joe Orton's 'Black Farce' in the 1960s. Today even a comic dramatist writing for the popular commercial theatre such as Alan Ayckbourn uses 'dark' themes; and this radical development is the focus of the following chapters.

At the same time, comedy is a highly conventional genre. As the response to Bernard Shaw's early plays showed, it arouses stock responses. The serious point of *Arms and the Man* was lost in the 1894 audience's laughter, and their applause convinced Shaw that his attack on romantic sentimentality had failed. Similarly in *Pygmalion* twenty years later, the force of standard comic patterns turned Shaw's ending upside down (see above, pp. 26–28 and 31–33). In English comedy from Shakespeare to Sheridan, marriage generally symbolizes the renewal of society; and the heroine is united with the hero, after overcoming all tribulations and obstacles. So Shaw was unable to persuade the public that his heroine specifically chooses not to do so – as the 1956 musical version of *My Fair Lady* graphically demonstrated, pandering to the popular taste by having her return to the hero's arms at the end. Indeed the expectation of marriage in comedy is so fixed that later dramatists can deliberately play off against it, from Noel Coward's deliberately scandalous *ménage à trois* in *Design for Living*, or its even more perverse echo in Joe Orton's *Entertaining Mr Sloane*, to the total breakdown of all relationships at the end of Patrick Marber's *Closer*.

Comedy is also consciously traditional. Although almost all playwrights tend to claim that their work is a clear departure from their immediate predecessors – most vociferously Shaw, whose early work was so obviously based on nineteenth-century models – those writing comedies have generally stressed the continuities with earlier comic drama. Thus in the Seventeenth Century Ben Jonson pointed to Aristophanes as his model, while Wycherley borrowed from Molière, who himself had reworked themes from Terence; and later Congreve defended his comedy by reference to Jonson.

Similarly, at the close of the Nineteenth Century Wilde's verbal wit and highly structured plots are a deliberate echo of Congreve, updating the eighteenth-century 'Comedy of Manners'. He was followed by Maugham, who explicitly described himself as an 'improviser' on well-known plots and situations, and placed his early plays directly in the tradition of Restoration comedy. More recently Arden has referred to the comic elements in his work as Aristophanic, while in 1970 Christopher Hampton based his first comedy, *The Philanthropist*, on Molière's *The Misanthrope*. Ayckbourn has adapted one of Sheridan's plays (*A Trip to Scarborough*, which Sheridan himself had adapted from Vanbrugh). Stoppard, who is very much an inheritor of Wilde's verbal comedy, incorporates scenes from his 1895 classic *The Importance of Being Earnest* in *Travesties* (1974) and brings Wilde himself on stage in *The Invention of Love* (1997); while Bond has used general eighteenth-century comedy in an even more polemic way in *Restoration* (1981: see above, pp. 173–75). Even an iconoclastic contemporary like Orton overtly echoes his predecessor, Ben Travers, and stated that his aim was to restore farce to its 'Aristophanic state' of deliberately 'vulgar sexuality and satiric fantasy'.[1]

The lines were already set right at the beginning of the century. On the one hand conscious artifice becomes a dominating aesthetic principle (following the line set by Oscar Wilde in the comedies he wrote between 1892 and 1895) – on the other stands an essentially realistic approach, where actuality is the touchstone against which illusory ideals are measured (epitomized by the Irish dramatist John Synge's 1907 classic, *The Playboy of the Western World*). These contrasting positions, explicitly rooted in a long tradition of satire and appealing to classic models – on one hand Congreve and Sheridan; on the other Molière and Jonson – mark out the two main directions pursued with increasing extremism by comic playwrights during the course of the century.

At the same time, such a traditional emphasis does not mean that comedy is 'safe', or necessarily supports the status quo in society. In fact, up to the present era satire was always the most politically acute form of drama. Jonson had been imprisoned for a play lampooning the Jacobean court; and when Walpole imposed government censorship on the English stage in the Eighteenth Century, his target was comedy. It is also no accident that where theatrical riots occurred – as they have done notably in the Restoration period, at some nineteenth-century continental stagings of Beaumarchais' *Marriage of Figaro*, and in the early days of the Abbey Theatre in Dublin – almost all of them were provoked by performances of comedies.

The deflationary effect of comedy is a particularly explosive way of challenging social ideals. Where a straight political attack may be recognized as legitimate argument, ridicule tends to be felt as personally insulting. In addition, when a playwright denies the kind of pre-set expectations, on which the comic effect is largely based, or applies humorous techniques to inappropriate topics, the contrast seems deliberately offensive. So, as with Orton and Barnes, at its radical extreme English comedy is specifically designed to outrage audiences.

4.1 Somerset Maugham (1874–1965): popular comedy versus social criticism

CHECKLIST OF MAUGHAM'S MAJOR PLAYS

A Man of Honour, 1903	*The Constant Wife*, 1926
Lady Frederick, 1908	*The Letter*, 1926
Smith, 1909	*The Sacred Flame*, 1928
Our Betters, 1917	*The Breadwinner*, 1930
The Circle, 1921	*For Services Rendered*, 1932
East of Suez, 1922	*Sheppey*, 1933

Somerset Maugham is better known today as a novelist. But with a total of thirty-two plays staged from 1899 (*Marriages Are Made in Heaven*) to 1933 (*Sheppey*), and with no fewer than four plays running simultaneously in London in 1908, Maugham also set the tone of Edwardian comedy and counts as its leading exponent. The style of his early comedies derives from Oscar Wilde, as does his ironic claim that they were 'trivial pieces' with no other aim than to 'hold an audience'.[2] At the same time there is a dark side to even his lightest plays. This creates an internal conflict between their conventionally comic surface, and their attack on the type of society represented by the audience: a conflict that becomes increasingly sharp until it dominates his later work, eventually destroying the comedy.

The tension is characteristic of the era, reflecting the draining of Victorian confidence over the first decade of the century and the loss of traditional moral standards following the devastation of the First World War. Maugham's drama is very much identified with that period. By the late 1920s his plays had lost their popular appeal; and although he continued writing novels for another thirty years, after the failure of *Sheppey* Maugham completely abandoned the theatre.

The serious aspect of his work is directly expressed in his first full-length play, *A Man of Honour*: performed in 1903 by the Stage Society (which also championed Bernard Shaw) with Granville-Barker in the lead role. Ruled by moral principles, a gentleman marries a barmaid, whom he has made pregnant but does not love. This 'honourable' behaviour is a recipe for disaster. Unable to gain his respect, she drowns herself, leaving him with suicide as the only reputable way out of social disgrace. Literally with a gun at his head, he finds the courage to reject this deadly morality and go on living. The play was praised for its uncompromising realism in exposing the human cost of class distinctions, and the sexual double standard – themes that recur in Maugham's comedies, linking his drama to Shaw as well as Granville-Barker.

Indeed, Maugham's claim that his dialogue represents 'not what [his characters] would naturally say in the circumstances, but what they would say if they knew how to put into words their true and considered thoughts' almost exactly restates Shaw's rejection of 'verisimilitude' for 'veracity'.[3] Both focus on the destructive effect of idealism, yet Maugham has an essential pessimism that distinguishes him from Shaw. Like Chekhov, he qualified as a doctor; and his medical training gave him a materialistic determinism that discounted any possibility of changing the human condition. This pessimism is reflected in an early novel like *Liza of Lambeth*, with its graphic depiction of poverty in the London slums where he had worked as a medical student. It also underlies his comedies – although almost all his plays are set in the middle-class world of his theatre audience, or high society.

It is partly this pessimism that led Maugham to reject the Shavian drama of ideas, stressing that 'the appeal of drama is to the emotions rather than to the intellect'; and his denial that theatre could ever be an appropriate art-form for 'an original thinker', is a clear attack on Shaw. The difference between Maugham and Shaw is indicated by *The Breadwinner* (1930) which, like *Candida* (1897), is a comic inversion of Ibsen's *A Doll's House*. Shaw reverses Ibsen by having the wife choose to stay, instead of leaving her family in the search for emancipation, since 'in the real typical doll's house it is the man who is the doll'. In Maugham's play it is the husband who walks out on his clinging wife, to find a new life as a travelling salesman whose wares are romance – corresponding to Maugham's concept of comedy as 'an artificial thing' where 'only the appearance, not the reality of naturalism is in place'.[4]

The way Maugham combines such apparently frivolous artifice with serious social themes can be seen in *Smith* (1909), where the situation is exactly the same as in *The Man of Honour*: a member of the upper class marries a serving girl. But here the focus is on high society, not the consequences of a misalliance; and the man is already an outsider before the marriage, having just returned from years in the colonies. The opening scenes present a conventional comic picture, where (as in Restoration drama) one of the characters points out that having 'no morals and no conscience' seems irrelevant so long as one 'has a very neat gift for repartee and a very keen sense of humour'.[5] The outsider's disapproval of these glamorous figures initially makes him appear a kill-joy, while the self-effacing serving girl is overlooked – by the audience no less than her employers – as a nonentity with the most common of all surnames, Smith, and (being a maid) no personal name. Maugham's intention is clearly to manipulate spectators into approving this picture of high society through the lightness of tone, so that when the viciousness of these characters' behaviour is made plain, the spectators are forced to question their own attitudes.

The turning point comes when the news that a child has died comes while its mother is playing cards. The woman is typical: having married for money, social engagements have a higher priority than caring for her sick baby. Its death provides a harsh contrast to the empty frivolity and egoism, jolting the audience out of their complacent acceptance of the apparently comic surface. In finding amusement in such figures, the spectators are identified with those who 'prefer the selfish pleasures'; and the effectiveness of this technique can be indicated by the reviewer who complained that 'I do not remember anything [in previous drama] . . . so brutal as the whole conceit whereby in the middle of a bridge party the death of a child is introduced as a dramatic element'.[6]

The moral standard by which society is judged comes from the colonist; and his condemnation of these people as 'wantonly cruel and selfish' acts as a catalyst for one of the 'heartless' women, who had been prepared to barter herself for a wealthy husband. Now she recognizes the worthlessness of her life, and decides to emigrate to Australia where she can find fulfilment in work. This opposition of the metropolitan centre and the world outside – in which the harsh conditions of Africa or Canada test the values of the class system, or offer a healthier alternative, is typical of Maugham's comedy. It recurs in *The Explorer* (1908), *The Promised Land* (1913) and even *The Circle* (1921). Equally typical is the way Maugham reverses a class-conscious audience's social assumptions. The serving girl not only turns out to have the virtues of honesty and humanity, so signally lacking in her socially respectable employers. In addition, at first she refuses the colonist (who is her employer's brother) on the ground that no member of the upper classes could be 'good enough', and only consents to marry him at the end because he can demonstrate by his actions that he is no gentleman.[7]

Despite the intentionally discomforting central incident, *Smith*'s success as a comedy was due as much to Maugham's use of stock character types – shop-soiled spinster, lounge-lizard lover, rough diamond from the outback, farmer's pure daughter – as to the balance between wit and sentiment in the traditional courtship action. Although this absence of psychological exploration makes the humorous resolution possible, it apparently sacrifices any serious point. Yet on another level it is precisely this lack of depth that carries the real attack. As the colonist explicitly comments: 'It took me some time to discover that you weren't real people at all. You're not men and women, but strange sexless creatures, without blood in your veins.' The audience goes through the same process of discovery. Thus the limitations of the comic form itself become the vehicle for criticism, demonstrating that 'England is full of people as flippant and frivolous and inane' as 'the marionettes in a child's theatre'.[8]

The way this works can be seen still more clearly in *Lady Frederick* (1908), the most popular of Maugham's early plays, where both the characters and the plot parody conventional comedy. He deliberately conceived the title-figure heroine as a cliché, 'the adventuress with a heart of gold . . . the charming spendthrift and the wanton of impeccable virtue'.[9] At the same time the standard courtship theme is extended towards farce. Not only do both the first two Acts end with her receiving proposals, but in Act III each of these offers of marriage are repeated, then followed by two more. In fact, with the exception of a footman and Lady Frederick's brother, every male in the cast wishes to make her his wife. Similarly, epigrams represent the emptiness of a meretricious existence where show displaces substance, while the central scene is a demonstration of the gap between social illusions and reality.

Here, in order to cure a youthful suitor of his infatuation, Lady Frederick receives him in her dressing room where the cold light of morning shows her face *'haggard and yellow and lined'*. As he watches, hair pieces are pinned on; cosmetics rejuvenate her complexion; lipstick transforms her mouth into a 'Cupid's bow' – and her question 'You don't mean to say you thought it natural?' reflects as much on the audience's response to theatre, as on the young man's unsophisticated idealism. Like him, the spectators have accepted the image of elegance and beauty for two whole Acts. The make-believe of the stage doubles for the sham of society. But instead of dismantling appearances, the sequence shows illusion being built up, in exactly the same way that the play reintroduces sentimental idealism on a different level: 'behind that very artificial complexion there's a dear little woman called Betsy who's genuine to the bottom of her soul'.

In the same way, the endings of these early plays undercut their social criticism, by supporting the most conventional clichés. Although the only personal relationships possible in this society are solely economic, and Lady Frederick is faced with 'marriage or bankruptcy', the rich husband she is forced to accept turns out to be 'a man who loved me though he knew me through and through'.[10] Similarly in *Jack Straw* (also 1908) even Maugham's theme of misalliance is trivialized. A hotel waiter, who masquerades as the Archduke of Pomerania in a joke devised by snobs to humiliate a *nouveau riche* family, and becomes engaged to their daughter – to the horror of the snobs who devised the practical joke (and by implication to the equal disapprobation of the class-conscious audience) – is revealed to be in fact the missing Archduke. Romance is reaffirmed, snobbery ratified. Yet the effect is cynical, these clichés being so obvious that they become mere technical devices, empty of meaning. Maugham's dual vision all too accurately reflects the social climate of the time. The audiences' applause may be a measure of their moral bankruptcy; but his plays are accomplices in perpetuating the class system that they attack.

Consensus is still preserved in *Our Betters* (written in 1915, though only staged two years later in New York and not produced in London until 1923), even if the criticism of society is made unmistakable by basing the charac-ters on clearly recognizably and highly visible people of the time: Consuelo Vanderbilt – who had recently renounced her position as Duchess of

Malborough – Emerald Cunard and her toy-boy Gordon Selfridge. Indeed, Maugham effectively drew attention to the parallels by the disclaimer printed in the programme for the 1923 London première: 'Owing to various rumours which were circulated when the play was produced in America, the author wishes to state that the characters in it are entirely imaginary.' Their blatant materialism and adultery is symptomatic of the viciousness of a society that degrades all who aspire to it. But at the same time, this attack was rendered 'safe' by restricting it to 'outsiders'. All are American women, whose wealth has purchased aristocratic titles through marriage. So the English spectators' prejudices are confirmed, and the display of shameless immorality is reduced to titillation.

However, after the First World War, Maugham's plays become increasingly problematic. The shift is already clear in *The Circle* (1921), the only one of Maugham's plays that has been regularly revived. A variation on Wilde's *Lady Windermere's Fan*, this focuses on a young wife's decision to run off with her lover, despite the ostracism and isolation this will mean – graphically represented by the fate of her mother-in-law, who made the same 'mistake' a generation earlier – and the ruin of her husband Arnold's political career (like that of his father, Champion-Cheney, before him) if she leaves him. This 'Modern Comedy' has many of the same elements as Maugham's earlier and more conventional plays. English society is measured against a young man from the colonies, freed from class attitudes by his work as a planter in Malaysia; and the dramatic tone is no less light. This outsider's criticism that these Establishment 'People seem . . . so insincere' is countered by the riposte that 'I don't think you want too much sincerity in society. It would be like an iron girder in a house of cards' – a rejection of seriousness that is ironically mirrored in the artificial style of the play.[11] Yet the challenge to the audience's moral norms was overt enough to provoke a vociferously hostile reception on the opening night.

The hypocritical insincerity of society, 'full of people doing things they don't want to do because other people expect it of them', is epitomized by the false generosity which Champion-Cheney persuades his son to adopt as a way of blackmailing his young wife into staying in a loveless marriage. By offering her freedom – the divorce she asks for, even an allowance if she does leave him – Arnold intends to put her under an obligation that her integrity will not allow her to accept. In addition, Lady Kitty and Lord Porteous (Arnold's divorced mother and the man she ran away with) are brought in to serve as an awful example of the dictum that 'there is no more lamentable pursuit than a life of pleasure'.[12] Since their passion has decayed into indifference, they are intended to show the wife that love is not worth the sacrifice of social position.

Still by comparison with this cynical manipulation, even the flawed relationship of the superannuated adulterers looks moral. Champion-Cheney, the spokesman for morality, has surreptitiously purchased sex through a series of increasingly younger mistresses ever since Lady Kitty left. So the socially condemned romantic choice becomes the only valid alternative. It not only reflects Maugham's personal position – having just left his own wife for a homosexual lover – but is implied to be a positive way of removing the corrupt ruling classes. Both Lord Porteous and Champion-Cheney were potential Prime Ministers before the scandal of one running away with the other's wife caused their resignation from government, and reduced them both to marginal figures. Now Arnold in turn will be forced to abdicate his control of the nation by his wife's elopement.

In addition to the moral shock of promoting adultery not only as the fulfilment of romantic idealism, but also as a source of social change, the audience is manoeuvred into a false position that exposes conventional prejudices. These are initially confirmed by the caricatured presentation of the elderly divorcees as worn-out roué and scarlet woman ('*dyed red hair and painted cheeks*'). At first sight their physical appearance undercuts the idealistic vision of Arnold's young wife, which is deliberately expressed in all too obvious sentimental clichés – 'My heart ached for that poor lonely woman ... When you've loved as she's loved you may grow old, but you grow old beautifully ... She had the world at her feet ... And she gave up everything for love.' The contrasting reality sets up her father-in-law, the original wronged husband, as a voice of reason to identify with – 'I never heard that she was lonely, and she certainly isn't poor ... how you let your imagination run away with you!'[13]

Thus, the spectators are led to associate themselves with the representatives of social respectability; and this is reinforced by the title of the play. *The Circle* raises expectations that the young lovers will be shown as repeating the disastrous experience of the older pair. Indeed, the notion of circularity is stressed, which on the surface supports the rationalist's claim that since 'We are the creatures of our environment', two women in the same social situation will therefore have identical fates.

However, what the action in fact demonstrates is the counter-assertion that 'You can do anything in this world if you're prepared to take the consequences, and consequences depend on character.' Instead of underlining similarities, the parallel illustrates an essential difference between the two generations. It is, of course, not 'a coincidence that her hair should be the same colour as mine', as Lady Kitty remarks of her young counterpart. Since hers is dyed red, while the other's is natural, the new departure has to be understood as the real thing and its precursor as only a false image.

> LADY KITTY My hair is not naturally this colour . . . it's white, prematurely of course, but white. I always think its a symbol of my life. Are you interested in symbolism? I think it's too wonderful.[14]

In these terms, sacrificing social position for the possibility of emotional fulfilment is unambiguously presented as the action of 'a woman of courage and endurance and sincerity'. Yet whether the young lovers will find lasting happiness working in the colonies is left open – particularly in light of later plays such as *East of Suez* (1922) or *The Letter* (1926), which show the actual experience of expatriate couples as bleak and destructive.

Even if the hope of social renewal far away from the corrupt metropolitan centre remains uncertain, this in no way diminishes the necessity for rejecting moral codes. Maugham's intention is not to prove the viability of an alternative system, but to provoke. Not only is an audience's approval of adulterous elopement – which the drama is clearly designed to elicit – directly contrary to their assumed ethical beliefs and social standards. Any spectator who dismisses Maugham's thesis is put in the position of supporting the view that 'principle . . . can always be sacrificed to expediency'.[15] In addition, the ending is overtly discomforting. Mistakenly believing his moral blackmail to be irresistible, Champion-Cheney laughs in triumph – while the Porteous pair, whose encouragement has persuaded his daughter-in-law to run off with the outsider, join in. And the laughter on stage forces the audience to question what they might be laughing at. It associates them with either the elderly adulterers they had initially despised, or the unprincipled egoist they had earlier identified with, who is turned into an object of ridicule by his ignorance of his own discomfiture.

In the later phase of his theatrical career, Maugham turned to bleakly serious themes. *The Sacred Flame* (1928) and *For Services Rendered* (1932) both retain elements of his earlier drama, revolving around high society adultery and marriages between people from different classes. However, in each play one of the central figures is a war-cripple; and the wit of the dialogue has become a last-ditch defence against suffering. The situation in the first is a variation on Ibsen's *Ghosts*, with the mercy-killing of a paraplegic son by his mother explicitly challenging the validity of any 'standard of right and wrong'. The other echoes Chekhov's *Three Sisters*, with the ex-officer (who offers one sister her only chance of escape from a life of self-sacrifice) shooting himself instead of being shot in a duel.

After the suicide of the blind war-hero, who has become convinced that the 'honour and patriotism' for which he sacrificed himself is only empty rhetoric to disguise the 'vanity . . . greed and . . . stupidity' of rulers who still 'haven't learnt a thing', the final tableau of peaceful family security in *For Services Rendered* is savagely ironic. The complacent father's assurance (as ignorant of the true state of affairs as the equivalent character at the end of *The Circle*) that 'the world is turning the corner and we can all look forward to better times in the future. This old England of ours isn't done for yet and I for one believe in it and all it stands for' is followed by his now mad daughter's hysterical singing of 'God Save the King' '*in a thin cracked voice . . . The others look at her, petrified*'.

For Services Rendered was a counterblast to Noel Coward's *Cavalcade*, which had been staged as an elegiac hymn to patriotism the previous year. The disquieting mix of comic elements and tragic treatment alienated the public, and indeed the attack on audience sensibilities is far more direct than in Maugham's earlier work. Yet, as he pointed out himself, even this play

might have been [re]written to achieve popularity. Any dramatist will see how easily the changes could have been made. The characters only had to be sentimentalized a little to affect their behaviour at the crucial moments of the play and everything might have ended happily.[16]

Notes

1 Maugham, preface to *Collected Plays*, London, 1931, I, p. xvi; Orton in *Plays and Players*, November 1978, p. 13.

2 Maugham, preface to *Collected Plays*, I, pp. xiii–iv.

3 *Ibid.*, Preface to III, p. xiii; *Prefaces by Bernard Shaw*, London, 1938, p. 609.

4 Maugham, prefaces to *Collected Plays*, I, p. xiv, and II, p. xvi; Shaw, cited in Mander and Mitchenson, *Theatrical Companion to Shaw*, p. 43; Maugham, *The Summing Up*, London, 1938, p. 58.

5 *Collected Plays*, I, pp. 122.

6 *Ibid.*, p. 159; *Sunday Times*, 3 October 1909.

7 *Collected Plays*, I, pp.174, 203.

8 *Ibid.*, I, p. 202.

9 *Ibid.*, preface to I, p. ix.

10 *Ibid.*, I, pp. 67–74 & 89, 21 & 80.

11 Maugham, *Plays*, London, 1932, IV, p. 21.
12 *Ibid.*, pp. 21, 38.
13 *Ibid.*, pp. 24, 17–19.
14 *Ibid.*, pp. 37, 89, 46, 76.
15 *Ibid.*, pp. 22, 63.
16 *Collected Plays*, III, pp. 197, 164, 181 and preface, p. xvi.

4.2 Noel Coward (1899–1973): comedy as social image

CHECKLIST OF COWARD'S MAJOR PLAYS

The Young Idea, 1923	*Design for Living*, 1933
The Vortex, 1924	*Blithe Spirit*, 1941
Fallen Angels, 1925	*Present Laughter*, 1942
Hay Fever, 1925	*This Happy Breed*, 1942
Bitter Sweet, 1929	*Peace in Our Time*, 1947
Private Lives, 1930	*Relative Values*, 1951
Cavalcade, 1931	*A Song at Twilight*, 1965

By contrast with the Edwardian comedy of Somerset Maugham, Noel Coward rejected any suggestion that a moral might be drawn from his plays. Indeed, he went so far as to lump Maugham with Pinero, the dramatist Shaw had labelled as representing the worst type of nineteenth-century sentimental conformism, dismissing both as dated because the plots of their 'Drawing-Room Dramas' were based on 'vanished moral attitudes'. As the self-appointed spokesman of the turbulent twenties, Coward proclaimed that 'Those high-toned drawing-room histrionics are over and done with ... The narrow-mindedness, the moral righteousness and the over-rigid social codes have disappeared.' Maugham reciprocated by criticizing Coward's drama as materialistic and intrinsically immoral.[1] Yet Coward was as much Maugham's follower as his rival.

Just as in Maugham's *Smith*, *The Promised Land* and *The Circle* (1909, 1913, 1921), the outsiders of Coward's early plays escape from the stifling rigidity of English society in order to survive – although their type of refuge is significantly different, salvation for Coward's characters being the sybaritic liberty of Italy (Gerda and Sholto in *The Young Idea*, 1921, produced 1923) or Paris (Larita Whittaker in *Easy Virtue*, produced 1924), rather than the strenuous simplicity of the colonies. Indeed, the derivative elements of Coward's first play clearly mark his starting point. The situation and aspects of the characters in *The Young Idea* explicitly echo Bernard Shaw's *You Never Can Tell* (1899), while the plot is a mirror image of *The Circle*. Written immediately after the production of Maugham's play, *The Young Idea* is a deliberate inversion. In Coward a young couple manipulate their step-mother into eloping with a colonial through exaggerating his declarations of devotion, whereas in *The Circle* a young wife is persuaded to run off by her parents-in-law despite the calculated generosity of her husband.

Perhaps the most misleading aspect of Coward's work is his pose as a socially disengaged amoralist, whose sole purpose is to entertain. Various commentators from Kenneth Tynan to John Osborne have considered Coward's public image – the appearance of upper-class elegance, inscrutable poise, cocktail party wit elevated to the epigram – to be the most brilliant of his artistic creations. Like Oscar Wilde, Coward is judged to have put his genius into his life; and, as with Wilde, its theatricality has been recognized on the stage, with Coward having gained the rare accolade of becoming a dramatic character in his own right (in a revue, *Cowardy Custard*, 1972, and a musical, *Noël and Gertie*, 1989). Coward also notoriously put his personality into his plays – writing major roles for himself to act – and the characters he played were a pose that disguised the reality of his life.

The implicit corollary to this celebration of himself as a star performer, of course, is that Coward's plays are taken to be meretricious fakes, highly polished surfaces empty of deeper human experience.[2] Certainly, as a closet homosexual, Coward lived central aspects of his life as an open pretence. In particular his reputation as a matinee idol hardly reflected his actual sexual preference. However, his comedies were not only vehicles for creating his public persona. They express the ambiguity of the performing self.

Display is also self-exposure; and while promoting the star image, in which glamour serves as a survival strategy, Coward's plays question the inherent self-obsession of stardom. At the same time, living up to this image imposed strategies that make his own comments on the significance of his plays particularly deceptive. The real subject of the first instalment in his autobiography (published at the egocentrically early age of thirty-eight) is how he found himself increasingly living a lie, in cultivating the patina of fame; and the last really revealing insight is his 1926 recognition of 'how warily I would have to go' to preserve his hard-won initial success. Stardom implies that display is an end in itself. Any wider purpose undercuts the validity of performance, and in adopting the glittering mask Coward liked to declare that his only motive as a dramatist 'was to write a good play with a whacking good part in it for myself'.[3]

However, this remark relates to *The Vortex*, which makes it immediately suspect. By any standards this is a significant play, which in 1924 challenged social conventions. It extended the theatrical range in the same way as Osborne's *Look Back in Anger* would do just over a quarter of a century later, creating an equivalent effect of shock and instant recognition. Similarly, *Cavalcade* caught the national mood of 1931 in a way that no other play during the Twentieth Century succeeded in doing, and was credited with directly contributing to the Conservatives' landslide victory in the polls two weeks after its opening. Yet Coward protested that 'during rehearsals I was so very much occupied in the theatre and, as usual, so bleakly uninterested in politics that I had not the remotest idea . . . there was going to be an election at all!'[4] In light of the social effect of these plays, such comments are at best disingenuous.

In fact, while still on his way to stardom and shortly before adopting its mask, he published a statement of purpose that directly contradicted this pose. Rejecting such press labels as 'Disgusting, Daring or Outrageous', in 1925 Coward had stressed that his aim was not to win notoriety or cater to popular demand, but to revolutionize the theatre by dealing directly with 'the hard facts of existence', to 'concentrate on . . . psychological impulses' and to 'enlighten' not simply 'amuse'. Even here a degree of self-consciousness gives an ironic twist to what he called the 'reckless exposition of my youthful credo'.[5]

However, Coward's apparent reversal of this serious stance a decade later was only a change of tactics (accompanying star status), following the principle that is summed up in *Private Lives* (1930):

ELYOT (*seriously*): You mustn't be serious, my dear one, it's just what they want.
AMANDA Who's they?
ELYOT All the futile moralists who try to make life unbearable. Laugh at them. Be flippant. Laugh at everything, all their sacred shibboleths. Flippancy brings out the acid in their damned sweetness and light.[6]

From such a perspective, any straight attack on society is inevitably subsumed by it; and even the most undogmatic moral that can be drawn from a play becomes inherently authoritarian. The only solution is to negate the root quality of seriousness itself, as Oscar Wilde had done in *The Importance of Being Earnest*. It is no coincidence that Coward's character who represents social norms in *Design for Living* (1933) is named Ernest; and towards the end of his career he acknowledged the parallel with Wilde in a musical version of *Lady Windermere's Fan: After the Ball* (1954), which avoided even literary seriousness by trivializing Wilde in its note of burlesque.

It is a common mistake to take Coward's comedies at face value, over-looking the element of Wildean paradox. Since his approach goes beyond ridiculing the moral mentality to promote by example a completely oppo-site scale of values, the more frivolous his work seems the more profound its implications actually become. The ambiguity of Coward's remark in an interview on his seventieth birthday is entirely in keeping: 'I have no great social causes. I can't think of any off-hand. If I did, they'd be very off-hand.'[7]

Indeed, plays like *The Vortex* or *Cavalcade* indicate how misleading the appearance of trivial entertainment in fact is. *Cavalcade* was hailed as providing 'a theme worthy of . . . our national theatre', while Coward de-fended his first major play, *The Vortex* (1924), against the censorship of the Lord Chamberlain as 'little more than a moral tract': a description which, although tongue-in-cheek, is indeed accurate.[8] These should be seen not as aberrations in their more conventionally serious tone, but as touchstones for his lighter work.

The Vortex presents high society as an ethical and emotional wasteland. The unsavoury pair of main characters represents the apogee of a culture where appearances substitute for values. Florence is renowned for her phys-ical beauty, although this has been replaced by cosmetics and hair dye as she ages; and she takes increasingly younger lovers to validate her self-image. Her son Nicky's artistic sensitivity is the product of drugs, while his sup-posed musical talent, at best erratic, is displayed with the sole purpose of attracting flattery and admiration. However, as in Shaw's vision of a soci-ety headed for the shipwreck of the First World War, the only alternative to this 'heartbreak' hothouse is 'horseback hall', and Coward's uncultured characters are even more despicable than the poseurs.

The surface glitter of theatrical performance is exploited so that 'one gets carried away by glamour, and personality, and magnetism' in the opening act. What the audience admires is then revealed as perverted and corrupting, by the introduction of a normal element: Nicky's fiancée, Bunty. She repre-sents the kind of healthy ordinariness, with which spectators can (initially) identify, being described as '*an excellent type . . . Very average*'. Her rejection of his milieu is designed to disillusion the audience; and the way this works is explicitly spelled out by the characters' on-stage reaction in the second act:

BUNTY I hate the atmosphere.
TOM I don't know how I've stood it for so long.
BUNTY You didn't notice it until I came, any more than I noticed Nicky's atmosphere until you came.

However, the boyishly asexual Bunty not only represents sanity, but saniti-zation. She is well matched with Tom, Florence's current toy-boy, described in a stage direction as '*good at games and extremely bad at everything else*'.[9] Indeed, she ends up in his arms. So spectators are forced to revise their opinions yet again. By any standards the drug addict and his adulterous mother are more dramatically interesting; and the climactic night-long con-frontation between the two combines echoes of Hamlet's bedroom assault on his mother with a variation on Oswald's agonizing revelation to his mother in Ibsen's *Ghosts*.

The drug abuse and sexual corruption seemed a revelation at the time, and were sufficiently shocking to provoke the first actress cast as Florence to with-draw from rehearsals. Perhaps more dated now than any of Coward's other work, the play's original effectiveness was clearly related to its impression of social reality. This was fostered by the way Coward adopted the attributes of his protagonist, performing the role off as well as on stage. He had him-self photographed (supposedly 'at work') lying in bed, a picture of elegant decadence. And he exactly mirrored the '*hectic and nervy*' quality of the part by giving 'one of those effective, nerve-strung, *tour-de-force* performances, technically unstable, but vital enough to sweep people into enthusiasm'.[10]

The moral attitude of the play is too obtrusive. Yet the double-edged opposition between the dull norm and an immoral glamour becomes a standard polarization in Coward's major comedies, while the reversal in sexual pairing, where each character ends up with an antagonist's partner, forms their typical structure. As Coward developed a unique dramatic voice any moral becomes highly ambiguous, but the underlying social criticism follows up the line established here: 'it's the fault of circumstances and civilization – civilization makes rottenness so much easier . . . How can we help ourselves? – We swirl about in a vortex of beastliness.'[11]

By contrast, the moral attitude of *Cavalcade* has been consistently misun-derstood. Highly praised as a eulogy of the national spirit when first per-formed in 1931, today it tends to be reviled as 'chauvinistic nonsense'. On the surface, one of the review headlines seems to sum up the whole play: 'A STUPENDOUS CAVALCADE: Noel Coward Devises Drury Lane's Greatest Drama: Vast Crowds in Amazing Stage Pictures'.[12] And it is largely because simplification is expected from this kind of visual pageant, that *Cavalcade* has been misread as the most simplistic form of patriotism.

Inspired by a photograph in an old *Illustrated London News* of a troop-ship leaving for the Boer War, reproduced in its second scene, *Cavalcade* was indeed conceived on an epic scale. The original production required a total company (back stage staff as well as actors) of over 250, and elaborate stage machinery for its unbroken flow of contrasting scenes. Running from the last day of the Nineteenth Century to New Year's Eve in 1929, the visual sweep of the story (as well as the sensational stage effects) was particularly stunning at the time, and contrasted vividly with the bleak Depression era. An opulent Edwardian ballroom waltz is followed by the swirling street life of an open-air market, with a girl dancing to a brass band that drowns out the costerboys' penny whistles. Visual highpoints of a whole range of acclaimed productions – from Henry Irving's *Corsican Brothers* in 1880, which set a mirror image of the Lyceum auditorium on stage, to Granville-Barker's staging of *Votes for Women!* (1906), which culminated in a Trafalgar Square Suffragettes' rally – are outdone in scenes on a musical comedy stage (including the whole of the music-hall audience), at a fashionable seaside resort (complete with bandstand and sudden thunderstorm), and in Trafalgar Square packed with revellers.

The automatic assumption that spectacle overwhelms sense has devalued *Cavalcade*, even as a document of an era. Yet, although some scenes are entirely without dialogue, the spectacle is in fact secondary.

The turning point of the play is encapsulated in the most economical of dramatic gestures. After seeing her son off on a troop train to France for the last time, the focal figure, Jane Marryot, turns away to light a cigarette in public: an action as precise in its statement in 1931 as Timothy Findley's imitation of it in *The Wars* (Canada 1986), where the respectable female pro-tagonist stalks out of a religious service to drink brandy on the church steps. Similarly, Queen Victoria's funeral is one of the key events in *Cavalcade*. But instead of showing the procession, Coward restricts the scene to a single family's response as they watch from their upstairs drawing room. The true focus of the action is defined by his comment that the suit-ability of the historical subject was determined not by its grandeur, but by its 'scope for intimate characterization against a background of crowd scenes'.[13]

A selection of specific individuals, the upper-class Marryots and their servants, the Bridges, represents the whole of English society. The com-bined experience of these two families provides the standards by which the grandiose pageant of history is judged; and particular weight is given to the women, who are seen as more objective commentators in being excluded from the political process. Private values repeatedly undercut public beliefs –

ROBERT ... We've had wars before without the world breaking.
JANE My world isn't very big.

– while even the spectacle and the crowd scenes, which incorporate the
official line, become increasingly less affirmative.

A powerful, if sombre, chiaroscuro is created. Massed waltzing couples
in the glittering light of chandeliers are set against the endless line of soldiers marching uphill through 1914 to 1918, '*out of darkness into darkness.
Sometimes they sing gay songs, sometimes they whistle, sometimes they march
silently, but the sound of their tramping feet is unceasing. Below the vision of
them, brightly-dressed, energetic women appear in pools of light, singing stirring
recruiting songs.*' However, this use of strongly ironic contrasts always places
the weight of emotion on the individual, alienated from these masses. It is
their personal pain with which the spectator empathizes: the single small
child encouraged to dance by the crowd, ignorant that her father has just
been killed in a traffic accident; Jane Marryot, having just received news of
her son's death in the last days of the war, who is caught up in the victory celebration '*like a sleepwalker through dense crowds of cheering, yelling people.
They push and jostle her... She stands there cheering wildly, with the tears
rolling down her face.*'[14]

History may be a colourful pageant for the uninvolved audience, or a cause
for general celebration. But for the individual participants it is a disaster.
Hopes are consistently betrayed, and love is particularly vulnerable. The
independence gained by the butler as the purchaser of a Public House brings
him to alcoholism and early death. As the Marryot's eldest son and his newly
wed bride move away from the ship's rail, their light-hearted speculation
about how long their happiness will last is silently answered by the name
revealed on a life-belt. Their idyllic honeymoon is on the ill-fated maiden
voyage of *The Titanic.*

Coward took *Cavalcade*'s title from the type of horseback procession that
had paraded imperial glory at Victoria's Jubilee celebrations. Yet the action
makes this apparent fanfare to triumphant nationalism ironic. Almost the
whole weight is on the downward progress over the first three decades of the
new century, to its low point in the symbolic '*Night Club-* CHAOS' finale.
This accelerating decline is not seen as a change from the era that comes
to an end with the old Queen's death, but as a continuation, fuelled by the
militarism that both founded and perpetuated the Empire.

Even at its height in the opening scenes, the imperial theme is presented
negatively. The call of duty, which takes both master and servant off to

the Boer war, produces the hysterical jingoism of Mafeking night; and the embarkation for South Africa is paralleled with the later departure of the troop train for the western front in 1918. Although 'The Bugle Call, dear, the Red, White and Blue' is an expression of real patriotic conviction, even at the beginning it is spoken as a conscious cliché. The sentiment becomes increasingly suspect as the off-stage colonial war is turned into a cruelly pointless nursery game of 'soldiers' (which also suggests the psychological effect on children of officially sanctioned violence), then replayed (with Boche – the insulting First World War name for Germans – substituted for Boer) when the children grow up. The final New Year's Eve salute 'to the hope that one day this country of ours, which we love so much, will find dignity and greatness and peace again', once much quoted, has been taken out of context by recent critics as evidence for Coward's reactionary support of the status quo. However, interpreting this as an affirmation of imperialistic pride in national greatness is ruled out by the earlier part of the Marryots' toast: 'to our sons who made part of the pattern and to our hearts that died with them'. Children are literally a nation's future, and of the representative four in the play, three have been killed while the sole survivor has paid for her entry into high society as a star dancer by prostitution.[15]

For all that, the toast in which the last scene culminates is accompanied by the whole company singing 'God Save the King' – and at least on one night when George V attended, the 1931 performances certainly aroused 'Great Outbursts of Loyalty: National Anthem Fervour'. Part of the emotional argument of *Cavalcade* is that there must be something splendid about an ideal that so many people are willing to die for; and even if this is illusory, the lives that were sacrificed as the price of empire themselves confer value on it. Set against the pain of Jane Marryot's bereavement, and her progressive disillusion with the imperial cause, which is underlined by its corrupting effect on society as a whole, this creates the play's tension of forces. Yet in terms of the 'pattern' of the complete action, the final vision of a Union Jack glowing through the darkness is more ambiguous than the original audiences assumed. It symbolizes the 'spirit of gallantry and courage' exemplified in the main characters. However, even the fact that it is capable of evoking such an admirable spirit hardly justifies the 'unbelievable Hell' of this clearly self-destructive society.[16]

Although Coward played up to the public response in a jingoistic curtain speech at the première (which he later regretted), his subsequent declaration that in preparing the play he had 'not one moment to waste on patriotic fervour' is supported by the action.[17] True, the emotional pull of music that includes 'Nearer My God to Thee' as a valediction for those drowned when the *Titanic* sank, or 'Land of Hope and Glory' to mark the Armistice of 1918, tends to swamp the distinction between the inner spirit of the people and their nation's global role. Yet the imperial ethos is shown to be inseparable from militarism, and the key voice of Jane Marryot strongly dissents from this 'Cavalcade'.

The play should not be confused with a propaganda film like Coward's *In Which We Serve*, written and produced in the very different circumstances of 1941–2. Rather, it extends the theme of Coward's immediately preceding and unproduced play, *Post-Mortem*, which is directly comparable to *Journey's End*, R.C. Sherriff's classic anti-war drama. *Cavalcade* replaces the deeply felt but unfortunate didacticism of *Post-Mortem* with a structural symmetry that carries the same message subliminally. Upper and lower classes are juxtaposed. Both suffer equally, but the possibility of creating a transcending social unity (symbolized in Fanny Bridges' engagement to the younger Marryot) is destroyed by the war that claims his life. Each public event is balanced against a personal scene, clearly establishing an equation between the triumph of the flag and personal tragedy.

The theatrical resources that are required to stage *Cavalcade* may be one reason why it vanished from the theatre for fifty years. Another is the persistent misinterpretation fostered by the public response to the first production, which distorted Coward's point about the sacrifices exacted in the name of patriotism into populist flag-waving. Neither reason justifies its exclusion from the repertoire: a 1981 production mixing amateurs with a small nucleus of professionals demonstrated that even such an epic show could be mounted without an exorbitant investment; and in 1985 it was performed to critical acclaim in North America where any patriotic appeal was largely irrelevant.

Indeed *Cavalcade* has been restaged twice with triumphant success at the Shaw Festival in Canada (1995 and again in 1996), and despite being ignored for so long, it has become part of popular culture in a way few plays achieve. The *Titanic* scene has become a cinematic cliché (re-used for example in the Monty Python film, *The Time Bandits*), while the 1970s *Upstairs, Downstairs* television serial borrowed some of the characters' names as well as the central idea, and the toast to the future has been adopted (unacknowledged, as well as out of context) as a pre-election rallying call by Mrs Thatcher. The play has even been absorbed by the apparently antithetical left-wing theatre in Joan Littlewood's *Oh, What a Lovely War* (1963: see above, pp. 121–22), which took its cue from the 1914–18 march sequence in *Cavalcade*. Indeed the use of Pierrots as soldiers in *Oh, What a Lovely War* is directly paralleled by a pastiche of 'Journey's End' in Coward's 1932 revue of *Words and Music*, where the slaughter of the First World War is represented by a chorus of clowns 'pelting each other with coloured paper streamers'. As musical and spectacular in its own day as the Lloyd Webber/Trevor Nunn extravaganzas of the 1980s, *Cavalcade* was also a considerable technical achievement.

So it is not surprising that Coward chose to head the first volume of his collected plays with *Cavalcade*, out of chronological order, particularly since it also provides a compendium of his most characteristic techniques. Specific scenes were clearly developed from satiric numbers in his musical revues, for instance 'The English Lido Beach' from *This Year of Grace* (1928), while the 'Twentieth Century Blues' from the finale recapitulates the whole action of *The Vortex*. The symmetry and structural balance *Cavalcade* displays are the hallmark of his most distinctive comedies from *Hay Fever* in 1925 to *Blithe Spirit* in 1941. In these the detachment is more obvious, though even the emotional darkness of *Cavalcade* is lightened by constant comic touches – which range from an ironic objectification of social attitudes on the stage-within-a-stage of the music-hall scene, to the broad slapstick of a fat lady trapped in a collapsing deck chair during a thunderstorm at the seaside. The bittersweet tone of these comedies is an extension of the conflicting emotional juxtapositions in *Cavalcade*. Indeed this tone becomes programmatic as the title to a 1929 play, *Bitter Sweet*, and forms a more accurate description of Coward's work than the song from that comedy – 'The most I've had is just/A talent to amuse' – which tends to be taken as his own estimate of his achievement'.[18]

Coward epitomizes the Jazz Age of the 1920s and 1930s. Yet as with his song 'Twentieth Century Blues', he rejects its values even in voicing them. Even though his revue, *On With the Dance* (1925), helped to define the hectic tone of the era, at the same time it was recognized that 'the speed of the change from scene to scene, of the performance of each number, is feverish, burlesquing the speed of our overheated life'.[19] Together with his most polished comedy, *Private Lives* (1930), the serious theme and sweeping scope of *Cavalcade* won Coward a reputation as the leading national dramatist, confirming his star status. His self-display, the ironic ambiguity of his drama, and its satiric attack on moral norms is summed up in two plays that focus on artists and the function of theatre: *Hay Fever* (1925) and *Design for Living* (1933).

The best example is perhaps Coward's much misunderstood comedy, *Design for Living*, which was explicitly intended as a star vehicle for Lynn Fontanne, Alfred Lunt and Coward himself. Deliberately exploiting and promoting the glamour of three equally matched popular stage-idols, it traces the relationships of Gilda, an interior decorator whose art is lifestyle, with a painter and a playwright (played, of course, by Coward) from their bohemian beginnings to artistic fame.

Discovered by Ernest, their art dealer acquaintance, in bed with Leo in the Paris apartment she shares with Otto, and later with Otto in Leo's London bed, Gilda marries Ernest, leaving Otto and Leo to embrace each other. Then as soon as they appear in Ernest's New York apartment she rejects him, to form a *ménage à trois* with her original partners. The theatrical effect was intended to mirror the characters' own emotional state:

... It was 'Gala' all right – strong magic!
GILDA Coloured lights, sly music, overhanging trees, paper streamers – all the trappings.[20]

With all this continual swapping of sexual partners in every conceivable permutation, plus its declaration that for artists all that counts is the professional quality of their art – quite independent of normal social or moral constraints – it was all too easy to label the action as not only self-indulgent, but sensationalistic. Indeed, the West End/Broadway star system, with its hype of physical attractiveness and rumoured promiscuity, is so obviously projected in the play that *Design for Living* instantly became the subject of pastiche and satiric cartoons on opening in New York.

As in *The Vortex*, the fictional painter, playwright and aesthete's 'lives are diametrically opposed to ordinary social conventions'. These accepted standards of behaviour are incorporated in the brazenly patronized figure of 'Little Ernest' who, as an art dealer, literally lives off their creativity. Dismissed as 'gentle and prim', this average representative of ordinary society is reduced to a slapstick patsy, literally tripped up at the height of his moral outrage to fall flat on his face.

At the same time, the action has demonstrated exactly how accurate his condemnation is when he accuses them of 'a ruthless egotism, an utter disregard for anyone's feelings but your own'. The audience are not intended to completely share his final disgust at 'the unscrupulous, worthless degenerates that you are! ... irresponsible and abominable', which is clearly excessive. But the artists are hardly meant to be taken as role models. As we are explicitly shown in a brief sequence between the jaded playwright, an interviewer and a photographer, the demands of celebrity corrupt the creativity it rewards, while Coward's spokesman is reduced to declaring: 'cash in ... and see how much we lose by it ... Success in twenty lessons! Each one more bitter than the last!'[21]

So, as a title, *Design for Living* was intended to be ironic, even interrogative, rather than prescriptive. The lesson of Gilda's socially respectable marriage to Ernest is that being 'sane' equals 'dead' (as she says just before she leaves him). Yet the vitality that distinguishes the anti-social artist is a form of insanity, and the final laughter has an alienating, manic quality. The slapstick treatment of Ernest is organized to get an automatic laugh from the audience – who then find their laughter being echoed from the stage in a highly discomforting and exaggerated form. Collapsing, intertwined on a sofa, the three stars '*break down utterly and roar with laughter. They groan and weep with laughter, their laughter is still echoing from the walls as* – THE CURTAIN FALLS.'[22]

The final grouping is not an image of community but exclusiveness, and in closing out Ernest also it excludes the audience, who are literally the society he represents. The alternatives on offer are equally unendorsable. Ernest's declaration that 'your values are false and distorted' is countered by Gilda's 'only from your point of view'.[23] All moral standards have been relativized to the point of meaninglessness. It is the stars' frivolity, their refusal to treat the issue seriously that maddens Ernest; and the only solution offered by *Design for Living* is purely aesthetic. The symmetrical patterning of the plot covers a void that it does not attempt to disguise, while being too artificial in its exact duplications and parallels to serve as a substitute for reality.

The reviews of the play Leo has written, which are read out in *Design for Living*, summarize typical criticisms of Coward's own works: 'witty' but 'disgusting' and 'decidedly thin'. Yet 'Change and Decay', the title of Leo's play, is indeed an accurate interpretation of the social trends depicted in the three artist-figures. Looking back on his comedies between the wars, Coward's defence against the accusation of superficiality was that 'they mirrored, without over-exaggeration, a certain section of the social life of the times'.[24]

This claim to realism is slightly misleading. Coward clearly heightens the behaviour of his characters and maximizes the contrasts between them, both for comic effect and to show the essence of social attitudes. Also the permutating sexual relationships, which substitute for plot, obey the comic laws of multiplication and repetition rather than psychological accuracy. However, he does replace the elaborately epigrammatical wit of traditional comedy with apparently natural, throwaway dialogue, which has a characteristically modern ring. At the same time he cuts away conventional dramatic structures, which contributes to the deceptive impression of superficiality. *Hay Fever* (1925) for example, as Coward himself pointed out, 'has no plot at all, and remarkably little action. Its general effectiveness therefore depends upon expert technique from each . . . member of the cast.'[25]

The way in which acting substitutes for action, and the language of gesture for verbal communication in Coward's work, is externalized within *Hay Fever* by the game of 'Adverbs', where a word is to be guessed from the manner of the person who performs it. Following the same principle, what actually takes the place of a cause-and-effect plot is an arbitrary sequence of illusory, and at one point even overtly scripted, activities.

Each member of an artistic family has independently invited a guest for a country weekend, and all exchange partners (as in *The Vortex* or *Design for Living*). Judith Bliss, a superannuated actress contemplating a return to the stage, takes over her daughter's prospective boyfriend from the Foreign Office and magnifies a single kiss into an adulterous passion that must be declared. Her husband meanwhile is persuading a *femme fatale*, whom their son has invited, that a little flirtation has committed her to elope with him. This places Judith in the role of injured wife, which she swaps for the chance to play a tragically magnanimous wronged lover on finding her own young guest in her daughter's arms. Her painter-son's completely unjustified announcement of his engagement to a flapper, whom his father is studying as a type for his next novel, then evokes the sketch of an aging mother abandoned by her children. Finally, the whole family plays out the climactic scene of her last stage success, a highly coloured but cardboard melodrama called 'Love's Whirlwind'.

This also happens to be the title of one of the outworn plays that the histrionic Arkadina had been famous for in *The Seagull* (performed by the Moscow Art Theatre during Coward's visit to New York in 1922). The parallel signals the way *Hay Fever* plays off the 'theatrical' against the 'real', just as Chekhov does. But where the dramatic references in *The Seagull* are used to contrast with the realistic approach of the play as a whole, in Coward the type of drama mentioned mirrors the nature of his own play. Even more explicitly than Leo's 'Change and Decay' reflects the subtext of *Design for Living*, 'Love's Whirlwind' sums up the frenetic whirligig of pretended passions in *Hay Fever*. Here the role-playing is echoed too in the titles of David Bliss's clichéd novels from 'The Sinful Woman' to 'The Bold Deceiver' and 'Broken Reeds'.[26] In this endless regression, everything reduces to theatre. Even Bliss has the ring of a stage name – emphasized by its blatant irony. 'Bliss' may be what this glamorously artistic family represents to the outside world, but it is the opposite of everything their guests actually experience.

Despite its theatricality, this is one of Coward's few comedies that depicted recognizable people in a real-life social milieu, being specifically based on a weekend of word games and histrionics at the house of the Broadway star, Laurette Taylor, whose 'evenings got such a reputation for *dread* in America that hardly anyone ever went at all. And [as Coward was quick to underline] I see their point.'[27] The theatricalization of life thus becomes an attack on the artificial values of a corrupt civilization.

Hay Fever is *The Vortex* transposed into a comic mode by the element of pretence. The harsh reality of the earlier play is rendered harmless by being only make-believe. Judith's weekend guest is no less juvenile and athletic than Florence's stud in *The Vortex* – but although he may be star-struck (unlike his earlier counterpart) his infatuation is never physically fulfilled. The 'normal' quartet, having paired off appropriately, walk out on their hosts – literally on tip-toe, behind the backs of the family – who are too preoccupied arguing over trivia (whether the father's fiction depicts the street map of Paris accurately) to even notice the departure of their guests. There is no pain for these artists in any of the revelations or discoveries that have occurred, since their adulteries, elopements and engagements only existed in their own fevered imaginations.

At the same time, even though this means that the attack on modern manners has no emotional cost, no one escapes censure. The cross-section of ordinary people from the outside world are exposed as victims of habit by the unconventional behaviour of the artists. Manipulable, they lack any moral centre; and the fact that they have turned to the Blisses as fashionable models, mistaking their superficial glamour for true values, is a symptom of a deeply unnerved and disoriented society. But if (as each declares) they 'never realize how *dead* I am until I meet people like you', the artists admit that their 'vitality' is 'entirely spurious'. Both sets are revealed as poseurs – even though the Blisses are in a sense what society has made them, and are simply living up to the expectations of their public.

Unlike *Design for Living*, where artistic talent is a justification for moral licence, here creativity is no excuse. The kind of pictures and novels produced by the Bliss family, as well as Judith's stage performances, are 'sadly superficial' and 'very bad', even in their own estimation.[28] Their only superiority is in the awareness of the roles they are playing; and although they can evaluate themselves objectively, this self-preoccupation blinds them to the needs and feelings of others. Close kin to Cocteau's *monstres sacrées*, both their art and their impromptu roles are a send-up of the trite sentimental melodramas of the 1920s – exactly the kind of play that Laurette Taylor made her name in.

On this level, *Hay Fever* is a satire on the transience of artistic fashions. Although nothing loses its topicality so quickly, the general point remains just as relevant. Directing the 1964 National Theatre revival, Coward found a contemporary equivalent for the largely forgotten Laurette Taylor. He made the play an ironic showcase for outdated stellar display by casting Edith Evans (identified with Wilde's Lady Bracknell by her classic performance in *The Importance of Being Earnest*, which had been filmed in 1951) as Judith Bliss. However frivolous on the surface, this parody of theatrical personalities has serious implications.

The '*universal pandemonium*' the Blisses are responsible for at the end is a foretaste of the society-wide 'CHAOS' that ends *Cavalcade*. Its cause is the absence of real values in contemporary life – as Coward indicates when the discomforted guests condemn their artistic idols, by whom they have been victimized and embarrassed, as 'the most infuriating set of hypocrites I've ever seen . . . You haven't got one sincere or genuine feeling among the lot of you – you're artificial to the point of lunacy.'[29] This is clearly intended to articulate the reaction of the average spectator to the Blisses; but the accusation is even more true of the ordinary characters, with whom the audience are associated. Metaphorically at least, they have been whoring after false gods, and are even more culpable, being blind to their own poses.

Private Lives (1930) presents the same material in a more polished and less dated form. In denying public values, the title spells out the principle behind all Coward's work, whether an epic like *Cavalcade* or the frothy burlesque of *Hay Fever*. The primacy of personal fulfilment is asserted in this case, over the socially sanctified ties of matrimony – by justifying Amanda and Elyot, who abandon their new spouses on the first day of their respective honeymoons and run off together. The underlying message appears reassuringly conformist, since their two marriages are as yet unconsummated (officially at least, this being the first night after their weddings, however often they might have been to bed with their respective spouses beforehand!) Indeed, having previously been husband and wife, they can argue that their new commitments are really invalid:

ELYOT . . . Catholics don't recognize divorce. We're married as much as ever we
were . . .

However, this claim that 'living in sin' is something the most orthodox moralist could hardly object to, becomes blatantly specious when they admit that, as far as religious beliefs go, they have 'absolutely none'. If neither Heaven nor Hell have any reality, then only the judgement of the World matters.

AMANDA We may be alright in the eyes of Heaven, but we look like being in the hell of a mess socially.[30]

But even this sort of sanction is demonstrably irrelevant.

By limiting the scenes entirely to private spaces, and restricting the characters to the four principals, as well as giving an overwhelming majority of the speeches to Amanda and Elyot themselves, the play affirms that society has no hold on the individual. In short, it subverts all moral standards. Even the gospel of egoism that *Private Lives* promotes is shown to be as much a symptom of a decadent society, as an antidote to it.

The play is deliberately plotless, having 'no further action after Act One'. It is also specifically trivial, its main interest according to Coward being 'from the point of view of technical acting' (like *Hay Fever*). In fact, with Coward and his co-star Gertrude Lawrence in roles recognizably based on their own stage personas, what the satiric mirror of *Private Lives* reflects is not so much society, as itself.[31] There seems to be almost no external reference point in the drama. Even the characters were indistinguishable from the actors, and (in the words of Coward's *alter ego*) the 'situation [was] entirely without precedent'. To that extent, the 1930s reviewers were correct in their criticism that the play displayed 'an unsurpassed gift for combining entertainment with nothingness'.[32] However, as the epitome of frivolity, it implies that the audiences who were entertained are equally purposeless. Coward's denial that the comedy has any significance beyond the 'talent to amuse', which he had flippantly claimed as his only value in *Bitter Sweet*, is in fact ironic. The famous exchange on global affairs represents his technique in miniature.

AMANDA ... How was it?
ELYOT The world?
AMANDA Yes.
ELYOT Oh, highly enjoyable.
AMANDA China must be very interesting.
ELYOT Very big, China.
AMANDA And Japan –
ELYOT Very small.

11 Anti-romantic comedy: Noel Coward and Gertrude Lawrence in Coward's *Private Lives*

At first glance such self-obsession reduces the outside world to meaning-lessness; and the lines are funny precisely because the characters seem abnormally egoistic. Yet a very different expectation has already been set up by Amanda's use of the same verbal formulas – 'Very flat, Norfolk' – as a deadpan gibe at Elyot's new wife. And it is later revealed that Elyot's geographical indifference is a measure of the real depth of his feelings: 'My heart broke on that damned trip round the world . . . completely unexciting because you weren't there to see [the sights] with me.'[33]

In fact, the whole play is structured on the perception of incongruities. Conventional romantic comedies end with the marriage of all eligible couples, signalling social renewal through sanctified union. Coward's love story reverses the pattern and inverts its symbolic significance, opening with marriages that immediately fall apart – then holding up as the ideal a relationship where quarrels are proof of passion, while peaceful amity betrays indifference. Having announced that if their abandoned mates should walk in on them, they will 'Behave exquisitely' (in context an insult, rather than signalling reconciliation), Amanda and Elyot do the exact opposite:

> . . . *they trip over a piece of carpet, and fall onto the floor, rolling over and over in paroxysms of rage.* VICTOR *and* SIBYL *enter quietly through the open door, and stand staring at them in horror. Finally* AMANDA *breaks free and half gets up,* ELYOT *grabs her leg, and she falls against a table, knocking it completely over.*
> AMANDA (*screaming*) Beast; brute; swine; cad . . .
> *She rushes back at* ELYOT *who is just rising to his feet and gives him a stinging blow, which knocks him over again.*[34]

Coward's version of the battle of the sexes is even more literal than Strindberg's, but here too everything goes by opposites. As an emotion that by definition breaks all restraints, love cannot be present without loss of self-control. So the degree of Amanda and Elyot's violence corresponds to the intensity of their passion; and in emphasizing their equality as sparring partners, the fight shows how well suited they are romantically. The question posed by Act I – having been driven to divorce before, can they stay together? – is answered. The traditional Jane Austen process of ascertaining lasting compatibility has been turned inside out. Their official mates, who support the 'acceptable' view of love as sentimental, soothing and harmonious, are made to look even duller nonentities than the social representatives in his other comedies.

However, in contrast to Coward's usual pattern, where creative individualists are sharply divided from ordinary members of the public, here there is no indication that either Elyot or Amanda are artistically talented. Love can afflict anyone. Reversing the pattern of *Hay Fever*, it is they who quietly exit, while the normal pair finally become dramatically interesting as they take up the same verbal abuse and physical quarrelling. Like Elyot and Amanda, strong feelings liberate even Victor and Sybil from stultifying social conformity. They finally become 'real' people, substantiating the claim made at the beginning of the play by Coward's *alter ego*, Elyot, that

very few people are completely normal really, deep down in their private lives. It all depends on a combination of circumstances. If all the various cosmic thingummys fuse at the same moment, and the right spark is struck, there's no knowing what one mightn't do . . . [35]

Typically, even this sort of throwaway statement seemed too unambiguously affirmative to Coward, who paired *Private Lives* with a one-act parody of the play: *Some Other Private Lives* (also 1930).

In a sense all Coward's mature comedies could be called 'Private Lives'. They are variations on the same theme, as in *Blithe Spirit* (1941), where death replaces divorce, with the ghost of an ex-wife coming between a newly married couple; and in almost all of them the value of individual experience is asserted against society. The tensions between his characters and their world are irreconcilable. Even when Coward, responding to the changing sexual climate, went 'public' about the most private area of his life in *A Song At Twilight* (1965), the same opposition is present. As Hugo Latymer (made up to look like Somerset Maugham), Coward acted out his own dilemma of an aging author, who has hidden his homosexuality as the price of fame. Yet, while the play itself took him 'out of the closet', his protagonist refuses to remove the mask that hides his real self from society. Where this tension is missing – as in the sentimentalized suburbia of *This Happy Breed* (written in 1939, but not performed until 1942), the mythologized England of *Relative Values* (1951), or patriotic wartime songs like 'London Pride' – Coward's work becomes unconvincing, however sincere.

Even in his dazzling series of revues, the frothy wit expresses a feeling of existential insecurity, and the question posed in one of his theme songs is characteristic: 'Cocktails and laughter, but what comes after . . . '? Coward's comedy depends on dissonance, as in his best-known lyric: 'Mad dogs and Englishmen'. There the pastiche of imperialism is so effective that the utter contempt Coward expresses for 'the Britishers' abroad is often overlooked, just as the song 'Don't Let's Be Beastly to the Germans' was misunderstood as a pacifist plea when it was first broadcast in 1943. In fact it is a withering ridicule of both the enemy and the appeasers:

Let's be meek to them –
And turn the other cheek to them
And try to bring out their latent sense of fun . . .
But don't let's be beastly to the Hun.

The sharpness of ironic bite is in direct proportion to the urbanity of the tone, with the lightness of the metre and the rhyming precision transposing hatred into humiliating scorn. The continuing effectiveness of Coward's wit was underlined by the popularity of *Cowardy Custard*, an anthology of songs intercut with excerpts from his plays, which was greeted in 1972 as 'a revelation . . . an evening of some of the most devastating satire I have ever heard'.[36]

The significance of Coward's work lies as much in its style as in its thematic material; and he stressed that those plays brought to the fore in the first volume of his collected works were not simply 'the most representative'. They are 'the most successfully experimental'.[37] In addition to the multimedia epic of *Cavalcade* and the introspective convolutions of *Design for Living*, his selection included comedies like *Hay Fever* and *Private Lives*. Since these have become accepted as standard classics of the genre, their technical novelty tends to be overlooked. But it is particularly their dramatic minimalism in reducing plot to situation, psychology to role-playing, and action to performance, that mark Coward's contribution to modern comedy.

This reductive approach, as well as the obliquity in Coward's dialogue, leads straight to Harold Pinter (discussed below, pp. 328ff.). Language is a weapon of attack for Coward's characters, while for Pinter's it is more frequently a defensive disguise. But in the plays of both the subtext frequently contradicts the sense of the speeches – as in *Private Lives*, where the denial of emotion establishes its presence, or expressions of hatred are the coinage of love. Both playwrights have the actor's sensitivity to the importance of what is left unsaid, and a keen ear for the fossilization of language. Indeed, the linguistic concern of the artists in *Design for Living*:

LEO Sherry's a very ludicrous word, isn't it, when you begin to analyse it?
OTTO Any word's ludicrous if you stare at it long enough. Look at 'macaroni'.

is directly picked up by Pinter's gangsters in *The Dumb Waiter* (1960):

BEN Go and light it.
GUS Light what?
BEN The kettle.
GUS You mean the gas...
How can you light a kettle?
BEN It's a figure of speech!...
It's common usage!...
GUS Macaroni Pastitsio. Ormitha Macarounada.[38]

The suspect quality of words translates into an underlying sense of anarchy in Coward's lyrics as much as his comedies, where serious questions are given trivial answers. His best work gives a disturbing impression that reality itself is irrational, and the search for significance irrelevant, so that (like the characters in his plays) 'we none of us ever mean *anything*'.[39] Such a statement exactly foreshadows Samuel Beckett; and it was precisely the Absurdist qualities of *Hay Fever* that made it the choice for a National Theatre showcase in 1964.

More than in any of Coward's other plays, in *Hay Fever* eccentricity becomes the rule. The actress, having destabilized her daughter's diplomat boyfriend by offering herself to him, repeats the gesture by giving away her daughter, husband and son. This duplication raises the comic stakes each time; but it also makes the action seem progressively less extraordinary, although increasingly extravagant. The same use of parodistic exaggeration and zany multiplication, together with the disintegration of language into cliché – 'Masses and masses of words!... They're great fun to play with' – reappear in Ionesco, or a piece of home-grown Theatre of the Absurd, such as N.F. Simpson's *One Way Pendulum* (1959).

Preposterous irrationality is shown to be perfectly normal in *Hay Fever*, as with the discovery that the Blisses keep a barometer inside a grand piano: it fell off the wall and broke when tapped by the diplomat, whose sense of responsibility has been so shaken by the humiliations of the night before that he would rather hide the pieces than explain. The same technique forms the basis of Tom Stoppard's *After Magritte* (1970), where even the most bizarre events turn out to have a logical explanation (see pp. 397–99 below).

The conspicuous violation of approved behaviour in the Blisses' rudeness to their guests, which ranges from ignoring their presence to yelling insults at their faces, is characteristic of Joe Orton's farce in the mid-1960s. Although Orton's characters are flatter and more extreme, they too generally fall into groups of outsiders and insiders, each of which consider the other to be abnormal, even actively insane – and the logic of this had already been set out in *Hay Fever*. When asked, 'Do you suppose they know they're mad?', one of Coward's characters replies: 'People never do.'[40]

However, the comparison to Orton's iconoclastic farce also indicates the underlying conventionality of Coward's comedy. *Hay Fever* reflects the loss of direction and disillusion expressed in the hectic pace of the 1920s' 'bright young things'. But instead of promoting social disintegration, the way this collapse in public values is depicted on the stage increases a spectator's awareness of accepted standards. Coward's isolating and fragmented family meals depend on the absent image of conviviality and communal celebration symbolized by the rituals of food. We laugh precisely because the blindly egocentric rudeness of the Blisses, or the violence of their argument over tea and toast, are presented as incongruous with normal behaviour.

In the final analysis, Coward's comedy reinforces the average values of society. As a result, his work suddenly seemed dated with the theatrical revolution ushered in by Osborne's *Look Back in Anger*. Like Terence Rattigan, though even more unjustly, he was rejected as an Establishment figure by the new wave of British dramatists who arrived in the mid-1950s, and dominated the scene well into the 1970s. However, more recently there has been a revival of interest in his work, with major productions at the National Theatre; and leading contemporary playwrights as different as David Hare and Alan Ayckbourn have paid indirect homage to his example with one replaying the scene of *Hay Fever* in *Amy's View* (1997), and the other updating Coward's version of the battle of the sexes from *Private Lives* in *Things We Do For Love* (1998).

Notes

1 Coward, *Play Parade*, II, London, 1939, pp. viii–ix. See Maugham, *The Summing Up*, London, 1948, pp. 154–5 – though Maugham also provided an introduction to the American edition of Coward's *Bittersweet and Other Plays*, New York, 1929.

2 The point is persuasively argued by John Lahr, *Coward the Playwright*, London 1982. Lahr also notes that 'Only when Coward is frivolous does he become in any sense profound' – but limits the function of this frivolity to a mere gesture of 'freedom' (p. 3).

3 Coward, *Present Indicative*, London, 1937, pp. 270, 209.

4 Coward, *Play Parade*, I, London, 1934, p. xi.

5 Coward *Three Plays*, London, 1925, pp. viii–ix, and *Play Parade*, I, p. ix.

6 *Play Parade*, I, p. 520.

7 Coward, in *The New York Times*, 16 December 1969.

8 *Daily Mail*, 1 November 1931; *Present Indicative*, p. 227.

9 *Play Parade*, I, pp. 202, 224, 173.

10 *Play Parade*, I p. 196; *Present Indicative*, p. 229. To argue, as Lahr does, that 'Charm was not only the subtext of *The Vortex*, but the object of the exercise' (*Coward the Playwright*, p. 25), implies that the moral resolution is simply an insincere flattery of the public's complacency.

11 *Play Parade*, I, p. 239.

12 *Evening Standard*, 14 October 1931; Simon Trussler, *Plays and Players*, November 1964, p. 7. An article such as 'Twentieth Century Muse, Alan Strachan assesses the plays of Noel Coward', *Plays and Players*, May 1973, pp. 22ff, is typical of critics who acknowledge Coward's comedies as 'classics', yet find the supposed reactionary jingoism and apparently anti-intellectual spectacle of *Cavalcade* so embarrassing or distasteful that they can only defend the one by completely ignoring the other. Strachan was one of the creators of the 1972 biographical revue *Cowardy Custard*, yet his critical assessment of 'the plays of Noel Coward' fails to mention *Cavalcade* at all.

13 Preface, *Play Parade*, I, p. viii. Coward also considered the French or Russian Revolutions as possible subjects; and these might have made his aim more obvious, since they are generally accepted as being emblematic of events crushing individuals.

14 *Ibid.*, pp. 59, 60, 68–9.

15 *Ibid.*, pp. 2, 7, 73. Scene 3 of Part II has already shown what Fanny Bridges' 'having the most wonderful offers' (p. 67) actually means.

16 *Daily Mail*, 1 November 1931; *Play Parade*, I, p. 73.

17 Preface, *Three Plays*, p. viii.

18 *Ibid.*, p. 124. 'A Talent to Amuse' is quoted in the first sentence of Mander and Mitchenson's introduction to *Coward: Plays One*, London, 1979, as well as forming the title of Sheridan Morley's biography, (London, 1969). However, rather than being sung by one of Coward's *alter egos*, the song expresses the sentimental failure of 'a humble Diseuse' (*Play Parade*, I, p. 123).

19 *The Morning Post*, 1 May 1925.

20 *Play Parade*, I, p. 363. In *Present Indicative* the sole motive for *Design for Living* is stated to be 'that when all three of us had become stars of sufficient magnitude to be able to count upon an individual following irrespective of each other, then, poised serenely upon that enviable plane of achievement, we would meet and act triumphantly together' (p. 159).

21 Preface to *Play Parade*, I, p. v, and pp. 460, 463, 425.

22 *Ibid.*, pp. 455, 464.

23 *Ibid.*, p. 462.

24 *Play Parade*, I, p. 374 and preface, V, London, 1958, p. xxxii.

25 *Play Parade*, I, pp. xi–xii.

26 *Ibid.*, pp. 321, 261, 271, 310.

27 Coward, cited in Charles Castle, *Noel*, London, 1972, p. 48.

28 *Play Parade*, I, pp. 302, 310.
29 *Ibid.*, pp. 339, 319.
30 *Play Parade*, I, pp. 506, 507 and 514.
31 *Play Parade*, I, p. xiv; *Present Indicative*, p. 376: a spectator, who knew Coward and Gertrude Lawrence well, commented 'I could not always tell when you were acting and when talking to one another' (T.E. Lawrence, as quoted in Lesley Cole, *The Life of Noel Coward*, London, 1976, p. 139).
32 *Play Parade*, I, p. 534; *The Times*, 25 September 1930.
33 *Play Parade*, I, pp. 497–8, 494, 515–16.
34 *Ibid.*, pp. 519 & 528.
35 *Ibid.*, p. 480.
36 *Plays and Players*, September 1972, p. 44.
37 Preface, *Play Parade*, I, p. vii. Coward, of course, was in an almost unique position for putting new theatrical ideas into practice, since he composed the music for his plays, and set their interpretation on the stage by directing them, as well as by taking the lead role.
38 *Play Parade*, I, p. 429 and Pinter, *The Room and The Dumb Waiter*, London, 1966, pp. 47, 58.
39 *Play Parade*, I, p. 307.
40 *Play Parade*, I, pp. 313, 323.

4.3 Ben Travers (1886–1980): society as Farce

CHECKLIST OF TRAVERS' MAJOR PLAYS

A Cuckoo in the Nest, 1925	*A Bit of a Test*, 1933
Rookery Nook, 1926	*Banana Ridge*, 1938
Thark, 1927	*Corker's End*, 1968
Plunder, 1928	*The Bed Before Yesterday*, 1975
Dirty Work, 1932	

Farce, with its roots in the satyr plays of Classical Greece and the physical comedy of medieval playlets, has traditionally focused on conjugal conflict and infidelity. Over the Nineteenth Century it became a tool for social satire in the vaudevilles of Labiche, which caricatured the rising French bourgeoisie's pursuit of marriage for money, and the increasingly cynical bedroom comedies of Feydeau, who used the spectacle of sexual hypocrisy to expose social snobbery. Its physical action and hectic pacing produced a picture of man as the helpless victim of circumstances, trapped by objects as much as social conventions, that was particularly suited to silent film, and reached its high point in the clowning of the Marx Brothers, Harold Lloyd and Charlie Chaplin. At the same time, farce has tended to come to the fore in periods of conspicuous materialism, or when sharp social divisions are in a process of breaking down.

These aspects combined to give the genre a specific modern resonance. Since the 1920s it has rivalled the musical as the staple of West End commercial theatre; and its English popular form was developed by Ben Travers, who was almost an exact contemporary of Noel Coward. Born shortly before Coward towards the end of the Victorian era, Travers did as much to set the tone of English comedy between the wars. Like Coward, he was still writing well after the theatrical revolution of the mid-1950s; and although his work was not eclipsed in the same way, it has been ignored by critics, for whom Farce is not a serious dramatic form.

Yet in his nine 'Aldwych farces', so-called because they occupied the stage of the Aldwych Theatre uninterruptedly from *A Cuckoo in the Nest* in 1925 to *A Bit of a Test* in 1933, Travers established a pattern that is still as effective over half a century later. In 1964, when short of money, the Royal Court revived *A Cuckoo in the Nest* (with John Osborne as the outraged husband) to finance its season of serious plays by Chekhov, Brecht, Osborne, Shakespeare and Beckett: a clear acknowledgement of Travers' continuing power to attract audiences. In 1976 there were three of his plays on the London stage: revivals of *Plunder* (1928), which was the first modern play to be performed in the new National Theatre building, and of *Banana Ridge* (1938) with Robert Morley; in addition to his last play *The Bed Before Yesterday*, which opened in 1975 with Joan Plowright. The calibre of such performers, and the accolade of a National Theatre production, confirm the artistic respectability won by Travers' handling of a genre that is normally dismissed as the most simplistic type of entertainment. His work therefore deserves the same attention as more academically respected dramatists such as Joe Orton or Peter Barnes.

Perhaps more than any other kind of play, Farce depends on performance; and Travers' characteristic pattern was largely determined by the requirements, capacities or even physique of a fixed troupe of actors. As co-stars, Tom Walls, specializing in red-nosed or disreputable men-about-town, and Ralph Lynn, whose 'monocled fatuity' was directly descended from 'the Edwardian 'nut' ', required the same number of laughs in any shared scene. Robertson Hare played 'the intimidated little male relative' of *Rookery Nook* (1926) so effectively that, as Travers admitted, 'the farces thereafter generally had to contain a situation in which he stood between an inexorable Walls and a more plausible but no less ruinous Lynn, to be fleeced of his fair repute, of his cash, of his trousers'.[1] Each of the young actresses providing the sexual attraction displayed a virginal naivety, while the other regular female member of the cast was a natural focus for jokes about corpulence. These provided the basic elements of the pattern: a balance of contrasts in which no one character dominated the stage; the victimization of haplessly inoffensive (male) and predatory or social climbing (female) figures; together with the essential innocence of the obligatory romantic entanglement.

Travers was consciously following what he defined as 'the formula for farce', modelled on Pinero's early stage-craft: 'Act 2 – the sympathetic and guileless hero is landed into the thick of some grievous dilemma or adversity. Act 1 – he gets into it. Act 3 – he gets out of it.' What distinguishes his work is the combination of absurd improbability with characters who are 'recognisable types of human beings. The funniness must be in the situations and circumstances . . . and these are only funny because the characters are so recognisably human'.[2] Their names derive from the tradition of Restoration Comedy, and are used for deliberately crude puns, innuendo or verbal analogy – D'Arcy Tuck, Cherry Buck, Clive Popkiss, Willoughby Pink, Lionel Frush, Poppy Dickey. They may sound ludicrous. Yet the more eccentric their predicament, the more normal their reactions.

Forced by a series of accidents to spend the night in the same bedroom with another man's extremely sexy French wife (and even to sign the hotel register as her husband) in *Cuckoo in the Nest*, a man's only thoughts are how to preserve their respectability. Rather than any adultery, no one gets any sleep at all. Offering refuge for the night to a beautiful young girl who has been thrown out of her house in nothing but her silk nightdress (now soaking) by her violently Prussian stepfather, the man's one concern in *Rookery Nook* (1926) is getting a proper dress for her. She may be seen coming out of his bedroom by the serving woman – or found wearing his pyjamas when his wife returns. Yet the man's increasingly frantic attempts to avoid being suspected of infidelity, as much as the girl's innate innocence, prevent even the thought of sexual pursuits. His predicament is complicated by the young lady borrowing the frock of a chance caller (an obviously promiscuous village wench), who is then trapped in the bedroom instead of the girl from next-door – unknown to the man – and confirms the worst suspicion of both his wife and his sister-in-law when she prances out in nothing but her (salaciously frilly) underclothes. Even so, once the young girl returns, having retrieved her own dress, her self-evident purity is enough to resolve the situation.

The standard setting, which recurs with variations in almost all Travers' Aldwych farces, is a two-level interior with stairs leading to a balcony (under which an observer can lurk unseen from numerous bedrooms opening off it) and a multiplicity of doors for complicated games of sexual hide-and-seek. Yet the only time two unmarried characters share the same bed in any of these plays is when an uncle and nephew have dared each other to stay in a haunted room – and then there is a third man hiding beneath the bed. Even when seduction is indeed intended, circumstances always conspire to prevent it. Although this avoidance of actual sex has been ascribed to the censorship that prevailed in pre-war theatre, there are too many dramatic advantages to think that the limitation was anything but self-imposed. Noel Coward's comedies of the 1920s and 30s deal openly with adultery, while even Travers' late play, *Corker's End* (1968), could still be described as a perpetually interrupted love scene.

In fact, the main source of Travers' humour is the incongruity between the obvious innocence of his protagonists, and their unambiguously compromising situations – which is inevitably given the worst possible interpretation by all representatives of society from their marital partners to their servants. As the father-in-law of *A Cuckoo in the Nest* typically points out, 'this lady friend of yours is foreign and very attractive, and the two together are generally looked upon as a foregone conclusion'; and when advised to 'tell' his wife 'the truth' (i.e. admit his infidelity) the husband's reply is all too accurate: 'Impossible. She wouldn't believe it' (the fact that he has managed to preserve the most rigorous propriety being inconceivable in the context).[3] The only way out is deception: thus compounding the suspicions of the self-righteous characters, and intensifying their attempts to expose immorality. This creates the plot complications, from which much of Travers' humour comes. In addition, since there is nothing but a non-event to be discovered, a happy resolution is easy to achieve.

This is, at least on the surface, a world without consequences. Significant issues may underlie the farce: Travers intended *A Cuckoo in the Nest* as 'a comment . . . on the contemporary state of the divorce laws', while *Banana Ridge* (1938) is based on the typically Strindbergian problem of doubtful paternity.[4] Yet all the husbands and wives of the first are reconciled, instead of ending up in the divorce courts; and in the second none of the putative fathers, who are being blackmailed into supporting an illegitimate child, turns out to be the true progenitor.

Similarly in *Plunder* (1928), where the plot revolves around a jewellry theft, the stolen goods are revealed to be the legal property of one of the thieves. Even Death is no more than an object of humour. Offering to fetch bed-linen to a supposedly haunted room, the skeletal butler in *Thark* (1927) terrifies his listeners with a voice of doom: 'I'll come after you with the [winding-] sheets.' In his hands a compromising letter is presented as 'only the last post'. Yet his sinister appearance and sepulchral voice is merely due to a morbid fixation on his name ('Death' turning out to be his real surname, although his superstitious employer prefers to call him Jones). Initially, perhaps, this butler's ghastly presence serves as an uneasy reminder of the true frivolity of the farce itself; but his actual dramatic function is to expose the self-importance and materialism of the characters, which is expressed as a rationalistic refusal to believe in ghosts. He only has to say 'Ah! [*In a terrifying tone*]' for all the others to collapse like a row of skittles: a typical example of the way Travers resolves his farcical point in meticulous choreography.[5] This type of physical imagery contains the meaning as much as the humour of Travers' plays, since his dialogue is deliberately empty to reflect the vapid nature of his characters. All the plays begin in convincing realism, with solidly middle-class interiors; and this picture of decorum and respectability disintegrates as the action begins to speed up. Farce becomes a dissolving agent, removing the props of social stability.

Similarly, moral principles are revealed as a cover for unpleasant egoism, or an excuse for mean-minded vindictiveness. So the question, 'To any decent-minded person there's nothing wrong in your sleeping on the floor of my room, is there?', brings the automatic response: 'Yes, but where's the decent-minded person?'[6] The only reliable motive is self-interest, and the most effective bond is not emotion but money. Misjudged innocents may recover their reputations at the end of each play, spouses may return to their arms, harmony be restored: all of which overtly affirms conventional norms. But the goings-on have effectively demonstrated respectability to be a sham. The social order that apparently triumphs is not only contingent, but hollow – as at the climax of *Thark*, in which the upper-class country-house setting literally collapses around the characters in a thunderclap and howling wind. And these destructive forces clearly stand for the spectators' response: the 'thunder' of applause and 'gale of laughter' (which is punned on in the title of Travers' autobiography, *Vale of Laughter*) that liberates the audience from social constraints.

This challenge to society is most explicit in Travers' 1928 classic, *Plunder*. Its country-house settings epitomize upper-class privilege and establishment wealth. Yet none of the characters has any right to their position. The abominable ex-housekeeper's justification for disinheriting the legitimate heir of her senile employer, whom she married on his deathbed, is demonstrably false. Her claim that the old man had been abandoned by his grand-daughter

12 Physical choreography and farcical terror: Mary Brough and Ralph Lynn (left) with Robertson Hare and Tom Walls (centre) in Travers' *Thark*

is contradicted by her admission of intercepting any letters between them; and her marriage turns out to be bigamous since she knew her first husband to be still alive. An aristocratic young man, who moves in the best circles, is no less fraudulent. He finances his status by professional crime; and the girl he introduces as his sister is merely his accomplice. The grand-daughter's fiancé is clearly the fortune-hunter everyone else takes him to be, and has no scruples about joining in the jewel theft, which forms the mainspring of the action. The jewellry in question, 'stolen' by the fake widow, is to be restored to the rightful heir by robbery: a plan hatched by the professional thieves for their own purposes. Even the grand-daughter – although yet another of Travers' images of feminine innocence – is prepared to connive at almost any crime.

Love is a dubious weakness exploited by the predators, and family loyalty is represented by the ex-housekeeper's blackmailing brother. Willing to keep quiet about her bigamy, but only for a large share of the proceeds, the disreputable brother's accidental killing when he interrupts the robbery is applauded by all. Yet the supposedly virtuous characters escape being arrested for murder only by resorting to the same tactics. Using their discovery of the ex-housekeeper's bigamy to blackmail her in turn, they force her to declare that her brother was the thief.

This buys off the corrupt forces of the law, who agree that no crime has been committed. The audience is clearly intended to accept this 'happy ending' as justice, since it is the means by which all the problems are solved and the grand-daughter's inheritance is restored. But clearly such a resolution is only achieved by sleight of hand; and it raises more issues, precisely because of the neatness with which such dubious knots are tied. If society is based on 'plunder', those who applaud are implicated as accessories after the fact. The audience are as guilty as any of the characters.

Unlike the standard Travers' pattern, there is an actual crime with serious consequences. But raising the stakes from the discovery of fictitious infidelity in his other plays, to the very real possibility of the hangman's noose – following a principle which anticipates Pinter: that 'only the maximum of menace could provide the maximum of laughter' – is simply an intensification of his usual practice.[7] In those other plays, however innocent the entanglement, the fear of being found out is no less; and it is the emotional state of the endangered characters that measures the seriousness of the situation. *Plunder* is also unusual in that the vital fact of the housekeeper's bigamy is initially kept hidden from the audience. Elsewhere in Travers' work, nothing is concealed from the spectators. Whatever the confusions and mistaken judgements of the characters, we always know the truth already, and so are made to feel superior.

In fact Travers takes every opportunity to heighten the audience's complacency. Hence the caricature of foreigners, or the grotesque portrayal of social inferiors. The explosively named Prussian father-in-law of *Rookery Nook* draws on all the chauvinistic clichés. Square-headed and bespectacled, he is a physical-fitness freak and violent disciplinarian, whose speeches are the crudest of stage-German from 'Fürchterlichkeit. Sturm und Drang. (*Pronounced*: *Fear-ster-lick-kite . . .*)' or 'Herr Gott! I vill make for you hot like hell', to 'I vin – Deutschland über Alles!' Similarly, the bigamous housekeeper in *Plunder* is so ugly that the only explanation for the elderly invalid to have married her is 'He must have been blind', and so fat that her clothes could be sold 'to a man who makes circus tents', while country labourers (as in *A Cuckoo in the Nest*) are Mummerset village idiots. As the downtrodden manservant in *Thark* puts it: 'my first duty is to remember my place'.[8]

As a satiric strategy, injecting an attitude of superiority into an audience cuts both ways. It exposes the same egoism and unthinking prejudices that are objects of ridicule on the stage. It also helps to win the spectators' assent for the subversive subtext of Travers' farces. However, it reinforces the very smugness that is attacked by his plays.

Its effectiveness also depends on the existence of a clearly defined social stratification to such a degree that Travers had to present his last play as a conscious period piece, since by the time *The Bed Before Yesterday* was written in 1975 English society was far more fluid than it had been before the war. However contemporary the tone of its subject – a frigid widow, who comes to experience the joy of sex through exposure to the promiscuity of liberated females – the action is set back in the 1930s when the class-consciousness, which his earlier plays relied on, was still prevalent. The setting is explicitly dated; and although the heroine has greater psychological depth than any of his earlier protagonists, the characterization relies on outmoded responses in the recognition of class types: the '*gentleman fallen on evil days*', whom she purchases as husband-of-convenience; her divorced cousin, who takes in lodgers to provide herself with lovers and '*is a good stage lower in the social scale*'; or the 'silly bounder' who '*enjoys using expressions and words which were in those days considered obscene*'.[9]

Turning back the clock in the auditorium is less easy than on the stage. When performed in 1975, all the figures surrounding the heroine of *The*

Bed Before Yesterday came across as blatant caricatures. As Joe Orton had remarked a decade earlier, after receiving poor notices for *The Erpingham Camp* (1967), 'the whole trouble with Western Society today is the lack of anything worth concealing'.[10] Without a relatively rigid society with identifiable moral codes, the classic farcical pattern developed by Ben Travers lost the overlap with reality that gave the laughter its point.

Even so, his plays from the 1920s and 30s have remained popular. Still frequently revived on the stage, they have been turned into films, and even a musical – *Popkiss* (*Rookery Nook*), 1972 – and seven of the Aldwych farces were adapted for television in 1970. The pattern Travers set was followed by the Whitehall farces in the 1950s mounted by Brian Rix: such as John Chapman's *Dry Rot* (1954), or Ray Cooney's *One for the Pot* (1961). Yet by the Swinging Sixties a far more radical form was required; and this was provided by Joe Orton.

Notes

1 Travers, *Vale of laughter*, London, 1957, p. 124.
2 *Ibid.*, pp. 139, 92–3.
3 Ben Travers, *Five Plays*, Harmondsworth, 1979, p. 74. J. C. Trewin is an example of using the censor as an excuse for Travers, in defending his work against Brian Rix's accusation of dated coyness (see *Plays and Players*, February 1976, p. 17).
4 *Vale of Laughter*, p. 130.
5 *Five Plays*, pp. 277, 268 & 283.
6 *Five Plays*, p. 53.
7 *Vale of Laughter*, p. 154.
8 *Five Plays*, pp. 169–171, 323 & 327, 236.
9 *Five Plays*, pp. 405, 422 & 438. Even enthusiastic reviews found the characterization of the minor figures artificial 'with their absurdity on the surface' (*Drama*, Spring 1976, p. 39) and 'lack[ing] the plausibility of the main situation' (*The London Times*, 10 December 1975).
10 *The Orton Diaries*, ed. John Lahr, New York, 1986, p. 219.

4.4 Joe Orton (1933–67): Farce as confrontation

CHECKLIST OF ORTON'S MAJOR PLAYS

Entertaining Mr Sloane, 1964   *Crimes of Passion*, 1967
Loot, 1965   (*The Ruffian on the Stair/*
What the Butler Saw, 1969   *The Erpingham Camp*)

Farce gained fresh relevance in the 1960s with Joe Orton's explosive, but short-lived eruption on to the English stage, which paved the way for Peter Barnes (see pp. 352ff. below) and influenced Howard Brenton's first short satirical pieces at the end of the decade. Savage and irreverent, Orton caught the sexual permissiveness and growing political dissent of the time. Yet although he struck a distinctive new note, his work was also a continuation of earlier trends.

Indeed, his first major farce, *Loot* (1965), clearly echoed Ben Travers' 1928 classic, *Plunder*, in its title as well as basic elements of its plot: a nurse who cuts the family out of her patient's will; a double robbery that brings police investigation; the threat of arrest for murder, and the use of blackmail to provide a resolution. At the same time, where Travers satirically presented this frenetic criminal activity as normal, Orton exaggerated it to the point of absurdity. The nurse is not just guilty of bigamy, but wholesale massacre – which is treated by the representative of law and order as a minor aberration: 'Seven husbands in less than a decade. There's something seriously wrong with your approach to marriage.'[1] Similarly, the blackmail and bribery in Orton's play involve not just one, but all the characters, including the bereaved husband and the police inspector.

Even in Orton's last, most fully developed farce, *What the Butler Saw* (1969), there are echoes of Travers' *Rookery Nook* in a hapless husband's attempts to find a dress for a naked girl and the substitution of another, very different type of character for her. But again the situation is extended way beyond anything credible by multiplication and sexual reversals. Orton declared himself to be 'a great admirer of Ben Travers, in particular'. Even so, he rejected the bowdlerization by which farce had become socially acceptable: 'French farce goes as far as adultery, but by Ben Travers's time it was only *suspected* adultery, which turns out to have been innocuous after all'. Reacting against what he saw as having 'become a very restricted form' Orton parodied Travers' formula for Farce by taking it to extremes.[2] So, while Orton was clearly working in the same tradition, he is also demolishing a recognizable type of theatre; and this iconoclasm corresponds to his overall aim, which was to be provocatively outrageous.

The first lines of Orton's earliest play, *The Ruffian on the Stair* (radio 1964, revised as part of a double bill, *Crimes of Passion*, 1967), had already set the characteristic tone of his drama, with its open homosexual suggestion:

MIKE ... I'm to be at King's Cross Station at eleven. I'm meeting a man in the toilet.
JOYCE You always go to such interesting places.[3]

Entertaining Mr Sloane (1964) revolves around a competition between brother and sister for the sexual favours of an amoral youth. This already objectionable situation is milked for obscene possibilities. Not only does the frumpish middle-aged sister see the youth as her own illegitimate son, transposing carnal seduction into incest. When he beats her father to death (to avoid arrest for murdering the old man's employer) filial feeling becomes merely an excuse for the sister and her homosexual brother to blackmail each other into covering up his crime. Their awareness of each other's complicity then serves as a bargaining chip in arranging a *ménage à trois* with a vicious murderer.

This attack on traditional pieties of the family, and the denial of romantic ideals in making the seduction grotesque (the 'girl' being fat, twice the age of the youth – and with false teeth: an Orton trademark) is made doubly offensive by the conventional surface of the play. The setting of seedy naturalism, and the use of a sentimental comedy formula for a perverse action that the characters treat as perfectly acceptable behaviour, is designed to intensify the shock effect. Instead of nastiness being relegated to the woodshed, it is uncovered beneath the ordinary living-room carpet.

As his characters declare, for Orton 'sexual licence' was 'the only way to smash the wretched civilization'; and explicitness replaces innuendo in his subsequent plays. Instead of being merely imaginary, as in *Entertaining Mr Sloane*, in *Loot* incest is linked to necrophilia, with a son being required to strip his mother's corpse naked. What the son calls 'a Freudian nightmare' in that play then becomes an actual rape of mother by son in *What the Butler Saw*. But 'licence' on the stage is not just intended as a liberating image. Its primary function is to arouse the most violent reactions possible in the average (by definition bourgeois) audience: 'Sex is the only way to infuriate them', Orton noted when determining to 'hot up' the first draft of *What the Butler Saw*: 'Much more fucking and they'll be screaming hysterics in next to no time.'[4] At first his plays were remarkably successful in provoking such an extreme response – even if critical appreciation of their stylistic qualities had already defused their shock potential less than a decade later, turning them into 'modern classics' by the 1975 Royal Court Orton season.

In 1964 *Entertaining Mr Sloane* was greeted with revulsion by most reviewers; and Orton contributed to the furore (under various pen-names, including 'Edna Welthorpe' – borrowing Terence Rattigan's symbol of the average middle-class philistine spectator). He deliberately sought to exacerbate public outrage by attacking any acceptance of his play through writing tongue-in-cheek letters to the press: such as, 'In finding so much to praise in ... a highly sensationalized, lurid, crude and over-dramatized picture of life at its lowest, surely your dramatic critic has taken leave of his senses'. And through 'Edna', who claimed to be 'nauseated by this endless parade of mental and physical perversion', Orton scripted the kind of audience reaction he wanted for his drama: 'Today's young playwrights [referring specifically to himself] take it upon themselves to flaunt their contempt for ordinary decent people. I hope that the ordinary decent people of this country will shortly strike back!'[5]

This wish was fulfilled when public rejection forced the first production of *Loot* in 1965 to close before it reached London – although it won the award for Best Play of the Year in 1966 – and *What the Butler Saw* was greeted with booing and hisses in Brighton and at the London opening in 1969. The violence remained verbal, but the antagonism between stage and audience was comparable to the Dublin riots over Synge's *Playboy of the Western World* or Sean O'Casey's *The Plough and the Stars*. The actor playing Orton's protagonist recalled 'a guilty sense of exhilaration in fighting them [the spectators]. They really wanted to jump on the stage and kill us all.'

Orton turned Farce into a weapon of class warfare: as he once remarked to an admirer, 'I'm from the gutter ... And don't you ever forget it because I won't.'[6] The sharp incongruity between subjects like death, incest or insanity, and their comic treatment was the detonator. His humour is always deployed strategically.

The key to Orton's approach is his way of treating conventionally tragic or disgusting situations as a source of comedy. This both trivialized public standards of seriousness, and used the audience's laughter to challenge their moral principles. In *Loot*, for example, a funeral is turned into knockabout slapstick (indeed, the original title was *Funeral Games* – which Orton re-used for a 1968 TV play satirizing the Church). Dumped out of her coffin to make place for stolen money, a murdered woman's body is exposed to every indignity in a running gag. Stripped naked, deprived of false teeth and glass eyes, shoved upside down in a cupboard, swathed in a mattress-cover and paraded as a dress-maker's dummy, the corpse becomes the prize in a game of hide-and-seek between her son and his undertaker-accomplice, the nurse who has murdered her and is wearing her dress, her husband whom the nurse plans to marry, and a corrupt police-inspector in disguise.

In the same way, verbal elegance is combined with scatalogical crudity, stylish epigrams with derisive aggression: 'Why don't you shut your mouth and give your arse a chance' (*Entertaining Mr Sloane*); 'It's Life that defeats

the Christian Church. She's always been well-equipped to deal with Death'
(*Funeral Games*); 'Have you taken up transvestism? I'd no idea our marriage
teetered on the edge of fashion' (*What the Butler Saw*).[7]

The contrast between presentation and subject is the key element in
Orton's brand of Farce. An observation about unemployed actresses
discussing the penalties of old age defines his theatrical approach – 'It was
a very sad scene because it was played in such a cheerful way' – and he
extended this approach into every aspect of performance. On one hand,
his dramatic situations are a collage of recognizable clichés borrowed from
B-grade movies, sitcoms and popular entertainment, corresponding to his
perception that 'in naturalistic plays, I couldn't make any comment on what
kind of policeman Truscott is [in *Loot*], or the law, or the big general things
of the Establishment'. Yet although he structured his plots as a controlled
frenzy (his own term for them) in order to project an image of anarchic
insanity, Orton continually stressed the need for realism. Presenting his
dead mother's dentures as 'the originals' to the shocked actor playing the son
in *Loot*, he remarks 'you're not thinking of the events in the play in terms of
reality, if a thing affects you like that'. Then, when the first production of the
play failed, he put it down to Peter Wood directing *Loot* for laughs instead
of 'perfectly seriously'. Orton's advice to the Royal Court about staging *The
Ruffian on the Stair* summed up his principle of contradiction: 'The play is
clearly not written naturalistically, but it must be directed and acted with
absolute realism. No "stylization", no "camp". No attempt to match the
author's extravagance of dialogue with extravagance of direction.'[8]

At the same time, Orton's view of life, as reflected in his diaries, is curiously
myopic. Politics are dismissed as irrelevant, the only positive action being:
'Reject all the values of society. And enjoy sex.'[9] His own homosexuality and
promiscuity is presented as a norm, universalized by his almost exclusive
focus on relationships with other homosexuals. These run the whole social
gamut, from Establishment figures, through the theatrical profession, to
migrant labourers, in a record of frenetic sexual activity completely divorced
from sentiment. Orton's one-sided selectivity implies that the (at the time
banned) homosexual subculture equals the whole of society. When recording his one foreign holiday in his diary, he presents every male in Morocco
as homosexual; and the only difference between Africa and England is stated
to be that the law drives this 'natural' activity underground in Britain. By
extension, heterosexual impulses, and indeed any feelings for others beyond physical lust, are either duplicity or self-deception. Respectability is
hypocrisy. All moral principles are fraud. The logical result of such an egoistic

view was Orton's brutal murder at the hands of his homosexual companion in 1967.

The premise of the diary form as literary genre (frequently misleading) is authenticity: an impression heightened in Orton's case by the sensationalism of his early death, and by the almost immediate publication of a biography (based in turn largely on Orton's diaries) which was turned into a quasi-documentary film in 1987 (the film's title of *Prick Up Your Ears* being a typical double meaning that Orton had considered as a possible play title). This process of canonization accurately reflects its subject's self-absorption, in which his own atypical personal experience is taken as universally representative.

In Orton's diaries, life is seen as validating art; and Orton's vision is directly reflected in his plays. His dramatic figures have no characteristics other than egoism, and all moral standards are inverted. Sexual deviation is seen as the norm, killing acceptable, and 'a bang on the nose . . . human contact'. Any innocence is presented as stupidity, all authority revealed as the source of chaos; and egalitarian principles only mean that everyone is equally corrupt. The whole of society is 'a madhouse. Unusual behaviour is the order of the day . . . It's democratic lunacy we practise'; and 'All classes are criminal today. We live in an age of democracy.'[10]

This universality of the abnormal and dishonest, which Orton's dialogue proclaims, is affirmed by his characters at the end of each play. Yet there is always one innocent who actually believes in the moral principles denied by the others, and who has to be disposed of in order to 'keep up appearances' (the typical closing line of *Loot*). In *Entertaining Mr Sloane* the senile puritanical father is killed because he insists on informing the police that his children's love-object is a murderer. In *Funeral Games*, a distraught man searching for his vanished daughter, who lies buried under the coal in her husband's cellar, is hauled away to a lunatic asylum to avoid the discovery of a faked murder. The pattern is clearest in *Loot*. The murdered woman's husband – 'a law abiding citizen' who likes 'to be of assistance to authority' and refuses to credit any 'stories which bring officialdom into disrepute'[11] – is arrested on a trumped up charge and carted off to prison where an 'accidental' death has been arranged for him, with the connivance of his son, to prevent him confessing to his priest about the crimes of the others.

Significantly, all these representatives of middle-class moral standards are father figures, the conventional symbol of authority. Their removal, clearing the way for a celebration of a new (dis)order, projects the destruction of restrictive social norms that Orton hoped to achieve through his drama.

This wish-fulfilment is most obvious – and least convincing – in *The Erpingham Camp* (first staged as the second half of *Crimes of Passion*, 1967), where an isolated holiday camp/prison is presented as a microcosm of society. The immediate reference of the title is to the Butlin's Holiday Camps dotted around the coasts of England, the down-market equivalent to today's Club-Med, where working-class families had their vacation activities regimented by staff dressed in bright red jackets. It also plays off the term 'camp', relating to over-the-top homosexual display.

In this play establishment complacency and repressive morality lead to a popular uprising, and total overthrow of the corrupt power structure. But the parody is so exaggerated that it reduces the revolution to fantasy. Erpingham, the megalomaniac and puritanical Director of this institution, dons the stock corset worn by overfed husbands of nineteenth-century French Farce beneath his white tie and formal tail-coat, topped off with a gardenia-buttonhole, in a parody of the classic scene from Brecht's *Galileo* (which has become almost a recurring cliché in more recent British drama). There the character of the liberal Cardinal changes as he is dressed in rigid traditionalism of papal robes – but here the clothing ceremony merely exaggerates Erpingham's cartoon-personality. He has named the camp after himself; and his symbolic status is made all-too explicit when he is hit by a bottle:

PADRE ... (*White-faced*). You've struck a figure of authority!

As in Orton's other plays, the primary target is hypocrisy – blatantly represented by the clergyman's criminal seduction of teenage girls during 'evangelical forays'. It infects the revolutionaries, with their slogan of 'Have a bash, for the pregnant woman next door!' (the riot having begun with a hysterical expectant-mother's face being slapped), as well as the authorities' declaration, in one of Orton's funniest lines, that: 'We'll have a couple of verses of "Love Divine All Loves Excelling", Padre. It's fire-hoses, tear-gas and the boot from then on.' But Erpingham's power is as hollow as his appearance. Faced with the outraged masses marching on his command-centre, the only way of restoring order that he can think of is a farcical display of traditional moral values: organizing a pageant based on Raphael's painting of 'Pope Leo turning back the Hordes of Attila', with the girl-molesting Padre and a vulgarly promiscuous camp entertainer standing in for Holiness and Virginity. Not surprisingly this empty image of moral authority fails to halt the mob, and the camp is literally demolished.

The red glare of fire fills the room. Distant strains of 'La Marseillaise' are heard.
With revolutionary banners flying they stream through the mists of a bloody dawn!
There is a sound of wood and glass being smashed.[12]

However, there is no hint of political consciousness in the insurrection. All
this rhetoric is deliberately inflated. The triumph of the masses is pure anarchy. The girl and the Padre are both raped, while Erpingham's ignominious
death when the floor gives way beneath him brings the instant restoration of
the status quo. Since these revolutionaries have no idea what type of society
they want to put in his place, the brutal camp security guard (who has been
manipulating the whole uprising) takes over.

What the Butler Saw (1969) gathers all these elements together. The social
microcosm here is a psychiatric clinic, where madness is exploited rather
than cured, following the epigraph from *The Revenger's Tragedy*: 'Surely
we're all mad people, and they/Whom we think are, are not.' Each of the
characters becomes convinced that all the others are insane, despite their
repeated assertions that 'There's a perfectly rational explanation for what is
taking place. Keep calm. All will be well.'[13]

   (As another indication of continuity in the tradition of farce, one might
note that the same source has been mined by Alan Ayckbourn, although
instead of taking an epigraph from Tourneur's Jacobean tragedy, Ayckbourn
transposes the whole theme into a modern context. But, like Orton, he casts
the singular tragic action into the multiplying mould of Farce with his 1991
double play, *The Revengers' Comedies*.)

   What the Butler Saw takes off from an amalgam of stock clichés: the casting
couch; seduction disguised as medical examination; a wife's unexpected return. The rapid pace, proliferating parallels and multiple reversals create an
extravagant impression of absurdity, yet in itself, each incident is completely
logical. A prospective typist takes off her clothes because the lascivious doctor, whom she wants to please as her future employer, persuades her that a
physical examination is necessary for anyone who wants to work in a psychiatric institution (*mens sana in corpore sano*, etc.). When this 'interview' is
stopped by his wife's unexpected appearance (*coitus interruptus*), the doctor's
natural response is to hide her discarded clothing. And when a government
medical inspector mistakes her for a patient because she is naked, the doctor is forced to support this diagnosis in order to prevent his licence being
removed. Her claim to be a secretary then becomes interpreted as a delusion
that justifies her being certified as insane.

At first sight the insistence by the doctor's wife that he hire a hotel page-boy to fill the post is eccentric in the extreme – until we learn that, having copulated with her in a hotel linen cupboard the previous evening, the page boy is blackmailing her into finding him employment. And his motive for making this unlikely demand (since the boy has no secretarial qualifications whatsoever) is quite rational. He needs a hiding place, which the clinic will provide since – having gone on to seduce a party of school-girls later in the night – he is on the run from the police for sexually molesting minors. So, when a police sergeant comes in search of the secretary to retrieve public property (part of a demolished civic statue that she picked up and put in her handbag), it is logical for the boy to put on a dress and wig belonging to the wife, and impersonate the girl, falling in with the doctor's last-ditch plan for covering up his own unethical behaviour in order to avoid arrest. Eluding her medical custodians, the maltreated secretary then seizes on the page's discarded livery as the only available clothing in which she can escape from the institute. When the boy discovers her dressed as him, he persuades the doctor that the solution for all their problems is to drug the Sergeant in order to remove his police uniform: the only way of getting out of the clinic being for the boy to masquerade as a policeman and take the fake page (as himself) into custody. The dress he has been wearing is then put on the Sergeant to preserve the 'decencies', and the Sergeant's unconscious body is hidden in the shrubbery.

This manic complexity is not only an essential part of Orton's humour. The effect of such an accelerating confusion of roles and identities discredits the logic behind it. Reason and madness merge. The doctor, who accurately protests that 'I'm not mad. It only looks that way', is forced to admit that any description of the external facts reverses all standards of normal and abnormal. The truth would only make things worse when the medical inspector comes on them disposing of the unconscious Sergeant, before the boy has had time to switch out of his female clothes. So he is introduced to the inspector as the doctor's wife since he is wearing her dress, while the supposed pageboy (the secretary) takes refuge in the doctor's embrace:

PRENTICE I'm not a pervert!

RANCE How would you describe a man who mauls young boys, importunes policemen and lives on terms of intimacy with a woman who shaves twice a day?

PRENTICE I'd say the man was a pervert.

RANCE I'm glad you're beginning to face the realities of the situation.[14]

Following this line, all the permutations of transvestism are milked for every possible sexual relationship – although, with the exception of the pageboy's offstage episode with Mrs Prentice in the hotel, no sex actually occurs.

In this sense, as well as in the use of cliché and the hectic tempo of the action, as Orton pointed out, *What the Butler Saw* is 'a conventional form' of Farce: 'one should prove that one can do it, like Picasso proved that he could paint perfectly recognisable people in his early period'. Even the title is traditional, having been used as far back as 1905 (when a comedy titled 'What the Butler Saw' was presented at Wyndham's Theatre), and comes from the most well-known type of pier-end peepshow machine: one showing a keyhole, through which a French maid could be watched stripping to her suspender-belt while a gentleman sheds his pin-stripe trousers. The sexual display is literally that: exhibitionism. It is summed up in the notorious phallic image that concludes the play, where the vital missing part of Sir Winston Churchill's larger than life-size statue (dismembered by a terrorist bomb) is held aloft as an example of the national spirit – but one that even manages to insult the veterans of the war against Hitler by reducing their motive for fighting to sublimated homosexual desire:

RANCE (*With admiration*) How much more inspiring if, in those dark days, we'd
    seen what we see now. Instead we had to be content with a cigar – the symbol
    falling far short, as we all realize, of the object itself.[15]

Offering symbolic surrogates for real sex is a fair definition of pornography; and in the dialogue Orton suggests that pornography not only caters to 'depraved appetites', but provides 'an instrument for inciting decent citizens to commit bizarre crimes against humanity and the state'. As a description of the play's aims, this exemplifies the unresolved contradiction in Orton's attitude to both his audience and his use of immorality.

The attack on authority figures, ranging from the 'National Hero', Winston Churchill, to the Government Inspector, Rance, is more directly challenging. Rance's position as 'a representative of order' and 'the forces of reason' is undercut by making him the cause of the 'chaos' he condemns. The moral status of the Establishment is ridiculed by his interpretation of everything in terms of the most lurid case histories. Any exercise of power is discredited by his manic progress from issuing certificates of insanity, to pouncing with strait-jackets on everyone who comes his way, or shooting all those he considers dangerous lunatics (including the policeman). The ending is consciously Euripidean, with the bleeding Sergeant in leopard-spotted dress descending as a parodistic *deus ex machina* to liberate the exhausted and injured figures. Trapped in the security bars designed to prevent the lunatics from escaping (clearly representing the cage of morality that drives a conformist population demented by repressing sexuality), they follow him up a rope ladder '*into the blazing light*'.[16]

What this final tableau celebrates, as in Orton's previous plays, is anarchy. However, at the same time as rejecting all social restraints and conventions, Orton claims traditional justification for the sexual explicitness of his work and its flouting of taboos: 'farce originally was very close to tragedy, and differed only in the *treatment* of its themes – themes like rape, bastardy, prostitution'.[17] The ending of *What the Butler Saw* is an exact rendering of this mixture.

The ironic image of redeemed humanity ascending into a saner heaven – though actually the oppressively moral world of reality that they have been temporarily liberated from by the farce – from the madhouse of furtive sex (defined solely as rape, blackmail or gender-bending perversion), derives from the apotheosis that crowns Classical Greek tragedy. And Orton combines this with the waving of a monstrously Aristophanic phallus. Similarly, the joyful recognition scene, which immediately precedes this coda and resolves the conflicts of the plot, would be a tragic outcome in conventional moral terms. The discovery of long-lost children is the ultimate disaster (although in the play presented as the opposite), since the revelation that the pageboy and the secretary are Mrs Prentice's illegitimate twins, fathered during a wartime blackout in the same hotel linen cupboard by the man she eventually married, is simultaneously an exposure of 'Double incest'.[18] Typically too, following through Orton's concept of traditional farce, the comic affirmation of this outcome is designed as the ultimate outrage to a middle-class audience's standards.

Orton's work is also traditional in another sense. He linked his style to Sheridan, Congreve and, in particular, Oscar Wilde. In Wilde's fate he saw his own experience of being a homosexual, an outsider, and imprisonment (Orton had been given a short sentence for defacing books from a public library); and there are clear echoes of Lady Bracknell in exchanges like

PRENTICE It's a fascinating theory . . . Does it tie in with known facts?
RANCE That need not cause us undue anxiety. Civilizations have been founded and maintained on theories which refused to obey facts.

His most effective lines echo the paradoxes of Wilde and Shaw in the use of inversion to capture unacknowledged truths, as with 'Love thy neighbour . . . The man who said that was crucified by his.'[19] The epigraph to *Loot* is taken from Shaw, while in addition to borrowing the situation of the missing dress from Ben Travers, the recognition scene of *What the Butler Saw* is lifted directly from the discovery at the end of *The Importance of Being Earnest* – although Orton travesties the Wildean resolution through exaggeration.

Indeed, the degree to which Orton was consciously extending the comic tradition becomes increasingly clear within his work. As the self-referential comments on symbolism and pornography indicate, *What the Butler Saw* parodies itself, and it does so through the pastiche of other plays. To underline the point, attention is drawn to the set as a typical artifact of Farce: 'Why are there so many doors. Was the house designed by a lunatic?'; and the action is continually presented as a literary cliché: 'Isn't that a little melodramatic, doctor? . . . Lunatics *are* melodramatic. The subtleties of drama are wasted on them'; or 'We're approaching what our racier novelists term "the climax".'[20]

Orton was equally sensitive to contemporary influences. His first play borrowed heavily from Harold Pinter, with its threatening stranger forcing his way into a woman's home (as in *The Room*, 1957) and question-and-answer interrogation (as in *The Birthday Party*, 1958). But the subliminal violence in Pinter's early comedy of menace is extended into on-stage murder, while Orton always supplies logical explanations for the Pinteresque elements of indefinable personality and reversal, in which the 'ruffian' becomes the victim. If Joyce is called Madeleine – or Sarah – in *Ruffian on the Stair* (radio 1964, staged 1967), it is because these were her trade-names as a prostitute. A stranger's completely motiveless assault on her and attempted rape turn out to be the result of her husband Mike's activities. As an Irish hit-man, his meeting at King's Cross Station, mentioned in the opening lines, was conspiratorial (not simply lavatorial or homosexual). It led to the killing of the stranger's brother/lover, whom he cannot live without – and since the stranger's religious principles forbid suicide (though not homosexual incest), his attack on her is designed to manipulate her husband into shooting him. In Orton, menace only seems arbitrary until the facts are revealed. This conjunction of absurd action with rationality, which is basic to all Farce, distinguishes his approach from Pinter's; and the extent of the difference can be seen in the moralistic subtext underlying Orton's work.

Paradoxically, considering their strongly anti-moral stance, on one level Orton's farces are morality plays. For instance, *Funeral Games* and *The Erpingham Camp* both deal explicitly with cardinal moral qualities. The first was originally commissioned, as an ironic exposé of Faith and Justice, for a television series on the 'Seven Deadly Virtues' (a title that indicates Shaw's continuing influence on the English dramatic scene, since it comes from the Don Juan in Hell scene of *Man and Superman*). The second was written for a companion 'Seven Deadly Sins' series, to illustrate Pride. In Orton's world, ethical principles are merely counterfeit, propaganda lies propping up an immoral society.

Where his plays are most effective is in challenging all the ways society categorizes individuals, particularly in terms of gender and sexual orientation. Moral attitudes – and in *Loot* or *The Erpingham Camp* the religion on which morality is based – are not only assaulted through the subjects he chose to dramatize, but undermined by the complexities and confusions of Farce that make the audience (as bourgeois representatives) accomplices through humour. At the same time, the fantasy elements in his work devalue its social criticism, making a negative statement even out of the imperative to attack the society that victimized him as a homosexual. Indeed, in carrying his principle of inversion to its extreme the morality – for which society apparently stands indicted in his plays – always turns out to be positive and applauded. Orton's brand of Farce is not so much subversive, as a declaration of war. It embodies the anarchy it celebrates.

Notes

1 Orton, *Complete Plays*, London, 1976, p. 215.
2 Orton, in *Plays and Players*, November 1978, p. 13.
3 *Complete Plays*, p. 32.
4 *Ibid.*, p. 209; *The Orton Diaries*, London, 1986, p.125.
5 Letters published in *The Daily Telegraph*, reprinted in *The Orton Diaries*, p. 281.
6 *The Orton Diaries*, pp. 256, 54.
7 *Complete Plays*, pp. 74, 317–18, 373.
8 *The Orton Diaries*, pp. 232, 211, 47; Orton, 1967 letter, cited by John Lahr in the introduction to *Complete Plays*, p. 20.
9 *The Orton Diaries*, p. 251.
10 *Complete Plays*, pp. 329, 412, 333.
11 *Ibid.*, pp. 274, 216–17.
12 *Ibid.*, pp. 303, 292, 310, 314 & 315.
13 *Ibid.*, p. 383.
14 *Ibid.*, pp. 418 and 417.
15 *Complete Plays*, pp. 447, 427–28. Ignoring the fact that Farce is primarily a visual medium, critical analysis of Orton's work tends to follow John Lahr in emphasizing its literary quality, picking up on the assertion in Orton's novel (*Head*

to Toe, London, 1971, pp. 148–9) that 'words were more effective than actions; in the right hands verbs and nouns could create panic'. (see Lahr, Introduction to Orton's *Complete Plays*, pp. 8–10). However true this may be of the novel, as in the closing sections of *What the Butler Saw*, it is the visual imagery that dominates Orton's plays.

16 *The Orton Diaries*, p. 242; *Complete Plays*, pp. 417 & 438, 448.

17 Orton in *Plays and Players*, November 1978, p.13.

18 *Complete Plays*, p. 446.

19 *Ibid.*, pp. 383, 340.

20 *Ibid.*, pp. 376, 427 & 447.

4.5 Samuel Beckett (1906–1989): interior space and play as image

CHECKLIST OF BECKETT'S MAJOR PLAYS

Waiting for Godot, 1953	*Not I*, 1973
Endgame, 1957	*That Time/Footfalls*, 1976
Krapp's Last Tape, 1958	*Ohio Impromptu* 1981
Happy Days, 1961	*Rockabye*, 1981
Play, 1963	*Catastrophe*, 1982
Cascando, radio 1963	*What Where*, 1983
Come and Go, 1965	

Samuel Beckett has dominated the theatre over the last four-and-a-half decades as much as Bernard Shaw did in the first half of the period. Yet he was only secondarily a dramatist. Beckett began with poetry, and devoted the first half of his career to a series of major experimental novels written between 1934 and 1951: *Murphy* and *Watt* (written in English), *Mercier and Camier*, and the trilogy *Malloy*, *Malone Dies* and *The Unnamable* (which first appeared in French). He only turned to the theatre as 'a diversion' to clear a block in his novel-writing. *Waiting for Godot* was begun after *Malone Dies* in 1948, specifically 'as a relaxation, to get away from the awful prose I was writing at the time'.[1]

The major themes and images that form the core of Beckett's drama had already been developed in these novels, which were influenced stylistically by James Joyce. Beckett's switch from third-person narration in his pre-war fiction to first-person narratives, is crucial for the development of his plays. Indeed, to some extent Beckett's novels are interchangeable with his play-scripts. Passages from the novels were transferred straight to the stage in Jack MacGowran's one-man show, *End of the Day* (1962, retitled as the more typically Beckettian *Beginning to End* for TV video), embodying 'a composite character of the intellectual tramp' that had become Beckett's theatrical trademark.[2] Similarly, the American experimental theatre group, Mabou Mines, has adapted Beckett's novellas for performance, staging *The Lost Ones* (1975) and *Company* (1983), as well as *Mercier and Camier* (1979) and *Worstward Ho* (1986).

As this type of interchange indicates, Beckett blurs the distinctions between literary genres. His voice is unusually consistent; and the narrow focus of his work makes his vision immediately identifiable. These qualities have gained his work a uniquely influential position not only in British, but also European and American drama. When *Waiting for Godot* appeared in London in 1955 (two years after its Paris première), it had an almost immediate impact. Unlike most first plays, Beckett's characteristic themes (already explored though his earlier novels) were fully articulated, while the form was in no way derivative.[3] It marked a clear break with the dramaturgy of the 1940s, and conditioned the subsequent work of practically all English and Irish playwrights. In addition to Beckett's specific influence on Pinter and Stoppard, who have consciously adapted his theatrical approach, his example established a new frame of reference for contemporary theatre, continually redefining accepted ideas of what is 'dramatic'.

Indeed, a measure of his influence is the change in the way his work is viewed. So where *Waiting for Godot* seemed initially incomprehensible to its first English audiences – and the reviewers – in the mid-1950s, its meanings are now seen as self-evident.

On one level, Beckett's drama can be seen as an extension of the symbolist line in poetic drama from W.B. Yeats to T.S. Eliot; and his starting point was the same in rejecting 'the grotesque fallacy of realistic art'.[4] The context for many of his characters is Eliot's poem *The Waste Land*, which Beckett echoed in his first poem, 'Whoroscope': a dramatic monologue in which the speaker is Descartes. J.B. Priestley anticipated Beckett's focus on time and perception in the 1930s, while Beckett's bleak depiction of existence parallels the symbolic nihilism of John Whiting in the early 1950s. Yet it is not hard to see why his primary influence has been on comic dramatists.

Beckett's typical figures through almost all his plays are tramps – clearly based on the quintessentially comic image of Charlie Chaplin. Indeed the characters of his first-performed, most frequently staged and still best-known play, *Waiting for Godot*, are comic archetypes on several levels. The primary pair of Vladimir and Estragon are not only a doubling of

Chaplinesque tramps: as Didi and Gogo, they are also circus clowns, explicitly performing comic turns. Like Pozzo and Lucky, they wear Charlie Chaplin bowler hats, while their dialogue is patterned on music-hall crosstalk. They tell each other stock jokes – 'You know the story of the Englishman in the brothel?' – and their actions are explicitly related to

> . . . the pantomime
> ESTRAGON: The circus.
> VLADIMIR: The music-hall.
> ESTRAGON: The circus.

For 'recreation' they perform a classic hat-swapping sequence; and the play ends with a typically farcical image, when incompetently trying to hang themselves, one takes off the cord he uses as a belt and stands there quite unconscious of the fact that his oversize trousers have fallen down about his ankles. For Beckett, as he remarked about the ending of O'Casey's *Juno and the Paycock*, the value of Farce is its effect of 'disintegration' and 'dehisence'; and his comedy is always set against a sense of existential nihilism. Yet this too corresponds remarkably well with the way playwrights like Peter Barnes, who dominated one line of British comedy in the 1960s and 1970s, merged farce with grotesque violence. (See pp. 359–62.) Indeed there are points even in *Godot* that clearly anticipate this kind of dark humour: Estragon, *'convulsed with merriment'* crying out 'He'll be the death of me!' catches the contradiction perfectly, as does the exchange:

> *Vladimir breaks into a hearty laugh which he immediately stifles, his hand pressed to his pubis, his face contorted.*
> VLADIMIR: One daren't even laugh any more.
> ESTRAGON: Merely smile. *(He smiles suddenly from ear to ear, keeps smiling, ceases as suddenly.)*[5]

Beckett's Existentialism also makes his plays highly intellectual; and this too has marked the development of contemporary British drama. It carries over into the philosophic comedy of Tom Stoppard – and hardly coincidentally it is in a play which revolves around philosophers, *Travesties*, that Stoppard pays explicit tribute to Beckett's influence in the final line: 'Wham, bam, thank you Sam'.

Perhaps the mark of a pioneer into new literary territory, Beckett's work is far more rigidly abstract in its philosophical nature than either his followers, or the Shavian discussion or thesis plays that represented the earlier form of intellectual drama, and leads logically to studio exercises written for academic seminars like *Rockaby* or *Ohio Impromptu* (both 1981). His drama not only expresses a specific and clearly identifiable set of ideas, but embodies typically intellectual qualities. Combining progressive thematic abstraction with increasingly simplified images, its hallmarks are consistency and a uniquely uncompromising search for ways of defining the essential human situation. References to outside events – whether the Holocaust, Hiroshima, or autobiographical details from Beckett's life – oblique to begin with, are gradually omitted altogether.

Even when Beckett turns to specific political themes in his last two playlets, *Catastrophe* (1982) written for an international programme protesting Vaclav Havel's imprisonment, and *What Where* (1983) which deals with torture and the totalitarian state, the focus is so generalized that their relevance depends solely on the audience's prior knowledge. 'Make sense who may. I switch off' declares the voice of a dead clown at the end of *What Where*, after the identical figures of Bam, Bem, Bim and Bom have each disposed of one another in the search for an unspecified secret ('where?').[6] Although paralleling the politicization in Pinter's plays of the 1980s, when he was most involved with PEN, *One for the Road* (1984) and *Mountain Language* (1988 – discussed below, pp. 331–33), these Beckett pieces are even more abstract. They are miniaturized models of psychological victimization, images in a mental limbo. As in the preceding series of monologues, from *Not I* in 1973 to *Rockaby* in 1981, Beckett's work becomes literally a 'theatre of the mind'. Corresponding to this, its stylistic values are precision and economy.

At the same time, since one of Beckett's philosophical premises is that ascribing any meaning to existence falsifies reality, his plays are designed to be experienced and not intellectually comprehended. To this end, any apparent statement in the dialogue is contradicted, or made ironic by its context. For instance, the declaration that 'Time has stopped', which seems to explain the characters' predicament in *Waiting for Godot*, provokes an immediate response of '*cuddling his watch to his ear*. Don't you believe it.' Conversely, the passage of time – signalled by the appearance of a few leaves on the bare tree that is the sole indicator of place – becomes ironic in terms of Beckett's substitution of circular repetition for dramatic development, which led one reviewer to describe *Godot* as 'a play where nothing happens twice'.[7]

This reciprocal undercutting can be seen at its simplest where word and action are opposed, as in the last couplet of each Act of *Waiting for Godot*:

'Well shall we go?/Yes let's go./*They do not move.*' More subtly, the final line of 'I can feel the rings' in *Come and Go* (1965) is denied by the costume description specifying that the fingers of the three women in the play be visibly bare.[8] This process of cancelling out also extends to Beckett's overall dramaturgy. His plays are closed compositions. Either characters finish in exactly the same positions as the beginning – or the stage image is isolated and internalized, complete in itself. But closure is always balanced against the absence of any resolution to the action.

The two Acts of *Waiting for Godot* are part of a potentially infinite series, in which the same tramps as 'all mankind' reappear each day/at every performance. Similarly, the final directive in *Play* (1963) is '*Repeat play*', ending with a marginally varied reprise of the opening lines; and the only progress within this duplication is one of diminishing returns, which is characteristic of all Beckett's plays. As he advised, the second run-through of *Play* should 'express a slight weakening, both of question and of response, by means of less and perhaps slower light and correspondingly less volume and speed of voice', suggesting 'an indefinite approximation towards' running down.[9]

This process is given metaphoric significance by the opening lines of *Endgame* (1957): 'Finished, it's nearly finished, it must be nearly finished. (*Pause.*) Grain upon grain, one by one . . . the impossible heap.'[10] Christ's last words on the cross are combined with a philosophical paradox proving that the universe is infinite, and with post-Newtonian physics. In the Classical Greek philosopher Zeno's demonstration, subdividing a finite quantity of millet and transferring half the remainder to the other pile over and over again would never produce a single heap, because the number of grains moved each time diminishes in a geometrical progression. This parallels one of the basic laws of thermodynamics, which asserts that while heat (life) constantly dissipates, absolute zero (death) will never be attained, since the smaller the differential, the slower the process becomes. Entropy is seen as a universal common denominator, and Beckett applies it to time. Zeno's 'impossible heap' is stage centre in the following play, *Happy Days* (1961), translated into grains of sand that pile up around the female protagonist, like sands from an hour-glass.

Beckett's figures are at an ever more extreme edge of their existence, but not one achieves an ending. This is reflected in the temporal setting or the lighting specified for his plays: typically late evening or grey halftones, a neutral state of non-darkness. Just as the characters of *Godot* 'don't seem able . . . (*long hesitation*) . . . to depart', so even the apparent finality of 'Nothing is left to tell' in *Ohio Impromptu* is undermined by its context. As a sentence in a story narrating the reading of the text that is read out aloud, it signals a continual regression of mirror-images.[11] And this avoidance of closure is a refusal of conclusions, both literal and intellectual.

The high degree of philosophical integrity in Beckett's work has particular academic appeal, while its elliptical concentration – coupled with ambiguity, and the avoidance of any definable statement – leaves his plays open to any number of different interpretations. The combination has created a whole scholarly industry, generating a confusing mass of commentary that significantly outweighs Beckett's total writings. This search for meaning in itself creates an impression that his work is obscure, which in turn seems to justify such elucidation. But the critical process is in a very real sense incompatible with the work it analyses. 'Crritic!' (with its derogatory extended guttural stress) is the ultimate term of abuse for Beckett's characters. His response to all this scholarly activity is the typically reductive 'No symbols where none intended', backed up with disclaimers that parody the academic pursuit of symbolism by identifying names like Godot, Hamm and Clov with the most basic everyday objects: boot (*godillot*), hammer and nail (*clou*). Beckett's position 'is to refuse to be involved in exegesis of any kind. And to insist on the extreme simplicity of dramatic situation and issue . . . My work is a matter of fundamental sounds (no joke intended).'[12]

This description is indeed accurate. Beckett's ideas may seem difficult to accept because of their radical negation of conventional values. But they are unequivocal, even limited, and repeated in all his writing, from early essays on 'Dante . . . Bruno. Vico . . . Joyce' and 'Proust' (1929 and 1931), which set out both the existential vision and aesthetic principles explored in his plays.

Nature is indifferent in Beckett's work; God absent, or at best unknowable. Although biblical images abound as the common currency of hope, prayers go unanswered – and when characters pray (as in *Endgame*) the effect is bitterly parodistic: 'Nothing doing!/The bastard! He doesn't exist!' So life has no transcendental meaning. 'We are alone'; and socially defined aspirations are no less illusory than religious justifications. On a universal scale, civilization is reduced to debris, while material circumstances are irrelevant to the human condition. Birth and death are the defining facts of existence, diminishing the variables of individual experience to insignificance: 'The essential doesn't change . . . Nothing to be done' (which forms the recurrent motif of *Waiting for Godot*).[13]

All Beckett's plays present versions of the same stark image, increasingly distilled to fundamentals. Even Pozzo, the figure in *Godot* most closely associated with self-deceiving social values, reaches the final insight that 'They give birth astride of a grave, the light gleams an instant, then it's night once more.' This is picked up in the opening words of *A Piece of Monologue* (1980), 'Birth was the death of him. Again'; and the same perception of human transience forms the total statement of *Breath* (1969). In this characteristically self-negating piece of wit (the humour lying in its context as a derisive contribution to Kenneth Tynan's erotic revue, *Oh! Calcutta!*), there are no characters or dialogue, only

1 Faint light on stage littered with miscellaneous unidentified rubbish. Hold about 5 seconds.
2 Faint cry and immediate inspiration and slow increase of light together reaching maximum in about 10 seconds. Silence and hold about 5 seconds.
3 Expiration and slow decrease of light together reaching minimum together (light as in 1) in about 10 seconds. Silence and hold about 5 seconds.[14]

Even the reality of the external world is problematic, being filtered through imperfect senses and interpreted according to received ideas. This makes the question of perception and awareness a central issue in Beckett's drama. Evasion of consciousness is seen as the normal state, since 'Life is habit. Or rather life is a succession of habits, since the individual is a succession of individuals', progressing through different roles and relationships. At the same time there are 'periods of transition that separate consecutive adaptations'. These 'represent the perilous zones in the life of an individual, dangerous, precarious, painful, mysterious, when for a moment the boredom of living is replaced by the suffering of being'.[15] The function of art is to arouse this awareness.

These aspects of perception are directly explored by two consecutive works that are pivotal in Beckett's development: *Play* (1963) and *Film* (1965). *Film*, framed by close-up shots of an open eye, takes its motto from Bishop Berkeley, the eighteenth-century philosopher who answered the empiricist claim that any object out of sight and mind had no reality by asserting an all-seeing God to validate existence. But Beckett reverses Berkeley's '*Esse est percipi*' (To be is to be perceived) by demonstrating that 'All extraneous perception suppressed, animal, human, divine, self-perception maintains in being.' The unnamed protagonist is divided between his own inner vision (E = eye), externalized in the camera lens, and the object (O = himself) on which it is focused. Typically, this highly abstract theme is given concrete form by reflecting its own medium. The central tramp-like figure – as played by Buster Keaton – is an immediately recognizable clown of the silent screen, while the action echoes the classic chase sequences of early comic films.

Like all Beckett's characters, the aim of 'O' is to escape – '*blindly*' – from 'the anguish of perceivedness', into the state of 'non-being' designated by his zero label. When the camera switches to his own (blurred/unwilling) perception it registers O's awareness of being watched, focusing on the eyes of passers-by in the street (who are equally horrified to find themselves under scrutiny), or of the pet animals in the room to which he flees. This 'illusory sanctuary' is both a crumbling tenement, and the tomb/womb or interior of the skull that recurs throughout Beckett's work.[16] 'O' can eject the dog and cat (in a classic music-hall farce sequence). He can cover window and mirror, with their connotations of outside viewers and insight, or destroy the memory of his past selves in tearing up family snapshots (a cliché reused in *A Piece of Monologue*, and representing the individual as 'a succession of individuals'). Yet he is still transfixed by his own consciousness. As in *Ohio Impromptu*, the final image is of identical *alter egos* staring at each other.

The role of the camera lens in *Film* – acting simultaneously as the self-awareness of the protagonist and, since the spectators' perspective is inseparable from its focus, as the audience's awareness – is replaced by a spotlight in *Play* (1963). Three impassive heads protruding from funereal urns and facing '*undeviatingly front*', the characters are reduced to disembodied minds. Provoked into speech as the light switches from one to the other, their inter-cut monologues illustrate the process of blotting out 'the suffering of being' with 'the boredom of living'. This is all too obviously represented by the triteness of their history: an 'eternal triangle' of adultery, from which any residual meaning has been removed. Not only is each insensible to the supposed objects of their lust or jealousy, but the past tense and repetition of their speech drains off all passion, while their toneless monotone denies any emotional truth. Even the pretence of personal involvement vanishes when the fragmented story is abandoned unfinished, unable to preserve them from awareness of the 'eye ... Opening and shutting on me' or to convince them of their reality. Without the relationship that defines their being through the eyes of the other two, nothing guarantees their existence but the spotlight, which contradicts their self-images as individuals by revealing '*Faces ... lost to age and aspect*'.

The key question is 'Am I as much as ... being seen?'[17] And it is the fear of nothingness that provokes the repeat of the play, like a record endlessly stuck in the same groove, echoing Yeats's image of ghosts dreaming-back their dead lives in *Purgatory* (1938).

Both *Film* and *Play* are programmatic. They excavate underlying themes in the preceding plays, and serve as a springboard for Beckett's later work.

In *Happy Days* (1961) Winnie, buried to the neck in her isolated sand-pile, can still exist if 'Someone is looking at me still. (*Pause.*) . . . Eyes on my eyes (*Pause.*)', which repeats the tramp's declaration, alone with his sleeping companion in *Waiting for Godot*, that 'At me too someone is looking, of me too someone is saying, He is sleeping, he knows nothing.'[18] If God is a pious fiction, then His role – in theatrical terms that of an outside observer, ratifying the characters by an awareness of their existence – is supplied by the audience.

Similarly, as the titles of *Film* and *Play* imply, in Beckett's work the medium is the message. One of Beckett's earliest statements of artistic principle asserted the primacy of

direct expression . . . if you don't understand it, Ladies and Gentlemen, it is because you are too decadent to receive it. You are not satisfied unless form is so strictly divorced from content that you can comprehend the one almost without bothering to read the other . . . Here form is content, content is form. Not about something.

And in *Play* – where, as the title suggests, the performance is the action – the remembered experience of the trio is identified with the theatrical context and by extension with game-playing. The ostensible dramatic subject, their lives, has no intrinsic significance. As one reflects, 'I know now, all that was just . . . play. And all this? . . . when will all this have been . . . just play?'[19]

'Just Play' could stand as the subtitle for all Beckett's earlier theatre. Even in *Waiting for Godot* (1953), which contains more activity and a larger range of figures than any subsequent work, there is so little to grasp on the level of plot or character that several of the first reviewers summed up the lack by quoting 'Nothing happens, nobody comes, nobody goes, it's awful.'[20]

On the surface the two tramps, Vladimir and Estragon, are waiting for a purpose – code name, Godot – just as the other pair in the play have an aim in travelling, Pozzo's goal being a market fair at which Lucky can be sold. But the basis of this drama is the denial of expectations: for the audience as much as the characters. The single tree is a parody of a stage-set. Suspense, or even dramatic development, is ruled out by continually replaying the identical sequences of words, as much as by having the second half of the play repeat the first. Salvation or purpose, equalling thematic resolution as well as meaningful significance for the characters' actions, is indefinitely postponed: promised for a tomorrow that can never be reached because the present is always today. Even the negative ending of suicide proves impossible; and its tragic connotations are deflated by the slapstick crudity of Estragon's trousers falling round his ankles.

There may be extreme physical changes in the other, socially oriented pair of Pozzo and Lucky from one act to the next; but these are not the result of aging. Rather than measuring the passage of time, they illustrate how the temporal process discredits human pretensions. The differences represent the inner truth behind the earlier appearances. The picture is the same, but portrayed in metaphoric terms. Pozzo's loss of balance and sight, which reduces him to helpless dependence on his now dumb retainer, reveals his assumptions about man's existential status ('Made in God's image!') as inherently blind and untenable. The rope that shackles slave to master is shown to run both ways.

Even the apparent contrast between the two pairs of characters is ambiguous. Vladimir and Estragon are equally bound together by a common need for companionship – as well as being umbilically tied to the absent Godot by their mutual desire for something to give their waiting purpose. One appears intellectual and volatile, the other sensual and supine. But this only mirrors the body/mind division of Pozzo and Lucky; and at times each of the tramps takes on the role of his opposite number.

In the second half it becomes clear that all their activities, even including breathing, are simply 'exercises' to 'pass the time'. Their relationship itself, embodied in their philosophizing, their arguments, abuse and embracing, is no more than a diversion 'that prevents ... thinking'. Their situation too, literally defined by the thoughts they as characters express about it, is revealed as mere 'recreation' since everything they say resolves into verbal games of question and contradiction. In the first act Pozzo presents his self-admiring oration, Lucky's dancing and display of 'thinking' specifically for their entertainment. Everything reduces to performance, as the tramps replay their own daily meetings, or 'play at Pozzo and Lucky' – transposing Lucky's anguish into a farcical mime of hat-swapping, modelled on a Marx Brothers routine from *Duck Soup* and directly comparable to the dog-and-cat sequence in *Film*.[21]

By extension all human occupations, summarized in Lucky's monologue as 'sports of all sorts', are only pastimes. And this applies as much to the audience as to the characters. The set is a stage, with toilets 'End of corridor on the left', and as such it becomes explicitly a playing space: 'the Board'. In attending the theatre to be entertained, to pass the time and perhaps find insights from seeing their lives reflected in drama, the spectators are no different from the tramps: 'We always find something, eh Didi, to give us the impression we exist.' But in this case the entertainment is deliberately minimal. Lucky's dance is incompetent, his vaunted thought incoherent. The

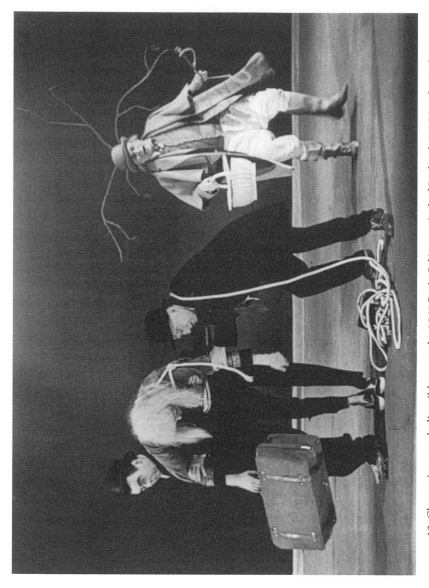

13 Clowns in a symbolic wilderness: the 1961 Paris Odéon revival of Beckett's *Waiting for Godot*

tramps evaluate Pozzo's emotional histrionics (presented as a set-piece of classic acting) to be 'awful./Worse than the pantomime./The circus'. Yet they themselves are like poor actors without a script, forced into improvisation that continually breaks down into cliché routines. In terms of performance, as much as for the performers,

the hours are long, under these conditions, and constrain us to beguile them with proceedings which . . . may at first sight seem reasonable, until they become a habit.[22]

The game-playing and theatricality is still more overt in *Endgame* (1957). Again there are two complementary pairs of characters, and at least a reference to a boy who (like Godot's messenger) might be approaching from somewhere else. But the situation is even more static. Only one of the four is able to move; a claustrophobic interior replaces the empty landscape of *Waiting for Godot*; and there is no possible exit since outside 'the earth is extinguished'. The action is again structured on analogies and repetitions. However, it is more limited in being restricted to a single run-through, which cuts the variation between the two halves of the earlier play. Instead, the ending simply returns the characters to their first positions.

Clov, the servant without whom the blind and paralysed Hamm cannot exist, announces his departure in his last lines. Yet he remains standing by the door (which in any case leads only into the even more enclosed cube of his kitchen) '*impassive and motionless, his eyes fixed on Hamm*', in exactly the same posture as at the beginning.[23] The lids have been replaced on the dustbins in which the legless Nagg and Nell are incarcerated. In his final gesture Hamm covers his face with the same bloodstained handkerchief that is revealed when Clov removes the dust-sheet, which hides Hamm's immobile figure at the opening. The only thing missing from the opening tableau is the dust-/winding-sheet. But this sheet merely represents the stage-curtain, an interpretation confirmed by Beckett in his 1967 Berlin production. Clov's initial actions literally set the stage, and his gathering up of the sheets marks the start of the performance: an ironic parallel to the symbolic folding of the cloth in Yeats's poetic dance plays.

The status of the action as no more than a dramatic 'entertainment', to be repeated for the next audience, is confirmed by continuous theatrical reference in the dialogue. When Hamm rhetorically enquires 'Why this farce, day after day?', the response is 'Routine', and his answer to what keeps Clov with him is 'The dialogue'. Very much the ham actor, he indulges in formal speeches, aspires to soliloquy and labels a throw-away line 'An aside, ape! Did you never hear an aside before?', while Clov refers ironically to

318 The comic mirror

his non-departure as 'This is what we call making an exit'. In stage terms (as Hamm points out) silence equals dramatic suicide. So the function of speech is not to communicate, but (as in *Play*) simply to enable the characters to exist by prolonging the performance. They ridicule the notion that their figures might come to signify anything. Indeed the constant repetition, both within the play itself and from performance to performance, or from one production to another, gradually wears away any intrinsic meaning, until 'the words that remain ... have nothing to say'.[24]

As a result, style becomes the only value, with the characters' past experience or present emotions being presented as fictional stories and set exercises: displays of histrionic (dis)ability. And this self-reflexive theatricality is paralleled by the chess imagery that Beckett emphasized in his definitive 1967 Berlin production. Clov was made to move in zigzags, the knight's two squares forward and one to the side, while Hamm's role was explained to the actor as 'the king in this chess game that was lost from the beginning. He knows from the start that he has made nothing but senseless moves': a 'bad player' but not a 'poor loser', since 'he plays [these moves] out with almost ironic detachment, conscious of their pointlessness'.[25] Significantly, this particular 'endgame' – the technical term for the final phase in chess – typifies Beckett's evasion of endings. The two white pieces (Nagg and Nell) are immobilized, while the opposing side (identified by the red faces of Hamm and Clov) is reduced to the one combination of pieces where checkmate is impossible.

Beckett's constant directives to the actors were 'more monotony' and 'simpler movements ... everything as economical as possible'. Moves and positions were plotted mathematically, so that, for example, in the prayer sequence the three pairs of hands and bowed heads formed exact equilateral triangles. Such symmetry – specifically representing 'Pythagorean' ideals of harmony and proportion, but doubly ironic when applied to this disintegrating universe of cripples and amputees – was reductive. It emphasized the artificial nature of the drama as a game, as well as corresponding to the rationality of chess. Indeed, the dual image of game-playing and theatre-performance is the key to *Endgame*, which Beckett defined as 'plain play. Nothing less. No thought of puzzles and solutions.' It encompasses everything from Hamm's opening 'Me ... to play', up to his penultimate sentence: 'Since that's the way we're playing it ... lets play it that way'.[26]

In a meaningless universe, the only affirmative activity is one that has no ulterior meaning: i.e. a non-professional game. And chess is not only the game closest to being completely symbolic and intellectual; it can be played against oneself, as (in both senses of the expression) Hamm does here, or as a purely mental exercise. This was reflected in the first 1957 production of *Endgame* by Roger Blin's interpretation of the bare-walled 'shelter', with its two eye-like windows through which Clov peers at the outside world, as the inside of a skull. From such a perspective, the four figures represent elements of the psyche in a monodrama; and carrying this principle of mental game-playing to its logical conclusion, Beckett's occupation in his role of author/director is the same as his characters. As he commented in an unusually frank reply to actors' queries:

There are so many things. The eye is as unable to grasp them as the intelligence is to understand them – Therefore one creates one's own world, *un univers à part*, in order to withdraw . . . to escape from chaos into an ever simpler world. Even Clov has this need for order – I have progressively simplified situations and people, *toujours plus simples*.

. . . the link between the individual and things no longer exists – One must create a private world for oneself, in order to satisfy . . . one's need for order. That for me is the value of theatre. One can set up a small world with its own rules, order the game as if on a chess-board – Indeed, even the game of chess is still too complicated.[27]

It is therefore hardly surprising that the function of the author becomes problematic for Beckett. As with contemporary political dramatists like Edward Bond or Howard Brenton, the writer-figure is central to Beckett's work. Estragon's rags define him as a poet. Hamm is above all a raconteur composing a quasi-autobiographical novel of a Beckettian sort, whose working method – 'babble, babble, words, like the solitary child who turns himself into children, two three, so as to be together, and whisper together in the dark' – exactly describes the process of *That Time* (1976), as well as being reflected in the reader/auditor double of *Ohio Impromptu* (1981).[28] It also applies to radio-plays like *Krapp's Last Tape* (1958) and *Cascando* (1963), which are Beckett's most explicit dramatizations of his position as a writer.

The title figure of *Krapp's Last Tape* presents the author as one of his own universalized tramps: a disreputable white-faced clown with purple nose, who slips on a cliché banana-peel. The reverse of Beckett's symbiotic pairs, where complementary characters form a single fully rounded personality (most obviously in the 'O' and 'E' of *Film*, or the May/Amy pairing in *Footfalls*: 1976), here isolated man is set against images of his own past.

The divided self is projected in the gap between the artist and art-work. Wordsworth's well-known definition of poetry, as emotion recollected in tranquillity, exactly describes Krapp's working method. But Beckett inverts the Wordsworthian unity of man and nature, experience and creative expression. In contrast to the Romantic ideal, thought and feeling, literary production and personal memory, are shown to be irreconcilable. The dichotomy is underlined because the subject of Krapp's (un)creative labours is himself, while the emotions he records or calls up are mechanically reproduced on a tape-recorder. And the connection between character and author is direct, as well as ironic, since the 'Shadows of the opus . . . magnum' dictated year by year – officially Krapp's biography – incorporates incidents from Beckett's own life.[29]

The Reel (Box 3 – spool 5), which Krapp replays as a starting point for recording the present episode of his life, speaks of his artistic inspiration: 'the light of the understanding and the fire'. But the words he puts on tape now are a rejection of previous experiences, which he reduces to fragmentary inconsequence by switching between tapes, reeling backwards or re-recording. Present experience invalidates previous insight, so that there is 'Nothing to say, not a squeak. What's a year now? The sour cud and the iron stool.' His name, like that of many Beckett characters, contains ironic multiple meanings. It denies significance to his art (labelling it as fundamental noises in a literal sense), as well as being self-contradictory since the symptom of Krapp's imaginative constipation is verbal diarrhoea.

All that the endless spools of tape achieve is repetition on an ever more minimal level, as with the 'Bony old ghost of a whore' that replaces Krapp's recorded memory of romantic love. 'Be again, be again' is his final injunction to himself; and the form of the play implies that this is all an artist can achieve. The one thing the tape-recorder does is to cancel out time, while Krapp's present recording of reflections on the revolving reels of past memory is set on a *'late evening in the future'*.[30]

Cascando (1963: originally written for radio, but staged by Mabou Mines in 1976) shifts the focus from the figure of the artist to Beckett's creative process. The script is divided between OPENER – the artist's critical faculty that selects, organizes, considers audience response – the narrative VOICE or artistic imagination, and MUSIC representing unconscious expression. The theme is the telling of a story, encapsulated in a name: Woburn, which is described as 'An image, like any other'. What VOICE recounts are glimpses of this image, depicting Woburn as yet another of Beckett's tramp-like characters, stumbling towards a shore and drifting out to sea in a boat without oars or rudder. But this fragmentary narrative is little more than a subtext to the search for expression.

Woburn's fictional journey is simultaneously the writer's exploration of his material. The categorical imperative for an author is communicating his perception of existence. Complete achievement would fulfil his function, making any further creativity redundant, and allowing the artist to 'rest no more stories . . . no more words'. But, like Godot, Woburn is a Platonic form that can never be realized. The requirement is to 'see him . . . say him . . . to the end'. Yet although there are 'thousands and one' possible variations, no single version is capable of encapsulating the total vision. Since each initially appears 'the right one', the assertion that 'this time I have it . . . I've got it' is automatically denied. The process that makes up the play opens with a non-beginning ('I resume'), and closes with a typically inconclusive 'it's him . . . it was him . . . I've got him . . . nearly –'.[31]

The absolutism of this aesthetic concept, in which the purpose of art is to express the process of its own composition and the image created is a projection of the artist, forms an exact correlative for the philosophical abstraction of Beckett's themes. It leads logically to the later plays, pared down to single poetic images, which can only be described as 'theatre of the microcosm'.

Cascando illustrates Beckett's principle that 'to be an artist is to fail' because 'unable to act, obliged to act, he [the artist] makes an expressive act, even if only of itself, of its impossibility, of its obligation'. The original title of *Cascando* – *Calendo*, a musical term equivalent to *diminuendo* – points to another aspect of Beckett's work. Reflecting on Proust, he had stated that 'the only possible spiritual development is in the sense of depth. The artistic tendency is not expansive, but a contraction. And art is the apotheosis of solitude. There is no communication because there are no vehicles of communication.'[32] This precisely outlines the pattern of Beckett's theatrical development.

Even in his early plays – which still use conventional dramatic idioms, if only ironically – surface elements are increasingly stripped away. Physical movement becomes restricted. Dialogue gives way to monologue. Already in the second half of *Waiting for Godot*, instead of dancing Lucky can only stumble and collapse. In *Endgame*, out of the same number of characters three are paraplegic, and the fourth moves with difficulty: '*Stiff, staggering walk*'.[33] Where Clov is still upright, the one mobile figure in *Happy Days* (1961) can only crawl and his speech is limited to fifty-three words, of which all but one are in the first half of the play. In *Come and Go* (1965), where three women each in turn impart significant information to another about the third, the same short sequence of sentences is repeated three times; but what is being said about each of the women when they temporarily leave the stage is inaudibly whispered, removing the core of the 'drama'.

The same progression is intensified in *Not I* (1973) and *That Time* (1976). After the heap of sand/time in *Happy Days*, that buries Winnie to the waist in the first half and rises to her neck in the second, come the truncated urns from which the heads protrude in the timeless purgatory of *Play*. Then in *Not I* the sole character is reduced to a mouth, speaking to the almost motionless cloaked back-view of her *alter ego*, while in *That Time* there is nothing but a decapitated face listening impassively to his own (recorded) inner voices. Drama is cut down to 'dramaticule' – the subtitle of *Come and Go* – then further distilled in the titles for collections of the later playlets to 'Shorts', 'Ends and Odds' or 'Occasional Pieces' (a bilingual pun combining *pièces d'occasion* or 'commissioned plays', with 'trivial fragments').

Beckett has outlined his own evolution as a dramatist in a marginal note about producing *That Time*: 'To the objection, visual component too small... answer: make it smaller on the principle that less is more'. This piece, which he described as 'on the very edge of what is possible in the theatre', is a compression of his work as a whole. As well as being a companion piece to *Footfalls*, it reproduces thematic fragments from other plays. In particular, the overlap of recorded memories from widely separated time frames echoes *Krapp's Last Tape*, while the single image of an old man's head, floating in darkness, parallels the disembodied mouth of *Not I* (a title which itself is taken from his 1953 novel *The Unnamable*). And in another marginal note Beckett commented that the text of *That Time* read not like a new work, but as 'something out of Beckett'.[34]

When directing *Endgame* Beckett singled out 'Nothing is funnier than unhappiness' as the most significant line in the play. And the way he continually repeats the same dramatic images and themes follows the same principle: 'it's like the funny story we have heard too often, we still find it funny, but we don't laugh any more'.[35] At the same time, as this statement indicates, repetition itself creates subtle changes. As well as increasingly limiting audience response, Beckett uses repetitions to chart a progression towards economy and simplification within an ever-tighter focus.

Although still later pieces like *Rockaby* or *Ohio Impromptu* (both 1981) reintroduce movement, however minimal, this is offset by geometrical rigidity. The 'Slight. Slow' inclinations of the rocking chair of the first playlet is explicitly mechanical, 'without assistance from W', the single unstirring woman sitting in it. In addition, since the chair is placed '*facing front downstage slightly off centre audience left*', this motion is towards and away from the spectator, rather than lateral.[36] So instead of mobility, the effect is of hypnotically recurring shifts in perspective on a motionless figure. In the other piece the two identical old men, seated opposite each other, are restricted to single hand-gestures. One knocks on the table with his left hand to control the flow of narration (like OPENER in *Cascando*) from the second, who turns the pages of the book from which he reads with his right hand. The single hat, placed exactly at the centre between them, reinforces the impression that these figures are mirror images. But again the perspective is turned. L (the Listener) faces front on the right, while his counterpart R (the Reader) is in profile at the left end of the table. And in both pieces the slight disequilibrium implicitly denies the stasis reached at the end of the texts.

Increasingly, Beckett's theatre presents the audience with a double negative. 'Nothing is more real than nothing', the epigraph from *Malone Dies*, applies to all his work. The observation that 'There's no lack of void', ironic in *Godot*, becomes more literal with each phase of his career.[37] Like Cordelia's 'Nothing' in *King Lear*, existential reality turns out to be inexpressible. Each half of the Beckettian paradox cancels the other, leaving isolated images that reflect only themselves and refer back to Beckett's previous images.

In his early novel *Murphy* (1938), Beckett outlined three ascending levels of consciousness: 'light' that comprises 'forms in parallel' to the 'physical fiasco' of the external world (equivalent to Plato's Cave), the 'half-light' of abstraction, and 'the dark of absolute freedom' populated by pure forms.[38] Plays such as *Endgame* or *Happy Days* correspond to the first level. There is social interaction between the characters, however truncated, and their actions have recognizable analogues in everyday activities. *Come and Go* and *Play* can be seen as transitional works. Although the reference to external life remains, it is either reduced to ritual, or emptied of significance. His later drama – *Not I*, *That Time*, *Footfalls* and *Rockabye* – explores the inner world of half-light.

All these post-1970 pieces present isolated figures in the moment of death. As plays of fragmented memory, the incidents and personal emotions related by these almost disembodied relics of humanity to themselves, or overheard in the fleeting voices of their deceased parents, are purely mental images. The 'other' is no more than a mirror of the self. Amy and May are anagrams of each other in *Footfalls*; the silently listening daughter of *Rockabye* is identical to her mother in attitude and dress. Even though tied by the nature of the stage medium to physical objects (as in *Breath*), or to the irreducible minimum of a single actor, the characters become ghost-figures, like the single on-stage female in *Footfalls*: 'Faint, though by no means invisible, in a certain light . . . a pale shade of grey', and explicitly wearing 'the costume of a ghost . . . worked like a cobweb'. When the actress asked 'Am I dead?', Beckett's reply was 'you're not really there'.[39]

Similarly, the action of Beckett's plays becomes abstracted to musical structures. The OPENER, VOICE and MUSIC of *Cascando* are orchestrated into a trio, with each counter-pointing the others in a developing pattern of combinations. Thus in the opening sequence the solo tones of OPENER, followed by VOICE, combine and speak against the MUSIC, modulating into VOICE with MUSIC, then all three together. And this is echoed in the closing variation, where the OPENER is followed by VOICE with MUSIC against the OPENER, leading to all three together and finally resolving in VOICE with MUSIC alone. Exactly the same orchestration occurs in *That Time*. The three contrasting voices of the old man's consciousness, and his previous selves as boy and adult, are interwoven, although they retain their spatial separation and discontinuity.

This musical use of language for poetic resonance is already present in the verbal patterning of *Waiting for Godot*:

ESTRAGON All the dead voices.
VLADIMIR They make a noise like wings.
ESTRAGON Like leaves.
VLADIMIR Like Sand.
ESTRAGON Like leaves.
    Silence.
VLADIMIR They all speak at once.
ESTRAGON Each one to itself.
    Silence. . . .
VLADIMIR They make a noise like feathers.
ESTRAGON Like leaves.
VLADIMIR Like ashes.
ESTRAGON Like leaves.
    Long silence.

In Beckett's early plays such passages are interludes. His later and shorter pieces are almost wholly orchestral, substituting musical qualities for drama – as in *Ghost Trio* (television, 1977), named after Beethoven's fifth piano trio. Here the musical form is transposed into the viewer's perspective, as well as the structure of the scenes. The three brief episodes of 'Pre-action', 'Action', 'Re-action' are each shown from three set camera positions. The situation is a residual echo of the essential action in *Waiting for Godot* and *Endgame*: an unidentified male figure waiting in a womb-like room; the arrival of a small boy who '*shakes head faintly*', denying the man's silent question. As ghosts, they inhabit a dead world – 'No shadow. Colour: none. All grey. Shades of grey' – and the only voice is a monotone female whisper, either in the man's head or on the tape-cassette in his hand, accompanied by brief passages from the slow movement of Beethoven's score, played out of sequence.[40]

Musically, *That Time*, or even *Cascando*, resemble a coda rather than a full composition, while in *Footfalls* and *Rockabye* rhythm is limited to a metronome beat in the audible footsteps back and forth across the stage (again 'a little off centre'), or in the visual rhythm of the rocking-chair. As with the brief piano excerpts in *Ghost Trio*, dramatic presence is eroded to the residual image retained momentarily on the retina when one's eyes are closed. This is a frequent effect in Beckett. It is produced by rapid alternations of light and dark during *Play*: '*Faint spots simultaneously on three faces. Three seconds... Spots off. Blackout. Five seconds. Strong spots simultaneously on three faces. Three seconds*'.[41] And the slow fade called for at the end of *Come and Go*, as the three female figures sit in silence with interlaced hands, creates the same impression.

This evolution towards absence may be entirely consistent with Beckett's declared principles. But it can also be seen as a reaction to the change in theatrical climate created by his own work, and perhaps even as a response to the academic industry growing around it. In 1955, when *Waiting for Godot* reached the English stage, the standard drama of the time was Noel Coward and Terence Rattigan, or the later quasi-poetic comedies of T.S. Eliot. These shared fourth-wall naturalism, drawing-room dialogue, well-made plots and socially situated characters: a form of dramatic representation that had remained unchanged since the turn of the century. At that time John Osborne and Harold Pinter were still repertory actors, Tom Stoppard a provincial drama critic. Beckett's play heralded a revolution to come and the impact was immense. However, barely a decade later its principles had become an accepted part of theatre language, and *Godot* (staged by the National Theatre in 1988) was soon acknowledged as a classic.

This not only made it possible for Beckett to advance the frontiers of drama to new levels of minimalism. It also required the exclusion of whatever dramatic elements remained, since his earlier reductionism was so quickly accepted and widely imitated, if his work was to retain its *avant-garde* status. And it is hardly coincidental that the direction Beckett has taken emphasizes

the values prized by his academic supporters. Indeed, he is recorded as commenting 'Oh, God, tomes are going to be written about this', when inserting
the word 'lacrosse' (with its pun on rites of passage and the Crucifixion) into
Footfalls. Although ambiguous, like all Beckett's humour, this represents a
complete reversal of his earlier statement that 'I'm not interested in the effect
my plays have on the audience. I simply produce an object.'[42]

However, the net result has been a withdrawal from the stage. After *Happy
Days*, Beckett's plays have increasingly been performed in smaller theatres
for short runs. Indeed, his late work is clearly designed for very limited
numbers of spectators, since their geometry is only effective in a narrow
perspective. From the extended sightlines of a large auditorium the careful
'off-centre' positioning of the figures in *Footfalls* and *Rockabye* would not be
visible. In the same way, close proximity to the stage for the whole audience
is required by Beckett's stress on nuances of facial expression, or his whit-
tling down of the human figure to fragments of anatomy: the disembodied
'*white face*' of the Listener that provides the sole visual image in *That Time*,
isolated in darkness 'about 10 feet above stage level midstage off centre ... as
if seen from above' – or the equally elevated mouth of *Not I*, which is only
'*faintly lit from close up and below*' and has been amputated even from the
head of the speaker. This visual restriction goes along with the extreme
brevity of the scripts. Beckett's process of radical negation has effectively
nullified his drama. What remains are variations on a single concentrated
and poetically charged image. And even this eludes understanding, since as
he stated of *Not I*, Beckett is 'not ... concerned with intelligibility', but with
working on the 'emotions of the audience rather than appealing to their
intellects'.[43]

Notes

1 Beckett, cited in Dierdre Blair, *Samuel Beckett, A Biography*, New York, 1978,
   pp. 361, 381.
2 Jack MacGowran, cited in Blair, *Samuel Beckett*, p. 555.
3 Although *Waiting for Godot* came after *Eleutheria* (1947), which echoes the
   rebellion against bourgeois society in Roger Vitrac's surrealist *Victor ou les Enfants
   au Pouvoir* (1928), Beckett refused to have the earlier play produced and kept it
   unpublished.
4 Beckett, *Proust*, New York, 1970, p. 57.
5 *Waiting for Godot*, New York, 1954, pp. 11b, 23b, 8b.
6 Beckett, *Collected Shorter Plays*, London, 1984, p. 316.

7 *Waiting for Godot*, p. 24; *The Nation*, 14 February 1959, p. 144.

8 *Waiting for Godot*, pp. 35 & 60; *Come and Go*, in *Modern Drama*, 19 (1970), p. 260 (the fullest text of the play).

9 *Waiting for Godot*, p. 51; Beckett, letter to George Devine, cited in Blair, *Samuel Beckett*, p. 567.

10 *Endgame*, New York, 1958, p. 1.

11 *Waiting for Godot*, p. 31; *Three Occasional Pieces*, London, 1982, p. 32.

12 *Waiting for Godot*, p. 48; *Watt*, New York, 1959, p. 254; letter to Alan Schneider, cited in Blair, *Samuel Beckett*, p. 470.

13 *Endgame*, p. 55; *Proust*, p. 49; *Waiting for Godot*, pp.14ff.

14 *Waiting for Godot*, p. 57; *Three Occasional Pieces*, p. 11; *Breath and other Shorts*, London, 1971, p. 11.

15 *Proust*, p. 8.

16 *Cascando and Other Short Dramatic Pieces*, New York, 1967, pp. 75, 85.

17 *Proust*, p. 8; *Cascando and Other Short Dramatic Pieces*, pp. 45, 61, 54.

18 *Happy Days*, New York, 1961, pp. 49–50; *Waiting for Godot*, p. 58.

19 Beckett, 'Dante . . . Bruno. Vico . . . Joyce', in *Our Examination for Incamination of Work in Progress*, Paris, 1929, p. 13; *Cascando and Other Short Dramatic Pieces*, p. 54.

20 *Arts*, 27 January 1953, and *The Sunday Times*, 7 August 1955.

21 *Waiting for Godot*, pp. 15, 49, 44, 41. (For a more extensive treatment of this aspect, see Ruby Cohn, *Just Play: Beckett's Theatre*, Princeton, NJ, 1980.)

22 *Ibid.*, pp. 47, 29, 23, 55, 44, 51.

23 *Endgame*, pp. 81, 82.

24 *Ibid.*, pp. 32, 58, 77, 81.

25 *Materialen zu Becketts 'Endspiel'*, Frankfurt, 1968, pp. 83, 114. (My translation.)

26 *Materialen . . .*, pp. 107, 73, 103, 6; *Endgame*, pp. 2, 84.

27 *Endgame*, p. 3; *Materialen . . .*, pp. 90–1.

28 *Endgame*, p. 70.

29 *Krapp's Last Tape*, London, 1959, p. 13. (For a comparison between Krapp's memories and Beckett's biography, see Blair, *Samuel Beckett*, pp. 490ff.)

30 *Ibid.*, pp. 15, 17, 18, 9.

31 *Cascando and Other Short Dramatic Pieces*, pp. 9 & 18.

32 'The Duthuit Dialogues' (1949), in *A Samuel Beckett Reader*, ed. John Calder, London, 1983, p. 210; *Proust*, p. 57.

33 *Endgame*, p. 1.

34 Beckett, cited in James Knowlson and John Pilling, *Frescoes of the Skull: The Later Prose and Drama of Samuel Beckett*, New York, 1980, p. 219, and in Enoch Brater, *Beyond Minimalism: Beckett's Late Style in the Theatre*, Oxford, 1987, p. 38.

35 *Endgame*, pp. 18–19 (and see *Materialen . . .*, p. 50).

36 *Three Occasional Pieces*, London, 1982, pp. 18–19.

37 *Three Novels by Samuel Beckett,* New York, 1965, p. 192; *Waiting for Godot,* p. 42.

38 *Murphy,* New York, 1957, pp. 111–13.

39 *Ends and Odds,* London, 1977, p. 36; Beckett, cited in Walter Asmus, 'Rehearsal Notes for the German Première of Beckett's *That Time* and *Footfalls*', in *Journal of Beckett Studies*, Summer 1977, p. 92; Billie Whitelaw, cited in Brater, *Beyond Minimalism,* p. 60. (For a more positive interpretation of the relationship between the three levels of interior reality and Beckett's aesthetics, see Sidney Homan, *Beckett's Theaters,* Lewisburg, 1984, pp. 12ff.)

40 *Waiting for Godot,* p. 40; *Collected Shorter Plays,* pp. 253, 248.

41 *Cascando and Other Short Dramatic Pieces,* pp. 45–6.

42 Beckett, cited in *The Times,* 9 January 1985, and in Colin Duckworth, *Angels of Darkness,* London, 1972, p. 17.

43 *Ends and Odds,* pp. 23, 13; Beckett, cited in Blair, *Samuel Beckett,* p. 625.

4.6 Harold Pinter (1930–): power plays and the trap of comedy

CHECKLIST OF PINTER'S MAJOR PLAYS

The Room, 1957	*Betrayal,* 1978
The Birthday Party, 1958	*One for the Road,* 1984
The Caretaker, 1960	*Mountain Language,* 1988
The Homecoming, 1965	*Party Time,* 1991
Landscape and *Silence,* 1969	*Moonlight,* 1993
Old Times, 1971	*Ashes to Ashes,* 1996
No Man's Land, 1975	

Born at the same time as Osborne and John Arden, and sharing much the same childhood background as Arnold Wesker (who also came from a Jewish family in the same area of London, and experienced the fascist demonstrations of the late 1930s), Harold Pinter was a central figure in the generation of post-1956 playwrights. However, in contrast to the naturalistic diatribe of Osborne's *Look Back in Anger,* which set the theatrical agenda for the movement, when it was first produced Pinter's work seemed confusingly unpolitical.

His early plays, such as *The Room* (1957) and *The Birthday Party* (1958), were rejected as obscure. However, his 1959 one-act piece, *A Slight Ache,* had clear echoes of Samuel Beckett's novel, *Malloy;* and his use of a tramp as the central figure in *The Caretaker* (1960) was seen as derivative of *Waiting for Godot,* first performed in London five years before. So Pinter became identified with the Theatre of the Absurd: a label popularized by Martin Esslin's influential study (published in 1961), which lists Pinter as a follower of Beckett and Ionesco.[1] However, this interpretation of his work became increasingly hard to justify, given the specific and recognizable social contexts of *The Homecoming* (1965) or *No Man's Land* (1975), although both were initially treated as examples of Absurdist Theatre – and in later short pieces like *Mountain Language* (1988) and *The New World Order* (1991) the political basis of his early plays was clarified by the explicit brevity of scenes in which the manipulation of language is linked to state violence, with mental torture substituting for physical abuse.

At the same time, partly because of his use of ambiguity almost all Pinter's plays up to the 1990s, when he became involved with PEN and the cause of political prisoners, are cast in unmistakable tones of comedy. *The Lover* (1963) and *Betrayal* (1978) both use conventional comic material; and it is not coincidental that Pinter's influence is clearly discernible in Joe Orton's farces. Indeed there are strong comic aspects to his drama, which led Noel Coward to see parallels between Pinter's work and his own comedy. As early as 1961 Coward singled Pinter out from the 'New Movement' (which in general he dismissed as 'pseudo-intellectual' or 'self-consciously propagandistic'), praising in particular his technical strengths: 'He uses language marvellously well . . . a superb craftsman, creating atmosphere with words that sometimes are violent and unexpected'.[2] Pinter in turn has reciprocated by directing a revival of Coward's *Blithe Spirit*. Similarly *Betrayal*, which Pinter dedicated to Simon Gray, is a variation on the social satire of *Otherwise Engaged* (which Gray had dedicated to Pinter in 1975). In fact, throughout the early part of his career, Pinter translated the themes of his supposedly existential plays into overtly comic revue sketches, with completely ordinary people and typically everyday situations. And his career could almost be said to be bracketed by satiric revue sketches, with two contributions to shows at the Lyric Hammersmith (indeed with the same actress, Sheila Hancock, performing in both shows): the first, 'The Black and the White' for *One to Another* in 1959; and 'God's Own District' for *Then Again* in 1997 being his last piece. Then, too, his linguistic influence can be seen both in the plays of the leading contemporary American dramatist, David Mamet, and more relevantly in the comedies of a young playwright like Patrick Marber (who has also acknowledged a debt to Mamet) – a sympathy that Pinter has reciprocated by directing Mamet's *Oleanna* for the Royal Court in 1993.

Although echoes of Beckett can be found in most of Pinter's plays, particularly in his experiments with interior monologue, *Landscape* and *Silence*

(1969), for Pinter the only direct influence of Beckett's work on his own is 'something of its texture'.[3] He shares Beckett's interest in Proust, with *Old Times* (1971) and *No Man's Land* (1975) picking up on themes from his screenplay for *A la recherche du temps perdu* in their treatment of memory; and a similarity to Beckett emerges in the evocatively enigmatic treatment of death in *Moonlight* (1993). But his dramatic world is always firmly grounded in contemporary society. *A Kind of Alaska* (1982) is a good example of his approach, and a measure of Pinter's difference to Beckett. Although on the surface its avoidance of coherent characterization and logic might seem to link it with Absurdist Theatre, it is a clinically accurate depiction of sleeping sickness and the disorientation of a patient revived by a recently discovered drug, L-Dopa. His early plays use almost exactly the same technique, with their apparent illogicality either mirroring the confused state of characters in a particular social situation, or reflecting the characters' method of dealing with threats to their independence.

The misinterpretation of Pinter's work is partly due to his rejection of all 'didactic or moralistic theatre' as 'sentimental and unconvincing'. His essential pessimism, together with the emphasis in his early plays on 'dealing with . . . characters at the extreme edge of their living, where they are living pretty much alone', contributed to his social commentary being overlooked.[4] However, the openly political subjects of his more recent work (*One for the Road*, 1984; *Mountain Language*, 1988) does not represent a change of theme, only a shift of attitude.

According to Pinter, the avoidance of specific political references in his early plays was the result of looking on 'politicians and political structures and political acts with . . . detached contempt. To engage in politics seemed to me futile.' Yet the standpoint in his later 'politically engaged' drama remains the same. His political involvement represents a moral commitment, rather than a belief that the stage can change the world; and this distinguishes his work from the more propagandistic approach of Arden and Edward Bond over the same period:

what old Sam Beckett says at the end of *The Unnamable* is right on the ball. 'You must go on, I can't go on, I'll go on.' . . . Me writing *One for the Road*, documentaries, articles, lucid analyses, Averell Harriman writing in the *New York Times*, voices raised here and there, people walking down the road and demonstrating. Finally it's hopeless. There's nothing one can achieve. Because the modes of thinking of those in power are worn out, threadbare, atrophied. Their minds are a brick wall . . . still one can't stop attempting to try to think and see things as clearly as possible.[5]

This parallels Tom Stoppard's argument that art cannot have a direct effect on society, only create the moral climate for eventual change. The political potential that Pinter sees in art is even more minimal: merely bearing testimony. Yet there is still a continuum between drama and political action. His plays contain a surprising number of figures related to the arts: a concert pianist (*The Birthday Party*), a would-be interior decorator (*The Caretaker*), poets (*No Man's Land*), publishers and an author (*Betrayal*). These characters are normally victimized, reflecting the oppressive conformity imposed by society, or hinting at the fate of so many artists under totalitarian states; and this theme carries through into the practical arena, with Pinter's public efforts to free imprisoned writers through PEN (the political organization of Poets, Playwrights, Editors, Essayists, and Novelists).

However confusing his work appeared at first, the plot-lines of even Pinter's full-length plays are all exceptionally simple. Indeed, each can be summed up in a single sentence. An unsociable boarding-house resident is terrorized by two sinister men who have come in search of him, reduced to blind violence at a birthday party thrown for him by his landlady, and taken away by them the next morning, incapable of speech or resistance but 'reoriented' and 'integrated' in a respectable suit and white collar (*The Birthday Party*, 1958).[6] An old tramp is offered a caretaker's job by a man who reveals he has been lobotomized in a mental institution and by his brother, each of whom claim to own the London slum house in which the tramp has been given refuge, only to be thrown out when he tries to play one off against the other (*The Caretaker*, 1960). When an expatriate university professor brings his wife home to introduce her to his North London family, she takes the place of her dead mother-in-law, enters into sexual relationships with both his brothers, and finally rejects her husband for life as a prostitute (*The Homecoming*, 1965). A man, struggling to keep his wife's affections against a woman from the past – her former flat-mate who (though on stage) is present only in their minds – finds himself replaying a humiliating scene that his wife claims to remember, which leaves him as the rejected outsider (*Old Times*, 1971). A down-at-heel poet tries to insinuate himself into the house of a successful colleague, but is prevented by the pair of servants who organize the celebrity's life and cater to his homosexual desires, leaving both writers in a limbo of creative impotence (*No Man's Land*, 1975). Friendship and love are exposed as mutual betrayals by a wife's affair with her husband's business partner (who had been best man at their wedding) when her husband manipulates her into admitting her adultery in order to justify his own philandering, and she in turn deceives her lover by concealing from him that her husband has discovered their relationship (*Betrayal*, 1978).

Even from such brief descriptions it is clear that all these plays are variations on the subjects of dominance, control, exploitation, subjugation and victimization. They are models of power structures. But the narrow focus – Pinter's typical cast being three, forming the smallest unstable relationship in which changing alliances can be formed and individuals isolated – depicts these political themes in purely personal terms. It is the psychology of politics rather than the social effect that is analysed; and this reduction of politics to a worm's eye view of the boot that crushes it, is typical of all Pinter's dramaturgy.

After *The Homecoming* there is a switch from characters at the very bottom of the economic scale, to figures from a 'respectable' stratum with whom the average audience could more easily identify, so that the wider relevance of Pinter's drama becomes more obvious. However, the same political realities are also there in his earlier plays. Although *The Birthday Party* was originally dismissed as incomprehensible and wilfully obscure, the action was not intended to be 'an unnatural happening' or 'all that surrealistic'. As Pinter put it, menacing figures 'out of nowhere . . . arriving at the door, [is something that] has been happening in Europe in the last twenty years. Not only in the last twenty years, the last two to three hundred.'[7] And in *Ashes to Ashes* (directed by Pinter himself in 1996 and partly inspired by a recent book on Albert Speer, Hitler's minister for Industry) the theme of the Holocaust surfaces openly. Once it is recognized, the reference to the Gestapo justifies the apparent illogic of the victim's interrogation – in Hitler's Germany the Jews' 'crime' was literally being born and by (Nazi) definition their existence as such contaminated the state, which are precisely the accusations levelled at Stanley in the play. Yet Pinter deliberately removes the issue of anti-Semitism by making one of the *Birthday Party* interrogators Jewish, and, as in *Party Time* or *Ashes to Ashes*, translates the actual situation of Germany in the 1930s or 1970s Turkey into a contemporary (and apparently incongruous) British context. Historical examples are secondary to the mentality that makes police states possible.

Hence Stanley, hiding from unspecified persecutors in *The Birthday Party*, attacks his possessive landlady with the same verbal techniques that are later used to destroy him, while his abductors threaten each other. His insensitivity, emphasized by Pinter when he directed the play in 1964, echoes Meg's blindness to what is going on around her. Lost in an incongruously romantic self-projection of being 'the belle of the ball', she ignores the way Goldberg and McCann terrorize Stanley during the party she has organized for him;

and the next morning she is not even aware that he has been taken away. By contrast fear keeps her husband Petey silent, the mere hint of a similar fate stopping any protest at what is being done to his lodger.

At the same time, Stanley's attempt to evade his pursuers is precisely what makes him incapable of withstanding the forces they represent. His contradictory vagueness about his background, profession, name and birth-date can be seen both as a defence-mechanism to keep himself from being identified, and as a nonconformist's assertion of individuality against the categorizing impulses of society. However, it is also a type of escapism, which according to Pinter means that

Stanley *cannot* perceive his only valid justification – which is he is what he is – therefore he can certainly never be articulate about it... he need only admit to himself what he is and is not – then Goldberg and McCann would not have paid their visit, or if they had, the same course of events would have been by no means assured.[8]

The only articulate character in *The Birthday Party* is Goldberg, whose control of his henchman as much as the victimized boarding-house popula-tion is expressed in verbally expansive monologues that are sinister precisely because of their self-indulgence. Domination is sought or evaded linguis-tically; and Pinter's deliberate avoidance of specific political references is a way of showing the roots of tyranny in ordinary everyday behaviour.

The same format recurs in Pinter's later, more overtly political plays. *One for the Road* (1984) is a repeat of Stanley's brain-washing in miniature. A man is reduced to conformity (torn clothes replaced by a new suit, sharing a drink with his interrogator) through physical and mental torture. The context is explicitly state terrorism – arrest by soldiers who vandalize his home, rape his wife and kill his son – but the setting is a conventional business office, nationality is left blank, and the closest we get to a reason for this torture is the interrogator's claim (in a very English metaphor) that 'you're on a losing wicket, while I can't put a foot wrong... [As] the man who runs this country announced to the country: We are all patriots, we are as one, we all share a common heritage. Except you, apparently.' That final word leaves everything wide open.

The point is even clearer in *Mountain Language* (first performed in 1988 and revived in 1991 as a double bill with *Party Time*, directed by Pinter himself). Again while the actual setting is left completely undefined, the action is immediately recognizable with an officer and a sergeant in an un-specified state using bureaucratic double-talk to victimize two wives waiting outside an unnamed prison for news of their missing husbands (a pair being the minimal multiple for all the women of the world's 'disappeared'). Like Stanley, the wives are inarticulate, though here it is because their 'mountain language', representing individual expression and mental independence at its most basic – and therefore least specific – level, has been banned. In both plays language is the attribute of authority, 'the voice of God', defined by those in power who do almost all of the speaking; and this is the principle behind all Pinter's dialogue.[9] *Party Time* is still more oblique, while explicitly inspired by his discovery, during travels for PEN, of two parallel societies in Turkey (one in charge, the other in prison). This is reflected in a glittering cocktail party, which to start with we are meant to take at face value as music plays and snatches of conversation about island resorts and health clubs are heard above the clink of glasses. The ominous subtext gradually becomes clear as one woman, nostalgically reminiscing about vanished friends she used to play tennis with, announces how happy she is not to be associated with them any longer, while another is violently cut off by her husband when she worries about her brother – who appears in a final blackout as a young prisoner, clearly a victim of the regime represented by this élite gathering, to describe the experience of being thrown into solitary confinement. And in *Ashes to Ashes*, while the reference to Hitler's death camps is shockingly clear in the woman's revelation about her factory-owner lover – 'the man I had given my heart to . . . I watched him walk down the platform and tear all the babies from the arms of their screaming mothers'[10] – there is no indication whether this describes the sadistic lover she is speaking to either actually or metaphorically, the memory of a previous relationship, or a purely imaginary experience reflecting the mental trauma of the century.

In each case politics is subsumed in psychology; and the major change in these later plays is the replacement of a variable hierarchy of fear by a stark opposition of the powerful versus the speechless. Their unlocated and generalized situations are equivalent to the use of ambiguous obliqueness in Pinter's early work, implying that the audience's security is no less illusory than that of his characters. The fate of the victims could be our own. And this becomes explicit in his own production of *Party Time* where the clothing, accents and mannerisms of the elegant society, barely insulated from the troops on the streets outside, were clearly those of fashionable London and the British Establishment. By contrast in the short eight-minute piece, *The New World Order* – written as one of a series of curtain-raisers to a 1991 International Festival of Theatre production of Ariel Dorfman's powerful play about Latin American dictatorship and retribution for political torture and the 'disappeared' – the extremely abstract image of a gagged prisoner verbally threatened by urbane interrogators is given its political reference solely by the theatricality context. Indeed Pinter's aim is clearly to generalize the specific foreign setting of Dorfman's play by inserting (very brief) references to the Gulf War and making the world 'clean for democracy'.

As Pinter commented in refusing to provide an explanatory note for the first production of *The Birthday Party*, 'everything to do with the play is in the play . . . Meaning begins in the words, in the action, continues in your head and ends nowhere . . . Meaning which is resolved, parcelled, labelled and ready for export is dead.' Each of Pinter's dramatic situations is designed to have 'any number of implications', so that each spectator can apply it to his own experience. However, the absolute division between We (the suffering) and They (the tools of dictatorship), that makes *One for the Road* or *Mountain Language* identifiably political, also simplifies the audience's response. Our sympathy is aligned exclusively with the victims, whereas in the earlier play Goldberg and McCann were both 'Our mentors. Our ancestors' as well as 'Them. Fuck 'em', placing the audience itself in an ambiguous position.[11]

This discomforting ambivalence is exploited through Pinter's manipulative use of comedy. In *The Birthday Party* the growing atmosphere of menace and the destruction of Stanley's personality is conveyed by riddles, children's games, music-hall cross-talk routines – all of which are intrinsically humorous – and this was accentuated by the acting style called for by Pinter in his own 1964 production, so that 'each line was greeted with gales of laughter'.[12] Even the sinister intruders are also standard comic types: the stage Irishman and Jew. McCann whistles 'The Mountains of Morne', utters stock laments like 'Tullamore, where are you?' and sings romantic ballads. Goldberg sentimentalizes his 'old mum', a wife he has abandoned, childhood innocence and 'gefilte fish', while being given to philosophical conundrums and exaggerated ethnic expressions like 'Mazeltov! And may we only meet at Simchahs!'

As cliché characters they have interchangeable names. McCann answers to Dermott or Seamus; Goldberg to Nat, Simey or Benny – and even at their most threatening, the form of dialogue is designed to evoke laughter from an audience:

GOLDBERG What have you done with your wife?
MCCANN He's killed his wife!
GOLDBERG Why did you kill your wife?
STANLEY (*sitting, his back to the audience*). What wife?
MCCANN How did he kill her?
GOLDBERG How did you kill her?
MCCANN You throttled her.

GOLDBERG With arsenic.... Why did you never get married?

MCCANN She was waiting at the porch.

GOLDBERG You skedaddled from the wedding.

MCCANN He left her in the lurch.

GOLDBERG You left her in the pudding club.

MCCANN She was waiting at the church...

GOLDBERG Why did the chicken cross the road?

STANLEY He wanted...

MCCANN He doesn't know. He doesn't know which came first!

GOLDBERG Which came first?

MCCANN Chicken? Egg? Which came first?

GOLDBERG and MCCANN Which came first? Which came first? Which came first?

STANLEY *screams.*[13]

The form is that of the one-liner joke (who was that lady I saw you with last night?/That was no lady, that was my wife), reeled off by incompetent clowns

14 Interrogation among the cornflakes: the hierarchy of victimization in Pinter's *The Birthday Party* (Royal Shakespeare Company, 1964, directed by Pinter)

who take several repeats to get the line right ('porch'/ 'lurch'/'church'), and confuse even the most familiar riddle. Their rapid patter, illogical contradictions, and impression of bewildered improvisation are all comic. With Stanley almost silent, his reactions hidden by his positioning, he becomes a straight-man whose cues have been misplaced through the ineptness of his partners; and the focus is on the duo of (literally) stand-up comedians, out-of-control actors reduced to desperate hamming.

The theatrical slant makes the context appear harmless, allowing us to enjoy the humour, until Stanley's scream forces a shocked re-evaluation. But the effect is not simply to remind the audience that this is a frightening interrogation. Enjoyment has made us accomplices. In our acceptance we have demonstrated the inhumanity that makes such a system of terror possible. This implies its existence in our society, and echoes the torturer's justification of 'The Necessary and the Possible' which, according to Goldberg, 'went like a bomb' in Bayswater.[14]

Pinter's work has been seen as an objective form of super-realism, marked by 'the myopically detailed, obsessive quality of his observation', where his 'fanatical accuracy' in transcribing everyday speech exposes the way conventional representations over-simplify actuality. However, the symbolic weight given to everyday objects undermines the naturalistic surface in Pinter's plays – like the toy drum which registers Stanley's mental distress in *The Birthday Party* by the increasingly uncontrolled rhythms of his playing, until he puts his foot through it signalling his total breakdown; or the spectacles that represent his nonconformist vision, which are snatched away and broken, to be replaced with ones to make him 'see straight'.[15] Pinter's realism is always subordinated to his manipulation of the audience. The opening breakfast sequence of *The Birthday Party*, for example, with sour milk on the cornflakes and trivia from the daily paper, may be meticulously ordinary. But in performance the banality is comic, so that our recognition of its truth to life is combined with a sense of superiority, which leads us to identify with Stanley's patronizing harassment of Meg. And this establishes the attitude (through a relatively inoffensive situation) that subsequently puts us on the side of the interrogators.

A short play like *The Dumb Waiter* (1960) provides a clear view of Pinter's early dramaturgy. A variation on the subject of *The Birthday Party*, it expands on hints in the Goldberg/McCann relationship by showing that the menacers themselves are not immune from the system they serve. One of the pair of thugs turns out to be the victim they have been hired to murder.

At first the situation looks normal: a couple of ordinary workmen killing nothing but time as they wait for someone to tell them what job they have been hired for. Only one third of the way through the performance are we given any clue about the nature of their job, when one takes out a revolver.

As in the preceding play, the scene opens with cups of tea and selections read aloud from the newspaper. Although the reported trivia here is violent, any overt tension between the characters is limited to comically confused arguments about standard expressions like whether 'light the gas' or 'light the kettle [is] common usage'. Even more explicitly than Goldberg and McCann, Gus and Ben are theatrical clowns, reminiscent of Laurel and Hardy, and the opening sets a tone of farcical slapstick:

tying his shoelaces, with difficulty... GUS... rises, yawns and begins to walk slowly... He stops, looks down, and shakes his foot.
BEN *lowers his paper and watches him.* GUS *kneels and unties his shoe-lace and slowly takes off the shoe. He looks inside it and brings out a flattened matchbox. He shakes it and examines it. Their eyes meet.* BEN *rattles his paper and reads.* GUS *puts the matchbox in his pocket and bends down to put on his shoe. He ties his lace, with difficulty.*[16]

The same action is then repeated with the other foot and a flattened cigarette packet, the exactness of the repetition compounding the absurdity and underlining the gag.

Even when their true profession becomes clear, the effect is one of gangster-parody, rather than a real threat, as they struggle to prevent discovery by attempting to fulfil impossible orders for increasingly exotic food, brought down by a service lift in the wall (the dumb waiter of the title). The gap between 'Marcaroni Pastitsio. Ormitha Macarounada' or 'One Bamboo Shoots, Water Chestnuts and Chicken. One Char Sui and Beansprouts', and what they have available to send up is ludicrous in its extremity: three biscuits (mouldy), one bottle of milk (sour), Eccles cake (stale) and a chocolate bar (melted) – or the packet of tea-leaves that can't be boiled because they don't have a shilling for the gas meter, let alone matches. Even their rehearsal of the killing is made farcical by the amount of care necessary to get the simplest cliché of the genre right. But again with the final reversal the audience are forced to question their responses; and there was nothing obscure about the political implications – at least on a general level. As Pinter later commented:

It was quite obvious to the actors [of the TV production] that the chap who is upstairs and is never seen is a figure of authority. Gus questions this authority and rebels against it and therefore is squashed at the end, or is about to be squashed. The political metaphor was very clear to the actors and director of the first production in 1960. It was not, however, clear to the critics of the time.[17]

The Dumb Waiter also established the minimal dramatic model of three players that remains standard for Pinter up to *No Man's Land* (1975) and *Betrayal* (1978), even if here the dominant figure (literally as well as metaphorically over their heads) is off stage. Similarly in *The Lover* (1963), another two-hander, the pattern is retained by one of the pair projecting himself into a different role: the figure of the title, who is the opposite of everything he represents as a husband. However, in *The Caretaker* (1960) the triangular relationship is undisguised, and all the possible alternations are explored. On one level each of the three characters is attempting to gain exclusive possession of the room where the action takes place, by playing one of the others off against the third. Equally each seeks to establish an emotional bond with a second through persuading him to reject the odd man out. But in the need/dependence versus ownership/power equation, both halves cancel out. The aims are self-defeating.

The Caretaker is yet another study in victimization – mental (Aston, with his psychiatric history), physical (Mick, leather-jacketed and unpredictably violent), emotional (Davies, the elderly tramp). But in response to the criticism of his earlier plays, Pinter stressed the focus on personal relationships and denied that the characters were 'symbols of anything'. What he described as the 'battle for positions' still contained wider social implications: 'The violence is really only an expression of the question of dominance and subservience, which is . . . a repeated theme in my plays'. However, the switch from symbolic power structures to depicting them in completely naturalistic terms proved equally open to misinterpretation. Since Pinter's tramp was almost automatically identified with the tramp figures of Beckett's *Waiting for Godot*, the room tended to be seen as an Absurdist limbo with no possible social relevance. As a result, *The Caretaker* produced much the same critical response as *The Birthday Party* where 'the characters appear[ed] to be mentally deficient and what it all means is anyone's guess'.[18]

Everything in the play is ambiguous, particularly the central character. Davies may really be named Jenkins; and the existence of papers to prove his identity becomes increasingly dubious as he procrastinates about fetching the references from Sidcup, even though these alone will give him the security he craves by qualifying him for the job of caretaker. His declared intention of going is contradicted by the (justified) fear that if he leaves the room there will be no chance of getting back in. His claims of a cultured or military past are belied by his odiferous uncleanliness, weakness and timidity. Given the slum setting, the job itself is no more than a fantasy-carrot.

Even Aston, who is clearly meant to be accepted by the audience as an ordinary and average person on the basis of his charity, kindness and unassertive predictability, is not what he seems. This socially accept-able normality is discredited by his revelation that electric shock treat-ment has left him a mental cripple: a version of Stanley's future after the Goldberg/McCann organization has finished with him. The shocking na-ture of the process that has reduced Aston to conformity implies that social conditioning is the equivalent of political oppression. But this too turns out to be ambiguous.

In performance the length of Aston's monologue, when he describes what has been done to him, is in itself convincing. Yet, according to Pinter, 'it isn't necessary to conclude that everything Aston says about his experiences in the mental hospital is true'. Hence, the image of himself that Aston presents can be seen as a performance. And indeed the way he represents himself as brain-damaged becomes the decisive factor that ensures the tramp's expulsion when, presuming on the belief that he is superior to his benefactor, Davies commits himself to an alliance with Mick. Once Mick withdraws support, Davies is isolated. On this level the action is merely a cruel game, in which the brothers select suitable victims from the street to exercise a sadistic fantasy of power; and the one time they are seen together, at the end of the play, supports such an interpretation: '*They look at each other. Both are smiling faintly.*'[19]

If Aston is acting a role, then promoting himself as a scapegoat prefigures Davies' fate. But it also plays on the audience's preconceptions, which are the true focus of the play. Whatever intrinsic significance the action holds is secondary to the way it evokes, then undercuts stock responses, in order to challenge the way we normally view things. The root cause of social oppression is how we categorize others, denying their individuality by type-casting – which is also the basis of standard theatrical characterization. Pinter attacks both through the lack of definable information. As he stated in a programme note for *The Dumb Waiter*, a month before the opening of *The Caretaker*:

The desire for verification is understandable, but cannot always be satisfied ... A character on the stage who can present no convincing argument or information as to his past experience, his present behaviour or his aspirations, nor give a compre-hensive analysis of his motives is as legitimate and as worthy of attention as one who, alarmingly, can do all these things.

At the same time, for Davies and Aston as much as for the overtly aggressive Mick, ambiguity is deliberate. It is a device for attack as much as a method of defence, since to be pinned down makes one vulnerable, yet the unknown is a threat. Their evasive self-contradiction also produces comic ironies. The way these characters exploit Pinter's proposition that a 'thing is not necessarily true or false; it can be both true and false' is creative and therefore a source of humour. This is compounded by farcical incongruity in the gulf between their proposed aims and the available means (the '*few short planks of wood*' and a non-functioning saw, versus the grandiose restoration plans of both Aston and Mick). Flattering self-projection becomes comic self-betrayal (Davies' claim to a military career, versus his evident cowardice and unreliability). Melodrama turns into ludicrous bathos: heavy breathing in the dark and assault by a frightening machine turns out to be trivial – 'just doing some spring-cleaning . . . There used to be a wall plug for this electrolux. But it doesn't work. I had to fix it in the light socket.'[20] However, this ordinary explanation is either a lie or evidence of abnormality, given the cluttered and filthy state of the room. It is thus a real threat, turning the tables on the audience yet again.

Similarly the tramp is both an object of pity, as victim, and a comic type: the braggart whose false pretensions are exposed. Even his insecurities are expressed comically – as in a confusion of categories like 'if you can't tell what time you're at you don't know where you are' while the techniques used to victimize him continually merge into stock comedy routines. For instance, the sequence where Aston offers Davies his bag, which Mick snatches away, is extrapolated into the Marx brothers' routine with a hat (also borrowed by Beckett in *Waiting for Godot*):

MICK *grabs it.* ASHTON *takes it.* MICK *grabs it.* DAVIES *reaches for it.* ASHTON *gives it to* DAVIES. MICK *grabs it.*
    Pause.
ASHTON *takes it.* DAVIES *takes it.* MICK *takes it.* DAVIES *reaches for it.* ASHTON *takes it.*
    Pause.
ASHTON gives it to MICK. MICK *gives it to* DAVIES. DAVIES . . . *drops it.*[21]

After which we discover that the bag is not Davies' property after all.

Even the ending, however tragic for the tramp, has a distinctly comic aspect. If his exclusion from the room is seen, in Esslin's terms, as an expulsion from paradise, then the contrast between that ideal state and the living conditions depicted on the stage are simply laughable – buckets to catch the drips from a leaking roof, sacking for curtains, a mound of mechanical junk on an iron bed, piles of old newspapers, a cracked china Buddha. On another level, however, this heap of redundant objects that hems in the characters, and provides the explicit motive for their conflict, satirizes a materialistic society that defines people in terms of their possessions, distorts relationships into a competition for illusory wealth, and imprisons their lives in accumulations of useless and potentially dangerous detritus. The comedy is double-edged. As Pinter commented,

I did not intend it to be merely a laughable farce ... where the comic and the tragic (for want of a better word) are closely interwoven, certain members of the audience will always give emphasis to the comic as opposed to the other, for by doing so they rationalize the other out of existence ... As far as I'm concerned, *The Caretaker* is funny, up to a point. Beyond that point it ceases to be funny, and it was because of that point that I wrote it.[22]

It has sometimes been assumed that this point is a temporal one in the action of the play – first half comic, second serious – when in fact it relates to perception. What may appear funny, viewed superficially, is simultaneously menacing, despicable or inhumane in terms of what the characters are experiencing. The comedy becomes a test of sensitivity that condemns those who laugh; and this is made explicit at various points in the dialogue. Terrorized by Mick, Davies' response is

> He's a real joker, that lad, you can see that.
> *Pause*
> ASHTON Yes, he tends ... to see the funny side of things.
> DAVIES Well, he's got a sense of humour, en' he?

and the double meaning of funny/abnormal underlines this uncomic humour in respect to Aston's mental illness:

> he's funny ...
> MICK   What's funny about him?
> *Pause.*
> DAVIES Not liking work.
> MICK   What's funny about that?
> DAVIES Nothing.
> *Pause.*
> MICK   I don't call it funny.
> DAVIES Nor me.[23]

Pinter's aim is to make the audience re-evaluate their assumptions about themselves, and hence to question the society of which they are representatives.

The problem with manipulative comedy is that once one tone has been set, the sort of violent contrast employed by Orton or Barnes is needed to shift an audience's perspective. However, the kind of juxtapositions made possible by the open artifice of farce would have required sacrificing the naturalistic credibility that makes Pinter's 'point' (at which the comic elements cease to be funny) so effective. Echoing Shaw's complaint about the response to *Arms and the Man*, Pinter attacked the uninterrupted laughter that greeted *The Caretaker* as a form of 'cheerful patronage', by which the audience evaded participation through 'uneasy jollification'. To avoid this, in subsequent plays Pinter gives his characters an increasingly identifiable social background.[24] This prevents them from being seen as clown figures. But (with the exception of *The Homecoming*) it also rules out the gratuitous violence of his earlier work, since this would look out of place in a normal context. Instead, sex is employed to undercut complacent acceptance of the comedy. As Orton's farces had demonstrated, perversion can be more disturbing than physical brutality. So *The Homecoming* (1965) focuses on incest and prostitution, while there are open references to lesbianism and homosexuality in *Old Times* (1971) and *No Man's Land* (1975).

The *Homecoming* is the best example of this phase in Pinter's work, and (perhaps because moral attitudes were still sharply defined in the mid-1960s) it provoked more outrage than the plays he wrote during the following decade. The most offensive aspect was the actions of the single female character: Ruth's seduction of both her husband's brothers while taking over the role of their mother; the way she agrees to their proposal for setting her up as a prostitute to pay her way in the family economy; her abandonment of the young children she has left behind in America. Pinter intended these to be the expression 'of despair which gives her a kind of freedom. Certain facts like marriage and the family for this woman have clearly ceased to have any meaning.'[25]

However, reviewers were 'troubled by the complete absence from the play of any moral comment', or expressed discomfort with what they saw as the protagonist's nymphomania – while spectators walked out of performances on the pre-London tour in disgust, or were recorded as 'fuming: "They're exactly like animals!"' In this last case, the response was perceptive, since

Peter Hall had built the production around the image of a 'human jungle' to reflect the 'deeply animalistic [quality in] the people's reactions to each other and they way they treat each other'.[26]

At the same time, as a parody of the standard 'meet-the-family' type of drama (mirrored in the title of T.S. Eliot's *The Family Reunion*), *The Homecoming* is in many ways Pinter's funniest play with its demolition of sentiments like 'home, sweet home', and satiric reproduction of clichés such as 'woman's place is in the home'. As with almost all his other plays, the title is both a literal description of the dramatic situation, and takes on a very different meaning by the end of the action. The opening sets up an almost typical 'homecoming', which echoes the Prodigal Son pattern in the unannounced return of an expatriate – who has made good teaching at an American college – to introduce his family to/impress them with the elegant wife he has married. They may arrive in the middle of the night; there may be no one to greet them. But Teddy stresses that everything is normal: 'Nothing's changed. Still the same . . . They're very warm people, really. Very warm. They're my family.'[27]

Exploiting the double meanings of this reassurance, the comedy lies in the incongruity between normal expectations and what actually happens. The technique is particularly clear at the start of the second act, where the men light cigars, sip coffee from tiny cups and compliment Ruth on her cooking. Yet this sophisticated picture of 'Happy Families' has already been discredited by every word spoken before the interval.

A typical example is the old father Max's sentimental eulogy of his dead wife, who taught her children

every single bit of the morality they live by . . . And she had a heart to go with it . . . I remember the boys came down, in their pyjamas, all their hair shining, their faces pink, it was before they started shaving, and they knelt at our feet, Jessie's and mine. I tell you it was like Christmas . . .

The idealized memory contrasts with everything we have heard before. His true feelings have already been shown by his contemptuous 'it made me sick just to look at her rotten stinking face', while the kind of 'morality' that the family actually live by is revealed in the acrimony and insults of every exchange, whether son to father or brother to brother, and epitomized in the gratuitous violence when the geriatric Max

hits JOEY *in the stomach with all his might.* JOEY *contorts, staggers across the stage.* MAX, *with the exertion of the blow, begins to collapse. His knees buckle. He clutches his stick.*

SAM *moves forward to help him.*
MAX *hits him across the head with his stick.*

His teenage son may be the victim here (together with his elderly brother), but young Joey has already been shown to have the same predelictions in his attempt to intimidate Ruth with stories of beating up women. Max's angry description of his family as 'crippled . . . three bastard sons, a slutbitch of a wife' and 'a lazy idle bugger of a brother', which immediately follows his eulogy is all too accurate.[28]

They are, in their own words, 'a lot of dogs', fighting for dominance. Only able to assert himself through (failing) physical force, the father loses his position to the younger males who, it is implied, may in fact be bastards rather than his own sons. But in this kind of biological competition, it is the woman who actually has control through her ability to withhold or dispense sexual favours. Realizing this, Ruth claims a local background in which she was 'a photographic model for the body' (with strong overtones of the Christine Keeler/Profumo sex scandal of the time).

Prostitution fits her for the role of maternal provider in the dual sense of economic, as well as emotional supporter of the family. It also picks up on Max's gratuitous insult, when he insisted on mistaking her for 'a filthy scrubber . . . I've never had a whore under this roof before. Ever since your mother died.'[29] The ambiguous implication here is fulfilled by Ruth, transforming an ordinary cliché (not even after his wife's death has Max been unfaithful) into its opposite (Max is a pimp, who ran the boys' mother as a prostitute).

Surface appearances have no necessary relationship to the reality underneath. Awareness of the distinction is crucial, since the gap can be used to manipulate others; and Ruth's suitability for the role she assumes is demonstrated by her instinctive comprehension of this principle:

I . . . move my leg. That's all it is. But I wear . . . underwear . . . which . . . moves with me . . . it . . . captures your attention [. . .] My lips move. Why don't you restrict . . . your observations to that? Perhaps the fact that they move is more significant . . . than the words which come through them.

Throughout, the characters' physical actions contradict the socially acceptable platitudes uttered, until by the end the contrast becomes black farce. When the most 'normal' member of the family (the boys' uncle Sam, who has been reduced to serving as chauffeur for Max's street-cruising wife: an elderly version of Aston, unassertive and neutered) collapses with a heart attack, his death is completely ignored by everyone. Ritual expressions of leave-taking are accompanied by Ruth kissing one brother-in-law then lying in an embrace with the other on the floor, while her husband looks on without reaction. Her parting words to him – 'don't become a stranger' – are followed by the graphic final image of one brother kneeling with his head on her lap in a blasphemous Piéta pose, while the father crawls over Sam's corpse, moaning for a kiss.[30]

At the same time, this gap between surface and substance is carried through into a series of reversals. Family relationships are revealed to be games of hostility, but the violence expresses dependency. In exchanging the relative autonomy of a wife with her own children in America for debasing exploitation as a prostitute, the woman's position as victim becomes the source of her power. Those with social or cultural superiority lose in the conflict between an upwardly mobile married woman and an uneducated working-class man, or a self-assured intellectual versus a crude thug. But their apparent defeat actually signals their ascendancy – even in the case of Teddy, who on the surface is unwillingly compelled to give up his wife.

In the London first production Teddy's part was played as 'the campus intellectual who'd opted out of any kind of responsibility in human terms', so that he was seen as being forced to retreat with empty dignity: the normal man neutered. However, in New York:

when he went at the end, leaving his wife, he was not in any way a victim or martyr. He was the biggest shit of all. He was leaving them with their deserts. He was leaving her with her deserts ... he brings his wife back to the jungle to have her tested by the laws of the jungle ... He goes back, in a way, confirmed in the family's hatred of women. In that sense, he's victorious.[31]

Following through on this metaphor, the play is a satiric attack on society, and the audience. An ordinary family are revealed as animals – but their brutality, which at first seems unnatural, is shown to be the norm. It expresses the underlying nature of the system in which they live; and the pair of outsiders (who at first seem their prey, normal by comparison and apparently vulnerable) turn out to be the most vicious of the predators. By laughing, the spectators affirm this picture of society. All the characters are products (in a literal biological sense) and active purveyors of prostitution. Any business contract or personal relationship is a bargain between pimps and whores, since this is the only kind of transaction shown. As sexual competition, love is a commodity to be bartered or sold; and the quality required for success in such a system is defined by Teddy as 'a way of being able to look at the world. It's a question of how far you can operate on things and not in things', maintaining 'intellectual equilibrium' by viewing others as 'objects. You just . . . move about. I can observe it.'[32]

This kind of objective detachment also describes the relationship between auditorium and stage in almost any kind of dramatic performance. Particularly in comedy, where laughter at the characters tends to rule out empathy with them, spectators have already taken up the callous attitude that is condemned as inhuman in Teddy. At its simplest, a clown slipping on a banana-skin is funny because we ignore the human pain involved, just as Max and the others ignore the death-throes of his brother. Mirroring the audience's enjoyment of dramatized suffering or brutality in the characters' 'unnatural' behaviour, is intended to bring home the degree to which society reduces people to objects.

As in his earlier plays, Pinter is taking comedy to the point at which it no longer seems humorous. But using the conditions of performance as an object lesson marks an advance in his dramaturgy, which is reflected in the open theatricality of *The Homecoming*. The bargaining over Ruth's rights and obligations as a prostitute is a parody of the marriage contract scene in *The Way of the World*, while the dynamics of oppression and submission are translated into a struggle for the acting space, in which the character who dominates is the actor who up-stages the others.

The same vision of a society composed entirely of whores and pimps recurs in *Betrayal* (1978), although more disguised by the shift from impoverished criminals to respectable literati, who (like Teddy in *The Homecoming*) holiday in Venice. If the essence of prostitution is intimacy without emotion, this is what the reversed structure of the action displays. All varieties of love – friendship, marriage and an adulterous affair, even the parent/child relationship – have been shattered by continual betrayals over the ten-year time frame, cancelling each other out and leaving the characters emotionally destitute.

By beginning with the end, and working backwards to the first moments of seduction (the seeds of which are planted at the wedding reception), the characters' passion is revealed as a meretricious pose. They have no religious or political commitment. Love is the only value remaining to them: the world-well-lost cliché. Yet any emotion is corrupted from the start by the deception it involves, revealing manipulation at the heart of even the most personal sphere in the society they represent. It is an essentially comic viewpoint; and *Moonlight*, Pinter's next full-length play fifteen years later, could be seen as a coda to this dismantling of the façade of 'Happy Families'.

Caught at the moment of final dissolution, the family is irretrievably shattered, its members isolated in their various limbos. The father on a lingering deathbed is alienated from his wife both by temperament and class (in her words, he is 'coarse, crude, vacuous, puerile, obscene, brutal... Most people were ready to vomit after ten minutes in your company') as much as by memories of another woman who has been her lover as well as his. Haunted by the ghost of his long-dead daughter in the garden eternally bathed in the moonlight of the title, he has been abandoned by his sons – unemployed and stuck in the bedroom of an unlocated flat – who he excoriates as 'A sponging parasitical pair of ponces, sucking on the tit of the state'.[33] The close proximity of the three areas on a stage emphasizes their isolation, and makes each seem claustrophobic. The fey image of the daughter is poetically evocative, the dying father is angry and despairing, while the overall tone is elegiac. Yet much of the dialogue – music-hall patter, word games and pretentious clichés collapsing into bathos, or exaggerated insults, even the non-communication between the separated circles of characters that embodies a desperate longing for emotional contact – is typical of comedy and bracingly funny.

This conflicting mix of comic technique and discomforting agony – whether undefined menace in his early plays, power-games among people, political threat, or as in *Moonlight* an existential void – is characteristic of all Pinter's work. And the comic elements always serve to highlight essentially serious themes. So in *Betrayal* the unusual, reversed structure of the action serves the same function as the clown figures or overt theatrical reference of Pinter's previous plays. Its artificiality corresponds to the fake life style of the characters. But in revealing the outcome, our conventional interest in *what* happens is replaced by questions of *how*. By switching attention to behavioural motivation, Pinter focuses more precisely than ever before on the mechanics of exploitation, the politics of betrayal.

In fact Pinter is the most consistent – and in a sense limited – of modern British playwrights in his subject matter, all his plays being variations on the same theme. This is marked by repeated patterns in characterization. The complementary figures of Mick and Aston from *The Caretaker* are mirrored in the Lenny and Joey pairing in *The Homecoming*. As thugs Lenny-and-Joey also echo Ben and Gus of *The Dumb Waiter*, who repeat the Goldberg/McCann pairing of *The Birthday Party*. The same pairing recurs as well as in the brutal servants, Briggs and Foster, in *No Man's Land* – where the struggle of the ineffectual poet Spooner to belong, and his final rejection, is a replay of Davies. The geriatric and dying fathers in *The Homecoming* and *Moonlight* have similar abusive personalities (a comparison underlined by the casting of Ian Holm, who had acted the pimp son in the original production of the first play, as both vindictive fathers). The relationship explored in *Landscape*, haunted by a former lover, is echoed in *Ashes to Ashes*. The relationship in *Old Times* explores the same dynamics as *The Lover*, while *Betrayal* can be seen as an extension of its companion play, *The Collection*. Even within each play patterns are duplicated. The couple who wish to rent *The Room* are younger versions of its married occupants. In *The Homecoming*, Ruth's three children (who will be brought up by their father alone) exactly duplicate the family structure of the older generation.

Similarly, Pinter's starting point for *One for the Road* (1984) – 'I had an image in my mind of a man with a victim. And I was simply investigating what might take place' – is (with a change of sex) identical to that of an early revue sketch like 'Applicant' (written in 1959, radio production 1964). Indeed, this image could be used to describe the basic situation of almost all his work from *The Birthday Party* on. However, although the behavioural patterns are the same throughout, the comedy has vanished as Pinter's political view has sharpened – or perhaps in response to his recognition of the writer's inability to influence political change, which is reflected in the impotent literary figures of *No Man's Land*. Instead of focusing on the point 'where the comic ... ceases to be funny', his more recent plays demonstrate that 'it's past a joke'.[34] And this approach is also the basis of the type of comedy that Peter Barnes developed.

Notes

1 Esslin has since changed his interpretation of Pinter as an existentialist and primarily symbolic dramatist (*The Theatre of the Absurd*, Harmondsworth, 1968, pp. 265ff.), presenting his plays – no less misleadingly – in terms of psychological archetypes representing the transition from adolescence (see *Pinter: A Study of his Plays*, London, 1977, pp. 84, 107–8, 119 & 153).

2 Coward, *The Sunday Times*, 15 January 1961, and *The Sunday Telegraph*, 22 May 1966.

3 Pinter, interview, *New Theatre Magazine*, January 1961, p. 9.

4 *Ibid.* and with Tynan, BBC, 28 October 1960.

5 Pinter, interview in *Los Angeles Times*, 29 October 1985, and with Nicholas Hern, *One for the Road*, New York, 1986, p. 20.

6 *The Birthday Party*, London, 1965, pp. 83–4.

7 Pinter, BBC interview, 3 March 1960.

8 *The Birthday Party*, p. 87; Pinter, 1958 letter to Peter Wood (director of the first production of *The Birthday Party*) printed in *Drama*, winter 1981, p. 5.

9 *One for the Road*, London, 1984, pp. 13, 9.

10 *Ashes to Ashes*, London, 1996, p. 53.

11 Pinter, letter to Peter Wood, p. 4.

12 *Plays and Players*, August 1964, p. 28.

13 *The Birthday Party*, pp. 60, 43, 56, 49–52.

14 *Ibid.*, p. 57.

15 John Russell Taylor, *Anger and After*, Harmondsworth, 1968, p. 304–5; *The Birthday Party*, p. 82.

16 *The Room and The Dumb Waiter*, London, 1966, pp. 47–8, 35.

17 *Ibid.*, pp. 58 & 60; Pinter, interview in *One for the Road*, p. 8.

18 Pinter, interviews, BBC, 28 October 1960, and in *Paris Review*, Fall 1966, pp. 31, 30; *Theatre Review*, June 1958, p. 21.

19 Pinter, in *Paris Review*, p. 28; *The Caretaker*, London, 1968, p. 75.

20 *The Caretaker*, pp. 6, 45.

21 *Ibid.*, pp. 62, 39.

22 See Esslin, *The Theatre of the Absurd*, p. 101; Pinter, *Sunday Times*, 14 August 1960. (For a fuller treatment of Pinter's comic characterization, see Elin Diamond, *Pinter's Comic Play*, Associated University Presses, 1985, pp. 65f.)

23 *The Caretaker*, pp. 40, 49–50.

24 Pinter, in *The Sunday Times*, 14 August 1960.

25 Pinter, in *Vogue*, 1 October 1967, p. 245.

26 *The Sunday Times*, 6 June 1965; *New Statesman*, 11 June 1965; Sir Peter Hall, in John Lahr, *A Casebook on Harold Pinter's The Homecoming*, New York, 1971, p. 11.

27 *The Homecoming*, London, 1966, pp. 22–3.

28 *Ibid.*, pp. 46, 9, 42, 47.

29 *Ibid.*, pp. 11, 57, 42.

30 *Ibid.*, pp. 52–3, 80.

31 Peter Hall, in Lahr, *Casebook*, pp. 29–31.

32 *The Homecoming*, pp. 61–2.

33 *Moonlight*, London, 1993, pp. 20, 36.

34 Pinter, interview in *One for the Road*, pp. 14, 11; and in *Sunday Times*, 14 August 1960.

4.7 Peter Barnes and Trevor Griffiths: the politics of comedy

Peter Barnes and Trevor Griffiths are contemporaries of Harold Pinter and Joe Orton, all four having been born in the early 1930s. However, where Pinter had already made his mark by 1958 and was associated with the new wave of dramatists that swept the English theatre in the 1950s, Barnes only reached the stage towards the end of the following decade and Griffiths in the 1970s. Like Pinter, Barnes was at first misleadingly labelled as an Absurdist – his nihilism coupled with farcical exaggeration, which expressed a radical and highly politicized attack on the Establishment, being so extreme that his work seemed grotesque fantasy, bearing no relationship to social reality. Griffiths on the other hand was recognized as a political dramatist from the start. Even though produced by Establishment theatres (the National and RSC), his early plays appeared at the same time as those of the younger generation following the radicalization of the theatre at the beginning of the 1970s, and clearly shared similar concerns.

Griffiths' first play *Occupations* (1970, RSC 1971) is directly comparable to the work of Howard Brenton or David Edgar. Indeed it directly anticipates Brenton's *Weapons of Happiness* (1976: see above, pp. 208–12) in using the example of a 1920 strike at the Fiat motor company in Italy to explore the ideological theories of Antonio Gramsci: a drama critic and co-founder of the Italian communist party, who developed the earliest concept of a Marxist role for theatre in bourgeois society. Griffiths' typical plays (his first major success, *The Party*, NT 1973; *Real Dreams*, USA 1984, London 1986) are debates on the philosophy and tactics of Marxist revolution, naturalistically presented. However, in contrast to the approaches of Brenton, Edgar and David Hare, Griffiths' approach was self-critical and objective from the start. While their drama attempted to revolutionize society, he focused on the problematic nature of parlour revolutionaries, showing them in a satiric light that reflects the ironic double meaning of a title like *The Party*.

Even if his plays deliberately avoid offering political solutions, they ask 'How do we transform this husk of capitalist meaning into the reality of socialist enterprise? The socialist future?'[1] Exactly the same question forms the basis of *Comedians* (1975). Although, like Pinter, Griffiths' plays are seldom classified as comedies – and their political message has always been obvious, sometimes indeed verging on straight propaganda, as in *Thatcher's Children* (1996) – from *The Party* to *Who Shall Be Happy...?* (1995) – his work includes comic figures or techniques, and *Comedians* is one of the key plays redefining the nature of contemporary British comedy. Of all Griffiths' stage work this is also the one play that has achieved a continuing place in the theatrical repertoire: for instance, being revived in an all-female version in 1986. It places him with Orton and Barnes, rather than among the straight political dramatists of the 1970s. And as a perhaps coincidental sign of this, key moments of both *Comedians* and Barnes' *Laughter* centre on Jewish jokes told in Nazi death camps.

Where Griffiths projects a Marxist future through theoretical debate, Barnes takes the other side of the political coin. His plays attack the evils of the existing system, and ransack European history for analogies to demonstrate the need for change. Medieval popes and the Spanish Inquisition, the Wars of the Roses, Ivan the Terrible's despotism and Nazi death camps are all shown as the logical extension of behaviour patterns imposed by social inequality. Focusing on the aristocracy and the role of religion in justifying exploitation, Barnes defined his aim as creating 'an anti-boss drama for the shorn not the shearers'.

Barnes' first play *Scelerosis* (1965) was a fairly conventional satire on British colonialism; and his distinctive style of comedy, combining macabre humour, Gothic shock effects and fierce parody in violent switches of mood, owes much to Orton's example. *The Ruling Class* (1968), which established these characteristic elements, includes clear echoes of Orton's *Loot* (1965) and *Crimes of Passion* (1967) – particularly in the prologue with its transvestite suicide for sexual kicks and the protagonist's experience of a religious revelation in a public urinal. More generally Orton's influence can be seen in the complete absence of empathy in Barnes' characters where egoism is 'the only affection you can rely on', and in Barnes' parodistic use of literary collage.[2] Like Orton, Peter Barnes and Trevor Griffiths view society from a specifically working-class perspective; and both share Orton's aim of using comedy as a declaration of class war. But each moves beyond Orton in using humour as a political weapon.

Peter Barnes (1931–): attacking the audience

CHECKLIST OF BARNES' MAJOR PLAYS

Scelerosis, 1965	*Red Noses*, 1985
The Ruling Class, 1968	*Sunsets and Glories*, 1990
The Bewitched, 1974	*Corpsing*, 1996
Laughter, 1978	*Dreaming*, 1999

As the Inquisitor-General in Barnes' *The Bewitched* (1974) points out, 'Nothing's more vital than our prejudices, those opinions we accept unexamined. Wi'out prejudices no religion, no morality, no submission.' This outlines Barnes' basic principle. His plays seek to attack unquestioned assumptions through exposing the relationship between traditional values and repression. The tone is set by the hymn that opens his first major play,

The Ruling Class (1968): 'The rich man in his castle, the poor man at his gate. God made them high and lowly, and ordered their estate.'[3] The point is that this is a traditional hymn of the Anglican Church; and the issue is what sort of religion could have created such an unjust situation. Barnes' analysis demonstrates that 'God' is a totem, created by the rulers as a way of justifying and perpetuating an unnatural situation, which brings out the worst side of human nature.

In *The Ruling Class*, this is explored through following the progress of Jack, a mad earl, whose social status has 'naturally' led him to believe himself 'the ruler of the Universe' (pride and religious mania being presented as equivalent 'delusions of *grandeur*'). Improving on the purely spiritual salvation provided by 'J. Christ Mark I', his 'new Dispensation of Love' redeems 'the *body* as well'. This horrifies his family and fellow aristocrats, because its logical consequence is that 'riches, pride and property will have to be lopped off . . . Love makes all equal. The mighty must bow down before the pricks of the louse-ridden rogues.' A doctor, brought in to 'cure' him, argues that 'No God of *love* made this world. I've seen a girl of four's nails had been torn out by her father. I've seen the mountains of gold teeth and hair and the millions boiled down for soap.'[4] And once convinced that his idealistic vision has no basis in reality, Jack's saintly behaviour reverts 'back to normal'. Allowing himself to be married off to his dead uncle's mistress to preserve the family reputation, and taking up his seat in the House of Lords, he wins vociferous applause from his peers by advocating the reintroduction of flogging and the death penalty.

In fact this extreme change of personality simply expresses Jack's redefinition of himself as 'God the Law-giver, Chastiser and Judge'. As before, he practises what he preaches. No longer the 'God of Love', he swaps free sex for blood-sports, shooting a poacher as well as a (heavily symbolic) dove. The God of society and the devil are interchangeable; and he reveals himself as 'Jack from Hell, trade-mark Jack the Ripper!' The play's premise is that this makes him, in the words of his wife – just before he slaughters her – 'one of [the Establishment], only more so'.[5]

The attack on religion is intensified in Barnes' next pair of one-act plays: *Leonardo's Last Supper* and *Noonday Demons* (1969). In the first, society is presented as hell, which is where Leonardo believes himself to be when he revives from a cataleptic coma. Ironically, it is the devilish greed, viciousness and violence of the undertaker's family that persuade him he is alive – Barnes' contention being (as Leonardo puts it) that 'S'natural to mistake the living world for Hell, the difference is so slight when men are piked and gutted in either place.' As the artist who created the drawing of the Divine Proportion, Leonardo da Vinci stands for the spiritual potential in humanity. But he is also the anatomist who filled sketchbooks with studies of cadavers, and this aspect of his art is reflected in the squalor of the charnel-house. At first the undertakers believe that this body, which comes back to life on their dissecting slab, must be a devil. When Leonardo persuades them he is human, they realize that there is more profit to be made from selling parts of his corpse than all the money he can offer. So they kill Leonardo to promote the trade in cosmetic and pharmaceutical products (manufactured from dead bodies). 'New men' of the Renaissance, they are prototypes of the modern capitalist.

Similarly, the pair of medieval saints in *Noonday Demons* each mistakes the other for a devil. Competing in mortifying their flesh and inducing miraculous hallucinations to prove their sanctity, they end by strangling each other in a paroxysm of violence. The dirt and pain of their starving existence looks an extreme of misery to modern eyes. Yet when they project themselves into the present – in a blasphemous replay of Satan offering Christ the kingdoms of the world – they see the commercialized urban existence of twentieth-century man as immeasurably worse than their self-induced sufferings: 'Tis a vision o' Hell.'[6]

Although Barnes' focus is always on the present, almost all his plays take their examples from little-known periods of the past. But this does not mean that his drama is limited by factual considerations. As he has recently put it, 'History is not history unless it is imagined ... The ghosts are all here and now and with us always'; and the principle that he works on is that 'an audience will always accept the version of history that they are told. They don't compare it to their own lives in the same way that they do with modern plays, and the suspension of disbelief is much easier.'[7]

The Bewitched (1974) returns to the attack on the class system. Depicting the modern Establishment had confused Barnes' general point in *The Ruling Class*, because the grotesque exaggeration used to represent the innate evil of the system seemed to distort the familiar social reality. So here Barnes took a documented historical example, where the ruler was not only at the very peak of the hierarchy but obviously aberrant, being a physically deformed epileptic idiot, and the religious establishment a by-word for cruelty. Carlos II of Spain is generally accepted as the tragic result of generations of inbreeding due to the belief that royalty, being divine, were different from ordinary people; and Barnes shows this hapless emperor as literally 'possessed' by the position he has inherited (epitomized by the image of his autocratic mother's dead hand clutching him from the grave).

His courtiers' flattery expresses the true nature of the system: this graphically subhuman ruler is indeed 'the true representative, the very image o'
[God's] monarchy o'er all creation'.[8] Any society unquestioningly obedient
to such a being, and obsessed by perpetuating the grotesque order he represents, could truly be called 'bewitched'. So they believe themselves to be,
when their increasingly desperate efforts to produce a 'legitimate' heir for
the throne leads the machiavellian palace priest to smuggle a virile nobleman into the Queen's bedchamber, dressed as a maid. The arrival of the
impotent Carlos, his malicious and suspicious jester (in the nobleman's discarded clothes), and the vengeful Queen Mother turns this assignation into
a farcical but terrifying game of hide-and-seek around the royal bed in the
dark – which convinces them all that sorcery is at work. Similarly, since it is
impossible to admit any flaws in a monarch, although the emperor's crippling deformities are clearly the cause of his impotence, his wife's inability to
become pregnant is explained as the result of black magic. So a group of nuns,
who are believed to be possessed by the devil and therefore capable of recognizing the devil's servants, are interrogated by the power-mad Inquisitor to
discover who is guilty of casting a spell on Carlos. These religious hysterics
indict the whole court in a universal conspiracy of witchcraft.

The point is bleakly ironic. The patently false accusation, which no one
denies, is all too true on a deeper level: Carlos, the priests who serve the
state, the aristocrats who profit from it, and the common people who collaborate in their own victimization, are all indeed suffering from a malignant
enchantment, spell-bound by the evil system in which they believe. This is
demonstrated by the nobles' willingness to accept the most agonizing tortures as the price of maintaining their privileges. Since their position derives
from Carlos, having their limbs crushed or their bodies crippled by the
bloodstained hands of the Inquisition is welcome – it makes them more like
him.

Barnes has already set up a satiric equation between the pretensions of
these Spanish grandees (notorious for being the proudest of all aristocrats)
and their submission to any humiliation. Their tortured physical condition
graphically represents the dehumanizing effect of social inequality, even
on those who supposedly benefit most from it. They finally achieve what
earlier they had hypocritically pretended, in a comic mimicry of Carlos'
physical disabilities:

The perfect harmony o' the dance glorifies the perfect harmony o' God's universe . . . Today, Sire, we practice the 'Pavan', . . . mirroring the natural authority o'
its dancers . . .

CARLOS ... *reverses and skids about in a series of extraordinary spastic lurches, arms
  and legs jerking uncontrollably and ending once again on the floor ...*
TORRES Your Majesty hath a natural sense o' rhythm ...
With their MAJESTIES *in the lead,* [the Courtiers] *wobble, lurch, do the splits, skid,
spin with poker-faced dignity ... in their grotesque cavortings. The music grows faster,
until the climax is reached with the male dancers all simultaneously keeling over onto
the floor with a crash.*[9]

As the dancing-master points out, dance was a traditional image of aristocratic ideals. So Carlos' epileptic fit is both a burlesque of hierarchical
order, and an expression of its true nature. Anything but harmonious, it
is reduced to ridiculous farce by the courtiers' parody. In all Barnes' plays,
crude physical reality is used to demolish the ideology that supports social
inequality; and the end of *The Bewitched* takes its cue from Goya. We
watch the birth of Carlos' successor, an even more freakish monstrosity with
'*a small elephant's trunk hanging down ... in place of a nose*', while 'a new age:
the Age o' Reason' is proclaimed. As in *Noonday Demons*, historical progress
without a fundamental change in the established order is presented as an
accelerating degradation. So the final image of *The Bewitched* is '*a huge,
grinning imbecile's face projected over the king*'.[10]

This is made explicit in Barnes' next play, *Laughter* (1978), which measures
the bureaucratic horror of Nazi death camps against the personalized cruelty
of an archetypal tyrant, Ivan the Terrible. Throughout Barnes' drama his
characters are the damned. In an endless parade of death and mutilation, they
are beaten with chains, broken on the rack or crushed on the wheel, blinded,
dismembered, drowned in excrement, shot, strangled, buried alive, burnt
at the stake, or herded into the gas chambers – and the ultimate indignity
is treating their suffering as comedy. Only the inhuman, the imbecilic and
the insane survive; and although Barnes takes his most graphic examples of
cruelty from the past, history is shown to be a record of increasing pain. As
the angel of death tells Ivan the Terrible:

You made death too personal, arbitrary, a matter of chance: too much like life. In the
coming years they'll institutionalize it, take the passion out of killing, turn men into
numbers and the slaughter'll be so vast no one mind'll grasp it, no heart break 'cause
of it. Ah, what an age that'll be. How confidently they'll march on to extinction ...[11]

The catalogue of tortures in Barnes' plays is so overwhelming that it has
sometimes been mistaken as a universal statement about the meaninglessness of existence – for instance in the first production of *Dreaming* (Royal
Exchange, Manchester, 1999) the whole stage had a glass floor, under which

the bones of slaughtered humans were piled, skeletons twisted by death agonies. But this interpretation overlooks the tone of outrage in making human agony the subject of Farce. Instead of implying a Beckettian 'Nothing to be done', the violence is a protest against the status quo. The nuns' cry of 'Blind chance rules the world!' in *The Bewitched* is only intended as true in the sense that Barnes denies any controlling divinity.[12]

Most of the plays include a positive alternative: the gospel of love that society rejects. The 'madness' of which Jack is 'cured' in *The Ruling Class* would resolve the dichotomy of body and soul and achieve social equality, if it were put into practice. Even Carlos in *The Bewitched* has a fleeting perception that since 'man's ... the one creature able t' profit from his errors' a future is possible in which

We'll live wi'out orders and obediences
Wi'out limits t' heart and mind.

And *Red Noses* (written in 1978, first staged 1985) proposes revolution by the oppressed as the way forward. Medieval proletarians, drafted as corpse bearers during the Black Death, deliberately spread infection 'to wipe the slate clean, turn the world underside up ... Plague time heralds a new dawn sun rising in the West'.[13] However, they fail because they lack the affirmative vision that the strolling players who wear the red noses of the title can provide.

In his recent plays over the last decade Barnes extends this positive potential. *Sunsets and Glories* (1990) presents an even more explicit example of the potential for good in the short reign of the hermit-pope, Saint Celestine. The play is a conscious revisiting of his earlier work. Themes are repeated from *The Ruling Class* (a holy 'fool', who unexpectedly finds himself at the apex of the political hierarchy), *Noonday Demons* (a battle between two women, both dressed as the Angel Gabriel), and *The Bewitched* (the farcical treatment of the thirteenth-century king and queen of Naples; the distorting flattery that leads courtiers 'to learn to speak without tongues' in imitation of a power-figure whose tongue has been cut out by the Turks). The humour in the play is also typically grotesque – as when, in an echo from Antonin Artaud's Surrealist piece *The Spurt of Blood* (staged by Peter Brook in his 1964 'Theatre of Cruelty' season) '*God's massive foot stamps down from the flies squashing* [the previous Pope] *flat with a loud squelch.*'[14]

According to Barnes, 'My plays are about good people in positions of authority ... How can you be truly good when you have responsibility and power. The two are mutually exclusive. The plays are illustrations of this perennial theme.' However, *Sunsets and Glories* marks a striking departure. While the theme is demonstrated in the dying words of his predecessor – 'Goodness drained from me when I became supreme Pontiff' – the hermit Morrone, elected Pope Celestine, is uncorrupted by his position. In one striking image (reversing the scene in Brecht's *Galileo* so frequently copied by other British playwrights) the new Pope steps '*right out of his magnificent but oversize white robe. The robe itself is so stiff, it is left standing upright but without* MORRONE *in it*'. Rather, his removal from the Papacy and eventual murder is a measure of the evil in such a social structure. By putting the intrinsic goodness of the sainted Celestine on the stage, Barnes counters the (historically successful) attempt by those in power to 'blot out his ex-ample and his name, else men and women will know how near they came to Paradise'.[15] Unjust privilege is assumed to be untenable once ordinary people (the audience) realize that an alternative exists.

In a sense his next work, four linked playlets under the title of *Corpsing* (1996), reverted to the Epilogue of *Laughter* in exploring the connections between laughter and death in the theatre (where getting a laugh is called 'slaying them in the aisles' and the title comes from the expression used whenever an actor gets an involuntary fit of giggles). Indeed in the first vignette a jinxed actress is driven to suicide by the jokes of an over-cheerful neighbour. But despite its deathbed scene and dire title of 'Last Things', the fourth playlet is valedictory: a husband-and-wife acting team, lying in transition between life and death, reminisce about their past on the West End comedy stage with touching amusement.

Similarly Barnes' last play of the century, *Dreaming*, appears to return to the world of *The Bewitched* and *Red Noses* in its ragged band of wanderers in the aftermath of the Wars of the Roses, whose path from the Battle of Tewkesbury in 1471 is marked by mass slaughters of peasants around them and punctuated by their own deaths as they are killed off one by one. Here again theatre is presented as a potential threat to authority, in the shape of a seedy group of strolling players and a vengeful Richard of Gloucester – eliminating the Beaufort family as possible rivals for the throne in the run up to his career as archetypal villain in *Richard III* – who complains 'People put words into my mouth, the wrong words usually.' And indeed his subversion of Shakespeare's well-known text is comic (from his opening words, 'Now is the summer of my deep content' to 'Why can I never find a horse?!') while, as in Barnes' earlier plays, characters literally die laughing.[16] But the newly dead also give farewell speeches of hope; Christ steps down from his cross to join ordinary mortals; and the soldier-hero, who almost accidentally finds himself opposing Richard, comes to realize his journey is a spiritual progress towards love. After returning home to find his wife and daughter murdered and his home destroyed, he meets and marries a Beaufort heiress, whom he takes to be his dead wife returned to him. The battle against historical facts is one he can never win – the future in which Richard is crowned king cannot be changed – yet the ending offers an image of purity and hope beyond the reach of Richard's forces of destruction. Silently holding his wife's hand, he freezes to death on a mountain-top in the snow that obliterates all the mangled bodies of the slain: a statue dedicated to love, looking out over the unwritten white page of the future, that could serve as a beacon for the present.

Barnes sees theatre as a catalyst with the potential to 'fuse telephone wires and have a direct impact on reality' (a phrase that echoes Orton); and *Red Noses* explores how this might work.[17] The red-nosed clowns are used to demonstrate the difference between humour that perpetuates a system of social injustice – metaphorically represented by the Plague and a politically activist type of comedy. While employed to distract the dying from their predicament with jokes, the comedians have the Pope's approval. When designed to offer consolation to the suffering, comedy may have entirely humane motives. But its primary function is to divert the audience from the reality of their situation. However, when the clowns parody a nativity play, ridiculing the religious ideals that sanctify the status quo, this type of comedy is considered so subversive that the Pope orders their immediate execution. By offering themselves as sacrificial participants in a real-life version of Herod's Massacre of the Innocents through their protest, the comedians reveal the true nature of the power structure.

The aim of *Laughter* is also to define this revolutionary humour, as the author-figure who introduces the play announces:

Gangrene has set in. Comedy itself is the enemy. Laughter only confuses and corrupts everything we try to say. It cures nothing except our consciences and so ends by making the nightmare worse . . . Laughter's the ally of tyrants . . . An excuse to change nothing, for nothing needs changing when it's all a joke . . .

He rejects the stock farcical elements of the custard pie in the face, the whirling bow-tie and squirting buttonhole-carnation – all of which he is subjected to during the speech. Although these pratfalls are the only thing that saves the introduction from puritanical sermonizing, they are intended as a demonstration of how conventional humour undercuts serious issues:

in the face of Atilla the Hun, Ivan the Terrible, a Passchendaele or Auschwitz, what good is laughter?!
His trousers fall down to reveal spangled underpants.[18]

The major question is how humour can have any relevance in the context of such horrific realities. The double play that follows, which presents two of these extremes of human brutality, exploits the incongruity of laughter and tragic sufferings. By subjecting these to comedy the spectators' horror at the cruelty of tyrants is heightened, and their disgust for those who co-operate in the system intensified.

Ivan pins his chancellor's foot to the floor to get him to speak 'wi' feeling'. He sings out 'Now ring dem bells! I say ring dem bells!' as he pulls down on the legs of a prince impaled on a stake to drive the point up through his bowels to his brain. Similarly, the twentieth-century German bureaucrats, working in the ministry that supplies concrete and cyanide for the extermination camps, put on paper hats and blow toy squeakers to block awareness of their function. Even the victims in the gas chambers – putting on a camp-entertainment as 'the Boffo Boys of Birkenau', in ragged prison uniforms with undertakers' top hats and canes – present their fate as a music-hall turn:

they perform a simple dance and patter routine, to the tune of 'On the Sunny Side of the Street' ...
BIMKO According to the latest statistics, one man dies in this camp every time I breathe.
BIEBERSTEIN Have you tried toothpaste?
BIMKO No, the Dental Officer said my teeth were fine, only the gums have to come out.[19]

All too literally, as they realize, 'this act's dead on its feet'. In this context humour ceases to be funny, the comic is no relief. Yet the play implies that farce can still have a subversive function when the form is divorced from conventional comic content. As the bureaucrats discover, certain types of 'Jokes carry penalties' ranging from 'five years hard labour' for ridicule of Ribbentrop, to the death penalty for one-liners like 'Listen, listen, what do you call someone who sticks his finger up the Fuhrer's arse?! ... Heroic ... No, a brain surgeon!' And this encapsulates Barnes' dramatic approach.

The jokes are designed to fall flat as Ivan's court fool, stabbed for the quip that 'In Holy Russia we never hang a man wi' a moustache. We use a rope.' So in *The Bewitched*, bedroom farce, exaggerated into absurdity, turns into sinister screams in the dark – while in the cells of the Inquisition, the figures of authority sing an anachronistic parody of 'The Saints Go Marching In' with the cries of the tortured providing the rhythm:

We'll sing a holy chorus when they're screaming on the rack.
We try to make them Christians but they all get cardiacs . . . [20]

The pun implicit in the contrast between the title of *Laughter* and its subject of slaughter, two words identical but for a single letter, is typical. Barnes works through the fusion of opposites, both within and (in his characteristic pairing of one-act double bills) between plays. He has defined his aim as juxtaposing discordant techniques, using 'soliloquy, rhetoric, formalized ritual, slapstick, song and dance' to create 'a comic theatre . . . where everything is simultaneously tragic and ridiculous'. Form and content conflict. When characters announce 'happy endings' (as they do at the close of each act in *The Ruling Class*) these are shown to be the worst of all possible outcomes. Any romantic sentiment in particular is immediately undercut, so that a request of 'Woo me, say something beautiful' brings a response of the crudest physical reality like 'Labia, foreskin, testicles, scrotum'.[21]

If the basis of comedy is the perception of incongruity (as the nineteenth-century philosopher Bergson suggested in his classic study of *Comedy*), then Barnes has accentuated this principle to the point where it becomes reversed. In his work incongruities deny the validity of laughter in order to generate perception. Yet however iconoclastic his approach, like Orton, Barnes claims a traditional genealogy. He labelled his first major play *The Ruling Class* 'A baroque comedy', and like Orton or Travers has paid tribute to the tradition of Farce in adapting one of Feydeau's plays (*The Purging*). But where Orton looked to Aristophanes and Oscar Wilde, Barnes' models are Ben Jonson and the German Expressionist, Frank Wedekind. He has adapted plays by both for modern productions (most notably Wedekind's savage satire *Lulu*); and there are clear echoes of Jonson in his own drama. There is a striking similarity of names between Volpone's servant Mosca, and Lasca in *Leonardo's Last Supper*. One of the key speeches is modelled on Volpone's opening prayer to lucre, while – like the charlatans in Jonson's *The Alchemist* – both the charnel-house businessmen and the con-men saints of *Noonday Demons* transmute excrement into gold.

Even his use of the grotesque has a traditional sanction, corresponding to Bakhtin's concept of Carnival, in which hierarchies (aesthetic as well as political) are inverted to break taboos by focusing on 'vulgar' bodily functions, physical appetite, excremental and genital imagery, violence, abusive language and 'crude' or 'impure' artistic forms (particularly Farce). Indeed, with Barnes' interest in the Middle Ages, it would be surprising if he had not come across Bakhtin's influential study of *Rabelais and his World* (first translated into English in 1968) where these ideas relating to the Roman Saturnalia and the medieval 'Feast of Fools' are developed. But Barnes seems to have extended comedy into a *cul de sac*. His plays, with their Brechtian use of history, have been successful in Germany; but apart from *The Ruling Class* they failed almost completely on the British stage.

Barnes was hailed as 'an entirely new talent of a very high order' by leading critics, when *The Ruling Class* first appeared in London. They labelled it 'one of those pivotal plays . . . in which you can feel the theatre changing direction', and called *The Bewitched* 'one of the major works in our modern classical canon'.[22] Yet in striking contrast, the majority of the reviews were sharply derogatory; and both works were shunned by the public. Although *The Ruling Class* transferred very briefly from the Nottingham Playhouse to the West End, and was made into a film with Peter O'Toole, none of his subsequent plays transferred to the commercial theatre. The first productions of each closed within weeks, and there have been no major revivals, though *Noonday Demons* was restaged briefly at a small London theatre in 1991. Popularity is a dubious measure of dramatic significance – even though it has more relevance to comedy than other forms – but it took seven years for *Red Noses* to find a production. In the decade from 1978 to 1988 Barnes wrote nothing for the stage; and it is perhaps significant that when he finally returned to the theatre with *Sunsets and Glories*, the black humour of the earlier plays was considerably less shocking, while the attack on society was outweighed by an affirmation of the human potential for goodness – a positive view also evident in the ending of his most recent play, *Dreaming*.

   The fate of his plays is partly due to Barnes' political concern, which leads to the highly symbolic nature of their depiction of society. His aim was to create a 'drama that made the surreal real, that went to the limit, then further'. But the grotesque magnification, which this produced, disguised the relevance of Carlos II's Spain, or medieval saints. Reacting to the way audiences seemed to ignore his point, the ending of *Noonday Demons* translates the action into self-referential terms, fulfilling the devil's threat that

You'll be resurrected in the second half o' the twentieth century as a stage freak. Your agonizing abstinence'll be treated as a subject for laughter . . . just another figment of your author's grotesque imagination.[23]

The perception is all too accurate. The vision in the plays is so extreme that it becomes reduced to pure theatre.

The urgency of changing society was clearly fuelled by Barnes' failure to reach a wide audience in the 1960s and 1970s. This explains the way he reuses the same material in plays throughout those decades. For example, the situation in which a character is faced with an identical but opposite *alter ego* is found in both *The Ruling Class* (confrontation between two madmen who share the same delusion of being God), and *Noonday Demons* (two saints, each believing the other to be the devil). It also recurs in *The Bewitched* (two priests, both claiming to be the sole representative of God), and *Laughter* (Ivan and a false Tsar). With each rejection by the public, his treatment of this narrow focus becomes increasingly extreme, further alienating those he aims to convert. And this points to a deeper problem in Barnes' treatment of the audience.

His main thematic concern in all his plays up to *Sunsets and Glories* or *Dreaming* is not tyranny (nor, despite his recent emphasis, the perversion of goodness by power) so much as the psychology of submission. According to the elderly retainer in *The Ruling Class*, 'You get into the habit of serving. Born a servant . . . from a nation of servants. Very first thing an Englishman does, straight from his mother's womb, is touch his forelock.' In the following plays the message is illustrated in progressively more grotesque terms. A prisoner on the rack gasps 'Twas a great honour, Your majesty' when Carlos accidentally tightens the screw on a royal tour of the torture chambers in *The Bewitched*. The dying prince screams 'God save the Tsar!' as Ivan drives the stake through his body in *Laughter*. The point of such examples is not the helplessness, but the active complicity of the sufferers. Their screams are 'the voice o' the people aching to obey' because they value permanence and certainty (even the certainty of slaughter), above personal responsibility and the unknown risks of freedom.[24]

From this viewpoint, there is nothing unique or specifically Germanic about the functionaries who organize Auschwitz, or the victims who acquiesce in their own extermination. In having 'always preferred strong government to self government', the Nazis are meant to be seen as simply an extension of the norm: 'National Socialism is part of the great conservative tradition. . based on solid middle class values', and propagated by religion that teaches 'obedience . . . as a principle of righteous conduct'.[25]

Thus the spectators, as representatives of the common people, are not only the sole potential for changing the system (the ruling classes being, as in Edward Bond's plays, more insane and inhuman the greater their power – see above p. 160). They are also guilty. The unpopularity of Barnes' plays might be equated with a refusal to acknowledge the truth of his statement – and that in turn would call for stronger medicine, even punishment. So his attack on the public becomes increasingly explicit.

In his first play the audience are treated as voyeurs. They are merely witnesses to murder, and have stockings thrown to them during a strip-tease. Although the implied demand is for action instead of (the conventional) passive acceptance of the dramatic situation, insults are defused by comedy, as when the mad earl is married off to his uncle's mistress:

'Therefore if anyone can show just cause why they may not be lawfully joined together, let him now speak, or else hereafter forever hold his peace.'
CLARE, DINSDALE *and* SIR CHARLES *stare deliberately at the audience. Silence.*
TUCKER Load o' British jelly-meat whiskers! Stand up on your tea-soaked haunches and stop it. Piddling half-dead helots.
SIR CHARLES Quiet, man. Show some respect.

In subsequent plays, where the violence becomes increasingly graphic, while physical deformity, extremes of suffering, or even genocide are presented as objects of humour, the audience are being viscerally assaulted. The tone at the end of *Laughter* is typical. The point that the builders of the gas chambers are 'ordinary people, . . . you, me, us' is not only underlined – the bureaucrats responsible

march Down Stage to sing at the audience with increasing savagery . . .
This is a brotherhood of man . . . Oh aren't you proud to be in that fraternity.
The great big brotherhood of man. Sing! Everybody sing!
. . . *an unseen chorus joins the finale in the darkness.*[26]

Barnes deliberately locates his drama 'on the outer limits of farce where everything is pushed to extremes of pain and cruelty'.[27] But as a propaganda tactic, alienating the audience is self-defeating; and Griffiths' *Comedians* (1975) can be seen as a commentary on this brand of comedy.

Trevor Griffiths (1935–): comedy as a weapon

CHECKLIST OF GRIFFITHS' MAJOR PLAYS

Occupations, 1970	*Real Dreams*, 1984
Sam, Sam, 1972	*The Gulf Between Us*, 1992
The Party, 1973	*Thatcher's Children*, 1993
Comedians, 1975	*Who Shall Be Happy . . . ?*, 1996

Picking up from his prologue to *The Party* (1973), where the figure of Groucho Marx introduces 'Poppa Karl', Trevor Griffiths' *Comedians* is (rather too literally) a lecture-demonstration on the political nature of humour. As aspiring stand-up comics, the pupils in an adult-education class are used to present a variety of examples. Gathering for a final session before their passing-out 'examination' – a try-out with a live audience, evaluated by a London agent – the material they work up covers the spectrum from off-colour limericks, and standard Irish or Jewish one-liners, to shaggy dog stories. Risqué, superficially daring, these jokes are designed to draw automatic laughs from an audience, who are then implicitly rebuked by the teacher's criticism of this type of humour. Only one student, Gethin, a bitterly cynical Welshman, refuses to co-operate.

Two main positions are articulated. Eddie Waters, the retired comedian teaching this night-class in the industrial wasteland of Manchester, argues that comedy should be subversive.

We work *through* laughter, not *for* it . . . A joke releases the tension, says the unsayable, any joke pretty well. But a true joke . . . has to do more than release tension, it has to *liberate* the will and the desire, it has to *change the situation*.

At the same time, his view is apolitical: humour should be therapeutic, undermining bigotry and revealing healing truths. In the first production this part was played by a well-known stand-up comedian, Jimmy Jewel, which gave his pronouncements added weight.

By contrast, for the examiner – also a one-time comedian and Eddie Waters' old professional antagonist, who awards union membership that opens the night-club circuit to the successful pupils – any comic is marketing a commodity that supports the status quo:

the people . . . demand, we supply. Any good comedian can lead an audience by the nose. But only in the direction they're going. And that direction is, quite simply . . . escape.[28]

The pupils he approves are those who betray their teacher's standards by exploiting stereotypes that foster racism, and sexist innuendo.

However, neither the competitive tension between the pupils nor the conflict between these two exponents of contrasting types of traditional humour is Griffiths' central focus. The real conflict is between the play's structure, and a completely different style of comedy that opposes both of these viewpoints. The play itself deliberately uses the most conventional comic techniques. The way the students are characterized evokes stereotypical responses in the audience: the Irish jokes are told by Irishmen, the Jewish by a Jew; the Welsh nonconformist looks like a street-corner lout. And when at the end a new pupil enters to sign up for the next class, he is a Pakistani who adapts a Jewish caricature to fit Muslims. In addition, a disapproving school-caretaker provides a running joke that punctuates the action.

For Griffiths, 'the question why we laugh at certain things becomes a metaphor for the question why we live the way we do'.[29] In performance the jokes that elicit laughter in *Comedians* are the stereotypes, even though we (and the pupils) have been shown how demeaning and ugly such distortions are. Then, when the class moves to a local club for their final test before the public, the theatre audience are cast in the role of the working-class bingo group, unwilling to have their pursuit of cash interrupted. Placed like this in a false position, our/their response determines the characters' fate; and Griffiths manipulates the spectators through specifying the degrees of nervousness in the novices, and of professionalism in their presentation. As stand-ins for a commercialized system that has been exposed as corrupting, listening to jokes that appeal to the most despicable prejudices, we are forced to question our reactions. But the comfortable solution of lining up behind the liberal-progressive principles of the teacher, rather than the reactionary materialism of the talent-scout (seated indicatively left and right of the forestage), is denied by the final comic turn presented by Gethin, the angrily frustrated Welsh pupil.

Violent and confrontational, this provides the other pole in the play. Unlike the verbal humour of the other students' presentations, where the humour is largely derived from their incompetence, this is a mime that breaks all the rules. It climaxes in a physical assault on two life-size dummies, dressed to represent the Establishment (in its role as typical first-night audience; a reference underlined by the student addressing his performance not to the public, but to the dummies). To underline the point, this attack on the audience ends with a defiant rendition of 'The Red Flag'. Uncompromising and brutally shocking, it is a microcosm of the type of humour developed by Barnes:

GETHIN ... Laugh you buggers, laugh! (... *squeezing their bodies up and down and voicing their laughter for them. Then very suddenly.*) Here. (*He takes a flower out of his pocket ... pins the flower – a marigold – with the greatest delicacy between the girl's breasts ... a dark red stain, gradually widening, begins to form behind the flower.*)[30]

The effect, summed up in the student's appearance which combines the white-face of a clown with the shaven hair of a skinhead, is intended to be simultaneously funny and chillingly threatening.

The post mortem on the pupils' nightclub turns in the last Act reveals that Waters stopped performing after hearing a fellow comedian telling Jewish jokes following a tour of Buchenwald. His perception that the death-camp 'was the logic of our world... extended', the end-result of the stereotyping on which conventional comedy is based, renders him impotent as a comic. In such a context – exactly paralleled by Barnes in *Laughter* – 'there were no jokes left. Every joke was a little pellet, a... final solution. We're the only animal that laughs.' Gethin's refusal to compromise, using the techniques of comedy as a revolutionary tool that challenges the socially conditioned sources of laughter through smashing accepted categories, is the only way forward.

But rejection of the system also means being repudiated by it. The hard-line student will never have the opportunity to perform to the public since his material is judged 'Not viable... repulsive... And aggressively unfunny.' This was indeed an accurate anticipation of the critical response to Gethin's act: its disturbing emotional charge led the reviewers to reject it as a positive alternative, since 'Prejudice seems... no better for coming from the Left than the Right. In fact it is worse, since we look to the Left to break barriers.'[31]

In fact his revolutionary character's fate foreshadows Griffiths' own marginalization as a dramatist. After *Comedians*, Griffiths (like Barnes) withdrew from the theatre for almost a decade. Turning to television as a better medium for reaching a wide working-class public, his next stage play, *Real Dreams*, was not written until 1984, and was specifically designed for an American audience. As in the case of Barnes too, Griffiths' recent return to mainstream theatre with *Piano* (an adaptation of *Platonov* for the National Theatre, 1990) compromises with popular taste, using characters and situations from Chekhov as a basis for comedy; and his other plays during the 1990s were all staged in small provincial theatres, with only *Who Shall Be Happy...?* reaching London. In a sense one of the characters in *Thatcher's Children* – a panoramic polemic on the effect of fourteen years of extreme conservative rule, written to mark Margaret Thatcher's resignation in 1993 – shows what happens to the Pakistani would-be comic after the end of *The Comedians*. The son of an Asian construction-worker in Leeds, who dreams of being a stand-up comedian, is framed by the police, jailed for arson, and instead joins the 'greed' society by becoming a drug dealer.

In fact, the whole issue of comedy raised in *Comedians* was intended to be secondary. It is a metaphor for political activism in terms of British society as a whole; and this is emphasized by the pun on educational and social class, as well as by the way the bingo club presentation within the play duplicates the performance of the play itself. For Griffiths, *Comedians* was a study of the 'pressures to conform ... which in the case of comedians are commercial pressures'. The dominance of such conformist influences ruled out the democratic socialist solution of reforming the system from within. Although this Shavian attitude (represented by Waters) might be 'principled ... in broad terms, progressive ... liberating, which is also what being a comedian is about', it had been superseded by 'a younger tradition, very violent, very angry, very disturbed' (symbolized by Gethin). The message of the play was that 'We've got to restate in our own terms what the world is like, what the world can be like.'[32]

However, this level of meaning was completely ignored by the reviews. Their focus was exclusively on the analysis of humour in *Comedians* – partly because of the dominating effect inherent in the use of theatre itself as a metaphor, which reappears in his next most popular play: *Who Shall Be Happy...?* (appearing first on television in 1994, then staged at the Belfast Festival in 1995 and directed by Griffiths himself in London in 1996). Focusing on Danton as an emblem of socialist ideals betrayed, imprisoned in 1794 and awaiting the guillotine as the French Revolution consumes those who fought for it, this (like Howard Brenton's *Weapons of Happiness* as early as 1979, David Edgar's *Maydays* in 1983 or David Hare's *Absence of War* just two years earlier) explores the failure of Griffiths' generation of radical playwrights and the defeat of Communism. As Danton puts it in a direct address to the 'Little white faces in the dark', the audience are living through 'the meticulously managed death of history'. In place of 'new-minting the coins of hope ... We have been yet busier reissuing the banknotes of despair' – though the ideals of Liberty, Equality, Fraternity will live on – and the title takes a line from the play, 'who shall be happy if not everyone?' But the whole political point is portrayed in terms of theatre, with Danton (symbolically named only 'The Prisoner') trying to escape death by persuading his guard that he is not himself but a different prisoner, an actor whom he claims is indistinguishable from the real Danton and has been placed in another cell as a decoy to foil any rescue attempt. He acts the actor, explaining that his ability to imitate Danton so convincingly comes from having researched the revolutionary leader in order to play his role earlier on the stage. And in this multiplication of representational mirrors pretence becomes the reality: as Danton acknowledges, 'Our lives are very much like theatre ... indifferently written and scandalously short of rehearsal'.[33] Revolutionaries, in succumbing to hypocrisy, turn into performers.

This theatricality links Griffiths, along with Barnes despite the extremism that has so severely diminished the appeal of Barnes's epic work, to mainstream British drama. The same overt reference to the stage, which heightens the artifice of performance and gives it metaphoric significance, has come to characterize the best of contemporary comedy. It is reflected in the plays of Alan Ayckbourn and Michael Frayn, as well as Tom Stoppard, although their work is completely opposed to the revolutionary stance promoted by Barnes and Griffiths.

Notes

1 Griffiths, interview in *Theatre Quarterly*, 6, no. 22, p. 46.

2 Barnes, introduction, *Collected Plays*, London, 1981, p. viii, and p. 352.

3 *Ibid.*, pp. 320, 22.

4 *Ibid.*, pp. 24, 25 & 28, 72.

5 *Ibid.*, pp. 91, 90 & 115.

6 *Ibid.*, pp. 145, 177.

7 Introduction, *Sunsets and Glories*, London, 1990, p. v, and Barnes, Programme Note for *Sunsets and Glories*, Leeds, 1990.

8 *Collected Plays*, p. 320.

9 *Ibid.*, pp. 215–16.

10 *Ibid.*, p. 338.

11 *Ibid.*, pp. 338, 145, 177, 365.

12 Beckett, *Waiting for Godot*, New York, 1964, p. 7 (and *passim*); Barnes, *Collected Plays*, p. 305.

13 *Collected Plays*, pp. 328–9; *Red Noses*, London, 1985, p. 16.

14 *Sunsets and Glories*, pp. 81, 1. See Artaud's *Spurt of Blood* in *Modern French Theatre* (ed. Michael Benedikt and George Wellwarth), New York, 1966, 225 and 226.

15 Programme Note to *Sunsets and Glories*; *Sunsets and Glories*, pp. 10, 85. The hermit/papal robe image reverses the well-known sequence in Brecht's *Galileo*, where a cardinal's personality changes as he dons his robes of office.

16 *Dreaming*, London, 1999, pp. 7, 30.

17 *Collected Plays*, p. viii.

18 *Ibid.*, p. 343.

19 *Ibid.*, pp. 349, 352, 410–11.

20 *Ibid.*, pp. 411, 395–6, 360, 265.

21 Barnes, *The Frontiers of Farce*, London, 1977, p. vii; *Collected Plays*, pp. 122, 387 & 98.

22 Harold Hobson, *The Sunday Times*, 2 March 1969, Ronald Bryden, *The Observer*, 2 March 1969, Martin Esslin, *Plays and Players*, 21 (June 1974), p. 36.

23 *Collected Plays*, Preface, p. viii, & p.161.

24 *Ibid.*, pp. 31, 262, 352, 376.

25 *Ibid.*, p. 385.

26 *Ibid.*, pp. 56–7, 409.

27 *The Frontiers of Farce*, p. viii.

28 *Comedians*, London, 1976, pp. 20, 33.

29 Griffiths, cited in Oleg Kerensky, *The New British Drama*, London, 1977, p. 201.

30 *Comedians*, p. 51.

31 *Ibid.*, p. 64; *New Statesman*, 28 February 1975.

32 Griffiths, in *Gambit*, 29 (976), p. 31, and *New Theatre Voices of the Seventies*, p. 132.

33 *Who Shall Be Happy...?*, London, 1995, pp. 6, 24, 52, 16.

4.8 Traditionalism and theatricality: Alan Ayckbourn and Michael Frayn

During the 1980s British comedy became truly popular – and populist – once more, sidelining the politicized violence of Barnes and Griffiths. The two dramatists who set the tone and have continued to dominate the broader reaches of the comic stage, Alan Ayckbourn and Michael Frayn, both reject the radicalism that fuelled the development of farce from Joe Orton to Peter Barnes – as indeed does the other major comic dramatist, Tom Stoppard. As Ayckbourn put it, in terms directly applicable to Trevor Griffiths' *Comedians*, 'I'm on a crusade to try and persuade people that theatre can be fun; but every time I start doing that, some hairy bugger from the left comes in and tells them it's instructive, and drives them all out again. If I want to be instructed, I go to night-school.' Frayn in turn deplored the 'didactic drive' of the 1970s on the grounds that it replaced drama by ideology.[1]

Unlike Orton, who treated tragic material as farce for shock effect, Ayckbourn and Frayn make farce a way of exposing the insensitivity of stock responses through showing potential tragedy beneath the comic surface, even though in *The Revengers' Comedies* Ayckbourn is playing directly off Tourneur's Jacobean *Revenger's Tragedy*. And in contrast to the symbolically grotesque picture of society in Barnes, their focus is always on a personal, in-dividual level. In this they were adopting conventional characterization; and in stressing entertainment as sufficient motive for writing, Ayckbourn and Frayn are not only consciously setting themselves apart from the political drama that was sweeping the English stage at the beginning of the 1970s, when they established their reputations. They were also underlining a return to traditional comic values.

As a side effect, this emphasis on entertainment also leads to their work being generally undervalued, in removing it from the sphere of academic criticism, which tends to measure the significance of drama by intellectual content or political commitment. These are easy to pin down in print, unlike the electricity of purely theatrical moments that characterizes Farce; and analysing, or even imposing, serious ideas confirms the value of the critic. Conversely, prolific output and wide popularity – achieved so notably by Ayckbourn – tend to be looked on as superficial, while commercial success is suspect. As a result Frayn and, until recently, Ayckbourn have attracted less critical attention than contemporaries like Harold Pinter or John Arden, even though Ayckbourn's work in particular has reached a far wider audience.

However, entertaining the public does not rule out realism or sharp commentary on social pretensions and contemporary morals – both of which underlie their comedy. Ayckbourn should be seen as a modern-day Noel Coward, in his brilliantly terse dialogue, acute observation of how people behave, and unsentimental humour. Like Coward, Ayckbourn's comic tone is astringent and frequently bitter. His move downmarket from the elegantly wealthy and artistic characters of Coward's plays in the 1930s, to the typically lower-middle-class manners on which his comedy focuses, is a symptom of the more democratic present. And his 1998 *Things We Do For Love* is a rewrite of Coward's 1930 classic, *Private Lives*, though in far more violent and sexually explicit terms. Similarly Frayn, who has translated all of Chekhov's major comedies for the English stage – a strikingly successful adaptation of *Platonov* (under the title of *Wild Honey*) in 1984, as well as *The Seagull* in 1990, *The Cherry Orchard* in 1994 and *Three Sisters* in 1997 – strikes a Chekhovian note in plays like *The Two of Us*, his early sequence of four one-act playlets for Lyn Redgrave and Michael Briers, or *Here* (1993), where an atmosphere of elegiac sadness suffuses the characters, reduced from Chekhov's country estates to an unfurnished one-room flat, who vainly attempt to construct a space where they can live in the moment, here and now.

At the same time their popularity has been accompanied by a genuine flair for theatrical experiment. Each has continually broken new ground in stage presentation. So it is hardly surprising if two of the best-known plays by both dramatists have the theatre itself as their setting. Frayn's *Noises Off*

(1982) takes the technical term for behind-the-scenes activity that breaks the theatrical illusion as its title. It juxtaposes backstage action against the rehearsal and performance of a mirror text: 'Nothing On', a highly artificial farce, which echoes Ben Travers' *Rookery Nook*. The characters are stock figures on two overlapping levels. As actors they are the drunken old-stager 'who first "trod the boards" in A MIDSUMMER NIGHT'S DREAM with the Ben Greet Players'; the shortsighted sex symbol who is blind without her contact lenses; the fading television star investing in her own show to finance retirement; or the insecure lover-boy whose jealousy misinterprets everything he sees. And they are cast as Shavian Burglar (à la *Heartbreak House*), and dumb blonde; comic servant (duplicating the TV soap role in which the aging actress made her name), and sophisticated seducer.

The catalyst on both back- and on-stage levels is the director. Lloyd's casual affairs with both the sex symbol, and the assistant stage manager (hired because her father's firm is sponsoring the production) who finds herself pregnant, are a real-life version of the on-stage characters' sexual activities. And this behind-the-scenes promiscuity progressively disrupts the performance that he has so carefully organized in the rehearsal.

As backstage events increasingly come to resemble the scripted action, Lloyd's predicament becomes the main farce, rather than the performance of 'Nothing On'. The Act I dress rehearsal (of which we only get to see the first Act) demonstrates the tenuous fragility of the ordered precision on which the performance of farce depends. Lines are forgotten, entries missed, doors jam at crucial moments or won't close; and the comedy misfires completely. It is the incompetence of the actors, not the antics of the characters, that is funny. But the director is still (barely) able to push the cast through until the curtain falls:

LLOYD I'm starting to know what God felt like when he sat out there in the darkness creating the world. (*Takes a pill*) ... Very pleased he'd taken his Valium.
BELINDA He had six days, of course. We've only got six hours.[2]

In the second Act, when the perspective is reversed, showing us the set from behind, the humour comes from mistaken motives and a series of emotional crises (typical of Farce) that afflict the actors in the wings. The complete silence imposed on them by the on-going performance just the other side of the thin scenery, magnifies their misunderstandings and frustrations into hysterical comedy.

A plate of sardines (which provides the running gag of the front-stage play) is tipped by the jealous lover over the head of his mistress, when he finds her in an apparently compromising position. Conversely, flowers and a bottle of whisky, brought by the director to buy off the angry dumb blonde he has abandoned, who is threatening to walk out on the production, become running gags in which he is the fall guy. The whisky, passed from hand to hand to keep it from the old soak, is finally given to him by the dumb blonde, left holding it when her cue comes. Mayhem results when, unable to find the drunkard for his scene, a fire-axe is fetched to break down the door of the toilet, in which he is (wrongly) believed to be hiding with the bottle. The flowers are repeatedly given to the wrong woman – even being carried on stage in place of the blonde's dress, which calls for some swift improvisation. Then, after being sent out three times to buy replacement bunches from the local florist, when the stage manager returns with a cactus (cash having run out) the jealous lover rams it into the director's bottom.

'Noises Off' outdoes 'Nothing On' in every way. The activity behind the scenes results in double the number of men with trousers round their ankles (including the director, to have the cactus spines removed), and two semi-nude girls instead of the one in 'Nothing On'. The chaos distorts the unseen performance, finally eclipsing it, when the assistant stage manager's jealous misery can no longer be contained by the backstage code of silence. Her declaration that Lloyd has made her pregnant, coming just after the curtain-lines (which are greeted with a deadly silence from the imaginary audience of 'Nothing On'), is heard throughout the theatre. As Frayn comments: 'The fear that haunts [the cast] is that the unlearned and unrehearsed – the great dark chaos behind the set, inside the heart and brain – will seep back on to the stage . . . Their performance will break down, and they will be left in front of us naked and ashamed.'[3]

This fear is realized in the final Act, some months later in the tour, when the mayhem behind the scenes has indeed spread on to the stage. The ubiquitous sardines become an equivalent of banana skins for actors to slip on, or custard pies to be ground in their faces by other actors during the scenes. As the performers hit each other over the head, or are tripped down the backstage stairs from the 'bedroom' as they exit, the stage manager is forced to enter as a stand-in for one after another, only to have each injured actor stagger into view while he is still on the set. This culminates in no fewer than three comic burglars appearing when the old soak misses his entry. Believing him to be drunk, the stage manager dashes on stage to say his crucial lines – as does the director, believing the stage manager is already on in another role – followed by the drunken actor himself. Under the pressure of such physical chaos the dialogue, uncertain at the best of times, disintegrates.

In desperation the cast drag down the curtain between them and the audience.

In Ayckbourn's *A Chorus of Disapproval* (1984), life copies theatre even more directly. There are striking surface similarities with *Noises Off*: the 'old die-hards' in the company are claimed to be 'original walk-ons in *Chu Chin Chow*' (a record-breaking Oscar Asche musical that ran from 1916 to 1921), while the director has given way to such Peter Brook-like excesses as *The Sound of Music* on trampolines.[4] Instead of a parody of contemporary popular comedy performed by professional incompetents, here a familiar classic – John Gay's eighteenth-century *The Beggar's Opera* – is being presented by amateurs. There is also the same breakdown of backstage relationships as in Frayn's play. However, rather than building up to a final catastrophe, in a typically Ayckbourn reversal the final scene of the drama is played as an opening prologue.

Even so, in *A Chorus of Disapproval* the community off-stage is not the self-reflexive world of the theatre (as it is in *Noises Off*), but the town of Pendon: the imaginary microcosm for Britain, which is the setting for most of Ayckbourn's plays about ordinary middle-class society. In addition the correspondences between the piece being performed, and the actors' personal lives, is far more complex than in Frayn's play. Ayckbourn uses the original songs of *The Beggar's Opera* as a specifically theatrical frame for events surrounding the production, to universalize the small-town gerrymandering that forms the subject of the outer play. Gay's mock-heroic depiction of eighteenth-century high society as highwaymen not only mirrors the personal lives of the cast; it is set up as an ironic contrast.

The celebration of Macheath's satiric salvation from the gallows and joyful reconciliation is played out by a chorus who would like nothing better than to hang the actor in the lead role. So the prologue opens with enthusiastic applause (from the imaginary Pendon public) and, following the curtain-calls, a congratulatory tribute to the 'one individual without whom none of this [the successful performance] could have happened . . . our very special Macheath, Mr Guy Jones'.[5] This is immediately set against the communal rejection and isolation that greets him when the curtain comes down, typifying the amalgam of comic humour and human pain in contemporary farce. The subsequent action then shows exactly how the (theatrical) triumph has come to be a (personal) tragedy, from Guy's first nervous audition as the least experienced and most recent recruit to this provincial operatic society, through ever more important roles – corresponding to his growing sexual involvements with the different women in the cast – up to his theatrical apotheosis, which also marks his utter moral and social debasement.

The rumoured expansion of a multinational plant in the town, which will turn waste ground into valuable property, motivates the plotting that promotes Guy – once the cast find out that he is employed in the firm's ambiguously 'obscure department called Alternative Forward Costing' – from the one-line part of Crook-Finger'd Jack to Filch, and finally to the hero-villain of the piece, as he becomes increasingly central in the off-stage activities of the cast. The parallels between the eighteenth-century whores and thieves, and the modern property speculators and their adulterous wives, substantiate the director's assertion that *The Beggar's Opera* is 'as vital and relevant as it was then'.[6] But they also contrast Restoration hedonism with the mercenary promiscuity of today in a way that undermines both. The comparison both exposes the way Gay's ballads make the despicable glamorous (the theatre as false image) and reveals the currently fashionable and trendy as meanly hypocritical.

All the Pendon people, except Guy, have analogues in the operatic roles. Some are deliberately switched: the over-protected rich girl (corresponding to Polly Peachum) being cast as Lucy, while a building contractor's wife who has the part of Polly in fact behaves as the prostitute, Jenny. But most of the parallels are exact. The initial Macheath is a de-romanticized counterpart of Gay's anti-hero. A violent and hostile misfit, who is involved in the production only because he is the boyfriend of an influential couple's daughter (the girl playing Lucy), he flaunts his copulation with the barmaid/stage manager, and vanishes after assaulting the director. The grasping and callous manager of a local factory, who owns the land in question and slips Guy money for tipping him off about its potential value, is a real-life Peachum (disguised in the minor part of the Gaoler). The speculative house-builder is no less unscrupulous than his stage-part as Macheath's henchman, Filch, in bribing Guy first with his promiscuous wife (cast as Polly Peachum), then with his role – which he values far more than her – in the hope of inside information about the plans of Guy's firm. Even the director turns a blind eye to his own wife's love affair with Guy for the same reason.

With the two wives of other men squabbling over a pair of underpants (belonging to the husband of one, donned by Guy in mistake, and left behind after visiting the other), instead of the two women Macheath has married coming to blows over their bigamous husband, Guy's situation is a farcical mirror of Macheath's. yet his innocence makes him a complete fake in the part. His complete incomprehension of the local corruption that he becomes sucked into, is comic in the incongruities it produces – as when, having no idea that he has been asked to a wife-swapping party, he invites a seventy-year-old widow as his 'partner'. Even more than this, his naivety is self-destructive. The root of Guy's problems is an all too common desire to make a good impression, which makes him reluctant to admit that his job is too junior to know what managerial decisions are being made in the company. He accepts all the bribes at face value, mistaking the money for generosity, the women's availability as a sign of his own sex appeal, and the operatic roles as a measure of his theatrical talent, without being able to keep his side of the implied bargains. In turn, his ignorance that anything is being required of him, is mistaken as simply a way of raising the stakes, provoking still more valuable bribes (and worse outrage) when he fails to supply the desired information.

Ironically, it is because he always acts with the best of motives, that he loses everything. Feeling morally obligated by the professed friendship of the director prevents Guy from making a commitment to the director's wife. So he loses the woman he loves, only to find himself out of a job as well as an object of contemptuous hatred when the news breaks that his firm, rather than expanding, is closing down the plant. Macheath's hanging during the performance almost becomes a real lynching; and only the mock reprieve required by *The Beggar's Opera* produces a happy ending, which is overtly artificial.

In both *Noises Off* and A *Chorus of Disapproval* the apparent distinction between theatrical performance and real life is denied. Although both reduce popular drama (in the form of commercialized entertainment and amateur rep) to parodistic farce, each resolves its characters' problems in terms of the theatre it satirizes. The stage substitutes for reality. So it is hardly coincidental that in affirming the artifice of comedy both plays refer back to a long tradition: from Ben Travers in the 1930s, through Ben Greet or Oscar Asche in the 1920s, to John Gay in the Eighteenth Century.

Like Joe Orton, and even Peter Barnes, Ayckbourn and Frayn emphasize precedents for their work. Ayckbourn's points of reference include Sheridan (to whom he has paid homage in a musical adaptation of *A Trip to Scarborough*), Pirandello and Ionesco, as well as Harold Pinter, whose work he was exposed to early on in his career, having played the lead in the second production of *The Birthday Party*. Ayckbourn's work combines these influences with Travers (to whom *Taking Steps*, a variation on *Thark*, was dedicated in 1979, and whose *Tons of Money* was the first production Ayckbourn directed for the National Theatre), P.G. Wodehouse and Buster

Keaton, in a virtual compendium of modern comedy. Similarly, as well as playing off Travers in *Noises Off,* Frayn clearly links his work to Chekhov. Some of his plays have also been compared to Pirandello, and he has acknowledged Ayckbourn's influence on his work. Indeed it was Ayckbourn who directed a revival of *Wild Honey* (Frayn's adaptation of *Platonov*) at his theatre in Scarborough. In addition, both have expressed admiration for Noel Coward.

The continuity of tradition, however radical the subject matter, is the defining hallmark of British comedy. What Ayckbourn and Frayn have added to these models is the technical experimentation, which culminates in *Noises Off* and *A Chorus of Disapproval.* This open theatricality – where people are presented as performers; their characters are those of their roles, and their social context a stage set; so that everything relates to drama – is the logical extension of trends established at the beginning of the century. It forms the background for comic dramatists as diverse as Somerset Maugham at the beginning of the period, up to Trevor Griffiths, as well as the contemporary pyrotechnics of Tom Stoppard.

Alan Ayckbourn (1939–): comic ambiguity and middle-class moralities

CHECKLIST OF AYCKBOURN'S MAJOR PLAYS

Relatively Speaking, 1967	*A Chorus of Disapproval,* 1984
How the Other Half Loves, 1969	*A Small Family Business,* 1987
Time and Time Again, 1970	*Man of the Moment,* 1989
Absurd Person Singular, 1972	*The Revengers' Comedies,* 1991
The Norman Conquests, 1973	*Time of My Life,* 1992
Absent Friends, 1974	*Communicating Doors,* 1994
Bedroom Farce, 1975	*Comic Potential,* 1998
Joking Apart, 1978	*Things We Do For Love,* 1998
Sisterly Feelings, 1979	*House* and *Garden,* 1999
Intimate Exchange, 1983	

Ackybourn is by far the most prolific of all twentieth-century British dramatists, outdoing even Bernard Shaw. Known for being able on occasion to complete a play in just six days, he has written around 55 plays – even Ayckbourn himself is unsure of the total – ranging from straight comedy through musicals (including an early unsuccessful adaptation of P.G. Wodehouse, *Eh Jeeves* with Andrew Lloyd-Webber). And he takes Shaw on directly in at least one play, *Comic Potential* (1998) which updates *Pygmalion*, one of Shaw's most lasting successes. He also (again like Shaw) directs most of his own work, starting practically at the beginning in the Stephen Joseph Theatre, Scarborough – which has been dedicated almost exclusively to his work – and later increasingly in London, which gives him the advantage of setting the interpretation of his plays. Since they are all performed first in Scarborough, he is also the only British playwright to straddle both the provinces and the West End.

Peter Hall justified the inclusion of Ayckbourn's work in the National Theatre repertoire as 'an accurate reflection of English life...a very important social document'; and titles like *How the Other Half Loves* (1969), *Absurd Person Singular* (1972) or *Men on Women on Men* (a musical revue, 1978) and *Woman in Mind* (1986) summarize Ayckbourn's thematic concerns.[7] Sexual politics and the deforming impact of social conditioning on the suffering individual – in particular the effect of marriage on women, and their sexual objectification by men – are a recurring basis for his comic actions. Their humour is based on the exaggeration of recognizable behaviour, which reveals the psychological cost of class distinctions and modern lifestyles. Indeed he could be said to have given such a definitive picture of cheerful failures and neurotic fantasists, the upwardly mobile with small ambitions and low moral standards, bored suburbanites and insecure housewives, tyrannical parents and weak-kneed or hollow-hearted adulterers, insouciant philistines and sad or abused women that he has literally created the image of British middle-class life. He has gained a reputation as 'the laureate of the petit bourgeoisie, the rhapsodist of provincial life'.[8] Yet at the same time the structure of his plays is often artificial and mechanistic, or the situation is exaggerated – even fantastically incredible, as with the premise of *Body Language* (1990) where in a reprise of P.G. Wodehouse's *Laughing Gas* the heads of two women, simultaneously decapitated by the whirling blades of a helicopter, are sewn back on to the wrong bodies. Indeed several of his plays are set in a sci-fi future, notably *Henceforward* (1986) and *Comic Potential* (1998) which are both set in a cybernetic dystopia with robots as characters, *Communicating Doors* (1994) where in 2014 sex is all virtual – 'mouse in one hand and a joy-stick in the other' – and prostitutes are state employees while London, like Sarajevo, is a burning and balkanized war zone. *Woman in Mind* is a dream play; and ever responsive to the latest fads, *Wildest Dreams* (1990) depicts the magic fantasy of Dungeons and Dragons. Yet the human dilemmas are always very close to home. In Ayckbourn's words, 'what one is trying to portray is normality, but you've got to have something to contrast it with, and indeed to upset it'.[9]

His approach is well-represented by the title of *Joking Apart* (1978). For Ayckbourn, humour is not important in itself, but for the serious problems that emerge behind it (as well as for being a tool for exposing the lack of compassion in the average spectator's laughter at the comic surface). The type of action he creates, with its manic multiplication and cross-purposes, its displays of social ineptitude and incongruous fantasies, is carefully constructed to evoke continuous laughter. Yet beneath this comic structure his themes are bleak, even potentially tragic. Marriages split apart; love is obsession, betrayal, self-deception or manipulation, but always pain (in *Things We Do For Love* a woman's cries of sexual passion are mistaken for weeping). Suicide is repeatedly attempted – from one of his first plays, *Absurd Person Singular*, through to his most recent work to date, *House* and *Garden* (1999), which contains a characteristic catalogue of alcoholism, mental breakdown and sexual abuse, as well as the break-up of no fewer than four marriages. Murder or accidental death is increasingly common in his plays – with the title figure being drowned in *Man of the Moment* (1989), a father killed in a car crash in *Time of My Life* (1992) or an elderly millionaire, who has just confessed to having his two wives murdered, expiring on stage in *Communicating Doors* (1994), and serial killings in *The Revengers' Comedies* (1991) as well as a duel where even a refusal to fight leads to death when one of the duellists throws his pistol on the ground and it goes off.

In his best plays, where the characters are more than stereotypes and catch our sympathy, Ayckbourn's comic ingenuity creates an extreme tension with such dark themes, which evokes a complex emotional response. Indeed the questionable nature of an audience's laughter at the characters' predicaments is underlined by the way comparable expressions of pleasure are treated on stage. So in *Absent Friends* (1974) the laughter of the characters is always inappropriate. When one of the group exclaims how happy they all are, his jovial assumption makes another of them weep hysterically. In the same play, a young man, whom everyone believes is heartbroken by the tragic death of his fiancée, laughs with complacency as he remembers the romanticized perfection of his lost love. The echoing laughter of the person listening to him, whose own marriage is breaking up, modulates from derision to despair:

COLIN *laughs.* PAUL *laughs.* COLIN *stops laughing.* PAUL *continues. It's hysterical, almost manic, uncontrollable laughter.*[10]

His plays are all premised on people's complete failure to communicate with each other, and their total inability to perceive each other's suffering. And by putting his audiences in the same position Ayckbourn is subjecting us to 'lessons in feeling' (Osborne's phrase – though here the technique is far subtler than the diatribes of *Look Back in Anger*).

As the most extreme expression of personal suffering, suicide is a particularly appropriate test for spectators' responses. Apart from *The Revengers' Comedies* where a man is about to throw himself off Albert Bridge, but instead comes to rescue a woman who had jumped shortly before only to find herself caught in the girders, notably all Ayckbourn's would-be suicides are female. Trapped in loveless marriages, crippled by emotional neglect or rejected by heartless lovers, they are mute, reduced to acting out their agony. As victims they call on our pity and compassion. Yet because – like all Ayckbourn's characters – they are inept and fail repeatedly, their increasing desperation leads them to try ever more incongruous methods. For instance in *House* and *Garden* a wife faced with the break-up of her marriage because of her affair with a married lover, who has now callously abandoned her, tries to hang herself during a garden fete, then drowning (in an ornamental pond that is far too shallow) and finally throws herself in front of a lawn-mower. So in Ayckbourn's plays, the greater the suffering, the more hysterical the spectator's laughter becomes. And the intended reaction is illustrated by a Scarborough playgoer, who is reported to have told Ayckbourn, 'If I'd known what I was laughing at, I'd never have started laughing at all.'[11]

The technique was already fully exploited in the first Act of *Absurd Person Singular*, where the farcical highpoint is produced by the increasingly desperate suicide attempts of a distraught housewife during a party in her own home – gestures of abject despair, all of which are unconsciously foiled by her uncomprehending guests. The comedy lies in the contrast between their socially prescribed responses, and her obsessive misery. Her first gambit, which takes her to the window ledge, is treated seriously. But the multiplying methods of self-destruction become increasingly farcical. Found with her head in the gas oven, groping for sleeping-pills dropped down the sink, or trying to hang herself with a washing line from the light-fixture, her guests mistakenly assume that she is cleaning the stove, clearing a blocked drain, or changing the light bulb. The focus, achieved through her catatonic silence throughout, is on how her husband and guests react. They illustrate the way numbing routine gets substituted for personal commitment, egocentricity and self-aggrandizement dehumanize us, or normal standards block out our ability to see what is really happening around us.

The incongruity of a party guest scrubbing a stove in evening-dress is a test of the spectator's sensitivity. Do we see it as evidence of a callous obsession with cleanliness – or does it reflect the degree to which this woman too has been trapped and defined by marital roles? The hostess' social-climbing husband, who uses the backs of her unread suicide notes to draw diagrams demonstrating his technical expertise as a building contractor, is an extreme example of the contemporary materialistic ethos that he espouses: 'No place for sentiment. Not in business . . . when the chips are down it's every man for himself and blow you Jack'. He gets soaked while taking the drain apart, while the bank-manager who finances his shoddy housing developments is almost electrocuted in trying to fix the light. The conformists are reduced to figures of fun in variations on the custard-pie-in-the-face. But we are constantly reminded of the human cost of Farce. This is summed up in the play's final apocalyptic image. The most egoistic of all the characters triumphs; and the dominance of the worst human attributes is signalled by his ability to impose a megalomaniac game of 'forfeits' on the party-goers:

Under his increasingly strident commands, the dancers whirl faster and faster whilst accumulating bizarre appendages . . . He screams at the dancers in mounting exhortation bordering on the hysterical
That's it. Dance. Come on. Dance. Dance . . .[12]

Each Act of *Absurd Person Singular* is set on Christmas Eve on successive years, with the same group celebrating at the house of each couple in turn. The psychological state of the would-be revellers, which grows more depressing from year to year, is contrasted with the festive season. Exactly the same incongruity appears in a play like *Time of My Life*, set entirely in a restaurant and portraying a disastrous family celebration, which hollows out the cliché of the title. And this way of exposing the gap between social ritual and reality is typical of Ayckbourn's work.

His farce typically revolves around dinner parties, birthdays, wedding anniversaries, reunions, country fetes, Christmas festivities: cliché occasions of joyful celebration and social unity, all of which fall apart – as indeed more tangible man-made objects also tend to do on his stage. The incompetence of the home handymen in the kitchen of *Absurd Person Singular* carries forward into other plays. A husband spends hours building a dressing-table from a do-it-yourself kit, only to have the wobbly object of his pride collapse in pieces the first time it is touched (*Bedroom Farce*, 1975). Bookshelves tumble down when a scrapbook is thrown against them in *Things We Do For Love* (1998). In *Just Between Ourselves* (1977), a wife whose nervous

breakdown causes her to break glasses, spill cups and drop saucers, is introduced by her crassly insensitive husband with 'You ever want a demolition
job doing ... she's your woman (*He laughs...*)'.[13]

Sam Beckett once remarked that Sean O'Casey was 'a master of
knockabout in this very serious and honorable sense – that he discerns
the principle of disintegration in even the most complacent solidities, and
activates it to their explosion ... from the furniture to the higher centres'.[14]
And as in the classic final line of *Juno and the Paycock* where a drunkard
looks round his devastated home and announces 'th' whole worl's ... in a
terr ... ible state o' ... chassis!', here too physical destruction is the symptom
of a collapsing society.

In an everyday context the most disruptive element is an innocent mav-
erick; and this kind of figure is a typical catalyst in Ayckbourn's plays.
Frequently this odd man out takes the stock form of the 'sexual Flying
Dutchman', whose predatory fornication undermines bourgeois marriage.[15]
But then he is anything but an idealized Don Juan: as in *The Norman
Conquests* (1973), where Ayckbourn's seducer is sleazy, scruffy and incapable
of even fulfilling his sexual promises. His attractiveness for the women is
merely a measure of their frustrated existence. Their marriages are so empty
that even the most degrading and transient opportunity for escape becomes
eagerly embraced. In fact, throughout *The Norman Conquests* the attack
on romantic illusion, the display of human misery and individual desperation, together with the discomforting endings in each play of the trilogy,
deliberately undermine the comic surface.

Love of course is the most traditional theme of comedy, which is also the
one genre where female characters – representing fecundity, social continuity
or redemptive forces – generally dominate the dramatic action. It is no
accident that Shaw wrote his best roles for women, and has been adopted as
a proto-feminist. In exactly the same way Ayckbourn's women characters
are always stronger than their male counterparts and partners or, when
victimized, more central. And this becomes increasingly obvious in his later
plays. Even when a woman is a mechanical robot, as in *Comic Potential*
where the central figure is an 'actoid' constructed to replace real actors in
formulaic TV sitcoms, she not only learns to be human but emerges as
both wittier and more resourceful than the young scriptwriter who teaches,
and comes to love her. Clearly modelled on Shaw's Eliza Doolittle – though
here the focus is explicitly on what it means to be human, rather than on
class distinctions, with the studio's motto being 'Nothing personal' and her
recurrent cry of 'there's no real me', while her Professor Higgins uses the

Book of Genesis to teach her to read[16] – she becomes a rebellious Eve, asserting female independence by knocking down a pimp. And the theme crystallizes in *Communicating Doors*, where a prostitute and two endangered wives join hands across the decades to change the past and save their lives, and become a literal symbol of the saving grace in female unity when they form a human chain over a hotel balcony. However, love does not fare nearly so well in Ayckbourn's plays.

Even at its most romantic and sentimental, as in *Comic Potential*, there is little chance of fulfilment since for all her newfound personal identity the robot remains trapped in her Barbie Doll mechanical body. Ayckbourn's cynical view is most explicit, as one might expect from the title, in *Things We Do For Love*, which presents a whole range of different passions: none desirable. At its lowest – literally on the three-level stage in the basement, where a pitiful loser expresses hopeless adoration of his landlady on the floor above by dressing in her cast-off clothes and painting a huge mural of her naked body on the ceiling – love is debasing and pornographic. She in turn sits rigid and alone in her soulless central flat, in retreat from her obsession with her boss, which she still harbours even though their brief affair was years in the past. For this textbook case of terminal repression, 'We all have a choice: live alone or compromise.' But her isolation crumbles when an old school-friend appears (fleeing from a violent husband) along with a new fiancé. Not only is she subjected to the friend's idolization – a continuing schoolgirl infatuation – but finds herself falling for the fiancé, even though he is the opposite of everything she believes in. Their lust, consummated upstairs (the heaven of forbidden bliss), is not only a cruel betrayal of her friend but also of herself. As she shrieks, 'You've turned me into an animal', and they beat each other up in a horrifying scene of physical battering.[17] In Noel Coward's *Private Lives* the battle of the sexes causes no damage, except to the furniture. Here the woman is covered in obvious bruises. The things we do for love are degrading, selfish and cruelly hurtful. Bedroom farce has become an extreme of domestic abuse.

Despite its popular appeal, such 'black farce' (Ayckbourn's own label for his drama) requires a sophisticated response. It plays off the expectations of the audience, revealing suffering individuals behind stock characters, or a painfully recognizable common experience in a cliché situation. The delicacy of this balance can be indicated by the way *Bedroom Farce* was received when it was staged in 1977 at a London theatre identified with re-vues and strip shows. Although the action is indeed confined to bedrooms, the different couples have no physical contact, and there are no immoral goings-on, sexually compromising situations, or even risqué jokes. The denial of expectations that had been specifically aroused by both the Feydeauesque title and the venue, meant that 'on Saturday nights it was hell; [the auditorium] was full of the Navy, screaming and whistling and shouting; "Get 'em off!" '[18]

Such manipulation of standard dramatic material, under-cutting conventional Farce, is accompanied by highly original forms of theatrical experimentation. But while always startling, Ayckbourn's innovations in stage presentation and dramatic structure are never simply arbitrary: rather they challenge the way audiences perceive what they see, as in *Man of the Moment* (1989), where the audience are continually required to re-evaluate the action before their eyes on every level of a multi-layered drama. On the surface the situation is a typical story from the tabloid press: the drowning of a one-time bank robber in his own swimming-pool on the Costa del Sol. Although it is claimed as accidental death, almost everyone present has a motive for killing him. But if it is murder, this may be entirely justified, given his past and violent personality. In addition to asking the audience to decide what the facts are, the play overturns the moral categories of hero and villain. The public enemy is now a public benefactor, having made a career as a TV personality influencing misguided youths away from crime and donating his fees to charity. The hero who tackled him single-handed during the hold-up is a complete nonentity, grateful to the man who disfigured the girl he has married (since he was unable to compete with the boys attracted to her when she was beautiful) and indeed responsible for her shooting, which was caused by his intervention. Yet even this set-up is overturned. Instead of being a confrontation between two opposing people staged for a television show, all the characters are revealed to be actors, making a film about the criminal's death. Nothing that we have watched is real.

Ayckbourn achieves the same effect in other plays by varying the dramatic context or structure in strikingly unusual ways. At its simplest normal expectations are reversed, as in *Absurd Person Singular* where the foreground party of each Act is off-stage and the focus is on what conventionally remains unseen in such a context: the kitchen. Or, in *Things We Do For Love*, where the action takes place between three apartments in a house, we see only the head and shoulders of the transvestite postman in the basement and just the feet of the lovers upstairs. This technique is extended by presenting simultaneous actions in different settings that coexist on the same stage (*Bedroom Farce*) – or where different time frames overlap as with *How the Other Half Loves* (1969), in which two separate dinner tables on consecutive evenings merge to illuminate class contrasts by juxtaposition. In several other works the same action or time frame is divided between different plays. So a trilogy like *The Norman Conquests* (1973) separates out the interconnected events of a single weekend in the same family house, each piece showing events in a different location – dining room, living room, garden – while in the double play *House* and *Garden* (1999), performed simultaneously in real time on neighbouring stages in Ayckbourn's home theatre at Scarborough and (in 2000) at the National Theatre, every exit from one setting is an entry into the other, giving a double perspective that illustrates how much lies beneath an everyday surface, impinging on it unseen with disintegrating effect.

Playing with time also becomes a plot device. In *Communicating Doors*, where a hotel closet leads not to the next room but to the past, carrying the characters from 2014 to 1994 (the date of the performance) then back to 1974, allowing the characters to avoid a dystopian future by changing the past. Similarly the action of *Time of My Life* splits into three, with one couple gradually working their way back to the first time they met, and a second couple moving forward to the break-up of their marriage, ending with the whole family at the beginning of the party we had been watching at the start of the play. The effect here, as in J.B. Priestley's *Time and the Conways*, reveals the frailty of human happiness – and indeed Ayckbourn paid specific tribute to Priestley in his programme-note for the 1993 London production.

Ayckbourn also expands such surrealistic openings-out of time and space (with all their comic potential) into multiple actions. In *Sisterly Feelings* (1979) and *Intimate Exchanges* (1983) different combinations of events and relationships depend on (supposedly spontaneous) choices made by the actors during any given performance – and in one of his children's enter-tainments, *Mr A's Amazing Maze Plays* (1993), the audience vote for which route the characters should take. The text of *Sisterly Feelings* offers four variations, depending on the toss of a coin in the prologue and a decision by either of the sisters during the action. From there, Ayckbourn went on to the ultimate in complexity with *Intimate Exchanges*. Alternative plots are developed 'from one tiny little moment – whether a woman decides to smoke a cigarette or not – into two separate scenes, four choices of third scene, eight choices of fourth and sixteen choices of fifth scene'.[19] In all of these permutations, further complexity is added by having the two actors play multiple roles.

As with all Ayckbourn's other plays, the theatrical experimentation is directly related to the central issues. 'That particular device' of flipping a coin was selected for *Sisterly Feelings* 'precisely because [the play] was about choice', while the multiplying variations of *Intimate Exchanges* are intended to exemplify the infinite possibilities for change in people's lives. At the same time, what each play really proves is, as Ayckbourn acknowledged, the opposite: that 'circumstances did it . . .' In writing, the different plots were set down, and 'it was only afterwards that one put on the decision-making process'. And, in fact – denying the apparent value put on free will – 'it doesn't make all that much bloody difference anyway', since the only real switches are in which character pairs off with whom, not in the quality of the eventual relationship. This underlying determinism in the structure of both plays was also reflected in production, where in practice the characters' choices had to be pre-selected for the actors before the curtain went up. So in *Sisterly Feelings* one of the different variations was played in turn for each of four performances, with only the fifth night being 'free' in the sense of the actors deciding which alternatives to take as they played.[20] As a result, instead of actual freedom, what each play demonstrated was the freewheeling scope of theatre itself.

Michael Frayn (1933–)

CHECKLIST OF FRAYN'S MAJOR PLAYS

The Two of Us, 1970	*Look, Look*, 1990
Alphabetical Order, 1975	*Here*, 1993
Donkeys' Years, 1976	*Now You Know*, 1995
Clouds, 1976	*Copenhagen*, 1998
Liberty Hall, 1979	*Alarms and Excursions*, 1998
Noises Off, 1982	

Frayn may have written fewer plays than Ayckbourn – he has a double life as a journalist, working for the *Guardian* and the *Observer*, as well as doing a series of television documentaries for the BBC, writing novels and screenplays (including a highly successful vehicle for John Cleese of Monty Python fame, *Clockwise*) – but he forms part of the same movement in post-political British comedy. Even when he deals highly political topics, his emphasis remains on the personal. So for instance the plot of *Now You Know* (adapted from one of his novels) turns on the leak of a secret report proving that the Government has lied about a case of racist police brutality and covered up the murder of a black immigrant: very much like the climatic event in Brenton and Hare's play *Pravda*. Yet here the leaked document is little more than a fulcrum to expose the fact that everyone has private secrets as well as prejudices and shows that the sort of openness demanded in the public sphere can only be disastrous when applied to individual relationships. Indeed the underlying content of his comedies is comparable to Ayckbourn, although defined in more universal terms so that his drama sometimes comes to seem an illustration of general concepts about life.

According to Frayn, what his plays 'are all about . . . is the way in which we impose our ideas upon the world around us. In *Alphabetical Order* it is by classification, in *Make and Break* by consumption'; and he has returned to this theme in *Constructions*, a collection of philosophical essays focused on the way we attempt to find meaningful order in the chaos of chance events. As this implies, Frayn's comedy is highly intellectual; and by comparison with Ayckbourn, Frayn seldom resorts to futuristic fantasy. Instead he has pointed to recognition as the basis for humour, where a play makes 'audiences . . . laugh because of its relevance to [their] own problems'.[21] And even when – as in one of his latest plays, *Copenhagen* (1998) – the characters are all presented as dead, in an afterlife of memory, Frayn takes pains to justify the historical accuracy of the action.

Where Ayckbourn typically focuses on the family, Frayn deals with organizations: the news media, a manufacturing industry, commercial theatre, or by extension the scientific community. A more explicit microcosm of contemporary society than Ayckbourn's middle-class homes, the newspaper library of *Alphabetical Order* (1975) is overwhelmed by the accretion of trivia in the piles of yellowing newsprint. While the instant redundancy of all the facts recorded in these clippings satirizes the illusory nature of what our news-fixated culture considers important, the confusion of the library files is presented as organic: a sign of individualism surviving even in what is – taking newspaper slang literally – a morgue. So (as in Ayckbourn's *Absurd Person Singular*) any attempt to impose order is revealed as a compulsive obsession. It dehumanizes an idealistic and attractive young woman, newly hired as assistant librarian, whose instinct for tidiness becomes a way of taking control. Gradually undermining the position of her unmethodical superior, her organization of the clippings carries over into the personal lives of the reporters. She institutes rules about how they use the material, cajoles them into dressing (and thinking) respectably, and wins over the most intellectually nonconformist among them when she becomes his lover.

Everything she does is in response to their request (although it goes beyond what she was hired for) and can be justified as being for their own good). But, by imposing normal standards of behaviour, she reduces these incompetent but individualistic drones to slaves of the system. As the aging message-boy comments, looking at the reformed and now apathetic reporters, 'People get what they've always wanted, and what they've always wanted turns out to be not what they want at all.'[22]

The same is true for the monstrous young woman – and even for the audience. At first she appears a figure of sanity, to be applauded in bringing cleanliness and order to the chaos. Once the priggishness and ambition behind her crusade for greater efficiency becomes clear, we long for her comeuppance. However, just when she reaches her goal of complete dominance, the announcement comes that the newspaper has been closed down, bankrupted by its previous ineptitude. Then she becomes, momentarily, an object of pity. On the other hand, the down-trodden reporters' reaction to unemployment is to celebrate their liberation by turning her carefully organized files into confetti:

LUCY We've been collecting waste paper all these years. (*She sweeps the cuttings out of John's folder*) . . .
WALLY (*singing*) Over my shoulder goes Vietnam!
GEOFFREY Over my shoulder goes Sex!
NORA Vandalism! I must say, this is rather fun!

Beyond being a rejection of the organizing pressures that the young librarian stands for, the reporters' 'vandalism' is an attack on the larger political or moral categories that shape modern life. The values promoted by social structures, and represented by the kind of event reported in the press, are exposed as no more than 'dead leaves'.[23] But this anarchic revolt is capped by a real revolution, when the young librarian persuades the staff to run the paper themselves. Accusing them of hurting her maliciously, in destroying what she has invested so much time and effort in creating on their behalf, she uses guilt feelings to blackmail them into a management takeover. There is no place for spontaneity, and no escape once they have become managers of the system that imprisons them.

The outcome of the comedy is as bleak as in any of Ayckbourn's plays; and Frayn's treatment of humour is no less ambiguous. Following on from Beckett, laughter is just as suspect as it is in Barnes or Griffiths, although Frayn's comic treatment avoids their polemic edge. When Frayn's characters laugh, as for instance in *Alphabetical Order*, their reaction follows his theory in signalling that they have suddenly come to recognize their predicament – but it is explicitly presented as a totally inappropriate response to their predicament:

LUCY (... *starts to laugh again*) ... I'm sorry. It's not funny!
NORA It's not at all funny.
JOHN It's what one might call tragic irony. (*He starts to laugh.*)[24]

By extension the audience's laughter is equally inappropriate, and this challenge is reinforced by the way Frayn experiments with stage presentation to subvert audience expectations and question they way they perceive what they are watching.

For instance in *Look, Look* (1990) – which extends the theatrical critique of *Noises Off* – spectators are faced with an on-stage audience apparently watching them, although it turns out that they are looking at a play-within-the-play. However startling to the reviewers, who compared *Look, Look* to Pirandello, this mirror image of the spectators is another bow to theatrical tradition as a reprise of a celebrated Victorian *coup de théâtre*, the scene in Sir Henry Irving's *Corsican Brothers* where the 1890s audience were presented with an accurate copy of the Lyceum Theatre in which they were seated, complete with spectators.

As a technique this sort of experimentation is very similar to Ayckbourn, but there is less sense of mechanical trickery and sleight of hand, since Frayn's often highly unconventional staging is so closely related to the subjects of his plays: the way news reportage categorizes events (*Alphabetical Order*), or the difference between socialist and capitalist views of the world – as in *Clouds* (1976), which reflects Frayn's disorienting experiences as a journalist in Cuba. As this implies, Frayn's dramatic structure is designed to echo psychological states; and the advertising slogan of the building firm that manufactures prefabricated houses in *Make and Break* (1977) as '*TOTAL INTERNAL ENVIRONMENT*' could stand as a motto for his drama as a whole.[25] Far more than Ayckbourn, Frayn's plays focus on the nature of art itself and the way drama, or other forms of literature, impinges on the world – as in *Liberty Hall* (1979), where a writers' collective takes over the Queen's residence at Balmoral Castle. His scenic experiments are also intended as an overt expression of the intellectual concepts of the plays themselves: most obviously in *Here* where a blank white box on the stage represents the *tabula rasa* of young lovers at the beginning of their relationship, or *Copenhagen*, with isolated characters circling each other in limbo, reflecting the structure of an atom.

His later comedies are increasingly philosophical, and *Copenhagen* (1998) – while it has a happy ending of a sort, and focuses on exactly the same scientific theories as Stoppard's *Hapgood* ten years earlier – is straight intellectual drama. The characters of *Here* (1993) are tormented by the search for authenticity and by the endless possibilities of life, unable to make decisions about the furnishing of their empty flat since possessions represent experience. Everything becomes a metaphysical discussion; and as one cries, they are going round in circles, to the extent that several critics commented that they made Hamlet look like a model of decisiveness, while at least two of the reviews were presented in the form of discussions. *Now You Know* (1995) resolves into a series of debates about honesty versus secrecy, while *Alarms and Excursions* offered a series of vignettes on the dehumanization of life by modern technology, with even the communications industry making any attempt at communicating impossible. One reviewer even called on the philosophy of Berkeley and Kant to explain the deeper implications of the farce, since *Copenhagen* – produced just four months before – had so firmly established Frayn's reputation as a playwright of ideas.

Revolving around Heisenberg's uncertainty principle and Bohr's theory of complementarity, which together with the Copenhagen Interpretation of quantum mechanics provided the basis for nuclear physics, every aspect of the play is designed to embody the concept of the universe defined by modern science. The characters responsible for ushering in the atomic age are seen in terms of their own theories. They 'live inside an atom', and as Heisenberg remarks:

Copenhagen is an atom. Margrethe [Bohr's wife, who transcribed all his theories] is its nucleus ... Bohr's an electron. He's wandering about the city ... I'm a photon. A quantum of light. I'm dispatched into the darkness to find Bohr. And I succeed, because I manage to collide with him.[26]

Even their status as ghosts parallels Schrödinger's imaginary cat, alive and dead at the same time.

Complementarity is constantly used to define a theme in which 'physics ... is also politics' and the two opposing scientists are mirror images of each other, while the Uncertainty Principle (or in the more precise term Frayn suggests in his Postscript to the play, indeterminability) correlates to memory – Heisenberg and Bohr cannot even agree whether they spoke together in German, Danish or English; and when both conclude they did their best work together, Margrethe asserts that each made their fundamental discoveries while alone. Uncertainty also defines the central action, a visit made by Heisenberg to his old mentor Bohr in September 1941 during the German occupation of Denmark: potentially a crucial turning-point in the Second World War, and much discussed by historians, but about which tantalizingly little is known for sure.

This visit is replayed in a series of inconclusive variations by the remembering ghosts of the long-dead protagonists, whose afterlife is like the half-life of radiation. The key question is Heisenberg's motive as the leader of the Nazi nuclear programme. Was he looking for Bohr's sanction to develop an atomic bomb – trying to get an agreement through Bohr's contacts in the American scientific community, that if he avoided working on it for Germany then the Allies would refrain too – or more subtly, subconsciously hoping that Bohr would make the moral choice for him by either showing him the solution (which he may have known but suppressed) to a mathematical problem that would make fission practicable, or by not doing so justify his (possibly willed) blind spot and thus deny Hitler such a weapon? Nothing can be determined with certainty, except that these particular scientists had the power of God to decide the fate of all the two thousand million people in the world, since following the principles of quantum physics the act of observing any event changes its nature. And anyone's motives, particularly Heisenberg's given the contradictory pressures he was under during the war, are equated with the theory of light, which is either (or both) a wave or a particle depending which you test for. Still, just as an electron can only be tracked by its effects, so the survival of London, Paris, Amsterdam – which would have been targeted as the Allies advanced, and utterly destroyed if Hitler had the atomic bomb to hand – can be seen as the effects of Heisenberg's meeting with Bohr. As Frayn puts it in the final words of the play:

Our children, and our children's children. Preserved, just possibly, by one short moment in Copenhagen. By some event that will never quite be located or defined. By that final core of uncertainty at the heart of things.

And the fact that Heisenberg apparently never considered tackling the crucial mathematical equation is represented as a reversed image of an atomic explosion, in which his 'tiny failure' had saving consequences that doubled and redoubled exactly like the chain reaction of nuclear fission, but with the opposite effect. This is also contrasted with the fact that the Allies did develop the atomic bomb and use it to destroy Japanese cities.

The play was given added coincidental relevance by opening within hours of the announcement that Pakistan had just tested its first atomic bomb. But what makes *Copenhagen* so striking is the way Frayn transmutes physics into the human dimension. As Bohr says it is the philosophical implications of science that matter – the same is true for Frayn himself, one of his earliest books being titled *Against Entropy* (1967) – and the play demonstrates that quantum physics have 'put men back at the center of the universe'. Reversing the traditional subordination of people to an omnipotent God or the determinism of classical mechanics, the fact that on a subatomic level observation itself changes reality means the universe is not objective. It exists only 'within the limits determined by our relationship with it. Only through the understanding lodged inside the human head'. Frayn also suggests this should lead to a 'new quantum ethics', recognizing that applied (as here in the play) to people, the Uncertainty Principle makes standard moral judgements unjustifiable. There is no attempt to deny the 'darkness inside the human soul' identified with Hamlet's Elsinore.[27] Yet paradoxically in the face of its discussion of Fascist tyranny, the Holocaust, and the nightmare of the Atomic Bomb, the play affirms the potential of individuals.

It also challenges the whole traditional basis of drama. If, following the principles of particle physics, we can only be aware of our own existence through observing the reactions of others to our presence, while uncertainty means that motivation cannot be determined even by ourselves, then all conventional characterization is false. On all levels *Copenhagen* is very much a play for the contemporary age. Much like Stoppard's *Arcadia*, it not only addresses modern science but is structured to express a new vision of life that corresponds to the latest scientific principles.

Notes

1 Ayckbourn, cited in Ian Watson, *Conversations with Ayckbourn*, London, 1981, pp. 108–9; Frayn, *Plays: One*, London, 1985, p. viii.
2 Frayn, *Plays: One*, London, 1985, p. 376.
3 *Ibid.*, p. xiv.
4 *A Chorus of Disapproval*, London, 1986, p. 33.
5 *Ibid.*, p. iv.
6 *Ibid.*, pp. 38, 33–4.
7 Sir Peter Hall, *The Sunday Times*, 1 June 1986, p. 42.
8 *The Sunday Times*, 13 February 1994.
9 *Conversations with Ayckbourn*, p. 115.
10 Ayckbourn, *Three Plays*, London, 1977, p. 112.
11 Cited in *The Daily Telegraph*, 5 March 1998.
12 Ayckbourn, *Three Plays*, pp. 37, 93.
13 Ayckbourn, *Just Between Ourselves*, London, 1978, p. 3.

14 Beckett, *The Bookman*, LXXXVI, 1934 (reprinted in *Sean O'Casey: a Collection of Critical Essays*, ed. Thomas Kilroy, Prentice Hall, 1975).

15 Ayckbourn, *Three Plays*, p. 47.

16 Ayckbourn, *Comic Potential*, London & New York, 1999, pp. 50, 108, 99.

17 Ayckbourn, *Things we do for Love*, London & New York, 1998, pp. 11, 112.

18 *Conversations with Ayckbourn*, pp. 124 & 162.

19 Ayckbourn, cited in Michael Billington, *Alan Ayckbourn*, New York, 1983, p. 166.

20 *Conversations with Ayckbourn*, pp. 155, 153.

21 Frayn, *Plays: One*, pp. x, xiii; see also *Constructions*, London, 1974.

22 Frayn, *Plays: One*, p. 52.

23 *Ibid.*, pp. 68–9.

24 *Ibid.*, p. 63.

25 *Ibid.*, p. 257.

26 Frayn, *Copenhagen*, London, 1998, pp. 60, 70–1.

27 *Ibid.*, pp. 73–4, 94, 60.

4.9 Tom Stoppard (1937–): theatricality and the comedy of ideas

CHECKLIST FOR STOPPARD'S MAJOR PLAYS

Rosencrantz and Guildenstern are Dead, 1966

Enter a Free Man 1968,

Jumpers, 1972

Travesties, 1974

Night and Day, 1978

The Real Thing, 1982

Hapgood, 1988

Arcadia, 1993

Indian Ink, 1995

The Invention of Love, 1997

Tom Stoppard has become without doubt the most interesting and respected English comic dramatist writing today. Like Harold Pinter's, his plays were originally seen as belonging to the Theatre of the Absurd, although their overt theatricality and technical experimentation anticipate the developments in the comedy of Alan Ayckbourn – whose first major success occurred within a year of Stoppard's breakthrough in 1966. This was also the year Joe Orton's *Loot* was performed. Unlike Ayckbourn or Orton, however, Stoppard's focus is consistently metaphysical. Like Frayn, his drama deals with philosophical issues rather than social problems (Ayckbourn), or sexual polemics (Orton); and the intellectual nature of his comedy make Stoppard very much the contemporary equivalent of Shaw.

In this his work is comparable with Pinter, whose early plays centred around such questions as the relationship between 'the Necessary and the Possible' or 'being and non-being'.[1] But Stoppard's highly distinctive tone is very different from Pinter's style. Where Pinter's 'Comedy of Menace' works through revealing sinister undercurrents in everyday situations and verbal elusiveness, Stoppard uses verbal wit, visual humour and physical farce to illustrate clearly defined topics: free will versus fate; the existence of God; the function of art; the nature of freedom and the responsibility of the press; the existential implications of modern physics. The virtuoso dialogue of his plays and the brilliant inventiveness of their theatricality have tended to obscure the serious intentions underlying his comedy, with the result that when (like Pinter) overtly political themes surfaced in Stoppard's work after *Every Good Boy Deserves Favour* (1977), this was taken as an aberration or a radically new departure.

This play is explicitly based on an actual case of a Russian dissident in a psychiatric prison – while the television play *Professional Foul* (1978), with which it is published, was written for Amnesty International's Prisoner of Conscience Year, and reflects the 1977 arrest of the playwright (and future President) Václav Havel for petitioning the Czech government to obey the Helsinki Agreement on human rights which Czechoslovakia had signed. Both pieces also seemed to mark a change in being directly linked to Stoppard's background as the son of a Czechoslovakian doctor (only naturalized as English when his mother remarried in 1946 after his father had been killed by the Japanese in Singapore). Yet the fantastical juxtaposition of philosophy and acrobats in a typical earlier Stoppard comedy, such as *Jumpers* (1972), is also found here in the incongruity between these subjects and the controlling images: an orchestra (*Every Good Boy* was commissioned by André Previn for performance with the London Symphony Orchestra), and a football match. In the same way Stoppard had used a documentary basis in *Travesties* (1974), where James Joyce's lawsuit over an amateur theatrical production in Switzerland is combined with Lenin's departure for the Finland Station and the First World War.

Again as with Pinter, Samuel Beckett's influence on Stoppard has been over-emphasized. In particular, he has been typecast by the play that made him a major dramatist overnight: *Rosencrantz and Guildenstern are Dead* (1966, NT, 1967). It was labelled 'a theatrical parasite, feeding off *Hamlet*, *Waiting for Godot*, and *Six Characters in Search of an Author* – Shakespeare provides the characters, Pirandello the technique, and Beckett the tone'.[2] Although *Rosencrantz and Guildenstern are Dead* was not imitating

Shakespeare or Beckett, but provided a critique of both by conflating them, this view influenced the reception of Stoppard's following plays.

In fact, Beckett's influence is less direct than even Stoppard's ironically backhanded tribute at the end of *Jumpers* suggests. 'No laughter is sad and many tears are joyful. At the graveside the undertaker doffs his top hat and impregnates the prettiest mourner. Wham, bam, thank you Sam.' Not only is this an explicit reversal of Beckett's perspective – 'For each one who begins to weep somewhere else another stops. The same is true of the laugh', so that 'Nothing is funnier than unhappiness' – it changes the bleak existentialism of 'Astride of a grave and a difficult birth. Down in the hole, lingeringly, the grave-digger puts on the forceps' into a comic affirmation of human vitality.[3] The reference to *Waiting for Godot* is parodistic. For Stoppard the value of Beckett was that he redefined the theatrical experience (discussed above, p. 307). The impact of John Osborne's *Look Back in Anger* in 1956 motivated the younger authors of the 1960s to write for the stage (see above, p. 86) – but it was Beckett's plays which were stylistically crucial to the revolution in English drama that followed. They had a liberating effect, opening up new possibilities to the stage.

This is reflected in the way Stoppard reviewed Beckett's work in his early career as journalist. Stoppard's perception of the way Jack MacGowran's one-man compendium of Beckett (*Beginning to End*, 1962) portrayed man 'caught between memory and desire. Everything is cancelled out' could well describe the structure of his own play *Travesties* (1974). Similarly, Stoppard's appreciation of the way 'in Beckett everything counts, nothing is arbitrary' carries through to become the basis of his own style. Yet Stoppard's reviews clearly reject the minimalism inherent in Beckett's vision, as with his criticism of *Happy Days* (1961): 'The statement has left theatre behind . . . dramatically it is not enough'.[4] There is a decisive difference in both Stoppard's choice of dramatic material, and the way he treats it.

More specifically relevant to Stoppard's approach is his appreciation of the way Richard Attenborough's film *The Angry Silence* blended 'entertainment and education as completely as a row of chorus girls explaining Einstein's theory of light'.[5] This not only points to the characteristic combination of philosophically significant issues with intellectually trivial theatrical ingredients: an incongruity that itself is the basis for much of the comedy in Stoppard's plays. It is also picked up in specific stage images that span his career. Ros and Guil (the modern, democratic and clown-like foreshortening of Shakespeare's Rosencrantz and Guildenstern) punctuate speculations on determinism by spinning coins. The juxtaposition of Einstein and chorus girls is repeated almost literally when Lenin's theory of value is expounded by a stripper in *Travesties*, and with variation in *Hapgood* (1988) where the theory of light is explained by glamorous spies. Similarly in *Jumpers* the intellectual gymnastics of moral philosophy are accompanied by a pyramid of acrobats, who also form a chorus line background for song-and-dance acts revolving around the significance of the first Moon Landing, together (again) with a still more eye-catching strip-tease act – performed on a swing.

Other models can be seen in Stoppard's earliest play, *Enter a Free Man* (TV, 1963 – first staged in 1968), which Stoppard referred to as 'The Flowering Death of a Salesman'. An essay in play-writing before the development of his idiosyncratic style, its characters and situation are drawn from naturalistic comedy and expressionistic social drama – specifically Arthur Miller's attack on the destructive dreams imposed by an inhuman, materialistic system, and Robert Bolt's *Flowering Cherry* (1958) – a play dealing with a conformist, who sees himself as an anarchistic rebel, but is incapable of living up to his fantasy. Although Stoppard almost immediately moved away from the naturalism of this 'meet-the-family' type of drama, *Enter a Free Man* establishes the basic elements of his comedy.

The quality of imagination in Stoppard's play comes from the Ben Travers tradition of intellectual farce celebrating eccentricity as a national charac-teristic, crossed with the arcane mechanical fantasy of Heath Robinson or Rowland Emmett drawings – which was also picked up by John Whiting's *A Penny for a Song* (1952). Unable to shed his chains, Stoppard's 'Free Man' is obsessed with impracticable inventions: a reusable envelope (gum on both sides of the flap), an alarm clock hooked up to a tape-recording of 'Rule Britannia', or a water-cooled machine-gun that will boil tea for the soldiers while it is being fired. The original title, *A Walk on Water*, reflects his nature as a 'holy fool' – described by Stoppard as 'unsinkable, despite the slow leak' – but any attempt to translate his imaginative liberty into real life is disastrous. The network of pipes installed in his living room to water the potted plants whenever it rains, which works on the 'Sponge Principle', floods the house because the only mechanism installed is one that turns the system on.

Stoppard's 'Free Man' would be at home in the Absurdist comedy of N.F. Simpson's *One Way Pendulum* (1959), where the lunatic Groomkirby family are each attempting to put a different personal obsession into practice. The cowed Mr Groomkirby, who longs for authority, is building a life-size Old Bailey courtroom inside his tiny semi-detached council house, so that he can preside as a judge. His death-fixated son is training Speak-Your-Weight machines to sing the 'Hallelujah Chorus' – planning to use them in a concert at the North Pole, and so tilt the globe by the weight of people attracted there, starting a new ice age and thus giving him a legitimate excuse to wear black in perpetual mourning for his victims. In Simpson's play these fantasies take over reality in Act II, merging in a dream-world, where the son is on trial before his hanging-judge father for mass-murder, while the mother's matter-of-fact acceptance of her family's oddities makes normality itself seem even more irrational.

By contrast, in *Enter a Free Man* realism dominates the second Act, requiring us to see human pathos in the previously two-dimensional figures. Although the switch in focus pulls this first play of Stoppard's apart, the mix of zany fantasy and realistic reference becomes characteristic of his work – and points to a fundamental difference with N.F. Simpson's Absurdism. Where Simpson's characters are typical of the lunatic world they inhabit, Stoppard's 'Free Man' is the outsider, whose idiosyncratic individualism challenges a conformist society that is unable to accommodate it. Stoppard's later plays extend and develop Simpson's brand of exaggerated logic. But it is always set against social norms, and in the context of recognizable or even documentary actuality: the carnage of the First World War and the Russian Revolution in *Travesties*, astronauts and the manipulation of democracy by ideologues in *Jumpers*, political scandal in *Dirty Linen* (1976), spy trials and Star Wars research in *Hapgood*, Lord Byron and the switch from Neo-Classical to Romantic sensibility at the beginning of the Nineteenth Century in *Arcadia* (1993), the British Raj in *Indian Ink* (1995).

Stoppard's short early piece *After Magritte* (1970) illustrates the technique. The opening tableau is bizarrely surrealist. In a bare room with all the furniture piled up against the door, an old woman lies on an ironing board, a black bathing-cap on her head and covered in a towel, with a bowler hat on her stomach and one foot resting against the surface of a steam-iron. A girl in a ball-gown crawls nose-down across the floor; and a half-naked man in thigh-length waders is blowing out a light bulb; while a policeman peers in through the window. As the family set the room to rights, what had appeared absurd is revealed to be the result of perfectly ordinary behaviour. The mother, stretched out on the ironing board because of a bad back, is about to take a bath; the girl is picking up ball-bearings scattered over the floor from the broken counter-weight of the light fixture; her husband is stripped to the waist because his shirt is about to be ironed, and he has donned waders to avoid electrocuting himself while plugging the iron into the light-socket. He is blowing on the lightbulb because it is too hot to unscrew; and the furniture has been cleared out of the way because he and his wife have been practising for a professional dance competition, which explains her elaborate dress.

While moving the furniture back into place, however, the family argue about a retrospective exhibition of Magritte's paintings (mounted at the Tate in 1969), which they dismiss as 'rubbish' on the grounds that it 'just wasn't life-like', although they are quite ready to accept the most extraordinary explanations for something that happened in the street as they left the art gallery. The woman claims to have been threatened with a cricket bat by an escaped convict in striped prison clothes with his face covered by a surgical mask and a black visor, carrying a stolen handbag and playing hopscotch in the road. Each of the others has seen something different: the criminal was a one-legged invalid hobbling on a cane, with a beard and the black spectacles of the blind, carrying a tortoise – or a football player in a striped team shirt, with shaving cream on his face and a football in his hand.

The two situations come together with the entry of the eponymously named PC Holmes and Inspector Foot, who in turn each have their own theories about the scene they observed through the window.

> FOOT (*without punctuation*) I have reason to believe that within the last hour in this room you performed without anaesthetic an illegal operation on a bald nigger minstrel about five-foot-two or Pakistani and that is only the beginning![6]

A fuse blows, leaving the characters literally as well as intellectually in the dark; and while PC Holmes is searching for the fuse-box, the Inspector confides in the audience that he himself was the man in the street. Once more the explanation is 'normal' – to the point of exaggeration. While shaving he noticed that the meter by which the family's car was parked had expired. Wanting to improve the public image of the Police, he dashed out of his home, picking up his wife's purse for change to put in the meter and (since it was raining) an umbrella that he waved to attract their attention. In his hurry he had jammed both feet into the same leg of his pyjamas; and he was wearing sunglasses because of a headache.

When the light comes back on, PC Holmes finds the family of 'suspects' and his Inspector in yet another set of bizarre positions – which appears as extraordinary to him as the original tableau had to the audience. The contention that 'there is obviously a rational explanation for everything', is demonstrated by illustrating that 'the activities in this room have been broadly speaking of a mundane and domestic nature bordering on cliché'.[7] Nothing is stranger than reality.

Like much of Stoppard's work, the play takes its title literally. It is 'After Magritte' both since everything that happens follows a viewing of the Magritte exhibition, and because the opening and closing tableaux are modelled on Magritte's classic painting *l'Assassin menacé*. It is also 'After Magritte' in the sense of commenting on his pictures. While making the audience question the logic of normality, the outcome shows Surrealism as an accurate representation of everyday activities. Indeed Stoppard has emphasized that the background situation

> was based on fact . . . somebody I know had a couple of peacocks in the garden, and one escaped while he was shaving . . . he had to cross a main road to catch it, and he was standing in his pyjamas with shaving cream on his face holding a peacock when the traffic started going by.[8]

The point is that what we take to be reality is only a mind set. Even the most extravagantly fantastic spectacle turns out to be ordinary once the context is understood. This is the key to Stoppard's approach; and *After Magritte* also sets the focus on perception that continues to be central in Stoppard's work from the 1960s to his most recent play, *The Invention of Love* (1997), and is the main theme in *Hapgood*. Indeed exactly the same image is used in *Jumpers*, where a police inspector is faced with '*a man holding a bow-and-arrow in one hand and a tortoise in the other, his face covered in shaving foam*'.[9] Challenging the way we see what we see underlies the displays of overt theatricality that are the hallmark of his plays. Hence their tendency – as again in *After Magritte* – to take literature or painting, rather than life, as their point of reference. Although this is sometimes criticized as a retreat into artifice, in fact it is a method of exploring the way art conditions society's behaviour through its ability to define reality.

The theme is already clear in *Rosencrantz and Guildenstern* (1966). If the title-figures are at first reminiscent of Beckett's clown-like tramps, '*passing time in a place without any visible character*', the Beckettian explanation for their predicament – that 'time has stopped dead' – is the only rationale explicitly rejected.[10] They may repeatedly find themselves waiting for Hamlet; but Hamlet is hardly Godot. The problem is their inability to escape him, not his failure to appear. Similarly, they may look like the minor figures from Shakespeare; but they are outsiders in the world of *Hamlet*, confused by its premises, and with an identifiably modern sensibility. So, instead of locating

Ros and Guil historically, their Elizabethan dress becomes literally a costume;
and the continual theatrical references in the dialogue make their context
the stage, not a social milieu.

Thus the dominating element in the action is not the plots and coun-
terplots of Claudius and Hamlet, in which they become enmeshed, but
the penniless troupe of travelling players whom they meet on their way to
Elsinore. Hailed as 'An audience!' by these actors, Ros and Guil later find
themselves in the same position of passive onlookers at the court. When they
do become participants in the 'plot' – whether of *Hamlet* or the Players –
they acknowledge their status as 'actors', performing for a public, since they
explicitly recognize the presence of (contemporary) spectators in the auditorium. For example, when the Player-King – unable to sell them a theatrical
performance and having lost at gambling with Guil – offers his 'Queen' to
pay the debt, the innuendo is based on the Elizabethan convention of a boy
actor taking female roles:

GUIL *looks around, at the audience.*
GUIL You and I, Alfred – we could create a dramatic precedent here . . . [11]

And this theatricality is in a very real sense the subject of Stoppard's play.

The opening sequence, where tossed coins invariably turn up 'heads' in a
brilliantly extended running joke, establishes the arbitrary nature of Ros and
Guil's universe. Here neither statistical laws of probability and diminishing
returns, nor economic principles like self-interest and the redistribution of
wealth, apply. The explanations they are left with are 'divine intervention',
or alternatively that 'within un-, sub-, or supernatural forces *the probability*
is that the law of probability will not operate as a factor'. But the metaphor
of the stage has already been established: 'GUIL (*flipping a coin*) There is
an art to the building up of suspense.'[12] They are literally characters from a
play, whose fate is already known to all the audience. Theirs is not the real
universe but the artificial world of drama, a point emphasized by the way
the play has been produced.

The original National Theatre staging used the same costumes for the
court that had been used for its opening production of *Hamlet* in 1963.
But the contrast with the contemporary attitudes of Ros and Guil and the
modern tone of their dialogue, showed up the elaborate court costumes
of the interpolated *Hamlet* scenes as exaggeratedly artificial. It also made
the speeches lifted from Shakespeare sound like phoney rhetoric: an effect
emphasized by speeding up the delivery of the lines as the court swept on
and off the stage.

Specifically, the context that Ros and Guil find themselves in is the drama of 'the blood, love and rhetoric school', in which the travelling players specialize:

Tragedy, sir. Deaths and disclosures, universal and particular, denouements both unexpected and inexorable, transvestite melodrama on all levels including the suggestive. We transport you into a world of intrigue and illusion . . .

Hamlet, of course, is one of these 'homicidal classics'.[13] What makes it particularly appropriate for Stoppard's purpose is the intellectual doubting of Shakespeare's hero that led the critic Jan Kott to call Hamlet 'our contemporary', together with the ambiguity in its treatment of predestination and providence.

It is the concept of fate that elevates the otherwise melodramatic action of 'homicidal classics' into tragedy. This imposes a moral logic on even the bleakest aspects of existence, thus transforming death into an affirmation of order. (Conversely it was the absence of any pattern of poetic justice that made *King Lear* 'too painful to be endured' for a traditionalist such as Dr Johnson.) The traditional tragic vision is not just a dramatic convention, it justifies the most disastrous conditions of life and presents human sacrifice as admirable. It is also inherently élitist in focusing exclusively on the sufferings of the powerful, privileging kings and queens over the common people, whose deaths are generally irrelevant. Although Stoppard later denied that he had any particular theme in mind – 'That's why, when the play appeared, it got subjected to so many different kinds of interpretation, all of them plausible, but none of them calculated' – these values are specifically what *Rosencrantz and Guildenstern* attacks.[14]

Stoppard reverses the traditional perspective of tragedy, turning the most minor figures in Shakespeare's play into the central focus, and shows their deaths as farcically senseless and unjust. The consistent topic of the play is introduced by the Players who (being the actors performing it) already know its ending, and so speak from 'Precedent':

GUIL Chance, then.
PLAYER Or fate.

Actors – playing on the word's double meaning as 'stage performers' and 'doers' – are 'the opposite of people'. As represented by dramatic characters like Ros and Guil, real people cannot determine their own destiny. The arbitrariness of their situation leads to the conclusion that 'We've been caught up. Your smallest action sets off another somewhere else and is set off by it . . . There's a logic at work – it's all being done for you, don't worry'.[15]

The true significance of this capsule definition of the tragic net is then provided in the central sequence, when the Players illustrate Ros and Guil's fate (in the sense of final outcome). As they explain:

PLAYER Do you call that an ending? – with practically everyone on his feet? My goodness, no – over your dead body.

GUIL How am I supposed to take that?

PLAYER Lying down . . . There's a design at work in all art . . . Events must play themselves out to aesthetic, moral and logical conclusion.

GUIL And what's that, in this case?

PLAYER It never varies – we aim at the point where everyone who is marked for death dies . . . Between 'just deserts' and 'tragic irony' we are given quite a lot of scope for our particular talent . . .

GUIL Who decides?

PLAYER *Decides? It is written* . . . We're tragedians, you see. We follow directions – there is no *choice* involved. The bad end unhappily, the good unluckily. That is what tragedy means.

Following this line, fate is not the expression of providence. The apparent moral logic of a tragedy is purely aesthetic; and the *deus ex machina* is explicitly the dramatist, who plays god with his theatrical creation. The tragic image of existence only relates to reality in the universality of death – the point at which Shakespeare overlaps with Beckett – so that the ideals of justice or spiritual values incorporated in tragedy are as illusory as the stage presentation of dying: which the Players do '*tragically*; *romantically*'.[16]

Stoppard's action undercuts the Shakepearean vision on every level. The action of *Hamlet* is doubly distanced, becoming not only fragmented into incomprehensibility, but a play-within-a-play, in which the climax is played out by tragedians who have shown themselves to be 'a comic pornographer and a rabble of prostitutes'. Minor figures are turned into the protagonists, while the aristocratic hero is relegated to marginal status as an object of curiosity, or at best a subject of enquiry. His 'To be, or not to be' soliloquy (perhaps the most famous speech in English literature) is reduced to silence, and explained as a symptom of madness: 'intimations of suicide . . . amnesia, paranoia, myopia . . . And talking to himself'.[17] Perhaps the most serious questioning of all, a play accepted as the greatest of Shakespearean tragedies is transformed into Farce. The deaths that form the tragic high point are revealed as theatrical trickery – and their rationale is summed up in an

epigrammatic phrase derived from Oscar Wilde: 'the bad end unhappily,
the good unluckily'.

Wilde himself appears in *The Invention of Love* (1997) along with his lam-
pooned *alter ego* from Gilbert and Sullivan's *Patience*. However, the relevance
of Wilde to Stoppard's drama was already clear in *Travesties* (1974), where a
performance of *The Importance of Being Earnest* is superimposed on historical events. Extrapolating on a documented incident in Zurich in 1917 – an
amateur production involving James Joyce that ended in a law-suit with a
minor consular official – scenes from Wilde's play are combined with the random coincidence that both Lenin's lodgings, and the café home of the Dadaist
Cabaret Voltaire, were on the same Zurich street: Spiegelgasse. Stoppard's
pastiche illustrates Wilde's principle that 'Life imitates Art far more than Art
imitates Life'; and the relationship between these contradictory elements is
the thematic focus, which turns on the question of perception.

Stoppard's first title, 'Prism' (punning on the name of Wilde's governess
who mistook a novel for a baby), points directly to visual distortions. These
are underlined by Stoppard's emphasis on defective eyesight, both the narrator and Joyce needing spectacles, while the dapper Rumanian Dadaist,
Tristan Tzara, sports a monocle. Astigmatic or monocular, the play exploits
a kind of dramatic double-vision, with the action being filtered through, as
well as literally 'framed' by the uncertain, self-asserting memoirs of a now
senile 'Carr of the Consulate'.[18]

The result of these juxtapositions is fragmenting and multiplying double
images. The doddering present-day Carr reappears as he was, or imagines
himself to have been, half a century before. Lenin contemplates disguis-
ing himself as a Swedish deaf-mute to leave for Russia – an instance of
historical fact being more absurd than any fiction. He also stands for the
missing Ernest of Wilde's comedy (being both puritanical and significant:
i.e. 'serious' in the political sense), since he is still unknown and using a
different name, Ulyanov: as Carr protests, 'don't forget, *he wasn't Lenin
then! I mean who was he!* as it were'.[19] Joyce (named Augusta instead of
Augustin in the baptismal registry) appears as Lady Bracknell. Tzara and the
young Carr become Jack and Algernon, wooing under pseudonyms (each
claiming to be either the other or his younger brother, as they do in *The
Importance of Being Earnest*), while their girl-friends – Gwendolyn and Cecily
in real life as in their amateur dramatic roles – are linked respectively with
Joyce/Lady Bracknell (as his amanuensis) and Lenin/Ernest (as his political
convert).

The double lives of Wilde's characters become a metaphor for the creative imagination. Down a Memory Lane that becomes an alleyway of mirrors – the literal translation of Spiegelgasse – Carr's myopically dislocated view of the past subsumes both an explicitly Joycean 'free association', and the Dadaist principles of spontaneity and simultaneity.[20] Similarly, Joyce's novel of *Ulysses* and Lenin's polemic on 'Imperialism', mixed up in a parody of Miss Prism's substitution of her romantic manuscript for the baby Ernest, are interchangeable. So are Joyce's multilingual wordplays and Tzara's Dadaist word collages (which, although nonsense in their English transliteration, are comprehensible French when spoken), while in a typical Stoppardian pun none of the characters can 'distinguish between poetry and . . . belle-litter'.

However, this comic confusion of opposites does not cancel out. The result is a synthesis, as in an earlier treatment of the unreliability of memory and the subjectivity of perception, *Artist Descending a Staircase* (written for radio in 1972 and first staged in 1988). There Stoppard attacks the *avant-garde* for lacking traditional values, but the play's structure is as modernist as its title. The Dadaism, Cubism and Futurism represented by three artists in their first exhibition, which they grandiosely title 'Frontiers in Art', is rejected as 'frivolous and not very difficult to do', compared to 'the infinitely more difficult task of painting what the eye sees'. Their self-absorption causes the suicide of the blind muse, Sophie. The one artist who loves her and takes up the realistic principles she argues for, capturing her essence in what the other two despise as 'post-Pop pre-Raphaelite', is killed by tripping (or being pushed by them) down the stairs. However, the scenes move back down through time from the present to 1914, then back up again in graduated steps that are 'set temporally in six parts, in the sequence ABCDEFEDCBA', mirroring Marcel Duchamp's Cubist picture of *Nude Descending a Staircase*.[21]

In *Travesties* these conflicting artistic positions are extended into three mutually exclusive antitheses. Joyce is the traditionalist; and his mythologizing continuity that connects 'Troy to the fields of Flanders' gives spiritual significance to the transient chaos of events. The revolutionary artist Tzara's aim is to liberate the imagination, by demolishing the illusory temple of aesthetic forms. Lenin epitomizes the revolutionary, for whom 'Art *is* society' and politics a materialist equivalent to poetry. Yet Tzara sees living as an artistic act, while even Lenin's rejection of aesthetic values implicitly acknowledges the humanizing effect of art: 'music . . . makes me want to . . . pat the heads of those people who while living in this vile hell can create such beauty. Nowadays we can't pat heads or we'll get our hands bitten off.' And this synthesis mirrors the contradictory position of Oscar Wilde: the aesthete, whose life embodied the fundamental paradox of *The Importance of Being Earnest* that 'in all important matters, style, not sincerity, is the essence' – and who was also the radical author of 'The Soul of Man Under Socialism'.[22]

The same combination of opposites is evident in the overall form of Stoppard's play. The structure of *Travesties* follows its narrator's parodistic declaration (combining Tzara's dadaist manifestoes with a pun on the popular song, 'My heart belongs to daddy') that 'my art belongs to Dada'. As a collage of fantasy and fact, history and present day memory, in which scenes from Wilde, Lenin's speeches, arguments about art and intellectual strip-tease, all reflect and undercut each other, *Travesties* follows typical dadaist principles. Yet at the same time the prismatic perspective, through which the action is presented, offers a practical demonstration of Joycean mythologizing. It transforms the chaotic and bloody conflicts of the First World War and the Russian Revolution, which are representative of the dehumanizing mass movements of twentieth-century life, into 'a tale of heroes, of a golden apple, a wooden horse, a face that launched a thousand ships...' – or rather into an old man's highly coloured and completely idiosyncratic memories. At the same time, as in Joyce's *Ulysses*, Stoppard's self-elected protagonist is insignificant and unheroic, while global warfare is reduced to a trivial squabble over a pair of trousers. As a whole, the play answers the question with which it ends: in Stoppard's paraphrase, 'whether the words "revolutionary" and "artist" are capable of being synonymous, or whether they are mutually exclusive, or something in between'.[23] The revolutionary function of art is aesthetic, creating social change through changing the way reality is perceived.

Indeed, the nature of drama is a recurrent subject of Stoppard's plays, which are as self-reflexive in the number of artist or writer figures they contain, as in their overt theatricality. In addition to the painters, poets and novelists in *Artist Descending a Staircase* and *Travesties*, there are philosophers and social scientists in *Jumpers* (1972) and *Professional Foul* (TV, 1977), dramatists in *The Real Thing* (1982) and *Rough Crossing* (1984), even theatre critics in *The Real Inspector Hound* (1968), to say nothing of a whole orchestra in *Every Good Boy Deserves Favour* (1977). And artists continue to appear in all Stoppard's plays over the last decade: a poet, a biographer and a painter in *Indian Ink*; critics and a poet (albeit absent) in *Arcadia*; burgeoning to the whole spectrum of writers, from a popular humourist to great Victorian cultural essayists, plus a poet, journalists and a playwright in

The Invention of Love. Through these figures Stoppard pursues an on-going argument about the nature of his drama, and its social function. His statement is consistent throughout: art can only work obliquely. Even *Night and Day* (1978), which deals with directly political issues of journalistic freedom and the potential for creating change through factual reportage, demonstrates that a play is different in kind and effect from documentary activism: 'one is doing a short-term and one a long-term job . . . art can't do what *World in Action* does'.[24]

As a defence of press freedom, and an attack on journalistic abuses, *Night and Day* illustrates the point. Even more obviously than in Stoppard's other work, this is a play with a message, which is summed up in the final declaration:

People do awful things to each other. But it's worse in places where everybody is in the dark. It really is. Information is light. Information, in itself, about anything, is light. That's all you can say, really.

Set in an African ex-colony (symbolically using the cliché description of Africa as the 'dark continent'), which is ruled by a more intelligent version of Idi Amin, equally brutal but educated at the London School of Economics, the play pits two representative journalists against each other. Wagner is the unprincipled professional, prepared to sell out anyone for a scoop, and biased by (lower) class prejudices. Milne, who has been expelled from the Union of Journalists for refusing to support a strike and whom Wagner despises as 'the Grimsby scab', is an unpolitical idealist and Stoppard's spokesman, inspired by the conviction that 'a free press, free expression – it's the last line of defence for all the other freedoms'.[25] Both are competing for Ruth, the wife of the engineer whose telex is the only way of getting their reports out of the country. Once a victim of the Press's capacity to destroy individual privacy, she surrenders herself to Milne in her imagination, and to Wagner in despair over Milne's death.

Exposing the facts has real potential to unseat governments or correct injustices. However, in the play true reporting is censored by the forces of repression; and these come more from the Left than from the Right. State oligarchy in the form of the African dictator, whose definition of a 'relatively free press' is a newspaper edited by his relatives, is finally unable to prevent the news getting out. On the other hand, the print union's threat of a protest strike means that a story, important enough to get a journalist killed, will never appear. Wagner suppresses the scoop for which Milne sacrificed his life, which would never be printed anyway – and his own report is a sanitized version of the facts that will hardly bring international pressure to bear on the dictator.

However, the real focus of the play is on freedom in a far wider sense. The journalists are blinkered by the myths of their profession, which get the young idealist killed and the hard-bitten cynic beaten. Ruth is unfree in almost every way. She is fettered as much by the fashionable stylishness and wit she adopts, as by her isolation in this alien country and the social rigidity of neo-colonial privilege. She is also trapped by marriage, and crippled by sexual repressions – which even her affairs with the two journalists are not capable of breaking. Yet Wagner is also engaged in the search for truth, while Ruth learns to express her inner self. The values of the play are not those of political activism, but personal freedom. Its focus is on the way Ruth's personal perceptions change when confronted (like the audience) by moral questions, demonstrating Stoppard's point that 'art . . . is important because it provides the moral matrix, the moral sensibility, from which we make our judgments about the world'.[26]

The way this moral matrix relates to politics already occupied centre-stage in Stoppard's second full-length play, *Jumpers* (1972), where the shabby philosopher-protagonist is engaged in wrestling with the subject of 'Man – Good, Bad or Indifferent'. Attempting to demonstrate the existence of these ethical categories, George's lecture continually regresses to the question 'Is God?' There is, of course, no way of proving such a proposition. So the most he can assert is a negative:

I don't claim to *know* that God exists, I only claim that he does without my knowing it, and while I claim as much I do not claim to know as much; indeed I cannot know and God knows I cannot. (*Pause.*) And yet . . .[27]

His position is literally a pathetic fallacy, since reason (the premise of his argument) is not only incongruous with faith, but in the world around him the evidence for any belief at all is collapsing.

The play is an anti-utopian fantasy, set against the background of the Moon Landing. This 'giant step for Mankind' (not American, but in Stoppard's fictional world British, and presented as an example of human depravity) has not only destroyed traditional poetic ideals – already re-duced to outdated romantic clichés in the Moon/June pop songs of George's wife, Dotty. It has also shattered all the traditional moral certainties, since mankind (in a speech that repeats an earlier treatment of the same subject in Stoppard's television play, *Another Moon Called Earth*, 1967) is now no longer the still centre of God's universe . . . Man is on the moon, his feet on solid ground, and he has seen us whole, all in one go, *little – local* . . . and all our absolutes, the thou-shalts and thou-shalt-nots that seemed to be the very condition of our existence, how did *they* look . . . Like the local customs of another place. When that thought drips through to the bottom, people won't just carry on.[28]

And the consequences are already present in the election of a totally pragmatist 'radical-liberal' government, which has taken over the news media and 'rationalized' the Church, backed by an intellectual establishment who have relativized all moral principles into irrelevance. The Moon Landing symbolizes this ethical void. The legendary heroism of Scott's 1910 British Antarctic expedition, when Lieutenant Oates sacrificed himself in a vain attempt to save his companions, is turned into an archetype of expedient self-interest, with a latter-day Oates being callously abandoned by the Astronaut Captain Scott since their damaged space-craft only has the capacity to lift one of them back to earth.

The same expediency is also the basis of the detective story plot, in which Dotty becomes the prime suspect. This begins and ends with the identical murders of two Rad-Lib supporters because each has become converted to spiritual values, which discredit all that the party stands for. In the prologue a professor of logic is shot down to prevent him recanting on the empiricism that legitimizes the new government, his pragmatic Scottish beliefs having been shattered by seeing their effect in the astronauts' selfish fight over their damaged spacecraft. Trying to get rid of Duncan McFee's corpse, which finds its way into her bedroom, preoccupies Dotty, leading her to enlist the support of the university's vice-chancellor, who is responsible for having him murdered, and providing a running gag throughout the play. In the epilogue a government-appointed atheist Archbishop of Canterbury is killed because, as a contemporary Thomas à Becket, he finds himself forced into religious faith by his official role.

As such an overview indicates, all the various levels of the play's action are interconnected. Even the question of whether Dotty is having an affair with the University vice-chancellor, Sir Archibald Jumper, who is also the leader of the Rad-Lib party, parallels George's existential enquiry. It is a practical illustration of his philosophical problem: 'How the hell does one know what to believe?' As a psychiatrist, Archie's claim to be giving Dotty a medical examination when discovered in her bedroom, is backed up by a dermatograph machine. The close-up of Dotty's naked body, which this throws on the television screen that covers one wall of her bedroom, could support either hypothesis. Indeed Stoppard makes the situation deliberately ambiguous:

GEORGE Well, everything you do makes it *look* as if you're . . . (*Pause*)
ARCHIE Well, what would it have *looked* like if it had *looked* as if I were making a dermatographical examination?

This echoes Wittgenstein's reply (earlier quoted by George) to the proposition that it would be '*natural*' to suppose the sun moved round the earth, since that was how it looks, which he refuted with the question: 'what would it have looked like if it had looked as if the earth was rotating?'[29]

When *Jumpers* was first produced, the impression of nihilism was so overwhelming that these interconnections were overlooked; and Stoppard's point was misinterpreted because the form did not fit into conventional patterns. In place of the standard 'drama of ideas' as a serious treatment of social issues, Stoppard had created a new theatrical category by taking 'the *play* of ideas' literally – both in using intellectual abstractions playfully, and embodying mental gymnastics in physical images.

As a result, the reviews of *Jumpers* generally applied the wrong standards to its mental gymnastics. Confused by Stoppard's approach – 'A metaphysical conundrum?' 'A surrealist farce?' – most reviewers found 'no . . . way to lock the jigsaw arabesques together'. His highly theatrical representation of logical syllogisms and circular arguments in the multiple reflections of the mirror-background for the prologue, and the dizzying revolve that spun the action from one scene to another, were taken as evidence for 'anarchy at the core of the text'. The response even to the 1976 revival was similar, with the 'fractured narrative' being seen as 'appropriate to a world of crumbling values'.[30]

Yet the underlying coherence of *Jumpers* affirms the existence of precisely those ethical values, which seem so signally lacking in the world depicted – just as the murder-victims' reversion to religious belief implies the reality of the principles that George cannot prove in the lecture he is writing. The whole action is based on puns and coincidence, which in themselves are ways of connecting apparently unrelated things. In addition to the overlaps between the Moon Landing, the bungled murder investigation, the adulterous bedroom farce, and George's on-going lecture-demonstration, there is a unity of metaphor.

Everything is brought together in 'the INCREDIBLE – RADICAL!! – LIBERAL!! **jumpers**!!'[31] These acrobats, clothed in the same yellow as the astronauts' space-suits, are members of the University faculty. Presented at

15 Acrobatic entertainers and romantic symbols: the finale of Stoppard's *Jumpers*

first simply as entertainment for Dotty's party, like the stripper who performs on a trapeze, they are the regimented henchmen of political dictatorship, who set opponents up to be killed, and eventually dispose of the bodies. They are also an image of intellectuals, 'jumping' from one fashionable attitude to another. Their human pyramid represents false hierarchies – form over content, political expediency determining principles – which parallels man's 'jump' to the moon. This in turn, having emptied romantic symbols of meaning, extenuates Dotty's infidelity, as well as finding a parodistic echo in George's 'leap' of faith.

As Peter Wood, the director associated with almost all Stoppard's work, commented: his 'are plays of ideas but the ideas are riding on a story. And because the two levels are so interrelated, a director [or indeed reader] has got to get the ideas right in order to get the story right'.[32] The future society represented by *Jumpers* is a cautionary object lesson, designed to provoke ethical responses from its audience. Its apparent nihilism has an affirmative purpose. But, rather than using a spokesman to define the 'right' response, the whole question of morality is raised in a way that requires the audience to ask what their own values are.

Thus the play contains a villain – the Mephistophelean vice-chancellor who has turned the University chapel into a gymnasium. The action reveals him to be an updated Richard III; and he was performed as a melodramatically sinister figure. But there is no hero.

Stoppard's moral apologist repeatedly rejects his wife's calls for practical help with the body in her bedroom, in order to concentrate on the abstract ethics of his lecture. He is as infected by the egoistic culture as the pragmatists he opposes. This was emphasized by Peter Wood's direction, which brought out George's 'capacity for self-parody, comic frenzy and operatic despair . . . a continuously writhing knot of insecurity and suppressed antagonism . . . a windmill of disconnected intelligence' – thus undercutting his intellectual claims.[33]

The philosophical issues Stoppard raises are significant. Professor A.J. Ayer, the leading logical positivist, recognized elements of himself in the characterization of George, as well as acknowledging that his ideas form the position George is arguing against. Indeed, he took the play's philosophical basis seriously enough to publish a rebuttal in *The Sunday Times* (9 April 1972), extracts from which were reprinted in the National Theatre programme for the 1976 revival. Yet the way George seeks to prove his argument turns it into Farce. His example is not only irrelevant, but it comically confuses different categories. In addition to the palpable incongruity of demonstrating abstract ideas by using physical objects, George mixes up two of Zeno's philosophical paradoxes with Aesop's fable about the hare and the tortoise.

The Ancient Greek philosopher Zeno's proofs of infinity (denied by the astronauts' perspective of an enclosed world) propose: A. That in a race where a tortoise is given a head start, it cannot be overtaken even by Achilles (the fastest runner in the world) since whenever he catches up, the tortoise will have moved marginally ahead; and B. That an arrow in flight is motionless, since in any given instant (by definition the smallest and therefore indivisible element of time) it occupies a particular point in space, and cannot be in two places at once. George's demolition of Zeno's theories, involving a pet hare and tortoise (nicknamed Thumper and Pat), as well as a bow and arrow, span the whole action. At the beginning, distracted by Dotty's cry of 'Fire!' – her previous calls of 'Help', 'Murder', 'Rape' and 'Wolves' having had no effect – his arrow misses the target and vanishes. When, later, he is unable to find the hare and Dotty (exasperated that the animal is more important to him than her predicament) claims to have eaten it, this convinces George that 'she somehow killed McFee, as sure as she killed my poor Thumper'.[34] Then, just after the vice-chancellor has supposedly proved that discovering the truth is a logical impossibility, a final denouement is provided by George's discovery of blood dripping from the top of the wardrobe. Climbing on a chair, he finds his missing hare transfixed by his lost arrow and, dismayed, in stepping down he crushes the tortoise with an appallingly audible crunch.

The demonstration may have all too literally misfired, but it is a graphic image of ideas having an effect on reality. George, weeping and calling (in his turn) 'Help! Murder!', for the first time abandons even the pretence of intellectual objectivity, and recognizes his moral failure in putting theories of Good and Evil before the needs of the individual: in particular Dotty. The ruins of his experiment not only disprove Zeno, but provide ironic evidence that philosophical abstractions do affect reality. The play's premise is that accepted ideas define how people behave, and so mould society: as Dotty remarks, 'Democracy is all in the head'.[35]

Like so many of Stoppard's other plays, *Jumpers* demonstrates a Shavian belief in the effectiveness of drama as a vehicle for influencing public attitudes. The detective story plot, with its farcical display of social corruption where the policeman is persuaded to participate in the activities of his suspects, offered incongruous bribes, and finally blackmailed into accepting (against all the evidence) that the dead professor of logic committed suicide inside the plastic garbage bag used to dispose of the body, parodies Joe Orton's *Loot* (1965 – see above, pp. 296 and 298). Orton's farce stands as the extreme example of a play that undercuts moral values. As a counterplay, *Jumpers* shows the type of world that follows from such a nihilistic vision, and works to reverse the intellectual trend underlying it.

In *The Real Thing* (1982), Stoppard returned explicitly to the question of 'the moral matrix' – as he does again in *Indian Ink* and *The Invention of*

Love – though here the literary model is his own drama. The action demonstrates that emotional reality does exist beneath the artificial surface of the opening play-within-a-play, 'House of Cards': a title embodying the two-dimensional lack of human depth that has frequently been criticized in Stoppard's work. This self-defence is paralleled by an attack on the assumption (exemplified by Arden, Bond and the radical Agitprop movement of the 1970s) that only direct political activism makes theatre significant.

Stoppard's example of this left-wing theatre is a television docudrama. Written in prison by a semi-literate soldier, and recounting his own actions and arrest as an anti-nuclear protester, the television script is a rather over-literal demonstration that open commitment makes drama socially ineffective. Private Brodie's dramatization lacks any credibility because it is so one-sided. As 'the real thing' (at least in one definition) its dialogue is crude and unliterary, exactly mirroring the ordinary and uneducated nature of its author. But this unsophisticated language reduces its representation of society to simplistic slogans.

In fact drama's relationship to reality is always symbolic; and ironically Brodie's assault on the political Establishment – setting fire to memorial wreaths at the Cenotaph – is purely theatrical. Instead of a real action, it is no more than an empty gesture; and even Brodie's political motivation turns out to be pretended, since he was only hoping to impress a TV actress (Annie) whom he met on the way to the march. Stoppard's *alter ego*, the professional playwright Henry, points out the flaw by listing Brodie's themes:

war is profits, politicians are puppets, Parliament is a farce, justice is a fraud, property is theft . . . It's all here [in Brodie's script] . . . patriotism is propaganda, religion is a con trick, royalty is an anachronism . . .

His point is that social structures and institutions are not objects which can be changed by action, but ideas coded in language. So change can only be achieved on the level of personal behaviour, through conditioning individual perception. This depends on verbal precision, which is the opposite of such radical clichés:

Words don't deserve that kind of malarky. They're innocent, neutral, precise, standing for this, describing that, meaning the other, so if you look after them you can build bridges across incomprehension and chaos . . . If you get the right ones in the right order, you can nudge the world a little . . . [36]

The Real Thing is a point-by-point illustration. Emotional truth, and its expression in the characters' personal relationships, is the reality to which the title refers. The playwright-protagonist's speeches are displays of wit that continually focus on the accurate use of words, while his own drama ('House of Cards') provides the model for the love triangles around which the plot revolves. Initially we take this scene, in which Max supposedly discovers proof that Charlotte is deceiving him with her lover Henry, as 'the real thing' – only to discover they are actors on a stage. In real life Henry is married to Charlotte, whom he is deceiving by an affair with another actress, Max's wife Annie. The same scene is replayed in very different keys when Max discovers Annie's infidelity, and when Henry (now married to Annie) forces her to admit she has been spending the night with Billy (the actor playing Brodie).

Adultery can be comic or tragic, depending on how the characters / people react to discovering their partners' sexual deception. But the 'real thing', people's emotion, can only be articulated through 'completely artificial' dialogue. Indeed, Henry – who finds it impossible 'to write love . . . it just comes out embarrassing. It's either childish or it's rude' – has to use lines from Strindberg's *Miss Julie*; and his actress wives both transpose their roles from *'Tis Pity She's A Whore* into affairs with their leading actors. Simultaneously emphasizing the influence of art on life and the importance of form, this double imaging follows the principle behind 'The House of Cards' and lifts 'adultery out of the moral arena [to] make it a matter of style', while the 'real' play answers the question 'What selves? What's left? What else is there that hasn't been dealt out like a deck of cards?'[37]

Stoppard's comic emphasis on the surface was expressed through theatricality in his earlier work; and critics tended to deplore its absence in the more realistic themes of his plays during the late 1970s and early 1980s. Yet even in *The Real Thing*, the foregrounding of the stage is retained in the Pirandellian paralleling of the inner and outer play, as well as in using members of the theatrical profession as characters. Despite this *The Real Thing* is as much a thesis play as *Night and Day*; and Stoppard's comedy is most effective when its social commentary is oblique, overturning preconceived value systems by embedding conventionally serious issues in apparently trivial forms and – in the tradition of Oscar Wilde – inverting the superficial and the serious. At the same time both the 'play' of ideas and thesis drama often seem to rule out emotional involvement; and in his last two plays to date, *Indian Ink* (performed in 1995, but originally an award-winning radio play, *In the Native State*, broadcast in 1991) and *The Invention of Love* (1997), Stoppard turns explicitly to the theme of passionate emotion and, more precisely, its expression.

On the surface a sentimental love story – indeed dedicated to Felicity Kendal, his then lover and the star in several of his plays – *Indian Ink* focuses on the mutually liberating relationship between Flora, an emancipated and (according to a District Officer in the India of 1930 at the start of Mahatma Ghandi's passive campaign of civil disobedience) 'politically sensitive' poet, and a young Indian painter. On a wider level this is a metaphor for the English love-affair with 'the Raj' and India's fascination with England. Flora, who has made her reputation on erotic poetry and suffers from tuberculosis, finds authentic emotion in the last days before her early death. The colonized 'Other', Nirad Das, whose art is overwhelmed by English models, learns to value his native heritage through her love.

But beyond that the play explores the nature of history and the way the past is rewritten, both through Flora's modern reliving of the experiences of a well-known Victorian lady traveller, Emily Eden whose 1839 reminiscences recorded in *Up the Country* are quoted in the final lines, and by combining the 1930s story with the lovers' descendants (together with a myopic American biographer whose profession is 'the worst possible excuse for getting people wrong') attempts to find the truth of their relationship 50 years later.[38] It is also a study in perception, symbolized in the 'secret' painting Das does of the nude Flora, following the example of Goya, who painted his Maja both naked and clothed. Contrasting cultural visions, this depicts her body in a European style against a traditional Indian background.

These themes are extended in *The Invention of Love*, where the contrast is between classical Rome, conjured up through its poetry, and the Victorian age represented by Oscar Wilde and A.E. Housman, the leading classicist of the time and the poet of 'The Shropshire Lad', backed by Ruskin and Walter Pater, the two leading art historians of the period, as well as a cunningly oblique reference to Alice in Wonderland. This is paralleled by a contrast between youth and age – with the dead Housman (AEH) transported to an Elysium that turns out to be 'the Oxford of my dreams, re-dreamt', where he meets his earlier self as an 18-year-old freshman. As such it is a reprise of *Travesties* (indeed the main roles in both plays were initially performed by the same actor, John Wood), and is structured in a similar way – although Housman's uncomfortable memories are all too accurate, unlike those recalled by 'Carr of the Consulate' – with the action mirroring what AEH describes as his own mental state:

archaism, anachronism, the wayward inconsequence that only hindsight can acquit of *non sequitur, quietus interruptus* by monologue incontinent in the hind leg of a donkey class ... and the unities out of the window without a window to be out of ... [39]

In a typically Stoppardian extended pun, based on the Oxford habit of referring to the Thames where it flows through the University as the Isis,

16 Visual puns and philosophic comedy: Charon's ferry meets *Three Men in a Boat* against a background of literary values in Stoppard's *The Invention of Love*

Charon's ferry meets Jerome K. Jerome's three men in a boat (here doubling for Housman and two undergraduate friends, one of whom forms the unrequited passion of his life). Even the subtitle of Jerome's well-known book, *To Say Nothing of the Dog*, carries through in a bedraggled stray rescued by the three, which replaces Cerberus, the triple-headed hound guarding the Underworld, and becomes the object of a demonstration that in Latin it is only word-order that decides who loves whom. The whole play revolves around this multiple elision.

As well as being a popular comic writer, Jerome is the journalist whose articles incited Lord Queensbury to leave the card 'to Oscar Wilde, posing as a Sodomite' that led to the famous series of trials. In addition we are reminded that Wilde started his London career writing for the *Pall Mall Gazette*, whose editor W.T. Stead is presented as personally responsible for the Criminal Law Amendment Act of 1885 outlawing child prostitution (to which an amendment was added criminalizing 'indecency' between males) under which Wilde was convicted.[40] This provides the context for Housman's unacknowledged lifelong love for a fellow undergraduate who was his polar opposite: a scientist and athlete; and the play culminates in a discussion between AEH and Wilde.

We have been continually reminded that the first love poems ever written were Roman (possibly Catullus who wrote to Lesbia – a suggestive name to contemporary ears) and that 'Nowhere was the ideal of morality, art and social order realized more harmoniously' than in Plato's Greece, which also (anathema to a Great Victorian like Ruskin) honoured love between men. During this climactic dialogue, which reaffirms that 'before Plato could describe love [in this reference homosexual], the loved one had to be invented' by poetry, Wilde asserts that the artist is 'the secret criminal in our midst... the agent of progress against authority', and poses the question whether Housman's self-denial is a betrayal. And whether Wilde's self-destruction is noble because it liberated future homosexuals from the closet, making 'art a philosophy that can look the twentieth century in the eye'. But the real issue throughout the play is the complete reversal of values that has taken place from Greece and Rome to the Victorians, who in believing themselves heirs of classical civilization have redefined virtue as 'what women have to lose, the rest is vice'.[41] It is all a matter of perception; and Stoppard gave this dominant theme its fullest expression in an earlier play, *Hapgood* (1988).

Here Stoppard's typical role-playing, mirror images, and confusion of illusion with reality are drawn from outside the theatre. The spy story employs comparable elements of disguise, doubles and deception; and this genre provides the overall metaphor for the play as well as the plot. The action revolves around the Star Wars secret of 'anti-matter' – i.e. the opposite of ordinary physical reality. The information may have been passed to the Russians, if the Russian scientist who has developed it is a Soviet plant instead of a defector, or if there is a mole among the British agents. Hapgood, the title character, who is the Russian's British 'control', is also his lover; and their son is used as a ploy to untangle the truth. She also takes the role of her bohemian, anti-establishment twin sister – and then has to take the role of her sister pretending to be herself – to entrap her subordinate, whom she suspects of being a double agent. He turns out to be not only the opposite of what he appears, but operates by using an identical 'twin' to evade detection, and has 'blown' her 'network . . . inside out'.[42]

There is a lot of talk about how things are seen, and the structure of the play itself follows the intellectual discussion of Newtonian versus Einsteinian theories of light, and the photo-electric effect. This is explicitly related to the characters' search for truth (and by extension, to the way spectators view the play). In the scientist's analogy between the action and a laboratory experiment:

Every time we don't look we get wave pattern. Every time we look to see how we get wave pattern, we get particle pattern . . . Somehow light is particle and wave. The experimenter makes the choice. You get what you interrogate for.

But this is misleading. Stoppard's focus is on 'the only real mystery in physics', which his scientist defines as

the missing rung. Below it, particle physics; above it, classical physics; but in between, metaphysics. All the mystery in life turns out to be this same mystery, the join between things which are distinct and yet continuous, body and mind, free will and fate, living cells and life itself . . .[43]

The whole play is set up as a test of perception for both characters and audience, in which there is no single correct solution. The structure of the scenes is designed as an equivalent of the square root of sixteen – to which, as the physicist points out, there are 'two correct answers. Positive and negative' – and the action embodies this in the permutation of 'doubles' and twins, where one person can be two characters, or vice versa.

Stoppard always provides the key to interpretation within each play: the Players' dumb show in *Rosencrantz and Guildenstern*, the acrobats' pyramid in the prologue of *Jumpers*, the final open question in *Travesties*. In *Hapgood* it is the proposition that 'the act of observing determines the reality', as Peter Wood's 1988 production emphasized.[44] The settings continually required the spectators to re-evaluate their perception through *trompe l'oeil*, distortions of scale, or deceptive perspectives. Thus the boarding-school building in the background to the rugby-match scenes (where Hapgood, her Russian, and her civil-servant boss watch her son), which at first glance appeared convincingly three-dimensional, was a flat cardboard cut-out. The photographer's studio (in which Hapgood plays the part of her own sister) contained an eight-foot-long toothpaste tube, monstrously out of scale. At the zoo (a typical 'meet' for spies) the characters gazed idly through the bars of a cage while talking – but the blank reverse of the notice identifying what is inside indicated that it was the audience who were the animals on show.

Yet if all this forces us to question reality, it also refers back to the artifice of the stage, where actors are not the characters they represent and all scenery is fake. In the theatrical context only what is unreal is true, and game-playing is the most significant activity.

Following this line, the spy plot of *Hapgood* is openly pieced together from stock elements of the genre, while the dialogue is composed of jargon. As the physicist, who reads 'only . . . spy stories', points out: 'they all surprise in the same way . . . I don't mind. I love the language . . . Safe house, sleeper, cover, joe . . .' The denouement itself is a cliché. The undercover war between opposing intelligence services is revealed to be a form of co-operation (as in the more cynical novels of Len Deighton or Le Carré). Its sole purpose is 'keeping each other in business', since the Star Wars secret to be guarded, or betrayed, has no possible practical value.[45] People are killed and love betrayed for an illusion.

On one level this represents the true nature of existence. Quantum mechanics, particle versus wave theories of light, Heisenberg's indeterminacy principle, are all used to explore 'metaphysics'. The point is much the same as in *Jumpers*: 'mathematics deny certainty, they reveal only probability and chance, and Einstein couldn't believe in a God who threw dice'. However, like the spy story, Stoppard also presents modern physics as intellectual games. Thus Euler's advanced mathematics is used to solve the puzzle of the Konigsberg bridges, which is explicitly duplicated ('*if not replicated*') in the opening scene of the play.[46]

In fact, the whole play is structured on game-playing, using the Kiplingesque image of spying as 'the Great Game', but taking the metaphor literally. As Hapgood warns her suspect colleague: 'you're street smart and this is a board game. In Paris you bounced around like Tigger, you thought it was Cowboys and Indians.' However, even more than in Stoppard's previous work, these are intellectual sports. The game of betrayal and state secrets is specifically compared to playing chess without a board against an absent opponent. The games the characters play are all of this sort: imaginary cards, where one player does not even know what game it is until the other calls out '*Snap!!*', or off-stage (and therefore in theatrical terms equally imaginary) football.

The dramatic action is also conceived as a series of games. Find the 'double', detect the twin, identify the father, discover a lost door-key: all are variations of Hunt the Thimble. The opening sequence is a double level Shell Game, switching both a row of swimming-bath cubicles (marked by towels) and the identical briefcases deposited inside them (marked by a radioactive spray), with the missing radio-bleeper in place of the traditional coin under the row of upturned cups. At the same time it is also a version of Musical Chairs, in which the person caught holding the bag when the music stops (or when the 'bug' goes off the air) is out. Even the shooting-range set-up is a familiar arcade/computer game (marketed as 'Hogan's Alley'), with illuminated '*cut-out villains*' appearing randomly within three arches, which the player must shoot before they 'kill' him, interspersed with '*civilians*', whom he must spare – though, in keeping with the abstraction of the other games, the text offers blue and green targets as an alternative.[47]

This level to the play was pointed up by the initial stage picture in the London production. The movements of the trackers in the '*short radio play*' that serves as prologue were projected with winking coloured lights on to a London street map in clear imitation of a recently issued cops-and-robbers board game called 'Scotland Yard'.

As so frequently in Stoppard's plays, the marginal becomes the major focus. The frame turns out to be central. Playing is everything. The comedy reflects itself, yet in doing so it raises significant philosophical issues. And this is particularly true of *Arcadia*, perhaps the best of all his plays, where form and content are inseparable.

Arcadia (1993) focuses on contemporary science just as much as *Hapgood*. But in place of particle versus wave theories of light, or Heisenberg's indeterminacy principle – both of which are also explored by Michael Frayn's 1998 play *Copenhagen* (see pp. 390–92) – Stoppard directs our attention here to chaos theory, fractal geometry and the laws of thermodynamics. These are combined with English landscape gardening, the history of aesthetics in the switch from rationalist Neo-classical ideals to Gothic Romanticism, Lord Byron and academic biography, making this one of Stoppard's most multi-layered plays. It also gathers together many of the themes from his other plays. The laws of thermodynamics and relativism, and the question of fate versus free will had already made an appearance in *Rosencrantz and Guildenstern*; poets and the reciprocal influence of art and social conditions in *Travesties*; the impact of science (in the more tangible form of the moon-landing) on worldviews in *Jumpers*. Even the tortoise and hare from *Jumpers* reappear (the hare here being shot by Byron). In the same way the theme of biography looks forward to *The Invention of Love*, where it is dismissed as 'the mesh through which our real life escapes', while the juxtapositioning and overlap of past and present anticipates *Indian Ink*.[48]

The two time frames of the play – 1809 in the days leading up to a fire that kills Thomasina on the eve of her 17th birthday, and at the same country house in the present day – replicate each other, in much the same way as the fractals she is said to have discovered, where repeating (or in mathematical terms, iterating) an equation with the solution to one being fed back into the next produces a constant geometrical pattern. In its simplest terms, as explained by Valentine, a computer expert in the contemporary scenes, the numbers translate into graphs, each graph being identical but formed from 'a small section of the previous one, blown up. Like you'd blow up a detail of a photograph, and then a detail of a detail, and so on, forever.' He is using the method to find an explanation for historical changes in the grouse population, as recorded in the family game-book. But the point of using it as a structure for the play is that it corresponds to the workings of nature, since (according to the Royal Society Research Professor cited in the programme for the original production) 'complicated, irregular or fluctuating behaviour – weather patterns, marginal rates of Treasury Bonds, colour patterns of animals or shapes of leaves – can be generated by the simplest of rules . . . the mathematics of chaos offers new and deep insights into the structure of the world around us'.[49]

In the same way the relationships between the characters in each time frame mirror each other, with variations that expand during the play. In both there is a teacher (Septimus, the family tutor/Bernard, a university professor) who publishes slashing reviews that outrage a writer (the incompetent poet, Chater/the non-academic historian Hannah) and is loved

by the daughter of the house (Thomasina/Chloe). In each, one of the family
(Thomasina/Valentine) is fascinated by 'the behaviour of numbers' and
using the same type of mathematics, although in the past the mathematician is also 'the genius of the place', while in the present the genius is his young
brother (Gus) who gave up speaking at the age of five. In each too, Byron is
absent, but very much on the minds of everyone else – and, as well as the
tortoise which is assumed to be still alive after 184 years, one character is identical in both time frames: the young boy Augustus/Gus (played by the same
actor). In addition, the same patterning recurs from scene to scene in the
historical frame, with the stage directions to one stating that it is 'A reprise',
while the description of the previous scene reminds us that 'We have seen
this composition before.'[50] At the same time in the present-day scenes, mim-
icking the expanding graph of fractals, whenever characters from either era
put anything on the table, it remains there, in a multiplying collection of
objects.

One of these is an apple – offered by the shy Gus to Hannah; picked up
in 1809 by Thomasina, who uses a leaf from it to plot an equation that will
demonstrate 'nature is written in numbers', then by Valentine to explain
how a 'picture of this leaf' could be made by iterating the right algorithm.
The apple, of course, is simultaneously emblematic of Newtonian physics
(in popular iconography one falling on Newton's head in an orchard led
to his discovering the law of gravity) and of Eve's seduction of Adam in
Eden: as Valentine puts it, 'The attraction that Newton left out. All the way
back to the apple in the garden.' And indeed the Biblical Garden of Eden,
or its classical equivalent Arcadia, is one of the controlling images in the
play. The title is picked up in the landscape of Sidley Park, with Hannah
describing the formal Italianate 1730s garden as having been 'Paradise in
the age of reason'; and the Lady Croom of 1809 seeing herself surrounded by
the picturesque naturalism of Capability Brown's garden that has replaced
it as being 'Here . . . in Arcadia' – which leads Thomasina to recall the title of
Poussin's famous painting (reproduced in the NT programme) where the 'I'
of *Et in Arcadia ego*! refers to death.[51] Indeed this reminder of mortality –
also inherent in the Biblical story where Eve's apple is a symbol of both sex
and death – is reflected in all the game shooting (and duelling) that goes on
in these idyllic surroundings; and even more centrally in the immolation of
Thomasina on the verge of sexual awakening, as well as in the implication
of her mathematical discovery.

For Hannah, the 1809 remodelling of the park into a Romantic wilderness,
complete with fake ruins and a hermitage, marks 'The decline of reason to

feeling', which makes the landscaper with his steam-engine (in Septimus' phrase) 'the serpent' in 'the scheme of the garden'. And it is the steam-engine, as well as stirring jam into a bowl of rice-pudding), that brings Thomasina to deduce the principle of entropy by revealing that 'the heat equation . . . only goes one way', which as Septimus realizes means that 'we are all doomed'. (Newtonian physics assumed that energy is conserved and therefore the universe is stable because it is limited to the laws of motion, but once the laws of thermodynamics are taken into account then 'the Improved Newtonian Universe must cease and grow cold'.)[52]

This seems a bleak vision of existence; and indeed the play is frequently seen as a statement of existential despair. Thomasina dies, unfulfilled; and we are told that Septimus spends the rest of his life alone in the hermitage, cov- ering mountains of paper in an (apparently) insane attempt to disprove her equations. Yet the final waltz, which unites couples from both time frames, is highly ambiguous. The pairings are patently incongruous – the dumb Gus with Hannah twice his age, and Thomasina with Septimus who has already refused her advances – but it is still a traditional image of harmony. Indeed while entropy (like all human life) may be a one-way passage to extinction, the Newtonian physics it displaced is totally deterministic and rules out free will. And Thomasina's 'New Geometry of Irregular Forms' offers a posi- tive alternative, since mathematically it is the opposite of entropy: 'In an ocean of ashes, islands of order. Patterns making themselves out of nothing.' There is also another form of creation that the play stresses. 'The action of bodies in heat' (the definition of thermodynamics) is also a description of sexual activity, which preoccupies all the characters in both time frames.[53] Their behaviour may be disastrous because, whether Septimus being se- duced by the promiscuous Mrs Chater in the gazebo or the modern-day Bernard copulating with Chloe in the hermitage, they pursue sex without loving while love, either in Thomasina's feelings for Septimus or the pre- tended engagement between Valentine and Hannah, remains unconsum- mated. However, sexual attraction is asserted as a force that escapes from all deterministic laws of physics, and the flame that consumes Thomasina is an emblem of passion. In the play it is only the candle she takes to her bed, which burns her up physically – but the clear implication is that this would not have happened if Septimus had accepted her invitation to go to bed with her, changing her historical fate by exchanging the candle for burning emotion.

Other things also get burnt during the play: all Septimus' endless pages of mathematical proofs, letters that would prove the truth about Byron; and a comparison is made to the burning of the library at Alexandria in which so much of the literature and scientific writings of the classical age were destroyed. However, Stoppard takes much the same view of the latter event as Shaw in *Caesar and Cleopatra*. The present-day scenes demonstrate that ideas never die, and 'Mathematical discoveries glimpsed and lost to view will have their time again.' Even if direct historical evidence vanishes, the truth (as with Byron's supposed duel over Mrs Chater) can still be intuited. More, facts are 'trivial' since 'It's wanting to know that makes us matter.' And Stoppard deliberately transforms history, most significantly in the figure of Thomasina. She – and the Byron connection – is clearly inspired by a real mathematical genius of the period, Ada, Byron's daughter who was born in 1815 and introduced the binary system (on which computer mathematics are based) in place of Charles Babbage's decimal system. But although Ada too died relatively young, she lived to marry at twenty, becoming Countess Lovelace and bearing two children. As the figure of Wilde remarks in *The Invention of Love*, 'Truth . . . is the work of the imagination.'[54] So the play itself, with its fractal-like structure that finally breaks through the entropic logic of time in the merging of past and present, becomes the ultimate affirmation of the positive value in human existence.

As Stoppard put it, while defending his position in *Artist Descending a Staircase*, art 'celebrates a world which includes itself – I mean, part of what there is to celebrate is the capability of the artist'. And his love of the theatre is given its fullest expression in his film of *Shakespeare in Love* – released at the same time as *The Invention of Love* was first performed – which not only celebrates the dramatist he has himself most frequently borrowed from, but the stage itself through standard jokes about performance taken literally (as when a nobleman's murderous pursuit is called 'slaying them in the aisles'). It is also directly embodied throughout his plays in the bravura display of theatrical fireworks, which are not an end in themselves, but a means of challenging the audience to re-evaluate their assumptions. Although art cannot determine how people act, beneath the complex surface of his comedies there is always a basic issue, corresponding to the principle of creating 'an utterly simple shape in order to ambush the mind with something quite unexpected about that shape by hanging it in a frame and forcing you to see it, as it were, for the first time'.[55]

This is a direct (but suiting our post-modern consciousness) more technically complex equivalent to the dialectics that Shaw introduced at the beginning of the century. Both are primarily dramatists of ideas. Some of

Stoppard's work, particularly perhaps *The Invention of Love*, qualifies for the label Shaw invented for his own 'discussion plays'. Indeed it would be possible to see Stoppard as the contemporary version of Shaw at the close of the century.

Notes

1 Pinter, *The Birthday Party*, p. 57 and *The Homecoming*, p. 52.
2 Robert Brustein, *The Third Theatre*, New York, 1969, p. 149. Although this has remained a standard view of Stoppard's work, reflected in *The Cambridge Guide to World Theatre* (e.g. 'in much of his later work, the influence of Polish and Czech "absurdist" writers can be felt' – p. 927), more recent interpretations have begun to challenge it: 'Ros and Guil share the predicament of the two tramps in *Waiting for Godot*. But their world is not in fact an absurd one. Because we enter the theatre knowing the outcome of Ros and Guil's lives . . . ' (Anthony Jenkins, *The Theatre of Tom Stoppard*, Cambridge, 1989, p. 40).
3 *Jumpers*, London, 1972, p. 87; Beckett, *Waiting for Godot*, New York, 1954, pp. 22, 58, and *Endgame*, New York, 1958, p. 18.
4 Stoppard in *Scene*, 26 October 1962, p. 19; 9 February 1963, p. 46, and 15 November 1962, p. 19.
5 Stoppard, *Bristol Evening News*, 8 March 1960.
6 *After Magritte*, London, 1971, pp. 37, 31.
7 *Ibid.*, pp. 32, 44.
8 Stoppard, cited in Hayman, *Tom Stoppard*, London, 1978, p. 86.
9 *Jumpers*, London, 1972, p. 43.
10 *Rosencrantz and Guildenstern are Dead*, New York, 1970, pp. 11, 16. (See Beckett, *Waiting for Godot*, p. 24: 'Time has stopped'.)
11 *Ibid.*, pp. 21, 32.
12 *Ibid.*, pp. 16 17, 12.
13 *Ibid.*, pp. 32–3, 23.
14 Stoppard, *Theatre Quarterly*, 4, (May–July 1974), p. 6.
15 *Rosencrantz and Guildenstern are Dead*, pp. 66, 25, 39–40.
16 *Ibid.*, pp. 79–80, 124.
17 *Rosencrantz and Guildenstern*, pp. 117, 27.
18 *The Complete Works of Oscar Wilde*, London, 1966, p. 992; *Travesties*, London, 1975, p. 25.
19 *Travesties*, p. 81.
20 *Ibid.*, p. 30. For these positive qualities, which apparently contradict the self-negating basis of Dadaism, see Robert Motherwell (ed.), *The Dada Painters and Poets*, New York, 1967, pp. 35–6 and 80f. – a work that Stoppard lists as one of his sources (*Travesties*, p. 15).

21 *Artist Descending a Staircase*, in *Albert's Bridge and Other Plays*, New York, 1977, pp. 95, 81, 73.

22 *Travesties*, pp. 43, 62, 74, 89; Wilde, *Complete Works*, p. 1,205.

23 *Travesties*, pp. 25, 43; and Stoppard, interview in *Theatre Quarterly*, 4 (May–July 1974), p. 12.

24 Stoppard, interview in *Theatre Quarterly* 4 (May–July 1974), p. 14.

25 *Night and Day*, London, 1979, pp. 92, 39, 58. Stoppard admits that 'Milne has my prejudice, if you like. Somehow, unconsciously, I wanted him to be known to be speaking the truth' (in *Gambit*, 10 (1981), p. 15).

26 *Night and Day*, p. 85; Stoppard, interview in *Theatre Quarterly* 4 (May–July 1974), p. 14.

27 *Jumpers*, pp. 46, 24.

28 *Ibid.*, p. 71.

29 *Ibid.*, pp. 71, 78 & 75.

30 *The Sunday Telegraph*, 5 February 1972, and *The New York Times*, 3 May 1974; *The Times*, 22 September 1976.

31 *Jumpers*, p. 18.

32 Programme note, National Theatre, 1976.

33 *The Times*, 22 September 1976.

34 *Jumpers*, p. 78.

35 *Ibid.*, pp. 81, 34.

36 *The Real Thing*, London, 1983, pp. 53–4.

37 *Ibid.*, pp. 40, 13, 63.

38 *Indian Ink*, London, 1998, pp. 78, 5.

39 *The Invention of Love*, London, 1997, pp. 104, 27,

40 A clear example of Stoppard shading historical fact to fit his dramatic theme. Although Stead and the *Pall Mall Gazette* were certainly part of the campaign, in fact it was initiated in 1879 by the Quaker activist, Alfred Dyer, who was publisher of *The Sentinel*.

41 *The Invention of Love*, pp. 17, 98 & 99–100, 79.

42 *Hapgood*, London, 1988, p. 87.

43 *Ibid.*, pp. 12, 49–50.

44 *Ibid.*, p. 12.

45 *Ibid.*, pp. 12, 47, 87.

46 *Ibid.*, pp. 49, 3.

47 *Ibid.*, pp. 44, 40.

48 *The Invention of Love*, p. 96.

49 *Arcadia*, London, 1993, p. 43; and Robert M. May, Royal Society Research Professor, University of Oxford and Imperial College, London, in the National Theatre programme, 1993.

50 *Arcadia*, pp. 67, 35.

51 *Ibid.*, pp. 27, 47, 74, 12–13.

52 *Ibid.*, pp. 27, 4, 87, 93.
53 *Ibid.*, pp. 76, 84,
54 *Ibid.*, pp. 38, 75, and *The Invention of Love*, pp. 95–6.
55 *Albert's Bridge and Other Plays*, pp. 100 & 101.

4.10 New Comic Voices: Patrick Marber (1964–)

While Stoppard, Ayckbourn and Frayn today form the establishment of contemporary British comedy, during the 1990s a younger and more subversive generation of writers emerged. Perhaps because the political protest of their predecessors seemed outdated by the fall of Communism in Eastern Europe, a surprising number of what might be called 'Thatcher's children' chose to depict their social criticism in comic terms. Even a playwright generally associated with agonized dramatizations of his personal psychiatric problems like Tom Kempinski briefly took up comedy with *Sex Please, We're Italian!* (1991), a parody of the 1971 farce *No Sex Please, We're British*, while a radical feminist like Debbie Isitt updated Trevor Griffiths' *Comedians* in *You Never Know Who's Out There* (1992), attacking homophobia and domestic abuse through a broken-down troupe – the rabidly misogynist so-called 'King of Comedy', a ventriloquist who can't go for a drink without his dummy, and an over-the-hill drag queen – on the North England cabaret circuit. And real-life contemporary equivalents of the radical in *The Comedians*, who had made their mark as stand-up comics in the previous decade, started writing plays in the 1990s.

Steve Berkhoff, who expanded from his earlier one-man presentation of East End yobs to attacking the theatrical tradition in the form of Hollywood extras (*Acapulco*, 1994) or Shakespearean parody (*Shakespeare's Villains*, 1998), is typical. Reaching wider audiences in the 1990s by dealing with a range of social figures, his short satiric pieces – in which he generally stars himself – and one-man monologues represent a cartoon line of comedy in which unlovely stereotypes are subjected to abuse in actions that hinge on sexual politics. Ben Elton is another example of an alternative comic who carried a reputation for one-man shows into West End plays (*Gasping* in 1990; *Popcorn*, first performed in Nottingham, in 1997; *Blast from the Past* in 1998), though unlike Berkhoff he has not acted in his own scripts. Again the figures are stereotyped in these plays and the dialogue deliberately vulgar – Elton co-wrote the scripts for the farcical television serial *Blackadder* – with a hypocritical exhibitionist lesbian hack and jokes like 'you … wouldn't recognize a good thing if it sat on your face and farted up your nose' satirizing the excesses of popular journalism (*Silly Cow*, 1991), or a tycoon who creates a monopoly on the air we breathe that leads to asphyxiation in the Third World as a farcical attack on capitalism with an environmentalist message (*Gasping*). And in his most popular play to date, *Popcorn* (adapted from his best-selling novel), Elton too takes on Hollywood, though more seriously than Berkhoff in satirizing the moral responsibility of violent films.

Yet even if the Tarantino-like movie director in *Popcorn* anticipates David Hare's similar unsympathetic figure in *Amy's View* (see pp. 230–31), here the director is a stereotype, arriving home, Oscar in one hand and centrefold model in the other – with his Hollywood trophy wife, who wants evidence for divorce, dragging along their daughter in pursuit. No less clichéd are two of his 'No. 1 fans', who are lying in wait for the director, and take him hostage together with family and bimbo. Trailer-trash psychopaths carrying the severed head of a security guard in a bag, they insist he provide them with a legal defence by publicly acknowledging responsibility for having 'inspired' their serial killings through films like his *Ordinary Americans*, which one describes (an analogy to *Four Weddings and a Funeral*) as 'Fifty-seven Murders, Plus People Taking Drugs and Fucking'.[1] Given topicality by the banning of the Cronenberg film *Crash* in England, and the legal suit in America against Oliver Stone for having incited copy-cat killing with *Natural Born Killers*, the play ends by indicting the audience for voyeuristic complicity in violence through trial-by-television in which the viewers can vote to save the director's life by switching off their sets.

But perhaps the most characteristic voice of contemporary English comedy comes from Patrick Marber, who also, as it happens, started off in stand-up comedy, and like Elton made his reputation as a scriptwriter for television shows like *The Day Today* (a parody of TV news) and the farcical hit series *Knowing Me, Knowing You*. With his first play, which he directed himself at the National, Marber caught the public ear. The production transferred to the West End; and the increasingly bleak tone of his stripped-down dramas, which have won prizes in both London and New York, seems to sum up the mood of the younger generation at the end of the millennium.

CHECKLIST OF MARBER'S MAJOR PLAYS

Dealer's Choice, 1995
After Miss Julie, 1996
Closer, 1997

Although lacking the political or sexual polemics of Griffiths and Joe Orton, beneath Marber's surface wit lies a dark cynicism that, in a comic mode, is very much the equivalent of Sarah Kane or Simon Ravenswood. There are also echoes of Pinter, but the most obvious comparison with Marber's dialogue is to the compressed, stunted language in the plays of the American dramatist, David Mamet. Since then Marber has acknowledged the influence by directing Mamet's *Old Neighbourhood* at the Royal Court (1998), although the parallels were already unmistakable given the subject matter of Marber's first play.

Mamet has described the way his characters act and the rhythms of his plays in terms of poker, and has quoted Thorstein Veblen to the effect that 'the more that jargon and technical language is involved in an endeavor, the more we may assume that the endeavor is essentially make-believe'.[2] And in *Dealer's Choice* (1995) Marber transfers this literally to the stage by centring the action entirely on a poker game – just as Mamet does in his film *House of Games* – which both mirrors and reveals the personalities of the players and the shifting power-relationships between them. In poker, as the characters state more than once, you 'play the man not the cards'; and there is the same fascination with the jargon of the game, as in the spiels of Mamet's real-estate salesmen. In addition Marber follows Mamet's *American Buffalo* or *Glen Garry Glen Ross* in focusing on an all-male society where dealings, whether in business or cards, become a vicious test of manhood.

Life is a gamble; and in this game, held in the basement of a restaurant after the customers have gone, everyone is a loser. Indeed in the psychology of gambling, compulsives play in order to lose, motivated – as Marber points out – by self-hatred or the need for respect, like the all too aptly named Mugsy who takes pride in being 'a good loser'. In fact in *Dealer's Choice* there are no winners. Even Ash, the professional cardsharp who plays only for money, turns out to live in poverty. Introduced as a beginner in order to clean up (and clear a gambling loan owed him by the son of the restaurant owner who runs the weekly poker game) he fails to win in the all-night poker session. And although he finally collects the £4,000 debt by blackmailing the father, he too needs the money to pay off a gambling debt incurred in a 'big boys' poker game where the stakes are far higher and the consequences of defaulting are serious, and where it is he who is the 'mug'. And since he will still be £1,000 short, he is at risk of being beaten up or killed. Similarly Steven, the owner of the restaurant and a successful entrepreneur who prides himself on self-discipline, deliberately throws a hand to allow Mugsy to pay his losses and allows the cardsharp to win the money his son owes on the toss of a coin, which he never even sees.

For these men poker is a substitute for love – as one remarks, 'poker without gambling is like sex without orgasm'– and it replaces family.[3] The restaurant owner can only relate to his son through the weekly game; all are divorced or incapable of sustaining a relationship with women; one gambles away the money to give his daughter a treat on the only day he is allowed to see her; another has lost what he'd saved to take his elderly mother on an outing. While psychologically accurate, Marber's insistence on the all-embracing nature of the addiction makes poker an image for contemporary England.

As in David Hare's 1995 play, *Skylight*, the restaurant business implicitly epitomizes consumer society; but here the focus is on monetary dealings. The play opens, as it ends, with a toss of the coin, described as 'business as usual'; and the depiction of the poker world 'divided between winners', defined as 'men of vision' who 'see a graveyard and think ... casino' and losers who 'can't see it as anything other than a graveyard', is also an image for the commercialism of the 1990s – a highly competitive but unproductive society fixated on the stock-market and state-run lotteries, where everyone wants riches without effort. Poker of course is a game of bluff and deception, which becomes self-deception; and everything Marber's characters do is a scam, fuelled by unrealistic dreams or unaffordable debt – just like the business-culture of mergers and takeovers. As one of the quotations about poker reprinted in the play-programme stated, 'The game exemplifies the worst aspects of capitalism that have made our country so great' (Walter Matthau). And though never explicit, this parallel is played on in the dialogue:

STEPHEN What do you think of Marx's theory of the inevitable decline of capitalism?
ASH Unlikely. Look at us.[4]

The dialogue is full of one-liners, from the response that Mugsy's dream of opening his own restaurant in a derelict Mile End public lavatory 'adds a whole new meaning to the term "convenience food"...', to 'What sleeps at the bottom of the sea and rapes mermaids? – Jack the kipper.' And the jargon of poker has a compelling attraction:

MUGSY You name it; Hold'em, Omaha, Irish, Lowball, Queen Follows ... Chicago, Hedgehog, Mugsy's Nightmare –
ASH What's that?
MUGSY I invented that one, it's five-card stud, hi-lo, two down, three up, whores, fours and one-eyed jacks wild with a twist, the twist being I'm the only one who understands it.[5]

But like the metaphor linking casinos with graveyards, naming the professional gambler Ash is no coincidence. Beneath the comic surface, as Marber states in the preface to the published text, '*Dealer's Choice* is a pessimistic play, a bleak comedy'; and his next play turned Strindberg's brutal portrayal of Darwinian selection in *Miss Julie* – first performed in 1889 – into a lament for the broken promise of social revolution.

A stripped-down version of the Naturalistic original, its laconic brevity, the hallmark of Marber's style, gives the action metaphoric weight. Updated to England on the night of the British Labour Party's landslide victory in the postwar election of July 1945, *After Miss Julie* (1996, adapted from a 1995 television version), the interaction between the spoilt daughter of a socialist Peer, who still 'despises the lower classes', and her father's servant newly returned from army service, becomes an image of class warfare. Julie may insist that 'the world is changing... there are opportunities now for self-improvement' – yet both are equally trapped by the long history of exploitation and inequality. This makes seduction little more than 'revenge... Your little class victory'; and the social system offers no way out but suicide.[6] Although this is, so far, the only explicitly political play of Marber's, its caustic and uncomfortable analysis underlies the apparently neutral portrayal of contemporary life in his comedies.

So in *Closer* (again directed by Marber himself for the National Theatre, 1997) the standard comic material of love and infidelity ruthlessly exposes a society where sex has become commodified and true feeling impossible. Even the way the characters are depicted as almost hermetically sealed off from the world around them is an image of isolation and dissociation that epitomizes the self-absorbed 'Me' generation of the 1990s. The four people seem to exist only in terms of their transient relationships to each other, in which all – except notably Alice, the young woman around whom the three others revolve – deceive and betray then swap partners. And this infidelity is indicated as habitual behaviour, with one of the women being a divorcee and one of the men dropping his previous girlfriend (who takes up with a poet, attracted ironically but significantly by the title of his book of poems, *Solitude*). Yet for all their obsession with finding love, they can achieve no more than physical intimacy. Demanding absolute emotional truth, all they can do is lie, since the language of love has become a cliché. And they are clearly intended to be representative.

As the description of the characters in the published text indicates, identifying each only as coming from town/suburbs/city/country, their backgrounds cover the whole of English society. In addition their professions relate directly to the theme of the play: a stripper (Alice), a photographer (Anna), a dermatologist (Larry) and a writer of newspaper obituaries who becomes a biographer (Dan). All in different ways stand for exposure, of oneself or others; the skin trade, and the substitution of surfaces for human reality; the resort to fantasy and image-making where improvements in the quality of life are fake, or at best cosmetic.

But the condemnation of contemporary society, irremediably damaged by the loss of a political idealism that is so complete no one is even aware of the lack, is completely subtextual. In this *Private Lives* for today, the dialogue has very much the same deadpan compression as Noel Coward:

ALICE Do you like it. . . in the *dying* business?
DAN It's a living.
ALICE Did you grow up in a graveyard?
DAN Yeah. Suburbia.[7]

The 'dying business' is (on many levels, including the 'small death' of coition) what the action is about. Yet in the immediate context it refers simply to Dan's work as a hack turning out sanitized obituaries; and although death is a recurring motif, until the final moments it only surfaces obliquely.

The play starts with the wandering free spirit, Alice, having been knocked down by a London taxi after exchanging a look with Dan – desire as a traffic accident – and it ends after her final break-up with him with her death: being run down by a car, presumably in an exactly equivalent encounter, on a New York street. The 'scar in the shape of a question mark' on her leg, possibly from initiating an earlier relationship in the same way, is indeed the 'mental disorder manifested in the skin' of self-mutilation (as the doctor suggests, even if in a very different sense).[8] Giving only contradictory information about herself, Alice is identified with her scar, as an existential question posed to this emotionally corrupt society, and represents hope, not just as the waif-like ideal of male fantasy but as the fleeting chance for a meaningful relationship. Yet even her name has been borrowed from a Victorian memorial for those who sacrificed themselves to save the lives of others: Alice Ayres, who died rescuing children from a fire in 1885. Now at the end of the millennium Alice becomes an equivalent icon through the photo Anna takes of her, titled 'Young Woman, London'; but although child-like, in the contemporary world she is betrayed by those who should save her. These characters may be obsessed with sex, but they are incapable of forming families. So their society, childless, literally has no future.

Notably there is no explicit political statement of the kind marking the earlier generation of playwrights like Edgar, Brenton and Hare – perhaps reflecting the way the 'New [in many ways neo-conservative] Labour' government had undermined any standard political rhetoric. Instead Marber builds up his social picture by incidental details, as well as through the highly patterned structure of the circular action and verbal repetition. But the culminative effect is a devastating indictment.

The green apple Alice bites in the opening moment, and the red half-eaten apple in the scene of 'Domestic Interiors' play off the primal sin in the Garden of Eden, as in Stoppard's *Arcadia*. However, here 'Paradise' is only a commercialized delusion – the label for private suites in a strip-club – while New York (the Big Apple) is 'a twenty-four-hour pageant called "Whatever You Want"'. They *celebrate* the sell-out' and 'the beautiful people' are 'all *whores*'. Similarly a 'Domestic Interior' is the art term describing the work of sixteenth-century Flemish painters who created the first images of ordinary homes and through them the whole idea of domesticity. Yet this scene-title relates to the parallel break-up of both marriages as a series of infidelities are revealed: in modern society, home life is an illusion undermined by guilt and betrayal. Even the smallest things in the play accumulate significance, like the toy Alice gives both her lovers – the Newton's Cradle with its swinging metal balls that knock each other out of contact, which becomes an image of the continually changing pairings in the play. Or the Aquarium, suggested as the title for Dan's biography of Alice and used as a rendezvous (at London zoo) – which stands for the fishbowl existence of the characters, not only obsessively stalked and spied on by each other, but under the gaze of the theatre-audience. As in the strip-club, 'Everything is a version of something else'[9] – and this forms the basis for Marber's thematic expression, in the same way that the use of blank cards in *Dealer's Choice* (specified in the stage-directions for the game) overtly signals that the focus is not on poker, but on what poker-playing reveals.

Closer is aggressively contemporary, as the key scene signifies in bringing the Internet on-stage. The words typed by the two men in their separate spaces either side of the stage, which appear on screens above each other's heads, graphically demonstrate the driving forces of the action: The replacement of emotional commitment by physical gratification; Egoism; the gap between language and truth, together with the absence of any real communication; Deception and manipulation. The chat-room they meet in is 'LONDON FUCK'; and cyber-sex – masturbation, both literal and when

17 Modern media and the betrayal of love in Marber's *Closer*

verbalized, fake ('Wait, have to type with I hand...I'm cumming right now...') – is fantasy unconnected with any real other, since one of the men is pretending to be a woman self-described as a female fetish ('Dark hair. Dirty mouth. Epic Tits... 36DD'), and in the aftermath of faked orgasm, the exchange reveals the reality of isolation and disjunction: 'Desire, like the world, is an accident. The best sex is anon. We liv as we dream, ALONE'.[10]

The Internet scene is not only shocking in its sexual content – it has the shock of up-to-date immediacy. Like other dramatists of the 1990s, Marber is very aware of the end of an era, but along with his other young contemporaries gives no sense that this will bring change. *Closer* depicts a sterile and atomized society, while the title-figure of *After Miss Julie* sees herself as Salomé – the *fin de siècle* icon of the 1890s – and in both the young girls who alone carry a promise of social renewal are destroyed. The approach of a new millennium is hardly a signal for hope.

Notes

1 *Silly Cow*, London 1998, p. 4; *Popcorn*, London, 1996, p. 48.

2 David Mamet, *Writing in Restaurants*, pp. 93–8 & 5.

3 *Dealer's Choice*, London, 1995, p. 76.

4 *Ibid.*, pp. 1, 10 and 21, 108; programme for the Vaudeville Theatre, 1995.

5 *Dealer's Choice*, pp. 62, 70, 53.

6 *After Miss Julie*, London, 1996, pp. 30, 22.

7 *Closer*, p. 2 – compare the patterning of the dialogue in Coward's *Private Lives*, p. 277 above.

8 *Closer*, pp. 96–7.

9 *Ibid.*, pp. 48–9, 63.

10 *Ibid.*, pp. 24–27.

Poetic drama – verse, fantasy and symbolic images

Poetic drama in the strict sense – plays with dialogue written in verse – has found little resonance on the British stage since the 1890s. The dominance of Bernard Shaw's definition of modernist theatre, and his attack on Shakespearean 'Bardolatry', was partly responsible for its eclipse. When the critic William Archer declared that verse substituted 'rhetoric for human speech' (echoing Ibsen), he was expressing a view that was widely held at the turn of the century.[1]

The use of verse on the stage had already become recognizably artificial by the mid-Nineteenth Century. The Romantic admiration for Shakespeare, which produced the derivative archaism of Keats' *King Otho* or Shelley's *The Cenci*, led to the picturesque escapism of Swinburne or the neo-Elizabethan inflation of Tennyson's *Becket* (1884). Even before naturalism established new criteria of authenticity, verse had been relegated to historical pageants: a dressed-up speech for costume plays. And the theatrical attempts of poets such as John Masefield or James Elroy Flecker only confirmed the gulf between verse and modern experience.

Masefield retreated from contemporary subjects (*The Tragedy of Nan*, 1908) to Roman and Biblical themes (*The Tragedy of Pompey the Great*, 1910; *Esther*, 1921); and although – following W.B. Yeats and Gordon Craig – he experimented with Japanese Noh and medieval Miracle Play models, his imagery remained purely verbal. The sensuous lyricism of Flecker's *Hassan* (1914, unperformed until 1923) has an exotic attraction that led to its revival as part of the 1951 Festival of Britain. But even when first produced, *Hassan* was received as a period piece, with its popularity due as much to the incidental music supplied by Delius and the ballets by Fokine, as to Flecker's romanticized Middle-Eastern legend.

Poetry, the traditional language for tragedy, was relegated to spectacle. Yet the naturalistic definition of modernism promoted by Shaw and Archer had clear limitations. In particular it was incapable of handling the 'passions' that the Nineteenth Century had seen as the soul of 'serious' drama. Concentrating on social issues, and appealing to reason, this type of modernism automatically tended to depreciate the spiritual aspect of existence. It was also increasingly challenged by continental influences. The French Symbolists of the 1890s were taken up by Oscar Wilde in *Salomé* (1891, first performed in England 1905), and Yeats. German and Scandinavian Expressionism, introduced to London during the 1920s by the Gate Theatre (where the plays of Kaiser, Toller and Wedekind, as well as Strindberg's later plays and O'Neill's early work, were staged by Peter Godfrey), provided an alternative model for dramatists in the 1930s. The symbolic Existentialism of Beckett, and the French Absurdism of Ionesco, which both appeared on the London stage in 1955–56, opened up new possibilities for English dramatists, which were directly opposed to the social confrontation initiated by Osborne's *Look Back in Anger* at the same time.

Although Shaw's principles have continued to shape the mainstream of British theatre, updated by Osborne, Arden and Bond, as well as Stoppard, these continental influences counterbalanced the dominance of Shaw. However, with the exception of Yeats at the beginning of the century, and T.S. Eliot and Christopher Fry in the late 1940s and early 1950s, the language of 'poetic drama' has not been verbal. Instead, structural equivalents were proposed. Poetry OF the theatre replaced poetry IN the theatre (Cocteau). At one extreme, an abstract geometry of moving shapes and light was used to create visual music (Gordon Craig). More conventionally, acted scenes integrated like images in a poem, have been proposed as a specifically theatrical form of poetry (Peter Brook). The first remained a largely unrealized ideal, although Craig's vision has been influential in terms of stage design. The second led to Brook's experiments with pre-verbal ritual in the 1960s, based on the theories of Antonin Artaud, which have carried over into David Rudkin's plays. However, in both these alternatives poetic attributes are completely divorced from verse.

Yet this 'poetry OF the theatre' shares common ground with modern verse dramatists, even those who (like Yeats) claim the 'sovereignty of words' over physical representation. Each rejects Naturalism. The naturalistic reflection of daily life is seen as limiting theatre (in T.S. Eliot's phrase) to 'transitory and superficial' subjects. Prose is equated with the prosaic, reducing existence to social/political terms that deny any archetypal or transcendental dimension – whereas 'the permanent and universal' is the province of poetry, epitomized in the expressionist 'call for a spiritual stage'.[2] In these terms, poetic drama need not be written in verse dialogue, which is only one of many non-naturalistic forms. The poetic vision can be expressed through mythic images and dream states, subjective explorations or existential universalization, symbolism and ritual.

Although this type of anti-naturalistic theatre puts particular stress on the unity of style and content, in defining poetic drama the form is secondary. What is significant is the area of experience with which it deals. This is generic and transcendental, as opposed to particular and social. It evokes subliminal states instead of making political statements. In this sense, whether dialogue is written in prose or verse is irrelevant, compared to dramatic focus and thematic intention.

5.1 The rejection of society: J. M. Barrie (1860–1937)

CHECKLIST OF BARRIE'S MAJOR PLAYS

Quality Street, 1902	*What Every Woman Knows*, 1908
The Admirable Crichton, 1902	*Dear Brutus*, 1917
Peter Pan, 1904	*Mary Rose*, 1920

At its most accessible and popular, this broadly defined kind of 'poetic' drama is embodied in fantasy, the classic example being J. M. Barrie's *Peter Pan* (1904). Although he co-directed a film with Granville-Barker in 1914, in which Shaw and William Archer made guest appearances, Barrie rejected the naturalistic social analysis that they championed as turning entertainment into 'a penance and the function of the dramatist . . . to that of the skeleton at the Egyptian feast'. His first play had parodied Ibsen; his review of Janet Achurch's *Hedda Gabler* concluded that 'to conceive of the Ibsen Drama gaining an extensive or permanent foothold on the stage is hardly possible'; and his work can be seen as a long rear-guard defence against it.[3]

Even *The Admirable Crichton*, hailed in 1902 as a penetrating social document, uses utopian fantasy to attack the class-structure. The injustice of master/servant distinctions are exposed – although disguised by traditional comic inversion: shipwrecked on a desert island, natural superiority makes the practical butler the 'Gov', while the aristocratic parasites are transformed into productive members of an arcadian society under his rule. Just when this utopia is about to be irrevocably ratified by Lady Mary becoming Crichton's wife, the arrival of a naval rescue-party restores the status quo; and renouncing her, he reassumes his earlier obsequious role.

Although it appeared a political cop-out when the play was revived in 1988, this 'happy' ending is clearly intended as ironic. The social positions to which the characters revert are now demonstrably untenable – while the traditional comic celebration, which affirms a new basis for society through marriage, is denied. Indeed, the radical intention of *The Admirable Crichton* was made explicit in Barrie's revised ending for a 1920 revival, where Crichton denounces social inequality on being forced back into subservience (instead of willingly reassuming his butler's role), 'foretelling' a great war leading to revolution. But this undercut the fantasy; and Barrie retained the original ending for the published text.

In *Dear Brutus* (1917), where 'a romance' is set against these wartime realities, the same sort of fantasy creates a permanent effect on the characters. Here the action and imagery of *A Midsummer Night's Dream* is embedded as an archetypal pattern in the action. (Indeed, Shakespeare's play is assumed to be so familiar that there are no explicit references to it in Barrie's text.) Adultery, social discord and self-disgust among the guests at an Edwardian house-party are resolved by the elderly host, who turns out to be Puck, 'all that is left of Merry England'.[4] He persuades them to take an after-dinner walk in a 'magic' wood. Losing themselves, each finds his or her dream; and they return one by one at dawn, sadder but wiser, determined to act on their new self-perception.

As in the earlier play, removing the fixed expectations and divisive customs of society liberates the people. The message is the same: nothing will change unless we change ourselves. But here the natural world in which the characters find themselves is purgatorial, rather than utopian, and subjective instead of geographical. Since the change is psychological, not in external circumstances, the reform is lasting. It also represents a return to traditional and spiritual values – Shakespeare being linked to subconscious desires through the significance of dreams.

The circular structure of *The Admirable Crichton* – where characters are returned to their opening state, while an intervening fantasy discredits the situation that had initially been accepted as normal – recurs in *Dear Brutus* and *Mary Rose* (1920). Both these plays, which Barrie labelled 'uncomfortable tales', also include dream children; and all three contain ideal worlds that are the opposite of existing society: a Robinson Crusoe atoll, a magic forest, and in *Mary Rose* an enchanted island. These elements come together in their pure form in *Peter Pan*, which epitomizes Barrie's work and became the standard by which he evaluated his other plays. According to an Edwardian contemporary, Barrie's 'popularity as a playwright surpassed that of all his

competitors. He only had two flops in his life.' Yet Barrie continually dispar-
aged his own success: 'ingenious enough, but not dug out of myself... an
artificial world' (*What Every Woman Knows*, 1908), 'What my work failed
in was robustness' (*Mary Rose*) – each play being found wanting in specific
contrast to the imaginative strength and realism of 'the Peter Pan Co'.[5]

By naturalistic criteria *Peter Pan* (1904) is sentimental escapism. But the
play's premise invalidates rational criticism and materialistic levels of experience. Childhood is presented as a Wordsworthian state of pre-social innocence, opposed to the adult world of everyday experience; and the child's-eye
view, through which everything is presented, is imposed on the audience.
Although generally regarded as children's entertainment, the play's intention
is rather to return parents to their childhood.

Set in an undefined past it is designed to evoke nursery memories. Pirates,
wolves with fiery eyes, redskins on the warpath and mermaids combing
their hair – like half-glimpsed wild beasts of fears in the shadows, the first
things to be seen in 'Never Land' – are the archetypal inhabitants of a child's
imagination from any age. Indeed, they were already traditional at the turn of
the century, and continue to be so primarily because of Barrie's play. Flying,
and the womb-like underground home of the Lost Boys, both have Freudian
resonances. Even the pretence of theatrical performance is mirrored in the
'pretend' children's games that are the basis of the action, with the roller-
blind on the nursery window through which Peter flies and which rises to
reveal the magical island, being '*what Peter would have called the theatre
curtain if he had ever seen one*'.[6]

The child's perspective highlights the gap between ideal and reality. It
glamorizes the family, centred round the loving mother figure as a vision of
beauty in evening gown, without concealing the poverty of mind as well as
purse in the society depicted. The father, '*fixed as a postage stamp*' and reduced to a cypher by his work, bribes his children into taking medicine, then
reneges on his bargain. Transposing the faithful family dog into a nurse may
be an inspired comic inversion; but it also implies that servants are treated
as dogs. Beneath the idealization of the mother, she is the agent of social-
ization for her children, '*tidying up their minds just as if they were drawers*'.
Above all, in terms of the play, the process of becoming a member of society
destroys the capacity for believing in any more ideal alternative. Growing
up means discarding imaginary illusions, adults being (by definition) no
longer able to perceive a figure like Peter Pan; and the purpose of the play
is to reverse this by bringing the play-world of infancy to life on the stage.
All that the children in the play require to enter this other world is that they

believe in it; and the performance becomes a test of belief for the audience. The whole machinery of pantomime is deployed to create a magical illusion, culminating in a direct appeal to the spectators: 'If you believe in fairies, clap your hands!'[7]

The island inhabitants gain a mythic reality as the epitome of popular images. As dots of coloured light, the fairies are pure essence, freed from the Victorian sentimentality of gauze and wings. Jas Hook, Captain of the Jolly Roger, is the quintessence of all pirates: cadaverous, black and sinister, with periwig and iron claw. At the same time, Barrie's stage directions emphasize that this magic world is a projection of Peter Pan's mind, animated by his consciousness. As his name implies, he is Pan, the pagan god of nature in the shape of a boy; and he embodies the play's repudiation of society. Ageless, he

ran away the day I was born . . . Because I heard mother talking of what I was to be when I became a man. I want always to be a little boy and to have fun.

And there is an echo of Huckleberry Finn in his final rejection, when the children offer him a home with their family. The prospect of school, followed by the drudgery of an office job, outweighs the emotional security of maternal love that has been his guiding desire throughout the action: 'No one is going to catch me, lady, and make me a man.'[8] Significantly, Captain Hook is presented as Peter Pan's *alter ego*. In this world of absolutes, innocence and evil are interchangeable; and Hook represents the demonic potential of society. (An Old Etonian from his final words as, defeated, he leaps into the waiting jaws of his crocodile nemesis calling out the school motto, Hook is the dark side of the upper-class Establishment.)

Never Land is the opposite of actual existence: specifically a dream, '*often half seen*' on the verge of sleep, and coexisting with the theatrical performance that ends with Peter playing pan-pipes '*on and on till we wake up*'. In the everyday world children are told fairy tales; on the island of imagination their ordinary life becomes the make-believe story. 'Wonderful thoughts' are enough to enable anyone to fly: they can liberate the audience from social restraints in their real lives, just as they free the children from physical constraints on the stage.[9] And to gain acceptance for his alternative vision, Barrie makes its vehicle as unthreatening as the dangers confronted by the children within it. Red Indians, crocodiles and the evil pirates – either friendly beneath their threatening appearance, or easily outwitted and routed – are reduced to games. In the same way, the play itself uses the unserious form of pantomime. Trivialized as children's entertainment, and thus rendered socially acceptable, it evades the censorship of reason.

Notes

1 William Archer, *The Old Drama and the New*, London, 1923, p. 47. The degree to which the modernist ethos – political, objective and scientific – and the values of poetic drama – existential, subjective and symbolic – were mutually exclusive can be indicated by the opposition between Shaw's dramaturgy and the Yeatsian dance-play, the most consistent and extreme attempt to create a new poetic idiom for the contemporary stage. Shaw's 'verbal fencing matches' embodying 'the bustle and crepitation of life' are the opposite of Yeats' ritualistic sublimation through 'self-effacing rhythm and language' (1907 letter to Fiona Macleod), which he recognized as 'the theatre's anti-self' (Open Letter to Lady Gregory, 1919).

2 W. B. Yeats, *Essays and Introductions*, London, 1961, p. 170; T.S. Eliot, *On Poetry and Poets*, London, 1957, p. 82; Walter Hasenclever, *Die Schaubühne*, 11 May 1916.

3 Barrie, in *The Times*, 21 April 1891.

4 Barrie, *The Admirable Crichton and Other Plays*, New York, 1926, pp. 16, 130.

5 *The Letters of J. M. Barrie*, ed. Viola Meynell, London, 1942, pp. vii, 21, 166, and Hesketh Pearson, *Theatre Arts*, July 1961.

6 *Peter Pan*, London, 1928, p. 4.

7 *Ibid.*, pp. 11, 7, 119.

8 *Ibid.*, pp. 31, 155.

9 *Ibid.*, pp. 46 & 160. (Barrie was persuaded to insert the business with 'magic dust' for fear that children might injure themselves in attempting to imitate his characters.)

5.2 J. B. Priestley (1894–1984): temporal dislocation and transcendence

CHECKLIST OF PRIESTLEY'S MAJOR PLAYS

The Good Companions, 1931	*Music At Night*, 1938
Dangerous Corner, 1932	*Johnson Over Jordan*, 1939
Laburnum Grove, 1933	*An Inspector Calls*, 1946
Eden End, 1934	*Ever Since Paradise*, 1947
Time and the Conways, 1937	*The Linden Tree*, 1947
I Have Been Here Before, 1937	*A Severed Head*, 1963

J.B. Priestley was in many ways the successor to Barrie, popularizing spiritual and metaphysical themes in a mainly conventional style. A contemporary of Noel Coward, who set the standard for social comedy between the wars, Priestley won a reputation, alongside T.S. Eliot, as the leading serious dramatist of the 1930s and 1940s. Indeed, far more than Eliot, Priestley's work is identified with its era. So he became the main object of attack in the theatrical revolution initiated by John Osborne in the mid-1950s, being singled out by the angry young protagonist of *Look Back in Anger* as 'like Daddy – still casting well-fed glances back to the Edwardian twilight from his comfortable disenfranchised wilderness'.[1]

The partial truth in this picture led to the disappearance of Priestley's plays from the London stage for the next twenty years, even though they remained a staple of repertory theatre. However, successful revivals of *An Inspector Calls* (West End 1973: first performed 1946) and *Eden End* (National Theatre 1974: first performed 1934), followed by West End productions of his comedies, brought Priestley back to critical notice. And indeed *An Inspector Calls*, in Stephen Daldry's spectacular 1992 production at the Old Vic, has proved to be one of the most popular modern plays ever: restaged in 1995 and still running at the turn of the new century, as well as a hit on Broadway.

Priestley's forty-nine plays range widely, from light social comedy and metaphoric political farce to static philosophical dialogue (modelled on the Charles Laughton performed-reading of the Hell sequence from Shaw's *Man and Superman*). Much of this work is derivative, with *The Roundabout* (1933) updating Somerset Maugham's comedy, *The Circle* (1921), while *Ever Since Paradise* (1946) echoes Shaw in its subtitle of a 'Discursive Entertainment', as in its ironic presentation of the battle of the sexes through Shavian debate. However, Priestley repudiates the theatrical line promoted by Shaw and Maugham in the series of plays that established him as the leading serious English dramatist of the 1930s. These are concerned – like Barrie's *Dear Brutus* or *Mary Rose* a decade earlier – with the redemptive presence of the supernatural in everyday life.

Like Barrie, Priestley switched between fiction and the stage. The dramatization of his novel, *The Good Companions* (in collaboration with Edward Knoblock, 1931), formed Priestley's first theatrical success, and *A Severed Head* (adapted with Iris Murdoch from her novel, 1963) his last. His characteristic theme, in which the external life of physical action and social responsibilities is set against a deeper subjective reality, echoes Barrie. Material existence is presented as transitory and illusory, by comparison with the world of dream; and his use of Shakespeare's *A Midsummer Night's Dream* as the basis for *Summer Day's Dream* (1949) is very similar to Barrie's treatment of the same source in *Dear Brutus* (see above, p. 439). For both Priestley and Barrie, Shakespeare's play represents spiritual values that are lacking in modern life. Although Priestley's view is darker, projecting a future of nuclear war and dictatorship, his updating has the same tendency to sentimental whimsy as Barrie. The Shakespearean archetype promotes sanity and utopian possibilities, converting the forces of blighting technology and military repression to a Rousseauesque environmentalism through the magic of nature.

Priestley's commitment to drama as an educative tool, concerned with serious ideas, parallels Shaw; and he shared similar political principles, lecturing to the Fabian Society on 'The Arts Under Socialism'. But the metaphysical vision of Priestley's 'Time Plays' is very different. These cover almost the whole of his theatrical career from *Dangerous Corner* (1932), to a television play of 1958, *Doomsday for Dyson*. Their apparently naturalistic surface is deceptive, moving towards overt symbolism as Priestley's major theme becomes more clearly elaborated.

Although generally working with naturalistic conventions to gain audience acceptance, Priestley always saw his drama as subversive. His aim was to undermine the conceptual basis of Naturalism – in particular its emphasis on material conditions and social existence as the only reality – and he protested that 'to regard me, as some professorial theorists . . . have done recently, as a typical playwright of the naturalistic tradition seems to me so absurd that I can only imagine that it is a judgement based . . . on ignorance'. For instance, there are plot parallels between Chekhov's naturalistic classic, *The Cherry Orchard*, and Priestley's *Eden End* (1934). Yet the subtextual expansion of surface action and use of atmospheric mood, which Chekhov had developed to increase the realism of his scenes, and to expose psychological depth in his characters, here point to a universe of pure symbols. If, as Priestley asserts, 'personality, the separate self, is an illusion' – a proposition that *Music At Night* (1938) was explicitly intended to demonstrate – then both the objective existence of society and individual impressionism is denied. Even *Dangerous Corner*, which Priestley dismissed as 'merely an ingenious box of tricks', implies as much.[2]

Quite apart from being the most frequently performed of his plays, *Dangerous Corner* repays analysis as the earliest and philosophically simplest of Priestley's 'Time Plays'. An apparent whodunnit, set in a country-house party typical of the genre, the plot revolves around a circular series of questions, each arising logically from the previous one. Money is missing, and one of the only three people who could have taken it commits suicide – who saw the dead man last? Was he really the thief? If he didn't steal the money, why did he shoot himself? Did he die by his own hand, or was he

murdered? Was whoever saw him last the murderer? The characters are conventional types: to the point that the female novelist, whose curiosity sets
things moving is described as '*your own idea of what a smart middle-aged
woman novelist should be*'.[3] In fact the triteness of these stock elements is
so blatant that the opening of a shot in the dark instantly became a cliché
(even here, in what was possibly its first use). The 'truth' revealed by the
investigation of the crimes is simply the opposite of the opening picture,
both being equally exaggerated.

The first impression after the blackout, of 'pairs of adoring husbands and
wives' in a 'charmed circle... a snug little group' is explicitly presented as a
Christmas-card pastiche: 'In these days almost too good to be true'. Instead
of the admired paragon he seems to be, the dead man turns out to have
been a drug-crazed rapist, while Olwen, the image of girlish innocence, is
finally discovered to be the murderer – although this too is inverted, since
rather than being a villain, she was the victim, shooting a dangerous maniac
accidentally and in self-defence. Similarly, the righteous avenger is shattered
by the revelations he has so singlemindedly pursued: 'my brother was an
obscene lunatic... my wife doted on him and pestered him. One of my
partners is a liar and a cheat and a thief. The other ... some sort of hysterical
pervert', while he recognizes the beautiful wife of one of his partners, whom
he has idolized, as 'a greedy little cat on the tiles'.[4] This final picture of universal corruption is so extreme that it stretches credulity as much as the
misleading first appearances. Clichés cancel out.

However, the audience have been warned that people are conditioned to
accept half-truths as reality, and that the pursuit of truth is as dangerous
as speeding into a dangerous corner unless (like the omniscient vision of
'God's truth') one is capable of seeing beyond the apparent facts. The play
demonstrates this by returning to the beginning after a second blackout.
This time, the opening shot in the dark is not a real-life murder, but only
the climax of a radio drama the characters have been listening to; and the
parallels between the broadcast (a detective story titled 'The Sleeping Dog')
and the previous action blurs the distinction between fiction and reality.
The naturalistic uncovering of dark secrets, and the acting out of violent
crime, are nothing but an illusion, a *trompe l'oeil*. The classic detective-story
twist here is that the murder never happened.

It is only one possible variant of equally imaginary circumstances. As
Priestley explained, 'All that happens between the two blackouts in the
play... is neither an actual happening nor yet somebody's dream, but a
What-Might-Have-Been, a sudden excursion for all the people concerned

into some other kind of time'. Catastrophe can be avoided by returning through time to an alternative course of events. However, the only reason why restoring the convivial status quo should be more real than the previous painful outcome, is that happy endings are the norm in popular fiction. Given the destructive sexuality, hypocrisy and crime that have just been exposed, it is a cover-up. Removing the consequences has done nothing to change the innate problems – unless personality is as variable as people's actions.

Yet personal consciousness is the controlling factor. This follows logically from the play's premise that reality is not empirical, but merely a concept defined by received assumptions. At the same time, Priestley is deliberately ambiguous when he asserts that 'You must suppose that Olwen alone, in a moment of agony, guessed this. You can even assume . . . that by a grand effort of will, she pulled them all back into our own world and time again.'[5]

Agonized by guilt, Olwen declares '(*with a certain hysterical quality*) . . . It *shan't* happen'; and this is the cue for returning to the beginning. Yet in fact the determining factor is mechanical and outside her control. In version 1 of the action, the radio stops functioning for no apparent reason; and this initiates the conversation that leads to the accusation of theft, with all that ensues. In version 2, one of the characters tunes in to a music programme; and instead of the discussion, they all take part in an impromptu dance (the conventional image of social harmony).

Priestley's point seems to be that no individual could determine such a shift – but then, in this particular context, the point goes by default. There are no individuals, since these characters are cliché figures. Indeed, personality as such is demonstrably unreal: an unfaithful wife explains that she 'wouldn't have looked at anybody else if [her husband]'d been – real. But he just isn't there.' Similarly the truth-seeker, whose ideal she was, rejects her with 'I don't know you . . . I'm saying good-bye to this. (*Indicates her face and body*.) That's all.'[6]

Priestley's fascination with Time as the new frontier for the human spirit, offering a replacement for outdated religious beliefs, was shaped by the speculations of the mystic P.D. Ouspensky, and the mathematician J.W. Dunne. The first proposed the coexistence of an almost infinite number of alternative time sequences; the second that there is a temporal plane on which the past, the future and the now of any given moment are simultaneously present. Dunne's 1927 *Experiment with Time*, which explored precognition in dreams, also offered support for the rejection of individuality as a subjective illusion.

As Priestley interpreted Dunne's conclusions: 'each of us is a series of observers existing in a series of Times. To Observer One, our ordinary fully awake sharp selves, the fourth dimension appears as Time'. It is on this second level that 'Observer Two' lives: 'the self we know in dreams', whose experience is outside the present and can only be tapped when the conscious mind is inoperative. In the further unknowable dimension of eternity a third-level observer exists, aware of both other selves, corresponding to the soul. Ascending the hierarchy of superior consciousness, individuality diminishes as particular experience gives way to an increasingly universal perspective. To this Priestley added the notion of recurrence taken from Ouspensky's *A New Model of the Universe*: each person endlessly re-lives their existence – giving us all the possibility of learning 'to live, evolve properly, and so . . . turn the circle into a spiral, and escape'.[7] The value of Ouspensky's mysticism to a Fabian Socialist like Priestley is that it reintroduces the categories of moral purpose and immortality without the need for a deity.

Whatever the credibility of this, as a working hypothesis it gave Priestley's plays a serious commitment, although it also produced major dramatic problems – as in *I Have Been Here Before* (1937), which explored these ideas directly. The omniscient figure was originally 'a transient from some other sphere'.[8] Making him a doctor with a foreign accent hardly gives this character credibility; and the thinness of his human disguise is indicated by the ordinary characters' suspicion that he is a German spy. The plot, which revolves around an unhappily married couple's chance involvement with a young man and leads to murder, is melodramatic. But suspense is removed by the alien doctor's knowledge of the tragic outcome, which he has witnessed in another temporal dimension and is therefore able to prevent. The sole motivation for anything these characters do – and even for their presence at the isolated Yorkshire inn, where they meet – is the contention that they have already lived through these events. All this makes it hard to identify with the stage world as a transcription of real experience; and when Priestley returned to the same theme in *An Inspector Calls* (1946), he rejected naturalistic surfaces for the conventional artifice of the thriller-genre in a variation on *Dangerous Corner*.

Again Priestley takes the standard detective-story assumptions about crime and punishment, good and evil, and uses these to represent the superficial view of life that blinds people to deeper realities. As in the whodunnit, nothing is what it seems. Like the earlier play, *An Inspector Calls* ends with a return to the opening situation. But here the effect is opposite, putting the stamp of determinism on the action and making it a projection of communal guilt, in which coming events cast their shadow before.

The action is set in 1912 on the eve of the First World War. But it has none of the nostalgia that characterizes Priestley's previous dramatizations of the Edwardian period, such as *The Good Companions* or *Eden End*. After economic depression and a second global conflict, the recurrence of time is now interpreted fatalistically, instead of as a possible window of opportunity. *An Inspector Calls* is a drama of repentance in which any acceptance of responsibility comes too late, and past exploitation of the poor brings future retribution – the destruction of civilization that has already occurred from the viewpoint of a 1945 audience, who are accused of still living the same blinkered materialistic existence as the pre-1914 characters.

The message brought by Priestley's policeman of the conscience is: 'if men will not learn that lesson, then they will be taught it in fire and blood and anguish'. And just as the characters experience their future, so the dramatic past is implicitly being repeated by the present audience, even after a second holocaust. When the Inspector unexpectedly enters their home, the Edwardian family simply cannot believe that his interrogation has any relevance to them. So they complacently dismiss him as a fake, only to find themselves – horrifyingly – acting out the crime of which they have been accused. In the same way, the enigmatic agent of justice (with all the supernatural connotations of the pun on ghost in Inspector Goole's name) is on his way to us. Heavily ironic references to the 'unsinkable' Titanic, or 'twenty or thirty years time – let's say in 1940' when 'you may be giving a little party like this' underline the contemporary point.[9]

The most effective of Priestley's 'Time Plays' is *Time and the Conways* (1937). The play is designed to give an audience the experience of Dunne's second-level observers – so opening their minds to an alternative and spiritual definition of existence. The opening scene, in which the Conway children prepare to act out a charade, offers a miniature example of Priestley's theme. Present and future overlap as Carol, the youngest child, dons '*an old shawl . . . some white hair – for the old lady. And . . . converts herself into a very creditable imitation*'. The shift in perspective, from which normal reality is seen as artificial, is indicated when they hold up '*some old-fashioned women's . . . clothes*', exclaiming 'Could you believe people *ever* wore such ridiculous things?' The implications of this heavily playful dressing-up are then explored in terms of the children's lives.

They speculate about being able to 'see around the corner – into the future'; and the unchronological sequence of the scenes gives the spectators precisely this ability.[10] The final Act is an unbroken continuation from the end of the first, while the middle Act jumps forward from 1919 to the present time of the performance. Presented as a precognitive dream, experienced but only imperfectly remembered by Kay, the most sensitive of the Conway children, this juxtaposition of their hopeful youth against their future reveals the gap between aspiration and achievement, promise and fulfilment. Our knowledge of what is hidden from the characters places us in a superior position. It also makes us see the happy family scene of Act I in a new light, when we return to it in Act III, creating emotional involvement through pathos.

The hope for a better life, celebrated in 1919 at the end of the First World War, is set against the bleak awareness that in 1937 the family (and the audience) are 'just before the next War'. In the second Act we learn that Carol will be dead before the end of the year, despite her vitality. The only outlet Kay's literary sensitivity has found is in hack journalism, while the social idealism of one sister has withered into frustrated hypochondria, and another is paying in misery for her wealthy marriage. By 1937 the family is literally as well as morally bankrupt; and returning to the party of 1919 shows us the seeds of disaster beneath their apparent happiness.

However, the obvious conclusion, voiced by Kay – 'Remember what we once were and what we thought we'd be . . . Better to die, like Carol, before you find it out, before Time gets to work on you . . . There's a great devil in the universe, and we call it Time' – is explicitly denied.

Time's only a kind of dream . . . now at this moment, or any moment, we're only a cross-section of our real selves . . . when we come to the end of this life, all those selves, all our time, will be us – the real you, the real me. And then perhaps we'll find ourselves in another time, which is only another kind of dream.

For the Conways, an awareness that they are 'immortal beings' is sufficient to transform despair into a sense of potential adventure; likewise, the structure of the play is designed to help an audience 'take a long view'.[11]

The opening of *Time and the Conways* presents a dark and empty stage, cut off from the light and music of human activity that filters through from beyond a curtained archway; and this metaphorical antechamber of consciousness forms the basis for the focal tableau that bridges each Act. At the end of the first Act Kay is left sitting alone, staring into the night, with the moon (carrying traditional connotations of dream and poetry) shining on her head through the windows. At the 1937 end of Act II the same picture is repeated with one essential difference – Kay '*stands there looking out, with head raised*' – and the final impression as the curtain falls on the 1919 conclusion to the play echoes this as the room returns to darkness. The lights fade, reducing the characters to '*no more than ghosts . . . the moonlight – and the faces of* KAY *and* ALAN *– still lingers; until at last there is only the faintest glimmer and the Conways have gone*'.[12]

The recurring pattern makes an audience acutely aware of perception, by challenging us to spot divergences within apparent parallels, although the ironies are over-obvious. At first glance, 1937 looks exactly the same as 1919: as the stage directions emphasize '*for a moment we think nothing has happened*'. However, switching on the light reveals that everything except the positioning of the single figure at the window is different, while in the return to 1919 what we have been shown as a false similarity between Acts I and II is reversed: '*the room and everything in it is exactly as they were before. Only* KAY *has changed*.'

This illustrates Priestley's concept of temporal reality, where 'everything is solidly there, whether we call it past, present or future'. In his terms, common experience (being restricted to the present) is analogous to 'travelling through a dark landscape with a searchlight, or . . . staring at a bright scene through a slit in a moving barrier'. All we have to do to see different sections of the continuum in any sequence is free ourselves from the limitations of a three-dimensional mind-set.[13] The relevance to the structure of *Time and the Conways* is obvious. But the naturalistic treatment of each time frame is inappropriate for representing the stream of consciousness, which underlies Priestley's metaphysical vision.

In a sense, despite the continuing popularity of his plays, Priestley never found a satisfactory dramatic form for his metaphysical view of life. Most of his 'Time Plays' lie uneasily in a middle ground between Naturalism and Expressionism. Indeed they can be performed in either style, as the contrast between the 1946 Moscow and London productions of *An Inspector Calls* showed.

Tairov's symbolic setting, in which a heavily ornamented ceiling sloped down to meet a sharply raked stage and a single door delineated the wall of the family living-room, opened up the perspective on the action with dim vistas beyond the brightly lit acting area. According to Priestley, this was effective in 'making everything cast a long shadow', whereas the detailed naturalism of the Old Vic staging, with the suburban house and its inhabitants 'solidly rooted in English life' prevented London audiences from grasping that the play's true focus lay beyond the immediate action.[14] As a result it was taken as a mere entertainment piece, with the unrealized substratum of spiritual meaning simply making the plot seem contrived. However, this disparaging

view of the play had to be completely revised when Stephen Daldry staged
it in 1992, and again in 1995. Returning to Tairov's non-naturalistic interpretation, Daldry's expressionistic lighting and graphic use of spectacle – as
in the final scene where the bourgeois doll's house, undermined by deceit
and moral corruption, literally disintegrated, suddenly collapsing in fragmented ruin on the stage – gripped audiences and revealed the true nature
of Priestley's drama, which operates here (as in many of his other plays) on
a spiritual level beneath an apparently materialistic surface.

Priestley's intention in the 'Time Plays' was 'to present dramatically a kind
of Everyman of my own generation', who 'would represent the deep distrust
of life felt by so many moderns'.[15] By contrast, Naturalism validates everyday
life. So, in the plays that followed *Time and the Conways* and *I Have Been
Here Before*, Priestley experimented with alternative stylistic models derived
from Thornton Wilder, Elmer Rice and the German Expressionists. *Music
At Night* (1938), *Johnson Over Jordan* and *Ever Since Paradise* (both 1939,
though the last was only performed in 1947) were attempts to find theatrical
equivalents for the stream-of-consciousness techniques that James Joyce or
Virginia Woolf had developed for the novel.

Music At Night uses a symphonic form 'to dramatise the mental adventures of a group of people listening to the first performance of a piece of
music'. Shifts between different levels of consciousness are represented by
fading music in and out, together with lighting changes. Dialogue modulates
from superficial cocktail-chatter, to trance-like delivery and counterpointed
soliloquies. The structure imitates the violin concerto, which provides an
accompaniment to the three 'movements' of the play, progressing from an
allegro to '*agitato – maestoso nobile*, which means . . . it becomes very agi-
tated – y'know, worrying about life, and then it turns all grand and noble,
just to end up with'. The musical score is assumed to control the characters'
moods. Its subliminal influence moves the action 'from the surface of the
mind to deeper and deeper levels of consciousness', finally demonstrating
that on the most intense level 'we are not the separate beings we imagine
ourselves to be'. However, as Priestley himself commented, 'trying to show
that personality, the separate self, is an illusion [is] a hopeless task in the
Theatre'.[16]

In response, *Ever Since Paradise* attempts to popularize his vision by ap-
plying it to the standard comedy of marriage. In terms of sex, the most
fundamental aspect of our lives, 'we're all sons of Adam' or 'daughters of
Eve'. At the same time, love can be presented as both an emotional reality,

and 'a cheat . . . ever since Paradise'. To gain acceptance for his ideas, Priestley acknowledges the intellectually suspect nature of his philosophical sources, while incorporating his time theories subliminally in the play's structure. Dunne's theories are parodied as 'this big *Now* . . . behind the little *Now*' (with 'Not just now thank you, some other time' as the characters' unanimous response to being asked to imagine themselves on the fourth dimension). Similarly Ouspensky's concepts are reduced to a *wonderful* talk on 'I AM THE GREAT ALL' by a spiritualist named Madame Rubbishky.[17]

The tone is light. But the multiple layers of the action give a sense of depth in much the same way as a hall of self-reflecting mirrors. Images multiply through setting up parallels between three different levels of characters: a married couple, whose story is presented by another pair as evidence for their arguments about whether the husband or wife is responsible for divorce; and the emotional interplay between a duet of pianists, who provide musical accompaniment for the action.

The dramatic frame is increasingly broken, with the married figures – who at first seem puppets, under the commentators' control – stepping out of their parts to watch the performance of the others, and the theatre audience also being brought in from time to time by direct address. Observing the actors in their 'example' the commentators (divorced some years previously) decide to remarry, while the pianists stop quarrelling and become engaged – and the rocky marriage of the pair in the inner play is saved by the divorced couples' intervention. The technique of *Ever Since Paradise* is extremely sophisticated. It anticipates Samuel Beckett's self-reflexive works, *Film* and *Play*, being based on the same contradiction between *cogito ergo sum* and *esse est percipi* – 'I think therefore I am' versus 'To be is to be perceived'.[18] Yet Priestley's stylistic advance is undercut by the comic clichés.

To some extent *Johnson Over Jordan* (1939) avoids the problems of the other two experimental plays, by presenting the action from the perspective of a protagonist who is central to every scene. Johnson is a typical, indeed deliberately ordinary character, who was immediately recognisable as 'the *Everyman* of our time'; and Priestley labelled his approach 'biographical-morality'.[19] Yet only the briefest naturalistic context remains as a prologue to establish the dream status of the action. As Johnson's face appears out of the darkness that envelops his funeral, the '*odd confused manner*' of his monologue, '*like a man in a delirium*', provides the spectator with a rationally acceptable explanation for an expressionistic depiction of modern life.

Priestley's techniques here are comparable to those of Auden and Isherwood's *The Ascent of F6*, performed two years earlier – a parallel underlined by the fact that Benjamin Britten composed the musical score for both plays. In each, external physical appearances symbolize a figure's moral essence. The dead Johnson's continuing materialistic preoccupation leads him to hell, in the form of the Universal Assurance and Globe Loan and Finance Corporation. Here a row of identical blank-faced functionaries shovel banknotes into a glowing furnace, desiccated millionaires are dwarfed by the enormous ledgers they frantically search through, while a *'ballet of clerks and secretaries comes rushing in, making strange shadows'*, dancing to the strident music of *'typewriters, adding machines, ringing of bells'.*[20] The furnace door becomes the entrance to the Jungle Hot Spot nightclub where customers have the faces of pigs, rats, vultures, gorillas – and correspondingly bestial behaviour. Figures multiply, objects expand and perspectives are distorted. All these elements are typical of Expressionist drama, with the depiction of Capitalism directly echoing Joan Littlewood's Agitprop ballet (discussed above, p. 74). Yet Priestley rejected the Expressionist label, which the critic James Agate pinned on the play. He argued that the defining quality of Expressionism was 'to flatten out character, to ignore the individual and concrete instance, and to find drama in the relations of purely symbolic figures'. By contrast he stated that his aim in *Johnson Over Jordan* 'was to show a real man in real relationships, but to do it outside time, to present it all, as in dreams, in a four dimensional manner'.[21]

In effect, however, this spiritual focus restricts the world of Priestley's play to image and idea. Succumbing to the animal side of human nature, Johnson regresses to primal Freudian patterns, stabbing his son and attempting to rape his daughter, whose individual identities are disguised from him by anonymous masks. Yet as a dead man he has no physical being. Both his actions, and all the other characters he meets, including his children, are only subconscious projections: 'Masks and shadows and dreams'. This frees him from moral responsibility. Simply the recognition that materialistic or animal desires are delusions is sufficient to gain forgiveness. So his final reward seems unearned.

Like the other individuals in the play, the 'Hell' of material reality is dismissed as 'mere appearance . . . a shadow', compared to the 'greater world' represented by *'a wide sky behind and in front of it two columns that might be part of some dateless temple. The whole effect should suggest humanity itself outside time.'* Corresponding to this, at the climactic points of *Music At Night* as well as *Johnson Over Jordan* the heightened dialogue modulates into formal verse. In both plays the group, or the archetypal protagonist, achieve salvation by simple affirmation. And *Music At Night* salutes 'the one mind that is ours yet infinitely greater than ours unresting until the whole world is aware of itself and wise' – even though the dialogue continually refers to the Nazi persecution of the Jews and the imminence of the war that was only a year away at the time of performance.[22] In hindsight the optimism seems facile. The expressionistic distortion of the factual surface, which Priestley uses to communicate subjective realities, is merely rhetorical. Negative images become reduced to caricature, while the utopian drive dissipates in lyricism.

Priestley's stylistic experimentation is comparable to Pirandello in its overt theatricality. His plays are the popular equivalent of Auden and Isherwood's poetic Expressionism, reflecting speculation about changing the present through the impact of the future on the past, which has recently found wide appeal in Steven Spielberg's science-fiction films. Like T.S. Eliot, his work focuses on inner or spiritual realities that underlie materialistic appearances. Even if, by the standards Eliot set for dramatic poetry, Priestley's verse is inflated and rhetorical, from Priestley's viewpoint 'My plays are meant to be *acted* not read. They are not literary (as Eliot's plays are, in my opinion, and Fry's) but at their best intensely and triumphantly theatrical.' At the same time, as Priestley put it, 'I took such dramatic technique as I possessed as far as it would go, using the most objective form . . . for material that was entirely and deeply subjective'.[23]

Despite its flaws, Priestley's work marks the loosening of Shaw's dominance over mainstream theatre. His achievement was to bring experimental techniques, symbolism, and existential themes on to the West End stage – where his 'time plays' still appear (the most recent examples being a 1990 production of *Time and the Conways* and the triumphantly long-running staging of *An Inspector Calls* by Daldry 1995).

Notes

1 *Look Back in Anger*, p. 8.
2 *The Plays of J.B. Priestley*, London, 1962, pp. vii–ix. The pre-eminent significance of the Time Plays for their author, and the place of even a slight piece like *Dangerous Corner* among them, is indicated by selecting these as the first volume of his

collected plays. (The other two volumes each cover the same creative time span, with the second being devoted to comedies and farce.)

3 *Ibid.*, p. 1.

4 *Ibid.*, pp. 1, 51 & 2.

5 Preface to the novelization of the play, Ruth Holland and J.B. Priestley, *Dangerous Corner*, New York, 1933, pp. vi–vii.

6 *Plays of J.B. Priestley*, I, pp. 52, 46 & 49.

7 Priestley, *Midnight on the Desert*, London, 1937, pp. 253, 277.

8 Priestley, *Rain Upon Godshill*, London, 1939, pp. 50–1.

9 *Plays of J.B. Priestley*, III, (London, 1950) pp. 311, 271–2.

10 *Plays of J.B. Priestley*, I, pp. 137, 136 & 133,

11 *Ibid.*, pp. 168, 176–7.

12 *Ibid.*, pp. 177, 197.

13 *Ibid.*, pp. 197, 178; *Man and Time*, London, 1964, p. 76.

14 *An Inspector Calls*, London, 1947, pp. vi–vii.

15 Priestley, *Rain Upon Godshill*, London, 1939, pp. 180–2.

16 *Plays of J. B. Priestley*, I, p. 386, preface, p. x, and 'A Note from the Workshop', in the Malvern Festival Programme, 1938.

17 *Plays of J. B. Priestley*, II, pp. 456, 516, 454, 490.

18 Samuel Beckett, *Cascando and Other Short Pieces*, New York, 1967, p. 75.

19 *Plays of J.B. Priestley*, I, p. x; Ashley Dukes, cited in Gareth Lloyd Evans, *J.B. Priestley – The Dramatist*, London, 1964, p. 44.

20 *Plays of J. B. Priestley*, I, pp. 276, 282–3.

21 Priestley, correspondence in James Agate, *Ego 8*, London, 1946, p. 94.

22 *Plays of J. B. Priestley*, I, pp. 313, 396 & 394.

23 Priestley, letter, cited in Gareth Lloyd Evans, *J.B. Priestley*, p. 222; *Margin Released*, London, 1962, p. 207.

5.3 Expressionistic archetypes: W. H. Auden (1907–73) and Christopher Isherwood (1904–89)

CHECKLIST OF MAJOR PLAYS

The Dance of Death, 1934 (Auden)

The Dog Beneath the Skin, 1936 (collaboration)

The Ascent of F6, 1937 (collaboration)

On the Frontier, 1938 (collaboration)

Paul Bunyan (opera), 1941 (Auden)

The Age of Anxiety, 1947 (Auden)

I am a Camera (adapt.), 1952 (Isherwood)

The Rake's Progress (opera), 1951 (Auden)

Even if the major impact of Bertolt Brecht's drama on British playwrights is usually dated to the 1950s, with the Berliner Ensemble's first appearances in London, already by the 1930s Brecht and German Expressionism had become the dominant continental influence, replacing French Symbolism (which had been adopted by W.B. Yeats or Gordon Craig at the beginning of the century). Sean O'Casey's combination of naturalistic scenes and expressionist vision in *The Silver Tassie*, staged in London in 1929, offered an example. The Marxist associations of the style were already leading to its adoption by the Workers' Theatre Movement (see above pp. 73ff.). So W.H. Auden and Christopher Isherwood were very much in tune with the time in developing an expressionist approach as the basis for a new form of poetic drama.

Picking up on Cocteau's proposition that 'There is a poetry of the theatre, but not in it', Auden's aim was to create a specifically dramatic 'poetry of action'; and the theatrical form was supplied by Isherwood, who had first-hand experience of the political polarization that underlay German Expressionist drama, as well as attending performances in Berlin – recorded in his novel *Goodbye to Berlin*, which was adapted for the stage as *I am a Camera* in 1952, and formed the basis for the Hal Prince musical, *Cabaret* (1966). The type of drama produced by their collaboration was echoed by T.S. Eliot's Christian verse-pageant, *The Rock* (1934), and influenced J.B. Priestley's experimental work at the end of the decade: particularly his quasi-religious *Johnson Over Jordan* (1939 – discussed above, pp. 452–54). In more general terms, their combination of revolutionary politics with religious fervour became the keynote for non-naturalistic drama of the period. As Eliot remarked in 1934: 'Only a cause can give the bond, the common assumptions between author and audience which the serious dramatist needs ... There are only two causes now of sufficient seriousness, and they are mutually exclusive: the Church and Communism.'[1]

Although ideologically incompatible with religion, the Marxism of the 1930s was as messianic as Eliot's Christianity; and the Auden/Isherwood plays increasingly take on a spiritual bearing. Even in Auden's first performed piece, *The Dance of Death* (1934), revolutionary politics were subsumed in archetypal symbols. This dramatic ballet used Agitprop elements, and some of the scenes parallel a Workers' Theatre Movement script such as Joan Littlewood's *John Bullion* (see above, p. 74). It is explicitly intended as

a picture of the decline of a class.
CHORUS Middle class.

ANNOUNCER Of how its members dream of a new life...But secretly desire the old, for there is death inside them. We show you that death as a dancer.
CHORUS Death for us.

Yet the revolution that finally disposes with Death is treated farcically; and class conflict is replaced by the opposition of transitory youth and beauty to moral and physical decay.

The Dance of Death is modelled in part on Brecht's *The Seven Deadly Sins of the Bourgeoisie* (performed in London as *Anna, Anna* in 1933 – and later translated by Auden into a ballet under the same title). But where Brecht updates medieval allegory as a tool for condemning Capitalism, Auden reverses the process. Instead, representative aspects of contemporary life – the pursuit of health in nature worship, the aspiration of Lindbergh's flight, the materialistic sensuality of a nightclub – are shown from a traditional quasi-religious perspective. This was underlined in the original production of the Group Theatre by pairing *The Dance of Death* with the Chester cycle *Flood*; and it was in terms of 'a return' to the technique of the medieval Mystery that Auden's ballet-play was seen as 'laying...the foundation of a new dramatic art'.[2]

The same qualities recur in Auden and Isherwood's three collaborative works. *The Dog Beneath the Skin* (1936) transforms Brechtian parable (specifically the Brecht/Weill opera, *The Rise and Fall of the City of Mahagonny*, 1930) into fairy-tale fable, with an upright hero (Alan Norman), a lost saviour-prince (Sir Francis Crewe) and marriage to a princess (the heiress of Honeypot Hall) as reward for the quest. Alan is literally the innocent abroad; and his journey through Europe, accompanied by the dog of the title, offers a symbolic survey of the moral state of Capitalism, which exposes its links with the rising tide of Fascism. We get 'a dog's-eye view' that strips away respectable façades to show 'people from underneath'. The political rationalism of Brecht's episodic play construction, in which each scene encapsulates a specific social point, is transposed into a picaresque panorama of false utopias. A city becomes a phantasmagorical Red Light district, in which

Plato's halves are at last united.
Whatever you dream of alone in bed,
...we will make it real instead.[3]

This is paralleled by Paradise Park, where all the figures represent different types of illusory idealism, which turn out to be escapist self-obsessions.

Against this symbolic backdrop, the action coalesces into images. At the
Nineveh Hotel the dancing girls are literally consumer-items, picked out
of the line-up by a gross diner for his meal, with 'the finger-nails served
separately as a savoury' – and when the innocent hero is seduced from his
quest by a glamorous film star, the woman of his dreams is a shop-window
dummy (on to whom Alan projects his own desires, speaking 'her' words in
falsetto). Although on one level they are political, condemning capitalism,
these images of corruption also represent a rejection of social existence.

Reality exists in the mind. Europe is a madhouse, inhabited by lunatics
who have succumbed to illusion, while the combination of whimsy with the
grotesque in the play implies that fantasy is indeed fact. As 'The Dog's Skin'
(temporarily vacated by its human inhabitant) points out in a soliloquy to
a clock, 'I'm an idea, you're an idea, everything's an idea'; and the ending
reinforces this. Alan discovers that the ideal hero, who was the object of his
search, has been with him all along (in the shape of the dog, with whom
he exchanges places to avoid arrest when he is unable to pay the bill for the
luxuries he has showered upon the seductress). Similarly, their return to
the romanticized village of the opening scene reveals that the ideal of rural
England is delusive.

Instead of acting as the saviour of the social order, Sir Francis rejects
his inheritance, and calls on the common people of the village to join
him in the coming war against the Establishment, since from 'a dog's-eye
view . . . such obscene, cruel, hypocritical, mean, vulgar creatures had never
existed before in the history of the planet'.[4] But this extreme condemnation is arbitrary, like the transformation of the village into a fascist camp
(where in one early version of the play – anticipating John Arden's ending
in *Serjeant Musgrave's Dance*, 1959 (see above, p. 140) – a machine-gun
is turned on the audience). Since the original England was a recognizably
sentimental picture, switching it to its opposite does not represent political actuality, but a change of vision. Everything in this dramatic world is
subjective; and the same is even more true of Auden and Isherwood's later
plays.

The human dog echoes *Peter Pan*, while as Isherwood himself realized,
there is a strong 'whiff of Barrie in his *Mary Rose* mood' in the super-
sensory trysts between the lovers from warring sides of *On the Frontier*
(1939).[5] The supremacy of imagination is even clearer in *The Ascent of F6*
(1937), where the journey is into the subconscious, culminating in physical
death on a clearly metaphorical peak; and the country reached is an amalgam of African natives, Tibetan monasteries and supernatural monsters.

Mountain-climbing is a symbol of spiritual achievement and self-conquest; the hero a sacrificial saviour-figure with the morality-play name of Ransome.

Real-life analogues for the hero were clear to audiences of the time. The international competition (waged against the all-purpose fascist country of Ostnia, which recurs in each of the other Auden and Isherwood plays) derived from Scott's race to the South Pole. The noble self-sacrifice of the sick Lieutenant Oates, walking out into the blizzard to give his comrades a chance of survival, is repeated in the suicide of one climber, while the deaths of Ransome and his last companion echo the tragic outcome of Scott's expedition. Ransome himself was based on T.E. Lawrence as a national hero who rejected society and combined a life of action with literary contemplation. The parallels were so obvious that Alec Guinness (who was later to re-enact the role more directly in *Ross*, Terence Rattigan's dramatization of Lawrence's life, 1960) researched Lawrence's biography as preparation for the part of Ransome in a 1939 revival of *The Ascent of F6*. Yet comparison with Rattigan's historical treatment shows the degree to which Auden and Isherwood's spiritual focus led to undramatic abstraction. In this confusion of allegories – signalled as much by the juxtaposition of weighty blank verse with parodistic doggerel and choral chants – everything cancels out; and the lack of substance is inherent in the subjective line of poetic drama.

The Group Theatre, for which Auden and Isherwood wrote, overlapped with the Poets' Theatre. This was founded in collaboration with Ashley Dukes' Mercury Theatre. It sought to resolve the opposition between literary verse and stage poetry in its emphasis on dance and music, and involved Eliot and Yeats. The proposed programme for the first season of the Poets' Theatre in 1935 was to include a pre-Canterbury production of Eliot's ritualistic *Murder in the Cathedral*, and an early version of *The Dog Beneath the Skin*, as well as two dance plays by Yeats, *A Full Moon in March* and *The Player Queen*.[6] Although this never came off, the Group collaborated with the Mercury Theatre on *The Ascent of F6*; and a tangible sign of its influence can be seen in the close association with Benjamin Britten, who composed the musical accompaniment for *The Ascent of F6* and *On the Frontier*, as well as other Group Theatre productions.

The Group Theatre was admired by Yeats as the extension of his own dramatic aims; and in addition to producing Eliot's experimental *Sweeney Agonistes* (1934), it fostered plays by Stephen Spender and Louis MacNeice. These shared the same quality of locating 'fact in fantasy' that formed the basis of Auden and Isherwood's work. Spender's only stage play, *Trial of a Judge* (1938), was one of the Group Theatre's most overtly political productions, dealing explicitly with the struggle between communists and fascists and the perversion of justice in Nazi Germany. But, as one reviewer perceived, Spender 'describes not the world of action but the mind that mirrors it'.[7] His Expressionistic stylization abstracts contemporary events to a ritual confrontation of Reds against Blacks that is indistinguishable from the two dream sequences, in which the court scenes of the play are presented.

The Group Theatre, which found its distinctive voice in Auden and Isherwood, closed with the war; and its final production in 1939 – a revival of *The Ascent of F6* – marks the end of symbolic Expressionism on the British stage. There was a short-lived attempt to revive the Group in 1950. But the poetic drama of the mind that it fostered in the 1930s had become the province of radio. Freed from the physical limitations of the stage, and the crudity of visual symbolism, the direct appeal to the ear and the imagination made radio an apt medium for subjective lyricism, which reached its fullest expression in the musically structured dreaming-back of Dylan Thomas' 'play for voices', *Under Milkwood* (1953).

Similarly, MacNeice's later verse plays were all written for broadcasting; and the link with Auden and Isherwood is clear in his most successful radio piece, *The Dark Tower* (1946), which incorporated the main aspects of *The Dog Beneath the Skin*: a quest, a naive hero seduced in his search through the phantasmagorical wasteland of society, together with Benjamin Britten's music. As MacNeice described it, this Pilgrim's Progress through Eliot's Wasteland, 'which does not admit of a completely rational analysis and still less adds up to any clear moral or message . . . has the solidity of a dream'. The advantages of a completely aural form were that it automatically created 'the stream of consciousness . . . subordinating analysis to synthesis', and appealing 'to more primitive elements' in the listeners. This is a capsule summary of the qualities that define modern poetic drama; and through radio Yeats' aim of focusing on words could finally be realized, without placing actors in barrels, since 'here and here alone can one listen to calculated speech divorced from all visual supports or interference'.[8]

Although verse drama, myths, and spiritual themes have continued to appear on the post-war stage, they tend to be objectively located in contemporary or historical contexts, as with the work of Christopher Fry or Peter Shaffer. David Rudkin's rituals of violence and Howard Barker's 'Theatre of Catastrophe' are the major exceptions. Through their work the very different *avant-garde* emphasis of French theatre, first introduced by Yeats, continues to influence British drama. Echoes of Auden and Isherwood's Expressionism can be found in John Whiting's plays, particularly *Marching Song* (1954) where there are parallels to *On the Frontier*. But the mainstream of poetic drama is represented by Eliot's attempt to create a religious theatre. This is typical in its merging of spiritual levels of experience with a specific social foreground.

Notes

1 *The English Auden: Poems, Essays, and Dramatic Writings* 1927–1939, ed. E. Mendelson, New York, 1977, p. 301; Eliot, *Rep*, October 1934, p. 5.
2 *Dance of Death*, prompt copy, p. 7 (cited in Michael Sidnell, *Dances of Death: The Group Theatre of London in the Thirties*, London, 1984, p. 77); *The New Statesman*, 3 March 1934.
3 *The Dog Beneath the Skin*, London, 1935, pp. 172–3, 57.
4 *Ibid.*, pp. 128, 146, 172–3.
5 Isherwood, cited in Sidnell, *Dances of Death*, p. 247.
6 For detail about the collaboration between The Group Theatre, Ashley Dukes and Yeats, as well as the reasons behind the failure to get the Poets' Theatre off the ground, see Sidnell, *Dances of Death*, pp. 266ff.
7 Louis MacNeice, *The Dark Tower*, London, 1947 (introduction), p. 21; Geronwy Rees, *New Writing*, II, 1939, p. 112.
8 MacNeice, Introduction to *The Dark Tower*, pp. 21, 10–11, 9 & 12.

5.4 T. S. Eliot (1888–1965): the drama of conversion

CHECKLIST OF ELIOT'S MAJOR PLAYS

Sweeney Agonistes, 1934	*The Cocktail Party*, 1949
Murder in the Cathedral, 1935	*The Confidential Clerk*, 1953
The Family Reunion, 1939	*The Elder Statesman*, 1958

Eliot's eminence as a poet and Nobel Prize winner raises expectations that his plays – even though comparable to the major achievements of other playwrights – have been unable to fulfil, making the assessment of his worth as a dramatist particularly difficult. The thematic universality and stylistic innovation of *The Waste Land* or *The Four Quartets* produce a unique poetic voice, at once deeply traditional and strikingly contemporary. Similarly, his essays have become classics of criticism. Analysing the state of drama over the early decades of the century, they have been more influential in reasserting the significance of theatre as a social catalyst, than any other theoretical writing since Shaw's journalism and prefaces at the beginning of the century. Eliot's plays, however – the practical realization of his critical principles – are rooted in their period to the extent that when *The Elder Statesman* was first performed in 1958 it already appeared dated: 'Pinero on stilts', in Tynan's derogatory phrase, 'the old story of the great man whose past catches up with him'.[1]

Indeed, Eliot's first experiments with drama are an integral part of the movement represented by Auden and Isherwood in the 1930s. *Sweeney Agonistes* was performed by the Group Theatre in 1934 (and again in a double bill with Auden's early morality play, *The Dance of Death*, in 1935), while *Murder in the Cathedral* was transferred from the cloisters to the commercial stage by Ashley Dukes' Mercury Theatre. In the era immediately following the Second World War, too, when serious new drama was restricted to J.B. Priestley's restatements of his 1930s themes or Terence Rattigan's naturalistic problem plays, the religious vision of Eliot's poetic drama set the standard. The association of verse with tradition and high-church culture, which he had promoted, influenced Christopher Fry, whose colourful imagery and poetic extravagance supplied a popular antidote to wartime austerity.[2] But this Establishment traditionalism relegated Eliot's plays to period pieces the moment the first post-war generation of playwrights stormed the theatre. Their old-fashioned impression was compounded by Eliot's adoption of the detective-story or drawing-room comedy format; and for a decade after John Osborne's *Look Back in Anger* in 1956, Eliot's plays vanished from the professional stage.

However, the standard theatrical genres of the time that Eliot used were a practical expression of his conviction that 'the music of poetry . . . must be a music latent in the common speech of its time'; and his plays share the same themes and images as his poems. The 'three [spiritual] conditions' that 'Little Gidding' explores as prevalent in modern society – 'Attachment to self and to things and to persons', 'detachment', and 'indifference' – are reflected in the characters of *The Cocktail Party* (1949). The symbolism of the 'rose garden' from 'Ash Wednesday' and 'Burnt Norton' reappears in *The Family Reunion* (1939) and *The Confidential Clerk* (1953). Indeed, drama can be seen as the logical development of his poetic aims. It was a practical expression of his Christian ideal of communion, extending outward in performance to create a community: both as a collaborative art, and in its participatory relationship with an audience. For Eliot,

The most useful poetry, socially, would be one which could cut across all the present stratifications of public taste – stratifications which are perhaps a sign of social disintegration. The ideal medium for poetry ... and the most direct means of social 'usefulness' for poetry, is the theatre.[3]

In addition, the artifice of stage performance exemplified his vision of modern people as 'hollow men', living in an illusory state. Its fake scenery paralleled the superficial nature of material realities (from a religious perspective), while the gap between the actor and his role mirrored the state of a population whose socially defined personas are divorced from their inner soul. So the theatre becomes a recurrent focus in all the plays Eliot wrote for the commercial stage. The dramatic form is used as a self-reflexive image for the alienated existence of characters, who find themselves 'Like amateur actors in a dream when the curtain rises ... dressed for a different play, or having rehearsed the wrong parts, ... ridiculous in some nightmare pantomime'. The protagonist of *The Family Reunion* returns from self-imposed exile resigned to 'Playing a part that had been imposed upon me' and taking his inherited place in society, only 'to find another one made ready – /The book laid out, lines underscored, and the costume/Ready to be put on'. The Elder Statesman, faced with the falsity of his public image, has to learn who he is 'off the stage, without his costume and make-up/And without his stage words'.[4]

On a wider level, Eliot's use of standard dramatic situations in *The Family Reunion*, *The Cocktail Party* and *The Confidential Clerk* also represented this illusory social existence. Audiences accustomed to seeing their world reflected in murder melodrama, or in comedies of sexual philandering or mistaken identity, could be shown its unreality by undercutting these conventional forms. In each case the surface action contrasts with a spiritual substructure that either contradicts or transforms its nature.

Eliot's aim was the spiritual transformation of society; and revitalizing recognizably banal types of social drama was intended as a theatrical equivalent – a model of what Eliot hoped to achieve. But the problem of borrowing from mainstream entertainment-theatre, was that his post-war comedies appeared increasingly conformist, with the poetry being sacrificed to reach a wide public. As a result, there seemed to be a sharp distinction between these later plays and his early, more overtly poetic non-commercial pieces: *Sweeney Agonistes* (written in 1926, and first performed in America in 1933) or *Murder in the Cathedral* (commissioned for the 1935 Canterbury Festival).

But this kind of borrowing occurred even at the outset of Eliot's career. In particular there are parallels with J.B. Priestley throughout Eliot's plays. Both adapted popular types of entertainment-theatre to serious themes, and shared the same approach of using a philosophic or mythic level of dramatic action to 'expose the underneath, or the inside, of the natural surface appearance'. The structure of Eliot's early pageant, *The Rock* (1934), which intercuts the building of a modern church with biblical and historical scenes, is based on theories of time dramatized by Priestley. As expounded by one of Eliot's cockney masons: 'the past, wot's be'ind you, is wot's goin' to 'appen in the future, bein' as the future 'as already 'appened'.[5] The way Eliot uses different levels of consciousness in *The Family Reunion* (1939) echoes Priestley's *I Have Been Here Before* (1937). And Priestley's alien doctor from the same play, who acts as spiritual mentor and resolves the ordinary characters' self-destructive passions, is closely related to Eliot's eccentric psychiatrist/ Guardian of *The Cocktail Party*.

Similarly, *Murder in the Cathedral* was a variation on the theme of the two preceding Canterbury Festival plays: Tennyson's *Becket* (1932 and 1933, first performed by Irving in 1893) and a blank-verse treatment of the same material by Laurence Binyon (1934). The stylization of *Sweeney Agonistes*, too, with its use of masks and continuous drumbeats to accentuate verbal rhythms, was explicitly based on Ezra Pound's Noh dramas and Yeats' 'Plays for Dancers'.[6] Even its fragmentary form corresponded to German Expressionist montage; and the 1934 Group Theatre production, which brought this out by quick cuts and blackouts, greatly impressed Bertolt Brecht.

This 'drama of modern life (furnished flat sort of people)' established the themes that Eliot returned to throughout his theatrical career. The disjointed, incomplete state of *Sweeney Agonistes* embodies the disintegration of contemporary consciousness. The twin epigraphs point to a dual focus, which is basic to all his plays: spiritual experience versus material existence; and the correlation of Greek myths of sacrificial rebirth with the Christian process of redemptive purgation:

ORESTES You don't see them, you don't – but I see them they are hunting me down,
    I must move on. (*Choephoroi*)

Hence the soul cannot be possessed of the divine union, until it has divested itself of the love of created beings. (*St John of the Cross*[7])

Society is presented as a wasteland of despair, in which man has regressed to animalistic primitivism, epitomized in jazz rhythms and a pop hit of the

18 The murderous wasteland: the ending of the Group Theatre production of
Eliot's *Sweeney Agonistes*

time, Bob Cole's 'Under the Bamboo Tree'. Plagiarism, in Eliot's use of this
song, is itself the expression of a debased culture, like the music-hall duos of
menacing gangsters and superstitious prostitutes who dance to it in the play.
For Sweeney, surrounded by shabby rented furniture and two-dimensional
figures, who lack any inner life, physical existence has been reduced to an
insubstantial nightmare.

In the twentieth-century world, Milton's Samson becomes Jack the Ripper.
Sweeney's corrosive sense of the lack of moral purpose leads him to identify
with a murderer, who is reported to have kept the corpse of his mistress
'With a gallon of lysol in a bath'. Since religious belief has atrophied to Tarot
card fortune-telling, the absence of the spirit means that a dead body is
indistinguishable from the living person. But once the material trappings
of urban civilization are seen as illusory, then reality is reduced to 'Nothing
at all but three things/ . . . Birth, and copulation, and death'. And if 'Life
is death', then killing becomes a liberating act. The logical consequence is
'Any man has to, needs to, wants to/Once in a lifetime, do a girl in'; and the
Group Theatre production ended in Sweeney chasing Doris with a cut-throat

razor.[8] Murder is simultaneously a symptom of spiritual death, the only way of rebelling against it, and its end result. As the modern equivalent of pulling down the temple of false gods, the urge to kill makes Samson Agonistes/'Apeneck Sweeney' the embodiment of the evil he attacks.

Eliot was consciously returning to the ritual origins of drama; and *Murder in the Cathedral* (1935) is the antithesis of this negative picture, designed as an antidote to the spiritual despair of modern life. This is signalled as much by the way Eliot incorporates elements of the liturgy in the verse, and by how the re-enaction of Becket's martyrdom is designed to be integrated with the Cathedral setting, as by the degree to which he modelled the versification on *Everyman*. The play as a whole is also presented as ritual by replacing plot with symbolic patterning, where all the historical figures and the contemporary actors embodying them

> . . . are fixed
> In an eternal action, an eternal patience
> To which all must consent that it may be willed
> And which all must suffer that they may will it,
> That the pattern may subsist, for the pattern is the action
> And the suffering, that the wheel may turn and still
> Be forever still.[9]

The image of the wheel comes from Dante. Man liberates himself from bondage to the senses on the revolving rim ('treading one endless round . . . in the hell of make-believe') by aligning his will with God as the unmoving axle, and so travelling down the spokes to the centre. And this forms the structure of the play. The physical 'substance' of political conflict, human passions and murder, being explicitly a 'strife with shadows', is relegated to an illusory existence.

The knights who slaughter Becket are on the external circumference of Dante's wheel; and the play's composition is circular. The action is framed by parallel choruses of ordinary citizens. The first half, the temptation of Becket, is mirrored by the temptation of the audience in the second, with Becket's sermon placed as a reflective pause in the centre. This parallelism was emphasized in the original production by using the same actors for the four Tempters and the four Knights, while the climax was choreographed to echo the same image in the passive martyr impaled by the spoke-like swords of the encircling killers.

The spectators are specifically instructed in their role: 'All things prepare the event. Watch', which links them with the chorus, for whom 'there is no action,/But only to wait and witness'. Unlike the many others who have died for their faith, a martyr is literally a witness to Christ's sacrifice in the sense that his death repeats the moral significance of the Crucifixion. A precondition is that martyrdom must be undertaken in the right spirit (hence the focus on Becket's motivation in the first act). But this is not in itself enough. What determines whether a man qualifies as a martyr is the spiritual effect of his killing on ordinary people. As Becket states in his sermon: 'A martyrdom is always the design of God, for His love of men, to . . . bring them back to His ways.'[10]

The chorus demonstrate this process in their progression from concern for their own material welfare and fear of disruption – through atonement for their passive complicity in the death of a saint, acknowledging their part in the sins of Man that the Crucifixion redeems – to their final affirmation of faith, expressing a new awareness in the spiritual meaning of existence. But in terms of the play's theme, Becket's martyrdom is only relevant to an age where (as the Fourth Tempter forecasts) the shrine has been pillaged and the saint merely a historical curiosity, if the theatrical re-enaction of his death has an equivalent spiritual effect on the modern audience.

The Chorus is Eliot's main tool for achieving this effect. It has a pivotal function within the play. It is the Women of Canterbury's despairing plea that enables Becket to overcome the paralysis of will induced by the Fourth Tempter's insinuation that pride is motivating him 'To do the right deed for the wrong reason'. Accepting their role in the pattern is what allows Becket to become 'the figure of God's purpose'. By acknowledging their guilt in the coming murder the choral group represents the sins of the world that Christ – and by extension martyrs like Becket – died to redeem. But, as 'the type of the common man', on stage throughout, the Chorus also serves to guide the spectators' response: 'It mediates between the action and the audience; it intensifies the action by projecting its emotional consequences, so that we as the audience see it doubly, by seeing its effect on other people.' The impassioned imagery, orchestral interweaving and sweeping rhythms of the choral verse is designed to carry us through the same emotional progression, while 'the use of platform prose' in the Knights' direct address to the spectators reinforces this identification by breaking through the historical distance 'to shock the audience out of their complacency'.[11]

When the Knights taunt Becket, their chanting is based on Vachel Lindsay's 'Daniel Jazz'. Equivalent to the jazz rhythms of *Sweeney Agonistes*, it represents the automatism and animalistic regression of the modern Waste Land. Together with the Knights' emergence as contemporary social types, it implies that the twentieth-century loss of faith is no less guilty of Becket's death than the historical characters. Their swords are as much our instruments, as those of the equally off-stage Henry II. Just as the Chorus is an accessory before the fact, so the spectators are accused of being accessories after it. At the same time the caricature, totalitarian echoes and speciousness of the Knights' self-justifications ensures our rejection of their claims that the martyrdom can be interpreted in purely secular terms (which corresponds to the deliberately misleading expectations of the detective-story title of the play). Similarly, the ritual patterning of the action is designed to impress on the audience a redemptive sense of order and inner significance in existence, corresponding to the Chorus' final spiritual affirmation.

In addition, the overlap between the actual site of the martyrdom and the stage was exploited in the original Cathedral production, to reinforce these thematic links between the modern public and the historical event. The performance, incorporating prayers, the introits, a sermon and the offering of body and blood in martyrdom, is metaphorically a Mass (the church service celebrating Christ's sacrifice), in which the Chorus serves as a choir, and the audience are placed in the position of the congregation. Becket's sermon is addressed to them; and their participatory role was reinforced by the staging in the second half. The Knights battered on the outside doors at the rear of the Chapter House, and marched up to the stage through the spectators. The Priests bearing Becket's body, followed by the Chorus bearing candles and singing the litany, did not simply exit behind the scenes. They moved out in procession around the great cloister, still heard and seen as the audience dispersed.

At the same time the external aspects of dramatic action are minimal. As the subject of all the previous dramas performed at Canterbury since the founding of the Festival, Becket's story was well known to the audience Eliot was addressing. But Eliot's treatment also denies any suspense: 'A man comes home foreseeing that he will be killed, and he is killed.' Even character development is ruled out by beginning the story immediately before the climax, while the four Tempters (as in Morality Play psychomachia) are projections of Becket's mind; and he co-operates with his murderers. Indeed, the whole play is based on the paradox that 'action is suffering/And suffering is action', derived from the Latin root of patience/passivity in the verb *patio*: to suffer. So the protagonist's usual dramatic function is reversed, his objective being to avoid willed activity – to such an extent indeed that the original actor of the role 'asked . . . how the positive character of Becket could be reconciled with so passive a protagonist?'[12] In addition, this absence of conflict is underlined by the geometrical structuring that substitutes for plot, as well as by the ritualistic 'freezing' of on-stage actors when not involved in a scene.

Such stasis is intrinsic to Eliot's association of religion with poetic theatre. The function of verse in drama was 'in imposing a credible order upon or-dinary reality and thereby eliciting some perception of an order *in* reality, to bring us to a condition of serenity, stillness and reconciliation'. By comparison to the value placed on eternity, any earthly concerns are irrele-vant – so that dramatic action becomes trivial. The compression of meaning in poetry embodies the nature of spiritual experience as 'The point of inter-section of the timeless/With time'.

In *Murder in the Cathedral* these qualities are an exact expression of the theme. But the same dramatic approach became problematic when Eliot, rejecting 'plays of *overtly* Christian purpose' as only preaching to the con-verted, turned to secular topics that would allow 'a Christian mentality to permeate the [commercial] theatre, to affect it and to influence audiences who might be obdurate to plays of directly religious appeal'.[13]

The same absence of conflict in his social comedies, and even *The Family Reunion* (1939) which was initially subtitled 'A Melodrama', leaves a void at the centre of the action. This transitional play combines elements of both *Sweeney Agonistes* and *Murder in the Cathedral*. It has a misleading detective-story frame, with a confession of murder, questioning of the suspect, and of a possible witness to the crime, as well as the appearance of a police sergeant. As in *Murder in the Cathedral*, the characters are divided into three levels of consciousness: a Chorus of ordinary people, fearful of revelation, who 'insist that the world is what we have always taken it to be'; initiates, like the Priests; and a sacrificial protagonist who 'must learn to suffer more'. As with Sweeney, the protagonist's guilt over the drowning of a girl leads to psychological alienation, and pursuit by the Eumenides. But this is 'not a story of detection,/Of crime and punishment, but of sin and expiation'.[14] Lord Harry Monchensey is simply replaying inherited patterns – the 'dream' of pushing his wife overboard at sea being a projection of his father's plan to drown Harry's pregnant mother in a well on the estate – and no murder has been actually committed.

Similarly in Eliot's last play, *The Elder Statesman*, where two blackmailers appear out of Lord Claverton's past, what they demand is acknowledgement of their existence, not money; and Eliot made Claverton's guilty secret equally imaginary. Manslaughter (a hit-and-run accident in the first draft of the script) is watered down to running over the body of a man already killed by another driver, while instead of embezzling money, Claverton's son becomes 'not a fugitive from justice – /Only a fugitive from reality'. By striking out any legal problem, Eliot emphasizes the distinction that 'crime is in relation to the law/And the sin is in relation to the sinner'.[15] But in removing the threat to the characters, this also reduces the motivation for their spiritual conversion.

This is also the case in *The Family Reunion*. Harry's situation is not re-solved by anything the characters do, but by his perception that 'It is not my conscience,/Not my mind that is diseased, but the world I have to live in.' This transforms the supernatural figures who pursue him from agents of divine punishment into 'the bright angels' of redemptive purgation, and allows him to break the curse of his family by simply walking away. The removal of criminal correlatives for sin internalizes the action, making it so abstract that there is no way of defining Harry's destination. His mother's (socially comprehensible) explanation that he might become a missionary – prefiguring the choice of the equivalent figure in *The Cocktail Party* – is explicitly denied. Indeed any concrete detail trivializes the resolution, as in Eliot's suggestion, reluctantly offered to help the actor, that 'he and the chauffeur go off and get jobs in the East End'.[16]

To offset this abstraction, Eliot developed techniques to create a 'double-ness in the action, as if it took place on two planes at once': a metaphoric quality that he saw as the defining characteristic of poetic drama. The du-ality of vision was given formal expression by establishing a subtext that paralleled the surface situation.

Each of his plays sets up a hierarchy of perception, originally formulated for *Sweeney Agonistes*, where a single character of 'sensibility and intelli-gence' addresses 'a small number of the audience, while the rest of the audi-ence would share the response of the other characters' who were 'material, literal-minded and visionless'.[17] Schematic élitism, such as this, diminishes in Eliot's later plays as the naturalistic context became more dominant, al-though it is still present as a way of privileging spiritual insight. So that in *The Family Reunion* or *The Cocktail Party* the saint/martyr's vision is shared in differing degrees by some of the other characters, offering contrasting perspectives.

Eliot combined this multiple focus with a 'mythical method', derived from James Joyce, which consisted in 'manipulating a continuous parallel between contemporaneity and antiquity' as 'a way of controlling, of ordering, of giving a shape and a significance to the immense panorama of futility and anarchy which is contemporary history'.[18] Those mythical parallels Eliot selected were already part of the theatrical tradition: Aeschylus' *Oresteia* in *The Family Reunion*; the *Alcestis* and *Ion* of Euripides in *The Cocktail Party* and *The Confidential Clerk*; Sophocles' *Oedipus at Colonnus* in *The Elder Statesman*. In each case they are disguised, in order to provide a subliminal pattern.

Adding the dimension of Greek tragedy, with its emphasis on fate, injects a sense of underlying patterns into the melodramatic, or conventionally comic plots that represent the vacuity of modern society. Each of these plays centres on a communal celebration; and (as in Harold Pinter's *The Birthday Party*) the gap between what the social gathering stands for, and what actually occurs, reveals the moral emptiness of people's lives. A birthday reunion signals the break-up of a family with the death of its matriarch, the non-appearance of two sons and her eldest son walking out. The guests at a cocktail party (already a standard example of superficiality and brittle pretence), which has been cancelled because the hostess has left her husband, are all unwanted or uninvited.

The archetypal parallels from Greek drama contrast with these images of social disintegration. Their hidden presence is signalled by breaking naturalistic expectations – and in turn the unnatural actions of the characters are justified by their correspondence to the myth. For instance, Eliot intended 'those who were at first disturbed by the eccentric behaviour of my unknown guest' in *The Cocktail Party* to recognize it as 'the behaviour of Heracles in Euripides' play', that tests Admetus after the death of his wife. At the same time, although the premise of Eliot's mythical substructures is that 'whether in Argos or England/There are certain inflexible laws/Unalterable, in the nature of music', his themes are defined by changes to the original stories.[19]

Where Agamemnon sacrifices his daughter, in *The Family Reunion* Harry's father has been persuaded not to dispose of his wife because it would mean killing his unborn child. The net that traps him is the web of family responsibilities; and instead of being butchered with an axe, his life was sapped by his wife's implacable will to preserve the status quo: 'To keep the family alive . . ./To keep me alive, and I live to keep them'. The sins are those of omission, and the curse lies in repeating the past rather than a developing pattern of vengeance. Similarly it is Harry's refusal to perpetuate the hell of unreality, symbolized by the country estate of Wishwood, that kills his mother. She is destroyed as much by her complete identification with it as by his departure; and her death represents the liberating destruction of a diseased society. So instead of fleeing in guilt (like Orestes), Harry's exit is to be seen as 'a triumph. The tragedy is the tragedy of Amy, of a person living on Will alone.'[20]

By contrast with Cocteau and Sartre, where the same mythic material is given contemporary relevance (*La Machine infernale*, 1934; *Les Mouches*, 1943), Eliot uses the stories of Oedipus or Orestes as analogues for a supernatural order unrecognized by the present. To be effective in lending universal significance to the particular and transitory activities of ordinary characters, the mythical cross-reference must remain subliminal. It corresponds to the 'fringe of indefinite extent, of feeling which we can only detect, so to speak, out of the corner of the eye and can never completely focus' that represents the proper 'range of experience' for poetic drama (as distinct from 'the nameable classifiable emotions and motives of our conscious life', which are expressed by prose and mirrored in his surface plots).[21]

The implications of this approach can be seen in the way Eliot treats the classical figures of the pursuing Fates in *The Family Reunion*. The key is their ambiguity in the *Oresteia*, where the intercession of the goddess Athena transforms them from punishing harpies – the Erinyes – to the Eumenides, or spirits of mercy. As he explained, 'the Furies are *divine* instruments, not simple hell-hounds ... [but also] "hounds of heaven"'.[22] This made them particularly appropriate to Eliot's theme of Christian Atonement; and they reappear in every one of his plays. But although their function stays the same, their nature changes from overt symbols to increasingly ordinary human characters.

Listed explicitly as 'THE EUMENIDES' in the cast of *The Family Reunion*, they are tangible embodiments of myth, physical visitants from a purely supernatural plane. At the same time, like Banquo's ghost, they can only be seen by those characters who are spiritually aware. Argos and England visibly overlap. Reflecting the various levels of action, the dialogue switches between colloquial and heightened verse, visionary trances, unconscious utterance and chanted incantation. But even with the shifts of consciousness in the play, the coexistence of two such different dimensions of reality proved to be incongruous on the stage. As Eliot commented, 'We tried every possible manner of presenting them ... and they are never right. They never succeed in being either Greek goddesses or modern spooks.' So in his next play, *The Cocktail Party* (1949), Eliot resolved this 'failure of adjustment between the Greek story and the modern situation' by concealing the plot's mythical 'origins so well that nobody would identify them'.[23]

Disguised as a psychiatrist, colonial envoy and interfering unofficial aunt in *The Cocktail Party*, the Eumenides interact with the social group whom they manipulate. However, their supernatural status is still preserved in making them 'strangers' (not only outsiders in a literal sense, but also in the metaphorical sense of having 'some sort of power' that marks them out as extraordinary). As 'Guardians' of ordinary people, they also embody the intrinsic self or moral core of the other characters, and act as the voice of conscience. The oddities resulting from this double status confused the audience when the play was first produced. So in *The Elder Statesman* (1958), where the equivalent figures are Intruders from the disreputable past, or in *The Confidential Clerk* (1953), where Pallas Athena takes the plebeian shape of 'a suburban respectable woman', even this duality is missing.[24] Completely integrated with the modern surface, in these last two plays the mythical level itself becomes unrecognizable. So it no longer serves as an ordering principle.

It is replaced by an external shaping of experience through imposing a geometrical symmetry on the surface plots. This is already present in *The Cocktail Party*. Not only does the missing wife have a lover, but he is in love with the mistress of the husband, whom he selects as his confidant, forming a quadrilateral equation. In addition the action is circular, beginning with the end of one party, and ending with the preparations for another. *The Confidential Clerk* takes this to an extreme. A husband and wife each have a misplaced illegitimate child; and both recognize him in the title figure. He in turn is revealed to have lost his real father, and chooses his clerical predecessor, whose own son was lost in the war, as his true (spiritual) parent. Where the original myth had a single child, the son of Apollo, believed dead by his mother who tries to kill him when adopted by her husband – Eliot adds an illegitimate daughter and a second unacknowledged son, accentuating the parallelism to a farcical level. And since the source is the least familiar of Euripides' plays, the automatic association is not with any classical archetype, but with W.S. Gilbert or Oscar Wilde.

The effect of this switch from subtext to formal structuring can be seen in *The Cocktail Party*, which contains both techniques. The myth of Alcestis, restored from death to her husband by Heracles, relates to the secondary figures of a married couple, representing the ordinary 'human condition' of compromise and 'the common routine'. Everyday equivalents are found – with the wife walking out on her husband, instead of dying, and a sanatorium substituting for Hades – so that the reference is purely metaphoric. Her return may be described as being 'To bring someone back from the dead', but this is only 'a figure of speech' using the platitude that 'we die to each other daily' in the sense of familiarity breeding indifference. As a result in the first production, according to Eliot, 'no one ... (and no dramatic critics) recognised the source'.[25] However, the Alcestis story has no relevance to the central focus of the play: the film-star socialite, who renounces human love for the path of martyrdom.

The incongruity of such a fate in the context of cocktail parties, the psychiatrist's couch and Hollywood films is betrayed by the grotesqueness of the girl being 'crucified/Very near an ant-hill' and eaten alive, as well as by the exoticism of its setting: darkest Africa, with echoes of Auden and Isherwood's *The Ascent of F6* (1937) in its superstitious heathens incited to cannibalism by foreign agitators. To make it persuasive, Eliot relies on the structuring of the action, which presents martyrdom as an equivalent to the more ordinary salvation achieved by the married couple. The two situations are balanced against each other. His father-confessor/psychiatrist-authority figure underlines that

Neither way is better
Both ways are necessary. It is also necessary
To make a choice between them ...
Both ways avoid the final desolation
Of solitude in the phantasmal world

The motive leading to one is the exact inverse of the other. Each starts with an awareness that 'one is always alone'. The ordinary man has 'ceased to believe in my own personality', while the saint has come to see 'that the world I live in seems an illusion'. And each is instructed to 'work out your salvation with diligence'.[26]

This equal emphasis on the two poles of the action corresponded with Eliot's overriding aim which, as in all his later work, was 'to bring poetry into the world in which the audience lives and to which it returns when it leaves the theatre' – so that 'our own sordid, dreary daily world would be suddenly illuminated and transfigured'.[27] In these terms, *The Cocktail Party* is his most successful play.

The alienated society of the opening is all too recognizable in the unanswered questions, unfinished stories and interrupted interviews of such a social gathering, as well as in the undernourishing or inedible food. These elements are transformed without introducing the openly supernatural figures, or symbolic trances of *The Family Reunion*. Trivia is replaced by reported martyrdom, which has deep emotional significance for all the surviving characters. Casual alcoholic consumption gradually modulates into spiritual libations. Barely distinguishable from prose, the dialogue exemplifies Eliot's principle that 'the chief effect of style and rhythm . . . should be unconscious'. Indeed the naturalistic surface is so complete that, as Eliot himself commented, 'it is perhaps an open question whether there is any poetry in the play at all'; and the first production was received simply as 'a superbly contrived conversation piece – lively, often cynical, sometimes profound'.[28]

Increasingly in Eliot's later plays, the social mode dominates, as the mythical subtext becomes more tenuous and the verse takes on the attributes of ordinary (if rather stilted) conversation. Yet ultimately, for Eliot, like his spiritually aware protagonists, 'What you call the normal/Is merely the unreal and unimportant'.[29] The effect of this religious perspective is intensified by the programmatic structuring of the action. In devaluing ordinary human concerns, the drama itself is undermined. The spiritual theme of *The Confidential Clerk* is reduced to a cliché by the artificiality of the plot, while the characters lack any convincing personal reality in *The Elder Statesman*.

Eliot's plays can be seen as a progressive series of experiments, each tackling dramaturgical problems revealed by his previous attempt to create a specifically modern form of poetic theatre. They were explicitly intended as a model for the next generation of dramatists; and indeed influenced Christopher Fry, whose lyric comedies also appeared in the immediate post-war period, as well as John Whiting, whose promising career in the 1950s was cut short by his early death. *The Cocktail Party* has been successfully revived (1967–68), and the continuing popularity of *Murder in the Cathedral* – produced by numerous amateur groups, as well as by the RSC (1972) – has led to it being called 'the third biggest box office draw in the world', while *Sweeney Agonistes* has proved strikingly theatrical with a jazz score by Johnny Dankworth and Cleo Laine (1965). However, the direction in which Eliot's experiments moved, gradually becoming almost indistinguishable from the popular dramatic forms that he intended to use as a basis for parody, implicitly demonstrated that traditional poetry was incompatible with conventional theatre. Indeed, formal verse has almost completely vanished from the contemporary stage; and – like Arden's *The Hero Rises Up* (1968) or Caryl Churchill's *Serious Money* (1987) – what few examples there are, use it as pastiche.

Notes

1 *Observer*, 31 August 1958.

2 For the association of verse drama with high-church views, see Findlater, *The Unholy Trade*, London, 1952.

3 Eliot, *On Poetry and Poets*, London, 1957, p. 31; *Complete Poems...*, New York, 1952, p. 142; *The Use of Poetry and the Use of Criticism* (1933), London, 1975, p. 153.

4 Eliot, *The Family Reunion*, London, 1963, pp. 21–2, 99, and *The Elder Statesman*, London, 1959, p. 83.

5 Eliot, introduction to S. Bethell's *Shakespeare and the Popular Imagination*, London, 1944; *The Rock*, London, 1934, pp. 15–16.

6 Eliot advised Hallie Flanagan, the first director of *Sweeney Agonistes* to 'see Ezra Pound's book and Yeats' preface and notes to *The Hawk's Well*' (cited in Hallie Flanagan, *Dynamo*, New York, 1942, p. 83).

7 Eliot, cited in *The Journals of Arnold Bennett*, 1921–29, ed. N. Flower, London, 1933, p. 52; *Complete Poems...*, p. 74.

8 *Complete Poems...*, pp. 80, 82–3. For a full description of the 1934 Group Theatre production, see Michael Sidnell, *Dances of Death*, London, 1984, pp. 100ff.

9 *Murder in the Cathedral*, London, 1965, pp. 32–3.

10 *Ibid.*, pp. 89, 25, 57. A fuller definition of martyrdom is given by D. E. Jones, *The Plays of T. S. Eliot*, London, 1960, pp. 64ff.

11 *Murder in the Cathedral*, pp. 52, 75, 91; Eliot, *The Listener*, 25 November 1936, p. 994; *On Poetry and Poets*, p. 81.

12 *On Poetry and Poets*, p. 80; *Murder in the Cathedral*, p. 32; Robert Speaight, in *T. S. Eliot: The Man and his Work*, ed. A. Tate, London, 1967, p. 183.

13 *On Poetry and Poets*, p. 94; *Four Quartets*, p. 32; Eliot, letter, cited in E. Martin Browne, *The Making of T.S. Eliot's Plays*, Cambridge, 1969, p. 312.

14 *The Family Reunion*, London, 1968, pp. 41, 87, 97.

15 *The Elder Statesman*, pp. 70, 89–90.

16 *The Family Reunion*, pp. 29, 107; Eliot, cited in Richard Findlater, *Michael Redgrave: Actor*, London, 1956, p. 50.

17 Eliot, *Selected Essays*, London, 1951, p. 229; *The Use of Poetry & the Use of Criticism*, Harvard, 1933, p. 147.

18 Eliot, *Dial*, November 1923, p. 483.

19 Eliot, letter, 13 March 1938, cited in Browne, *The Making of T.S. Eliot's Plays*, p. 107; *The Family Reunion*, p. 91.

20 *The Family Reunion*, p. 15; letter, 13 March 1938, cited in Browne, *The Making of T.S. Eliot's Plays*, p. 107.

21 *On Poetry and Poets*, p. 85.

22 Letter, 19 March 1938, cited in Browne, *The Making of T.S. Eliot's Plays*, p. 107.

23 *On Poetry and Poets*, pp. 95 & 83–4; letter, 19 March 1938, cited in Browne, *The Making of T.S. Eliot's Plays*, p. 107.

24 *The Cocktail Party*, London, 1958, pp. 58, 75, 67; character notes for *The Confidential Clerk*, cited in Browne, *The Making of T.S. Eliot's Plays*, p. 285.

25 *The Cocktail Party*, pp. 139, 72; *On Poetry and Poets*, p. 85.

26 *The Cocktail Party*, pp. 174, 141, 133 & 99, 110, 131, 128 and 145.

27 *On Poetry and Poets*, p. 82.

28 *Ibid*, pp. 73 & 85; *New Statesman*, 3 September 1949.

29 *The Family Reunion*, p. 85.

5.5 Appealing to the popular imagination: Christopher Fry and Peter Shaffer

After the Second World War, Martin Browne – the founding director of the Religious Drama Society for which Eliot's early Church plays were commissioned – revived Ashley Duke's Mercury Theatre to foster modern poetic and religious drama. In his view, the two were synonymous: 'Our aim is to stage plays by poets, but as poets are sensitive beings it is not surprising that they concern themselves with religious themes in time of world chaos.'[1] This programme resulted in an extension of the Group Theatre experiments from the 1930s – a typical example being Ronald Duncan's allegorical masque of temptation and resurrection, *This Way to the Tomb* (1945), which was heavily influenced by both T.S. Eliot's *Murder in the Cathedral* and Auden and Isherwood's *The Dog Beneath the Skin*.

However, Browne's Mercury Theatre also introduced a new poetic voice with Christopher Fry's *A Phoenix Too Frequent* (1946). Satirizing false ideals of sacrifice, this comedy showed a way out of the tomb. The euphoria of victory had not been matched by improvements in the conditions of life for the British population. Reflecting the drive for social justice, which fuelled the war-effort, a Labour government had just been elected. But the cities were bombed-out shells, food was still rationed – and the lightness and wit of Fry's play caught the public mood of the time.

Christopher Fry (1907 –): spiritual comedy and celebratory verse

CHECKLIST OF FRY'S MAJOR PLAYS

A Phoenix Too Frequent, 1946   *The Dark is Light Enough,* 1954
The Lady's Not for Burning, 1948   *Curtmantle,* 1961
Venus Observed, 1950   *A Yard of Sun,* 1970
A Sleep of Prisoners, 1951

Escaping to a fanciful Roman setting, *A Phoenix Too Frequent* celebrated love and new beginnings in highly coloured verse that seemed to offer fresh opportunities for poetry on the stage. The young Roman widow, who finds the potential for new happiness in a common soldier, instead of starving herself to death in her aristocratic husband's mausoleum, embodied the public's desire to put the darkness of the war behind them, and the hope of a brighter future in the union between social classes. But Fry's apparently secular perspective still contained the spiritual vision that defined the earlier poetic drama of Eliot; and his comedies were accompanied by straight religious plays.

From *The Boy with a Cart* in 1937, dramatising the legend of the Cornish St Cuthman and written – like Eliot's pageant *The Rock* three years earlier – in aid of a church building fund, up to *One Thing More,* celebrating Caedmon's songs and performed at Chelmsford Cathedral in 1986, Fry has continually returned to Festival plays. This attempt to reintegrate theatre with its religious roots always tended to become a retreat into mythical history, as in *Thor, With Angels,* commissioned (like *Murder in the Cathedral*) for the Chapter House at Canterbury in 1948. Dedicated to Martin Browne, the plot involves the legendary figure of Merlin in the conversion of Britain to Christianity with the tenth-century arrival of St Augustine. However, in *A Sleep of Prisoners,* performed as part of the Festival of Britain in 1951, Fry succeeded in creating a modern idiom through merging biblical vignettes with a contemporary context in dream sequences.

Designed for church presentation, again like Eliot's drama of martyrdom, the performance space of *A Sleep of Prisoners* is identical with the play's setting, where four captured British soldiers are imprisoned in a church. Plot development is replaced by a paradigmatic structure of parallel scenes to make 'Affairs . . . soul size./The enterprise/Is exploration into God.' A single physical action – one soldier's refusal to hate the (unnamed) enemy, which provokes an attack by another prisoner, who sees war as a fight against evil – is progressively modified by biblical archetypes. Warfare is equated with the primal murder of Abel by his brother Cain, then transformed into the story of Absolom and King David. This is followed by Abraham's blood-offering of his son Isaac, which is prevented by an angel – and finally by Shadrach, Meshach and Abednego, who are saved by faith from the fiery furnace. From a killing motivated by political necessity, and lamented by the man responsible, then a reluctant sacrifice narrowly avoided, the original violence becomes a redemptive purgation, in a 'design where each of the four men is seen through the sleeping thoughts of the others, and each in his own dream, speaks as he is, not as he believes himself to be'.

When they wake the soldiers have been converted by their subconscious experience, and all affirm the saving grace of love for one's enemy. The audience are clearly intended to follow the movement of these Everymen 'from division to unity': a humanistic version of salvation, where 'the answer is in ourselves . . . each individual has in him the elements of God'.[2]

These Festival plays express Fry's religious aims directly, while his one historical drama, *Curtmantle* (1961) deals with exactly the same subject as *Murder in the Cathedral*, but from the king's perspective rather than that of the martyr. However, it was his cycle of 'seasonal comedies' that seemed to offer a model for contemporary verse drama. The same themes of resurrection, and the triumph of love over death, are broadened and corroborated by romantic fulfilment. The optimism, which seems utopian in the violent and sacrificial context of *A Sleep of Prisoners*, is legitimized in these plays by a traditionally affirmative comic resolution. Similarly the verbal exuberance of colourful poetic images – which appears excessive and ornamental in a monumental religious tragedy like *The Firstborn* (1946), where the subject is the deliverance of the Israelites by Moses, and the Seven Plagues of Egypt – becomes a legitimate part of the celebratory tone in these comedies.

For Fry, 'comedy is an escape, not from truth but from despair, a narrow escape into faith'. And by embodying this spiritual vision in naturalistic stories of human love (rather than Christian Passion) he was able to present 'a world in which we are all poised on the edge of eternity . . . in which God is anything but a sleeping partner' in everyday life.[3]

The most distinctive and effective of these 'seasonal comedies' is *The Lady's Not for Burning* (1948). Its fifteenth-century characters are intoxicated with fantastical imagery, which is offset by the irony in their predicament. The lovers stand for contrasting forms of rationalism: a cynical soldier of fortune, who can find nothing beyond the 'tedium . . . of the humdrum' and the sordid physical facts of existence; and the scientifically minded daughter of a mathematical alchemist, who sees reality as limited to 'What I touch, what I see, what I know; the essential fact'. They discover 'the magnetism of mystery' through love – and the plot illustrates the irrational nature of life through explicitly contradictory and 'irresponsible events'.[4]

Being disillusioned by the apparent meaninglessness of the world, the man confesses to murder (and even to being the Devil) in order to get the witch-hunting townspeople to put him out of his misery. But the authorities refuse to hang him simply because he demands it, whereas the girl is condemned to be burnt because she denies being a witch and does not want to die. Mistaking the man's death-wish as a generous attempt to save her by sacrificing himself, the girl is unwillingly attracted to him, while he unexpectedly finds himself reciprocating her emotion. So when the murdered man, whose body she is supposed to have spirited away, turns out to have been merely sleeping off a drunken stupor and the lovers are allowed to slip quietly out of their prison, their perception of life has completely changed. The sunrise, which was to have signalled their execution, becomes the symbol of a new future.

The only magic is amorous bewitchment. The supernatural is dismissed as superstition, in order to affirm the miraculous nature of ordinary life. Rationalism leads to despair, while falling in love reveals the spiritual significance of existence. As one character remarks, 'What a wonderful thing is metaphor'; and Fry's use of verse both expresses and exemplifies this sense of wonder. Restating Eliot's association of prose with materialistic pragmatism, Fry argues that in 'a world as wildly unprosaic as this one is' – a proposition illustrated by the romantic vision of his comedies – 'poetry is the language of reality'.[5]

In Fry's definition of poetic drama 'the poetry and the construction are inseparate . . . for the poetry is the action, and the action – even apart from the words – is the figure of the poetry'. This echoes Jean Anouilh, whose plays Fry translated; and like Anouilh's '*pièces roses*', he relies on mood to achieve imaginative unity. So each comedy is keyed to a particular season: bitter-sweet April transition in *The Lady's Not for Burning*; the sensuality of summer in *A Phoenix Too Frequent* and *A Yard of Sun* (1970); autumnal ripeness and decay in *Venus Observed* (1950); elegiac nostalgia in the 'winter comedy' of *The Dark is Light Enough* (1954). The integration of poetic mood and action corresponds with Fry's thematic aim to infuse life with spirituality. Yet rather than enhancing daily existence, Fry's extravagant imagery and high-flown language inherently devalue it. His premise that 'what we *call* reality is a false god, the dull eye of custom', leads to an artificial heightening of the dramatic context, and undermines individual characterization.[6]

Like Perpetua, the heroine of *Venus Observed*, we are invited to 'Meet England . . . among the wisps/Of magic we still possess'. But this is a country very far from ordinary experience, with its towering observatory and neo-classical 'Temple of Ancient Virtues' on a ducal estate. The characters, from the star-gazing Duke of Altair down to his earth-bound gardener, are lovable eccentrics. The love-complications that lead to the burning of the observatory are based on the myth of Paris and the apple of discord; and to underline that these are not everyday activities, they occur on 'All Hallowe'en'. As here, the exotic settings of Fry's plays – the Roman cemetery of *A Phoenix Too Frequent*, the turning point between the dark ages and the Renaissance in *The Lady's Not for Burning*, or a Hungarian mansion during the revolution of 1848 (*The Dark is Light Enough*) – glamorize figures lacking personal identity. The characters are symbolic, like Perpetua, reflecting the desires of the audience. A modern-day Venus, she describes herself as 'any girl: Perpetua/Perpetual, making no gesture I can call/My own'.[7] And this effect is underlined by the lyricism of Fry's verse, which makes all his characters' speeches interchangeable.

As the language of spiritual perception, Fry's poetry becomes an end in itself. When Perpetua is encouraged 'To use longer sentences', she is immediately given a forty-four-line speech on the subject of syntax, all in a single extended sentence. Verbal pyrotechnics are consciously designed to display the richness of a spiritualized world in contrast to the impoverished materialism of a prosaic urban society, to the point of self-consciousness, as in the misanthropic idealist's attack on scientific rationalism in *The Lady's Not for Burning*:

We have given you a world as contradictory
As a female, as cabbalistic as the male . . .
Revolving in the ballroom of the skies
Glittering with conflict as with diamonds:
We have wasted paradox and mystery on you
When all you ask us for, is cause and effect! –
. . . How uneconomical
The whole thing's been.

However, the problem with this poetic inflation is that, in the same way as it blurs distinctions between the characters, it removes moral significance from the dramatic events. As Stephen Spender was the first to point out: 'The Fry method is to subdue the action of the characters to the charm and wit of the verse. The temperature of human behaviour is lowered to a point where things like robbery, fornication and murder are made to appear merely verbal, and one soon ceases to care about them.'[8]

In one sense, Fry represents the high point of modern attempts to revive verse drama. His tone is lyrical in the extreme; and by contrast to Eliot, with whom he was closely associated, Fry flaunts poetry. Immensely popular at the time, the imaginative vitality of his verse attracted actors of the stature of Edith Evans, John Gielgud and Michael Redgrave, while Laurence Olivier and Peter Brook directed his plays.

Yet the unreality of Fry's dramatic situations and the artificial nature of his comedy made his work seem dated, as soon as Osborne and Arnold Wesker introduced new standards of authenticity in the late 1950s. At the same time Samuel Beckett set completely different criteria for dramatic dialogue. So, although Fry continued to write over the next two decades, his work was marginalized. Apart from *The Lady's Not for Burning*, which has continued to retain its popularity – its title even being adopted by Mrs Thatcher, in her famous assertion that 'the Lady's Not for Turning' – his plays have only occasionally been revived, with *A Sleep of Prisoners* being staged in a series of London churches (1987).

As a result Fry has had little direct influence, although there are echoes of his poetic whimsy in John Whiting's early comedy, *A Penny for a Song* (1952: see below, p. 497). But Fry's position as a popular writer dealing with significant issues was almost immediately filled by Peter Shaffer. He can be seen as following Fry in many ways – and Shaffer's ' "total theatre", involving not only words but rites, mimes, masks and magics', fulfils a similar need for colourful vitality in a society that was increasingly seen as mechanistic and materialist during the 1960s and 1970s.[9]

Peter Shaffer (1926–): symbols of the divine

CHECKLIST OF SHAFFER'S MAJOR PLAYS

Five Finger Exercise, 1958	*Equus*, 1973
The Royal Hunt of the Sun, 1964	*Amadeus*, 1979
Black Comedy, 1965	*Lettuce and Lovage*, 1987
White Lies, 1968	*Yonadab*, 1988
The Battle of Shrivings, 1970	*Gift of the Gorgon*, 1993

Even though none of Shaffer's plays is in verse, his early comedy, *Five Finger Exercise* (1958), picks up on Eliot's attempts to integrate poetry and naturalistic comedy, in its subtext of hidden myth. Labelled by Shaffer as 'a semi-autobiographical play . . . well-made' in style, its apparently everyday characters are contemporary equivalents of Oedipus and Hippolyta; and it was interpreted as 'a new version of the Passion story'. Although lacking the specifically Christian vision of Eliot and Fry, Shaffer's most significant plays, *The Royal Hunt of the Sun* (1964), *Equus* (1973) and *Amadeus* (1979), have an equally strong religious basis. As he has pointed out, 'all three pieces share a common preoccupation with worship and man's attempts to acquire or murder a special divinity'.[10] This theme also leads Shaffer to the rejection of society, that is characteristic of more conventional poetic drama, in his preference for the passionate individual versus the moral conformist.

There is also another more specific link with Fry in *The Royal Hunt of the Sun*, where Shaffer uses a narrator, who looks back on betrayed idealism in the figure of his youthful self as a participant in the historical events he describes. Exactly the same technique for giving a moral perspective on the action was developed by Fry in *Curtmantle* (produced three years earlier), which – like Shaffer's play – deals with the sacrifice of a spiritual opponent for political expediency. Similarly Shaffer's basic situation in *The Battle of Shrivings* (1970) is a variation on *The Lady's Not for Burning*. In this battle of beliefs, a humanist saint (reminiscent of Bertrand Russell) is brought to despair of his rational idealism by an alcoholic and nihilistic poet (combining D.H. Lawrence's instinctive physicality with T.S. Eliot's vision of a social wasteland), who comes to affirm the life that he had denied. Despite their difference in age, the pair represent comparable attitudes to Fry's rationalistic 'witch' and cynical soldier. The spiritual polarization and its reversal in *Shrivings*, which is also reminiscent of the change in Fry's characters, is a hallmark of Shaffer's drama.

Shaffer also shares the stylistic ideal, emphasized by poetic dramatists from the Symbolists at the turn of the century, that reaches its fullest definition in Samuel Beckett's 'form is content, content is form. Not about something'. But in contrast to Beckett, where the dramatic medium is pared down to an irreducible and highly intellectual image, Shaffer incorporates his existential theme in colour, costume and ceremony, spectacle, choreographed movement and aural composition. The external elements of production become the core of play-scripts that 'demand elaborate physical actions to complete them'. Dialogue and characterization, the standard carriers of dramatic meaning, become secondary to the staging. By explicitly using 'gesture to enshrine idea', Shaffer's aim in each of his major pieces has been to create 'an experience that was *entirely and only theatrical*' (Shaffer's italics). As a result, from the first a continual refrain in reviews was the apparent superficiality of these plays, in which language failed to meet the demands of ambitious subjects, or the 'dazzling display' of visual effects seemed to cover a 'hollow centre'.[11]

Such criticism certainly applies to *Yonadab* (1988), where encasing the same theme of 'man's attempts to acquire or murder a special divinity' in an Old Testament story of incest and melodramatic revenge led to monumental cliché, so that the elaborate staging became a form of sensationalistic voyeurism. Conversely, the extent of Shaffer's reliance on non-verbal elements to convey inner depth is clearly revealed where they are missing from his drama, as in *Shrivings*.[12] By its very nature, Shaffer's major theme of irrational faith affirmed through negation is anti-intellectual – in each of his plays figures representing rationality are forced to abandon their logical position. So it can only be effectively communicated in emotional terms through symbols.

The way this works can be illustrated by *The Royal Hunt of the Sun*, where there are clearly distinct levels in the action. These are mediated through the reactions of an old and disillusioned narrator, reflecting on his participation in the conquest of Peru as an idealistic boy. The historical plot of 'how one hundred and sixty-seven men conquered an empire of twenty-four million' is the most superficial. Behind this epic adventure story stands 'the conflict of two immense and joyless powers'.[13] Spain, with its poverty and competitive individualism, is presented as the antithesis of Peru, with its material plenty, equality and authoritarian regimentation. On this second level the play refers to the dominating twentieth-century political systems, Capitalism and Communism.

Throughout the first half of the play the two are contrasted, with the ordered contentment and peace of the Inca regime discrediting the civilizing pretensions of the European invaders, whose dynamic aggressiveness and militancy in turn reveals this social utopia as mass spiritual enslavement. But these political opposites are in essence identical. 'The Conquistadors deified personal will: the Incas shunned it. Both in a deep sense denied man.' Since each civilization is one-sided, their good qualities are equally destructive. Thus the Catholic priest declares 'hunger a right' because 'it gives life meaning . . . happiness has no feel for men here since they are forbidden unhappiness'.[14]

Following this dialectical principle, the negative political layer of the play (the plot) is set against aesthetics (the staging). The conquest of Peru destroys the victors' integrity and ideals, as much as it reduces the conquered to unalleviated misery, while the plundering of the country's wealth corrupts even the Spanish homeland. In political terms the play is a bleak picture of total devastation. By contrast the theatrical presentation embodies a positive vitality. It also reintroduces the dialectic in very different terms. On one side is the continuous movement of the Conquistadors and their mimes of marching (through a jungle of savagery and death), 'the Great Ascent' (with the mountains representing aspiration as much as a physical ordeal) or the violent 'Mime of the Great Massacre' (a ballet of slaughter, with a scarlet cloth as a river of blood flowing out of the sun symbol of the Inca Empire to cover the stage). This is set against the emblematic stillness of the Inca god-king posed above them in the stylized golden sun-flower, and the exotic chanting or geometrically choreographed dances of the Indians: 'the active iron of Spain against the passive feathers of Peru'.[15] From the aesthetic viewpoint the action is not political, but sexual: penetration and rape. The opposition is between complementary male and female principles, or even body against soul.

This carries over into the personal relationship that dominates the second half of the play. As with Pozzo and Lucky in Beckett's *Waiting for Godot*, the Conquistador General and the subjugated Inca Emperor, whom he comes to love, are bound together by a rope in an image of mutual dependence. Pizarro is crude and aggressive masculinity personified, the epitome of physical activity – Atahuallpa ethereal and androgynous, representing both the exotically feminine Other (in the classic imagery of colonialism) and serene spirituality. But like other polarities in the play, these opposites are equated: 'both bastards, both usurpers, both unscrupulous men of action, both illiterate – they are mirror images of each other. And the theme which lies behind their relationship is the search for god.'[16]

To ward off attack by the armies around them, the small band of invading mercenaries are forced to behave as if they were the gods foretold by Inca legend, who Atahuallpa mistakenly believes will ratify his divine right to the throne he has usurped. Atahuallpa's faith in his own divinity converts the atheist Pizarro, appearing to offer the Conquistador General an escape from the moral dilemma of murdering the captive Emperor, whom he has given his word to protect, through belief in his resurrection after death. At the same time Atahuallpa is forced to recant and be baptized, in order to avoid death by burning and preserve his corpse to be revived by the sun's light. For Pizarro the hunts for gold or fame turn out to be equally illusory motives. The 'name that won't ever be forgotten . . . sung here for centuries in your ballads' becomes the infamy of a betrayer and butcher. Yet Pizarro comes to realize that he has 'gone God-hunting and caught one'.

On the surface, this too is denied. Christianity is presented throughout as hypocritical, cruel and death-centred, while sun-worship is just as much a betrayal of belief. The 'impossible' resurrection fails. Yet by doing so it produces a real miracle in restoring Pizarro to humanity. At the beginning, his 'frostbitten' soul is incapable of feeling. The relationship with Atahuallpa moves him to laughter, love and finally the only tears he has ever shed. The young narrator writes the word 'god' on Atahuallpa's fingernail; and in terms of the play, the divinity so conspicuously absent in Church and society is found in the individual spirit. This insight is hardly profound, but once again the meaning is carried by theatricality. In the final tableau, surrounded by masked and chanting Indians, Pizarro waits for sunrise with the dead Inca at his feet '*as if turned to stone*'. Just as his frozen figure breaks out into the violence of grief, so these rigid images of the human face appeared to become alive. As Shaffer pointed out, the audience projected the emotions of the moment onto '*the great golden funeral masks of ancient Peru*', so that their – in fact, unmoving – '*immense triangular eyes*' were credited with a whole spectrum of feelings: hope, expectation, amazement, disbelief and despair.[17]

Shaffer's enquiry into the existence of God is extended in his following plays. The starting point of *Equus* (1973) was an actual incident where a local boy viciously blinded six horses. But as with *The Royal Hunt of the Sun*, the factual event is less significant than 'the reverberations it set up'. These are explored through confrontations with a psychiatrist in the mental institution to which the boy has been committed. On the surface the play has the form of a clinical enquiry, with the whole cast visible throughout as both 'witnesses' and (in an explicit echo of Greek tragedy) 'a Chorus' on benches surrounding a bare wooden operating space. This performing area is lit by 'a battery of lights set in a huge metal ring', behind which a section of the audience fill the role of medical students on 'tiers of seats in the fashion of a dissection theatre . . . pierced by a central tunnel'.

However, the fenced wooden square 'set on a circle of wood' is also a sporting arena, as the stage directions indicate: not simply 'a railed boxing ring', but suggesting a more ancient and deadly blood sport. In a real sense, the mental struggle between analyst and recalcitrant patient that provides the surface conflict is only shadow boxing. The dominating animal figures superimpose the image of a bullfight over that of an operating table, transforming the backstage audience into spectators at a Corrida. And behind this lies human sacrifice, with the onlookers as atavistic worshippers – therapy being presented as a modern substitute for religion through the psychiatrist's 'very explicit dream' of cutting out children's entrails in a ritual of divination as 'a chief priest in Homeric Greece'.[18]

Shaffer's point is that the boy's 'act . . . lacked, finally, any coherent explanation'. Neither the repressive tensions created by Alan's devoutly Catholic mother and atheistic radical father, nor his childhood fascination with horses, is sufficient. His guilt and impotence, when a stable girl attempts to seduce him in the horse-barn, may be psychologically comprehensible. But the re-enaction of the crime is shocking precisely because none of these conventional interpretations justifies the violence. Instead the key factor is the link between religion, suffering and sexual sublimation, in which Jesus has been phonetically transposed into *Equus* (Latin for horse). Logic does not apply. Indeed, even with the horses identified as divinities, gouging out their eyes can hardly block the sight of 'a Jealous God' who 'sees you forever and ever'.[19]

The play underlines this by the immediate appearance of symbolic horses, '*dreadful creatures out of nightmare . . . archetypal images – judging, punishing, pitiless*'. The visual imagery is compelling, with the stylized centaurs formed from actors wearing skeletal silver horses' heads and hooves, creating an effect of magical transformation: a vital and potent force come to life. The central question of the play is not, why the crime was committed, but the call of 'Why Me? . . . Account for Me!' from the primitive and irrational religious urge in 'the black cave of the Psyche'.[20]

During the writing of *Equus*, Shaffer's interest shifted from the boy to the psychiatrist. As the only character to address the audience directly, the psychiatrist is also our representative: both a normal person with whom the average spectator can identify, and through his profession embodying the normative pressures of society. We are therefore intended to share his viewpoint as, in Richard Burton's analysis of the role, he 'gets sucked into his patient's torment almost against his will. He envies the boy for his passion; in the end it becomes his own.'[21] So, as Dysart comes to recognize that he is sicker than the patient he is required to heal, we realize (with him) that intellectual detachment disguises sterility, and that taking away the boy's pain means destroying the fundamental need for worship.

Dysart's name (with its connotations of dysfunction, dies, as well as Dis the Roman god of the underworld) implies that his rationalism is the death-principle. Its opposite, the mythic visions projected under hypnosis, form the positive pole of the play. Programme notes for the National Theatre production contained excerpts from Frazer's *Golden Bough*, while Jung's theories are central to Shaffer's dramatic concept: 'the cells of one's brain contain endless archetypal images that stretch back beyond the Stone Age'. Drawing on primitive associations of horsemen with gods, centaurs, or the white horse of Revelations, these universal myths are assumed to be part of everyone's subconscious. So details are left for the spectators to fill in, with 'the animal effect' being 'created entirely mimetically'. The actors' heads were visible beneath the equine masks, ceremonially donned in full view of the audience; and the absence of realism produced 'a stable of Superhorses to stalk through the mind'.[22]

The structure is simpler than in *The Royal Hunt of the Sun*, the whole action being centred on the developing relationship between psychiatrist/father figure and patient/surrogate son, Apollonian rationality versus Dionysiac instinct. Not only are all the events a case-history, presented from Dysart's memory. But the core scenes of the boy's erotic night-riding, and his sexual encounter with the girl that leads into the climactic blinding, are doubly distanced as imaginary replays of the past during therapy.

Shaffer has defined tragedy as 'a collision between two different kinds of Right', as distinct from 'a conflict between Right and Wrong'; and on the surface *Equus* presents a balance:

The normal is the good smile in a child's eyes – all right. It is also the dead stare in a million adults. It both sustains and kills – like a God. It is the Ordinary made beautiful: it is also the Average made lethal.[23]

But this equipoise is distorted by the way Shaffer emphasizes Jung's assertion that 'Neurosis is an escape from legitimate pain'. The neurotic and the norm are reversed. The socially respected psychiatrist and psychotic delinquent are mirror images: Dysart emasculated by the drabness of his marriage and using Greek legend as a substitute for the spiritual meaning missing from his 'normal' existence – the boy's impotence being the result of living out the primitive religious instinct. They are linked in mutual dependence, and the classic psychiatrist/patient transferral works both ways since Dysart's involvement – to the point of becoming the god's voice in the boy's mind – revives his own spiritual capacity in the process of extinguishing his patient's.

The way Shaffer defines the theme echoes *The Royal Hunt of the Sun*: 'the hunting of the human Psyche by the cult of a narrowly defined

Normality'.[24] Pizarro's conversion is repeated in more immediately accessible contemporary terms, while the tighter focus of *Equus* intensifies the emotional impact. At the same time it makes the oppositions seem simplified and programmatic, so that *Equus* verges on thesis drama.

In *Amadeus* (1979), which centres on the same false father-son relationship as *The Royal Hunt of the Sun* and *Equus*, Shaffer develops the role of the narrator in order to offset this tendency to polemic by creating ambiguity. The antithesis of the rational Dysart, the eighteenth-century court-composer Salieri is warped by jealousy, even insane; and instead of a case history, his memories are presented for a self-serving ulterior purpose. As a result, the play has provoked more argument than any of Shaffer's other work. Although *Equus* had been criticized by psychologists, their comments were limited to the type of treatment employed by Dysart, while *Amadeus* was attacked by historians, who questioned the theme of the play as a whole in challenging its historical authenticity.

Factual accuracy is only relevant if the main focus of *Amadeus* is seen as the relationship between genius and social norms, art and morality. On this level the play's statement is highly tendentious. Shaffer seems to be asserting that artistic creativity, as epitomized in Mozart, is completely divorced from intellectual capacity, ethical principles, personal dedication, or the values of society. These qualities are all dismissed, being embodied in Salieri – presented as a musical hack without artistic inspiration or originality – while his rival Mozart is characterized as an *idiot savante*, rude, insufferably arrogant, animalistic and infantile. Since this is a demonstrably misleading distortion of Mozart, as well as undervaluing Salieri's real (if more limited) talent, the point it supposedly demonstrates is discredited.

However, the real theme of *Amadeus* is not this but, as with Shaffer's other serious plays, the relationship between Man and God. His intentions are shown by the way biographical facts about Mozart's *Requiem* have been changed. This was commissioned by a Count Walsegg-Stuppach. Having developed the habit of paying for compositions to pass off as his own, Stuppach approached the ill and impoverished Mozart anonymously through his steward – the origin of the legend about a masked man involved in the composer's death – and the unfinished score was completed by Sussmayr: one of Mozart's pupils, who was also the lover of Mozart's wife, Constanza. In Shaffer's play it is Salieri who attempts to seduce a virtuous Constanza through blackmail; and Salieri himself who commissions the piece, disguised in a mask to become 'a Messenger of God stepping out of Mozart's confessed dreams'.[25] (And in the film version the dying Mozart, having unmasked this apparition, dictates the remaining music to Salieri, who thus contributes to the posthumous fame of the rival he has destroyed.) Everything expresses the egoism of the central figure.

Shaffer takes his title from Mozart's middle name, but its significance for the play is that Amadeus means 'loved by God'. Even more than in *Equus*, the narrator is the protagonist in his own story, the agent who controls and manipulates the action, as well as the only fully developed character. Salieri is a Mephistophelean Iago, whose jealousy of Mozart's musical genius (and sexual prowess) leads him to declare war on a divinity that he conceives as 'the God of Bargains', yet recognizes in the abstract perfection of music. This contradiction motivates the drama; and the exact terms of Salieri's original compact are crucial. His prayer was to be

a Composer! Grant me sufficient fame to enjoy it. In return I will live with virtue. I will be chaste. I will strive to better the lot of my fellows. And I will honour You with much music all the days of my life!

Fame as a composer during his lifetime is precisely what he is granted. But it is in recompense for music honouring a society he despises. Having 'sacramentalized their mediocrity', his ability becomes a punishment instead of a reward; and his tragedy is his awareness that 'A note of music is either right or wrong – *absolutely*! Not even Time can alter that: music is God's art.'[26] In short, the dichotomy between artistic genius and social morality flows from Salieri's 'bargain', and reflects his warped vision.

The ironies multiply. As the only character in the play to appreciate the greatness of Mozart's music, Salieri becomes the supreme communicator of its genius in justifying his destruction of Amadeus. He perceives the voice of God speaking through Mozart. Yet for Mozart music is an expression of the human spirit, at its most ennobling when celebrating the ordinary lives and common desires of 'real people'. To silence Mozart, Salieri encourages immoral or politically dangerous subjects for court operas, and suggests the use of secret Masonic ritual in a popular vaudeville to destroy him by alienating all his patrons. Yet these become the inspirations for Mozart's masterpieces. In driving his rival to starvation and despair, Salieri destroys himself. As he finally recognizes, 'We are both poisoned, Amadeus. I with you: you with me.'[27]

In fact, by determining Mozart's destiny, he takes on the role of the God he rejects, although his hubris is implicitly mocked by the petty meanness of his acts. Indeed, the whole frame of the play is ironic, Salieri being also presented as the playwright. His motive in recounting his crime is to gain the immortality denied to his music, which he sees as forgotten while Mozart's is played everywhere. By committing suicide he hopes to convince the audience that he was personally responsible for Mozart's death: 'After today, whenever men speak Mozart's name with love, they will speak mine with loathing! As his name grows in the world so will mine.'[28] His failure to kill himself only persuades his contemporaries (embodied in the two 'Venticelli' who represent rumour) that his self-accusation is evidence of a deranged mind. Yet in a sense this merely reflects his fears, since the play indeed establishes Salieri as a presence for the posterity his character addresses.

Unlike the 1898 Pushkin/Rimsky-Korsakov opera *Mozart and Salieri*, which also dramatizes the composer's death as the murder of genius from professional jealousy, the poison in this case is moral. As such it not only corrodes Salieri's soul, but is capable of corrupting his audience. Beneath the attractive elements of his personality – his comic greed for sweetmeats, urbane cynicism and above all his sensitivity to Mozart's music, which serve to encourage spectators into identifying with Salieri's view – Shaffer stresses his '*malignant slyness*' towards us. His claim on the modern public as accomplices and companions in mediocrity makes the play a test of contemporary values, using the characterization of Mozart as its touchstone.

Salieri presents Amadeus (as distinct from the historical Mozart) as 'an obscene child', whose excruciatingly high-pitched manic giggle and anal witticisms are designed to alienate the audience, just as his conceited arrogance antagonizes the musical aristocracy on whom he depends for his livelihood. The picture, based on a distorted and one-sided exaggeration of biographical facts – Mozart's scatological letters and documented fondness for puerile jokes – is a travesty. So much so, that Simon Callow who originally played the role found 'it was impossible to believe that the little beast I'd produced (in direct response to the text) had written a note of the music around which the whole play revolved'.[29]

At the same time, his anarchic and animal crudity makes Amadeus a representative of 'Natural Man', passionate and elemental, just as his operatic subjects are democratic: revolutionary qualities denigrated by a reactionary hierarchical Establishment, which labels them as crude and vulgar in order to defuse their political threat. Since the musical conformist Salieri has identified himself with the artificial and hypocritical Court (Shaffer's most disparaging condemnation of society as an embodiment of mediocrity that destroys creative potential) his epithet for Amadeus, 'the Creature', is doubly loaded. The portrait is drawn by Salieri, warped by his malice. If we accept it, then we have aligned ourselves with the forces of destruction, and deserve his final contemptuous salutation to 'Mediocrities everywhere – now and to come'.

Peter Hall noted while preparing the National Theatre production that 'There must be a tension between what the audience sees and what Salieri describes.' In performance this was created by using 'something akin to revue technique' to present Mozart's character, corresponding with Simon Callow's perception that in Shaffer's dramaturgy 'the mask of the face, ways of speaking, external details are the essence'.[30]

As in Shaffer's other work, the form is the key to the play's meaning. Even the theological theme is undercut, since Salieri's declaration of war on God at the end of the first Act can be seen not merely as a deceptive self-justification for his jealousy, but as megalomaniac fantasy. It marks the point where he is revealed as paranoic. From then on Mozart's music, which dominates the emotional mood, becomes increasingly distorted to echo Salieri's moral disintegration, signalling the inaccuracy of his vision.

In fact, the essential level of the play is musical. Described by Shaffer in musical terms as a fantasia, *Amadeus* is conceived as an opera. It is framed by an overture and a final coda, in which the orchestral qualities of the dialogue arc particularly clear, with the massed citizens as a chorus accompanying the solo voices of the two Venticelli. And the scenes are structured like musical passages with 'an opening Chorus, the whispers of the populace . . . a duet . . . a trio, and later a quintet. Salieri's monologues are the big arias.'

This opera/drama is specifically Salieri's 'last composition, entitled *The Death of Mozart*, or *Did I Do It?* . . . dedicated to Posterity' and opening with a traditional Invocation, in which the modern spectators are ironically substituted for conventional gods.[31] But the opera that Salieri presents is a pastiche of Mozart rather than his own. Mozart's father, projected into the double figure of the fearful accusing stone Commendatore of *Don Giovanni* and the godlike forgiving High Priest Sarastro from *The Magic Flute*, reflects the ambiguity of Salieri's relationship to Mozart. The issue of revenge versus justice and the motif of masks and intrigues in *Seraglio*, *Figaro* and *Don Giovanni* are built into the action. Salieri's eavesdropping, hidden by a high-backed wingchair, ironically mirrors the classic scene of Cherubino hiding in a bedroom chair. The infantile sexuality of Amadeus and his wife is transposed into the Papageno theme from *The Magic Flute*, symbolizing natural man. Salieri's blackmail of her echoes the blackmail of Constanza by the surrogate father Bassa Selim in *Seraglio*, and so on. The form of Salieri's composition involuntarily glorifies the rival whose destruction obsesses him (though even this might be seen as part of his plan, since the degree of immortality he can achieve depends on the continuing enthusiasm for Mozart's music).

All three plays feature disillusioned narrators, whose perspective represents the anti-spiritual wasteland of contemporary society, but whose testimony demonstrates the existence of the divinity they deny. Each is a drama of obsession, using memory scenes, flash-backs and dream sequences to explore subconscious reality. Each focuses on 'apocryphal imagery' to appeal to the spectator's subconscious: 'The Sun God dead in his square. The horse God dead in his stable. The God in music dying in his slum, watched by the worshipper who has destroyed him.'[32]

Shaffer borrows his staging eclectically from the *avant-garde* – *Equus*, for example, uses exactly the same metaphoric combination of bull-ring and dissecting theatre as Jerzy Grotowski's adaptation of Calderón's *The Constant Prince* (1968), which had seemed a revelation when it toured Europe two years before *Equus*. As with John Whiting or David Rudkin, Shaffer's focus on spiritual experience is combined with a rejection of social values, including religious institutions. Even a light farce like *Black Comedy* (1965) corresponds to the *avant-garde* search for alternative forms in non-western theatrical traditions, borrowing its inversion of light and darkness from a Peking Opera set-piece.

At the same time, where the poetic *avant-garde* is typically exclusive and élitist – withdrawing from the stage like Yeats, or sacrificing avant-garde principles as well as poetry in order to address a popular audience, like Eliot – Shaffer's work puts the *avant-garde* on the mainstream stage in an apotheosis of 'total theatre'. His major plays, *The Royal Hunt of the Sun*, *Equus* and *Amadeus*, have each attracted larger numbers of spectators worldwide than any other serious contemporary drama and been turned into commercial films – as well as receiving the accolade of productions by the National Theatre, and awards on Broadway. Indeed *Equus*, which has been counted as the most immediately successful British play in stage history, was the first play ever to win all the New York awards in a single year.

Notes

1 E. Martin Browne, *Theatre World*, February 1948, p. 28.

2 *A Sleep of Prisoners*, Oxford, 1951, pp. 49 and preface; Fry, *New York Times*, 14 October 1951.

3 Fry, in *Adelphi*, November 1950, p. 27, and *World Review*, June 1949, pp. 21, 18.

4 *The Lady's Not For Burning*, Oxford, 1950, pp. 64, 53, 57, 20.

5 *Ibid.*, p. 3; Fry, in *Saturday Review of Literature*, 21 March 1953.

6 Fry, cited in J. C. Trewin, *Drama*, I, 1988, p. 20; *World Theatre*, Autumn 1955, p. 52. (For a fuller discussion of the seasonal imagery, see Derek Stanford, *Christopher Fry: An Appreciation*, London, 1952, which reflects the admiration for Fry's form of poetic drama when it first appeared.)

7 *Venus Observed*, Oxford, 1950, pp. 54, 65.

8 *Ibid.*, p. 62; *The Lady's Not For Burning*, p. 54; Spender, *London Magazine*, December 1955, p. 80.

9 Shaffer, Author's Notes to *The Royal Hunt of the Sun*, London, 1964, p. ix.

10 Shaffer, cited in Oleg Kerensky, *The New British Drama*, London, 1977, p. 58 and John Carey, *The Listener*, 31 December 1970, p. 928; Shaffer, 'An introduction to … THE ROYAL HUNT OF THE SUN, EQUUS, and AMADEUS, *Amadeus*, London, 1984, p. x.

11 Beckett, in *Our Examination for Incamination of Work in Progress*, Paris, 1929, p. 13; Shaffer, Preface to *Equus*, London, 1973, p. vi and programme note to *The Royal Hunt of the Sun*, National Theatre, 1964; *New Statesman*, 17 July 1964, and *The Times*, 8 July 1964.

12 Accounting for the failure of *Shrivings*, Shaffer pointed to his reliance on quasi-Shavian argument, which accentuated 'the danger in my work of theme dictating event … rhetorical dialectic was beginning to freeze my characters into theoretical attitudes' (Preface to *Collected Plays*, London, 1982, p. xiv).

13 *The Royal Hunt of the Sun*, p. 1, and Shaffer, National Theatre programme note, 1964.

14 Shaffer, National Theatre programme note, 1964; *The Royal Hunt of the Sun*, p. 52.

15 *The Royal Hunt of the Sun*, pp. 25, 38; Shaffer, National Theatre programme note, 1964.

16 Shaffer, interview in *Plays and Players*, April 1964, p. 23.

17 *The Royal Hunt of the Sun*, pp. 7, 75, 31, 79.

18 Shaffer, interview in *The Sunday Times*, 29 July 1973; *Equus*, London, 1973, pp. 8 & 9, 24.

19 *Equus*, pp. 7, 103.

20 *Ibid.*, pp. 106, 74.

21 Richard Burton, interview in *The New York Times*, 4 April 1976.

22 Shaffer, in *Vogue*, February 1975, p. 192; *Equus*, pp. 13, 8. (The effectiveness of this overtly theatrical approach can be contrasted with the film version of *Equus*, where cinematic realism reduced the horses to physical objects and their blinding became simply horrifying, preventing any imaginative identification.)

23 'An Introduction …' in *Amadeus*, p. ix and *Equus*, p. 63.

24 Carl Jung, cited in Shaffer, *Vogue*, February 1975, p. 192; Shaffer, Preface to *Collected Plays*, p. xiv.

25 *Amadeus*, Preface, p. xxviii.

26 *Ibid.*, pp. 8, 11.

27 *Ibid.*, pp. 59, 93.

28 *Ibid.*, p. 100.

29 *Amadeus*, pp. 51, 20; Simon Callow, *Being an Actor*, London, 1984, p. 86.

30 *Amadeus*, pp. 51, 102; Peter Hall, *Diaries*, ed. John Goodwin, London, 1983, p. 455; Callow, *Being an Actor*, p. 95.

31 Schaffer, in *The New York Times*, 14 December 1980; *Amadeus*, p. 9.

32 Shaffer, in *The Observer*, 4 November 1979.

5.6 Apocalyptic visions in theatres of Cruelty and Catastrophe: John Whiting, David Rudkin and Howard Barker

The theories of Antonin Artaud, the French Surrealist, have been a seminal force in *avant-garde* theatre, and had almost as much influence on English drama as Brecht or Beckett (see pp. 113–15 and 307).

Artaud's scattered productions from 1926 to 1935 had outraged the Parisian public, and he brought a new intensity to acting in Abel Gance's film *Napoleon* and Dreyer's *Passion of Joan of Arc*. But Artaud's ideas only began to filter through on to the British stage in a significant way at the end of the fifties, a decade after his death. Published in 1938, his essays outlined a multidimensional and physical 'Total Theatre' that would purge Western society of its materialistic morality through a 'necessary cruelty' in exposing audiences to myths of 'gratuitous violence', producing 'images of energy in the unconscious'.[1] Artaud's concepts opposed every element of conventional naturalistic plays, borrowing from Oriental models – in particular the 'trance dances' of Bali – and calling for a return to the ritual roots of drama. This primitivist ideal tapped into the sources of the counterculture movements that reached their high point with the Flower-Power festivals of the Sixties; and *The Theatre and Its Double* had an almost immediate impact when translated into English in 1958.

Artaud's influence on British drama is usually dated from Peter Brook's exploratory 1962 'Theatre of Cruelty' season. Using the resources of the RSC, Brook's programme (which led to the 1964 RSC production of Peter Weiss' *Marat/Sade*) opened with Artaud's 1927 playlet, *A Spurt of Blood*. It included a short piece by Arden, and culminated in a part-performance of Genet's banned play, *The Screens*. But this directorial initiative had already been anticipated by dramatists such as Ann Jellicoe and David Rudkin. Indeed, Rudkin's first play, *Afore Night Come* (1960, RSC, 1962) was considered as possible material for Brook's experimental performances at the LAMDA Theatre Club; and Ann Jellicoe had paved the way even earlier with *The Sport of My Mad Mother* (1958).

Jellicoe defined *The Sport of My Mad Mother* as 'an anti-intellect play', being not only based on 'irrational forces and urges', but intended to 'reach the audience directly though rhythm, noise and music, and their reaction to basic stimuli'. The title refers to the Indian goddess Kali, a mother figure symbolizing the creation of new life through death and destruction. This dualistic divinity is given modern embodiment in the pregnant leader of a London teenage gang with blood-red hair '*falling from her brow like a Japanese lion wig*' and a '*dead white*' face. The whole action revolves around street violence, turning everyday activities into stylized patterns of sound and movement, which culminate in birth pangs of 'bloody organic confusion', and the death/castration of the male figures (who represent moral responsibility and control).

These symbolic rituals are set within an explicitly theatrical frame, stressing the pretence of performance to heighten its intensity and immediacy on the principle that 'If you increase the challenge to belief you also increase the theatricality.'[2] But the dichotomy between the theatricality and the hallucinatory, anarchic vision is too great; and the potentially explosive rituals are defused by turning the action into children's games. Although Jellicoe returned to a similar subject in *The Rising Generation* (1967) – refused by the Girl Guides' Association, which had commissioned the work, on the grounds of its orgiastic feminism – her most successful play was a social comedy (*The Knack*, 1961); and Jellicoe subsequently abandoned the professional theatre for community drama (see above, pp. 185–86).

John Whiting (1917–63): surreal dimensions of reality

CHECKLIST OF WHITING'S MAJOR PLAYS

A Penny for a Song, 1951	*Marching Song*, 1954
Saint's Day, 1951	*The Devils*, 1961

John Whiting was one of the leading theatrical innovators of the early 1950s, yet his work has clear links with both with the poetic traditionalists that preceded him, and with the more popular type of serious drama that followed. The last play before Whiting's early death, *The Devils* (1961 – an adaptation of Aldous Huxley's *The Devils of Loudon*, commissioned by the RSC) anticipated Peter Shaffer's *The Royal Hunt of the Sun* (1964) in its broad historical sweep and theme of religious obsession. The violence and mythic quality of its action also in some ways paralleled Artaud's prescription for a 'cruel' theatre, as did *Saint's Day* (1951). However, Whiting's starting point was very similar to Christopher Fry, whose influence can be seen in *Penny for a Song* (1951).

Set in the time of Napoleon, this whimsical fantasy celebrates English eccentricity by suffusing farce with sentimental mood in its depiction of a batty baronet's last-ditch plans to repel invaders. Dressed as the Emperor with phrase book in hand – to order the French armies back home when they land – he is mistaken for Napoleon by his own villagers; and when his hot air balloon descends straight down a well, they detonate the gunpowder stored in it to send him flying over the Dorset countryside: a comic apotheosis, which ends in a bucolic cricket match and the romantic ascent of the evening star.

In sharp contrast, Whiting's characteristic drama was experimental, and dealt with contemporary subjects. The tone had already been set in *Saint's Day* (written in 1948 as a 'technical exercise', since Whiting considered it out of tune with the theatrical climate of the time – accurately in light of the critical incomprehension when it was finally produced the same year as *A Penny for a Song*).

Like Eliot's *Family Reunion* (1939), which some of the speeches parody, *Saint's Day* presents a naturalistic surface that switches into another dimension. But here even ordinary existence is presented as surreal. The conventional country-house setting is a symbolic wasteland: '*an architectural freak*' minimally furnished with decaying objects and overshadowed by dead elms, that imprisons its inhabitants in the cold and barren atmosphere of winter (also the name of the dour servant). All who take up residence in this 'damned house' are refugees. The 'aged poet', whose birthday provides the title, has exiled himself to this isolated wilderness of the spirit, as has his grand-daughter's painter-husband, while the villagers with whom they are locked in a sterile conflict are burned out of their homes.

Everything in the play has a naturalistic rationale. The poet's self-imposed twenty-five years of silence is his revenge on a society that cast him out. The neglect and bareness of the room is the result of poverty; and the hatred of the villagers, fuelled by fear, has been earned by 'abuse, the result of hurt pride'.[3] Yet the singleness of tone and extremity of mutual isolations, together with the completeness of the final catastrophe, shifts apparent normality into an apocalyptic vision.

For Whiting (quoting the French surrealist Montherlant) 'external action, simplified as much as possible, is only a pretext . . . to express activities of the human soul with the greatest truthfulness, intensity and depth'. The events that mark the progressive stages of spiritual revelation in *Saint's Day* have an arbitrary logic. The death of the poet's dog – perhaps from natural causes, though the old man blames the villagers – blocks the last possibility of escape offered by a visitor. An admirer of the poet, who has organized a London dinner in his honour, even the well-intentioned outsider is trapped in the old man's fantasy of revenge when a loaded revolver goes off in his hand by mistake, killing the poet's pregnant grand-daughter. This unintentional act destroys the young visitor's belief that 'the power invested was for good'. His perception that 'We are here – all of us – to die. Nothing more than that. We live for that alone', causes a holocaust.[4] In fulfilling this vision, he destroys the faith of the local parson, who inadvertently sets fire to the village by burning his theological library in despair. Finally, he orders the hanging of the poet he had come to rehabilitate, together with the painter, at the hands of a marauding band of criminal soldiers.

Originally summoned by the poet as instruments of his war against the village, which they have been terrorizing, these escapees from a military prison are the equivalent of Eliot's Eumenides: agents of spiritual retribution (or rather damnation) in a world where God does not exist. As with the revolver-shot and the fire, 'The agency is human, not providential.' Fate is the sum of meaningless accidents; and the play demonstrates that 'it is not a question of finding but of losing the pieties, the allegiances, the loves'.[5] Self-destruction – stated to be the theme of the play by Whiting – is not only a condition of human life, illustrated in the characters' behaviour, but its ultimate purpose.

Saint's Day is an exploration of the soul that denies the existence of the spirit and attacks religion; and the form of the play mirrors its content. A symbolic universe is evoked by realistically depicted objects and people that, unlike the figures in Eliot's quasi-naturalistic plays, have no extrinsic significance. In contrast to Eliot, the language is not heightened by archaism. It is neither imagistic, nor formalized into verse. The poetic statement is created out of the overall structure and mood. As in Whiting's other play of nihilistic conversion, *Marching Song* (1954), which deals obliquely with the post-war Nuremberg trials for military atrocities, the double vision allows shifts in style and radical personality changes in the characters, without losing consistency.

These qualities anticipated Samuel Beckett's existential drama, an affinity that Whiting recognized on seeing *Waiting for Godot* (first performed two years after *Saint's Day*). And they led George Devine to declare that *Saint's Day* 'splits wide open the conventional forms of playwrighting and allies itself with the other modern arts in a way that no other play has done'.[6]

David Rudkin (1936–): visions of hell

CHECKLIST OF RUDKIN'S MAJOR PLAYS

Afore Night Come, 1960	*The Triumph of Death*, 1981
Ashes, 1974	*The Saxon Shore*, 1986
The Sons of Light, 1977	

It took Jellicoe 'some years to understand that [*The Sport of My Mad Mother*] is based upon myth and uses ritual'. By contrast, Rudkin declared from the first that 'Theatre is a ritual'.[7] Even so, like those of Whiting or Jellicoe, Rudkin's dramas of demonic possession, mythic sacrifice and spiritual redemption are firmly grounded in contemporary society, or in a specific historical context.

The Midlands orchard of *Afore Night Come* (1960) is on the bus line from Birmingham; and the performance of the play is intended to reproduce actuality as closely as is possible in the theatre. Local accents are closely observed; the action takes place in one setting and on a single day; sound effects include a crop-spraying helicopter; and the environment is extended out into the auditorium with the '*Proscenium arch disguised by shed-fronts with practical doors . . .*' Similarly, Rudkin's introduction to *The Saxon Shore* (1986) stresses that the 'only (conscious) bending of history has been to bring one . . . plantationer "Saxon" community beneath the Roman Wall itself'.[8]

However, in all Rudkin's plays atavistic violence and archetypal resonances undermine such naturalistic appearances. Increasingly horrific visions – in which multiplying victims are brutalized, brainwashed, sexually assaulted, dismembered or burnt alive – reduce the realistic frames of his plays to an illusion. 'The Black Country' is both a geographical place and a symbolic moral state; more than a physical frontier. Hadrian's Wall is a manichean divide with 'Rome this side, chaos that, Christ here, darkness beyond'.[9]

Afore Night Come and *Ashes* (1974), Rudkin's next play to reach the stage, preserve a recognizable social surface throughout, even if the underlying action makes the normality it represents highly questionable. The uneducated itinerant fruit-pickers of *Afore Night Come* echo the peasants of Tolstoy's *Powers of Darkness* (1888), with their inarticulate language and rudimentary concerns serving as a cliché of authenticity. So, on a different level, does the grotesque Irish tramp, whose avoidance of work and empty assumptions of superiority (like the similar figure in Pinter's *The Caretaker*) make him a scapegoat. The final climax of ritual murder is shocking precisely because it grows so unexpectedly out of the repetitive everyday work-activity that has filled the stage up to that point.

It throws previous comments and actions that had been accepted as ordinary into a completely different light. The foreman's attempts to get the old tramp away from the orchard, which at the time had seemed no more than a natural intolerance of outsiders, his reluctance to bring out knives for slashing rubber tyres to bind the tree-trunks, or the social bitterness of the exploited workers about

... this job. Things between boxes and bloody trees. Sacrifices.

TAFFY Whole world's a bloody human sacrifice. Slaughter-house, three quarters of the bloody world, to feed the privileged...

take on an altogether darker meaning. As do references from a simple-minded lunatic to being 'Baptized in the Blood of the Lamb' or 'marked with the mark of the beast', that initially appear comically incongruous.[10]

There are shades of Oscar Wilde's *Salomé* (1905) in the orgasmic clasping of the tramp's bloody head: severed after slashing a cross on his chest. But here this is a baptism in damnation, not an apotheosis. The confusion between different types of sacrifice signals a perverted religion, fuelled by brutalized and truncated beliefs. The tramp is killed as a surrogate for the Wandering Jew, desecrating the earth he walks on. Yet the seasonal rite for renewal of 'Trees gone bitter since last year' would require the blood of the youngest and healthiest, the student, who is indeed the expected victim.[11]

However, the murder of the old tramp is juxtaposed with an apocalyptic rain of pesticide from a helicopter, which sprays down on the labourers as their knives slash the sacrificial corpse. This gives quite a different symbolic meaning to their action. It implies that this superstitious violence is not only an expression of deep subconscious needs denied by society, and an assertion of primitivism in opposition to it, but also the end-product of a dehumanizing technocratic civilization. Similarly, the sense of underlying spiritual reality is largely communicated by biblical images, which Rudkin uses as the natural speech of rustic simplicity. Yet the dialect language can also be seen as a symptom of brutalized personalities, as in *The Sons of Light* (1965–6, reworked in 1969–1971, produced in a rewritten version in 1976, then as revised, the final text, 1977) where 'archaism' is explicitly 'a metaphor of... regression'.[12] And the motivating force for evil is religion (particularly Christianity as the official creed for the society of which this group of labourers in *Afore Night Come* is a reductionist microcosm). Significantly, the only figure to oppose the ritual of killing is the homosexual patient from a local lunatic asylum, who succeeds in saving the student. Positive values are embodied in a marginalized outcast, who has been condemned by society for sexual perversion.

The same inversion of moral norms and rejection of modern society recurs in *Ashes*, although the spiritual dimension was disguised by an emphasis on political content in the first production.[13] Dehumanizing science and the pressures of social conformity reduce an infertile married couple, obsessed by the desire to overcome their perceived inadequacy by becoming parents, to 'malfunctioning clinical objects' and animals. All other characters – doctors, medical ancillaries, adoption officers and a 'fecund neighbour' – are played by a single actor and actress: interchangeable and therefore faceless representatives of social repression. Religion is parodied when a pregnancy test finally proves positive – with a booming sound-track of orchestra and choir in Mahler's 'Veni, veni Creator Spiritus' and a *'pencil spot on desk now draped altar-like with white cloth, central on it a tall specimen-jar, chalice like... glows like Holy Grail'*. This is a false apotheosis: not only because it is followed by miscarriage (and incineration of the wife's surgically removed reproductive organs), but because the whole thrust of the action is toward discarding socially defined personalities.

In terms of the play's evolutionary theme, man can only survive through change. So perpetuating themselves through a child would reproduce the patterns of the past. Instead, the woman finds herself deprived of her sexual identity; and has to create a different personality. The husband (again a homosexual as positive figure) comes to reject his Northern Irish inheritance as 'tribal son', as well as 'fatherhood' and 'the myth of manliness'; and the ending, with *'all male personae shed'* is announced as *'A BEGINNING'*.[14] The documentary surface, autobiographical basis, and apparent focus on personal relationships made this Rudkin's most popularly accessible play.

But as well as developing the musical structure, archetypal overtones and hallucinatory intensity, which characterize his more obviously poetic work, *Ashes* contains all the elements of his later vision in embryo.

Anal sexuality, male/female transpositions, and religious repression are central to *The Sons of Light* (1976) and *The Triumph of Death* (1981). Children of the isolated, evangelically obsessed islanders in the earlier play have been abducted by a Caligari-like psychologist, who runs a subterranean concentration camp. This demonic power-mad figure exercises control by setting himself up as the Old Testament God of punishment. His experiments have turned the kidnapped children into 'demented and deformed' grotesques, boy-woman and girl-man; and he serves the mainland Establishment, who ship over their non-conformist or rebellious citizens for 'treatment'. These prisoners are sodomized by guards (led by '*a pornographic "black angel" ikon of bestial malehood*') as part of the process that atrophies their humanity and reduces them to completely socialized zombies, indistinguishable from the rock they quarry to make their prison. The convicts of the subterranean/subconscious concentration-camp and the primitive islanders above-ground are equally victims of the insane scientist's brainwashing techniques; and the new pastor denounces his congregation's belief in an evil god of 'Wrath. Only His chastisement can transfigure you? God? Ungod!'[15]

In *The Triumph of Death*, set in a generalized medieval period, these themes are even more graphic. Opening and closing with the excremental images of defecating religious figures (the 'Feminine' boy whose vision led to the Children's Crusade; and a transsexual Luther) the symbolic 'Dark Ages' are ruled by a monstrous female Pope, whose face is '*a farded skull of cancerous death. Crown a Triple Tower, from which diminished human figures imprisoned scream and reach*'. His/her principal agent is a nun, who changes sex to seduce the homosexual spiritual opponent of this demonic-Papatrix, finally being transformed into a repugnant parody of modern femininity as a medical doctor (following Rudkin's consistent rejection of science). Against these forces of morality/evil stands a Christ figure, who is revealed as '*Satan, Cernunnos, Pan, call Him what you will. Night*'.[16] Devil and God have exchanged places; the moral and sexual norms are reversed. So here, extending the pattern of Rudkin's earlier plays, homosexuality is glorified in Pan's coupling with a worshipper, sanctifying the body that 'Crosstianity' debases.

However, each of Rudkin's plays ends with an image of hope. The visceral and extreme violence, repellant and unremitting, is intended to be purgatorial. The brutality is presented as the effect of civilization, produced by the false values of repressive Christianity and materialism. These baleful influences can only be countered by shattering people's social conditioning – in itself an agonizing process – which offers the potential for liberation. The cremation of the wife's womb in *Ashes* recurs with the burning of a pagan Joan of Arc at the stake in *The Triumph of Death*, and with the 'pure . . . primal essence' of a murdered slave-soldier rising from the inciner-ated embers of his dismembered body in *The Sons of Light*, where a saviour descends into 'The Pit' and brings 'the tower of death to dust'.

This is Rudkin's most explicit image of regeneration. The pastor's son, taking on the role of a 'King of Love' (as the antithesis of the God of Death), urges the entombed prisoners 'Up! Into your proper Kingdom . . . Your light has come' during an apocalyptic earthquake. This 'Surrection' (the title of the play's final section – a word that merges political insurrection with spiritual resurrection) miraculously frees a schizophrenic idiot from her de-monic 'possession' by inherited behaviour patterns, symbolized in a '*mother-persona, barren, destructive*' and '*father-persona, repugnant, devouring*'.[17] The only exception to this optimistic pattern of transcendence through martyrdom is *The Triumph of Death*, where the Pan-Christ is defeated by the forces of evil. Here, the final apotheosis is ironic – Luther's face being printed on German banknotes, as an image of a distorted religion sanctifying twentieth-century Capitalism.

Rudkin has described his drama as aspiring to 'the quality of an archetypal myth'; and the plots of these plays are based on biblical fable and fragmentary Shakespearean or historical images, all of which combine suffering with salvation.[18] Noah's Flood and *King Lear* provide a symbolic subtext for *The Saxon Shore* (Ceiriad being Cordelia). The martyrdom of Joan of Arc (as the daughter of the lone survivors from the Children's Crusade) is replayed in *The Triumph of Death*, the Harrowing of Hell in *The Sons of Light*, and both plays revolve around the Massacre of the Innocents.

These archetypes chart a geography of the mind. Rudkin's dramatic settings are purely psychological landscapes, inhabited by symbols. Their subterranean geology is the strata of the subconscious. As self-admitted re-flections of the author's own 'psychic turmoil', the visionary horrors enacted on stage lay claim to an unusual degree of authenticity, which is designed to transmit their hysteria to audiences. Following Antonin Artaud, Rudkin's theatre is intended as 'the truthful precipitate of dreams'. Reviews of all his plays have repeatedly referred to Artaud, who appears as a character in

The Triumph of Death – in the demonic role of Joan's confessor from Dreyer's 1927 film, *The Passion of Joan of Arc* – and these 'images of energy in the unconscious and gratuitous crime on the surface' are intended to exercise a therapeutic Artaudian 'Cruelty' against the spectators.[19]

However, the subjective intensity necessary to create this effect also creates problems in structure and stage realization. Narrative continuity is sacrificed for the intuitive links, fluidity and transformations of dreams. As a result the actions of Rudkin's characters appear unmotivated. In addition, representing symbolic visions physically on the stage tends to make them look artificial, particularly since much of Rudkin's symbolism derives from German Expressionist film. The extremism of this 1920s style verges on farce, as in the dark-visored Germanic mad-scientist of *The Sons of Light*, and leads to simplification.

More damagingly still, Rudkin's inversion of good and evil becomes so absolute that it loses moral relevance. The total condemnation of all intellectual, material and scientific progress leaves regressive primitivism as the only positive value (embodied in the 'Iron Age' existence, to which the crippled refugees from the Children's Crusade revert in *The Triumph of Death*). The call to their daughter to

Open your eyes. Look at this world. What folk be in it? They have a Lord. Of Love. Nailed living to a tree ... Day, night and day they hammer in the nails again ... They live by something they call money, which is the shit of toil. The name of their true Master is the Devil. Lord of Death.

is clearly meant as a directive to the audience. Yet as members of modern society the public are by definition 'the undead' and damned:

The blind, the maimed, the crazed reach each to us. Soldiers returned. Then suddenly, severally, pause. Scent us anew.
BLIND LAD Smell death. Smell death here.[20]

Similarly, translating this political attack into subjective religious images drawn from the depths of the psyche undercuts each level. And there is equal confusion in an approach that exploits conventional reactions of shock and disgust in order to induce audiences to reject the morality that produces such attitudes.

Rudkin's is a drama of exorcism. However, the traumatic degree of human suffering and assault on audience sensibilities considered necessary to achieve this spiritual purgation has been counter-productive; and none of Rudkin's later plays has reached a wide public. Forging a poetic language from archaic prose to create a visionary and subjective inner landscape of violent ritual and emotive archetypes, they are undeniably powerful. Yet their obsessive intensity exposes internal contradictions in his spiritual and anti-social approach. Although Rudkin's treatment of sexuality links his work to feminist drama, it has become marginalized by his extremism, sharing the fate of Barnes' comedy. Indeed Rudkin is the poetic/religious counterpart to Peter Barnes (discussed above, pp. 352ff.) and their plays occupy the same time frame, defining a specific moment in British drama.

Howard Barker (1946 –): dreams of violence

CHECKLIST OF BARKER'S MAJOR PLAYS

The Hang of the Gaol, 1978	*Golgo*, 1990
Victory, 1983	*Scenes from an Execution*, 1990
The Castle, 1985	*The Europeans*, 1993
The Power of the Dog, 1985	*Hated Nightfall*, 1994
Crimes in Hot Countries, 1985	*Minna*, 1994
The Bite of the Night, 1988	*(Uncle) Vanya*, 1996
Seven Lears, 1989	*Und*, 1999

Barker's work is a continuation of Rudkin's, but with a wider scope. A contemporary of David Hare and Howard Brenton, Barker shares their left-wing convictions and his earliest plays, *Fair Slaughter* (1977), *The Hang of the Gaol* (1978), present a prison hospital or an official inquiry into a prison riot and the burning down of a jail as polemic images for the state of the nation. Yet even these contain a surrealistic element, which comes to overwhelm the political content of his later work. More radical – in particular stylistically – his rejection of modern society is psychological and visceral, rather than ideological.

Of his almost 30 plays over the last two decades, the only one specifically addressing a contemporary issue is *A Passion in Six Days* (1983, staged in the same week as the Labour Party Conference it attacked), which parodied the new leader, Neil Kinnock, as Brian Glint, 'a traitor to the Left', in a bitter lament for the betrayal of working-class values. A few others are set in the Twentieth Century: *No End of Blame* (1981) about an artist caught in the First World War who chooses political cartoons as the most immediate way of changing society but ends up in a mental asylum, and *The Power of the Dog* (1985) with a photographer filming battlefield atrocities as Stalin and Churchill divide up Europe at Yalta while the Russian Army takes over Eastern Europe at the end of the Second World War. But the clear sense of despair at the absence of any viable political alternatives in a society summed up by one of the characters in *A Passion in Six Days* as 'rotting decencies and murdered hope', together with dismay at the inhumanity of the modern world which led the photographer of *The Power of the Dog* to exclaim 'if the impossible is true, where does that leave – does an artist cope with that?', has led to an emigration from the present.[21] And even if plays like *The Last Supper* (1988), *The Love of a Good Man* (1993) or his most recent productions *The Early Hours of a Reviled Man* and *Und* (both 1999) have a contemporary context, they represent it as a phantasmagoria.

Starting with *Victory* (1983), which focuses on the defeat of the Puritans with the restoration of the monarchy in 1660, most of Barker's plays present historical subjects from an increasingly nihilistic perspective. So in *The Europeans* (written for the RSC in 1984, but only performed in 1993) the question asked is 'How do we escape from History? We reproduce its mayhem in our lives.' And history becomes reduced to myth in a nightmare of disintegrating archetypes. This is explicit in a play like *The Bite of the Night* (1988) where a classics teacher follows Helen through the eleven lost cities of Troy, only to find a series of barbaric epochs in each of which one of Helen's limbs is chopped away in a search for 'the essential Helen' until she ends up as an amputee on a trolley, pushed along by blind Homer: 'No Helen but what other people made of her.' In the programme essay Barker described this as a 'play for an age of fracture' and this is reflected by a non-sequential vision of history as an arbitrary construct where Nazi atrocities coexist with ancient Troy.[22]

By 1988 Barker had evolved his concept of a 'Theatre of Catastrophe', rejecting didacticism and the stereotypes of political theatre as 'an unacknowledged collaboration with the ruling order'. Calling instead for a tragic drama of ambiguity and imagination, where images of extreme violence expose the moral and social crisis by appealing to 'the abolished unconscious', his aim is to challenge a positive response from 'the unpredictability of the human soul' through stretching audiences 'to the limits of tolerance'.[23] This leads to actions filled with excruciating torture, mental agony and motiveless killing – as with the horrific catalogue of flogging, rape, infanticide, dismemberment, decapitation in *The Possibilities* (1988) – on stages that are bloodstained battlefields: literally with *The Love of a Good Man* (1993) which

19 Polemic images and the poetry of violent action: sacrificial babies in Barker's
The Bite of the Night

is set in the First World War killing-field of Passchendaele and the cemetery built over the corpse-filled mud.

These themes and techniques were already clear in *The Castle* (1985, restaged by the Wrestling School 1995), which is perhaps the most accessible expression of Barker's 'Theatre of Catastrophe'. The apparent medieval context of a knight returning from the Crusades is undercut almost immediately by his discovery that the women left behind have set up a feminist commune, breaking down all established/male order to free 'the ground, . . . religion, . . . the body' during his seven-year absence. And any sense of historical authenticity becomes increasingly eroded by anachronisms where medieval men in armour call on weapons from past and present – double-headed axes with Bofors guns and two-handed swords with heavy artillery – in an endless chronology of slaughter that culminates with the roar of jet warplanes streaking overhead. Together with the arms race embodied in the castle of the title, which 'makes war necessary' by making 'enemies where there are none', the feminism and the jets initially led reviewers to assume that the play was – like David Edgar's *Maydays* – about the women's protest camp outside the US Airbase at Greenham Common.[24] But even if this may be one reference, the imagery is too grotesque and the action too extreme for a simply political allegory.

A witch, who lures the master-builder constructing the castle into copulating with her, is chained to his corpse – which gradually disintegrates until she is dragging a skeleton around with her. The knight's wife, who has betrayed her lesbian lover first by submitting to her returned husband, then by becoming pregnant through seducing the Moslem prisoner responsible for designing the castle, kills herself by stabbing the baby in her womb. Her death is followed by a mass suicide of all the others who are pregnant. And this is treated as farce –

SOLDIER TWO. Mind yer 'eads!
SOLDIER ONE. Raining women!

– although, as the priest who cries out that they are bearing 'our future in their innards and they kill it' implies, this final vision is truly apocalyptic: the ultimate catastrophe.[25]

Everything relates to sexuality. In its natural state, with all fences demolished by the women, the curving hill is female (as the knight's wife explicitly remarks, 'A woman, this country') while the perpendicular walls and rigid circles of the castle, which the men build for the knight, graphically symbolizes a phallocentric view of life as well as embodying the emotional repression, hierarchy, mathematics and logic that are conventionally associated with masculine principles. Contrasted with the natural geometry of a flower, as well as with the supposedly feminine principles of equality, sexual liberation and non-rational language – exemplified in the elliptical ungrammatical speeches of the women, who are described as having 'freed' all vocabulary starting with 'the words for women's and men's parts' – this stone castle is 'not a house' but a 'magnet of extermination'. It is the reverse of all standard expectations. Not simply because 'It resembles a defence but is really an attack' and being a threat creates 'enemies where there are none', but through promoting a continual state of war: the arena that justifies masculine authority. Building it both transforms the landscape from a female to male shape, and imposes discipline through which the female utopia is nullified. As the witch urges the knight's wife, 'the more they bore into the hill the more we must talk love, the bond, fasten it'; but the walls literally change the climate, forming wind tunnels that generate gales and snow, and negating the witch's female power. However for the captured infidel Krak (named after the Crusader fortress of Krak des Chevaliers) planning this castle is also a revenge for the Knight's slaughter of his family since 'Its vertical profile, which I took further than any other architect, renders it utterly vulnerable' in the arms race it generates.[26] And it is the height of the phallic walls that make it possible for the women to take their revenge on males by destroying their future.

Even religion is reduced to an instrument of sexual domination, with the knight instituting 'the Gospel of Christ the Erect!' and after his death the priest offering the witch a 'Holy Congregation of the Wise Womb'. But as the knight had come to realize, the world depicted – the one ruled by men – could only have been created by 'an evil deity' or a lunatic God. The only alternative to apocalypse is a world without any government at all; and the quasi-medieval setting represents a purely psychological 'Dark Ages'. At the same time Barker states that *The Castle* and his other plays written for a 'Theatre of Catastrophe' are 'irreducible to a set of meanings'; and the abolition of logical or social analysis is intended to produce a 'terror' in the audience 'akin to the shock felt by an animal uncaged' that will serve as an antidote to 'an age of persistent meaning, of relentless indoctrination'. In its place (as the director of the 1995 production of *The Castle* asserts) is

emotional and linguistic seduction, secret, complex, sometimes fugitive, a tidal effect of beauty and violence.[27]

Questioning the role of the artist has been a recurrent feature of twentieth-century English drama, reflecting a need to intervene more directly in current issues or to redefine their own status as playwrights, and Barker's work includes more artist-figures than even Bond or Stoppard. These illuminate his aims. As in *The Power of the Dog* or *A Passion in Six Days*, photography of contemporary life (the naturalistic approach) or political cartoons (like the Agitprop theatre of the 1970s) is shown to be impotent. *Scenes from an Execution* (radio 1984; staged in 1990) demonstrates the effects of censorship and the cooption of the artist, here a female painter in seventeenth-century Venice, by society. And later plays dissect the sources of modern social drama by re-imagining the worlds of Lessing's *Mina von Barnhelm* (1767) – the German playwright Lessing being widely credited as the originator of bourgeois realism – and Chekhov. By exposing the reality of the Seven Years War, a background to Lessing's comedy which is barely mentioned in the original, *Minna* (1994) challenges the basis of Enlightenment reason, while *(Uncle) Vanya* (1996) depicts a helpless but tyrannical Chekhov, murdered by his own characters from the original play as the only way of preventing him from distorting their lives. In dismissing naturalism and social discourse, as these pieces do, Barker is also attacking the primacy of dialogue in drama, along with the rationalist values implicit in the verbal language of these classic texts. The contrast exposes his own theatrical approach: metaphoric, highly subjective and emotional, intrinsically poetic.

Indeed Barker has published seven volumes of poetry, and there are free verse scenes in several of his plays, including *The Castle*, while even in the prose dialogue, as one character remarks, 'words, like buckets, slop with meaning'.[28] However, on the stage it is the physical imagery, as much as the words, that carry the meaning; and the effectiveness of Barker's plays is partly due to the fact that he is possibly the only contemporary playwright with an acting company, the Wrestling School (formed in 1989 with an Arts Council grant), specifically devoted to performing none but his plays. As its name suggests, the Wrestling School has developed a distinctively physical style of performance; and in this, although their techniques are very different, Barker's work parallels the new form of theatre represented by Simon McBurney and the Theatre de Complicité, while the grotesque surrealism of his plays overlaps with Caryl Churchill, even if only a late play like *The Skryker* approaches the level of violence that is standard in Barker.

Notes

1 Artaud, *The Theatre and its Double*, New York, 1958, pp. 82ff. For an extended discussion of Artaud's influence, see my *Avant Garde Theatre 1892–1992*, London, 1994, pp. 126–30.

2 *The Sport of My Mad Mother*, London, 1958, pp. 5, 57, 86; Jellicoe, *Some Unconscious Influences in the Theatre*, Cambridge, 1967, p. 16.

3 *The Collected Plays of John Whiting*, London, 1969, I, pp. 91, 114.

4 Whiting, *The Art of the Dramatist*, ed. Ronald Hayman, London, 1970, p. 111; *Collected Plays*, I, pp. 164–5.

5 *Ibid.*, p. 139.

6 *Radio Times*, 3 October 1951.

7 Jellicoe, Preface to *The Sport of My Mad Mother*, p. 5 (1964), and Rudkin, *Plays and Players*, February 1964, p. 17.

8 *Afore Night Come*, in *Penguin Plays: New English Dramatists 7*, Harmondsworth, 1963, p. 75; *The Saxon Shore*, London, 1986, p. vii.

9 *The Saxon Shore*, p. 26.

10 *Afore Night Come*, pp. 116, 88.

11 *Ibid.*, p. 80.

12 Author's Note, *The Sons of Light*, London, 1981.

13 The interpretation of *Ashes* as 'a political metaphor for Ireland' was imposed by Charles Marowitz in a press handout, and was felt by the cast to contradict Rudkin's aims: see *Plays and Players*, March 1974, p. 23.

14 *Ashes*, London, 1978, Author's Note and pp. 25, 49, 12, 51.

15 *The Sons of Light*, London, 1981, pp. 44, 18, 31.

16 *The Triumph of Death*, London, 1981, pp. 1, 29,

17 *The Sons of Light*, pp. 57, 78, 66, 76, 7 and 9.

18 Rudkin, *Plays and Players*, May 1976, p. 26.

19 *Ibid.*, p. 25; Artaud, *The Theatre and its Double*, pp. 82ff.

20 *The Triumph of Death*, pp. 16, 8.

21 *A Passion in Six Days*, London, 1985, pp. 9, 18; and *The Power of the Dog*, London, 1985, p. 40.

22 *The Europeans*, London, 1990, p. 45; *The Bite of the Night*, London, 1988, p. 89; *Arguments for a Theatre*, Manchester 1993, p. 38.

23 *Arguments for a Theatre*, pp. 48–50, 52.

24 *The Castle and Scenes from an Execution*, London, 1985, pp. 7, 14.

25 *Ibid.*, pp. 39–40.

26 *Ibid.*, pp. 13, 30, 14, 19, 38.

27 *Ibid.*, pp. 22, 41, 32–3; *Arguments for a Theatre*, pp. 80–2; Kenny Ireland, Riverside Theatre programme, January 1995.

28 *The Castle*, p. 16.

5.7 Caryl Churchill (1938–): from the psychology of feminism to the Surreal

CHECKLIST OF MAJOR PLAYS

Owners, 1972
Objections to Sex and Violence, 1974
Light Shining in Buckinghamshire,
   1976
Vinegar Tom, 1976
Cloud Nine, 1979
Top Girls, 1982
Fen, 1983

Softcops, 1984
Serious Money, 1987
A Mouthful of Birds, 1987
Lives of the Great Poisoners, 1991
The Skryker, 1994
This is a Chair, 1997
Blue Heart, 1997
Hotel, 1997

Like most of the playwrights who came out of the 1970s counter-culture women's movement, Churchill is usually seen as a highly political writer. But although, particularly in her early plays she shares the same focus on revisionist history as Pam Gems, and her viewpoint is even more uncompromisingly feminist, her work centres on psychology rather than society. And where Gems (with the exception of *Blue Angel*), Micheline Wandor or Shelagh Stephenson are essentially naturalistic in approach, even if using unconventional structures, Churchill's drama is increasingly imagistic and surreal. She presents politics from a subjective perspective, and the characterization in her most typical plays (from *Cloud Nine* in 1979) culminating in the mythic nightmare of *The Skryker* (1994) is symbolic. The effect is frequently comic, even farcical. Yet in a very real sense Churchill's approach is poetic – indeed even her most directly political play, *Serious Money* (1987) which deals with the stock market and global Capitalism, is written in rhyming verse. And her dramatic structures have always been radical and dynamic, breaking out of conventional forms in much the same way as Whiting or Rudkin. As with other women playwrights, her intuitive and fluid shaping of character and action reflects a specifically female consciousness, but goes beyond that. It becomes visionary.

Her first full-length play, *Owners* (1972), borrows the transparent characterization of Orton's farce, where the speakers openly express the most anti-social motivations and desires, switching their attitudes without transition. (For a discussion of Orton's drama, see above, pp. 293ff.) This makes it possible for Churchill to set up a graphic reversal of conventional expectations of male/female behaviour. Wives are presented as active figures, while the males are completely passive. The dominant woman is a sterile egoist, prepared to burn down a house to evict the tenants, whose child she expropriates by forced adoption (both building and baby being equivalent forms of real estate in a competitive system, where the value of possessions is the power they confer over others). Churchill uses every emotional means to condemn her commercialism. The young mother she dispossesses is a childhood friend, whose husband she has also seduced and – when he refuses to abandon his wife – orders to be murdered; her own husband, emasculated and bankrupt, she reduces to a state of incapacity where he can only dream of killing her and even when he puts a pistol to his own head, he misses.

Although the mayhem and moral exaggeration is derivative, the play marks out Churchill's dramatic territory. The parallel drawn here between the ownership of property and people, which reduces individuals to objects, lies behind the equation of Capitalism with sexual exploitation in her later plays; and the exaggeration anticipates their subjective, alternative realities.

Even an otherwise conventional reinterpretation of history, like *Vinegar Tom* (1976), uses cross-gender casting in the epilogue, where the Elizabethan theologians responsible for writing *Malleus Malleficarium, The Hammer of Witches* appear, to draw a heavily ironic moral from the action. But these historical men are played by female actresses – dressed 'as Edwardian music hall gents in top hat and tails'.[1] Here this double incongruity is intended as straight parody, the action having already disproved the existence of the witchcraft that the sexist theologians condemn. It reinforces the condemnation of stereotypes, shown as the products of an ignorant fear of female sexuality, through ridiculing 'genuine' extracts from the sixteenth-century book that promoted the victimization of women, as both superstition and cross-talk patter. However the anachronism also has a hallucinatory effect.

Cloud Nine (1979) develops this sexual transposition, making it central to the action. Explicitly based on 'the parallel between colonial and sexual oppression', the play emerged from a workshop on sexual politics, which included 'a straight married couple, a straight divorced couple, a gay couple, a lesbian, a lesbian-to-be, at least two bi-sexual men'. The dramatic material reflects the sexual permutations of this selected group, as well as improvisations on 'power and role-reversal' and 'status exercises', where randomly shuffled cards determined the actors' gender or social position. The title itself came from the life story of the caretaker at the rehearsal rooms, beaten continually by her husband and victimized by a series of men until that year when she experienced her first orgasm in late middle age, leading her to assert that 'We're living on cloud nine today'.[2]

Churchill represents the artificial nature of sexual conditioning as farcical by having a Victorian lady performed by a man, her adolescent son by a woman, and (later in the play) a young girl by a man. This is paralleled with social conditioning through having a white actor as the black servant, embodying his adoption of the white rulers' values. These reversals are carried through into the children's behaviour, with the son being prevented from playing with a doll belonging to his younger sister (herself a life-size doll, a non-person to be moulded by society), while the girl's lesbian mother encourages her to play with toy guns.

The first Act in nineteenth-century Africa sets up a contrast between the rigidly correct Victorian family and repressed personal desires. The authoritarian father Clive stands for imperialist/paternalistic attitudes. But the moral standards he asserts are both incompatible with the cross-sexual casting, and undercut by the action. Even he is unable to live up to the principles he proclaims, forcing his sexual attentions on a neighbouring widow, while the lesbian governess (played by the same actress) tries to seduce his wife Betty. In turn, Betty (obviously male beneath her crinolines) lusts after Harry, a bold explorer with whom she wants to elope, although Harry is only using her as cover for homosexual relationships with both the (female) son, and the family's black servant.

Disintegrating surface appearances are patched up by forcing the explorer to marry the governess as the only way of avoiding exposure. But the untenable nature of this expedient is emphasized by the degeneration of the wedding into a fight between Betty and the widow. The image of marriage, as the epitome of sexual stereotypes that have already been shown as false, is extended into a tableau of colonialism, affirming that 'the empire is one big family'.[3] And this cliché illusion breaks down in turn as the white 'native', whose parents have been killed in a punishment-raid organized by Clive, raises a pistol to shoot him.

The only pairing that is heterosexual on the level of both plot and presentation is between a homosexual and a lesbian, while the outlawed relationships the other characters enact are 'normal' in terms of the actors. One of the 'boys' with whom the explorer copulates is (acceptably) female and the 'woman' the governess attempts to seduce is in fact a man, leaving the conventional husband and (male) wife as the only obviously 'unnatural' couple.

Divorcing male and female stereotypes from physiology was intended to 'physicalize the characters' psychologically ambivalent identities'; and this offers a key to Churchill's dramatic approach in which subjective states are externalized, creating a hallucinatory reality.[4] At the same time, the rapid pacing, overt artifice and satirical treatment of cliché make the attack on Victorian values in the first half of the play a brilliantly sustained piece of cartooning. The comedy defuses any moral outrage, involving spectators in a visionary fantasy as well as facilitating acceptance of the second Act, which literally brings home the demolition of sexual norms.

Set in London and the immediate present, the second part of *Cloud Nine* uses a double time frame to dismiss anachronistic attitudes by showing the younger generation – twenty-five years older, but a century later – achieving an alternative lifestyle. The cross-casting is repeated, but instead of juxtaposing genders it is now used to draw a contrast between Victorian and modern characters, with the earlier 'mother' becoming the son, and the 'son' taking the mother's part. Reversing the inversions of the first Act restores the correspondence between sex and role to indicate that the characters have become integrated individuals; and the audience are presented with a model of sexual liberation that goes against every conceivable taboo. The Victorian daughter (a doll in part one, now a mother herself) leaves her husband for another woman, and is joined by her brother, a homosexual who declares himself a lesbian, all three being 'sick of men'. Their aging mother leaves Clive too, preferring to live alone and assert that she is 'a separate person' through masturbation.[5]

As the theme song, promising that 'It'll be fine when you reach Cloud Nine', announces: 'it's upside down when you reach Cloud Nine'. Everything in the play works by opposites, including the proposed solution, which is given a utopian tone by the loose, atomized structure of the second half: a liberated style designed to reflect 'uncertainties and changes of society, and a more feminine and less authoritarian feeling', in explicit contrast to the 'male dominated and firmly structured' first Act.[6] At the same time, the cartoon fantasy of the first half – which carries through into the second with the grown man/little girl figure – undercuts the reality of the sexually liberated role models proposed by the play's ending.

The play is left open-ended, encouraging spectators to follow the emancipating principle proposed by the characters: 'if there isn't a right way to do things you have to invent one'. Betty, as the divided Victorian woman who comes to accept and approve the radically different lifestyles of her contemporary children, serves as a guide to audience response. But the effectiveness

20 Sex changes and the farce of gender roles: Antony Sher as a five-year-old girl in the Joint Stock production of Churchill's *Cloud Nine* (Act II)

of the final image, in which the now elderly/modern day Betty embraces her younger Victorian/male self, depends on the audience having been brought to the same point as Churchill, for whom gender divisions had become so irrelevant while working on the play that in rehearsing for the New York production she 'forgot' the actor playing Betty was a man, despite his beard and jeans.[7]

The utopian vision of *Cloud Nine* echoes *Light Shining in Buckinghamshire* (1976), where a historical basis is found for sexual liberation in the visionary radicalism of the seventeenth century. This play was intended as a corrective to the 'simple "Cavaliers and Roundheads" history taught at school', by showing the Civil War from the perspective of the Levellers and Ranters. As in her first play, *Owners*, Churchill makes a direct connection between liberty and the abolition of property, whether in sexual or material terms – and as in *Vinegar Tom*, the significance of this era is that from a Marxist viewpoint it marks the beginnings of modern Capitalism, and thus the point at which repressive sexual 'norms' were imposed. Dramatizing a transitional period offers the opportunity of presenting people who have not yet been subjugated by economic forces and gender roles, as well as exposing the roots of contemporary oppression. But here the picture of social injustice is set against the 'revolutionary belief in the millennium' that inspires the communistic wing of Cromwell's 'New Model Army'.[8]

The absolute equality that was demanded by the Ranters and Levellers defines the political ideal that underlies all Churchill's work:

We'll all live together . . . everything in common . . . we'll have no property in the flesh. My wife, that's property. My husband, that's property. All men are one flesh . . . We'll take the land, all the land, and Christ will come . . . in this sense. He will come in everyone becoming perfect so that the landlords all repent stealing the land.

However, this radical possibility has already been 'betrayed' – a recurring word in the play – by the parliamentary leaders, who are instrumental in setting up the capitalist system. The grass-roots idealists are crushed by the 'revolution' for which they have fought, the message being that any form of liberation requires a total change in society. The point, which is expressed at its simplest in the declaration that 'You can't separate fucking and economics' (*Cloud Nine*), is explored in Churchill's later plays.[9]

Top Girls (1982) again sets history against the present. But here, unlike *Cloud Nine*, the comparison demonstrates that changes in the position of women are superficial: literally a question of costume. The title is ironic. The opening dinner party, hosted by the new female director of the Top Girls employment agency – at the pointedly named Prima Donna restaurant – to celebrate her own rise to the top, gathers a whole range of 'famous women' from the past. For Marlene, who sees herself as their modern equivalent, these figures justify the competition for power in male terms. Their status supports her position, while at the same time providing the perspective for evaluating the contemporary model of success in Marlene.

Their stories encapsulate the exploitation of women through the ages. Yet their physical presence in the world of today gives the scene a dream quality. It is surrealist. In addition, as symbols brought to life they set the contemporary action that follows, where they reappear in modern analogues, in a non-realistic context. And this is intensified by the mix of history, apocryphal myth, and purely artistic or literary figures.

They fall into two distinct groups. Either they achieved fame through taking roles reserved for men – like Isabella Bird, the Victorian explorer, or Pope Joan, who (supposedly) reached the pinnacle of the exclusively male church hierarchy in 854 by posing as a man. Or they embody archetypal feminine qualities like Lady Nijo, the influential courtesan of a thirteenth-century Japanese emperor, and Griselda, the archetypal peasant cowgirl who married a prince and was celebrated for her patience by Petrarch, Boccaccio and Chaucer. Yet all their experiences are comparable; and their descriptions of achievement are simultaneously accounts of rape, personal deprivation and psychological battering. Griselda has won her position by allowing the sacrifice of her children. According to legend Pope Joan was stoned to death when the birth of a child revealed her as a woman. The only exception is the monosyllabic Dull Gret – the one figure, apart from the apocryphal Griselda, taken from art rather than history – whose story of revenge closes the scene. But she is the same as all the others in having lost her babies.

Churchill specifies that their speeches overlap as a way of demonstrating both their similarity, and their inability to learn from each other. However different their historical and cultural circumstances, each takes responsibility for herself. Yet, apart from Dull Gret, what unites them is submissiveness to the men in their lives – authoritarian fathers, sexist lovers, brutal husbands – and it is in the gruesome tribulations they have overcome that they find a common bond: attributes which repulse Marlene, who sees herself as independent of men.

Her assertion that 'we've all come a long way' rings hollow. As the doubling of these historical figures with modern counterparts in the subsequent play indicates, there has been no essential improvement in the female situation. Pope Joan reappears in a job-interview as a middle-aged middle-manager who passes as a man at work, having suppressed her sexuality to compete in a male-dominated world. The only revolutionary figure – Dull Gret with armour over her apron, painted by Brueghel leading a female invasion of hell and taken as the archetype of proletarian rebellion by Brecht – is updated as Marlene's teenage niece, whom Marlene dismisses as 'a bit thick . . . She's not going to make it.'[10]

Marlene's explicitly Thatcherite competitive ethos has no place for the uneducated and underprivileged, such as her niece/Dull Gret. But the cost of reaching the top in such a system is demonstrated by the revelation that this girl is Marlene's unacknowledged daughter, raised by her sister in the bleak working-class countryside (explored in Churchill's next play, *Fen*, 1983) from which Marlene has escaped. The pursuit of capitalist rewards has meant rejecting maternal instinct, human feeling and moral values. And the conclusion is bleak, the final line of the play being 'frightening' (also the last word of Pope Joan in the prologue). Female emancipation has come to mean adopting exactly those aggressive and predatory values which have for centuries oppressed women – significantly, in the prologue all the 'famous women' ignore the silent waitress. The only path left is the potential violence of a modern-day Dull Gret.

At the same time the structure of the play offers a model of alternative ways of thinking. Its complex mixture of styles, temporal dislocation, and overlapping speeches, extends the anti-authoritarian principles developed in the second half of *Cloud Nine*. Combining surreal fantasy with Shavian discussion and documentary case-histories, as well as naturalistic domestic drama (complete with kitchen sink and ironing-board), *Top Girls* breaks out of conventional methods of portraying life on the stage, and suggests new ways of seeing reality. Moving from a historical overview, through juxtaposed scenes of Marlene at work and the daughter's rebelliousness – both of which precede the opening dinner-party – the action takes us forward two days to the daughter's appearance in Marlene's office. It then closes with a political argument from twelve months earlier, creating a dynamic that is liberated from cause-and-effect logic.

The overall movement is from a general panorama to domestic particulars, and from the archetype to individuals. Within this gradually narrowing focus, the fragmented plot-line and stylistic contrasts create three short, interwoven plays, each of which provide different perspectives on a central theme. The action, concluding in the chronologically earliest scene, has a circular shape commonly associated with unchanging recurrence. But this is contradicted by an unresolved situation – whether Marlene will accept her daughter – which leaves the drama open-ended. The effect is to stress that every aspect of existence is interconnected, while ruling out all standard ways of putting things together.

This is the only one of Churchill's plays where all the characters are female, the point being that even 'top girls' replicate the exploitation of their own sex. In a single-gender context questions of male domination are irrelevant, as in the all-male *Softcops* (written at the same time as *Cloud Nine*, although only performed in 1984), which uses a historical survey of criminal punishment as a model for social coercion and shows men as equally victimized. The gender restriction in *Softcops* and *Top Girls* shifts the focus to the political and economic system. Feminism becomes a moral perspective instead of the subject.

This development reaches its full expression in Churchill's most successful play, *Serious Money* (1987), which attacks the stock market as the epitome of Capitalism. Bringing together themes and techniques from earlier plays, this 'City Comedy' presents a society on the edge of apocalypse. As in *Top Girls*, *Serious Money* uses an eclectic mix of styles; but here these are integrated rather than juxtaposed. Documentary detail, which gains a high degree of conviction from the immediacy of its material, is combined with symbolic theatrical forms that transcend topicality. The galloping verse of the dialogue and hectic pace of the action create a hallucinatory sense of hyper-reality.

Serious Money makes the operations of Capitalism completely surrealistic by basing its action closely on actual news events of the day. The 'Big Bang' of stock market deregulation took place during workshop research for the play, which incorporates the scandals that resulted. The plot mirrors the insider dealing of Boesky, the Guinness affair where stock values were illegally manipulated in a takeover manoeuvre (both explicitly referred to), even the boardroom battle that resulted in the collapse of Lehmann Brothers, as well as the diversion of foreign aid to private pockets (in a South American equivalent of Imelda Marcos), and the debt-for-equity rip off of the impoverished Third World. Yet all this intense financial activity is placed in a Morality Play context, with the corporate raider's target being 'Albion' (the traditional symbol for England), and the action taking on aspects of a grotesque dance of death displaying the Seven Deadly Sins.

The prologue, taken from Shadwell's *The Stockjobbers* (1692), also brings in a historical perspective. The comparison with Restoration Comedy not only implies that fraud is inherent in the system since the practice of artificially 'lowing and heightening of Shares' is unchanged, but also serves as a measure of the difference between past and present. Where Shadwell's Jobbers are a despised under-class whose aim is 'to turn the penny', their modern descendants are at the top of society and 'making serious money'. Bad has become worse; and this downward progress accelerates within the play, which revolves around the dispossession of the old Establishment by a 'hungrier and hornier' younger generation, who no longer pay even lip-service to moral values: 'It's like Darwin says, survival of the fit'. As bankers are ousted by traders, the motto of the London Stock Exchange *(Dictum Meum Pactum,* My Word Is My Bond) becomes 'My word is my junk bond', with the most aggressive and unprincipled reaching the top.[11]

In this cut-throat jungle the monstrous central figure of *Owners* has multi-plied, with de-sexed women mounting a gender takeover. Even more ruthless than their male competitors, they mark the ultimate low point of this moral recession. This is the only play of Churchill's that does not include a single child; and the focus on LIFFE – the London International Financial Futures Exchange – is ironic since the women's triumph, equated with 'a natural dis-aster', makes any future for society impossible. The rape of Albion may be (temporarily) frustrated by a government minister. But the epilogue fore-casts Boesky's female successor running for the American presidency, while the most corrupt of the stockbrokers heads 'the City's new disciplinary panel'. Political and legal checks have become co-opted by those they are intended to curb. However, on another level the change is only in style, exposing the reality of what went on behind the old façade. As one of the new men argues, 'It just don't look quite so pretty,/All the cunning little jobs,/ When you see them done by yobs'.[12] This echoes the central point of the play, stripping away hypocrisy to reveal crude materialism.

In the plot, which revolves round a young futures trader's investigation of her wheeler-dealer brother's death, the profit motive and the motive for murder are identical, so that the economic and personal levels of the action fuse together, with one corrupting the other. And the verdict of suicide, which is mutually agreed at the end, stands for the self-destructive nature of a society where money is the only value.

Sexuality is distorted. Personal relationships no longer exist. Indeed, the all-consuming activity of the markets denies any possibility of psychological depth, and limits emotion to greed and fear. The objects of this greed have become completely abstract, with commodities being replaced by 'paper' contracts for 'futures' – while even the buying and selling of money is su-perseded by trade in debt. Simultaneously people are reduced to objects: one-dimensional characters lacking almost any introspection and naked in their rapacity. Consequently, there is no basis left for anything beyond mutual exploitation. When a banker and a businesswoman try to arrange a romantic assignation, they find there is no time for even a quick drink in their moneymaking schedules. Bringing a brother's murderer to justice takes second place to finding where he 'stashed the loot'. Even religion has become just another commodity, with a trader offering to 'make . . . a market in divinity (any day)'. Morality is merely PR imagery, with one takeover tycoon being publicized as a 'White Knight' having 'cornered the market/In fatherly, blue-eyed, babies, worker's friend', while her opponent is promoted as a 'sexy' villain, 'Bad and glamorous'.

These grotesque confusions of categories are summed up in the song that closes the first act, where crude sexual lust merges with the frenzy of trading:

Out you cunt, out in oh fuck it
I've delt the gelt below the belt and I'm jacking up the ackers
My front's gone short, fuck off old sport, you're standing on my
knackers . . .
I'm the local tootsie playing footsie but I don't mind a bit
Cos my future trusts my money lusts as far as it can spit
And my sterling works on mouthy jerks whose bids are full of shit . . .[13]

At the same time, the vitality so evident here makes this vision of hell paradoxically attractive.

The gap between aims and achievement, language and action is the essence of comedy. These empty characters, whose only aim is simply going for the gold, no holds barred, are the obsessional type-figures of farce; and the doubling, which brings out underlying similarities, also makes it difficult to condemn them as individuals. Instead, the effect is ironic, with the actor who plays the murdered Jake also playing the revengeful loser, who blows the whistle on Jake's activities, as well as Jake's nemesis, the DTI inspector. The actress who plays his sister (an ambiguous agent of justice) is also the 'white knight', whose defence of Albion is only a ploy to win control for herself, while other characters are linked to portray varieties of calculated self-interest – summed up as 'ugly greed and sexy greed'.[14] The overtly artificial verse dialogue is also deceptively comic, with rhyming couplets not only expressing the unnaturalness of the characters' behaviour, but lending a light and frivolous gloss to the deadly loss of all human values.

Similarly, the speed and fluidity of short scenes, played simultaneously or with overlapping speeches, which echoes the exponential growth caused by deregulation, carries the audience irresistibly along. The moral inversion, where evil is admirable and social responsibility derisory, is projected in the two major images of share dealing as game-playing, and as drug-traffic. For the 'players' (using the language of the market) the deals and cheating are 'the most fun I've had since playing cops and robbers...a cross between roulette and space invaders'.[15] The sheer excitement of the game is as addictive for them as the cocaine they also trade in. And this conditions the audience's response. The energy, which gives zest to repugnant activities, insinuates that the spectator could also be a participant. The drama is indeed fun, 'play' in both senses; and its hectic stock-market scenes offer us the equivalent of the insider information that preoccupies the characters.

This was reflected in sharply divided critical reactions to the play. It was hailed as 'a wickedly accurate portrait of the cultural revolution which has been taking place in the City', and dismissed as 'a piece that's all things to all wo/men' being 'stuck in some moral no-man's land'.[16] But the apparent moral confusion is deliberate. By putting the audience into an untenable position of applauding the triumph of what would normally be condemned, *Serious Money* implies that all are guilty, and that even those not directly involved collaborate.

The excitement and wit also made the play a notable exception to most political or feminist drama of the time that typically preached to the already converted, by attracting those it attacked. The production drew people from the City; and investment bankers like Morgan Stanley International or Shearson Lehman booked whole performances for their staffs. As the director, Max Stafford-Clark, commented: 'If you capture accurately enough the world of the people you are depicting, then it's very flattering and they will come and see it, just as people did in the Restoration.'[17] At the same time, in an almost unique example of drama/audience dependence, this meant that when the stock market crashed later in the same year, the play closed.

With the fall of communism in 1989 – marked by Churchill with *Mad Forest* (one of the earliest English plays on the subject, appearing in 1990, along with Brenton and Tariq Ali's *Moscow Gold*) – the explicit Marxism of her earlier work disappears. *Mad Forest*, for example, reduces politics to the purely personal level, showing the Romanian uprising against Ceauşescu and the betrayal of its ideals by the communist functionaries who infiltrated the National Salvation Front through the eyes of ordinary men and women in Bucharest. As a result the imagistic surrealism and psychological qualities that underlie her work emerged more clearly. Moving beyond primarily feminist themes, she had already defined her focus as 'power, powerlessness and exploitation; people's longings, obsessions and dreams', rather than specific gender issues.[18]

And this development – implicit in *Softcops* or *Serious Money*, and already present in *A Mouthful of Birds* (1987) where the mythic tragedy of Euripides' *Bacchae* was reconstituted as a modern urban nightmare – led to plays like *This is a Chair* or *Blue Heart* (both 1997) where political events exist only as an irrelevant distraction to personal lives, or as dreams projected over the fears and neuroses of individuals. So in *This is a Chair* captions head-lining 'Pornography and Censorship', 'Genetic Engineering' or 'The War in Bosnia' counterpoint scenes of a family tensely quarrelling over dinner while watching TV, a couple who have been woken by an unexplained noise in the middle of the night, and a breathless woman breaking her date with a wait-ing man by explaining she has double-booked. And in *Heart's Desire* (the first piece in the double play *Blue Heart*) parents waiting in their ordinary kitchen for the return of their long absent daughter simultaneously imagine various possible alternatives: rampaging children enter instead; a lesbian lover appears to announce that the daughter will not be coming home after all; a monstrous ostrich flaps around the kitchen table; masked men break in and gun down everyone in the room – and each time the scene restarts, leaving the couple in exactly the same position. *Blue Kettle* (the second play) extends this in a series of images where language increasingly breaks down – with the words 'blue' or 'kettle' increasingly substituting for all other words the characters speak – as a young man searches for a substitute for his dying mother by approaching a whole series of women and persuading each that he is the illegitimate son they gave away for adoption at birth, in a demonstration of the compulsive need for alternative realities. But the play that most fully explores this obsessive dreaming of the powerless is *The Skryker* (1994).

Although there is no direct connection, this play picks up on some of the same rituals and dream material as Ann Jellicoe had experimented with almost 40 years before in *The Sport of My Mad Mother* (see p. 496 above). The language of the mythical Skryker, a 'shapeshifter and death portent' who dominates the play, is openly poetic, full (as the reviews noted) of Joycean word-associations and linguistic meldings that echoed the verse of Gerard Manley Hopkins. The effect is hypnotic:

May day, she cries, may pole axed me to help her. So I spin the sheaves shoves shivers into golden guild and geld and if she can't guessing game and safety match my name then I'll take her no mistake no mister no missed her no mist no miss no me no.

This surreal stream of consciousness is mirrored by the stage action which surrounds two sisters – Josie who has murdered her baby and been shut in a mental institution; Lily pregnant at the beginning, who abandons her baby to descend into the world of the subconscious. Everyone they interact with in their everyday lives is the shapeshifter in disguise. At first a monstrous black figure – her true shape, 'ancient and damaged', which she reverts to again at the end – the Skryker appears as another inmate of the asylum and an old woman dying in the hospital where Lily takes her sick baby, a paranoid bag lady, a lonely American woman in a hotel bar, a disturbed child, and an abused teenage runaway on drugs. In addition to this gamut of female suffering, she also appears as the Christmas tree fairy, corresponding to her guise as a spirit who fulfils wishes. And she is even a man obsessed by snuff movies and convinced he will 'witness unprecedented catastrophe', who is stabbed by Josie when he competes for Lily's love. Although there are other figures, these are all from the realm of folklore: Black Dog and Bogles, the Kelpie (seen cutting up '*the body of* WOMAN *who went away with him*') or a Hag who is 'chopped . . . to pieces, chipped . . . to pasties'; and even where recognizable figures from modern society enter they are subsumed in this alternative reality, like the ' BUSINESSMAN *with a* THRUMPIN *riding on his back. He doesn't know it's there*'.[19]

These folklore figures are the archetypes of the unconscious. As the Skryker says, 'Haven't I wrapped myself up rapt rapture ruptured myself in your dreams'; and her disordered speech is, on one level, a measure of the damage done to this internal level of existence – identified with the female, and with Nature – by the wasteland of modern urban life, commercialism and scientific progress. As the Skryker explicitly complains, television and aeroplanes are killing her, 'bloodmoney is the root of evil eye nose the smell hell the taste waste of money'. In Churchill's previous play, *Lives of the Great Poisoners* (1991: an operatic dance drama, also written for the Second Stride Company), the inventor of leaded petrol and CFCs was paralleled to notorious mass murderers from literature, history and the modern age – Medea, the seventeenth-century Marquise de Brinvilliers and Crippen. And here too she is concerned with the effects of pollution and global warming:

Drought. Apocalyptic meteorological phenomena. The increase of sickness. It was always possible to think whatever your personal problem, there's always nature. Spring will return even if it's without me . . . This has been a comfort to people as long as they've existed. But it's not available any more.

In *The Skryker* it is the mental consequences that are the focus. Both girls descend into the 'underworld' and Josie's insanity is increasingly echoed by her sister, whose 'mind's going out of control like when there's going to be

21 Psychological surrealism and dream archetypes embodied in Churchill's
The Skryker

an accident'.[20] And this is directly mirrored by the hallucinatory vision presented on the stage.

If the play is confusing it is because the grotesque figures – which in the original National Theatre staging by the Second Stride Company formed images out of Hieronymous Bosch – stand for conflicting things. Monstrous shapes are traditional in folklore, yet here their hideous appearance is implied to be both the result of ecological breakdown, and of mental disturbance. In addition they not only represent the (damaged) world of Nature, as well as the collective unconscious, but also the destructive social forces that threaten these vulnerable young women, and perhaps their unexpressed needs and desires. Yet ambiguity is an essential part of myth; and Churchill's aim is clearly to involve the audience on an irrational and psychological level.

All Churchill's work manipulates time and stage conventions, undermining received notions of personality, and challenging the way we perceive reality. In her earlier plays this appeared to be in the service of a political agenda, but the increasingly symbolic images drawn from the unconscious reveal even their sources as essentially poetic. But despite the emphasis on verse in *Serious Money*, as *Blue Heart* so clearly illustrates, the intended level of communication is beyond verbal language. Instead the focus on obsessions of power and the longings of the exploited, which is reflected in her shaping of the dramatic experience, leads to a type of purely physical theatre.

The written text of *The Skryker*, for example, is extremely short in comparison to standard full-length plays, with over half the performance time being filled with the choreographed movement and visual imagery that gave shape to suggestive and fantastic levels of reality outside the range of spoken words. And it is significant that Churchill is the only major dramatist who has continued to develop her plays collectively. Indeed collectivity is a key element, compensating for the increasing blackness of her vision. In plays like *Cloud Nine* and *Top Girls* (which came out of Max Stafford-Clark's workshop company at the Royal Court) – as did *Blue Heart* almost twenty years later – or in *Mad Forest* (which was created in a workshop with students from the Central School of Speech and Drama), the power of the community to marginalize individuals is set against the collective potential of the marginalized to subvert the power structure. And throughout the 1990s Churchill has collaborated with the experimental Second Stride Company whose staging is music- and dance-based.

As with *The Skryker* where words take on non-logical forms, the result is a style of performance drama or physical theatre, which has proved one of the most productive lines of development over the final decade leading into the millennium. In this it corresponds with the work of performance-artists like Simon McBurney. At the same time, the nightmare material of plays like *The Skryker* or *Lives of the Great Poisoners*, and the open surrealism of *A Mouthful of Birds* or *Blue Heart* are clearly echoed in the plays of Sarah Kane, who takes this hallucinatory treatment of everyday life to its extreme limits.

Notes

1 Churchill, *Plays: One*, London, 1985, p. 134.
2 *Ibid.*, p. 245; *The Joint Stock Book*, ed. Robert Ritchie, London, 1987, p. 139; *Cloud Nine* Workshop Diary I (unpublished) pp. 100, 106, 141.
3 *Plays: One*, p. 266.
4 Churchill, cited by Helen Keyssar in the *Massachusetts Review*, Spring 1983, no.24, p. 213.
5 *Plays: One*, pp. 307, 316.
6 *Ibid.*, pp. 312 & 246 (Preface to *Cloud Nine*).
7 *Ibid.*, p. 319; Churchill, cited Keyssar, *Massachusetts Review*, p. 210.
8 *Plays: One* (Preface to *Light Shining . . .*), p. 183.
9 *Ibid.*, pp. 234, 309.
10 Churchill, *Top Girls*, London, 1982, pp. 10, 33.
11 Churchill, *Serious Money*, London, 1987, pp. 13 & 53, 25, 105.
12 *Ibid.*, pp. 66, 110, 88.
13 *Ibid.*, pp. 85, 44, 91–2, 60.
14 *Ibid.*, p. 92.
15 *Ibid.*, p. 54.
16 *Times Literary Supplement*, 3 April 1987, *City Limits,* 16 July 1987, and *Time Out*, 15 July 1987.
17 Max Stafford-Clark, cited in *Vanity Fair*, December 1987, p. 76.
18 Churchill, in *The New York Times*, 22 November 1987.
19 *The Skryker*, London, 1994, pp. 1, 44, 46, 29, 35.
20 *Ibid.*, pp. 32, 12, 43.

5.8 Sarah Kane (1971–1999): the poetry of madness in violent dreams

CHECKLIST OF KANE'S MAJOR PLAYS

Blasted, 1995	*Cleansed*, 1998
Phaedra's Love, 1996	*4.48 Psychosis*, 2000

It is quite striking that Caryl Churchill's shift to open surrealism in *The Skryker* occurred less than a year before Sarah Kane's first play to hit the London stage. Taken together these mark a new development in feminist drama at the end of the millennium. At the same time, it is hardly surprising that, due to the physical and sexual violence depicted, Kane's work was initially seen extending the line of radical social criticism represented by Bond's *Saved* and Brenton's *Romans in Britain* – or that her first plays have been linked with *Trainspotting* (adapted for the stage from Irvine Welsh's novel in 1995) and Mark Ravenhill's *Shopping and Fucking* (produced in 1996, just after *Blasted* and *Phaedra's Love*) as part of a new style of radical political theatre.

The confusion was clear in the reviewers' extremely critical response to *Blasted* – with typical comments ranging from 'It might be a savage indictment of a society bereft of values and incapable of compassion, but it feels too relentless for that' to 'for all the talk of a violent world, the world shown here is not recognizable'. Partly because of the lack of any believable social context, the atrocities so graphically presented provoked outraged disgust; and even though *Blasted* ran for barely two weeks, the newspaper scandal was perhaps more vociferous than for any other play during the century, certainly matching the shock expressed over *Saved* or the moralistic condemnation of *The Romans in Britain*. And the director's response to the critics compounded the problem by stressing the play's social relevance, asserting that *Blasted* had been staged by the Royal Court because it offered an antidote to the 'fascination with and glamorization of violence' characteristic of contemporary culture and 'sold to us as entertainment' by the media, as well as addressing issues of 'nationalism, racism, emotional and physical abuse, sexual fantasy and the male urge to self-destruct'.[1]

However, unlike the two previous plays that had aroused this sort of controversy, *Blasted* was neither censored (as *Saved* had been at the same theatre in 1965) nor legally prosecuted (as *Romans in Britain* was in 1980), despite even more graphic depictions of child abuse – with a baby being eaten on stage, instead of stoned – and brutalizing homosexual rape. Of course censorship had long been abolished and certainly in the post-Thatcher era public attitudes may have been less repressive; yet as the newspaper *furor* shows, this lack of official reaction can hardly be seen as simply a sign of changing social values. In fact the non-involvement of the authorities or even the Arts Council (like the National, the Royal Court was a subsidized theatre) indicates the essential difference of *Blasted* as a play. Those earlier works had each presented a coherent attack on the situation in Britain at the time.

By contrast Kane's drama has no moral framework or perspective: indeed none of the elements – a plot-line to shape audience response, credible characterization, an identifiable setting – that conventionally give drama social relevance. Instead the action and the figures only have validity as symbolic expressions.

This is not to say the play has no basis in politics, or is alienated from its time. There are clear connections between *Blasted* or *Cleansed* and the radical modern British artists like Damien Hirst assembled by Saatchi for the notorious 'Sensation' exhibition. Indeed in directing her own production of *Phaedra's Love* (1996) Kane gave her mythical Greek queen and dysfunctional family identifiable overtones of British royalty – yet she also painted the ordinary populace as a voyeuristic, murderous mob, undermining any standard political point. Rather Kane can be seen as taking the feminist principle that 'the personal is political' to its extreme, where her own psychological turmoil becomes a register for the sickness of modern civilization – *SICK* being the title of Kane's earliest work, a trilogy of monologues (1994) performed in the provinces. In many ways her drama should be grouped with *This is a Chair* or *Blue Heart*, the plays Churchill was writing at the same time. Yet this parallel was disguised by the visceral impact of Kane's images, and the autobiographical subjectivity that increasingly emerged in her work.

The intensity and barely motivated violence of the atrocities performed in *Blasted*, together with the deliberate ambiguousness of the setting, signal that this is a dreamscape in which fragmented reflections of daily experience are projected in a heightened form. The context is both international and localized; continual references to Leeds and the clearly identifiable British accents of the protagonists being set against the anonymity of an expensive hotel room – representing the materialistic superficiality of a globalized culture. And in the same way, while life continues as usual with football-matches and room-service, a war is being fought on the streets outside: martial law putting down a civil rebellion, a military peace-keeping operation, or perhaps a colonial invasion. So when the wall of the hotel is demolished by a mortar-shell and the room dismantled as the floorboards are torn up, it represents the final disintegration of a corrupt civilization (an image repeated in *Cleansed* where, following the explosive destruction of another wall, flowers burst into bloom all over the stage).

All three characters in *Blasted*, even the most abusive, are victims; most obviously the waif of a girl who suffers from epilepsy, is unemployed, possibly retarded, and abused by the much-older man she is with. Either a prostitute he picks up regularly, or a girlfriend whose youth he has exploited, the man forces her to masturbate him and '*simulates sex*' (the stage direction a typical ambiguity) with a gun held to her head while she lies unconscious in one of her fits. Yet he too is in the last stages of lung-cancer, probably combined with cirrhosis of the liver – though in contrast to her ailments, as a heavy smoker who consumes a bottle of gin before breakfast, these are symptoms of self-destructiveness – and she in turn assaults him with violent sexual foreplay, scratching and biting, then performs oral sex on him at the climax of which she bites his penis, leaving him prostrate '*in pain, unable to speak*'. A tabloid journalist specializing in 'shootings and rapes and kids getting fiddled by queer priests' or the ritual torture and murder of teenagers by a serial killer (a report he dictates over the phone about the fate of a local girl travelling in New Zealand – even the most distant place is subject to equal horrors), this seedy man is also possibly an undercover government agent, or perhaps part of a right-wing death squad, and in fear of his life. Justifiably: since a Soldier bursts in, anally rapes him at gunpoint, then chews his eyes out and eats them. However, even this Soldier (unnamed – a universal figure embodying all types of military atrocities, who recounts exploits of group rapes and torture, grotesque killings and mass transportation of refugees in cattle-trucks) is a victim, merely taking revenge for the girl he loved: 'they buggered her. Cut her throat. Hacked her ears and nose off, nailed them to the front door' and 'ate her eyes'. He is '*crying his heart out*' during his rape, and blows his own brains out with the man's revolver during the night.[2]

Then too there are purely associative connections in the action, characteristic of the subconscious. The Soldier tells of watching fleeing women throw their babies to others in the hope of saving them; and the girl, who has escaped through the bathroom window, returns with a baby a woman has thrust into her arms. Almost immediately it starves to death; burying it under the floorboards, she abandons the man declaring 'I'm hungry'; and after indicating the passing of a week by rapid alternations of darkness and light, the man now '*weak with hunger*' disinters and eats the baby, then climbs down into the hole with its remains.[3]

Physical hunger, as an analogue for unsatisfied and unfulfillable desire, is also foregrounded in Kane's next plays. Hippolytus, the fat and incurably unpleasant son of Phaedra, stuffs himself continually with junk food as a substitute for the personal involvement he is unable to feel. Sex with endless women who pursue him is no enjoyment; even while being seduced by his mother he is totally affectless and '*eats his sweets*' throughout '*without taking his eyes off the television*'; only the threat of being burnt alive or lynched by the mob bringing a connection. 'Life at last' he exclaims, and his dying words are 'If only there could have been more moments like this'. In *Cleansed* a teenage boy yearning for an unattainable woman is force-fed a whole box of chocolates, paralleling the obsessive feeding of tokens into the slot of a peepshow booth; and in *4.48 Psychosis* the voice of the suicidal woman, the first of whose symptoms is listed as 'Not eating', describes her state as 'a consolidated consciousness . . . in a darkened banqueting hall'.[4] At the same time it is noticeable that, as in *Blasted*, almost all the horrific violence that marks Kane's plays is based on sex, or relates specifically to genitalia.

Phaedra hangs herself because of her son's indifference to sex with her. And in the final cataclysm Hippolytus, accused of raping her in her vengeful suicide note, is assaulted, disembowelled and has his genitals cut off and barbecued by the mob at the behest of his father Theseus who, not recognizing her, has already raped and slaughtered his daughter for 'Defending a rapist', then cuts his own throat out of remorse. In *Cleansed* one homosexual is beaten then impaled up the anus to get him to betray the name of his lover; and the pair are then punished for their relationship, one having his tongue cut out and being forced to swallow the ring he put as a pledge on his partner's finger, then having first his hands and later his feet chopped off, while the other, after being thrown down '*from a great height*' has his throat cut out of jealousy because he still continues to have sex with the amputee, who is then castrated, his penis being sewn on to the body of a girl significantly named Grace whose breasts are also chopped off to turn her into the brother with whom she identifies, dresses as, and has sex with.

All these appalling images are not only presented as irrational – barely motivated by sexual desires or perversions – but also in full view. Masturbation, oral and anal sex, incestuous copulation and rape are performed front stage and in the nude; even the aftermath of the surgical sex-change, with Grace lying '*unconscious on a bed . . . naked apart from a tight strapping around her groin* [later removed] . . . *and blood where her breasts should be*'. And particularly in *Cleansed* – even more violent and sexually explicit than *Blasted* – the shock effect is intensified by the compression of such actions, which occur in every scene throughout a play that is barely 40 pages of text including stage-directions. With such contraction, the overwhelming catalogue of atrocities becomes numbing. Yet there is a twentieth-century theatrical tradition justifying such assaults on audience sensibilities. Off-the-wall and in-your-face, these physical horrors echo the dark violence of David Rudkin's plays (see above, pp. 499ff.) but without the religious connotations underpinning his drama. And perhaps even more than Rudkin,

Kane is fulfilling all the requirements of Artaud's 'Theatre of Cruelty': 'a theatre in which violent physical images crush and hypnotize the sensibility of the spectator' bringing 'to birth images of energy in the unconscious, and gratuitous crime on the surface'.[5] Her drama is also intrinsically poetic – again in the sense of Artaud, who called for *action* to replace *written* poetry, and particularly formal verse.

The symbolism of that eyeless head of the man protruding from a grave in *Blasted* may have been disguised by the realism of the violence. But in *Cleansed* the action is clearly surreal; and this was underlined in performance through the stylization of the violence imposed by James MacDonald (the director of all Kane's plays at the Royal Court). The university setting also doubles as a mental institution run by an insanely malevolent doctor, in which the girl is subjected to shock therapy – '*An electric current is turned on.* GRACE's *body is thrown into rigid shock as bits of her brain are burnt out*' – and as a prison in which an illegitimate boy is incarcerated. The gymnasium is a torture chamber; the showers have been turned into peep-show cubicles; and the rooms are designated solely by colour: White (for the sanatorium), Red, Black. With deliberate incongruity sounds of cricket and football-matches counterpoint the violence. One of the homosexual's amputated hands is carried off by rats. When automatic gunfire shatters the gymnasium wall and spatters it with blood, a stage direction reads: '*Out of the ground grow daffodils. They burst upwards, their yellow covering the entire stage*'; and when Grace and her brother reach their sexual climax, and '*hold each other, him inside her, not moving. A sunflower bursts through the floor and grows above their heads.*'[6] Yet Grace's brother has been killed in the first scene through heroin being injected straight into his eye, his body burnt and his clothes given to the boy to wear. Grace physically becomes her brother, and in the same way doubles as the striptease dancer in the peepshow, whose name is also Grace. And after being beaten and raped, when her brother (who has held her head throughout) puts his hands on her blood seeps through her clothes where he touches, and simultaneously his body bleeds in the same places.

Horror and hope come together. *Blasted* ends with the girl, bleeding from between her legs – the sign of violent rape – feeding and mothering the eyeless man in the hole. More explicitly, in *Cleansed* bigger-than-life flowers bloom in the torture chamber. Shock treatment that destroys the brain to 'Burn you clean' is also sunlight that grows to a blinding intensity; and these contradictions culminate in the ending. Holding the handless arm of the castrated homosexual, who is now dressed in Grace's discarded female clothing, Grace/Graham '*smiles. The sun gets brighter and brighter, the squeaking of the* [dying] *rats louder and louder*'.[7] Though undercut, even parodied by technicolour exaggeration, the imagery points to a possible way beyond the violence of a degraded civilization, as does the gender-blending.

At the same time it is possible to see the language of Kane's plays as a type of free verse, even if this was disguised for the first audiences by a gritty, almost Pinteresque linguistic realism. The pared-down, truncated sentences of her one-line dialogue, frequently reduced to exchanges of single words, form stichomythic patterns, and build to rhythmic cadences. Present in earlier plays, this is most obvious in *Cleansed*, where the torturers are presented chorically:

VOICES She was having it off with her brother
        Weren't he a bender?
        Fucking user
        All cracked up
        Shit no
        Shit yes
        Crack crack crack

And Kane's last play, finished just a week before her death and produced posthumously in 2000, is unmistakably in the form of a free-verse dramatic poem. Written for various voices – or perhaps, given its highly personal and internalized subject matter, a single voice taking multiple roles – it has clear, almost melodic rhythms and a highly formal pattern of interior monologue interrupted by lists of symptoms and medications, or by (remembered or possibly imagined) sessions with a psychiatrist. The shaping is designed to mirror the content. As she puts it explicitly in the play:

irrational
irreducible
irredeemable
unrecognizable
derailed
deranged
deform
free form[8]

That list of echoing words is almost conventionally poetic; and the script contains echoes of Shakespeare, Beckett, Edward Bond and (another suicidal poet) Sylvia Plath.

With the exception of *Phaedra's Love*, which hints indirectly at Freudian psychoanalysis in its use of Greek mythology, all the bleak single-word titles of Kane's fully developed plays refer unambiguously to mental illness and psychiatric intervention in a sequence that plays off both drugs and electric shock therapy followed by chemical treatment: *SICK, Blasted, Cleansed*. Her final, posthumously produced piece, is (notoriously) an explicitly and agonizingly personal depiction of her state of mind in the period leading up to her suicide; and in hindsight it is also noticeable that all Kane's plays revolve around suicide. In addition to the soldier who blows his brains out in *Blasted*, the eyeless man first tries to shoot himself, then attempts to strangle himself, and ends up in a grave, while the baby is declared a 'Lucky bastard' for dying before he has lived.[9] Like Phaedra, the illiterate teenager in *Cleansed* hangs himself with the stockings of the woman he desires. Even the title of *4.48 Psychosis* refers (as the Royal Court programme noted) to 'the hour, in the middle of the night, when anguish hits the mentally unstable hardest'; and the whole play is an internal monologue charting the progress of clinical depression ending in death.

Yet even here the personal and the political connect. If the diagnosis is 'Pathological grief' then this comes from an awareness of 'sense interned in an alien carcass and lumpen by the malignant spirit of the moral majority'. If 'the future is hopeless' it is because 'We are the abjects/who depose our leaders'. There is no escape from complicity – 'Victim. Perpetrator. Bystander' – so the speaker is overwhelmed by personal guilt for all the political atrocities, social injustice and individual cruelties of twentieth-century history, since they are inextricable from the individual consciousness. As the script explicitly states, 'my mind is the subject of these bewildered fragments', and so:

I gassed the Jews, I killed the Kurds, I bombed the Arabs, I fucked small children while they begged for mercy, the killing fields are mine, everyone left the party because of me, I'll suck your fucking eyes out . . .[10]

And the speech ends with the repeated denial, 'I REFUSE'. But this existential refusal leaves only one solution, 'an ineffectual moral spasm/the only alternative to murder'. In this context the 'moral spasm' is expressed in suicide. However it is also an accurate description of Kane's plays. Sucking 'fucking eyes out', as she imagines herself doing (perhaps to her audiences?) is also a direct reprise from *Blasted*; and the focus on eyes – sucked out and eaten, or impaled with a hypodermic full of heroin (or indeed the intensity of light that blinds the spectators twice in *Cleansed*) – echoes one of the most powerful Surrealist images. These acts are variations on the eyeball cut open with a razorblade in the classic Salvador Dali–Luis Buñuel film of *Un Chien Andalou.*

Kane's description of herself as 'the child of negation' is reflected in her art and, tragically, in life. But *4.48 Psychosis* also proposes a positive value in madness. If, as the script asserts, 'We are anathema/the pariahs of reason' and rationalism (symbolized by the university-prison of *Cleansed*; associated with the dominant male mindset) is at the root of contemporary cultural problems, then liberating the irrational becomes the only valid alternative. And this is directly expressed in her plays, which are designed as a form of shock therapy for the public – but in contrast to standard medical treatment, 'where madness is scorched from the bisected soul', the violence of her images is intended to destabilize sanity, to free the subconscious.[11]

The process has clear dangers as the sad fate of the author, tipping from outrage to suicide (the ultimate form of protest) all too clearly shows. Yet Kane's own mental disturbance injects a compelling authenticity; and the extremism of her art helps to show the essential qualities of a movement that began in British theatre with the rediscovery of Artaud's theories in the late 1950s, and Peter Brook's 'Theatre of Cruelty' performances in 1962, leading up to a widespread phenomenon in the last years of the century. At the same time the visual emphasis in all Kane's plays, and the complete lack of any stage-directions, scenic indication, or speaker designations in her final piece – which therefore required a production evolved from improvisation and devising – also points to another type of broadly poetic theatre that came to the fore in the 1990s.

This can be loosely described as 'Performance Art', where physical action becomes the equal of verbal dialogue, or even the dominant mode of expression (and at its extreme – though this is rare in professional British theatre – replaces words altogether, as in the mime of Marcel Marceau). This approach has also been associated with feminist theatre from its beginning in the radical women's groups of the 1970s (see pp. 233–38 above) and, significantly, characterized Caryl Churchill's symbolist work in the 1990s; but its most prominent practitioner has been Simon McBurney and the Theatre de Complicité he founded. And while McBurney's work, being rooted in Commedia del'Arte and the clown mime of the French school of Jacques LeCoq, has a very different tone from Kane's plays, sublimating any violence, the most striking Theatre de Complicité pieces also have been surrealist visions.

Notes

1 *Evening Standard*, 19 January 1995, and *Jewish Chronicle*, 27 January 1995; James
   MacDonald in *The Observer*, 22 January 1995.
2 *Blasted & Phaedra's Love*, London, 1996, pp. 27, 31, 48, 47 & 50, 49.
3 *Ibid.*, pp. 59, 60.
4 *Ibid.*, pp. 81, 90, 103; and *4.48 Psychosis*, London, 2000, pp. 21, 3.
5 *Cleansed*, London, 1998, p. 39; and *The Theatre and Its Double*, pp. 82–3.
6 *Cleansed*, pp. 29, 27, 14.
7 *Ibid.*, pp. 28, 45.
8 *Ibid.*, p. 25; *4.48 Psychosis*, pp. 20–21.
9 *Blasted*, p. 57.
10 *4.48 Psychosis*, pp. 21, 12, 27, 29, 25, 39.
11 *Ibid.*, pp. 37, 26, 31.

5.9 Simon McBurney (1957–): devising a physical theatre

CHECKLIST OF THEATRE DE COMPLICITÉ'S MAJOR PLAYS

More Bigger Snacks Now, 1985	*The Three Lives of Lucie Cabrol*, 1994
Anything for a Quiet Life, 1998	*Out of a House Walked a Man*, 1994
The Street of Crocodiles, 1992	*The Vertical Line*, 1999

Although Simon McBurney would not formally qualify as a dramatist and
has done all his work in collaboration, he is always the author of record –
along with Mark Wheatley or the novelist John Berger – in scripting the
performances devised with his Theatre de Complicité company. He is usually
considered primarily as a director, having staged striking productions of
The Visit (1988), Dürrenmatt's grotesque satire on economic corruption,
Brecht's parable of social justice *The Caucasian Chalk Circle* (NT, 1997), and
Ionesco's surrealist farce *The Chairs* (1999). But apart from one, none of
the other 14 pieces performed by Theatre de Complicité from 1983 to 1999
was based on pre-existing play-texts. In fact he should be seen as an auteur
or deviser: a new type of playwright working with his or her own acting
company to improvise stage action out of which a script emerges.

Indeed Caryl Churchill's relationship with the Second Stride Company is
similar to McBurney's with Theatre de Complicité. If anything he has greater
control, having founded his own company, all of whom shared his training
with the French mime and mask expert Jacques Lecoq. Indeed he should be

seen in the same light as the Canadian director/actor/deviser Robert Lepage, who is generally credited as the author of his performance pieces.

A comparison to Peter Brook illustrates the point, particularly since in some ways McBurney's approach is similar, starting off from Brook's concept of the stage as an 'Empty Space'. Indeed one of McBurney's plays, *The Three Lives of Lucie Cabrol* – an adaptation of Berger's novella of peasant life, presented in minimalist terms (1992) – is very similar in its representational technique to Brook's adaptation of a documentary study of African tribesmen, *The Ik*, performed almost 20 years earlier. With this and his dramatization of African myth in its companion piece *The Conference of the Birds* (1976) Brook was working as a deviser, developing new dramatic material with his own group of actors in the same way as McBurney. But even though since 1970 Brook has produced plays with his own company, the International Centre for Theatre Research in Paris through which he has developed a highly expressive style of physical theatre, however unconventional their interpretation these have all been based on standard texts by Chekhov, Jarry or Shakespeare. While the scripts for some of his major productions – *Orghast* (1971) or *The Mahabharata* (1985) – were collaborative, in each case the poet Ted Hughes and the francophone playwright Jean-Claude Carrière wrote texts that then served as the basis for rehearsal. Apart from his two African pieces, Brook functions as a director.

By contrast McBurney is responsible for shaping much of the spoken dialogue as well as the stage action; and the speeches are developed in tandem with the acted situations, even if he is pursuing an essentially non-verbal, intercultural, and highly physical form of theatre. At the same time this means that the words are inseparable from the performance; and there are no published texts of Theatre de Complicité scripts.

To some extent McBurney's theatrical approach derives from the sixteenth-century Italian form of Commedia del'Arte; and the Theatre de Complicité links with this tradition of symbolic, stylized mime were openly acknowledged in his 1990 adaptation of a script by Ruzzante – *Il Bilora*, which he updated to contemporary London and re-titled *Help! I'm Alive*. However Commedia is merged with other specifically modern elements, represented by McBurney's productions of Dürrenmatt, Brecht and Ionesco: the political critique of modern society, and Surrealism.

Theatre de Complicité's early prize-winning performance-piece, *More Bigger Snacks Now* (1985), attacked consumer-society by showing its glitzy advertising images of glamorous wealth and jet-set travel as the fantasies indulged by a group of hungry, impoverished, unemployed squatters: their only escape from a grimy slum-room with its broken down couch. *Please, Please, Please* (1986) presented a bleak picture of bourgeois home-life, with empty family activities culminating in a disastrous Christmas celebration, while *Anything for a Quiet Life* dealt with deadening office routine, and *A Minute Too Late* (both 1988) parodied the rituals of death and funerals.

In each piece characters crippled by stunted desires and trapped by their inability to communicate were used to expose an underlying inhumanity in the modern world – but presented through high-energy and sometimes highly acrobatic performances, all these shows also offered an image of vibrant life and human potential. The office of *Anything for a Quiet Life* literally deconstructs, as the building itself disintegrates under the impact of manic farce, with aborted meetings, broken air-conditioning, clandestine affairs continually thwarted by circumstance and hierarchical games of 'pass-the-buck'. In *A Minute Too Late* the combination of embarrassment and grief, faced by the agonizing need to deal with hospital bureaucracy and the hypocrisy of Western funeral parlours, makes any 'normal' behaviour impossible.

Into its place comes physical clowning, taken to such a frenetic extreme that the picture of life appears hallucinogenic. As in Churchill's *Blue Heart*, language fails. But in McBurney's work action takes over in a way that is mirrored and made explicit in the situations presented on stage – as with the office-manager in *Anything for a Quiet Life*, dictating an outraged letter to his delinquent staff. Unable to get further than the standard opening of 'Dear colleagues . . .' he is driven into a desperate pantomime that becomes increasingly deranged as he mimes searching for words. Not surprisingly, the enthusiastic reviews, which greeted these Theatre de Complicité shows, were filled with terms like 'lunatic fantasy' or 'hilarious nightmare', 'inconsecutiveness' and 'anarchy', 'farcical and disturbing' – and repeatedly 'surreal'.[1]

It was a short step from this to Theatre de Complicité's major pieces like McBurney and Wheatley's *The Street of Crocodiles* (first performed at the National Theatre in 1992, restaged at the Young Vic Theatre in 1994, and in the West End in 1999) or *The Three Lives of Lucie Cabrol* (first staged at Manchester in 1994, transferred to the West End in 1995, and toured worldwide in 1996–7).

A staging of the life and stories of the Polish Surrealist Bruno Schulz, *Street of Crocodiles*, is a highly successful experiment in evolving a performance-style to match the Surrealism of Bruno Schulz's short stories, which (like

Kafka's novels) present life in terms of hallucinatory transformations and metamorphoses. Schulz, a Polish Jew who found himself employed by the German Gestapo to destroy books – including his own – that didn't correspond to the Nazi worldview, was shot by a Nazi Officer in 1942; and McBurney's script combines Schulz's dark and densely metaphorical stories with his life. It centres on Schulz's attempts to come to grips with his own father: an unsuccessful shopkeeper, who was also an eccentric visionary, fascinated by birds and keeping a whole aviary in his attic. Becoming an obsessive recluse, Schulz's father spent his last years in an insane asylum; and he figures in several of Schulz's stories.

As his character announces in the show, 'Matter is in a constant state of fermentation, it never holds the same shape for very long' – and this is mirrored on the stage, where books turn into fluttering birds and actors transform into furniture, or inanimate objects like the rolls of cloth stacked in the father's shop take on a life of their own. Perspectives are distorted; our vision of normality is destabilized. McBurney defined *Street of Crocodiles* as 'the drama of twilight: of shifting colors and juxtapositions of movement'.[2] Everything becomes fluid, in a kaleidoscopic series of transitions, framed by the ominous sound of marching boots and culminating in the execution of the author-hero. From Schulz's personal memories emerges a mental image of twentieth-century European history and the Holocaust.

McBurney's other major international success, *The Three Lives of Lucie Cabrol*, extended the same style. Again based on short stories, this time from *Pig Earth*, the first volume of John Berger's socialist *Into Their Labours* trilogy, it presents a picture of brutal peasant life in rural France, the survival of an outcast, and the triumph of the human spirit over poverty, hatred – even death (with Lucie's 'third life' taking place after her murder, when all the dead return as ghosts). Minimal scenery – a rickety table, a few planks, an old tin bathtub on a surface of brown earth scattered thinly over the stage – is animated by just seven actors who transform themselves from villagers marched off to war, or different members of Lucie's unsympathetic family, into the chickens scuttling in and out of Lucie's kitchen, pigs being slaughtered (their blood draining into the bathtub), cows in a barn, trees and the bushes from which Lucie picks berries, even a ploughed field.

Unlike the imaginary excess and phantasmagoria of *Street of Crocodiles*, the picture is of grim reality and hard subsistence living. Yet both the stark bareness of the staging and the brutality of the 'Pig Earth' existence it depicts are transfigured through the visual impact of mime and movement into a triumph of total theatre and, in the visionary ending, of spiritual

22 Hallucinogenic transformations with a world of books as pillow, sheets and bedtime-stories: McBurney's *The Street of Crocodiles*

transcendence. In each of these pieces the imagery is reduced to essentials, like the line of empty shoes in *The Three Lives of Lucie Cabrol* that represents all the people who have died, or creates a disorienting hallucinatory effect as when actors walked vertically down walls in *Street of Crocodiles*, forming visual poetry.

And one of Complicité's most recent pieces, *The Vertical Line* (devised in collaboration with John Berger: 1999), is a poetic meditation on the way we perceive past and future, and how art is used to cope with death. Moving right outside the conventional theatre, it was staged in a disused underground station in central London.

The audience were led down a long circular stairway to the abandoned platform and into the dark rail tunnel: a progress into the depths, which was also a journey back into the past. Combining surrealist symbolism with documentary images, spectators were faced with a graffiti-artist spraying an immense purple eye on one green-tiled wall of the entry-hall, while videos showing Berger himself and archaeologists in hard hats were projected on the walls of the staircase. Once down on the platform spectators lay on a line of empty mattresses, while a soundtrack from Second World War radio played, evoking Henry Moore's pictures of the London Blitz. This gave way to photos of Corsica, projected over the curving roof, and a spoken commentary by Berger about the upright stones, the first primitive 'statues', placed there in Neolithic times. Then filing into the tunnel, they stood in complete darkness, while Berger's voice conjured up unseen images of the Chauvet cave paintings – bears, horses, lions and human hands drawn by artists 32,000 years ago – and described their recent discovery in 1995.

The Vertical Line with its use of audio-visual collage and high-tech media possibly marks a new departure in McBurney's art. But the style of physical performance he developed with Theatre de Complicité – the minimum of props, on an almost bare stage – has infiltrated mainstream companies. His work has been shown at the Edinburgh Festival (as well as at major Theatre Festivals in North America) and at the National Theatre in London, where McBurney has become one of the regular directors. And McBurney, who describes Complicité as 'a theatre of bodily functions', has been widely credited with completely changing the nature of English stage-performance.[3]

As the *Daily Telegraph* remarked in 1999, 'It is no exaggeration to say that Complicité has expanded the possibilities of theatre, and a host of other companies have followed in its wake'.[4] In addition to the influence of this new, highly physical style of acting, McBurney has also taken the type of collaborative creation introduced by Max Stafford-Clark through Joint Stock, along with other experimental fringe groups in the 1970s, to a new level, redefining the playwright as deviser in a type of poetic drama where gesture and movement, rather than speech communicates meaning. And along with Beckett, Churchill and others experimenting with new forms, his work represents an on-going search for the kinds of meaning that will both reflect and express contemporary consciousness leading into the new millennium.

Notes

1 *The Independent*, 13 April 1998; *What's On*, 20 April 1988.
2 McBurney, *cit. The Tribune*, 21 April 1992.
3 McBurney, *cit. Mail on Sunday*, 6 March 1994.
4 Charles Spencer, in *The Daily Telegraph*, 21 January 1999.

Selected critical bibliography

(Works cited in the text are not included here, and can be found in the Notes to each section.)

2 DEFINING MODERNISM

George Bernard Shaw

Bloom, Harold, ed. *George Bernard Shaw*. Broomell, PA: Chelsea, 2000.

Carpenter, Charles A. *Bernard Shaw and the Art of Destroying Ideals: the Early Plays*. Madison: University of Wisconsin Press, 1969.

Dukore, Bernard F. *Bernard Shaw: Director*. Seattle: University of Washington Press, 1971.

Evans, T.F., ed. *Shaw: the Critical Heritage*. London: Routledge, 1976.

Gordon, David J. *Bernard Shaw and the Comic Sublime*. New York: St Martin's Press, 1990.

Holroyd, Michael. *Bernard Shaw: the One-volume Definitive Edition*. New York: Random House, 1998.

Hugo, Leon. *Edwardian Shaw: the Writer and His Age*. New York: St Martin's Press, 1999.

Innes, Christopher D., ed. *The Cambridge Companion to George Bernard Shaw*. Cambridge; New York: Cambridge University Press, 1998.

Innes, Christopher D., ed. *A Sourcebook on Naturalist Theatre*. London; New York: Routledge, 2000: 1–23, 189–248.

Peters, Sally. *Bernard Shaw: the Ascent of the Superman*. New Haven: Yale University Press, 1996.

3 SOCIAL THEMES AND REALISTIC FORMULAE

Harley Granville-Barker

Kennedy, Dennis. *Granville-Barker and the Dream of Theatre*. Cambridge: Cambridge University Press, 1985.

Purdom, C. B. *Harley Granville Barker: a Man of the Theatre, Dramatist and Scholar.* Westport, CN: Greenwood Press, 1971.

Salmon, Eric. *Granville-Barker: a Secret Life.* London: Heinemann, 1983.

John Galsworthy

Coats, Robert Hay. *John Galsworthy as a Dramatic Artist.* New York: C. Scribner's Sons, 1926.

Dupre, Catherine. *John Galsworthy: a Biography.* First American Edition. New York: Coward, McCann & Geoghegan, 1976.

McDonald, Jan. *The New Drama, 1900–1914: Harley Granville-Barker, John Galsworthy, St John Hankin, John Masefield.* Basingstoke: Macmillan, 1980.

Terence Rattigan

Darlow, Michael and Hodson, Gillian. *Terence Rattigan, the Man and His Works.* London; New York: Quartet Books, 1979.

Young, B.A. *The Rattigan Version; Sir Terence Rattigan and the Theatre of Character.* London: Hamilton, 1986.

Wansell, Geoffrey. *Terence Rattigan.* New York: St Martin's Press, 1997.

D. H. Lawrence

Malani, Hiran. *D. H. Lawrence: a Study of His Plays.* Atlantic Highlands, NJ: Humanities Press, 1982.

Preston, Peter and Hoare, Peter eds. *D. H. Lawrence in the Modern World.* Cambridge: Cambridge University Press, 1989.

John Osborne

Denison, Patricia D., ed. *John Osborne: a Casebook.* New York: Garland, 1997.

Ferrar, Harold. *John Osborne.* New York: Columbia University Press, 1973.

Trussler, Simon. *The Plays of John Osborne: an Assessment.* London: Gollancz, 1969.

Whitebrook, Peter. *John Osborne.* London: Richard Cohen, 1997.

Arnold Wesker

Dornan, Reade W. *Arnold Wesker Revisited.* New York: Twayne, 1994.

Leeming, Glenda. W*esker the Playwright.* London: Methuen, 1983.

– and Simon Trussler. *The Plays of Arnold Wesker: an Assessment.* London: Gollancz, 1971.

Wilcher, Robert. *Understanding Arnold Wesker*. Columbia, SC: University of South Carolina Press, 1991.

Brechtian Influences

Robert Bolt

Hayman, Ronald. *Robert Bolt*. London: Heinemann, 1969.

Peacock, D. Keith. *Radical Stages: Alternative History in Modern British Drama*. New York: Greenwood, 1991.

Turner, Adrian. *Robert Bolt: Scenes from Two Lives*. London: Hutchinson, 1998.

Joan Littlewood and Peter Nichols

Littlewood, Joan. *Joan's Book: Joan Littlewood's Peculiar History as She Tells It*. London: Macmillan, 1994.

MacColl, Ewan. 'Grass Roots of Theatre Workshop'. *Theatre Quarterly*. 4 (Jan–March 1973).

Parkin, Andrew., ed. *File on Nichols*. London: Methuen, 1993.

Worthen, William B. ' "Deciphering the British Pantomime": *Poppy* and the Rhetoric of Political Theatre'. *Genre*. 19 (1986): 173–191.

Christopher Hampton

Carson, Katherine. '*Les liaisons dangereuses* on Stage and Film'. *Literature/Film Quarterly*. 19.i (1991): 35–40.

Free, William N. *Christopher Hampton: an Introduction to His Plays*. San Bernardino, CA: Borgo Press, 1994.

Gross, Robert, ed. *Christopher Hampton: a Casebook*. New York: Garland, 1990.

John Arden

Gray, Frances. *John Arden*. New York: Grove, 1982.

Hunt, Albert. *Arden: a Study of His Plays*. London: Eyre Methuen, 1974.

Page, Malcom. *Arden on File*. London: Methuen, 1985.

Wike, Jonathan, ed. *John Arden and Margaretta D' Arcy: a Casebook*. New York: Garland, 1995.

Edward Bond

Hay, Malcolm and Philip Roberts. *Bond, a Study of His Plays*. London: Eyre Methuen, 1980.

Hirst, David L. *Edward Bond*. London: Macmillan, 1985.

Lappin, Lou. *The Art and Politics of Edward Bond*. New York: Lang, 1987.

Stuart, Ian. *Politics in Performance: the Production Work of Edward Bond, 1978–1900.* New York: Lang, 1996.

David Edgar

Bull, John. *New British Political Dramatists: Howard Brenton, David Hare, Trevor Griffiths and David Edgar.* London: Macmillan, 1984.

Painter, Susan. *Edgar, the playwright.* London: Methuen, 1996.

Page, Malcolm and Simon Trussler. *File on Edgar.* London: Methuen, 1991.

Swain, Elizabeth. *David Edgar: Playwright and Politician.* New York: Lang, 1986.

Howard Brenton

Boon, Richard. *Brenton: the Playwright.* London: Methuen, 1991.

Mitchell, Tony. *File on Brenton.* London: Methuen, 1980.

Wilson, Ann, ed. *Howard Brenton: a Casebook.* New York: Garland, 1992.

David Hare

Donesky, Finlay. *David Hare: Moral and Historical Perspectives.* Westport, CN: Greenwood, 1996.

Fraser, Scott. *A Politic Theatre: the Drama of David Hare.* Amsterdam; Atlanta, GA: Rodopi, 1996.

Homden, Carl. *The Plays of David Hare.* Cambridge; New York: Cambridge University Press, 1995.

Olivia, Judy L. *David Hare: Theatricalizing Politics.* Ann Arbor, MI: UMI Research, 1990.

Zeifman, Hersh, ed. *David Hare: a Casebook.* New York: Garland, 1994.

The Feminist Alternative:

Pam Gems

Carlson, Susan L. 'Revisionary Endings: Pam Gems's *Aunt Mary* and *Camille*'. *Making a Spectacle: Feminist Essays on Contemporary Women's Theatre* Ed. Lynda Hart. Ann Arbor: University of Michigan, 1989 : 103–17.

Reinelt, Janelle. 'The Politics of Form: Realism, Melodrama and Pam Gems's *Camille*.' *Women and Performance: A Journal of Feminist Theory*. 8 (1989): 96–103.

Wandor, Michelene. *Carry on, Understudies: Theatre and Sexual Politics.* London: Routledge, 1986: 161–6.

4 THE COMIC MIRROR

Somerset Maugham

Barnes, Ronald Edgar. *The Dramatic Comedy of William Somerset Maugham.* The Hague; Paris: Monton, 1968.

Towne, Charles Hanson. *W. Somerset Maugham: Novelist, Essayist, Dramatist.* New York: G. H. Doran, 1925.

Noel Coward

Briers, Richard. *Coward and Company.* London: Robson Books, 1987.

Cole, Stephen. *Noel Coward: a Bio-bibliography.* Westport, CT: Greenwood, 1993.

Gray, Frances. *Noel Coward.* Basingstoke: Macmillan, 1987.

Kiernan, Robert F. *Noel Coward.* New York: Ungar, 1986.

Ben Travers

Smith, Leslie. 'Ben Travers and the Aldwych farces'. *Modern Drama.* 27 (1984): 429–48.

Joe Orton

Bigsby, C. W. E. *Joe Orton.* London; New York: Methuen, 1982.

Rusinko, Susan. *Joe Orton.* New York: Twayne, 1995.

Shepherd, Simon. *Because We're Queers: the Life and Crimes of Kenneth Halliwell and Joe Orton.* London: GMP, 1989.

Samuel Beckett

Begam, Richard. *Samuel Beckett and the End of Modernity.* Stanford: Stanford University Press, 1996.

Birkett, Jennifer and Kate Ince, eds. *Samuel Beckett.* London; New York: Longman, 2000.

Blair, Diedre. *Samuel Beckett: A Biography.* New York; London: Harcourt Brace Jovanovich, 1978.

Blau, Herbert. *Sails of the Herring Fleet: Essays on Beckett.* Ann Arbor: University of Michigan, 2000.

McMullan, Anna. *Theatre on Trial: Samuel Beckett's Later Drama.* New York: Routledge, 1993.

Miller, Lawrence. *Samuel Beckett: the Expressive Dilemma.* New York; St Martin's Press, 1992.

Pilling, John. *Beckett Before Godot.* New York: Cambridge University Press, 1997.

Worth, Katharine. *Samuel Beckett's Theatre: Life Journeys.* Oxford, NY: Clarendon Press, 1999.

Harold Pinter

Bloom, Harold, ed. *Harold Pinter: Modern Critical Views.* New York: Chelsea, 1987.
Dukore, Bernard F. *Harold Pinter.* Basingstoke: Macmillan, 1988.
Knowles, Ronald. *Understanding Harold Pinter.* Columbia: University of South Carolina Press, 1995.
Quigley, Austin. *The Pinter Problem.* Princeton: Princeton University Press, 1975.
Regal, Martin S. *Harold Pinter; a Question of Timing.* Basingstoke: Macmillan, 1995.

The Politics of Comedy

Peter Barnes
Dukore, Bernard F. *The Theatre of Peter Barnes.* London; Exeter, NH: Heinemann, 1981.
– *Barnestorm: the Plays of Peter Barnes.* New York: Garland, 1995.

Trevor Griffiths
Cave, Richard A. *New British Drama in Performance on the London Stage: 1970–1985.* Gerrards Cross: Smythe, 1987: 213–48.
Garner, Stanton B. *Trevor Griffiths: Politics, Drama, History.* Ann Arbor: University of Michigan, 1999.
Poole, Mike and John Wyner. *Powerplays: Trevor Griffiths in Television.* London: BFI Publishing, 1984.

Alan Ayckbourn

Billington, Michael. *Alan Ayckbourn.* Second Edition. New York: St Martin's Press, 1990.
Dukore, Bernard F., ed. *Alan Ayckbourn: a Casebook.* New York: Garland, 1991.
Holt, Michael. *Alan Ayckbourn.* Plymouth: Northcote House, 1999.
Kalson, Albert E. *Laughter in the Dark: the Plays of Alan Ayckbourn.* Rutherford, NJ: Fairleigh Dickinson University Press; London; Toronto: Associated University Press, 1993.

Michael Frayn

Page, Malcolm. *File on Frayn.* London: Methuen, 1994.
Smith, Leslie. *Modern British Farce: a Selective Study of British Farce from Pinero to the Present Day.* Totowa, NJ: Barnes & Noble, 1989: 168–72.
Worth, Katharine. 'Farce and Michael Frayn'. *Modern Drama.* 26 (1983): 47–53.

Tom Stoppard

Andretta, Richard A. *Tom Stoppard, an Analytical Study of His Plays*. New Delhi: Har-Anand Publishers in association with Vikas Publishing House, 1992.

Gordon, Robert. *Rosencrantz and Guildenstern are Dead, Jumpers* and *The Real Thing: Text and Performance*. Basingstoke: Macmillan, 1991.

Jenkins, Anthony. *The Theatre of Tom Stoppard*. Cambridge; New York: Cambridge University Press, 1989.

Kelly, Katherine H. *Tom Stoppard and the Craft of Comedy: Medium and Genre at Play*. Ann Arbor: University of Michigan, 1991.

Patrick Marber

Karwonski, Michael. 'Classically Closer'. *London Magazine*. 38.3–4 (1998): 104–7.

5 POETIC DRAMA

J. B. Priestley

Braine, John. *J.B. Priestley*. New York: Barnes & Noble, 1979.

Cooper, Susan. *J.B. Priestley: Portrait of an Author*. London: Heinemann, 1970.

Hughes, David. *J.B. Priestley: an Informal Study of His Work*. London: R. Hart-Davies, 1958.

Klein, Holger M. *J.B. Priestley's Plays*. Basingstoke: Macmillan, 1988.

W. H. Auden and Christopher Isherwood

Carpenter, Humphrey. *W.H. Auden*. London: Allen & Unwin, 1981.

Lemming, Glenda. *Poetic Drama*. New York: St Martin's Press, 1989: 139–51.

Sidnell, Michael J. *Dances of Death: the Group Theatre of London in the Thirties*. London: Faber, 1984.

T. S. Eliot

D.E. Jones. *The Plays of T.S. Eliot*. London: Routledge, 1960.

Malamud, Randy. *T.S. Eliot's Drama: a Research and Production Sourcebook*. New York: Greenwood, 1992.

Sidnell, Michael J. *Dances of Death: the Group Theatre of London in the Thirties*. London: Faber, 1984.

Smith, Carol H. *T.S. Eliot's Dramatic Theory and Practice*. Princeton, NJ: Princeton University Press, 1963.

Appealing to the poular imagination

Christopher Fry

Leeming, Glenda. *Christopher Fry*. Boston: Twayne, 1990.

Wiersma, Stanley M. *More Than the Ear Discovers: God in the Plays of Christopher Fry*. Chicago: Loyola University Press, 1983.

Peter Shaffer

Gianakaris, C. J. *Peter Shaffer: a Casebook*. New York: Garland, 1991.

Klein, Dennis A. *Peter Shaffer*. New York: Twayne, 1993.

Macmurraugh-Kavanagh, Madeline. *Peter Shaffer: Theatre and Drama*. Basingstoke: Macmillan, 1998.

Plunka, Gene A. *Peter Shaffer: Roles, Rites, and Rituals in the Theater*. Rutherford: Fairleigh Dickinson University Press; London: Associated University Press, 1988.

Apocalyptic Visions

John Whiting

Hurrell, John D. 'John Whiting and the Theme of Self-destruction'. *Modern Drama*. (1965): pp. 134–41.

Robinson, Gabrielle S. *A Private Mythology: the Manuscripts and Plays of John Whiting*. Lewisburg, PA: Bucknell University Press, 1989.

Salmon. Eric. *The Dark Journey: John Whiting as a Dramatist*. London: Barne & Jenkins, 1979.

David Rudkin

Forian-Szabo, Ewa. 'David Rudkin: Strategies of Enslavement and Liberation'. *AUL*. 29 (1990) : 31–69.

Rabey, David Ian. *David Rudkin: Sacred Disobedience: an Expository Study of His Drama 1959–96*. Amsterdam, The Netherlands: Harwood Academic Publishers, 1997.

Howard Barker

Boireau, Nicole, ed. *Drama on Drama: Dimensions of Theatricality on the Contemporary British Stage*. Basingstoke: Macmillan, 1997: 30–58; 59–71.

Lamb, Charles. *Howard Barker's Theatre of Seduction*. The Netherlands: Harwood Academic Publishers, 1997.

Rabey, David Ian. *Howard Barker, Politics and Desire: an Expository Study of His Drama and Poetry, 1969–87*. Basingstoke: Macmillan, 1989.

Caryl Churchill

Fitzsimmons, Linda. *File on Churchill.* London: Macmillan, 1987.
Kritzer, Amelia H. *The Plays of Caryl Churchill: Theatre of Empowerment.* Basingstoke: Macmillan, 1991.
Rabillard, Sheila, ed. *Essays on Caryl Churchill: Contemporary Representations.* Winnipeg: Blizzard, 1998.
Randall, Phyllis, ed. *Caryl Churchill: a Casebook.* New York: Garland, 1988.

Sarah Kane

Sellar, Tom. 'Truth and Dare: Sarah Kane's *Blasted.*' *Theater.* 27.1 (1997): 29–34.
Stephenson, Heidi and Natasha Langridge. *Rage and Reason: Women Playwrights on Playwrighting.* London: Methuen, 1997.

For reviews of plays, current and revivals, produced between January 1981 and the present, see: *London Theatre Record.*

Index